Handbook of Research on Democratic Strategies and Citizen-Centered E-Government Services

Ćemal Dolićanin
State University of Novi Pazar, Serbia

Ejub Kajan
State University of Novi Pazar, Serbia

Dragan Randjelović
Academy for Criminalistic and Police Studies, Serbia

Boban Stojanović
University of Niš, Serbia

A volume in the Advances in Electronic Government, Digital Divide, and Regional Development (AEGDDRD) Book Series

Information Science REFERENCE
An Imprint of IGI Global

Managing Director:	Lindsay Johnston
Managing Editor:	Austin DeMarco
Director of Intellectual Property & Contracts:	Jan Travers
Acquisitions Editor:	Kayla Wolfe
Production Editor:	Christina Henning
Development Editor:	Allison McGinniss
Typesetter:	Amanda Smith
Cover Design:	Jason Mull

Published in the United States of America by
Information Science Reference (an imprint of IGI Global)
701 E. Chocolate Avenue
Hershey PA, USA 17033
Tel: 717-533-8845
Fax: 717-533-8661
E-mail: cust@igi-global.com
Web site: http://www.igi-global.com

Library of Congress Cataloging-in-Publication Data

CIP Data
ISBN: 978-1-4666-7266-6
eISBN:978-1-4666-7267-3
Print & Perpetual:978-1-4666-7269-7

This book is published in the IGI Global book series Advances in Electronic Government, Digital Divide, and Regional Development (AEGDDRD) (ISSN: 2326-9103; eISSN: 2326-9111)

British Cataloguing in Publication Data
A Cataloguing in Publication record for this book is available from the British Library.

For electronic access to this publication, please contact: eresources@igi-global.com.

Advances in Electronic Government, Digital Divide, and Regional Development (AEGDDRD) Book Series

Zaigham Mahmood
University of Derby, UK & North West University, South Africa

ISSN: 2326-9103
EISSN: 2326-9111

Mission

The successful use of digital technologies (including social media and mobile technologies) to provide public services and foster economic development has become an objective for governments around the world. The development towards electronic government (or e-government) not only affects the efficiency and effectiveness of public services, but also has the potential to transform the nature of government interactions with its citizens. Current research and practice on the adoption of electronic/digital government and the implementation in organizations around the world aims to emphasize the extensiveness of this growing field.

The Advances in Electronic Government, Digital Divide & Regional Development (AEGDDRD) book series aims to publish authored, edited and case books encompassing the current and innovative research and practice discussing all aspects of electronic government development, implementation and adoption as well the effective use of the emerging technologies (including social media and mobile technologies) for a more effective electronic governance (or e-governance).

Coverage

- Frameworks and Methodologies for E-Government Development
- E-Government in Developing Countries and Technology Adoption
- ICT Infrastructure and Adoption for E-Government Provision
- Adoption of Innovation with Respect to E-Government
- E-Governance and Use of Technology for Effective Government

The Advances in Electronic Government, Digital Divide, and Regional Development (AEGDDRD) Book Series (ISSN 2326-9103) is published by IGI Global, 701 E. Chocolate Avenue, Hershey, PA 17033-1240, USA, www.igi-global.com. This series is composed of titles available for purchase individually; each title is edited to be contextually exclusive from any other title within the series. For pricing and ordering information please visit http://www.igi-global.com/book-series/advances-electronic-government-digital-divide/37153. Postmaster: Send all address changes to above address.

Titles in this Series

For a list of additional titles in this series, please visit: www.igi-global.com

Revolutionizing the Interaction between State and Citizens through Digital Communications
Sam B. Edwards III (Green Mountain College, USA) and Diogo Santos (Federal University of Maranhao, Brazil & Dom Bosco University, Brazil)
Information Science Reference • copyright 2015 • 330pp • H/C (ISBN: 9781466662926) • US $195.00 (our price)

Emerging Issues and Prospects in African E-Government
Inderjeet Singh Sodhi (St. Wilfred's Post Graduate College–Jaipur, India)
Information Science Reference • copyright 2015 • 331pp • H/C (ISBN: 9781466662964) • US $175.00 (our price)

Handbook of Research on Advanced ICT Integration for Governance and Policy Modeling
Peter Sonntagbauer (Cellent AG, Austria) Kawa Nazemi (Fraunhofer Institute for Computer Graphics Research (IGD), Germany) Susanne Sonntagbauer (Cellent AG, Austria) Giorgio Prister (Major Cities of Europe, Italy) and Dirk Burkhardt (Fraunhofer Institute for Computer Graphics Research (IGD), Germany)
Information Science Reference • copyright 2014 • 508pp • H/C (ISBN: 9781466662360) • US $295.00 (our price)

Emerging Mobile and Web 2.0 Technologies for Connected E-Government
Zaigham Mahmood (University of Derby, UK & North West University Potchefstroom, South Africa)
Information Science Reference • copyright 2014 • 332pp • H/C (ISBN: 9781466660823) • US $205.00 (our price)

E-Governance and Social Inclusion Concepts and Cases
Scott Baum (Griffith University, Australia) and Arun Mahizhnan (National University of Singapore, Singapore)
Information Science Reference • copyright 2014 • 356pp • H/C (ISBN: 9781466661066) • US $205.00 (our price)

Design, Development, and Use of Secure Electronic Voting Systems
Dimitrios Zissis (University of Aegean, Greece) and Dimitrios Lekkas (University of Aegean, Greece)
Information Science Reference • copyright 2014 • 270pp • H/C (ISBN: 9781466658202) • US $195.00 (our price)

Digital Access and E-Government Perspectives from Developing and Emerging Countries
Peter Mazebe II Mothataesi Sebina (University of Botswana, Botswana) Kgomotso H. Moahi (University of Botswana, Botswana) and Kelvin Joseph Bwalya (University of Botswana, Botswana & University of Johannesburg, South Africa)
Information Science Reference • copyright 2014 • 356pp • H/C (ISBN: 9781466658684) • US $195.00 (our price)

Technology Development and Platform Enhancements for Successful Global E-Government Design
Kelvin Joseph Bwalya (University of Botswana, Botswana & University of Johannesburg, South Africa)
Information Science Reference • copyright 2014 • 511pp • H/C (ISBN: 9781466649002) • US $235.00 (our price)

IGI GLOBAL
DISSEMINATOR OF KNOWLEDGE
www.igi-global.com

701 E. Chocolate Ave., Hershey, PA 17033
Order online at www.igi-global.com or call 717-533-8845 x100
To place a standing order for titles released in this series, contact: cust@igi-global.com
Mon-Fri 8:00 am - 5:00 pm (est) or fax 24 hours a day 717-533-8661

List of Contributors

Aboelmaged, Mohamed Gamal / *Ain Shams University, Egypt* 374
Ahn, Michael J. / *University of Massachusetts, USA* 38
Alencar, Antonio Juarez / *Federal University of Rio de Janeiro (UFRJ), Brazil* 328
Alexandre, Celina / *University of Beira Interior, Covilhã, Portugal* 302
Aparecida dos Santos, Pamela / *Universidade Federal de Lavras (UFLA), Brazil* 231
Araujo, Renata / *Federal University of the State of Rio de Janeiro, Brazil* 92
Asquer, Alberto / *SOAS, University of London, UK* 20
Bermejo, Paulo Henrique de Souza / *Universidade Federal de Lavras, Brazil* 144, 231
Bogdanović, Dragan / *State University of Novi Pazar, Serbia* 265
Cappelli, Claudia / *Federal University of the State of Rio de Janeiro, Brazil* 92
Correa, Alexandre Luis / *Federal University of the State of Rio de Janeiro (UNIRIO), Brazil* 328
Couto, Rafael / *University of Beira Interior, Covilhã, Portugal* 302
De Decker, Bart / *KU Leuven, Belgium* 251
Engiel, Priscila / *Pontifical Catholic University of Rio de Janeiro, Brazil* 92
Falcone, Francisco / *IEEE Computer Society E-Government STC* 1
Felizardo, Virginie / *University of Beira Interior, Covilhã, Portugal* 302
Fernandes, Marcelo Carvalho / *Federal University of Rio de Janeiro (UFRJ), Brazil* 328
Garcia, Nuno / *University of Beira Interior, Covilhã, Portugal & Universidade Lusófona de Humanidades e Tecnologias, Lisbon, Portugal* 302
Gebba, Tarek R. / *Al Ghurair University, UAE* 374
González, Federico / *IEEE Computer Society E-Government STC* 1
Jiménez, Carlos E. / *IEEE Computer Society E-Government STC* 1
Lancieri, Luigi / *University of Lille1, France* 125
Lazarević, Konstansa / *State University of Novi Pazar, Serbia* 265
León, Carlos / *Universidad de Sevilla, Spain* 192
Martín, Antonio / *Universidad de Sevilla, Spain* 192
Martínez-Carreras, M. Antonia / *Universidad de Murcia, Spain* 107
Martins, Teresa Cristina Monteiro / *Universidade Federal de Lavras, Brazil* 144
McNutt, John / *University of Delaware, USA* 38
Milutinovic, Milica / *KU Leuven, Belgium* 251
Mishra, Gaurav / *Dhirubhai Ambani Institute of Information and Communication Technology (DA-IICT), India* 56
Novaković, Igor / *University in Pristina/Kosovska Mitrovica, Serbia* 353
Oliveira, Daniel José Silva / *Universidade Federal de Lavras (UFLA), Brazil* 231
Pires, Ivan / *University of Beira Interior, Covilhã, Portugal* 302

Puyosa, Héctor / *IEEE Computer Society E-Government STC* 1
Ramayah, Thurasamy / *Universiti Sains Malaysia, Malaysia* 73
Re, Jesús D. Jiménez / *Universidad de Murcia, Spain* 107
Sabugueiro, Daniel / *University of Beira Interior, Covilhã, Portugal* 302
Schmitz, Eber Assis / *Federal University of Rio de Janeiro (UFRJ), Brazil* 328
Šimić, Goran / *University of Defense, Serbia* 164
Solanas, Agusti / *IEEE Computer Society E-Government STC* 1
Sorge, Christoph / *CISPA and Institute of Legal Informatics, Saarland University, Germany* 214
Sousa, Paula / *University of Beira Interior, Covilhã, Portugal* 302
Stanković, Jelena / *University of Niš, Faculty of Economics, Serbia* 353
Thominathan, Santhanamery / *Universiti Teknologi MARA, Malaysia* 73
Zakaria, Mohamed R. / *Al Ghurair University, UAE* 374
Zoughbi, Saleem / *IEEE Computer Society E-Government STC* 1

Table of Contents

Preface xxi

Acknowledgment xxxii

Section 1
E-Government Adoption: Issues, Challenges, Experiences

Chapter 1
Smart Government: Opportunities and Challenges in Smart Cities Development 1
Carlos E. Jiménez, IEEE Computer Society E-Government STC
Francisco Falcone, IEEE Computer Society E-Government STC
Agusti Solanas, IEEE Computer Society E-Government STC
Héctor Puyosa, IEEE Computer Society E-Government STC
Saleem Zoughbi, IEEE Computer Society E-Government STC
Federico González, IEEE Computer Society E-Government STC

Chapter 2
Big Data and Innovation in the Delivery of Public Services: The Case of Predictive Policing in Kent 20
Alberto Asquer, SOAS, University of London, UK

Chapter 3
If We Build It, Will They Come? An Appreciation of the Microfoundations of E-Government 38
Michael J. Ahn, University of Massachusetts, USA
John McNutt, University of Delaware, USA

Chapter 4
Telecentres as a Medium for Good Governance in Rural India 56
Gaurav Mishra, Dhirubhai Ambani Institute of Information and Communication Technology (DA-IICT), India

Chapter 5
Ensuring Continued Usage of an E-Government Service in Malaysia: The Role of Perceived Usefulness and User Satisfaction 73
Santhanamery Thominathan, Universiti Teknologi MARA, Malaysia
Thurasamy Ramayah, Universiti Sains Malaysia, Malaysia

Section 2
Business Process Modeling for E-Government Services

Chapter 6
Raising Citizen-Government Communication with Business Process Models 92
Renata Araujo, Federal University of the State of Rio de Janeiro, Brazil
Claudia Cappelli, Federal University of the State of Rio de Janeiro, Brazil
Priscila Engiel, Pontifical Catholic University of Rio de Janeiro, Brazil

Chapter 7
Towards the Integration of E-Government Process in the University of Murcia: Business Process Strategy 107
Jesús D. Jiménez Re, Universidad de Murcia, Spain
M. Antonia Martínez-Carreras, Universidad de Murcia, Spain

Section 3
Harnessing the Citizen and E-Government Collective Intelligence

Chapter 8
Collective Intelligence in a Computer-Mediated Environment 125
Luigi Lancieri, University of Lille1, France

Chapter 9
Open Social Innovation..144
Teresa Cristina Monteiro Martins, Universidade Federal de Lavras, Brazil
Paulo Henrique de Souza Bermejo, Universidade Federal de Lavras, Brazil

Chapter 10
E-Government Documents and Data Clustering..164
Goran Šimić, University of Defense, Serbia

Chapter 11
Semantic Framework for an Efficient Information Retrieval in the E-Government Repositories 192
Antonio Martín, Universidad de Sevilla, Spain
Carlos León, Universidad de Sevilla, Spain

Chapter 12
The German Electronic Identity Card: Lessons Learned..214
Christoph Sorge, CISPA and Institute of Legal Informatics, Saarland University, Germany

Chapter 13
Sentiment Analysis, Social Media, and Public Administration 231
Daniel José Silva Oliveira, Universidade Federal de Lavras (UFLA), Brazil
Paulo Henrique de Souza Bermejo, Universidade Federal de Lavras (UFLA), Brazil
Pamela Aparecida dos Santos, Universidade Federal de Lavras (UFLA), Brazil

Section 4
E-Health: Issues and Solutions

Chapter 14
Privacy-Friendly Management of Electronic Health Records in the eHealth Context 251
Milica Milutinovic, KU Leuven, Belgium
Bart De Decker, KU Leuven, Belgium

Chapter 15
Early Warning System and Adaptation Advice to Reduce Human Health Consequences of Extreme Weather Conditions and Air Pollution 265
Dragan Bogdanović, State University of Novi Pazar, Serbia
Konstansa Lazarević, State University of Novi Pazar, Serbia

Chapter 16
E-Health: Current Status and Future Trends..302
Virginie Felizardo, University of Beira Interior, Covilhã, Portugal
Paula Sousa, University of Beira Interior, Covilhã, Portugal
Daniel Sabugueiro, University of Beira Interior, Covilhã, Portugal
Celina Alexandre, University of Beira Interior, Covilhã, Portugal
Rafael Couto, University of Beira Interior, Covilhã, Portugal
Nuno Garcia, University of Beira Interior, Covilhã, Portugal & Universidade Lusófona de Humanidades e Tecnologias, Lisbon, Portugal
Ivan Pires, University of Beira Interior, Covilhã, Portugal

Section 5
Government-to-Business and -Citizen Communications and Services

Chapter 17
Evaluating E-Government Initiatives: An Approach Based upon the Appropriation of Tangible and Intangible Benefits 328
Antonio Juarez Alencar, Federal University of Rio de Janeiro (UFRJ), Brazil
Marcelo Carvalho Fernandes, Federal University of Rio de Janeiro (UFRJ), Brazil
Eber Assis Schmitz, Federal University of Rio de Janeiro (UFRJ), Brazil
Alexandre Luis Correa, Federal University of the State of Rio de Janeiro (UNIRIO), Brazil

Chapter 18
Impact of Local Self-Government Institutions on Creating a Business-Friendly Environment: Multi-Criteria Analysis 353
Jelena Stanković, University of Niš, Faculty of Economics, Serbia
Igor Novaković, University in Pristina/Kosovska Mitrovica, Serbia

Chapter 19
Towards a Citizen-Centric E-Government Service Index Model: Developments and Impediments within the Egyptian Context 374
Mohamed R. Zakaria, Al Ghurair University, UAE
Tarek R. Gebba, Al Ghurair University, UAE
Mohamed Gamal Aboelmaged, Ain Shams University, Egypt

Compilation of References 396

About the Contributors 441

Index 454

Detailed Table of Contents

Preface xxi

Acknowledgment xxxii

Section 1
E-Government Adoption: Issues, Challenges, Experiences

Chapter 1
Smart Government: Opportunities and Challenges in Smart Cities Development................................1
Carlos E. Jiménez, IEEE Computer Society E-Government STC
Francisco Falcone, IEEE Computer Society E-Government STC
Agusti Solanas, IEEE Computer Society E-Government STC
Héctor Puyosa, IEEE Computer Society E-Government STC
Saleem Zoughbi, IEEE Computer Society E-Government STC
Federico González, IEEE Computer Society E-Government STC

The advent of Smart Cities is one of the greatest challenges and field of opportunities in the goal to achieve sustainable, comfortable, and socially responsible living environments. A large number of factors, spanning from government/administration/citizen interaction models, heterogeneous communication network, interoperability, or security determine the capabilities and functionalities that can be deployed. In this chapter, different factors in the implementation and adoption of E-Government within Smart City scenarios are described. The authors include the Interoperability Principle as a part of the Open Government concept and link this concept with the Smart Cities view. Then, they describe a new model of public organization that they call "Intelligent," characterized by the "Smart Government," and they propose a matrix with the elements of this model. Then, the authors analyze the technical and infrastructure dimensions of the matrix.

Chapter 2
Big Data and Innovation in the Delivery of Public Services: The Case of Predictive Policing in Kent...20
Alberto Asquer, SOAS, University of London, UK

This chapter aims to discuss the role of Information and Communication Technologies (ICTs)—especially of the so-called Big Data—in the innovation of public service delivery. After reviewing the relevant literature on innovation and innovation diffusion in the public sector and the rise of Big Data, the chapter presents a narrative of the case of the adoption and implementation of predictive policing in Kent County Police, UK, as an instance of (early) application of Big Data in public sector organizations. On the whole, the analysis of the case suggests that past conditions and adoption strategies play an important role in the introduction and acceptance of innovative work practices that exploit the potential of contemporary ICTs.

Chapter 3
If We Build It, Will They Come? An Appreciation of the Microfoundations of E-Government 38
Michael J. Ahn, University of Massachusetts, USA
John McNutt, University of Delaware, USA

This chapter explores the possible role of microfoundations (social, cultural, and institutional factors) as a determinant of electronic government. While earlier research has implied that microfoundations might be critical to e-government, this research presents an approach to assessing how technology interacts with societal factors in creating (or not creating) e-government success. The findings suggest that e-government development depends not only on strict technological and economic capacity but also on fertile social and institutional environment that facilitate the development of e-government. These findings support the basic premise that e-government does not exist in a vacuum and these soft factors and attributes create an environment that directs the outcomes of e-government. This enriches previous research on e-government acceptance such as Diffusion of Innovation Theory (Rogers, 1983) and the Technology Acceptance Model (Davis, 1989) and extends it to national and international realms.

Chapter 4
Telecentres as a Medium for Good Governance in Rural India 56
Gaurav Mishra, Dhirubhai Ambani Institute of Information and Communication Technology (DA-IICT), India

It has been established in literature that "good governance" has major implications for poverty reduction, equity, empowerment, and quality of life. Information and Communication Technology (ICT) is seen as potentially very influential for the cause of good governance. E-governance is seen as means to achieve tenets of "good governance". E-governance addresses core components of good governance by seeking to improve efficiency and effectiveness of government, relationships with communities, businesses, citizens, and NGO/civil societies for better provision of services, accountability, transparency, and social development. In the beginning sections of the chapter, ideologies behind good governance are discussed because e-government initiatives are presumably embedded in the "good governance" thinking in development. The chapter also focuses on the relevance of e-governance as a means to achieve "good governance." In rural areas e-governance services are mostly provided through telecentres; hence, the chapter also discusses the role and issues related to telecentres for e-governance service delivery.

Chapter 5
Ensuring Continued Usage of an E-Government Service in Malaysia: The Role of Perceived Usefulness and User Satisfaction 73
Santhanamery Thominathan, Universiti Teknologi MARA, Malaysia
Thurasamy Ramayah, Universiti Sains Malaysia, Malaysia

This chapter highlights the importance of continuance usage intention of a technology. Continuance intention is defined as one's intention to continue using or long-term usage intention of a technology. Although initial acceptance is important in identifying the success of an information system, continued usage is even more significant in ensuring the long-term viability of technology innovations and in enhancing the financial and quality performance of an organization. Therefore, this chapter aims to examine the continuance usage intention of e-filing system by taxpayers in Malaysia. The data were collected from 153 taxpayers in the northern region of Malaysia using survey method. The result shows a significant relationship between perceived usefulness and continuance usage intention. Surprisingly, perceived usefulness was found to be insignificantly related to satisfaction and satisfaction towards continuance usage intention. Implication of these findings to the Inland Revenue Board of Malaysia is also elaborated.

Section 2
Business Process Modeling for E-Government Services

Chapter 6
Raising Citizen-Government Communication with Business Process Models 92
Renata Araujo, Federal University of the State of Rio de Janeiro, Brazil
Claudia Cappelli, Federal University of the State of Rio de Janeiro, Brazil
Priscila Engiel, Pontifical Catholic University of Rio de Janeiro, Brazil

This chapter draws out the challenge of how to provide information to citizens with respect to organizational business processes, particularly public service processes. The aim is to discuss the issues concerning organizations' disclosure to citizens, particularly in describing how services are performed in these organizations. It relies on the idea that an urgent step to improve citizen participation in public matters, especially in public service delivery, is to provide citizens with ways to understand how and why internal processes must be conducted. The chapter reports on how business process models can be used for organizational communication and describes proposals to extend this communication to external actors. The conclusion presents remarks on challenges and future work.

Chapter 7
Towards the Integration of E-Government Process in the University of Murcia: Business Process Strategy 107
Jesús D. Jiménez Re, Universidad de Murcia, Spain
M. Antonia Martínez-Carreras, Universidad de Murcia, Spain

Several countries are adopting e-government strategies for adapting the administrative procedures to automated process with the aim of obtaining efficient and agile processes. In this sense, the European Union has published some directives which indicate the need for European countries to adopt e-government in the public administration. Additionally, the Spanish government has published laws and documents for supporting the adoption of e-government in the different public administration. Concretely, the University of Murcia has developed a strategy for the adoption of e-government using a service-oriented platform. Indeed, this strategy has evolved for the adoption of BPM for its administrative processes. The aim of this chapter is explaining the strategy for the adoption of business processes in the University of Murcia.

Section 3
Harnessing the Citizen and E-Government Collective Intelligence

Chapter 8
Collective Intelligence in a Computer-Mediated Environment 125
Luigi Lancieri, University of Lille1, France

The role of the computer in the emergence of collective intelligence is most of the time underestimated. Outside the fact that it allows the collaboration between individuals, it modifies the interactions and memorizes the traces of the activity. These specific features lead to computer services becoming full actors of the interaction with their own influence like individuals. The resulting symbiosis effect boosts significantly the outcome of the human collaboration. Thus, the objective of this chapter is to deepen our understanding of these mechanisms in order to improve the management of collective intelligence.

Chapter 9
Open Social Innovation..........144
Teresa Cristina Monteiro Martins, Universidade Federal de Lavras, Brazil
Paulo Henrique de Souza Bermejo, Universidade Federal de Lavras, Brazil

Social innovation and open innovation are two concepts that have gained prominence in the last decade. Small social innovations have the potential to change the global system, expanding through a collaborative process. Furthermore, the collaborative process is the main characteristic of open innovation. Social and open innovations are relevant and emerging; their relationship with each other has been neglected in the literature. Based on the study of social innovation and open innovation, this chapter proposes a framework about the "open social innovation" and demonstrates how it can be implemented through examples in Brazil and the US. Based on the literature review and these examples, it is evident that "open social innovation" is already a reality in many regions and is a combination of the two original concepts converging in collaborative process.

Chapter 10
E-Government Documents and Data Clustering..........164
Goran Šimić, University of Defense, Serbia

This chapter is about documents and data clustering as a process of preparing the information resources stored in the e-government systems for advanced search. These resources are mainly represented as textual data stored as field values in the databases or located as documents in file repositories. Due to their growth in number, search for some specific information takes more time. Different techniques are used for this purpose. Most of them include information retrieval based on a variety of text similarity measures. The cost of such processing depends on preparation of resources for searching. Clustering represents the most commonly used technique for such a purpose, and this fact is the basic motive for this chapter.

Chapter 11
Semantic Framework for an Efficient Information Retrieval in the E-Government Repositories......192
Antonio Martín, Universidad de Sevilla, Spain
Carlos León, Universidad de Sevilla, Spain

An enormous quantity of heterogeneous and distributed information is stored in e-government repositories. Access to these collections poses a serious challenge, however, because present search techniques based on manually annotated metadata and linear replay of material selected by the user do not scale effectively or efficiently to large collections. The artificial intelligence and Semantic Web provide a common framework that allows knowledge to be shared and reused in an efficient way. This chapter proposes a comprehensive approach for discovering information objects in large digital collections based on analysis of recorded semantic metadata in those objects and the application of expert system technologies. The authors suggest a conceptual architecture for a semantic search engine. They use case-based reasoning methodology to develop a prototype. OntoloGov is a collaborative effort that proposes a new form of interaction between citizens and e-government repositories, where the latter are adapted to users and their surroundings.

Chapter 12
The German Electronic Identity Card: Lessons Learned 214
Christoph Sorge, CISPA and Institute of Legal Informatics, Saarland University, Germany

Authentication is an important aspect of e-government applications, as in many cases the identity of a citizen has to be established before provision of a service. Germany is among the countries that have established an electronic identification and authentication infrastructure, based on an electronic identity card. The card enables both local and remote authentication to service providers and authorities. While privacy-enhancing technologies have been used to a large extent in its design and there are no known attacks on its security protocols, the eID card has been harshly criticized. Less than a third of the citizens requesting an identity card choose to activate the eID function. Using the example of Germany, this chapter discusses whether the establishment of an electronic authentication infrastructure makes sense and presents possible reasons for the German eID card's lack of success. In addition, the authors consider electronic signatures and their integration in an electronic authentication infrastructure.

Chapter 13
Sentiment Analysis, Social Media, and Public Administration 231
Daniel José Silva Oliveira, Universidade Federal de Lavras (UFLA), Brazil
Paulo Henrique de Souza Bermejo, Universidade Federal de Lavras (UFLA), Brazil
Pamela Aparecida dos Santos, Universidade Federal de Lavras (UFLA), Brazil

This chapter describes how sentiment analysis, based on texts taken from social media, can be an instrument for measuring popular opinion about government services and can contribute to evaluating and developing public administration. This is an applied, interdisciplinary, qualitative, exploratory, and technological study. Throughout the chapter, the main theoretical and conceptual formulations about the subject are reviewed, and practical demonstrations are made using opinion-mining tools that provide high accuracy in data processing. For demonstration purposes, topics that triggered the popular protests of June 2013 in Brazil were selected, involving million people across the country. A total of 51,857 messages posted on social media about these topics were collected, processed, and analyzed. Through that analysis, it can be observed that even after six months, the factors that motivated the protests continued generating citizen dissatisfaction.

Section 4
E-Health: Issues and Solutions

Chapter 14
Privacy-Friendly Management of Electronic Health Records in the eHealth Context 251
Milica Milutinovic, KU Leuven, Belgium
Bart De Decker, KU Leuven, Belgium

Electronic Health Records (EHRs) are becoming the ubiquitous technology for managing patients' records in many countries. They allow for easier transfer and analysis of patient data on a large scale. However, privacy concerns linked to this technology are emerging. Namely, patients rarely fully understand how EHRs are managed. Additionally, the records are not necessarily stored within the organization where the patient is receiving her healthcare. This service may be delegated to a remote provider, and it is not always clear which health-provisioning entities have access to this data. Therefore, in this chapter the authors propose an alternative where users can keep and manage their records in their existing eHealth systems. The approach is user-centric and enables the patients to have better control over their data while still allowing for special measures to be taken in case of emergency situations with the goal of providing the required care to the patient.

Chapter 15
Early Warning System and Adaptation Advice to Reduce Human Health Consequences of Extreme Weather Conditions and Air Pollution 265
Dragan Bogdanović, State University of Novi Pazar, Serbia
Konstansa Lazarević, State University of Novi Pazar, Serbia

The authors developed a multi-site Internet service to provide the public with real time information about local weather and air quality, how they may affect health, and how general population and different sensitive population groups can protect their health during periods of extreme weather conditions or increased air pollution levels. The information service is based on data obtained from the Republic Hydrometeorological Service of Serbia and Serbian Environment Protection Agency. Health warnings and recommendations are given separately for each AIQ and heat index or wind chill index value, for each sensitive population group, as well as for the general population. The project is currently implemented on the website of the Institute of Occupational Health Niš and will be offered to other healthcare institutions in Serbia. Evaluation of the system should enable redefinition of heat and wind chill indices and air pollution threshold values if necessary. This chapter explores the service.

Chapter 16
E-Health: Current Status and Future Trends...302
Virginie Felizardo, University of Beira Interior, Covilhã, Portugal
Paula Sousa, University of Beira Interior, Covilhã, Portugal
Daniel Sabugueiro, University of Beira Interior, Covilhã, Portugal
Celina Alexandre, University of Beira Interior, Covilhã, Portugal
Rafael Couto, University of Beira Interior, Covilhã, Portugal
Nuno Garcia, University of Beira Interior, Covilhã, Portugal & Universidade Lusófona de Humanidades e Tecnologias, Lisbon, Portugal
Ivan Pires, University of Beira Interior, Covilhã, Portugal

Due to higher life expectancy, the number of older people continues to increase, and with it the number of cases of chronic diseases. Estimates indicate that the percentage of people with at least one chronic disease living in modern societies can reach as much as 40%, making chronic diseases one of the major challenges for modern healthcare systems. In order to reduce healthcare costs, solutions based on information and communication technologies have emerged. The expansion of e-Health solutions is associated with the increased demand for flexible, comprehensive, and cost-effective chronic care models, and continues expanding, putting together a very comprehensive set of knowledge. This chapter presents an inclusive and widespread current state of the art of e-health solutions for chronic diseases, proposing a number of predictable future trends and scenarios.

Section 5
Government-to-Business and -Citizen Communications and Services

Chapter 17
Evaluating E-Government Initiatives: An Approach Based upon the Appropriation of Tangible and Intangible Benefits 328
Antonio Juarez Alencar, Federal University of Rio de Janeiro (UFRJ), Brazil
Marcelo Carvalho Fernandes, Federal University of Rio de Janeiro (UFRJ), Brazil
Eber Assis Schmitz, Federal University of Rio de Janeiro (UFRJ), Brazil
Alexandre Luis Correa, Federal University of the State of Rio de Janeiro (UNIRIO), Brazil

Over the last decade, governments around the word have made substantial investments in e-government initiatives with the aim of improving the efficiency and effectiveness of public services. While some of these initiatives are aimed at improving tax collection and reducing running costs, the main benefits that they provide are intangibles such as greater taxpayer satisfaction and increased transparency in government decisions. This chapter presents a method to analyse e-government initiatives. The method takes into consideration that these initiatives are frequently comprised of several projects that are divided into a number of subprojects. Moreover, it evaluates e-government initiatives through a balanced view of the tangible and intangible benefits they provide. All of this is made clear with the support of a real-world inspired example.

Chapter 18
Impact of Local Self-Government Institutions on Creating a Business-Friendly Environment: Multi-Criteria Analysis 353
Jelena Stanković, University of Niš, Faculty of Economics, Serbia
Igor Novaković, University in Pristina/Kosovska Mitrovica, Serbia

The chapter objective is to demonstrate application possibilities of Multi-Criteria Analysis (MCA) in the specific local economic development problem in Serbia that refers to assessment of Local Self-Government (LSG) institutions' capabilities to act in order to create business-friendly environments and increase entrepreneurial activities. The primary aim of the chapter is to formulate an adequate multi-criteria model for evaluation of institutional cooperation between business councils, as representatives of local authorities and the business community in observed LSG units. Results indicate inadequate quality and functionality of the business councils, although cooperation has been established between the business councils, as a local government institution, and representatives of business community. Data analysis is conducted using relevant statistical methods. For multi-criteria analysis of subjective preferences of Local Economic Development (LED) offices has been applied Analitic Hierarchy Process (AHP).

Chapter 19
Towards a Citizen-Centric E-Government Service Index Model: Developments and Impediments within the Egyptian Context 374
Mohamed R. Zakaria, Al Ghurair University, UAE
Tarek R. Gebba, Al Ghurair University, UAE
Mohamed Gamal Aboelmaged, Ain Shams University, Egypt

The purpose of this chapter is three-fold. First, it proposes a novel E-Government Service Index (ESI) that is a citizen-centric maturity model. Second, the model uses Egypt's E-Government services as an experimental arena to spot the maturity of the provided services and highlights e-government development in Egypt. Finally, the chapter explores the impediments of citizen-centric e-government implementation within the Egyptian context and recommends specific interventions within the frame of the proposed model.

Compilation of References 396

About the Contributors 441

Index 454

Preface

E-government is rapidly changing the way governmental services are provided to citizens and businesses. The increasing amount of data, regulations, policies, and their updates is resulting in a huge number of semi-structured heterogeneous documents including semantic and multilingual problems. On the other hand, globalization, migration, financial crisis, climate changes, and other natural hazards that may happen either locally or across the globe are putting new challenges to e-government (e.g. how to provide accurate information to citizens with respect to their constitutional laws and to businesses with respect to desired economic growth).

This book was motivated by the challenges that editors faced during the realization and management of the III44007 project1, the intentions of which are given in Randjelović et al., 2013; Šimić et al., 2014). This book focuses on e-government issues, challenges, and opportunities in modern era including but not limited only to citizen-centric requirements, adoption experiences, and technological opportunities. For years, these issues have been the focus of the e-government research community. This book gives a useful and comprehensive overview of such efforts and looks into the future.

WHAT IS UNIQUE ABOUT THIS BOOK

The 53 authors from all around the world give an excellent overview on what is going on in electronic government today. Their chapters address many actual and highly relevant topics as described in detail later on. During the preparation of the Table of Contents and especially writing this preface, the editors faced a number of ideas, topics, and different approaches mutually interconnected and cross-referenced. The aforementioned facts led us to conclude that this book has some unique characteristics. This book is unique in terms of its coverage, approaches, and comprehensive treatment of its subject matter. More specifically, this book aims to:

- Present a solid foundation for understanding the e-government challenges, adoption experiences, importance, benefits, and also prerequisites;
- Give a comprehensive overview of enabling technologies, their strengths, and weaknesses;
- Address existing challenges such as smart cities development, business process modeling in e-government, dealing with medical records, etc., and propose solutions;
- Offer a variety of application-oriented concepts and solutions, examples include B2G solutions, citizen-oriented climate changes warnings and advices, business process modeling in high education, etc.;
- Foresee trends and give visions about future research and expected results.

A large number of figures and real-world or running examples that the authors used to gain greater understanding and confidence in the presented research results represent special features of this book. In addition, the authors define a number of key terms mostly in their own way, whilst some of them have cited standardized and widely accepted definitions.

Behind unique characteristics of the book is the editorial team whose members are the symbiosis of professorship and research background, industrial and management experience, editorial background, and an extraordinary enthusiasm around the book project. As results, the editors engaged a huge Editorial Advisory Board with a dozen widely recognized experts from academia, industry, and standards body. In addition, many contributing authors are either experienced researchers or have backgrounds in topics addressed in this book.

BACKGROUND

Almost ten years ago, Reddick set up the goal of modern e-government (Reddick, 2005). The point was given to citizens' engagement in democracy. Instead of people on the streets, let governments make decision making more transparent. In addition, the starting point of every E-Business is the market, its needs, structure, mechanisms, and regulations (Dorloff & Kajan, 2012). We must also agree that target population (citizens, business, and the other government institutions) of a government interest might be seen as an important market whose needs should be met in the most suitable manner.

Since the time when the aforementioned paper by Reddick was published, many technological, social, and economic changes have occurred. The global economic crisis has stressed the world a lot; the use and influence of social networks and Web 2.0 has risen; and the Web itself, celebrating its 25th anniversary at the time this book was written, is going to reach its full potential in a reasonable future. In the meantime, many new e-government services have been developed, implemented, evaluated, abandoned, etc. Reviewing the literature, there are quite enough papers related to the guidelines and research in the e-government arena. Examples include papers about adoption (Belanger & Carter, 2009; Rashman & Randor, 2005), governance (Hartley, 2005), legal issues (Concha et al., 2012; Estevez & Janowski, 2013), ICT and public administration (Arendsen et al., 2014; Bertot et al., 2010; Danzinger & Andersen, 2002), etc. The comprehensive list of the most valuable papers on e-government may be found at ERGL (The E-Government Reference Library2) maintained by Dr. Hans Jochen Scholl at Washington University.

New Web technologies in forms of Web services (Papazoglou et al., 2007), Web 2.0 phenomenon and associated technologies (O'Reilly, 2009), Semantic Web as envisioned by its inventor (Berners-Lee et al., 2001), Web of things (Barnagi et al., 2013), and intelligent agents (Unland, 2012) give new opportunities for e-government issues and challenges. In addition, new challenges and opportunities behind new technologies are wide open for e-government business process modeling, enrichment, and monitoring. Despite some difficulties that have been recognized by the research community (Škrinjar & Trkman, 2013), there are several research efforts regarding Enterprise 2.0 that promise a new era of more efficient business (Errol et al., 2010; Faci et al., 2014; Kajan et al., 2014; Maamar et al., 2011, etc.).

A comprehensive overview of Web 2.0 opportunities and their added value in e-government is given in Chun et al. (2010). The authors emphasize added value preferences to e-government based on social media. These are information on source, service on demand, policy making with negotiation, and shared governance. Lee (2011) stated that the data is the most prominent value-added thing to e-business via

Web 2.0. This data comes every day over social networks, wikis, blogs, crowdsourcing, tagging, but also over mobile communications, with the emergent inputs taken by cameras, sensors, GPS, etc. As a result, we have a "Big Data" paradigm (Boyd & Crawford, 2013). Recent research shows that 2.5 x 10^{18} bytes of data is added every day, 90% of which is unstructured (Kim et al., 2014).

How can this data be organized, searched, retrieved, and used for better transparency and service delivery? Many research efforts are underway. They are based on natural language processing (Spies, 2015) and form so-called collective knowledge systems (Gruber, 2007). Such knowledge is also known as collective intelligence. That is the great opportunity to governments to listen to the people and take appropriate actions, using, for example, crowdsourcing (Brabham, 2008) or analyze sentiments expressed over social networks (an example is given in this book). This is a wide open research challenge and includes many topics such as data clustering, information retrieval, ontology matching, semantic issues, multilingual issues, etc.

In summary, this book covers many aforementioned aspects of e-government, as explained in the next section.

CONTENT AND FOCUS OF THE BOOK

Content and Organization

The 19 chapters of the book are grouped into 5 sections, which are briefly highlighted below. The 1st section, "E-Government Adoption: Issues, Challenges, Experiences," consisting of 5 chapters, sets up the general discussion about the main issues in electronic government from different angles. Starting with smart city challenges in the first chapter, this section further analyses various aspects of e-government adoption, such as predictive policing, dealing with big data and micro-foundations, governance, perceived usefulness, and user satisfaction, as well.

The 2nd section, "Business Process Modeling for E-Government Services," consists of 2 chapters that emphasize several multidisciplinary views and concepts of business process modeling in electronic government. Both chapters are focused around appropriate business process strategies for e-government. From a technological point of view, the section is based on BPMN requirements and technologies. From the applicability point of view, the first chapter in this section targets citizen understanding of business process models, while the second deals with business processes and their modeling that may be applied in high education. Overall, both chapters gave an inspiration view for business process modeling in e-government.

The 3rd section, "Harnessing the Citizen and E-Government Collective Intelligence," is the data-related heart of this book and the "middleware" between issues and challenges in e-government addressed in the two previous sections and application domains shown later, devoted to describe the added value possibilities of e-government services to the population.

Section 4, "E-Health: Issues and Solutions," has 3 chapters that concentrate on different aspects of data in electronic health. These aspects cover privacy-friendly management of medical records, observation of climate changes in order to advise people on how to take care of themselves, and an overview of e-health systems and devices for good life and health assistance. Despite that on the first sight these aspects are quite different, they have a common synergy: to help people to have good health as much as possible.

The 5th section, "Government-to-Business and -Citizen Communications and Services" also has 3 chapters. This section, despite different methodologies, is completely devoted to services in G2B and G2C domains. The first two chapters are focused around e-government investments, whilst the third chapter focuses on services maturity offered to citizens in the Egyptian context.

Topics Covered

This book addresses a large number of research topics in the arena of e-government. These are (in alphabetical order):

- Adoption
- Big Data, Business Process
- Citizen-Centered, Collective Intelligence, Crowdsourcing
- Data Clustering, Data Mining, Decision Making
- Electronic Health Record
- Governance
- ICT, Information Retrieval, Innovation, Interoperability
- Ontology
- Policymaking
- Sentiment Analysis, Service Delivery, Smart Cities, Social Innovation, Social Media
- Transparency

Topics listed are chosen by editors either as the most important or most frequent or most challenging. All chapters address at least three or four research issues, the most common of which are adoption, decision making, ICT, governance, social media, service delivery, etc.

In addition to their topics, the chapters are also differentiated by their attributes (i.e. by the ways they bring information and findings to readers). These vary from overall to very specific, analytical to experimental, with or without theoretical contributions and/or visions, etc. All in all, the variety of these attributes give a specific weight to the book content and quality.

A DEEPER VIEW OF THE SECTIONS

Section 1: E-Government Adoption – Issues, Challenges, Experiences

Chapter 1, "Smart Government: Opportunities and Challenges in Smart Cities Development," written by members of IEEE Computer Society E-Government Standard Technical Committee, gives an effective introduction to the book topics approaching and opening the fundamental questions about how to achieve sustainable, comfortable, and socially responsible living environments. The authors present the challenges faced when developing smart cities with special emphasis to interoperability. They presented the "SmartGovernment Ecosystem Matrix" in which the features of Open Government and Smart Cities will determine the *Smart Government* level and show the challenges and opportunities related to ICT adoption. Irreversible and mutually effective citizen-government communications lead to a complex form of governance that can be the best road to development on the national and regional levels. This is what we know as "smart governance," which is the immediate future of societies in this context.

Chapter 2, "Big Data and Innovation in the Delivery of Public Services: The Case of Predictive Policing in Kent," deals with adoption and implementation of predictive policing in Kent County Police, UK, as an instance of (early) application of Big Data in public sector organizations. Alberto Asquer highlights the opportunities of Big Data for designing and delivering more efficient and effective public policies and then introduces the predictive policing that is used as an early instance of Big Data application in Kent County (UK). The case shown in the chapter spots positive effects after a few months of experimentation. Furthermore, the author uses the case in order to analyze the difficulties during implementation of innovative practices. In summary, this chapter represents an excellent example of how new technologies and strategies mixed together may improve public services.

Chapter 3, "If We Build It, Will They Come? An Appreciation of the Microfoundations of E-Government," delves into the possible role of social, cultural, and institutional factors (microfoundations) as a determinant of electronic government. The authors, Ahn and McNutt, propose a theoretical framework consisting of six factors: social capital, financial capacity, social conditions, social values, citizen characteristics, and digital divide for measuring their influence to the quality of e-services and e-participation. Their findings confirm that the success of e-government does not solely depend on technological and financial resources. Instead, e-government should be viewed as nested within a broader social and institutional environment that influences the outcomes of e-government. As such, they suggest the aforementioned factors to be considered in e-government planning and development so that policymakers can make smarter and more successful choices.

Chapter 4, "Telecentres as a Medium for Good Governance in Rural India," written by Gaurav Mishra, focus on governance issues in rural areas, particularly in India. After discussion, what the "good governance" means or is supposed to be is emphasized in India, where good governance has been on the agenda of government reforms to achieve transparency, accountability, and improvement in various social development parameters. Pointing out that ICTs are recognized by governments throughout the world by their potential to improve economic and social progress, the author focuses on telecenters (community shared ICT services) as ways to deliver public services to rural areas. The chapter further gives a comprehensive overview of motivation, implementation, and sustainability challenges of such telecentres in rural India. The concluding section emphasizes that telecentres have become an appropriate medium for the delivery of government services in rural areas where citizens can access services irrespective of educational qualification or economic or social status.

Chapter 5, "Ensuring Continued Usage of an E-Government Service in Malaysia: The Role of Perceived Usefulness and User Satisfaction," provides a case study aiming to examine the continuance usage intention of e-filing system by taxpayers in Malaysia. An evaluation of the role of perceived usefulness and user satisfaction in ensuring the continuance usage intention of e-government services in Malaysia focusing on the e-filing system is given.

Section 2: Business Process Modeling for E-Government Services

The authors of Chapter 6, "Raising Citizen-Government Communication with Business Process Models," deals with delivering public services using business process models. The chapter is motivated by perspectives on the issues, controversies, and problems of presenting business process models to citizens and their effectiveness for understanding service delivery activities, responsibilities, rules, and outcomes. The authors focus on the design of service that may be understood by citizens, defining attributes of organizational transparency: *adaptability*, *intuitiveness*, *clarity*, *conciseness,* and *uniformity.* The business process design based on these attributes is demonstrated by two use cases, one devoted to research activities at a Brazilian university and the other intended for a specific student's needs. The approach has been tested using questionnaires of the target population. The authors argue that the given observations may explain how using process models and designing them for understanding can raise interaction among citizens and public institutions.

Chapter 7, "Towards the Integration of E-Government Processes in the University of Murcia: Business Process Strategy," provides another view and another use case for business process modeling in higher education. The aim of this chapter is to present a methodology for integrating e-government business processes over the SOA (Software-Oriented Architecture) developed in the University of Murcia, Spain. After a comprehensive overview of regulations set up by governments and available open-source tools, Re and Carreras focus on the business process strategy at the University of Murcia and on the Electra framework.

Section 3: Harnessing the Citizen and E-Government Collective Intelligence

This section starts with Chapter 8, "Collective Intelligence in a Computer-Mediated Environment," written by Luigi Lancieri. It brings an introduction to whole section devoted to harnessing collective intelligence in order to achieve better e-government outcomes. The author analyses several important aspects of collective intelligence and the role of modern media as well. He concludes that media can efficiently support the collective activity, modify the interactions between individuals, and finally, keep traces that are memory pieces witnessing the activity and interactions. Special emphasis is given to the strength of mediated services in order to make decision easily. Further, a critical approach regarding ethical and legal issues of interaction track use is also given. In the concluding remarks, Lainceri pointed out that, despite many open questions, everyone should understand that the opinion of the majority is crucial for good governance.

Chapter 9, "Open Social Innovation," draws our attention on a phenomenon that may be used as an entry point to address social needs. Social innovations manifest as changes in attitudes, perceptions, or behaviors, resulting in new social practices created collectively and intentionally targeted to a desired social objective, causing social change. On the other hand, open innovation by default is mainly devoted to business goals achievements. In this chapter, Martins and Bermejo explain how these two independent concepts interfere and how common synergy of both may be explored. It is supported by two examples, one from USA and another from Brazil. In the former case, crowdsourcing is used to harness the power of the Internet and social media through online engagement tools that connect public organizations and community members who might not be involved. In the later case, crowdstorming is used for greater societal involvement in the proposition, discussion, and evaluation of innovative ideas answering questions presented by governments and corporations.

The next four chapters deal with management, usage, and analysis of data populated either by citizens or by government. Chapter 10, "E-Government Documents and Data Clustering," by Goran Šimić, gives an excellent overview of unstructured text clustering. After the basic concepts, such as the text content representation, measure of document frequency, etc., the author concentrates on clustering taxonomies.

Further, text-clustering algorithms, such as K-Means and Fuzzy C-Mean, are presented. All are supported by the standard initiatives for content description and then by use case that describes clustering by ADVANSE framework. The chapter content is highly supported by 18 figures.

Chapter 11, "Semantic Framework for an Efficient Information Retrieval in the E-Government Repositories," written by Martin and Leon, deals with the another aspect of e-government data. Whilst the former chapter is devoted to data organization at most, this chapter is devoted to semantic information and knowledge retrieval in e-government repositories. Currently, there are no borders between these two concepts; they are mutually compatible and enhanced each other. This chapter specifically addresses the interoperability requirements, which further leads to ontology development and deployment. The presented use case illustrates the OntoloGOV prototype architecture intended to support semantic retrieval knowledge in Sevilla institutional repositories. The chapter finishes with a look at the research needs and offers perspectives.

In Chapter 12, "The German Electronic Identity Card: Lessons Learned," Christoph Sorge provides an analysis of the establishment of an electronic authentication infrastructure and presents possible reasons for the German eID card's lack of success. The background section covers the history of electronic identity cards and an overview of these in Germany, including security protocols, public-key infrastructure, security assessment, and adoption. Further, he focuses on costs and benefits of electronic identification infrastructure, discuses who should operate such an infrastructure, and analyses usefulness of electronic identity to e-government services. After a discussion devoted to electronic signatures, Sorge concentrates on lessons learned in Germany. He points out some reasons for limited adoption by German citizens. These include, but are not limited to, usability, trust, number of services supported, and the current state of the security of the overall system. As the conclusion, the author argues that the combination of a national identity card, an electronic authentication infrastructure, and an infrastructure for electronic signatures could still prove useful, but requires more investments and, in particular, the provision of beneficial services.

Chapter 13, "Sentiment Analysis, Social Media, and Public Administration," presents an interesting research on sentiment analyses over social media, particularly regarding FIFA World Cup hosted in 2014 by Brazil, but also related to other hot spots like health, transportation, education, etc. This research aims to propose a technique of sentiment analysis as a tool to allow public administrators to use information circulating on social media for strategic purposes. The presented findings motivated authors to argue that sentiment analysis can help public managers and elected representatives monitor public opinion on government and public services and create some improvements. In the end, the authors point to some limitations in their case study, such as the number of topics and terms defined.

Section 4: E-Health – Issues and Solutions

As Milica Milutinovic and Bart DeDecker highlight in Chapter 14, "Privacy-Friendly Management of Electronic Health Records in the eHealth Context," the main obstacles to electronic health record adoption are the privacy and security concerns of the users. In this chapter, the authors argue that the system presented provides a novel model that grants the users augmented control over their data. After outlining the system requirements, the authors present the underlying system architecture and its functionality. Protocols described allow e-Health systems to exchange records with medical organisations and other authorised healthcare providing entities. The proposed architecture also enables the patients to define their access control policies and to identify misuses.

Chapter 15, "Early Warning System and Adaptation Advice to Reduce Human Health Consequences of Extreme Weather Conditions and Air Pollution," written by Bogdanović and Lazarević, presents a meteorology warning system for citizens. The background section gives an overview of air pollution and pollutants and to their influence on human health. It also covers meteorological factors such as air temperature, atmospheric pressure, air humidity, etc. The main section presents the system functionality and gives some useful tips to users in order to prevent negative influences of extreme weather conditions and air pollution. The system is intended for general and vulnerable population groups in the cities of Serbia. At this stage, the system has been implemented on the website of the Institute of Occupational Medicine in Niš and will be offered in other towns in Serbia

Chapter 16, "E-Health: Current Status and Future Trends," focuses on e-Health solutions for chronic diseases, proposing a number of predictable future trends and scenarios. After the short background related to ICT in healthcare, the authors concentrate on telemonitoring and self-management of chronic diseases. A number of devices and systems used to support caregivers, care organizations, and patients are presented. Concluding remarks highlight some open research issues and future trends.

Section 5: Government-to-Business and -Citizen Communications and Services

Chapter 17, "Evaluating E-Government Initiatives: An Approach Based upon the Appropriation of Tangible and Intangible Benefits," deals with a method to better analyze e-government initiatives based upon intangibles and on the incremental fundings of ICT projects. The background section gives an overview of the research on tangible and intangible benefits and on incremental funding of ICT projects. Then the authors introduce the case of a parking space booking system, supported by another system, "motor-vehicle fining." In the former, the goal was to reduce unnecessary traffic across the center of particular city, whilst the later system intended to fine law-breaking drivers. Due to many complaints given to the major office, the city developed a third system. The authors then analyze benefits of each project, after dividing them into subprojects, and summarize the proposed method.

Chapter 18, "Impact of Local Self-Government Institutions on Creating a Business-Friendly Environment: Multi-Criteria Analysis," discuses multi-criteria analysis of the specific local economic development problem in Serbia. The problem analyzed is about creating business-friendly environments for new investments. After an introduction to the problem, the authors describe the existing legal framework that regulates institutional cooperation between the business community and local self-government. Further, they present a research methodology. The research was carried out on the sample of 56 cities and municipalities in Serbia, and it was based on a specific questionnaire (given in the appendix of the chapter). Using *analytical process hierarchy* method, the authors argue that the business councils in observed local self-government units in Serbia do not carry out their activities in an efficient and effective manner, and the authors propose an improvement of the local units' functionality by observing the concrete needs of the local economy.

Chapter 19, "Towards a Citizen-Centric E-Government Service Index Model: Developments and Impediments within the Egyptian Context," proposes a citizen-centric maturity model. After an overview of appropriate maturity models, the authors focus on a research model applied to Egypt as an example of a developing country. The model they present is the E-Government Service Index Model (ESI). They find that the Egyptian e-government portal offers 43 services via 23 service providers, but 6 of them have no presence at all, 6 are informative only, whilst the rest of the services are transactional. Further, the authors gave an overview of e-government development in Egypt, its readiness, and impediments to citizen-centric e-government implementation. The presented ESI model recommends specific interventions on e-government services that may help policymakers in Egypt develop a coherent strategic vision for the future to overcome the barriers to developing a successful e-government

WHO SHOULD USE THIS BOOK?

The target audience of this book is composed of researchers, teachers, practitioners, managers, and undergraduate and PhD students in various e-government programs. From a research point of view, the analysis of the e-government adoption problems, which are given in many chapters, many original results, the background and reference sections, etc. are valuable sources. From the educational point of view, the overview of problems and enabling technologies and many definitions of key terms present good teaching and learning material in one place. From the practical point of view, the experiences and use cases that are behind many chapter findings are of particular advantage.

Ćemal Dolićanin
State University of Novi Pazar, Serbia

Ejub Kajan
State University of Novi Pazar, Serbia

REFERENCES

Arendsen, R., Peters, O., ter Hedde, M., & van Dijk, J. (2014). Does e-government reduce the administrative burden of businesses? An assessment of business-to-government systems usage in the Netherlands. *Government Information Quarterly*, *31*(1), 160–169.

Barnagi, P., Sheth, A., & Henson, C. (2013). Web of things. *IEEE Intelligent Computing*, *28*(6), 6–11.

Bélanger, F., & Carter, L. (2009). The impact of the digital divide on e-government use. *Communications of the ACM*, *52*(4), 132–135.

Berners-Lee, T., Hendler, J., & Lassila, O. (2001, May). The semantic web. *Scientific American*, 29–37. PMID:11323639

Bertot, J. C., Jaeger, P. T., & Grimes, J. M. (2010). Using ICTs to create a culture of transparency: E-government and social media as openness and anti-corruption tools for societies. *Government Information Quarterly*, *27*(3), 264–271.

Boyd, D., & Crawford, K. (2012). Critical questions for big data. *Information Communication and Society*, *15*(5), 662–679.

Brabham, C. D. (2008). Crowdsourcing as a model for problem solving: An introduction and cases. *The International Journal of Research into New Media Technologies*, *14*, 75–90.

Chun, S. A., Shulman, S., Sandoval, S., & Hovy, E. (2010). Government 2.0: Making connections between citizens, data and government. *Information Polity*, *15*(1-2), 1–9.

Concha, G., Astudillo, H., Porrúa, M., & Pimenta, C. (2012). E-government procurement observatory, maturity model and early measurements. *Government Information Quarterly*, *29*(1), 43–50.

Danziger, J. N., & Andersen, K. V. (2002). The impacts of information technology in public administration: An analysis of empirical research from the "golden age" of transformation. *International Journal of Public Administration*, *25*(5), 591–625.

Dorloff, F.-D., & Kajan, E. (2012). Balancing of heterogeneity and interoperability in e-business networks: The role of standards and protocols. *International Journal of E-Business Research*, *8*(4), 15–33.

Erol, S., & Granitzer, M., Happ, Jantunen, S., Jennings, B., Johannesson, P., … Schmidt, R. (2010). Combining BPM and social software: Contradiction or chance? *Journal of Software Maintenance and Evolution: Research and Practice*, *22*(6-7), 449–476.

Estevez, E., & Janowski, T. (2013). Electronic governance for sustainable development — Conceptual framework and state of research. *Government Information Quarterly*, *30*(1), 94–109.

Faci, N., Maamar, Z., Kajan, E., & Benslimane, D. (2014). Research roadmap for the enterprise 2.0 – Issues & solutions. *Scientific Publications of the State University of Novi Pazar Ser. A: Appl. Math., Inform. and Mech.*, *6*(2).

Gruber, T. (2007). Collective knowledge systems: Where the social web meets the semantic web. *Web Semantics: Science, Services, and Agents on the World Wide Web*, *6*(1), 4–13.

Hartley, J. (2005). Innovation in governance and public services: Past and present. *Public Money and Management*, *25*(1), 27–34.

Kajan, E., Faci, N., Maamar, Z., Loo, A., Pljaskovic, A., & Sheng, Q. Z. (2014). The network-based business process. *IEEE Internet Computing*, *18*(2), 63–69.

Kim, G.-H., Trimi, S., & Chung, J.-H. (2014). Big-data applications in the government sector. *Communications of the ACM*, *57*(3), 78–85.

Lee, I. (2011). Overview of emerging web 2.0-based business models and web 2.0 applications in business: An ecological perspective. *International Journal of E-Business Research*, *7*(4), 1–16.

Maamar, Z., Hacid, H., & Huhns, M. N. (2011, March/April). Why web services need social networks. *IEEE Internet Computing*, 90–94.

O'Reilly, T. (2009). What is web 2.0? In Design patterns and business models for the new generation of software. Sebastopol, CA: O'Reilly Radar.

Papazoglou, M. P., Traverso, P., Schahram, D., & Leymann, F. (2007). Service-oriented computing: State of the art and research challenges. *Computer*, *40*(11), 38–45.

Randjelović, D., Kajan, E., & Dolićanin, Ć. (2013). An approach to governance and policy making architectural framework. *Scientific Publications of the State University of Novi Pazar Ser. A: Appl. Math. Inform. and Mech.*, *5*(2), 111–123.

Rashman, L., & Radnor, Z. (2005). Learning to improve: Approaches to improving local government services. *Public Money and Management*, *25*(1), 19–26.

Reddick, G. C. (2005). Citizen interaction with e-government: From the streets to servers? *Government Information Quarterly*, *22*(1), 38–57.

Šimić, G., Jeremić, Z., Kajan, E., Randjelović, D., & Presnall, A. (2014). A framework for delivering e-government support. *Acta Polytechnica Hungarica*, *11*(1), 79–96.

Škrinjar, R., & Trkman, P. (2013). Increasing process orientation with business process management: Critical practices. *International Journal of Information Management*, *33*(1), 48–60.

Spies, M. (2015). (forthcoming). Towards an open software architecture for interleaved knowledge and natural language processing. *Scientific Publications of the State University of Novi Pazar Ser. A: Appl. Math. Inform. and Mech.*, *7*(1).

Unland, R. (2012). Interoperability support for ebusiness applications through standards, services and multiagents systems. In *Handbook of research on e-business standards and protocols: Documents, data and advanced web technologies* (pp. 129–153). Hershey, PA: IGI Global.

ENDNOTES

1. "New information technologies for analytical decision-making based on the organization of experiments and observations, and their application in biological, economic and social systems" project III44007, funded by the Ministry of Education, Science and Technological Development of the Republic of Serbia.
2. http://faculty.washington.edu/jscholl/egrl/index.php.

Acknowledgment

We would like to thank all the people involved in the development and review process of the book, especially those who served on the EAB in an excellent, very useful, and inspirational manner. Many of the authors of the chapters contributed to the review process for chapters written by other authors. Thanks go to all those who provided constructive and comprehensive reviews. We would like to thank all the authors for their contributions.

We would like to express special thanks to the third group of researchers who took part in the review process by answering our personal call for help: Prof. Stephen Aikins from University of South Florida, Prof. Sanford Borins, University of Toronto, Dominic Chalmers from University of Strathclyde, UK, Prof. Wichian Chutimaskul from King Mongut's University of Technology, Prof. Radovan Čekanac from Military Medical Academy Belgrade, Prof. Luitzen De Boer from Norwegian Institute of Science and Technologies, Dr. Steve Drew from Griffith University, Dr. Francisco Flores, University of Huelva, Marian Harbach from Hannover University, Prof. Borisav Jošanov from Novi Sad Business School, Prof. Zoran Milošević from University of Niš, Prof. Andrzej Romanowski from Lodz University of Technology, and Athanasios Vasilakos from Kuwait University.

Special thanks go to Kayla Wolfe, Jan Travers, and Allison McGinniss at IGI Global for their great support. Special thanks also go to the publishing team at IGI Global, whose contributions throughout the whole process from the initial idea to the final publication have been invaluable.

Ćemal Dolićanin
State University of Novi Pazar, Serbia

Ejub Kajan
State University of Novi Pazar, Serbia

Dragan Randjelović
Academy for Criminalistic and Police Studies, Serbia

Boban Stojanović
University of Niš, Serbia

Section 1

E-Government Adoption:

Issues, Challenges, Experiences

Chapter 1
Smart Government:
Opportunities and Challenges in Smart Cities Development

Carlos E. Jiménez
IEEE Computer Society E-Government STC

Héctor Puyosa
IEEE Computer Society E-Government STC

Francisco Falcone
IEEE Computer Society E-Government STC

Saleem Zoughbi
IEEE Computer Society E-Government STC

Agusti Solanas
IEEE Computer Society E-Government STC

Federico González
IEEE Computer Society E-Government STC

ABSTRACT

The advent of Smart Cities is one of the greatest challenges and field of opportunities in the goal to achieve sustainable, comfortable, and socially responsible living environments. A large number of factors, spanning from government/administration/citizen interaction models, heterogeneous communication network, interoperability, or security determine the capabilities and functionalities that can be deployed. In this chapter, different factors in the implementation and adoption of E-Government within Smart City scenarios are described. The authors include the Interoperability Principle as a part of the Open Government concept and link this concept with the Smart Cities view. Then, they describe a new model of public organization that they call "Intelligent," characterized by the "Smart Government," and they propose a matrix with the elements of this model. Then, the authors analyze the technical and infrastructure dimensions of the matrix.

INTRODUCTION

Efficiency, effectiveness, sustainability, and citizen-centric services are obligations that governments need to fulfill. In order to achieve them, society and governments need to understand that everything is interconnected in our society nowadays. Concepts, actors and institutions, systems, environments, energy, citizens, infrastructures, information, policy and technology are elements or subsystems that are interweaved within a larger system, which needs to adopt the key of the governance efficiently. We refer to a system of systems within our current Information & Knowledge Society's context.

DOI: 10.4018/978-1-4666-7266-6.ch001

The evolution in population distribution is heading towards the increase in the amount of people living in large urban areas. This poses one of the biggest challenges for mankind: achieving sustainable cities as well as increasing the quality of life of such environments, in which the local government is the closest to citizens. Administrations have the responsibility to provide the best public services to citizens. They can more easily know and understand their needs, and foresee the best way to satisfy them. The local government is the government of cities and, in this context, it has the key to transmit and provide their services to the citizenship by using off-the-shelves tools for a true and real adoption of the governance paradigm.

The nexus between Government & Governance and Citizenship & Cities within the Information & Knowledge Society are keys of a new view of our world as a "system" in which its optimal status should be to achieve the highest degree of governance within a city, in which their benefits are maximized and their disadvantages are minimized. The first key, should be associated with the adoption of the governance paradigm from the Open Government and, the second one, should be associated with an intelligent way to understand our environment as a Smart City. Both together are the optimized level of a new ecosystem within the public organizations, characterized by an open & smart government, where ICT and interoperability are powerful tools. The implementation of a Smart City is a complex task that requires a multidisciplinary approach. In this chapter, we provide a holistic view following a top-down approach so as to present the characteristic elements of Smart Cities and the challenges that have to be faced in their deployment from an ICT & Infrastructure perspective.

In this chapter, different factor in the implementation and adoption of e-Government within Smart City scenarios will be described. We will include the Interoperability Principle as a part of the Open Government concept and we link this concept with the Smart Cities view. Then, we will describe a new model of public organization that we call "Intelligent", characterized by the "Smart Government", and we propose a matrix with the elements of this model. Then, we analyze the technical and infrastructure dimensions of the matrix.

From the Open Government to Smart Government

Transparency, collaboration, and participation are elements identified as Open Government principles included within the perspective of Obama (2009). In addition and related to IT adoption, from a public organization perspective, according to Jiménez & Gascó (2012) we can understand Open Government as an evolution of e-Government, in which the governance paradigm is achieved, and the ICT role and its degree of adoption is a key driver that has important implications. In fact, we are in front of key tools that give us the possibilities to transform into a reality, the term used since the 50's of the 20th Century (Parks, 1957): the Open Government. In this sense, according to Jiménez & Gascó (2012) "the Open Government is given by characteristics that turns it into an unprecedented fact, related with its openness high level (…) the new perspective, from our view, it is not based in the objectives but in its tools used to achieve it". In this sense, we see ICT as a driver, an integral driver that has transformed and (it is yet transforming) our society and all its elements. The level of change will depend on its degree of adoption.

Information and Communications Technologies, as drivers, mean an important view of the back office within the context of Open Government, but it is a "hide side", and we see the special need for focusing and analyzing this key side from the ICT as a driver. From this view, within the Open Government view there is a principle that harmonizes the key elements of governance and the back office, a key and critical factor for the achievements of e-Government in a broad sense, an element that has evolved from the technical view into a transversal view within public organizations: the interoperability.

We understand interoperability as the true key of the back office. European Union (2009) defines interoperability as "the ability of disparate and diverse organizations to interact towards mutually beneficial and agreed common goals, involving the sharing of information and knowledge between the organizations, through the business processes they support, by means of the exchange of data between their respective ICT systems". In fact, interoperability is one of the most complex elements related to Governance. From the perspective of e-Government, this element and all its dimensions have been keys in this area in last year's.

According to Jiménez (2013), we see interoperability as a required principle so as to have an integral concept for an Open Government, and strongly related to the three principles of the Obama memorandum. We understand that the Interoperability Principle is the projection of the open government philosophy within the back office, as well as intelligent governance. In fact, our view of an integral Smart Government is a new level from an incremental view driven by the ICT role, for the public organization, that we add to the three-level model that Gascó (2007) proposed. Based on that model, we add the fourth modernization phase, characterized by the inclusion of the achievement of the interoperability as a principle, as well as the inclusion of the variables that would define it as the public dimension of the smart cities for an smart governance. The transformation of a public organization will be based on four key principles: Interoperability, Transparency, Collaboration, and Participation (Table 1).

Now, we understand the concept of Open Government included within Smart Governance (Jiménez, 2013a) Indeed, we understand that there is no smart government without open government. Smart Governance should be characterized by an ecosystem composed by the evolution of the characteristics of both key components (Open Government and Smart City) linked into a new system within the public organization.

Related to governance, we should be able to decide how much "open" a government is. An indicator or a benchmark has to be adopted whereby a government can be measured as to how much "open" the same way we measure the e-readiness of e-governments.

One method in which the degree of governance of countries is by quantifying the World Governance Indicator (WGI), obtained by six dimensions of governance starting in 1996: Voice and Accountability, Political Stability and Absence of Violence/Terrorism, Government Effectiveness, Regulatory Quality, Rule of Law, and Control of Corruption, as described in Kaufmann et al. (2010). Adopting the WGI, for

Table 1. Public organizations model, modernization phases, and ICT-driver role

Organization	Modernization Phase	ICT Role
1. Bureaucratic	Initial. Target: Winning efficiency and effectiveness.	Automatization of workflows and reorganization of internal processes. (**eAdministration**).
2. Professional	Advanced. Adopting the public management perspective (emphasizing efficiency but citizen service too).	Without forgetting the previous phase, now ICT help to interact with citizens through websites and portals. (**eGovernment**).
3. Relational	Adopting the governance paradigm (a citizen isn't just a client but it participates within the governability processes and procedures).	Key related to transparency and accountability on one hand and, on the other hand related to institutional collaboration. (**Open Government**).
4. Intelligent	Adopting the Interoperability Principle maximizing efficiency.	Interconnected "ecosystem" and management (**Smart Government**)

example, one can see that on a scale of -2.5 to +2.5 world governments are rated through the World Bank governance indicator, and hence out of over 200 government in the world, one can see for example that Finland (+2.25) in 2011 rated as #1 in effective governance in the world while Somalia (-2.16) rated as the last, as stated by the WGI Cross Country Indicators (2011). Hence we cannot assume that with the proper technology and policy we can implement an open government in any country in the same way. There is a degree of freedom that implementation can proceed with. In some autocratic police states there is no way to implement a truly open government. It is logical to set two thresholds, for example, α and β, such that

$$-2.5 \leq \alpha,\beta \leq +2.5 \text{ and } \alpha<\beta$$

where all governments with an indicator below α are not ready for open government development, while countries with WGI higher than β can be seen as "too much open" to implement an open government with a reasonable amount of control. In fact, one can describe these countries as very open, least restrictions, and unless we view them as ideal states one is tempted to think there is no "need" for a government in such cases.

Smart Government and the Smart City View

A unique definition of Open Government (Wilson & Linders, 2011) or Smart City (Chourabi, et al., 2012) does not exist, but nevertheless there are key concepts and characteristics generally agreed, related with them.

A city is much more than its government, but its governance is one of its key elements in order to become smart. The concept of smart city is maybe the most novel concept dealt with in this

Figure 1. World governance versus open government opportunities

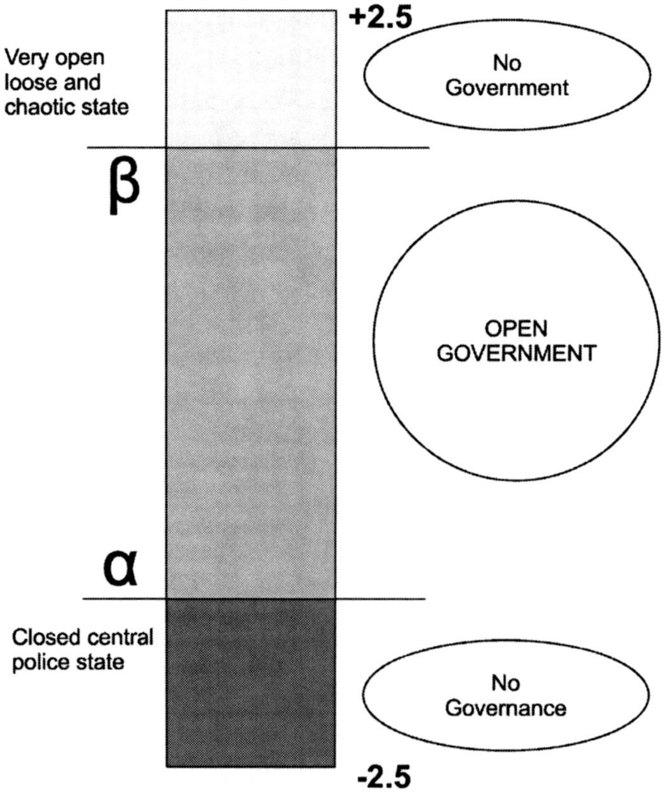

context. Related to the concept of smart city Chourabi, *et al.* (2012) it is conceptualized both in practical as well as in academic terms. There are some common variables that are included in different degrees, but it is stated that "it could be thought of as a large organic system connecting many subsystems and components". Related with the view of a city as a system and its smart characteristic Mitchell (2007) states the following "The new intelligence of cities, then, resides in the increasingly effective combination of digital telecommunication networks (the nerves), ubiquitously embedded intelligence (the brains), sensors and tags (the sensory organs), and software (the knowledge and cognitive competence)".

Related to the concept of smart city, among the major factors in controlling sustainability, energy and water consumption are the most relevant, without forgetting increased accessibility for all (Ando, 2008).Moreover, cities exhibit complex energy grids, in which common elements, such as city lighting or climate control systems can be optimized (Dugan, 2011). Transportation systems also account for a large part of energy consumption, with an impact on pollution levels as well as on the travel times and traffic congestion (Bodhani, 2012). Quality of living and the well being of the inhabitants cities is a one of the main goals to achieve, in which information systems play a key role. A large variety of communication networks, spanning from body and personal area networks to the holistic view of Internet of Things coexist and produce a huge amount of information.

In order to optimize resource management as well as to increase living quality, the concept of Smart City, as an interactive and dynamic urban ecosystem comes to place, completely integrated with environment (Zambonelli, 2012), in great deal possible due to the advances in communication networks (broadband access, mobile networks and Internet of Things), with the development of adaptive computer systems and the advent of advanced nanoelectronics to produce smarter devices (Feki *et al.*, 2013) and the unprecedented success and power of social networks and Web 2.0, as well as concepts as Open Innovation applied to public organizations (Chesbrough & Vanhaberbeke, 2011). Therefore, the combination of integral resource management as well as the increase in governance and participation can be considered the founding elements within the concept of Smart Cities.

From a back office perspective and related to the implementation of a Smart City strategy, it requires, as previously stated, the control and interconnection of a number of systems, from energy grids, water and waste management, transportation systems and communication systems, schematically depicted in Figure 2.

Related with its challenges, (Robinson, 2012) highlights:

1. The efficient electric energy generation and usage (which can be optimized by means of smart grids and smart metering techniques, efficient street lighting and building automation strategies);
2. Transportation Systems (hybrid technologies and full electric transport systems, intelligent traffic control systems and public transportation);
3. Water and waste management (close monitoring of water distribution networks and the deployment of water control systems, recycling strategies);
4. Communication systems (gather information and to provide variables for effective control, managing the communication networks typology –personal, by capacity, by end user access, by physical channel, hybrid, etc- that forms a high complex communication ecosystem);
5. Data handling and data processing (with the aid of the multiple communication systems, a very large amount of data is generated). But we have to pay attention in other dimensions and their important consequences, as

Figure 2. Representation of the systems involved in the adoption of a Smart City concept, in which Resource Management as well as Open Government are key drivers

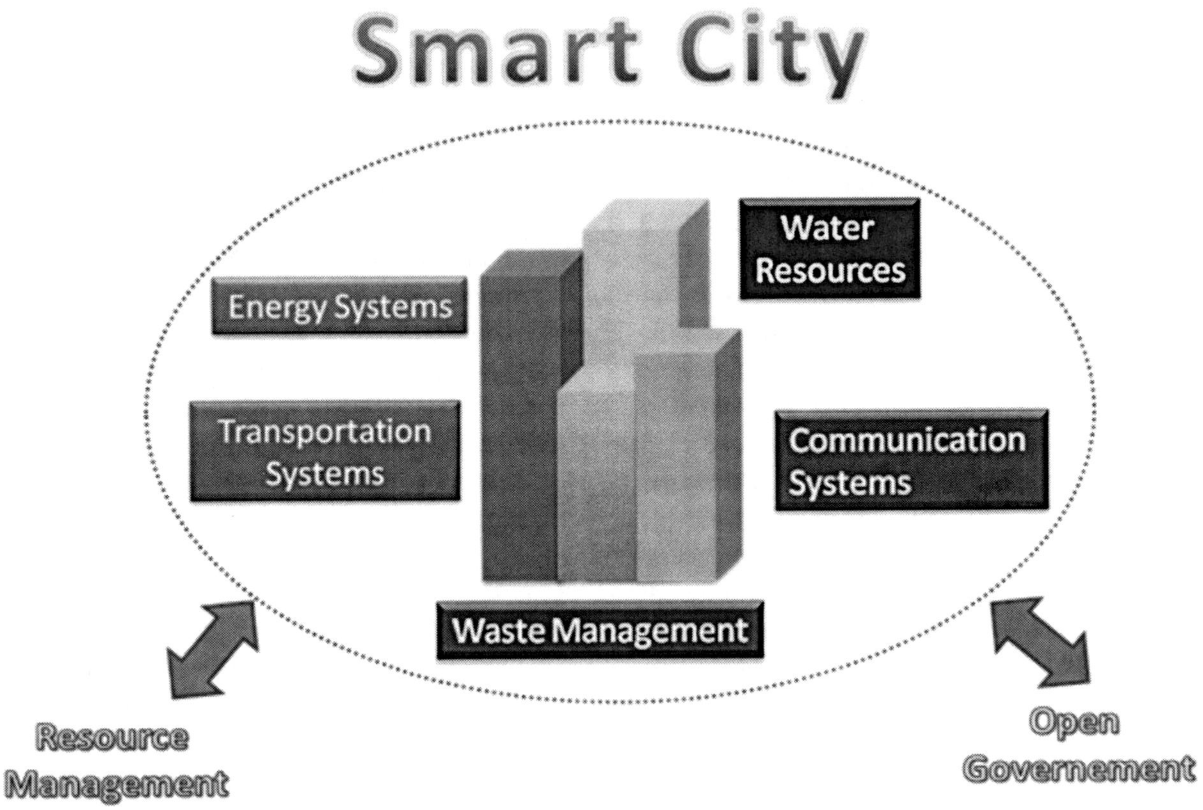

Gavaldà & Ribera-Fumaz (2012) shows, related the social impact of Smart City policies in the Barcelona City case.

Frameworks have been studied for governance of smart cities (Ojo et al., 2012). We consider interesting at this point, to include here the integrative framework that (Chourabi, *et al.*, 2012) propose for smart cities, a framework that we will use as a tool in order to specify key elements within our smart government ecosystem. As we stated previously, a transversal and integrative view is essential at this point. The framework employed proposes initially eight areas as basis: management and organization, technology, governance, policy context, people and communities, economy, infrastructure, and natural environment.

At this point and related with the areas of such framework, a new version is proposed herein which, on the one hand, technology and infrastructure are together and, on the other hand, governance and policy, both are within the same area. In addition, we identify people and communities with an area that we are naming "social". As stated in Chourabi, et al. (2012), we can associate different elements and critical factors to the six areas of the framework that we propose, where some of its factors could pertain to two or more different areas. Now, the framework's areas and factors proposed here are:

- **Organizational and Management:** Change management, conflicts management, organizational dimension of interoperability, or resources management.

- **Technology and Infrastructure:** Integration, technological dimensions of interoperability (Jiménez, Criado, & Gascó, Technological e-Government Interoperability. An Analysis of IberoAmerican Countries, 2011), green IT, smart grid, big data, security, or privacy.
- **Governance and Policy:** Institutional and inter-institutional collaboration, participation, transparency, or interoperability governance, where its legal dimension is included.
- **Social:** Digital divide, participation, communication, quality of life, or accessibility.
- **Economy:** Efficiency, costs, investment, or ROI.
- **Environment:** Natural conservation, sustainability.

In a way, open government is concerned with citizen and government collaboration whereas smart cities are concerned with improving quality of life of its inhabitants. This becomes a good combination that, in fact, according to Gartner group (Di Maio, 2012) it is envisaged that in post 2015 the evolution of open government and smart cities, should integrate into a so-called" smart government" where Public-Private-People Partnership (Ahmed & Ali, 2006) it would be an important element. In this regard the limitation of being local for cities or national disappears, and instead we consider a government that focuses on sustainability, agility and blending technologies such as information, operational and communications technologies. This is normally carried out across multiple domains in different process areas and jurisdictions to generate sustainable public value.

Certainly, the future of open government and smart cities lies within the smart government. This is the great challenge that will shape the development of governance in the next generation.

Holistic Approach

The analysis of Smart Governance and its relation with the concept of Smart Cities or even Smart Regions requires a multidisciplinary approach in order to fully understand and hence provide optimal solutions in terms of required resources as well as obtained results. Traditionally, aspects of governance models, public administration, social-economic implications and technological requirements are analyzed in a separate way. This can be in part due to the fact that until recently, technical developments were not easily accessible to the general public. In the last decade, there has been a strong adoption by the general audience of technological elements such as Internet, interactive devices and mobile devices, leading to a scenario in which technology is commonplace. Moreover, reduction in fabrication costs has enabled mass production and global availability of a wide range of personal computing devices and mobile communication devices, which in turn has opened the way to new forms of social interaction. Therefore, by considering the characteristics and performance of available technologies and their application to context aware scenarios, the economic, administrative and social impact can be derived. In this chapter, such multidisciplinary vision is applied in order to provide insight on the benefits and limitations that existing technology offers in the adoption of e-Government within Smart Cities.

The initial step is to describe the main variables that must be assessed in the establishment of a Smart Government framework, following a description of the elements and role of Information and Communication Technologies in such framework.

The Smart Government Ecosystem Matrix

Based in the smart city areas and factors abovementioned, as well as the open government principles, we propose the Smart Government as the highest modernization phase of the public organizations, evolved from Open Government. In this sense, we propose a Smart Government Matrix that would determine the mix of the key variables (Table 2). As we can see, the matrix is composed by the open government principles (where we have included the Interoperability Principle) as key drivers within the public dimension of smart city, as well as the key ties from the new smart city framework proposed. The relevance of the dimension is given, in qualitative terms, by the size of the corresponding dot within the matrix (i.e., larger dots imply bigger relevance). It is important to say as we stated initially in this chapter- that we are focusing the chapter's view mainly on the back office, thinking about the ICT role as key driver, which has the potentiality to transform public organizations. This is the reason that in this chapter, within our matrix we will specially highlight the Interoperability Principle of Open Government, and the Technology & Infrastructure Tie of the Smart City Framework[1] where, interoperability has an important technology component and weight.

Related with the consequences of the Interoperability Principle within the ecosystem, this element harmonizes all its actual concepts, elements and dimensions, integrated within different abstraction levels, where information is the true core, with a key role for public organization. This approach will harmonize many of the policies that could be readily interoperable not only from one city to another, but also from one region to another leading to a more inter-regional e-governance.

An up-to-down view of these interoperability ties embedded, is depicted in Figure 3, showing Interoperability Strategy (Public Policy); Interoperability Framework and its technical, organizational and semantic dimensions; the next ones would include elements as ontologies, open data or big data (related with semantics) leading in the end to a diversity of elements and datasets.

At this point, it is important to highlight that now we are viewing our ecosystem from a back office view, in which elements usually do not exhibit clearly defined boundaries and, there for gradual nexus with other elements must be considered. Within this complex framework, it is now possible to focus on the key challenges from a Smart Governance view, related to the elements within the matrix previously depicted in Figure 2.

KEY ELEMENTS AND CHALLENGES FROM ICT-DRIVER ROLE

From the back office and related to the technology and infrastructure tie and the interoperability principle, the key topics where special attention is required will be detailed: interoperability, architecture, cybersecurity, data processing, and semantics and privacy.

Table 2. Smart Government ecosystem matrix; technology and infrastructure tie

Open Gov Smart City	Transparency	Collaboration	Participation	Interoperability
Organizational & Management				
Technology & Infrastructure	•	•	•	•
Governance & Policy				
Social				
Economy				
Natural Environment				

Figure 3. Layers with some of its interoperability components

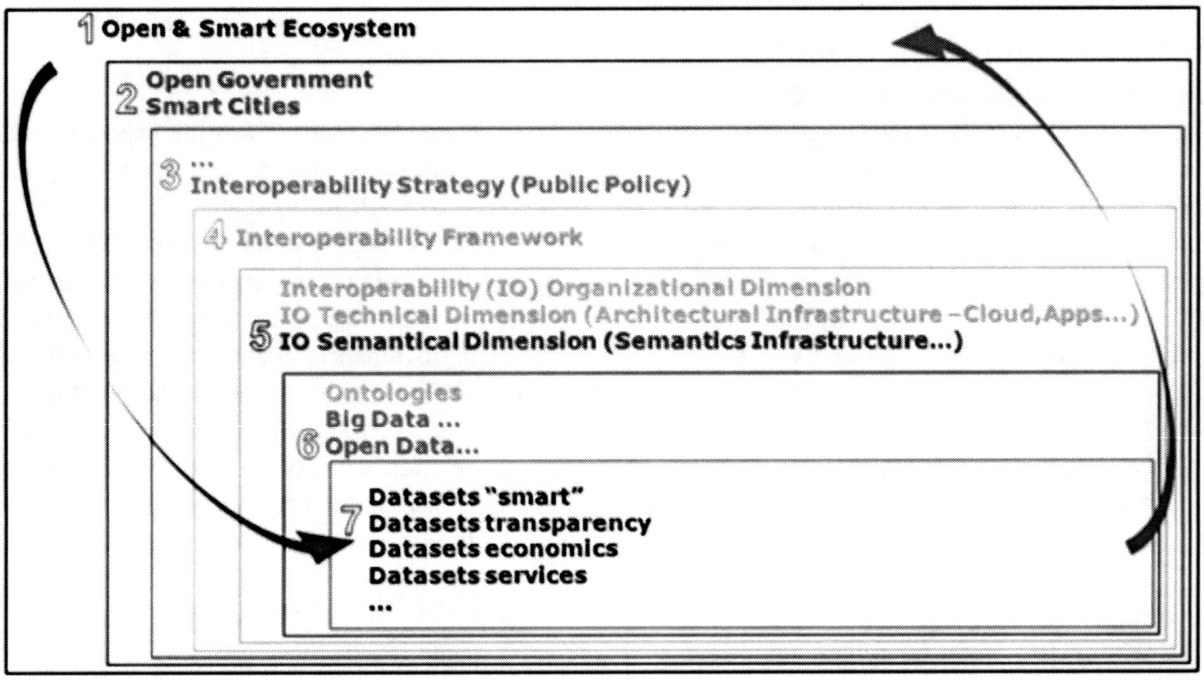

Interoperability

Interoperability components and its different dimension and elements play a key role. Several technological (but not only technological) setups would have to interface with a multitude of technical implementations across the government and city processes including inter-city arrangements. It is clear that unless they are fully interoperable the performance and outcomes would be deeply affected. One could say that interoperability is an integral part of the "smartness" of the city, and hence of the government. This could not be viewed in pure technical terms as other concerns of interoperability among regular information systems because of a major reason: governance also has to be interoperable. In other words, regulations, procedures and services have to be mapped interchangeably yet allowing e-governors to reconfigure peculiarities according to its needs. What is interesting to note at this point is that the "smartness of the government" through its agility and sustainability would allow citizens as well as government and city entities to have some degree of ability to fine-tune configurations to make interoperability work directly for their benefit, rather than waiting for systems to do so. This is the kind of seamless nature of smart governments.

There is still a significant way ahead to develop such interoperability, as there is need to develop and undertake holistic strategies addressing all related issues in a comprehensive manner. Related to a holistic view of interoperability the Iberoamerican Interoperability Framework (Jiménez et al. 2011) shows such view and the elements that would provide an excellent opportunity for countries of the region to develop technical e-government projects from different points of view, within groups of countries or sectorial policies. In large areas of similar cities and societies such framework is essential to adopt, considering smart governance of the region.

Systems Architecture

ICT infrastructure is the base in which other Smart City infrastructures layers are leaning. We can identify architecture with the "configuration" of systems and technologies. A flexible and secure coordination of ICT infrastructure is needed to connect among them urban infrastructures, service infrastructures and people. We could say that ICT architecture in place for Smart City has four major components or domains (Bartoli *et al.*, 2011):

- **Data/Information:** Includes information related to users, home, industry, business and services. Analysis of that information could be used to provide city intelligence to optimize resources or identify areas of improvements. Information could be any sort of data produced by human or devices likes sensor or computer systems.
- **Application:** Includes machine-to-machine application and human application being used for monitoring physical assets to support services, process, industrial production, home or building automation, geographic information systems, etc.
- **Network:** It is the communication infrastructure used to connect (communicate) information, application and city's management components by means of different technology to access and transport data and exchange information.
- **Management:** It is related to the management of city's information and application. It defines the relationship, rules and policies between information and application components.

In the case of Smart Cities the expected role of wired infrastructure is limited as the main backbone to handle heavy data traffic and people data exchange applications. Wireless access is supposed to continue growing taking advantage of its relative better cost position and expected technology improvement to tackle current challenges. Table 3 summarizes different access technologies.

Machine to Machine, M2M, end-to-end network enable devices or smart nodes to be communicated without human intervention. This concept implies different nodes interacting in an autonomous way following self-organization rules, it shall satisfy power efficiency and reliability requirements to seamless operates. A machine could be a device like a sensor which through a communication network interact with another machine, a computer, which extract, process gathered information and automatically controls and provide instruction to other machines like a final control element, a valve. M2M networks allow to coordinate applications and devices which could be public or private. The management component reinforces a security policy to restrict notification and access to sensitive or private data, information and/or control commands just to those smart nodes with the level of authorization and appropriate credentials.

Current wireless cellular solutions were designed for Human-to-Human communication.

Table 3. Access network; element connecting sensor and actuators

Access Network	Description	Available Solution
Satellite	Satellite communication	GPS, GIS.
Wired	Dedicated cabling between sensor/ actuator and gateway	Cable, DSL/ADSL, Fibre Optic, Power Line Communication (PLC).
Wireless cellular	Dedicated cellular link	GSM, GPRS, EDGE, UMTS, LTE, WiMAX.
Wireless capillary	Shared short range link/network	WLAN, ZigBee, IEEE 802.15.4x

Utilization for M2M connections requires a paradigm change. In (Dohler *et al.*, 2010) the authors summarize M2M challenges and work being done for leading technical task groups and standards developing organizations on cellular and capillary M2M, ETSI, 3GPP, IEEE and ITF. Table 4 shows current focus by technologies.

A wide range of applications (urban infrastructure, service infrastructure, industrial wireless automation, sustainability, life style, etc) shall be interconnected and here is where technical interoperability and standardization efforts are required in order to minimize technology fragmentation, avoid proliferation of particular solutions and develop secure and reliable cost-effective networks.

Cybersecurity and Threats

One of the success factors to realize Smart City benefits is the capability of its ICT system to collect massive data and transform that into information to take better decisions and optimize resource usage. Capturing data about people habits and behaviors using city infrastructure at public and home spaces is key to make a city smarter. Security and privacy of such data is a major challenge that must be properly addressed. People expect Smart City systems to be secure and to preserve their life private, therefore integration of security and (an absolute) confidentiality into ICT infrastructure design is a hard requirement, otherwise user will be reluctant to use the services provide by Smart City.

Potential threats and challenges could arise from system interconnection (collaboration of systems designed to serve to different purposes open new weaknesses that have not been considered when securing the individual systems); big data and large number of users (data is collected by smart devices and other types of ubiquitous sensors at public and private locations and data transmission could be intercepted); services customization (adapting services to each user needs or preferences by means of many configuration options and questions could threat privacy too).

As (Correia, 2011) states, it is important to work on countermeasures. Potential countermeasures or working areas to improve security are cryptography and key management for platforms with limited memory and computation capability, evolutionary trust models for scalable and secure inter-systems interaction, abstract and comprehensive security policy languages, self-monitoring and self protecting systems, development of methods for designing security and privacy into complex and interdependent systems, pseudo-anonymization techniques to decouple user's identity from data collection, advanced encryption and access control, interoperability of different identity management systems or development of privacy policy languages.

An important element to mention at this point is related to critical infrastructure cyber security. As previously stated, Smart City strategy requires the control and interconnection of city critical infrastructure (energy grids, water and waste management, transportation systems, communication systems).

From a view of performance criteria, enhanced sensors and Industrial Control Systems (ICS) data

Table 4. Standards Developing Organization and Technical Task Force groups

Cellular M2M	Capillary M2M
• ETSI for M2M architecture • 3GPP suite for Access network • IETF for network and transport protocols	• IEEE for physical and link layer protocols • IETF for network and transport protocols • ISA for control systems and ICS cybersecurity • ETSI for completing hybrid M2M solutions

security requires to carefully leverage security best practice from information and communication technology domain without compromise ICS performance requirements (Puyosa, 2008).

ICS security and in particular security of critical infrastructure like smart grids is getting more attention from governments agencies, researches and media since Stuxnet malware was discovered and dissected (Falliere *et al.*, 2011) and risk is being consider as real rather than a potential one. Stuxnet is the first ever PLC rootkit and was primarily written to reprogram an ICS by modifying code on PLCs; its authors are highly specialized on both ICT security and ICS programming and configuration.

Smart grid security and other key elements in this area have been studying by technical task groups and standards developing organizations are working on the development of it, including European Network and Information Security Agency (ENISA), National Institute of Standards and Technology (NIST), IEEE and ISA. (ENISA, 2012) recommends a set of minimum security measures to improve Smart Grid cyber security services. (NIST, 2010)is a comprehensive guideline advising how to develop a cybersecurity strategy for Smart Grid focused on prevention, mitigation, response and recovery. (Yan *et al.*, 2012) concludes on the needs to create the requirements of standards for Smart Grid cybersecurity. Convergence of guidelines into a set of standards is a decisive strategy to improve Smart Grid cybersecurity. A work to be done in parallel is to use available guidelines to test its goodness to rise security level and detect improvements.

An interesting topic here is the crisis management on Smart City and the need to protect critical systems. Smart City is capable to better deal with crisis situations by using its ICT infrastructure and analytical capabilities to coordinate multiple public agencies and citizens. Typical crisis management system, see Figure 4, uses different type of meters to sense some potential catastrophic events (storm water, earthquakes, tsunami, nuclear radiation, etc).

As an example, we could cite the government of Japan has developed a disaster resilience solution which involves observation systems, information gathering capabilities, data analysis and decision making aids, together with an intelligent warning system, all linked together in an interoperable manner (Japan Meteorological Agency, 2013).

Crisis management preparedness shall include communication network and power supply redundancy and backup to support operation of Smart City minimum services to deal with crisis management.

Data: Semantics and Processing

Very often researchers assume that the concept of open government implies open data. Scientifically and logically this is not true. An open government can have limitations on what open data is about, and certainly open data is a precondition for open government, but a truly open government relies on specific data sets that are supportive of certain domains which normally are not public, the least of which are security and privacy. Certainly, one of the main conditions for the success

Figure 4. Crisis management process on Smart City

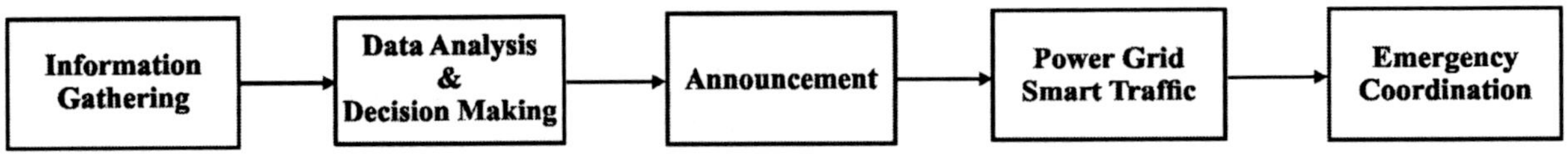

of open government is to have open data (Elhari & Bounabat, 2011) but, about open data, it will be necessary to understand what data should be opened, what formats it will have, what semantic level is required.

Internet of Things, Social Networks, e-Transactions, e-Government Information, Open Data, Scientific Data: Big Data. The quantity of information, (un)structured typology, diversity or high speed origination, and the need of processing it in real time, are key elements that will condition next years. The difficult of its processing and to obtain the value in the moment needed, it is a true challenge. As we have previously seen, related to data we are in front of a more important element that Open Data in the next years: the automatically generation of data, and the storage and processing of the information. It gives rise to the concept of Big Data -i.e., massive amount of data inherent to urban sensors and monitoring-that needs key issues of selecting which of these variables is relevant for control purposes, as well as the computational challenges related with real time processing of such massive data collection).

Efficient data processing on real time is addressed to be one of the key factors in the next years, and related with all areas. We could think on platforms to manage information based on cloud architectures and the automated information gathered from sensors, or other information that means unstructured data. Open Data and Big Data ("NoSQL") that goes from sensors until the information required when we speak on electronic forms, e-documentation, e-filling or e-Processes within a public organization, where the information that were before in paper format, now is all electronic. The analysis of this data gives us important value, but an efficient analysis is a challenge too. In this sense, semantics and algorithms it will play important roles next years (Feldman et al., 2012).

Privacy Invasion

Smart cities are equipped with a wide variety of means to gather information from citizens. Networks of sensors, video-surveillance cameras and radio-frequency identification (RFID) antennas are just a few examples of technologies and devices that allow the easy gathering of potentially sensitive data from citizens. This unprecedented gathering of citizens' data might endanger their privacy.

The fundamental right of individuals to privacy must be guaranteed. We believe that governments should embody the foundations to support the protection of individual privacy. To do so, first there is a need for identifying the possible privacy breaches, second the right countermeasures must be selected and, finally administrations must provide the means for the citizens to collectively protect their privacy.

Identifying Privacy Breaches in a Smart City

In Martínez-Ballesté *et al.*(2013) the authors identify five dimensions related to the privacy of citizens and, by extension, those dimensions are the ones in which privacy breaches might appear:

- **Identity Privacy:** This dimension is related to the privacy of citizens and users of Smart Cities' services that have to identify themselves in order to gain access to those services.
- **Query Privacy:** Citizens interact with technologies provided by Smart Cities. In many occasions, these interactions translate into queries that citizens send to the information systems of a Smart City.
- **Location Privacy:** Citizens' mobile technologies with self-location capabilities

can use their current location to obtain directions and information from Location-Based Services (LBS) providers (private or public). However, by sharing their location, citizens might endanger their privacy.

- **Footprint Privacy:** When citizens use the technical infrastructure provided by Smart Cities, they leave some of their information behind. Every transaction, action or query could be recorded. All the data collected from individuals is known as microdata and is stored in microdata sets.
- **Owner Privacy:** Owner privacy refers to the privacy-aware computation of queries across the databases from different autonomous entities and users.

Determining the Right Countermeasures

Once the privacy breaches are identified, it is possible to look for the right countermeasures to avert them. In Martínez-Ballesté *et al.* (2013) the authors summarize a number of Privacy Enhancing Technologies (PET) that could be applied to cope with the challenge of protecting the privacy of citizens in all the aforementioned dimensions.

Analyzing in detail all possible countermeasures related to PET is out of the scope of this chapter, however, for the sake of completeness we briefly summarize some relevant techniques that could be applied to mitigate privacy breaches in each dimension and we provide references for the readers interested in more detailed information about the suggested techniques.

It is apparent that using technologies based on Statistical Disclosure Control (SDC) (Hundepool, et al., 2012), differential privacy and Privacy Preserving Data Mining (PPDM) (Vaidya & Clifton, 2004) could help to mitigate the problem of Owner and Footprint privacy. With regard to Identity Privacy, it could be protected by well-known approaches such as Anonymisers, Peudonymisers, k-Anonymity and, Privacy-aware video surveillance (Martínez-Ballesté *et al.*, 2012).

By using off-the-shelf techniques like cloaking, collaborative masking (Solanas & Martínez-Ballesté, 2008) and random perturbations (Pérez-Martinez & Solanas, 2011), location privacy could be protected. Finally, private information retrieval (PIR) algorithms (Chor *et al.*, 1995) are adequate to guarantee query privacy.

Put Countermeasures in Action

It is apparent that, although it is not simple, we have many technologies that could help us protect our fundamental rights. However, it is far from easy to put them in practice. To do so, we believe that there is a need for a bottom-up approach in which the foundations consist of administrations that support the whole structure (Figure 5).

The key issues for the bottom-up approach to be successful could be summarized as follows:

- **User Awareness:** Governments must struggle to make citizens know which risks they are facing. Citizens must be aware of the privacy invasions that they could suffer if they do not take the proper actions. The role of the administration in this regard is paramount.
- **Collaboration Fostering:** Citizens have to understand that privacy is no longer an individual matter but a collective issue. As social beings we cannot understand our existence within a Smart City in terms of individuality and there are many privacy protection methods that would highly benefit from the collaboration of users (e.g. k-anonymity, collaborative location obfuscation, etc.).
- **Technologies Improvement:** Governments have to support the development of new and better techniques and devices to protect the privacy of the users of Smart Cities. There are many areas in which research has to be

Figure 5. Graphical scheme of the bottom-up approach to citizens' privacy founded on e-government

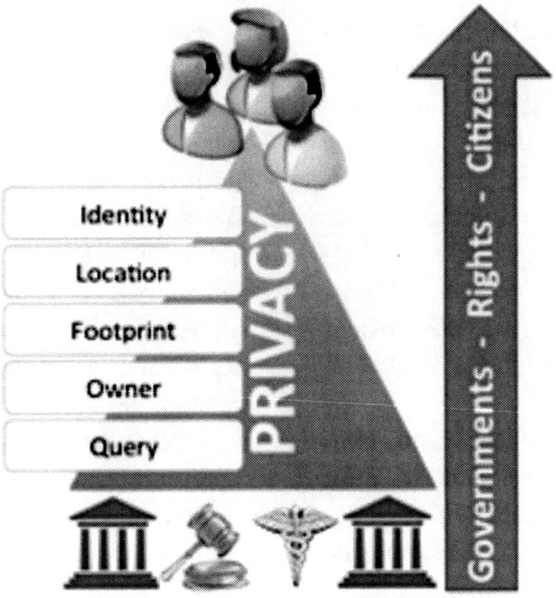

conducted, namely cryptography, artificial intelligence, behavior analysis, etc. Public administrations are responsible for the provision of funds to researchers in order to cope with the great challenge of advancing privacy enhancing technologies for the sake of human rights.

- **Law Enforcement:** Privacy enhancing technologies have to be applied by all actors involved in the management of citizens' data. Those actors might fail to fulfill the privacy requirements stated by law. In this case the administration must strongly address the issue and take legal action to avert further violations of citizen's privacy.

Opportunities and Challenges

As it has been stated, the implementation of a scenario in which Smart Cities and Smart Governance co-exist can be greatly beneficial for all of implied agents, from citizens, to administrative bodies and different levels of service providers. It can also be seen that it is multidisciplinary task, in which complex systems and procedures must be correctly synchronized in order to clearly provide an effective and efficient user experience. Therefore, opportunities as well as challenges to overcome can be observed, such as:

- Opportunities:
    - Higher degree of interaction from citizens with different government levels.
    - Increased efficiency in resource management.
    - Enabling truly participative citizenship, increase democratic levels.
    - Reduction of social exclusion with the aid of context-aware environments within the framework of Smart Cities and Ambient Assisted Living.
    - Increased user satisfaction in the use of public services, such as transportation systems, due to more efficient operation.
- Challenges:

- Resources must be allocated in order to provide technological as well as human resources in the implementation phase of Smart environments.
- Interoperability issues can limit the overall possibilities in system operation.
- Resistance to technological adoption, particularly in the case of more vulnerable population sectors (elderly, lower income), with a non-desired risk of increasing social exclusion gaps.
- Limitations in the collection and handling of massive amounts of data, which are a consequence of large deployed sensor networks and multiple systems operating to provide control of resources.

CONCLUSION

The development and sustainability of urban environments will lead to the adoption and evolution of Smart Cities and its governance. In this chapter we have added the "Interoperability Principle" to the three Open Government known principles of Transparency, Collaboration and Participation. This new principle adds a level in the model of classification of public organizations related to ICT adoption: the "Intelligent" organization, characterized by the "Smart Government" in which interoperability and efficiency are fundamental in the context of the smart city.

Based on this view, we have presented the "SmartGovernment Ecosystem Matrix" in which the features of Open Government and Smart Cities will determine the Smart Government level. Next, we have shown the challenges and opportunities related to the ICT adoption, mainly from a back office view for public organizations, in which the ICT role as a driver will be key. We pose challenges, not only in technical terms but also in the model of governance and active role of its inhabitants. A holistic approach has been followed in order to analyze the main characteristics involved.

The new challenging feature of the technology dependence is that the link between the citizen and the government has become not only irreversible but also mutually effective. This kind of partnership has yielded a new reality: we have to use technology in a much smarter way and on additional levels apart from citizen online services and support in form of advanced e-government applications. This directly leads to a complex form of governance that can be the best road to development on the national and regional levels. This is what we know as "smart governance", which is the immediate future of societies in this context.

Privacy is a fundamental right that has to be protected. Smart Cities are gaining momentum and their ability to gather private information from citizens has no precedent. Public administrations must be a strong foundation for the protection of citizens' rights, and they must play a fundamental role to guarantee that Smart Cities are not only smart but also respectful with the fundamental rights and social protection of their citizens. Otherwise, Smart Cities will hardly be a reality and they will face the opposition of their most valuable asset – their citizens.

Most of the current research that is going on about open government and smart cities faces certain arguments that would raise room for research and discussion. Arguments affect directly the technical nature of any implementation along, in addition of course to the policies that should be best adopted the overall smart government approach. We have analyzed the special focus of technological projection & governmental view, but other different are needed too. It has been usual linking Smart City with technological field, but social implications of technology other has important to study too, because technology can impact in positive or negative ways. This is the case of digital divide or ICT alphabetization. Extensive research is needed in order to test the model with empirical cases as well as define the weight of all elements of the matrix.

REFERENCES

Ahmed, S. A., & Ali, S. M. (2006). People as Partners: Facilitating people's participation in public-private partnership for solid waste management. *Habitat International*, *30*(4), 781–796. doi:10.1016/j.habitatint.2005.09.004

Ando, B. (2008). A Smart Multisensor Approach to Assist Blind People in Specific Urban Navigation Tasks. *IEEE Transactions on Neural Systems and Rehabilitation Engineering*, *16*(6), 592–594. doi:10.1109/TNSRE.2008.2003374 PMID:19144591

ATOS. (2011). *Open Cities. New Trends for Smart Cities.* Project co-funded by the European Commission within the ICT Policy Support Programme. Dissemination Level. Deliverable D2.2.21 V1.3.

Bartoli, A., Hernandez-Serrano, J., Soriano, M., Dohler, M., Kountourisz, A., & Barthelz, D. (2011). Security and Privacy in your Smart City. In *Proceedings of Smart Cities Congress 2011.* Barcelona: IEEE.

Bodhani, A. (2012). Smart Transport. *Engineering and Technology*, *7*(6), 70–73. doi:10.1049/et.2012.0611

Chesbrough, H. & Vanhaverbeke, W. (2011). Open Innovation and Public Policy in Europe. *Science Business.*

Chor, B., Goldreich, O., Kushilevitz, E., & Sudan, M. (1995). Private information retrieval. In *Proceedings of 36th Annual Symposium on Foundations of Computer Science* (pp. 41-50). Milwaukee, WI: IEEE.

Chourabi, H., Nam, T., Walker, S., Gil-García, J. R., Mellouli, S., Nahon, K., et al. (2012). Understanding smart cities: an integrative framework. In *Proceedings of 2012 45th Hawaii International Conference on System Sciences* (pp. 2289-2297). Hawaii, HI: IEEE.

Correia, L. M. (2011). *Expert Working Group on Smart Cities Applications and Requirements.* Lisbon: Univ.

WGI Cross Country Indicators. (2011). Retrieved from http://info.worldbank.org/governance/wgi/index.aspx#doc-cross

Di Maio, A. (2012). Smart Government: Sustainable, Affordable, Innovative. In *Proceedings of Worldwide Government Solutions Forum 2012*. Academic Press.

Dohler, M., Watteine, T., & Alonso-Zárate, J. (2010). *Centre Tecnològic de Telecomunicacions de Catalunya.* Retrieved from http://www.cttc.es/en/event/100423-machine-to-machi.jsp

Dugan, R. C., & McGranaghan, M. (2011). Sim City. *IEEE Power and Energy Magazine*, *9*(5), 74–81. doi:10.1109/MPE.2011.941867

Elhari, K., & Bounabat, B. (2011). Platform for Assessing Strategic Alignment Using Enterprise Architecture: Application to E-Government Process Assessment. *International Journal of Computer Science, 8* (1).

ENISA. (2012). *Appropiate security measures for smart grids: Guidelines to asses the sophistication of security measures implementation.* Retrieved from http://www.enisa.europa.eu/activities/Resilience-and-CIIP/critical-infrastructure-and-services/smart-grids-and-smart-metering/ENISA-smart-grid-security-recommendations

European Union. (2009). Decision Num. 922/2009/EC of the European Parliament and the Council of 16 September 2009 on interoperability solutions for European public administrations (ISA). *Official Journal of the European Union,* (L 260), 20-27.

Falliere, N. O., Murchu, L., & Chien, E. (2011, February). *W32.Stuxnet Dossier: V1.4.* Retrieved 2013 6-April from http://www.symantec.com/content/en/us/enterprise/media/security_response/whitepapers/w32_stuxnet_dossier.pdf

Feki, M. A., Kawsar, F., Boussard, M., & Trappeniers, L. (2013). The Internet of Things: The Next Technological Revolution. *Computer Magazine*, *46*(2), 24–25. doi:10.1109/MC.2013.63

Feldman, D., Sung, C., & Rus, D. (2012). The single pixel GPS: learning big data signals from tiny coresets. In *Proceedings of the 20th International Conference on Advances in Geographic Information Systems* (pp. 23-32). ACM. doi:10.1145/2424321.2424325

Gavaldà, J., & Ribera-Fumaz, R. (2012). Barcelona 5.0: from Knowledge to Smartness? *IN3 Working Paper Series*.

Hundepool, A., Domingo-Ferrer, J., Franconi, L., Giessing, S., Nordholt, E. S., & Spicer, K. (2012). *Statistical Disclosure Control*. John Wiley & Sons, Ltd. doi:10.1002/9781118348239

Japan Meteorological Agency. (2013). *Smart City Resilience. Learning from Emergency Response and Coordination in Japan*. Retrieved 2013-April from http://www.gsma.com/connectedliving/wp-content/uploads/2013/02/cl_SmartCities_emer_01_131.pdf

Jiménez, C.E. (2013a). "Smart Governance": Una aproximación al concepto de gobernanza inteligente. *Revista Perspectiva*. Dossier. Septiembre de 2013

Jiménez, C. E. (2013b). *Impacto de la Ley Reguladora del Uso de las TIC en la Administración de Justicia*. Barcelona: Centro de Estudios Jurídicos y Formación Especializada.

Jiménez, C. E., Criado, J. I., & Gascó, M. (2011). Technological e-Government Interoperability. An Analysis of IberoAmerican Countries. *IEEE Latin America Transactions*, *9*(7), 1112-1117.

Jiménez, C. E., & Gascó, M. (2012). Y ahora... gobierno abierto. Nuevos términos en la constante búsqueda por la transparencia y la rendición de cuentas. In *Proceedings of XVII Congreso Internacional del CLAD sobre la Reforma del Estado y de la Administración Pública*. Cartagena de Indias: CLAD.

Kaufmann, D., Kraay, A., & Mastruzzi, M. (2010). The Worldwide Governance Indicators. *Methodology and Analytical Issues*.

Martínez-Ballesté, A., Rashwan, H. A., Puig, D., & Paniza Fullana, A. (2012). Towards a trustworthy privacy in pervasive video surveillance systems. In *Proceedings of IEEE International Conference on Pervasive Computing and Communications Workshops* (pp. 914-919). Lugano: IEEE. doi:10.1109/PerComW.2012.6197644

Martínez-Ballesté, A., Solanas, A., & Pérez-Martínez, A. (2013). The Pursuit of Citizens Privacy: A Privacy-Aware Smart City is Possible. *IEEE Communications Magazine*, *51*(6), 136–141. doi:10.1109/MCOM.2013.6525606

Mitchell, W. J. (2007). *Intelligent cities*. Retrieved from http://www.uoc.edu/uocpapers/5/dt/eng/mitchell.pdf

Net!Works European Technology Platform Expert Working Group. (2011). *Smart Cities Applications and Requirements*. Net!Works.

NIST. (2010). *Introduction to NISTIR 7628 Guidelines for Smart Grid Cyber Security*. Retrieved from http://csrc.nist.gov/publications/nistir/ir7628/introduction-to-nistir-7628.pdf

Obama, B. (2009). Transparency and Open Government. *Presidential Documents, 74*(15), 4685-4686.

Ojo, A., Dzhusupova, Z., & Janowski, T. (2012). *e-Macao Report 199 - Intelligent Governance of Smart Cities.* Research-Practice Gap Analysis.

Parks, W. (1957). The open government principle: Applying the right to know under the Constitution. *The George Washington Law Review*, *26*(1).

Pérez-Martinez, P. A., & Solanas, A. (2011). W3-privacy: the three dimensions of user privacy in LBS. In *Proceedings of 12th ACM International Symposium on Mobile Ad Hoc Networking and Computing*. Paris: ACM.

Puyosa, H. (2008). Control systems vulnerability to cyberattacks. *Oilgas*, *41*(475), 71–75.

Robinson, R. (2012). *The Urban Technologist: A personal view of emerging technology and Smarter Cities.* Retrieved from http://theurbantechnologist.com/2012/08/07/five-roads-to-a-smarter-city/

Solanas, A., & Martínez-Ballesté, A. (2008). A TTP-free protocol for location privacy in location-based services. *Computer Communications*, *31*(6), 1181–1191. doi:10.1016/j.comcom.2008.01.007

Vaidya, J., & Clifton, C. (2004). Privacy-preserving data mining: Why, how and when. *Security & Privacy*, *2*(6), 19–27. doi:10.1109/MSP.2004.108

Vienna University of Technology. (2007). *European Smart Cities.* Retrieved from http://www.smart-cities.eu/

Wilson, S. C., & Linders, D. (2011). *The open government directive: a preliminary assessment. In Proceedings of iConference 2011* (pp. 387–394). New York: ACM. doi:10.1145/1940761.1940814

Yan, Y., Qian, Y., Sharif, H., & Tripper, D. (2012). A Survey on Cyber Security for Smart Grid Communication. *IEEE Communications Surveys and Tutorials*, *14*(4), 998–1010. doi:10.1109/SURV.2012.010912.00035

Zambonelli, F. (2012). Toward Sociotechnical Urban Superorganisms. *Computer Magazine*, *45*(8), 76–78. doi:10.1109/MC.2012.280

KEY TERMS AND DEFINITIONS:

Interoperability: The ability to exchange and use information, allowing systems and organizations to work together.

Smart City: A developed urban area that creates sustainable economic development and high quality of life by excelling in multiple key areas; economy, mobility, environment, people, living, and government.

Smart Government: The use of innovative policies, business models, and technology to address the financial, environmental, and service challenges facing public sector organizations. The concept of Smart Government relies on consolidated information systems and communication networks.

ENDNOTE

1 Note that this chapter is mainly focused in the 2nd row and the interaction with the new principle of interoperability included within the Open Government principles (identified in the 4th column of the matrix). A deep eranalysis of all elements of the matrix, exceed of the scope of this chapter.

Chapter 2
Big Data and Innovation in the Delivery of Public Services:
The Case of Predictive Policing in Kent

Alberto Asquer
SOAS, University of London, UK

ABSTRACT

This chapter aims to discuss the role of Information and Communication Technologies (ICTs)—especially of the so-called Big Data—in the innovation of public service delivery. After reviewing the relevant literature on innovation and innovation diffusion in the public sector and the rise of Big Data, the chapter presents a narrative of the case of the adoption and implementation of predictive policing in Kent County Police, UK, as an instance of (early) application of Big Data in public sector organizations. On the whole, the analysis of the case suggests that past conditions and adoption strategies play an important role in the introduction and acceptance of innovative work practices that exploit the potential of contemporary ICTs.

INTRODUCTION

In the next decades, we may witness the emergence of more challenging social, economic, and political issues than the governments have been used to tackle so far. Contemporary trends, such as the booming digitalization of social activities, the growing call for transparency and public participation, and the increasing stress on public finance will most probably call for more advanced ways of providing public services than is generally performed nowadays. Within such scenario, public sector organizations need to develop and cultivate the capacity to innovate their 'business processes' (the ways of delivering public services) and 'products' (the kind of quality of public services) if they are to enhance governments' capacity to cope with the expectations of citizens and local communities. One way to fulfill this requirement is to develop strategies for searching, adopting, and implementing new technologies that can be effectively employed in the delivery of public services.

Among current sources of technological change and Information and Communication Technologies (ICTs) in particular, the emergence

DOI: 10.4018/978-1-4666-7266-6.ch002

of so-called Big Data – that is, of datasets that are so large in size that they cannot be captured, stored, managed, and analyzed through typical database software – seems particularly relevant. Big Data are formed through the recording and storage of traces of various acts performed by several individuals over time, such as financial transactions, social media traffic, health records, and GPS coordinates, often by means of mobile tools (Manyika et al., 2011). Big Data are typically generated in digital format, are passively obtained as 'by product' of daily activities and interactions, are collected automatically when data is generated, and are geographically and temporally traceable (UN Global Pulse, 2012). Typically, Big Data are controlled by financial, telecom and Internet companies, although recently also the governments and non-profit organizations have increasingly paid attention to the creation and use of such datasets.

Various works have highlighted that Big Data provide enormous opportunities for designing and delivering more efficient and effective public policies (Bollier, 2010; Boyd & Crawford, 2012; Manovich, 2011). Big Data may enable public authorities to detect early signs of emerging phenomena (e.g., disease spread), monitor social behavior (e.g., response to emergency), measure behavioral or economic impact of policy measures (e.g., traffic congestions or credit card expenses), and pick the 'sentiment' of communities (e.g., through the analysis of blogging topics and crowd-sourcing). By means of advanced statistical and computational techniques, public sector analysts may unveil patterns and anomalies within these large socio-economic datasets that may not be ordinarily evident on the basis of 'conventional' information channels. Big Data, then, potentially enable the production of information that can be used for innovating processes and products of public sector organizations in ways that have not been accessible so far.

This paper aims to discuss the role of Big Data in the innovation of public service delivery on the basis of the case study of the adoption and implementation of predictive policing in Kent County, the UK, taken as an early instance of application of Big Data in the public sector. Originally developed in Los Angeles and Santa Cruz (California), predictive policing is a system for analyzing past offence records and providing police officers with indications of the likely areas and time of criminal activity on daily basis. The case will show the rationales for the adoption of productive policing, the organizational interventions made for inserting the technology into existing work practices, and the perceived effects on service delivery. More generally, the case study will provide some explanatory arguments that are used as a basis for discussing how public sector organizations may grasp the opportunities offered by Big Data for improving public service delivery (Albury, 2005; Hartley, 2005; Jun & Weare, 2010; Osborne & Brown, 2011; Rashman & Radnor, 2005).

Innovation in Public Sector Organizations: The Rise of Big Data

During the last decades there has been a growing interest towards innovation in the public sector. Several scholarly works have addressed issues about what innovation in the public sector is, what stimulates innovation and its diffusion, and what are the effects of innovation on the efficiency and effectiveness of public service programs (Albury, 2005; Altschuler & Behn, 1997; Borins, 1998; Hartley, 2005; Moore, 2005;Moore & Hartley, 2008; Mulgan & Albury, 2003; Osborne, 1998; Osborne & Gaebler, 1993). Innovation is typically regarded as an important mean to attain improvements in the provision of public services, both in terms of enhanced quality of service delivery and of increased responsiveness to the needs and aspirations of citizens and users (Moore & Hartley, 2008).

Information and Communication Technologies (ICTs) provide an important source of opportunities for innovation in the public sector (Heeks, 1999; Finger & Pécoud, 2003; Marche &McNiven,

2009). Contemporary ICTs techniques and tools have the potential for revolutionizing the structure, processes, and operations of governmental entities (Islam & Ahmed, 2007). A typical instance of application of ICTs to public sector activities is e-government that is conceived as a tool (Hood, 2006) that broadly consists of the use of ICTs for the provision of information and, in some occasions, for the actual delivery of public services. E-government plays an important role to improve the efficiency, effectiveness, transparency and accountability of the governmentand to potentially contribute to transform the internal and external relationships of public administration (UNDESA, 2003).

Innovation has been variously defined. Some scholars considered it as a process through which new ideas, objects and practices are created, developed or reinvented (Rogers, 2003; Kimberly, 1981). Others highlighted that innovation should be conceived within a particular role, group or organization (King, 1992), which constitutes a reference benchmark for assessing the novelty of the new idea, object or practice (Aitken & Hage, 1971; Hage & Dewar, 1973; Rogers, 2003). Other stressed that - differently from inventions (Bessant, 2003) - innovations should consist of new ideas that are effectively implemented and result in improvements over existing work practices (Tidd et al., 2005; van de Ven, 1986; Wolfe, 1994). Other, moreover, argued that innovations should be accompanied by an original, disruptive and fundamental transformation of an organization's core tasks, else the term could be misunderstood as any kind of change in organizational routines, or improvements, or modification of existing work processes (Lynn, 1997; Moore & Hartley, 2008).

Innovations may be of different sorts. Some innovations consist of the original ideation, design, and implementation of novel technological and organizational systems that result in an improvement of the work processes. Other innovations, instead, consist of the awareness, translation, and adoption of innovative principles and practices that have been already devised and possibly implemented in other organizations, which could be placed in other contexts, locations, or time period (Rogers, 2003; Thompson, 1965). When innovations are transferred from one organization to another, they may result in a more or less widespread diffusion among an organizational population. The diffusion of innovation, generally understood as 'a process in which an innovation is communicated through certain channels over time among the members of a social system' (Rogers, 2003: 5), typically takes place in an informal and unsupervised way. On some occasions, however, innovations are spread across organizations as the result of deliberate and orchestrated efforts from a central or authoritative source, who is interested in what is generally called a 'dissemination' of innovative principles and practices (Greenhalgh et al., 2004; Korteland & Bekkers, 2008). Both the diffusion and the dissemination of innovation rest on the adoption decision from the side of the organization that imports the innovative principles and practices. Sometimes, the importing organization plainly replicates the formal features of the innovation, while, on other occasions, it reinterprets the innovative principles and practices in an original way (Dolowitz & Marsh, 1998).

Innovations in the public sector are typically pursued as a way to attain at least three objectives (Moore, 2005). Some innovations are pursued in order to devise better methods for performing core, basic functions of the public sector organization. Other innovations are motivated by the desire to abandon a 'one size fits all' approach in favor of one that encourages adaptation and customization of organizational processes and services as a way to better meet the demands of the clients. Other innovations, finally, are stimulated by the aim to introduce new products and services that can be functional to performing part of the organizational mission that has not been dealt with so far, or to extend the current mission to additional areas or intervention. In the last sense, innovation plays a strategic role in repositioning the organization in its environment by changing the objectives and reconfiguring the population of stakeholders the organization has to cope with.

As observed by Osborne (1998), innovation is a dynamic process that may be hard to reduce within rigid classification schemes. Within the business literature, a distinction is often drawn between product and process innovations as potentially different forms of innovations. Osborne (1998) contended, instead, that public sector organizations tend to produce services, where the boundary between interventions on what is produced and how it is produced are generally blurred. In addition, public sector organizations may occasionally 'reverse' their inclination towards improvements of existing organizational processes and 'reorient' their efforts towards reinventing service delivery processes in relation to shifting policy goals and mandates.

Depending on whether innovation is directed to existing or new services of the public sector organization and on whether it is intended to serve the interests of existing or new clients, Osborne (1998) proposed four types of public service innovations. Innovations that focus on existing services for existing clients are called 'developmental', in the sense that they enrich and strengthen the delivery of public services within the present domain. Innovations that relate to new services for new clients are labeled 'total' and result in discontinuities within the existing organization, or possibly in the creation of a new organization. Those innovations that consist of new services for existing clients are referred to as 'evolutionary', while those that are formed of existing services extended to new clients are called 'expansionary'.

The identification of different types of innovation entails, apart from additional clarity about what constitutes innovation, questions about what stimulates one form of innovation or another one. In principle, public sector organizations seem to possess various means for pursuing innovation: they often enjoy the control of key assets, the possibility to exert authoritative powers, and the benefit of centrality within social and economic networks. Public sector organizations may often access state-of-the-art technologies and information about social and economic trends. They are in the position, therefore, to devise innovative ways for addressing public concerns by expanding the range of existing services and the target population of beneficiaries.

Yet, public sector organizations may lack leveraging on the resources at hand and miss opportunities for innovation. What stimulates innovation, then? What kind of institutional and organizational conditions facilitate the search for innovative principles and practices and their implementation? These questions have received a growing amount of attention during last decade (Walker, 2003; Moore, 2005). Jun and Weare (2010), in particular, argued that innovation originates from efficiency concerns, internal bureaucratic politics, external demand, and search for legitimacy with respect to peer organizations. Efficiency concerns may stimulate innovation as a way to buffer the organizational processes from external uncertainty. Internal bureaucratic politics may trigger innovative efforts because they affect the distribution of power and resources within organizations. External demand may result in innovative efforts if public officers aim to appeal to influential stakeholders who may be especially sensitive to service quality improvements driven by modern technologies. Finally, search for legitimacy may stimulate innovation as a way to enhance political legitimacy by meeting the social expectations about the organizational missions. In part, however, satisfying social expectations may also take the form of symbolic actions that are not accompanied by any substantive improvement in operational performance. In addition, innovations may be stimulated by vendors, who are plainly interested in persuading public sector organizations to purchase their technologies.

Jun and Weare (2010) argued that externally oriented motivations appear more influential than internal factor, and that the quality of internally developed innovations is generally superior to innovations that are imported from others' experiences. Also, innovation seems more likely to happen if it entails relatively modest risk and conflict with existing organizational values and customary behavior (Berry & Berry, 1999; Rogers, 2003) and if organizations possess slack resources and access to key expertise. On the contrary, innovation may be hampered by adversarial relationships with other organizational parts (Stoker & Wilson, 1986; Tolbert, Mossberger, & McNeal, 2008; Willem & Buelens, 2007) and by the lack of opportunities to learn from the experience of others (Tether, 2002).

Other works focused on the process of diffusion of innovations across organizations rather than on the stimulation of innovations within any particular organizational venue. In part, scholarly works highlighted the role of psychological factors that come into play in the decision to adopt (or not) innovative principles and practices (Bagozzi, 2007; Venkatesh et al., 2003). Some works focused on the role of social networks in transmitting information about innovations (Rogers, 2003; Valente, 1995), while others were concerned with the political factors that affect the diffusion process (Berry & Berry, 1990, 1999; Sapat, 2004) and cultural conditions that influence the adoption decision (Silverman, 1971; March & Olsen, 1989; Scott, 2001). Generally, reviewed works were especially sensitive – in a cultural or constructivist approach – to the 'social fitness' of innovation (Pollitt, 2002; Greenhalgh et al., 2004) with respect to the relevant stakeholders.

Additional works have especially focused on individual-level motivations for innovation adoptions. In part, innovation diffusion is related to the willingness of inventors, early adopters and intermediary organizations to share and spread knowledge about the innovative principles and practices. In part, however, the diffusion of innovation also depends on the adequate endowment of expertise and resources in the recipient organization (Rashman & Hartley, 2002; Downe et al., 2004), their size (Greenhalgh et al., 2004; Rogers, 2003), their receptivity to change and inclination to risk-taking (Greenhalgh et al., 2004), and the presence of policy entrepreneurship (Kingdon, 1995). Other factors relate to features of the organizational network (Dolowitz & Marsh, 1998; Scott, 2001; Rogers, 2003), such as perception of what other organizations are doing (Greenhalgh et al., 2004), the degree to which organizations are linked by interpersonal networks, geographical and cultural proximity (Berry &Berry, 1990; Dolowitz & Marsh, 1998), sense of affinity with other organizations (Berry & Berry, 1990) and interdependency (DiMaggio & Powell, 1991; Rogers, 2003).

The present literature review suggests that research on innovation in the public sector resulted in several theoretical findings so far, but also that not all questions about what innovation is, what stimulates innovation, and what triggers and sustains innovation diffusion have been answered. What seems required, for example, is a more explicit theoretical argument for explaining innovation (as an organizational process) and innovation diffusion (as an inter-organizational process) in relation to organizational-level, individual-level, and psychological-level factors and conditions. Features of individual psychology, such as attitude towards risk and leadership, may be relevant to account for features of individual behavior, such as manifest support or resistance towards innovation opportunities. Individual attitudes towards innovation, moreover, need to be combined with institutional and organizational conditions as a way to account for the adoption of innovations by a particular organization and their spreading across organizational ecologies.

Sources of technological change in ICTs, and in particular the rise of Big Data, provide several opportunities for innovation in the public sector (US Executive Office of the President, 2014). Big Data have been generally defined as those data that cannot be analyzed using traditional processes or tools (Manyika et al., 2011). In a more refined interpretation, Big Data are understood as the production and analysis of data that are characterized by large volume, rapid velocity (i.e., real time or nearly real time information), and sheer variety (i.e., formats that include text messages, images, readings from sensors, GPS signals, and more, and that originate from laptops, smart phones, tablets, and other devices), that require new forms of processing to enable enhanced decision making, insight discovery and process optimization (McAfee & Brynjolfsson, 2012). Big Data are data sets formed through the recording and storage of traces of various acts performed by individuals over time, such as financial transactions, social media traffic, health records, and GPS coordinates, often by means of mobile tools (Manyika et al., 2011).

The opportunities offered by Big Data lay in the possibility to analyze large amount of data for generating new insights and assist decisions. Big Data analytics – that is, the process of examining large amount of data through various advanced techniques – is expected to result in the discovery of relationships (i.e., correlations and patterns) between variables that are not necessarily formulated as ex ante hypotheses to test (Minelli, 2013; Ohlhorst, 2013; Sathi, 2012). These techniques enable the analysts to 'explore' large data sets without any committed interpretation of the information available. The algorithms of Big Data analytics, in fact, may return unexpected results in the form of unforeseen relationships between variables that have not been theorized yet. Big Data analytics, therefore, may stimulate the development of a new understanding of phenomena and, to some extent, of methods for anticipating consequential effects of events or happenings.

Big Data are expected to provide enormous opportunities for designing and delivering more efficient and effective public policies (Bollier, 2010; Boyd & Crawford, 2012; Manovich, 2011; OECD, 2013), in such ways as, for example, detecting early signs of emerging trends (e.g., disease spread), monitoring social behavior (e.g., response to emergency), measuring behavioral or economic impact of policy measures (e.g., traffic congestions or credit card expenses), picking the 'sentiment' of communities (e.g., mainstream micro-blogging topics and crowd-sourcing), and anticipating future behavior (e.g., predictive policing). By means of advanced statistical and computational techniques, public sector analysts may unveil patterns and anomalies within these large socio-economic data sets that may not be ordinarily evident on the basis of 'conventional' information channels, such as national census.

The emergence of Big Data, however, also poses new issues. These datasets and analytical capabilities call for a reconsideration of the role of the government within the system of public value creation, especially in relation to the use of governments' tools (i.e., nodality, authority, treasure, and organizational capacity) for orchestrating the exploitation of Big Data for designing, implementing, and evaluating public policies. In addition, questions arise with respect to who owns and controls Big Data, who supplies the information contained in Big Data and why they produce it, who demands the information hosted in Big Data and why they ask for it, and what strategy should governments follow to actively engage business companies and the civil society for making use of Big Data for public purposes.

As a way to contribute to this line of research, the present study contains a case study of innovation in the public sector based on Big Data where individual, institutional, and organizational features come into play for explaining the innovation adoption decision. The case under consideration is the adoption of predictive policing by Kent County Police in the UK, that is taken here as an (early) instance of application of Big Data to public service innovation. The case will show, in particular, that consideration for individual, institutional, and organizational features is important in order to explain early adoption of an innovation at a stage when it has not been widely diffused among public sector organizations yet.

PREDICTIVE POLICING IN KENT COUNTY

Origins, Adoption, and Implementation of Predictive Policing

Predictive policing provides an early instance of application of Big Data in the public sector. In essence, predictive policing consists of analytic techniques for anticipating future offences, especially in terms of identity of the offender, place where crimes will happen, and possibly the time when they will take place. As such, predictive policing can be understood as originating from a broader intellectual movement towards conceiving policing as a proactive activity to identify underlying crime problems and prevent offences, and away from the old fashioned reactive stance of detecting offenders and enforcing legislation (Eck &Spelman, 1987; Goldstein, 1979). So-called 'problem-oriented policing' consisted of encouraging policemen to discover the root cause of crime and to devise solutions to tackle them, especially in collaboration with local communities. Over time, application of this approach resulted in small but significant positive effects in reducing crime and disorder (Weisburd et al., 2008).

Predictive policing also builds on earlier efforts to assist the enforcement of laws with innovative techniques and managerial practices. These efforts included, for example, the ideation and adoption of CompStat at the New York Police Department (originally, in the Transit Police Crime Analysis Unit), a strategic management process to inform crime control services (Maple & Mitchell, 2000). Following a trajectory of increased professionalization and bureaucratization of police activity that took place in Western countries since the establishment of the London Metropolitan Police Force in 1829, in the second half of the twentieth century police service delivery strategy had come to rest upon three core functions, namely random patrol, rapid response to calls for service and reactive follow-up investigation of crime (Walsh, 2001). During last decades, the traditional ways in which police operated were partially adjusted to include larger community participation and support (Eck & Rosenbaum, 1994), together with greater decentralization and empowerment of patrol officers and operational supervisors. CompStat further enriched police activities by introducing business-like administrative policies assisted by a computerized information system that collected, mapped and analyzed crime statistics.

Predictive policing originates from research conducted at the University of California Los Angeles (UCLA) on pattern recognition and modeling (a line of research also related to military applications; Lewis et al., 2012).The technique spilled over to the police domain, especially along the collaboration between the Los Angeles Police Department (LAPD) and Dr Jeff Brantingham at UCLA and Dr George Mohler at Santa Clara University. Predictive policing was based on a technology that extracts patterns of behavior from past crime data and provides an identification of locations where crime and anti-social behavior are most likely to occur in the near future in a more accurate way than offered by alternative techniques, such as 'hot spot' policing and intelligence-led tactics. The technique resulted in a more efficient and effective use of patrol resources that are instructed to target 'hot spots' provided by the predictive policing system and communicated to police staff in daily briefing sessions.

In part, predictive policing was generally received with circumspect and suspicious attitudes, especially among police staff of early adopters in the US. Popularized in the press as a kind of 'Minority Report' style of crime prevention (after the film starring Tom Cruise), predictive policing elicited a cautious response that questioned the extent to which the technology really brought anything new to well established procedures for crime prevention and whether computer generated data provided any better information about crimes and offences than police staff 'on the road' already possessed. The police departments of Santa Cruz and of Los Angeles, however, acknowledged that the technique provided faster analysis of data, complementary inputs to those already possessed by experienced policemen, and a source of enhanced legitimacy for the police with respect to the local communities. The instructions received from predictive policing, moreover, enabled the police to deploy their staff resources in a more efficient way that resulted in positive effects on the value generated from taxpayers' money. Eventually, the police authorities that had adopted predictive policing techniques also reported a significant decrease of incidence of crimes (Friend, 2013).

Within a few years, other police officers in the world started to look at the early experience of predictive policing in the US with growing interest. Among them, in spring 2012 officers at Kent County Police (that already possessed some experience in pioneering innovative policing techniques, such as 'intelligence-led policing') read about predictive policing at LAPD in an article that had appeared in the specialized police press. After some preliminary information-gathering, they decided to undertake a trial project based on the analysis of several years' worth of crime data and human behavior for predicting the areas where offenses are likely to take place. The decision to explore the adoption of predictive policing was taken by Chief Constable Ian Learmonth, who argued that 'Predictive Policing helps address the root causes of crime and anti-social behavior rather than looking solely at the symptoms and will be used a tactical option as part of the force's current policing model. Predictive policing is the best example of old fashioned policing but using 21st century technology' (Kent Police website, 13th December 2012). Implementation of the project was assigned to Detective Chief Superintendent Jon Sutton. The system would produce 500 square feet 'hot spot' zones that are ranked into priority lists and communicated to policemen also through smart phones, tablets, and PCs.

After establishing contacts with the Police Departments of Santa Cruz and of Los Angeles and with the vendor company of the predictive policing software, Kent County Police became better informed of the technique and of how it could be employed. Kent Police possessed large amount of data that had been subjected, in the past, to some analysis, e.g., studies on repeated victimization. In a sense, then, the idea of using algorithms for inferring valuable information for crime prevention had been already contemplated within Kent Police cognitive domain. The prospect that predictive policing techniques could provide twice or three times more accurate predictions than calculations performed by analysts stimulated additional interest towards the technique. Accuracy, in fact, played an important role in determining whether crime prevention efforts gained any relevance in police patrol - provided that scarce police patrol resources could only be targeted to circumscribed locations and time periods only.

Having been persuaded of the merits of the predictive policing system, Kent Police (precisely the Chief Constable, Deputy Chief Constable and Assistant Chief Constable, the chief officer team and heads of profession, and the head of analysis) formed the decision to invest in the technology. A six-month trial period involved the deployment of the predictive policing system in the North Division of Kent County and a silent test of predictive accuracy in West Division. The adoption of predictive policing techniques called for the collaboration of staff involved in patrol activities. Generally, policemen tend to develop a detailed knowledge and understanding of the social system where they perform their duty. As a general attitude, in this respect, police staff that builds their expertise 'on the road' may find themselves skeptical (or cynical) with respect to automated or computerized systems that 'pretend' to substitute human expertise and judgmental capabilities with algorithms. A pivotal point within the adoption and implementation of predictive policing, then, exactly was the attainment of a buy-in from the side of the police staff, which should have been persuaded that predictive policing constituted an additional tool for better performing their duty, rather than a threat to their expertise.

The police staff were introduced to the predictive policing system with a series of presentations made by Steve Clark, Deputy Captain of the Police Department of Santa Cruz, and Professor Jeff Brantingham, one of the academics who pioneered the method. The initial attitude of Kent County Police staff was rather cautious at the outset, but it gradually turned into a more positive inclination. A relevant feature of the predictive policing system that apparently had a positive effect on individuals' attitudes was the perceived soundness and accuracy of the system. As Sutton put it:

[The predictive policing system] takes real life data so that gives us the evidence base and it takes in the theories that we've always worked to and acknowledged, [such as] repeat victimization [and] near repeat victimization. So everything in it is stuff that we'd rely on and that we'd recognize as a sound evidence base to work from. How that's put into this mathematical equation and then outputs is beyond my need to know. What I do need to know is, is it accurate and [that according to UCLA academics] it's probably twice, three times more accurate than how the analysts predict. So, if that's the case, then rather than us having random patrol and with our resources getting fewer we probably need to be more accurate. As accurate as we can be with the resources we have. (Interview, February 2013)

The system was presented as having a minimal impact on routine work of police patrol. In effect, the indications provided by the predictive policing system were used to partially redirect police time resources within their usual patrol practices. As Sutton put it, 'So we say, you know if you've got 15 minutes that's all we're asking you to do, just go and have a walk around this location, and you can make a difference in 15 minutes.' (Interview, February 2013). As such, the system was not perceived to pose any material threat to established police patrol practices. Rather, it was generally presented (and accepted) as a complementary tool that could assist in directing policemen's attention and time to most sensible areas.

The system, however, posed some threat to the analytical community within the police service. Analysts exactly possessed the kind of expertise and skills devoted to predict where crime would happen. The predictive policing system, in this respect, might be perceived as an algorithmic way to perform their same tasks, or even to perform it better than incumbent analysts. For crime analysts that had positioned themselves at the core of the intelligence function, the prospect that a piece of software 'dispossessed' them of part of their sources of distinctive contributions to the police force could be reasonably unwelcome. The police management, however, skillfully led the analysts to assess the merits of the predictive police system and to appropriate it as a component part of the repertoire of tools of their intelligence craft. As Sutton put it: 'It doesn't replace anything else, it's just another tool in the box, you know' (Interview, February 2013). More crucially, the analysts were charged of assessing the effectiveness of the system on the basis of the West District as controlled experimental design.

The main organizational venue for the implementation of predictive policing was the so-called 'tactical predictive policing board', where representatives of all interested parties met for discussing the development and application of the technique. At the operational level, the predictive policing system produced reports that were used in the morning briefing sessions. One of the elements of the briefing included a map that showed the location of 'hot spot' areas related to street crime, such as burglary, vehicle crime, violence, sexual offenses, robbery, criminal damage and anti-social behavior. In addition, a bi-weekly tasking coordination group regularly reviewed the past two weeks' performance and identified threats for the following two weeks and assigned resources to priorities. The content of the tasking coordination group could change over time, depending on the kinds of crime activity that the predictive policing system reports signaled as those most likely to happen.

Early testing of the predictive policing system resulted in positive impressions that assured the management to pursue the experimentation further. As Sutton put it:

It was a new idea, and we'd sold it quite well I felt, we were really engaged with it. It was a time of the year when [the staff] were able to engage with it, it was just before the Christmas period when some of the staff are off, and you have less staff to do the job. In those two weeks what [predictive policing] showed was that you could actually put more staff out on the ground in those locations [where they were needed] and we observed a significant change of performance. (Interview, February 2013)

Within a few months after the launch of the experimentation, Kent Police was able to spot early signs of positive effects. Information provided by the predictive policing software was regularly employed to instruct police patrols about where to target their presence. Showing up at 'hot spot' locations might have effectively contributed to reduce crime activity, although – to some extent – the information provided by the predictive policing software generally corresponded to well understood critical areas within the county territory that experienced policemen possessed. Anyway, the presence of police patrols in 'hot spot' areas seemed orchestrated in a way that made better use of scarce time and staff resources. As Sutton put it:

So we're a couple of months into it and we're starting to see signs of positivity in all these areas in terms of we're finding crime occurring in the middle of these locations. That's not to say we wouldn't have known that ordinarily, I think there's an element here that says we would have probably predicted some of this anyway 'cause they're in the usual places. There will be some that we wouldn't have ordinarily patrolled or known about, that's some of the work we need to understand. The fact that it almost can be seen as a resource allocation tool, so it does actually place people out, it gives them some focus as opposed to allowing officers to determine through instinct where to patrol, which may not be as accurate. (Interview, February 2013)

During the following months, the predictive policing system apparently delivered some tangible results. In August 2013, Kent Police announced that the trial of the system had delivered 6% reduction of street violence in Medway (BBC, 2013). In an effort to publicly exhibit the potentials of the system, on November 29th, 2013, police offers carried out foot police patrols that targeted areas where predictive policing anticipated that burglars might strike and that resulted in about a dozen people arrested (Kent Police web site, 2013). An operational review of the system conducted by Kent Police estimated overall 4% reduction of crime, and reported that the predictive policing system resulted 59% more likely to predict the location of a crime than Kent analysts (Kent Police, 2013).

Analysis of the Case

Having narrated the adoption of predictive policing in Kent County Police, this part of the chapter aims to explain the adoption and implementation of this innovative practice. First, an argument can be made that predictive policing counts as an instance of innovation in the provision of policing services, because of the employment of novel technological and organizational systems that resulted in an improvement of the work processes. The kind of innovation under consideration can be considered as a 'developmental' one in the classification of Osborne's (1998), insofar as the predictive policing system resulted in the provision of an existing service (crime prevention) to the same client population (residents of Kent County) rather than in the enlargement of the services and the expansion of the client population. The adoption of predictive policing, therefore, does not radically reconfigure existing scope of the service and practices. Yet, it is relevant to address the general issue of the role of Big Data in innovating service delivery practices in public sector organizations.

The case of predictive policing in Kent County seems especially pertinent to investigate important mechanisms of the diffusion of innovations in the public sector. The innovation diffusion process typically originates from organizations where innovations are invented and then spreads towards follower organizations. In understanding the dynamics of innovation and innovation diffusion, we may argue that different factors and conditions come into play in the adoption of innovative practices along the diffusion process. The invention of innovation, in particular, may be better explained by different factors, conditions, and mechanisms (such as, for example, individual expertise, motivations, and entrepreneurial spirit) with respect to the adoption of innovations at later stage (such as, for example, societal pressures to conform to what other organizations have already done). In this respect, the experience of Kent County Police can be understood as one of an 'early adopter' of the innovative practice.

Explaining why 'early adopters' of innovations implement the innovative practices is not trivial. Differently from the inventors, early adopters lack the kind of social recognition (i.e., appreciation) that is generally granted to those who successfully pioneer new methods and techniques. At the opposite, advocates of innovation in early adopter organizations may face internal hostility towards adopting practices that 'have not been invented here'. Differently from the follower organizations, however, early adopters lack the kind of social pressure (i.e., push to conformity) that mounts when an increasing number of peer organizations follow certain canons of conduct as a basis for gaining legitimacy. Yet, if there were no early adopters then no innovation, that is introduced in an inventor organization in the first place, would ever diffuse among followers. It seems relevant, therefore, to precisely investigate what led Kent Police County to adopt predictive policing because this can shed some light into a crucial stage of the innovation diffusion process.

Why, then, did Kent Police adopt the predictive policing technique? How did they implement it in such an apparently effective way? As a way to answer these questions, we consider five different component parts of the process of adopting the predictive policing system. First, predictive policing gained the attention of key mangers of Kent Police. Obviously, as predictive policing was not invented in Kent Police, then the introduction of the system into the early adopter would have not taken place if senior police officers had not noticed it as an experience that had taken place in other police organizations. In this respect, the activation of a network of police actors, in the form of publications and other means for circulation of information, plays an important role in the stimulation of attention towards what other peer organization did. At the individual level, we may argue that canons of professional identity include keeping one's informed of the experiences of other peers and devoting some effort to keep one's knowledge of emerging practices within the professional domain up to date. The activation of the professional police network, moreover, seems relevant to account for the ease of access to information about experiences of predictive policing in Santa Cruz and Los Angeles, as well as for the credibility granted to the sources.

A second component part of the adoption process relates to the identification of the potential for performance improvement in some dimensions. The evidence from the case study shows that Kent Police was especially interested in the accuracy of predictive policing system with respect to existing analytic techniques. The rationale for attention towards this particular performance dimension, in turn, relates to the limitation of organizational resources, namely in the form of police patrol hours available. If predictive policing lacked the promise of improvement in a dimension that was considered as relevant by Kent Police senior officers, then arguably they would have not devoted further attention to investigating the possibility to apply the system into their organization.

A third component part of the adoption process consists of an early feasibility assessment. The evidence from the case study shows that Kent Police already possessed some experience in the use of advanced analytic techniques, such as 'intelligence-led policing'. In this sense, the organization was well positioned to understand the innovative technique and incorporate it within their working practices. If senior police officers were not confident that Kent Police could engage in a meaningful dialogue with the inventors of the predictive policing system, then they could have stopped any further efforts to introduce the novel techniques and practices. Cultural proximity between the UK and the US, in addition, might have supported the belief that police practices adopted in Santa Cruz and Los Angeles could be translated into the Kent Police context.

A fourth component part of the adoption process consists of the generation of an 'internal proof' for the working of the innovation. Although predictive policing was not invented in Kent Police, the case study provides evidence that senior police officers intended to gain firsthand experience of the performance effects of the system. This aim was attained through the predictive policing trial period and, more significantly, through the controlled experiment design. Arguably, these interventions contributed to stimulate a sense of ownership of predictive policing and to counteract the possibility that the system could be ostracized because of being alien to Kent Police's intellectual and operational background.

Finally, a fifth component part of the adoption process consists of the safeguarding of a 'truce' that senior police officers made with police staff, especially with the analysts group. The case study evidence shows that, despite potential sources of apprehension that predictive policing system could dislodge the role that the analysts has within the intelligence function of Kent Police, analysts were generally supportive of the innovation. In part, this may be explained on the basis of the skillful efforts to frame predictive policing as not threatening to existing organizational practices. In part, this may be also accounted for by the participation of the analysts to the assessment of the effectiveness of the predictive policing system, which ultimately led them to appropriate the method and technique as part of their own repertoire of tools.

In explaining how these component parts of the adoption process contributed to the effective implementation of novel practices that enriched existing police patrol activities, we consider the role of the combination of social mechanisms of organizational learning and protection of identities and role. Organizational learning is a process that results in behavioral change as a consequence of performance feedback cycles (Argyris & Schön, 1996; Levitt &March, 1988). The case evidence suggests that Kent Police experienced an organizational learning process as policemen became gradually acquainted with the new technique and the 'tactical predictive policing board' and the tasking coordination groups started to meet regularly and provide inputs to the use of predictive policing information. In addition, a mechanism of protection of identities and roles (Wenger, 2007), that relates to staff's inclination to establish their expertise and contribution to crime prevention activities, could have affected policemen's attitude towards the new technology. The confinement of predictive policing as a mere additional tool to the repertoire of experienced policemen, in this respect, served the rhetorical purpose of downplaying the 'liability of newness' (Singh et al., 1996) of the new technology and therefore overcome the barriers of suspicion, skepticism and cynicism that part of the staff might have felt towards the predictive policing technology.

FUTURE RESEARCH DIRECTIONS

The analysis of the case of the introduction of predictive policing in Kent County provides some directions for pursuing further research on innovation and innovation diffusion in the public sector. First, additional case studies could be collected about the use of Big Data as a source of technological innovations that can help improving the performance of existing services provided the present clients as well as expanding the range of services and/or extending the reach of service delivery to additional clients. Second, additional efforts could be directed to better understand the adoption and implementation from 'early followers' of emerging innovation opportunities – as it was the case of Kent County Police with respect to the 'original innovators' of Santa Cruz and LAPD. 'Early followers', in fact, differ from 'late followers' in the spreading of innovations because the formers face uncertainty as to whether the innovation provides operational gains and lack the kind of legitimacy support that is generally acquired by innovations that have already diffused among an organizational population. Third, more research could be directed to investigate the managerial strategies that support the implementation of innovations, especially when the new technology might potentially be perceived as a threat to the expertise, skills and capabilities of part of the staff.

CONCLUSION

This chapter provided a case study on an instance of early adoption of Big Data technology for the innovation of crime prevention activities. The chapter argued that sources of technological opportunities may result in innovations within public sector organizations depending on the presence of favorable organizational and institutional circumstances. The scholarly literature on innovation and innovation diffusion, in fact, provides that innovations may not necessarily take place because of the prospect of improving operational performance only. Rather, the adoption and implementation of an innovation relates to a strategic process that entails the repositioning of the organization within its environment, the activation of linkages with new stakeholders (and, in relation to this, possibly also the dismantling of previously relevant contacts), and the management of expectations from the side of the part of the staff who could be most prone to consider the innovation as a threat rather than an additional tool for better performing their work.

The analysis of the case of the adoption of predictive policing in Kent Police provides some evidence that Big Data may contribute enhancing opportunities for innovation in public sector organizations. Opportunities offered by technological advancement, however, do not necessarily entail that public sector organizations are willing and able to innovate. Some public sector organizations may exert original efforts to invent novel services or approaches to deliver existing services in a more effective, efficient, and economic way. Others may follow inventors and early adopters by mimicking others' initiatives and importing techniques and practices that have spread among similar organizations. The particular contribution of this study, in this respect, has been the one to explain the conduct of an 'early adopter' of an innovation, namely of predictive policing. While Kent Police did not invent predictive policing, nevertheless it was one of the very early police bureaus in the world to follow suit the lead of the Police Departments of Santa Cruz and Los Angeles.

The analysis of the case suggests that five component parts of the adoption process seem especially relevant to account for the decision to introduce the technique to the organization and for the effective incorporation into existing organizational practices. First, individuals in senior positions should notice the opportunity offered by Big Data, possibly on the basis of information channeled through professional or policy networks. Second, the innovative technique and practice should hold the promise to deliver some improvement in any relevant dimension of organizational performance. Third, the early adopter organizations should positively assess the feasibility of introducing the innovation. Fourth, the early adopter may generate original evidence about the effectiveness of the innovation. Finally, senior managers should induce the organizational staff to assess the merits of the innovative technique and to accept the introduction of novel practices. If these activities are appropriately performed, then public sector organizations may effectively grasp the opportunities offered by sources of technological innovation generally, and Big Data in particularly.

ACKNOWLEDGMENT

I would like to thank Detective Chief Superintendent Jon Sutton of Kent County Police for the interview in February 2013.

REFERENCES

Aitken, M., & Hage, J. (1971). The organic organization and innovation. *Sociology*, *5*(1), 63–83. doi:10.1177/003803857100500105

Albury, D. (2005). Fostering innovation in public services. *Public Money & Management*, *25*, 51–56.

Altshuler, A. A., & Behn, R. D. (1997). *Innovation in American Government: Challenges, Opportunities, and Dilemmas*. Washington, DC: Brookings Institution Press.

Argyris, C., & Schön, D. A. (1996). *Organizational Learning: A Theory of Action Perspective*. Reading, MA: Addison- Wesley.

Bagozzi, R. P. (2007). The legacy of the technology acceptance model and a proposal for a paradigm shift. *Journal of the Association for Information Systems*, *8*(4), 244–254.

BBC. (2013). *Predicting crime 'cut Medway street violence by 6%'*. Retrieved 14th August, from http://www.bbc.co.uk/news/uk-england-kent-23689715

Berry, F. S., & Berry, W. D. (1990). State Lottery Adoptions as Policy Innovations: An Event History Analysis. *The American Political Science Review*, *84*(2), 395–415. doi:10.2307/1963526

Berry, F. S., & Berry, W. D. (1999). Innovation and Diffusion Models in Policy Research. In P. Sabatier (Ed.), *Theories of the Policy Process*. Boulder, CO: Westview Press.

Bessant, J. (2003). *High-Involvement Management: Building and Sustaining Competitive Advantage Through Continuous Change*. Chichester, UK: Wiley.

Bollier, D. (2010). *The Promise and Peril of Big Data*. Washington, DC: The Aspen Institute.

Borins, S. (1998). *Innovating with Integrity*. Washington, DC: Georgetown University Press.

Borins, S. (2001). *The Challenge of Innovating in Government*. Washington, DC: IBM Center for the Business of Government.

Boyd, D., & Crawford, K. (2012). Critical Questions for Big Data. *Information Communication and Society*, *15*(5), 662–679. doi:10.1080/1369118X.2012.678878

DiMaggio, P. J., & Powell, W. W. (1991). The Iron Cage Revisited: Institutional Isomorphism and Collective Rationality in Organizational Fields. In W. W. Powell & P. J. DiMaggio (Eds.), *The New Institutionalism in Organizational Analysis*. Chicago, IL: University of Chicago Press.

Dolowitz, D. P., & Marsh, D. (1998). Policy Transfer: A Framework for Comparative Analysis. In M. Minogue, C. Polidano, & D. Hulme (Eds.), *Beyond the New Public Management: Changing Ideas and Practices in Governance*. Cheltenham, UK: Edwards Elgar.

Downe, J., Hartley, J., & Rashman, L. (2004). Evaluating the Extent of Inter-organizational Learning and Change in Local Authorities Through the English Beacon Council Scheme. *Public Management Review*, *6*(4), 531–553. doi:10.1080/1471903042000303328

Eck, J. E., & Rosenbaum, D. (1994). The new police order: effectiveness, equity, and efficiency in community policing. In D. Rosenbaum (Ed.), *The Challenge of Community Policing: Testing the Promise*. Thousands Oaks, CA: SAGE. doi:10.4135/9781483327006.n1

Eck, J. E., & Spelman, W. (1987). *Problem-Solving: Problem-Oriented Policing in Newport News*. Washington, DC: National Institute of Justice, Police Executive Research Forum (PERF).

Finger, M., & Pécoud, G. (2003). *From E-government to E-governance? Towards a Model of E-governance*. Paper presented at the 3rd European Conference on E-government. Dublin, Ireland.

Friend, Z. (2013). Predictive Policing: Using Technology to Reduce Crime. *FBI Law Enforcement Bulletin*. Retrieved from http://www.fbi.gov/stats-services/publications/law-enforcement-bulletin/2013/April/

Goldstein, H. (1979). Improving Policing: A Problem-Oriented Approach. *Crime and Delinquency*, *25*(2), 236–258. doi:10.1177/001112877902500207

Greenhalgh, T., Robert, G., Macfarlane, F., Bate, P., & Kyriakidou, O. (2004). Diffusion of Innovations in Service Organizations: Systematic Review and Recommendations. *The Milbank Quarterly*, *82*(4), 581–629. doi:10.1111/j.0887-378X.2004.00325.x PMID:15595944

Hage, J., & Dewar, R. (1973). Elite Values Versus Organizational Structure in Predicting Innovation. *Administrative Science Quarterly*, *18*(3), 279–290. doi:10.2307/2391664

Hartley, J. (2005). Innovation in Governance and Public Services: Past and Present. *Public Money and Management*, *25*, 27–34.

Heeks, R. (1999). Reinventing Government in the Information Age. In R. Heeks (Ed.), Reinventing Government in the Information Age (pp. 9-21). New York: Routledge.

Hood, C. (1986). *The Tools of Government*. London: Chatham House.

Islam, M. M., & Ahmed, A. M. S. (2007). Understanding E-Governance: A Theoretical Approach. *Asian Affairs*, *29*(4), 29–46.

Jun, K.-N., & Weare, C. (2010). Institutional Motivations in the Adoption of Innovations: The Case of E-Government. *Journal of Public Administration: Research and Theory*, *21*(3), 495–519. doi:10.1093/jopart/muq020

Kent Police. (2013). *Predpol operational review – initial findings*. Kent County Police Corporate Services – Analysis Department.

Kent Police Web Site. (2013). *Predictive policing day of action targets burglars*. Retrieved 3rd December, from http://www.kent.police.uk/news/latest_news/131203_predpol_day_a.html

Kimberly, J. R., & Evanisko, M. J. (1981). Organizational innovation: The influence of individual, organizational and contextual factors on hospitals adoption of technological and administrative innovations. *Academy of Management Journal*, *24*(4), 689–713. doi:10.2307/256170 PMID:10253688

King, N. (1992). Modeling the innovation process: An empirical comparison of approaches. *Journal of Occupational and Organizational Psychology*, *65*(2), 89–100. doi:10.1111/j.2044-8325.1992.tb00487.x

Kingdon, J. W. (1995). *Agendas, Alternatives, and Public Policies*. New York: Longman.

Korteland, E., & Bekkers, V. (2008). The Diffusion of Electronic Service Delivery Innovations in Dutch E-policing: The Case of Digital Warning Systems. *Public Management Review*, *10*(1), 71–88. doi:10.1080/14719030701763195

Levitt, B., & March, J. G. (1988). Organizational Learning. *Annual Review of Sociology*, *14*(1), 319–340. doi:10.1146/annurev.so.14.080188.001535

Lewis, E., Mohler, G., Brantingham, P. J., & Bertozzi, A. L. (2012). Self-exciting point process models of civilian deaths in Iraq. *Security Journal*, *25*(3), 244–264. doi:10.1057/sj.2011.21

Lynn, L. (1997). Innovation and the Public Interest: Insights from the Private Sector. In A. Altchuler & R. Behn (Eds.), *Innovation in American Government*. Washington, DC: Brookings Institution.

Manovich, L. (2011). *Trending: The Promises and the Challenges of Big Social Data*. Retrieved from http://www.manovich.net/DOCS/Manovich_trending_paper.pdf

Manyika, J., Chui, M., Brown, B., Bughin, J., Dobbs, R., Roxburgh, C., & Hung Byers, A. (2011). *Big Data: The Next Frontier for Innovation, Competition, and Productivity*. McKinsey Global Institute.

Maple, J., & Mitchell, C. (2000). *The Crime Fighter: How You Can Make Your Community Free*. New York: Broadway Books.

March, J. G., & Olsen, J. P. (1989). *Rediscovering Institutions: The Organizational Basis of Politics*. New York: The Free Press.

Marche, S., & McNiven, J. D. (2003). E-Government and E-Governance: The Future Isn't What It Used to Be. *Canadian Journal of Administrative Sciences*, *20*(1), 74–86. doi:10.1111/j.1936-4490.2003.tb00306.x

McAfee, A., & Brynjolfsson, E. (2012). Big Data: The Management Revolution. *Harvard Business Review*, (October): 1–9. PMID:23074865

Minelli, M. (2013). *Big Data, Big Analytics, Emerging Business Intelligence and Analytic Trends for Today's Business*. Hoboken, NJ: John Wiley & Sons. doi:10.1002/9781118562260

Moore, M., & Hartley, J. (2008). Innovations in Governance. *Public Management Review*, *10*(1), 3–20. doi:10.1080/14719030701763161

Moore, M. H. (2005). Break-through innovations and continuous improvement: Two different models ofinnovative processes in the public sector. *Public Money and Management*, *25*, 43–50.

Mulgan, G., & Albury, D. (2003). *Innovations in the Public Sector*. London: Cabinet Office.

OECD. (2013). Exploring Data-Driven Innovation as a NewSource of Growth: Mapping the Policy Issues Raised by 'BigData'. *OECD Digital Economy Papers, 222*.

Ohlhorst, F. (2013). *Big Data Analytics: Turning Big Data into Big Money*. Hoboken, NJ: John Wiley& Sons.

Osborne, D., & Gaebler, T. (1993). *Reinventing Government: How the Entrepreneurial Spirit Is Transforming the Public Sector*. London: Plume.

Osborne, S. P. (1998). Naming the beast' defining and classifying service innovations in social policy. *Human Relations*, *30*(9), 1133–1154. doi:10.1177/001872679805100902

Osborne, S. P., & Brown, L. (2011). Innovation, Public Policy and Public Services Delivery in the UK: The Word that Would Be King? *Public Administration*, *89*(4), 1335–1350. doi:10.1111/j.1467-9299.2011.01932.x

Pollitt, C. (2002). Clarifying convergence: Striking similarities and durable differences in public management reform. *Public Management Review*, *3*(4), 471–492. doi:10.1080/14616670110071847

Rashman, L., & Hartley, J. (2002). Leading and learning? Knowledge transfer in the Beacon Council Scheme. *Public Administration*, *80*(3), 523–542. doi:10.1111/1467-9299.00316

Rashman, L., & Radnor, Z. (2005). Learning to Improve: Approaches to Improving Local Government Services. *Public Money and Management*, *25*(1), 19–26.

Rogers, E. M. (2003). *Diffusion of Innovations*. New York: The Free Press.

Sapat, A. (2004). Devolution and innovation: The adoption of state environmental policy innovations by administrative agencies. *Public Administration Review*, *64*(2), 141–151. doi:10.1111/j.1540-6210.2004.00356.x

Sathi, A. (2012). *Big Data Analytics*. Boise: MC Press.

Scott, W. R. (2001). *Institutions and Organizations*. Thousand Oaks, CA: Sage Publications.

Silverman, D. (1971). *The Theory of Organisations: A Sociological Framework*. London: Heinemann.

Singh, J. V., Tucker, D. J., & House, R. J. (1986). Organizational Legitimacy and the Liability of Newness. *Administrative Science Quarterly*, *31*(2), 32–44. doi:10.2307/2392787

Stoker, G., & Wilson, D. (1986). Intra-organizational politics in local authorities: Towards a new approach. *Public Administration*, *64*(3), 285–302. doi:10.1111/j.1467-9299.1986.tb00623.x

Tether, B. S. (2002). Who co-operates for innovation, and why an empirical analysis. *Research Policy*, *31*(6), 947–967. doi:10.1016/S0048-7333(01)00172-X

Thompson, V. (1965). Bureaucracy and innovation. *Administrative Science Quarterly*, *10*(1), 1–20. doi:10.2307/2391646

Tidd, J., Bessant, J., & Pavitt, K. (2005). *Managing Innovation: Integrating Technological, Market and Organizational Change*. Chichester, UK: Wiley.

Tolbert, C. J., Mossberger, K., & McNeal, R. (2008). Institutions, policy innovation, and e-government in the American states. *Public Administration Review*, *68*(3), 549–563. doi:10.1111/j.1540-6210.2008.00890.x

UNDESA (United Nations Department of Economic and Social Affairs). (2003). *E-Government Survey 2012: E-Government for the People*. New York: United Nations.

US Executive Office of the President. (2014). *Big Data: Seizing Opportunities, Preserving Values*. Washington, DC: The White House.

Valente, T. W. (1995). *Network models of the diffusion of innovations*. Cresskill, NJ: Hampton Press.

Van de Ven, A. H., & Rogers, E. M. (1988). Innovations and organizations: Critical perspectives. *Communication Research*, *15*(5), 632–651. doi:10.1177/009365088015005007

Venkatesh, V., Morris, M. G., Davis, G. B., & Davis, F. D. (2003). User acceptance of information technology: Toward a unified view. *Management Information Systems Quarterly*, *3*, 425–478.

Walker, R. M. (2003). Evidence on the Management of Public Service Innovation. *Public Money & Management*, *23*(2), 93–102. doi:10.1080/09540962.2003.10874830

Walsh, W. F. (2001). Compstat: An analysis of an emerging police managerial paradigm. *Policing: An International Journal of Police Strategies & Management*, *24*(3), 347–362. doi:10.1108/13639510110401717

Weisburd, D., Telep, C., Hinkle, J., & Eck, J. (2008). *Effects of Problem-Oriented Policing on Crime and Disorder*. Washington, DC: U.S. Department of Justice. doi:10.4073/csr.2008.14

Wenger, E. (2007). *Communities of Practice: Learning, Meaning, and Identity*. Cambridge, MA: Cambridge University Press.

Willem, A., & Buelens, M. (2007). Knowledge sharing in public sector organizations: The effect oforganizational characteristics on interdepartmental knowledge sharing. *Journal of Public Administration: Research and Theory*, *17*(4), 581–606. doi:10.1093/jopart/mul021

Wolfe, A. (1994). Organizational innovation: Review, critique and suggested research directions. *Journal of Management Studies*, *31*(3), 405–431. doi:10.1111/j.1467-6486.1994.tb00624.x

KEY TERMS AND DEFINITIONS

Big Data: Relatively large data-sets that originate from diverse sources and that are not analyzable through standard methods and tools.

Innovation: The process that results in the introduction of novel principles and practices in the work activities of an organization.

Innovation Diffusion: The process that results in the spreading of innovations across different organizations.

Predictive Policing: A technique for anticipating where certain kind of crimes are most likely to happen and informing crime prevention.

Chapter 3

If We Build It, Will They Come?

An Appreciation of the Microfoundations of E-Government

Michael J. Ahn
University of Massachusetts, USA

John McNutt
University of Delaware, USA

ABSTRACT

This chapter explores the possible role of microfoundations (social, cultural, and institutional factors) as a determinant of electronic government. While earlier research has implied that microfoundations might be critical to e-government, this research presents an approach to assessing how technology interacts with societal factors in creating (or not creating) e-government success. The findings suggest that e-government development depends not only on strict technological and economic capacity but also on fertile social and institutional environment that facilitate the development of e-government. These findings support the basic premise that e-government does not exist in a vacuum and these soft factors and attributes create an environment that directs the outcomes of e-government. This enriches previous research on e-government acceptance such as Diffusion of Innovation Theory (Rogers, 1983) and the Technology Acceptance Model (Davis, 1989) and extends it to national and international realms.

INTRODUCTION

Efforts to apply technology to government offer the public a host of potential benefits (West, 2005). These benefits range from providing virtual access to information and service for citizen to transforming the way that government functions (Kim & Layne, 2001; Andersen & Henriksen, 2006). As technology advances and the level of technology sophistication in the general population becomes more pervasive, expectations by both citizens and policymakers rise. Unfortunately, the success of e-government efforts doesn't always meet expectations. The recent experience of the United States with the website for the Affordable Care Act is just another reminder of a long litany of issues with the effectiveness of e-government. While there are certainly a host of potential reasons for any

DOI: 10.4018/978-1-4666-7266-6.ch003

e-government failure, one of the least recognized is a lack of potential fit with the microfoundations of government. Microfoundations is a popular and often controversial concept in the social sciences (particularly economics), but lacks a consistent usage in the literature on e-government. For the purpose of this study, microfoundations refer to the structures and relationships that underpin certain social processes or activities that influence how institutions operate. Here, these social structures, and processes work as the foundation (hence the term, microfoundations)for government and effective government operation depends on their characteristics.

Putnam (2000; 1995) famously argues that social capital provides the microfoundations for effective national and local government. There is considerable evidence that social systems either promote or inhibit innovation (Rogers, 1983). Some researchers talk about a culture of innovativeness (Boehmke & Skinner, 2012) in states. These are factors that are generally ignored in approaches that look at what technology can potentially do and assume that installing it is adequate. The problem is that many e-government advocates ignore the microfoundations of both technology use and government. This approach, sometimes call the "field of dreams problem" (if you build it, they will come), characterizes the approach of a number of both practitioners and academics. If planners and policy makers had access to these additional dimensions, they could make smarter and more successful choices.

Since e-government activities are conducted by governmental institutions, the microfoundations of e-government cannot be completely separated from those of government per se. Still, it is unclear that effective governments are necessarily better at e-government than ineffective ones. Technology competence doesn't always follow from excellence in other functions. This research will explore this dimension by offering a cross sectional consideration of the relationship between E-government quality and underlying value and governmental dimensions while controlling for the digital divide and per capita GNP. We will explore the following research questions:

RQ1: Is there a relationship between underlying social values, social conditions, citizen characteristics and social capital and e-government outcomes?

RQ2: Is this relationship (if any) affected by the digital divide and economic output?

Background

The growth of Electronic government represents a rapidly evolving force in the world today. From very humble beginnings e-government has emerged as substantial force in the growing information society and a major driver in the future of government. Unfortunately, some e-government projects fail to deliver on their promises. Some are technically flawed. Others are never implemented properly or just never used (see Dada, 2006; Heeks, 2003).

While there is substantial literature on the organizational aspects of e-government implementation, a considerable body of research on comparative e-government programming and a smaller amount of research looking at cultural factors in e-government there is a need to look further toward a more complete approach. Our model builds on six factors, each of which will be considered in turn. Our model includes Social Capital, Social Conditions, Social Values, Citizen Characteristics and Financial Capacity, and the Digital Divide. These are factors that previous research suggests much influence large scale social innovation. While previous e-government research has considered some of these factors, our model expands this approach. The overall model appears in Figure 1.

The model suggests that there are microfoundations (social conditions, citizen characteristics,

Figure 1. Theoretical framework

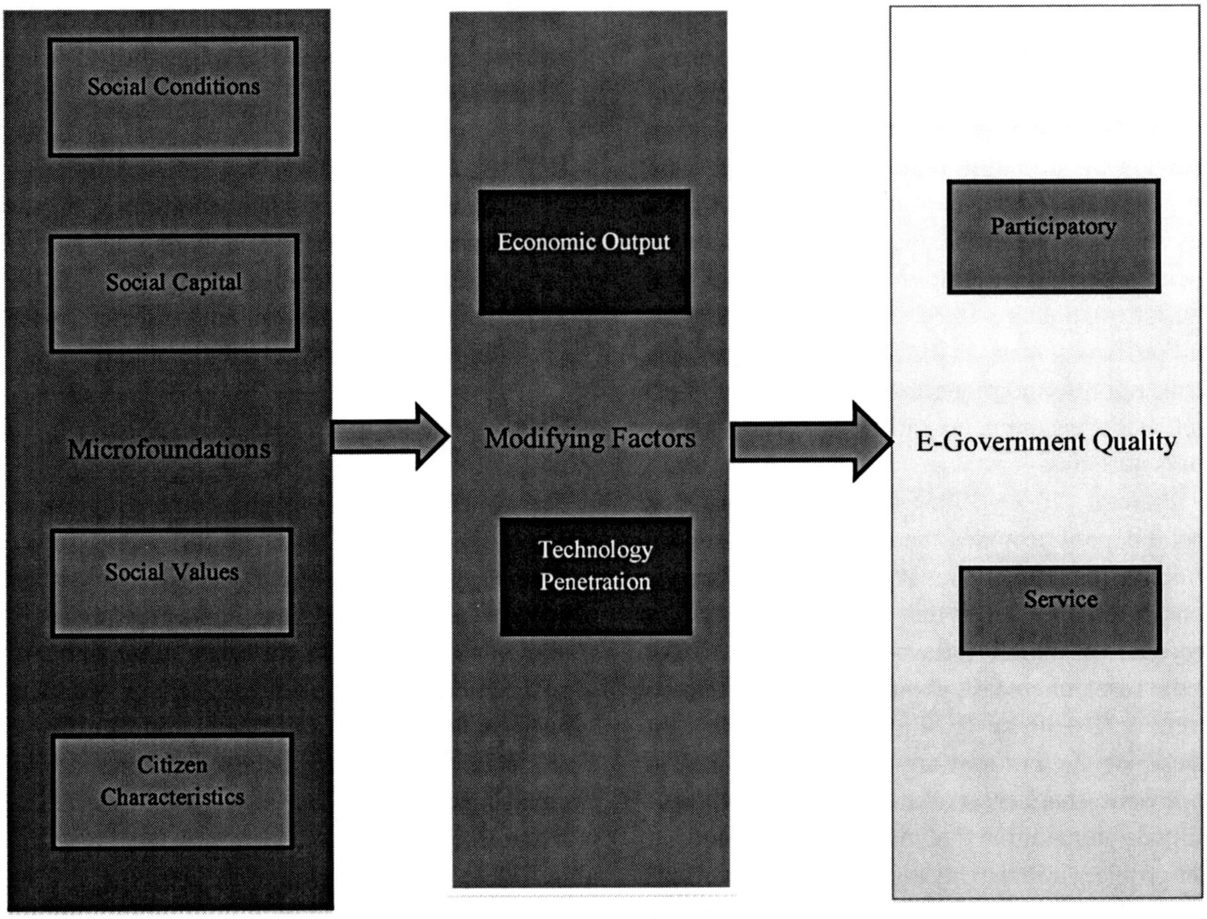

Social Values, and Social Capital), modifying factors (economic output and technology penetration) and outcomes. Each of these factors is considered below.

- **Social Capital:** The role of social capital in public programs and good government is one of the major intellectual forces in current public policy. The World Bank (2011), which initiated a major effort to promote social capital throughout the world, defines social capital as:

Social capital refers to the institutions, relationships, and norms that shape the quality and quantity of a society's social interactions. Increasing evidence shows that social cohesion is critical for societies to prosper economically and for development to be sustainable. Social capital is not just the sum of the institutions which underpin a society – it is the glue that holds them together.

While there are many approaches to social capital and many competing definitions, the approach pioneered by John Coleman (1988) and developed by Robert Putnam (1995; 2000) seems to be most useful in this context. Social capital is about networks, trust and relationships. It is about having the type of civic order that underpins the democratic process. It speaks to norms of trust and effective networks of relationships that enable social action. It also looks at civic groups, organizations, associations and so forth. Associations provide citizens with the opportunity to learn how to participate in a democracy. Without these opportunities, participation will not be as extensive. Social capital is seen as the microfoundations of government. Therefore, social capital is proposed as the foundation for an effective political system. This tradition builds on Putnam's (Putnam, Leonardi, & Nanetti, 1994) work with local governments in Italy. He eventually extended this analysis to much larger targets in his well-regarded "Bowling Alone" argument. (Putnam, 2000). Governments that are supported by higher levels of social capital are more likely to be successful as governments. This does not always result in more effective service delivery however. It also does not necessarily translate into more innovative government.

Putnam (2000) differentiates between bonding social capital (which makes groups more supportive of each other) and bridging (which reaches out to other groups). His recent work has examined the relationship between social capital and diversity (Putnam, 2007). Social capital theory also augers nicely with emerging literature on citizen participation and voluntary associations (Rainie et al., 2012) as well as the developing field of network studies (Rainey, Rainie & Wellman, 2012).

While Putnam's original research depends on traditional face to face social capital, there have been significant efforts to look at the online developments that parallel the factors involved in traditional face to face social capital (Rainie et al., 2012; Norris, 2002; Lee & Lee, 2010; Rainie, Purcell & Smith, 2011). Unfortunately, measuring online social capital from a macro perspective has not been completely developed.

Given the role of social capital in promoting effective government, there should be a positive relationship with successful e-government. This relationship should be particularly strong with those aspects of e-government that promote participation.

- **Financial Capacity:** The cost of e-government in terms of hardware, software, technical personnel and so forth can be considerable. This means that a lack of financial support could be considered a barrier (see Moon, 2002) to adequate e-government. Economic capacity is a prerequisite to effective taxation which is essential to effective government programming. This means that there should be a reasonably direct relationship between economic output and higher levels of e-government performance. This might be moderated by higher levels of income inequality. In a regressive tax situation, higher levels of inequality should result in smaller tax revenues. This is particularly true of consumption taxes. Since lower income taxpayers consume a greater portion of their income, the resulting aggregate tax payments should be greater. The GINI coefficient, while not without its problems, is one of the most accepted and used measurement tools for inequality.
- **Technology Penetration:** E-Government is only possible if there is a corresponding level of technology available in the general population. The digital divide will not only make it more unlikely that citizens will use the service (Belanger & Carter, 2006: 2009), it can also make it less likely that there will be political effort to develop e-government. Strictly speaking, the digital divide is more complex than technology penetration alone (McNutt, 1998). It includes skills and education needed to make full use of the Internet. This includes a number of factors that go beyond penetration. These are more difficult to capture and assess in an international situation because some of the components are relative to the society and economy of the individual nations.

- **Social Values:** Values are a critical element of culture. They reflect our worldviews and experiences as a people. They tell us what is right or wrong, good and bad, desirable and undesirable. They give rise to social norms and a variety of tools for social control. Social values tend to be stable over time. They typically evolve very slowly. While cultural change is possible, it is difficult to accomplish. Value change requires significant resources and a considerable time period to accomplish. The literature on social movements and social change offers examples of cultural changes that have occurred (for example changes in the role of women and changes in the orientation toward the environment). These required years to accomplish and considerable amounts of effort.

There has been a small amount of systemic literature linking e-government with cultural values (See for example Carter & Weerakkody, 2008; Khalil, 2011). Cultural Values about Freedom of expression & association, Rule of Law, Corruption will be important here, as well as values about use of technology would lead to better acceptance of E-government.

- **Citizen Characteristics:** Characteristics of the potential user population are critical factors. These include general satisfaction, role of government, and perception of technology and whether they use the Internet for politics. Depending on the population orientation, they can be barriers or facilitators. This is reflected well in Roger's (1983) work on the diffusion of innovation. Different populations groups adopt innovations at different rates and these groups are defined by education, socioeconomic status and social attitudes. He defines five successive adopter groups: innovators, early adopters, early majority, late majority and laggards. Innovators and early adopters are those with higher education, higher social economic status and who are more receptive to innovations while laggards tend to be those with lower education, social status and more traditionalistic attitudes.
- **Social Conditions:** Finally, the level of development of a given nation is critical. This factor looks at the sum of social and economic development present in a society. Level of Development refers to economic and social activity in a society. It is important here because it encapsulates the struggles that government and citizens have to contend with in their daily activities. Throughout history of social and economic development, the measurement of this concept has changed dramatically.

Early work tracked Gross National Product (GNP) with the idea that economic output would raise general conditions (Todero, 1985). The growing understanding that GNP was not a perfect measure of development led to a search for alternatives. This was especially true in light of the development communities basic human needs approach in the 1970s.

The Overseas Development Council's Physical Quality of Life Index (PQLI) (Morris & McAlpin, 1979) was an early attempt to define noneconomic development. This index combined adult literacy rate, life expectancy at age one and infant mortality rate into an index that placed nations from zero to 100. While this was a substantial improvement on merely using GNP as a measure of development, it considers a decided limited number of dimensions.

The United Nations Human Development Index was created in the early 1990s by a group of scholars under the leadership of economists Mahbub ul Haq and Amartya Sen (Klugman, Rodríguez, & Choi, 2011). The United Nations Development Program sponsors this effort and continues to maintain the series. This provides a much more comprehensive set of indicators that define development far more broadly. It includes both economic and noneconomic indicators and creates an index where national development can be summarized. Over the years, the index has evolved and been refined. While it is certainly not without its critics, it remains a well-regarded index.

The level of development index used in the United Nations E-Government Studies is the Human Capital Index (UN, 2010). According to the United Nations "The data for the human capital index relies on the UNDP 'education index' which is a composite of the adult literacy rate and the combined primary, secondary and tertiary gross enrolment ratio with two third weight given to adult literacy and one third to gross enrolment ratio.

- **E-Government Performance:** E-Government performance has been defined in a variety of ways. A variety of studies have yielded conflicting results on e-government quality. For the purposes of this study, we employed the United Nations approach which divides effectiveness into service effectiveness and participation effectiveness. The United Nations (2010) defines E-Government as:

E-government is defined as the use of ICT and its application by the government for the provision of information and public services to the people. The aim of e-government therefore is to provide efficient government management of information to the citizen; better service delivery to citizens; and empowerment of the people through access to information and participation in public policy decision-making.

The UN has attempted to build an international consensus around the included concepts that underpin e-government.

- **Summary of the Theoretical Framework:** In sum, our model attempts to explain why e-government performance happens in a country based on six factors: Social Capital, Financial Capacity, Social Conditions, Social Values, Citizen Characteristics and The Digital Divide. The dependent variable is divided into e-service and e-participation. We find that there is support for our approach in the general literature. Based on our discussion above, we would expect the following relationships would occur:

Hypotheses:

H1: Higher levels of social capital will be associated with higher levels of general e-government performance;

H1a: Higher levels of social capital will be associated with higher levels of e-participation e-government performance;

H2: Higher levels of Human Capital will be associated with higher levels of general e-government performance;

H3: Higher Levels of Internet Penetration will be associated with higher levels of general e-government performance;

H4: Higher levels of GNP Per Capita will be associated with higher levels of general e-government performance;

H5: Higher levels of inequality will moderate the relationship between Per Capita GNP and e-government performance.

H6: Higher Levels of support for Free Expression, Government Quality, Rule of law, corruption control, Work-Orientation, technology as a benefit and the role of government will be associated with higher levels of general e-government performance.

These propositions will be tested with empirical data.

MAIN FOCUS OF THE CHAPTER

This is a cross section relational study using secondary analysis. The United Nation's Rankings of E-Government Performance in 2008 is used as the dependent variable. The two subscales e-services[1] and e-participation[2] were used as dependent variables. Scores were taken from the 2008 UN E-Government Annual Report. Data for other variables were taken from the World Value Survey 2005-2006, CIA's World Fact Book, and World Bank Governance Indicators 2002. Data sources and measurements are outlined in Table 1.

- **Analysis:** All data was coded and cleaned. Several Ordinary Least Squares (OLS) regression models were fitted to the data. The results are presented in Table 2.

The results show that hypotheses 1 (social capital), 1a, 2 (human capital), 3 (Internet penetration), and 6 (social conditions, social values) are partially supported while hypotheses 5 (economic inequality), and 4 (economic output) were not supported. Some social capital variables such as happiness and trust had significant impact on the quality of e-government. Greater human capital (hypothesis 2) was associated with the quality of e-government services but not with e-participation, higher level of Internet penetration (hypothesis 3) was a significant predictor of high quality e-services and e-participation. Surprisingly greater economic output measured by GNP per Capita (hypothesis 4) and economic inequality (Gini index) had no influence on either e-services or e-participation. Measures of social conditions (hypothesis 6) such as free expression, government quality, rule of law, and social values such as the role of government and perception of technology as a benefit (technology approval) did not have any significant influence on e-government quality. However, one of social values variables, work-orientedness of

Table 1. Variables and sources

Predictor	Indicator	Measurement	Source	Mean	Std. Deviation
E-government Quality	E-Service Index	an index measuring the extent to which e-government services and websites are able to meet the needs of citizens, including e-information, e-services and e-tools. According to the UN report, it measures "the online presence of national websites, along with those of the ministries of health, education, welfare, labour and finance of each Member State." Range: 0-1(high quality)	UN E-Government Survey 2008	0.349	0.229
	E-Participation Index	an index evaluating the quality of online tool that "enables governments to dialogue with their citizens. By enhancing government's ability to request, receive and incorporate feedback from constituents, policy measures can be better tailored to meet the needs and priorities of citizens." Range: 0-1(high quality)	UN E-Government Survey 2008	0.191	0.215
Social Conditions	Human Capital Index	A composite variable of the adult literacy and secondary and tertiary gross enrolment ratio. Range: 0-1 (high human capital)	UN E-Government Survey 2008	0.766	0.216

continued on following page

Table 1. Continued

Predictor	Indicator	Measurement	Source	Mean	Std. Deviation
Social Values	Free Expression	capturing perceptions of the extent to which a country's citizens are able to participate in selecting their government, as well as freedom of expression, freedom of association, and a free media. Range: 0-1 (high freedom)	World Bank Governance Indicators 2002	0.487	0.283
	Government Quality	capturing perceptions of the quality of public services, the quality of the civil service and the degree of its independence from political pressures, the quality of policy formulation and implementation, and the credibility of the government's commitment to such policies. Range: 0-1(high effectiveness)		0.496	0.284
	Rule of Law	capturing perceptions of the ability of the government to formulate and implement sound policies and regulations that permit and promote private sector development. Range: 0-1 (high rule of law)		0.493	0.286
	Corruption Control	capturing perceptions of the extent to which public power is exercised for private gain, including both petty and grand forms of corruption, as well as "capture" of the state by elites and private interests. Range: 0-1 (less corruption - better control)		0.497	0.287
Citizen Characteristics	Work-Oriented	Indicate how important Work is in your life. 1 (Very Important), 2(rather important), 3(Not very important), 4(Not at all important)	World Values Survey 2005-2006	1.505	0.244
	Technology Approval	Answer to survey question "Would you say the world is better off or worse off because of science and technology?" Range: (worse off) 1 - 10 (better off)		6.671	0.772
	Role of Government	Answer to a survey question - choose between 1 (the government should take more responsibility to ensure that everyone is provided for) - 10 (people should take more responsibility to provide for themselves)		4.861	0.892
Social Capital	Trust	Answer to a survey question "Tell me whether you trust people you meet for the first time 1 (trust completely) - 4(do not trust at all)"	World Values Survey 2005-2006	2.988	0.262
	Happiness	Answer to a survey question "Would you say you are - 1 (very happy) - 4 (not at all happy).		1.905	0.231
	Politics Interest	Answer to a survey question "How interested would you say you are in politics? 1 (very interested) - 4 (not at all interested).		2.657	0.311

continued on following page

Table 1. Continued

Predictor	Indicator	Measurement	Source	Mean	Std. Deviation
Economic Output	Gini	Gini coefficient value. Range: 0-1(perfect inequality)	CIA World Fact Book	39.194	9.317
	Population	Natural Log of Population		17.056	1.696
	GNP per capita	Natural Log of GNP per capital		9.511	1.081

Table 2. Analysis results

	Dependent Var.	E-Service Quality			E-Participation Quality		
	Independent Var.	**B**	**Std. Error**	**Sig.**	**B**	**Std. Error**	**Sig.**
	(Constant)	0.213	0.63	0.737	1.579	1.143	0.18
Social Conditions	Free Expression	-0.264	0.162	0.116	-0.155	0.295	0.60
	Govt Quality	-0.151	0.33	0.65	-0.124	0.6	0.84
	Rule of Law	-0.325	0.35	0.361	-0.44	0.635	0.49
	Corruption Control	**0.604****	**0.287**	**0.046**	0.223	0.522	0.67
Social Capital	Happiness	**-0.274****	**0.129**	**0.044**	**-0.747*****	**0.234**	**0.00**
	Politics Interest	0.073	0.08	0.368	0.038	0.145	0.80
	Trust	**-0.175***	**0.088**	**0.058**	-0.124	0.16	0.45
Social Values	Work-Oriented	0.063	0.143	0.664	**0.444***	**0.259**	**0.10**
	Govt More_Less	-0.026	0.025	0.312	-0.06	0.046	0.20
	IT_Benefit	-0.002	0.035	0.964	-0.019	0.063	0.77
Citizen Characteristics	Human Development Index	**0.587****	**0.283**	**0.048**	0.382	0.514	0.46
Economic Output	Gini	0.003	0.002	0.301	0.006	0.004	0.21
	Population	**0.033****	**0.013**	**0.019**	**0.052****	**0.024**	**0.04**
	GNP per Capita	0.004	0.073	0.958	-0.13	0.132	0.33
Technology Penetration	Internet Access	**0.337****	**0.16**	**0.045**	**0.889*****	**0.29**	**0.01**
	Model Significance	>.001			>.001		
	Adjusted R-Squared	0.773			0.71		
	Valid n=	40			40		

citizens had positive influence on the quality of e-participation, and the level of social control on corruption (a social condition variable) had positive effect on e-service quality.

As shown in Table 2, some variables influenced both e-government services and e-participation while others influenced either e-services or e-participation system indicating that the quality of e-services and e-participation is influenced by a different set of social and institutional factors.

Variables such as internet access, population, and general happiness level of the population had consistent and positive influence on both e-services and e-participation where easy access to internet, greater population, and "happier" population translated into high quality e-government services and e-participation systems. This is consistent with existing literature where population is correlated with high e-government quality and easy access to internet contributes to the development of high quality e-government services and e-participation. The happiness index and its positive influence on e-government in general are interesting. Here, the negative and statistically significant coefficient indicates that nations with happier population tend to have higher quality e-services and e-participation. One possible explanation for this finding is that happiness here may reflect general quality of life in the country and where there is higher level of general satisfaction in life, both e-government services and e-participation systems tend to be of higher quality.

While Internet access, population and happiness had consistent and positive influence on e-government, the analysis also revealed that varying social, cultural, and institutional factors influenced the development of e-services and e-participation systems differently. As anticipated in hypothesis 2, greater human capital had statistically significant and positive influence on the quality of e-services, while not having any significant influence on the quality of e-participation. As indicated by the negative and statistically significant coefficient for Trust, greater level of trust in fellow citizens translated into greater e-government service, however, this has had no effect on the quality of e-participation. Interestingly, countries whose citizens did not value work and therefore gave low priority to their work and career in their lives ("work-oriented"), scored higher in e-participation quality. Conversely speaking, this means that when citizens value their work highly as a high priority in their lives and consequently commit large portion of their resources, including time and efforts on work and career, the quality e-participation system "suffers" –in a sense that they don't have time and energy to go participate in "e-participation activities," causing a negative pressure on the quality of e-participation system. The same variable, however, did not have any influence on the quality of e-services, arguably because the demand for e-government services remains relatively steady and subject less to citizen's voluntary participation.

In any type of relational study, the possibility of reverse causality of influence must be considered. This is a consequence of the design and a limitation of the study.

Issues, Controversies, Problems

Our findings illuminate some interesting facts about the role of social, cultural and institutional microfoundations on the development of e-government. First, the quality of e-service and e-participation are influenced by different factors. The quality of e-services were heavily influenced by happiness, trust (social capital), control of corruption, human capital, technology penetration and economic output while e-participation was influenced by fewer factors such as the general level of happiness (social capital), work-orientedness of citizens (social values), in addition to the common factors such as economic output and technology penetration.

The quality of e-services falls in the realm of service-oriented interactions with citizens as compared to more political or democratic interaction with citizens. This aspect of e-government requires technical skills and knowledge – such as the necessary hardware and software - as well as understanding of government processes and databases to enable online transactions. Therefore it makes sense that countries with high human capital tend to have high quality e-government services as such technical "hard skills" and knowledge necessary for e-service transactions would be more readily available in countries with greater human capital. On the contrary, an e-participation system is political in nature and its development is influenced by factors different from service-oriented applications (Ahn, 2011). In our analysis it is the general level of happiness and work-orientedness of citizens in addition to economic output and technology penetration that influence the quality of e-participation system.

Furthermore, conducting transactions online requires a certain level of trust such as trust in the online technology used in the online transaction (Belanger & Carter, 2008; Pavlou, 2003; Chang et al., 2005; Thomas, 1998) and this is reflected on the positive effect of trust on the development of high quality e-government services where high level of trust among citizens provides a foundation for the development of high quality e-services. Along the same line of argument, corruption is found to have a significant influence on the development of e-government services. This means e-government will not develop into sophisticated online systems for service transaction if the nations hosting e-government do not have sufficient control over corruption – an aspect of institutional trust. Corruption may reduce citizen's confidence in using e-government services and corruption may be an inhibiting factor in e-government development. Relatively corrupt national institutions would resist the prospect of transparency that may accompany with the adoption and development of e-government (Bertot, Jaeger, & Grimes, 2010; Kim, Kim, & Lee, 2009). In other words, corrupt nations are not likely to promote e-government.

It is interesting to observe that these same variables, social capital, trust, and corruption, did not have significant influence on e-participation services and it was not related to social conditions such as free of expression and association, the rule of law, or the quality of government. In fact, what appear to be critical in e-participation were higher levels of citizen's happiness and lower levels of concern about work and career. This may potentially indicate that the development of e-participation system is dependent on an environment where citizens are generally content and happy, and when they have free time and energy. When citizens are pre-occupied with work there is little room to involve themselves with e-government. At an individual level, it isn't whether or not the country has sufficient social capital, or democratic framework of expression, association or upholding the role of law, or corruption that improve e-participation system but rather if citizens have enough time and energy and willingness ("happy enough") to get online and engage in online dialogue with the government and other citizens.

Happiness and Internet access played significant role in the development of both e-government services and e-participation system. This is consistent with past research where population and access translate into demand for innovation (such as e-government) and this demand has a "demand-pull" effect on e-government development (Tolbert, Mossberger, & McNeal, 2003). Sufficient level of demand for online services and online participation is an important basic foundation for e-government.

However, it was perplexing that GNP per capita did not have a significant influence on the development of either e-government services or e-participation. One would expect that financial resource and economic environment would be expected to have a positive impact on e-government development. This is suggested by the literature as there is no consensus on the role of financial resource and economic environment on e-government. Some studies indeed found a positive relationship (Coursey & Norris, 2008; Streib and Wiloughby 2005) while others do not (West 2005; Tolbert, et al 2008). Our analysis shows that when controlled for other various social, cultural and institutional characteristics, the variable did not have any statistically significant influence on e-government, consistent with the latter findings.

Solutions and Recommendations

Our findings confirm that the success of e-government does not solely depend on technological and financial resources. Rather e-government should be viewed as nested within a broader social and institutional environment which influences the outcomes of e-government. Therefore these factors should be considered in e-government planning and development so that policy makers can make smarter and more successful choices. Fountain's technology enactment framework (2001) helps explain why this study suggests that e-government outcomes reflect social, cultural and institutional characteristics of the hosting country. General level of trust, the level of corruption in society, existence of social capital should be considered in developing e-services in addition to financial and technological capacity of the government adopting e-services. Quality of life, satisfaction the availability of citizen's individual resources and willingness to participate in online dialogue on public matters (as opposed to private matters – career and work) should be considered. Instead of simply creating e-participation services with an expectation that if you build it, citizens will come, a more nuanced approach is needed. Citizens may not log on and engage in dialogue when they are experiencing low quality of life and focused much on work and career. This stands in opposition to the public matters that e-participation aims to promote. The citizen participation literature has long suggested that available time is critical to participation but more than mere free time is needed.

FUTURE RESEARCH DIRECTIONS

One interesting observation from our analysis is that in general there are more countries with high quality e-government services while their e-participation service lags behind. The scatter plot in Figure 2 shows where each nation's e-government quality stands when e-service/e-participation quality ratio is compared. There is greater number of e-government cases where e-service quality outweighs that of e-participation quality.

This is a curious phenomenon as e-participation applications perceivably require substantially less economic and technical resources than providing online government service transactions. If the country could produce high-level e-government services, why do they lag behind? If they had the technical and financial capacity to create high quality e-services, what social and institutional variables prevented them from creating high quality e-participation systems? One possibility is the political will needed to engage citizen's in their own government. Examining this relationship and identifying key determinants of this trend would help further illuminate the role of social micro-foundations on the development of e-government. What factors influences some countries to end up with service-oriented e-government and some with e-participation-oriented e-government?

This study departed from traditional approaches to explaining e-government such as technology acceptance model (TAM) or diffusion of innovation (DOI) to focus on "soft factors" such as social capital, social value, social conditions and citizen characteristics as predictors of e-government quality. These theories deal with much lower levels of analysis (primarily individuals and organizations) so there is a possibility of integrating them in our approach. Building that type of micro-macro linkage could yield some exciting findings.

In addition, studying the changes in social and institutional values and their influence on the outcomes of e-government over time would further explain the role of social, institutional factors in influencing the direction of e-government outcomes.

Figure 2. E-service quality and e-participation quality correlation scatter plot

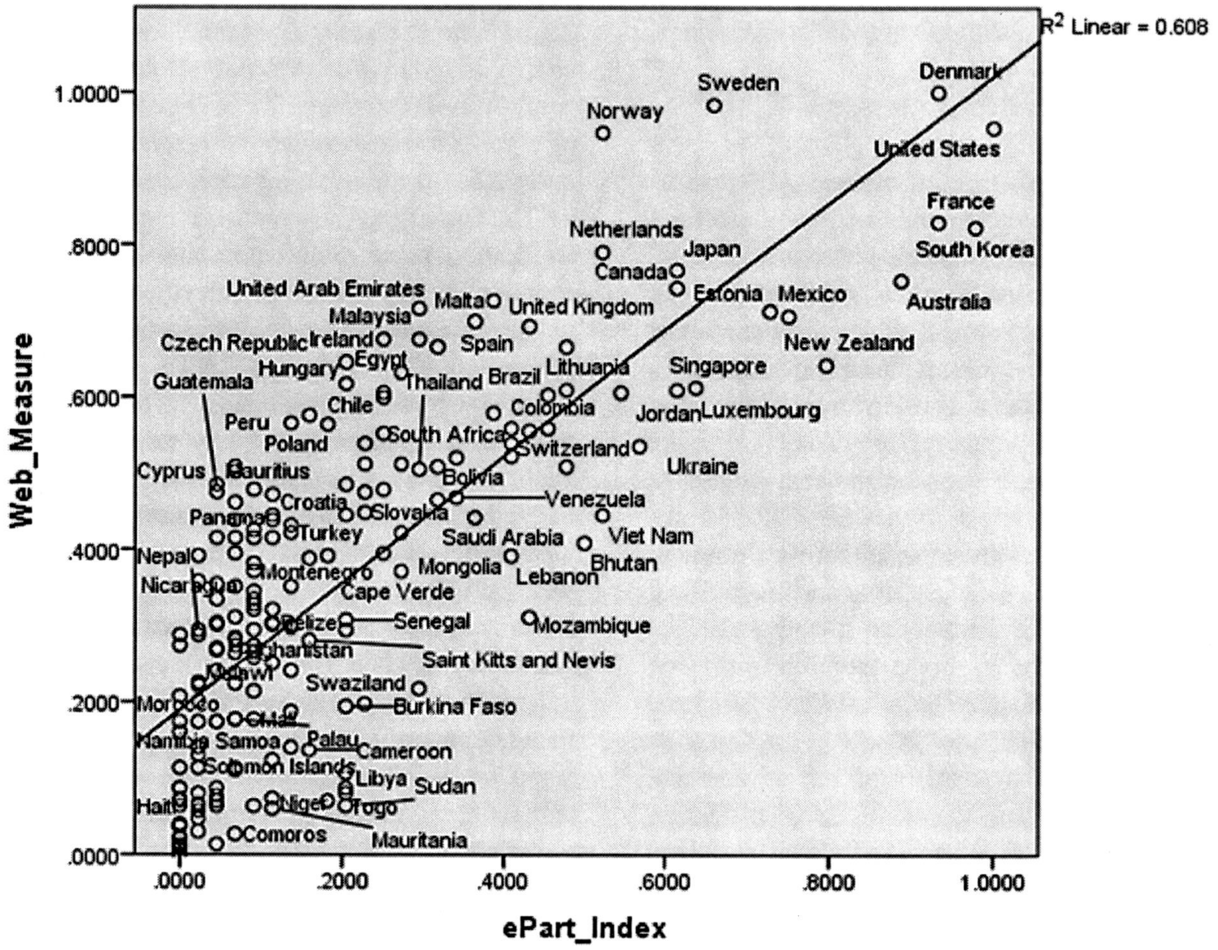

CONCLUSION

This study explored how social, cultural and institutional factors interact with technology in creating high quality e-government. We examined the role of social microfoundations of e-government such as social capital, social conditions, social values, and citizen characteristics, along with technology penetration and economic output in creating effective e-service and e-participation systems. We found various social and institutional factors played important role in developing high quality e-government: Human capital, trust, quality of life (happiness), and control of corruption provided an important foundation for more service-oriented e-government services while the development of e-participation was dependent on the general quality of life (happiness) and the extent to which citizens possess sufficient willingness to commit time and energy to e-participation system other than their private interest such as one's work and career. Lastly, this study also confirmed that essential demand for e-government as reflected in Internet accessibility (penetration) and population played a basic foundation for both e-government services and participation systems to grow.

The findings suggest that e-government development depends not only on strict economic capacity, availability and accessibility of technology, economic demand and supply for e-government services, but also on fertile social and institutional environment that facilitate the development of e-government such as trust, institutional transparency (corruption control), general quality of life, and human capital. These findings support our basic premise that e-government does not exist in a vacuum and these soft factors and attributes create an environment that direct the outcomes of e-government.

This study must be seen in light of its limitations. In any study utilizing secondary data, there is always the issue of unknown errors in the data. While the data sources used here are well respected and understood there is still the possibility of error. As a relational study, our research cannot establish that reverse correlation is not present. This is a limitation of most studies of this type. Finally, there are factors that are exogenous to the model. This is a limitation of this type of design.

REFERENCES

Ahn, M. (2011). Adoption of E-communication applications in U.S. municipalities: The role of political environment, bureaucratic structure, and the nature of applications. *American Review of Public Administration, 41*(4), 428–452. doi:10.1177/0275074010377654

Andersen, K. V., & Henriksen, H. Z. (2006). E-government maturity models: Extension of the Layne and Lee model. *Government Information Quarterly, 23*(2), 236–248. doi:10.1016/j.giq.2005.11.008

Belanger, F., & Carter, L. (2006, January). The Effects of the Digital Divide on E-Government: An Empirical Evaluation. In *Proceedings of System Sciences,* (*Vol. 4*, pp. 81c-81c). IEEE.

Belanger, F., & Carter, L. (2008). Trust and risk in e-Government adoption. *The Journal of Strategic Information Systems, 17*(2), 165–176. doi:10.1016/j.jsis.2007.12.002

Bélanger, F., & Carter, L. (2009). The impact of the digital divide on e-government use. *Communications of the ACM, 52*(4), 132–135. doi:10.1145/1498765.1498801

Bertot, J. C., Jaeger, P. T., & Grimes, J. M. (2010). Using ICTs to create a culture of transparency: E-government and social media as openness and anti-corruption tools for societies. *Government Information Quarterly, 27*(3), 264–271. doi:10.1016/j.giq.2010.03.001

Boehmke, F. J., & Skinner, P. (2012). State Policy Innovativeness Revisited. *State Politics & Policy Quarterly, 12*(3), 304–330. doi:10.1177/1532440012438890

Carter, L., & Weerakkody, V. (2008). E-government adoption: A cultural comparison. *Information Systems Frontiers, 10*(4), 473–482. doi:10.1007/s10796-008-9103-6

Chang, I., Li, Y., Hung, W., & Hwang, H. (2005). An empirical study on the impact of quality antecedents on tax payers' acceptance of Internet tax-filing systems. *Government Information Quarterly, 22*(3), 389–410. doi:10.1016/j.giq.2005.05.002

Coleman, J. S. (1988). Social capital in the creation of human capital. *American Journal of Sociology, 94*(s1), S95–S120. doi:10.1086/228943

Coursey, D., & Norris, D. F. (2008). Models of E-government: Are they correct? an empirical assessment. *Public Administration Review, 68*(3), 523–536. doi:10.1111/j.1540-6210.2008.00888.x

Dada, D. (2006). The failure of e-government in developing countries: A literature review. *The Electronic Journal of Information Systems in Developing Countries, 26.*

Davis, F. D. (1989). Perceived usefulness, perceived ease of use, and user acceptance of information technology. *Management Information Systems Quarterly, 13*(3), 319–340. doi:10.2307/249008

Fountain, J. E. (2001). *Building the virtual state: Information technology and institutional change*. Washington, DC: Brookings Institution Press.

Heeks, R. (2003). *Most eGovernment-for-development projects fail: how can risks be reduced?*. Manchester, UK: Institute for Development Policy and Management, University of Manchester.

International Bank for Reconstruction and Development. (2011). *What is social capital?* Retrieved from http://go.worldbank.org/K4LUMW43B0

Khalil, O. E. (2011). E-Government readiness: Does national culture matter? *Government Information Quarterly*, *28*(3), 388–399. doi:10.1016/j.giq.2010.06.011

Kim, S., Kim, H. J., & Lee, H. (2009). An institutional analysis of an e-government system for anti-corruption: The case of OPEN. *Government Information Quarterly*, *26*(1), 42–50. doi:10.1016/j.giq.2008.09.002

Kim, S., & Layne, K. (2001). Making the connection: E-government and public administration education. *Journal of Public Affairs Education*, 229-240.

Klugman, J., Rodríguez, F., & Choi, H. J. (2011). The HDI 2010: New controversies, old critiques. *The Journal of Economic Inequality*, *9*(2), 249–288. doi:10.1007/s10888-011-9178-z

Lee, J., & Lee, H. (2010). The computer-mediated communication network: Exploring the linkage between the online community and social capital. *New Media & Society*, *12*(5), 711–727. doi:10.1177/1461444809343568

McNutt, J. G. (1998). Ensuring social justice for the new underclass: community interventions to meet the needs of the new poor. In B. Ebo (Ed.), *The Cyberghetto or Cybertopia: Race, Class, Gender & Marginalization in Cyberspace* (pp. 33–47). New York: Praeger.

Moon, M. J. (2002). The Evolution of E-Government among Municipalities: Rhetoric or Reality? *Public Administration Review*, *62*(4), 424–433. doi:10.1111/0033-3352.00196

Morris, M. D., & McAlpin, M. (1979). *Measuring the Condition of the World's Poor*. New York: Pergamon Press.

Norris, P. (2002). *Democratic phoenix: Reinventing political activism*. Cambridge University Press. doi:10.1017/CBO9780511610073

Pavlou, P. (2003). Consumer acceptance of electronic commerce: Integrating trust and risk with the technology acceptance model. *International Journal of Electronic Commerce*, *7*, 69–103.

Putnam, R. D. (1995). Bowling alone: America's declining social capital. *Journal of Democracy*, *6*(1), 65–78. doi:10.1353/jod.1995.0002

Putnam, R. D. (2000). *Bowling alone: The collapse and revival of American community*. New York: Simon and Schuster. doi:10.1145/358916.361990

Putnam, R. D. (2007). E pluribus unum: Diversity and community in the twenty-first century the 2006 Johan Skytte Prize Lecture. *Scandinavian Political Studies*, *30*(2), 137–174. doi:10.1111/j.1467-9477.2007.00176.x

Putnam, R. D., Leonardi, R., & Nanetti, R. Y. (1994). *Making democracy work: Civic traditions in modern Italy*. Princeton University Press.

Rainie, H., Rainie, L., & Wellman, B. (2012). *Networked: The new social operating system*. The MIT Press.

Rainie, L., Purcell, K., & Smith, A. (2011). *The social side of the internet*. Pew Internet and American Life Project.

Rainie, L., Smith, A., Schlozman, K. L., Brady, H., & Verba, S. (2012). *Social media and political engagement*. Pew Internet & American Life Project.

Rogers, E. M. (1983). Diffusion of innovations (3rd ed.). New York: Free Press.

Streib, G., & Willoughby, K. (2005). Local Governments as E-Governments:Meeting the Implementation Challenge. *Public Administration Quarterly*, *29*(1), 78–110.

Thomas, C. W. (1998). Maintaining and restoring public trust in government agencies and their employees. *Administration & Society*, *30*(2), 166–193. doi:10.1177/0095399798302003

Todaro, M. (1985). *Economic development in the third world*. New York: Longman.

Tolbert, C. J., Mossberger, K., & McNeal, R. (2008). Institutions, policy innovation, and e-government in the american states. *Social Science Quarterly*, *84*(1), 52–70.

UN Public Administration Program. (2010). *Human Capital*. Retrieved from http://unpan3.un.org/egovkb/egovernment_overview/human-capital.htm

West, D. M. (2005). *Digital government: Technology and public sector performance*. Princeton, NJ: Princeton University Press.

ADDITIONAL READING

Ahn, M., & Bretschneider, S. (2011). Politics of E-Government: E-Government and the Political Control of Bureaucracy. *Public Administration Review*, *71*(3), 414–424. doi:10.1111/j.1540-6210.2011.02225.x

Barthold, C., & McNutt, J. G. (2009). The Emerging therapeutic system and the digital divide. Ferro E., Dwivedi Y.K., Ramon G, Williams M.D. (Eds.). Handbook of Research on Overcoming Digital Divides: Constructing an Equitable and Competitive Information Society. Harrisburg: IGI Books. doi:10.4018/978-1-60566-699-0.ch010

Bekkers, V. (2003). E-government and the emergence of virtual organizations in the public sector. Information polity 8, 89-101.

Bertot, J. C., & Jaeger, P. T. (2006). User-centered e-government: Challenges and benefits for government websites. *Government Information Quarterly*, *23*(2), 163–168. doi:10.1016/j.giq.2006.02.001

Bertucci, G. (2008). *From e-Government to Connected Governance*. New York: United Nations Department of Economic and Social Affairs Division for Public Administration and Development Management. http://unpan1.un.org/intradoc/groups/public/documents/un/unpan028607.pdf [accessed April 8, 2013]

Chadwick, A., & May, C. (2003). Interaction between States and Citizens in the Age of the Internet: "e-Government" in the United States, Britain, and the European Union. *Governance: An International Journal of Policy, Administration and Institutions*, *16*(2), 271–300. doi:10.1111/1468-0491.00216

Compaine, B. M. (2001). *The digital divide: facing a crisis or creating a myth?* Cambridge: MIT Press.

Gil-Garcia, J. R., & Martinez-Moyano, I. J. (2007). Understanding the evolution of e-government: The influence of systems of rules on public sector dynamics. *Government Information Quarterly*, *24*(2), 266–290. doi:10.1016/j.giq.2006.04.005

Gil-Garcia, J. R., & Pardo, T. A. (2005). E-Government success factors: Mapping practical tools to theoretical foundations. *Government Information Quarterly*, *22*(2), 187–216. doi:10.1016/j.giq.2005.02.001

Helbig, N., Ramón Gil-García, J., & Ferro, E. (2009). Understanding the complexity of electronic government: Implications from the digital divide literature. *Government Information Quarterly*, *26*(1), 89–97. doi:10.1016/j.giq.2008.05.004

Holzer, M., Manoharan, A., Shick, R., & Stowers, G. (2008). *U.S. State E-Government Report.* Newark, NJ: National center for public performance. Retrieved fromhttp://andromeda.rutgers.edu/~egovinst/Website/PDFs/US%20State%20Survey%20(Full%20Report).pdf

Kovačić, Z. J. (2005). The impact of national culture on worldwide e-government readiness. *Informing Science Journal*, *8*, 143–158.

Lee, J., Kim, H. J., & Ahn, M. J. (2011). The willingness of e-Government service adoption by business users: The role of offline service quality and trust in technology. *Government Information Quarterly*, *28*(2), 222–230. doi:10.1016/j.giq.2010.07.007

Margetts, H., & Dunleavy, P. (2002). *Cultural barriers to e-government.* UK: National Audit Office.

McConnaughey, J., Everette, D. W., Reynolds, T., & Lader, W. (1999). *Falling through the net: defining the digital divide.* Washington, DC: National Telecommunications and Information Administration, U.S. Department of Commerce.

McConnaughey, J., Nila, C. A., & Sloan, T. (1995). Falling through the cracks: a survey of the "have nots" in rural and urban America. Washington, DC: US Department of Commerce; Available at http://www.ntia.doc.gov/ntiahome/fallingthru.html

McNutt, J. G., & Brainard, L. (2010). Citizen Participation and Electronic Government in the States: Help or Hindrance? Paper read at the Urban Affairs Association 40th Conference Sustaining Cities in a Time of Globalization: Social, Economic and Political Realities. March 10 - 13, 2010, Honolulu, Hawaii

Milakovich, M. E. (2012). *Digital governance: New technologies for improving public service and participation.* New York, NY: Routledge.

National Telecommunications and Information Administration. (2004). *A Nation Online: Entering the Broadband Age.* Washington, DC: United States Department of Commerce.

Norris, P. (2001). *Digital divide.* New York: Cambridge University Press. doi:10.1017/CBO9781139164887

Schlozman, K. L., Verba, S., & Brady, H. E. (2010). Weapon of the strong? Participatory inequality and the Internet. *Perspectives on Politics*, *8*(2), 487–509. doi:10.1017/S1537592710001210

Scott, J. K. (2006). E" the people: Do US municipal government Web sites support public involvement? *Public Administration Review*, *66*(3), 341–353. doi:10.1111/j.1540-6210.2006.00593.x

Selwin, N. (2004). Reconsidering political and popular understandings of the digital divide. *New Media & Society*, *6*(3), 341–362. doi:10.1177/1461444804042519

Strover, S. (2003). Remapping the Digital Divide. *The Information Society*, *19*(4), 275–277. doi:10.1080/01972240309481

Van Dijk, J., & Hacker, K. (2003). The Digital Divide as a Complex and Dynamic Phenomenon. *The Information Society*, *19*(4), 315–326. doi:10.1080/01972240309487

Vehovar, V., Sicherl, P., Hüsing, T., & Dolnicar, V. (2006). Methodological Challenges of Digital Divide Measurements. *The Information Society*, *22*(5), 279–290. doi:10.1080/01972240600904076

Welch, E. W., Hinnant, C. C., & Moon, M. J. (2005). Linking citizen satisfaction with e-government and trust in government. *Journal of Public Administration: Research and Theory*, *15*(3), 371–391. doi:10.1093/jopart/mui021

West, D. M. (2005). *Digital government: Technology and public sector performance*. Princeton, NJ: Princeton University Press.

KEY TERMS AND DEFINITIONS

Gini Coefficient: The Gini Coefficient is a measure of inequality, usually income inequality. It measures the difference between a diagonal line and the Lorenz Curve. A Gini coefficient of zero is perfect equality while a Gini coefficient of one is perfect inequality.

Gross Domestic Product per Capita: GDP is the value of all of the goods and services produced internally by a nation over a one year period. GDP per capita is GDP divided by the population.

Internet Penetration: This means the portion of the population that has access to the Internet. It defines a portion of the digital divide.

Microfoundations: Microfoundations refer to the structures and relationships that underpin certain processes or activities.

Social Capital: Social capital refers to the institutions, relationships, and norms that shape the quality and quantity of a society's social interactions. Increasing evidence shows that social cohesion is critical for societies to prosper economically and for development to be sustainable. Social capital is not just the sum of the institutions which underpin a society – it is the glue that holds them together. Source: World Bank, 2011.

ENDNOTES

1 **Web Measure:** An index measuring the extent to which e-government services and websites are able to meet the needs of citizens, including e-information, e-services and e-tools. According to the UN report, it measures "the online presence of national websites, along with those of the ministries of health, education, welfare, labour and finance of each Member State."

2 **E-Participation**: An index evaluating the quality of online tool that "enables governments to dialogue with their citizens. By enhancing government's ability to request, receive and incorporate feedback from constituents, policy measures can be better tailored to meet the needs and priorities of citizens."

Chapter 4
Telecentres as a Medium for Good Governance in Rural India

Gaurav Mishra
Dhirubhai Ambani Institute of Information and Communication Technology (DA-IICT), India

ABSTRACT

It has been established in literature that "good governance" has major implications for poverty reduction, equity, empowerment, and quality of life. Information and Communication Technology (ICT) is seen as potentially very influential for the cause of good governance. E-governance is seen as means to achieve tenets of "good governance". E-governance addresses core components of good governance by seeking to improve efficiency and effectiveness of government, relationships with communities, businesses, citizens, and NGO/civil societies for better provision of services, accountability, transparency, and social development. In the beginning sections of the chapter, ideologies behind good governance are discussed because e-government initiatives are presumably embedded in the "good governance" thinking in development. The chapter also focuses on the relevance of e-governance as a means to achieve "good governance." In rural areas e-governance services are mostly provided through telecentres; hence, the chapter also discusses the role and issues related to telecentres for e-governance service delivery.

INTRODUCTION: GOOD GOVERNANCE

Good governance is a term widely used in public administration, political science and development literature. Good governance has become a political and economic conditionality for multilateral financing and programs for developing countries (Brillantes Jr & Fernandez, 2013; Weiss, 2000). There has been increased focus on good governance which is seen as important by major aid donors (Moore, 2006). According to Hyden, (2001), improvement of the political setups of developing countries is seen as a pre-requisite for development.

Governance can be understood as the government's ability to make and enforce rules, and to deliver services (Fukuyama, 2013). Governance refers to the institutional underpinnings of public authority and decision making (Grindle, 2012). 'Good governance' as a concept shows a positive connotation in relation to political systems. The opposite concept i.e. 'poor/bad governance' implicit a problem that countries need to avoid (Grindle,

DOI: 10.4018/978-1-4666-7266-6.ch004

2012). The consequences of non-performing government or poor governance can be wastage of resources, undelivered services and denial of social, legal and economic protection to citizens (Grindle, 2004). Poor governance can affect the countries socio-political, environmental and economic sustainability (Hellström, 2011). In literature, there is no clear consensus on what actually constitutes 'good governance'. There are varied dimensions on the concept of 'good governance'. According to Chandra and Yokoyama (2011), good governance should include a legal system that is effective, impartial and transparent. In addition, it should protect property and individual rights. The system should have public institutions that are stable, credible and honest; and government policies that favour free and open markets (Chandra & Yokoyama, 2011). Parameters, like, voice and accountability, political stability, absence of violence, effective government, regulatory quality, rule of law, and control of corruption constitutes integral part of good governance (Ott, 2010). Good governance definitions differ in the degree to which they imply particular policies or policy outcomes, for example, stable macroeconomic policy, reduction in poverty, openness to trade, decentralization, efficient revenue collection, widespread participation in development decision-making, or strong legislatures (Grindle, 2011). Concepts, such as accountability, transparency, participatory monitoring, voice, democratization, rule of law, access to information, social inclusion, women's empowerment, and civil society capacity development have been used as components of good governance in designing programmes in various sectors like infrastructure, environment, health and public sector reform (Bhargava, Cutler, & Ritchie, 2011). According to Weiss (2000), good governance tries to remove two undesirable characteristics of governance: the unrepresentative character of governments and inefficiency of non-market systems (Weiss, 2000).

As seen in the above paragraph, there are multiple dimensions on what constitutes good governance. However, largely there is consensus on the parameters of human rights in the development debate. This approach makes it clear that the poor have the right to a decent life and those rights are vehicles for empowerment (Hyden, 2001). Citizen engagement is held to be important for good governance as recognized by development actors (Bhargava et al., 2011). Good governance is considered problematic as a guide to development or poverty reduction as it covers many areas of the public sector, from institutes engaged in policy making to organizations which manage administrative systems and deliver goods and services to citizens (Grindle, 2004). Grindle (2004) believe that good governance requires change in political organization, representation of interests and a process for policy and decision making. When good governance is seen as means for poverty reduction these aspects are to be taken into consideration. According to Grindle (2004), reforms in judicial systems, public administration, public expenditure management, anti-corruption and decentralization are means to achieve good governance.

There are critiques to good governance which focus less on principles like accountability or equity but more on the ways these principles are achieved. Universal models developed by western donors are often questioned for their viability in different socio-economic, historical and cultural contexts (Grindle, 2011). Good governance has often been linked with aid criteria and developing countries are sometimes burdened with loans to meet these criteria for the further release of funds (Grindle, 2004). In some cases donors ignore violations of good governance to meet their objectives. Global funding organizations sometimes favour strong stakeholders and also may not follow principles of good governance. Weiss (2000) argues that although good governance has been on the radar of the international agenda, it has also been critiqued by UN systems. Effective political environment and open markets associated with good governance are seen as an intrusion by recipient countries. In addition, UN systems prioritize the need to capture the complex reality of governance and to strike a balance between private and public sectors. UN systems consider it important to go beyond democratic symbols and put forward necessary elements of public welfare. The World Bank may push an agenda of neoliberal policies while UN systems engage in local government and civil society. Another argument put forth by Grindle (2011) is that China, a country with poor governance, has shown development in three consecutive decades. This raises a question on the relationship between good governance and development.

Provisions of accountability, efficient delivery of services, and reduced corruption can certainly empower poor people to achieve the desired improvements in their livelihood. However, the key issue is which particular reforms of good governance can be introduced for poverty reduction. As argued by Grindle (2004), civil service reform may improve pay and working condition of employees but it has little to do with the poor. They further say that decentralization may indeed enhance decision making and make local government officers more accountable. But there are also objections that decentralization could lead to inequality in regional constituencies. One persistent danger with good governance is that governments may spend their precious time and money in reforms which may have little impact on poverty reduction. According to Grindle (2004), a better approach to good governance is to understand the problems, for example, the reasons for poor delivery of services, and find solutions to such problems.

It has been a challenge to bring about good governance in countries where governments do not cooperate, and lack basic legitimacy in the eyes of citizens, and are locked in conflicts and have less capacity and resources. Are there ways to reduce the burden on the administrative and managerial systems in countries with better legitimacy, focus on poverty reduction and capacity and human resources? (Grindle, 2004). Some approaches have been suggested in development discourse to tackle such challenges. The delivery of government services through NGO (Non-government organisation)/civil societies or empowering citizens to monitor government are among a few ways which have been suggested to address these issues (Grindle, 2004).

GOOD GOVERNANCE IN THE INDIAN CONTEXT

'Mahabharat'[1] is arguably the first Indian treatise on aspects of governance, containing cantos like *Rajdharama*[2], besides *Sabhaparvam*[3] and *Vanaparvam*[4] (Sharma, 2005). Good governance has been given importance by leaders of pre-independent and post-independent India. Jawahar Lal Nehru, the first prime minister, emphasized the challenge facing India, such as poverty, inequality of opportunities, ignorance and disease (Singh, 2008). This reflects the challenge of good governance for social development. Good governance has been related to and is closely connected with poverty reduction; hence its main aim is to enhance capabilities of the poor for better livelihoods and empowerment. In India, governance has not changed since Independence though there have been indications about the adoption of a citizen's charter, the laws on right to information and promoting accountability and transparency of government (Godbole, 2001). Corruption in India has broken the country and the seats of power represent failed promise of democracy (Miklian & Carney, 2013). According to Miklian and Carney (2013), to run a business in India means going through backdoor negotiations, payoffs to politicians and bureaucrats. Godbole (2001) argues that principles of good governance have been neglected in India and if these were followed, India would have not presented a picture of such squalor, filth, illiteracy and poverty even after nearly sixty six years of Independence.

The weak institutions of governance have an adverse impact on service delivery. Poverty reduction is a function of improvements in the quality and timely delivery of services to poor people of basic education, health, potable water and other social and infrastructural requirements (Singh, 2008). Throughout India, the government has failed to hold its bureaucrats and politicians accountable for transgressions and simultaneously failing to uphold collective promises (Miklian & Carney, 2013). According to Godbole (2001), good governance in India should focus on maintenance of law and order, administration of justice and socio-economic welfare of weaker sections, improving service delivery, decentralizing administrative, legislative and executive functions and finally, the rule of law.

In India, good governance has been on the agenda of government reforms to achieve transparency, accountability and improvement in various social development parameters. The enactment of laws on good governance, fiscal responsibility, budgetary management and the protection of whistle-blowers have been proposed in India's parliament in 2000 to move things forward in the direction of good governance (Godbole 2001).

In order to promote good governance as proposed by the government of India in 2000, steps have been taken to uplift backward classes in Indian society. The Indian parliament passed the National Rural Employment Guarantee Act (NREGA) in 2005 to promote the security of livelihoods in rural areas. NREGA is based on decentralized implementation; the principal authorities for the implementation of the Rural Employment Guarantee Scheme (REGS) are the local government (Panchayat) institutions at the district, block, and village level. Right to Information Act was passed in 2005 by the Government of India to ensure timely response to citizen requests for government information. This act has provided a new spectrum to citizens' participation in public affairs. Active citizen and civil society engagement in governance processes, including decision making, is essential to realize the objectives of good governance (Taqiuddin, 2011). He lists some administrative accountability measures taken by Indian government agencies for securing participation, they are:

- A law on community participation to institutionalize citizen participation in local decision making,
- Citizen charters stipulating standards of service delivery and penalty for non-compliance,
- Conventional and on line help line for grievance redressal,
- Arrangements for feedback on services,
- Whistle blower protection mechanism,
- Public service delivery legislation conferring right to public services with grievance officer to quickly investigate and grant relief,
- Ombudsman to independently enquire into complaints,
- Chief /vigilance officer who reports directly to the government,
- Integrity pacts for procurement,
- Third party inspection of quality of works and supplies, and
- Independent evaluation studies.

In India, reservation policies are in place to provide equitable distribution of economic resources and a worthwhile sharing of power at different levels in the running of the state affairs (Misra, 2013). According to Singh (2008), direct elections in villages have brought democratic consciousness and the need for democratic behaviour. Cutting down direct citizens' interface with the government is also seen as one of the measures for the reduction of harassment of citizens by government agencies. Repeated visits to government offices, complaints of harassment, wastage of time and money and corruption could be addressed through such single window systems as e-government centres (Godbole, 2001). An enhanced role of civil society/NGOs in policy and decision making has been found instrumental in the efficient delivery of services in India (Singh, 2008). In India, contractual relationships between government and civil society organization have increased in addition to new governance arrangements (Madon, 2009), and these relationships show signs of enhanced participation of civil society in government affairs, thereby, contributing to good governance.

India has initiated many e-governance projects under National E-Governance Plan (NEGP), Common Service Centres (CSCs) is one of them. India has therefore moved some steps forward towards good governance by promoting e-governance in its policy agenda.

E-GOVERNANCE AND E-GOVERNMENT

The terms e-government and e-governance are extensively used in literature. These two terms have different connotations. E-governance, according to Ndou (2004), is the public sector's use of the most innovative information and communication technologies, like the Internet, to deliver improved services to all citizens. Furthermore, its aim is to provide reliable information and greater knowledge in order to facilitate access to the governing process and encourage sustained citizen participation. According to Haque and Pathrannarakul (2013), e-government is the systemic use of ICTs to support the functions that a government performs for its constituents, mainly related to the provision of information and services. Al-Tawil and Sait (2007) define e-governance as the development, deployment and enforcement of policies, laws and regulations necessary to support the functioning of an e-government.

According to APDIP-e-Note-6 (2006), e-government is an integral part of e-governance. E-governance defines the way government institutions, businesses and citizens use e-government to achieve a better service delivery based transparency, accountability and public feedback mechanisms. The note further elaborates on e-governance services and suggests that these services involve interaction between citizens and the democratic processes such as online public hearings, electronic voting, feedback systems, complaint registration, signature campaigns and participation in decision-making. Continuous feedback and interaction enables citizens to demand better and efficient services and makes governments accountable. Thus, some of the main advantages included in these concepts include efficiency in government service delivery, transparency and accountability of government and empowerment of citizens. Based on these concepts it is foreseeable that e-government can provide automation and transformation in governance. These, in turn, can increase overall effectiveness and efficiency of governance.

E-GOVERNANCE FOR GOOD GOVERNANCE

As noted above, it has been established in literature that good governance has major implications for poverty reduction, equity, empowerment and quality of life. Information and communication technologies (ICTs) have the attributes of imparting added value to processes that give identity, form and relationships that characterize good governance, create an atmosphere of openness that identifies and stems corrupt behavior (Bertot, Jaeger, & Grimes, 2010; Okot-Uma, 2000). ICTs are primarily understood as Internet technologies and Internet-based applications, but they also include network technologies, databases, and electronic workflow systems (Schuppan, 2009). However, Geldof and Unwin (2005) argues that ICT is not limited to just Internet related technologies; it includes a whole range of information and communication technologies from written letters, and radio, to computers and mobile telephony. ICTs have provided new opportunities for growth and development worldwide. Governments throughout the world are making efforts to utilize the potential of these technologies to improve economic and social progress. ICTs support and transform external working of governance by processing and communicating data (Heeks, 2001). ICTs have become a key component of government initiatives and ICTs are used as servants to the master of good governance (Heeks, 2001). According to Rogers and Shukla (2001), e-governance seeks to realise processes and structures for harnessing the potential of ICTs at various levels of government and the public sector and beyond, for the purpose of enhancing good governance.

A better informed citizen can exercise his/her rights, make government accountable and for empowerment. The flow of information is regarded as essential for effective governance because the provision of government services mainly involves creating and communicating information (Gant, 2008). E-governance brings both efficiency and effectiveness gains to government - efficiency gains in terms of cheaper governance and quicker governance, and effectiveness in terms of better and innovative governance (Heeks, 2001). Therefore, e-governance addresses core components of good governance by improving the efficiency and effectiveness of government and improving relationships with communities, businesses, citizens and NGO/civil societies, which eventually leads to better provision of services, accountability, transparency and social development.

TELECENTRES AS A MEDIUM FOR E-GOVERNMENT SERVICES

As discussed earlier, ICT is seen as a very influential and enabling cause of good governance. And e-governance is the best means to achieve the objectives of good governance. There is extensive economic and social disparity between urban and rural areas in developing countries. Therefore, ICT based government initiatives are often motivated by the desire to alleviate poverty, enhance socio-economic status and empower rural men and women (Venkatesh, Sykes, & Venkatraman, 2013). For rural areas, telecentres have been utilized as a delivery channel for various ICT projects as discussed in the above section. Telecentres can reduce digital divide by making services available to large sections of society (Rogers & Shukla, 2001). Telecentres are today considered one of the most successful means to promote ICT diffusion in developing countries as they increase the access of people to ICT, particularly the poor and people living in remote rural areas (Gopakumar, 2006). Thus, telecentres seem to have the potential for an efficient and effective delivery of government services which is one of the components for good governance i.e. services for all. Another tenet of good governance, namely efficient and effective delivery of government services, can also be achieved through telecentres. Telecentres can provide better access to government information and also increase transparency in service delivery. Initiatives like Gyandoot and Drishtee in India have sought to increase the level of e-governance at the state level by negotiating with state governments to provide various services on the internet. Telecentres have the capability to increase the citizens' inputs into public sector decisions and actions thereby strengthening civil society and processes of democratization (Whyte, 1999). Madon (2009) has rightly pointed out that a telecentre can provide a shared public space for a rural poor community in the developing world. There is also optimism in literature about the potential of telecentres in promoting e-commerce related activities. Telecentres can also be used as marketing channels for farmers, artisans and others for better income. Transaction costs can also be reduced in accessing various government and e-commerce services through telecentres (Oestmann & Dymond, 2001). Next section focuses on concepts related to telecentres and their role in good governance.

TELECENTRE CONCEPTS

Telecentre is a word commonly associated with ICT for development projects. Telecentres provide public access to ICTs for educational, personal, social and economic development (Bailey, 2009; Harris, Kumar, & Balaji, 2003). Roman and Colle (2002) define telecentre as a public place where people can get a variety of communication services, and where a major part of the operator's purpose is to benefit the community. They regard the more narrowly focused cybercafés or Internet kiosks as important because of their potential to become telecentres. Oestmann and Dymond (2001) define telecentres as strategically located facilities providing public access to ICT-based services and applications. According to them, telecentres generally have facilities of telephone, fax machine, computer, printer, photocopiers, high speed telecommunication network, multimedia equipment and meeting space.

The idea of a community sharing computer technology emerged in the 1980s with the introduction of the telecottage in Scandinavia, the purpose of which was to fight against the marginalisation of remote rural places, and this was before the Internet (Roman & Colle, 2002). Roman and Colle (2002) further elaborate on the history of telecentres. According to them, in the mid-1990s a new breed of telecottages appeared in Hungary and these were built with the purpose of social and economic development. By 1994, there were more than 230 telecentres in Australia, Austria, Canada, Denmark, Finland, Germany, Ireland, Japan, Norway, Sweden, the UK and the USA (Oestmann & Dymond, 2001). The telecentre movement was part of a more robust movement and was marked with a variety of international organisations supporting the diffusion and adoption of ICTs and telecentres (Roman & Colle, 2002). According to Roman and Colle (2002), the telecentre movement had three assumptions:

1. Appropriate information can contribute significantly to development.
2. ICTs provide an important and potentially economical way for people to access that information.
3. Telecentres are a viable way to connect communities with information and communication technologies.

Telecentres are being established in communities with the objective of improving social and economic development and the empowerment of citizens. In addition, telecentres are seen as a delivery channel which has the capability of reducing digital divide in remote, rural and otherwise disadvantaged communities (Oestmann & Dymond, 2001). There is no definitive model for telecentres and they vary immensely in size, service delivery and infrastructure. The telecentre model depends on the location of telecentres (rural or urban), investments and support from public and private sector. Some telecentres provide only basic telecommunications services and are best referred to as 'phone shops' or 'public call offices' (PCOs) and India is one of the countries which has independently developed these, starting in urban or larger rural communities with low level of private telephone penetration and a large enough market for public access businesses to be commercially viable (Oestmann & Dymond, 2001). Telecentres may include educational and information services, for example, information on agriculture, weather, health, and government contact details.

SUSTAINABILITY OF TELECENTRES

Telecentres have been associated with sustainability issues in literature hence it is important to understand what sustainability means in the context of telecentres. Although sustainability is discussed widely in literature, there is no concrete definition of it. But sustainability in development is now generally regarded as the ability of a project or intervention to continue in existence after the implementing agency has departed (Harris et al., 2003). These authors further say that continuity is widely seen as a measure of sustainability and it has become one of the criteria for obtaining funds. Sustainability is the term used in literature to measure the success of any ICT for development project. Kumar and Best (2006) have proposed five types of sustainability namely financial, social, institutional, technological and environmental.

Financial sustainability refers to the capability of telecentres to generate sufficient income for meeting running costs (maintenance and operational). Financial sustainability is often regarded as a condition for the continued existence of the centre (Harris et al., 2003). In addition it should provide sufficient income to the operator/entrepreneur for his/her livelihood. Financial sustainability remains a challenge for telecentres as their purpose is not only to generate sufficient income but also to reduce digital divide by making services affordable to all sections of the society (Keniston & Kumar, 2003; Kumar & Best, 2006; Kuriyan, Toyama, & Ray, 2006). The tension between social and financial goals is inherent at the state, entrepreneur and consumer levels, making it difficult to run a financially self-sustaining ICT kiosk project that also meets social development goals (Kuriyan et al., 2006). Financial sustainability is most critical and even most difficult to achieve. This is because of the plummeting cost-power ratio of computers. The price of computers typically remains many orders of magnitude beyond the average annual incomes of telecentre users in developing countries (Harris et al., 2003).

Technological sustainability can be seen as the ability of the technology to withstand technological change both in software and hardware components for a period of time. In technologically sustainable centres change in technology may not affect the availability of products and services (Misund & Hoiberg, 2003). According to Bailur et al. (2007), technological sustainability is entwined with financial sustainability. This is because technical equipment usually entails both capital and recurrent costs, and if the technology is not updated the services may be less user-friendly and therefore less likely to be used.

Through social sustainability telecentres are able to meet the requirements of citizens. Social sustainability defines the usefulness of these centres to citizens. Unless the centres have any 'utility' to people their chances of being used remains bleak. Social sustainability is about whether access to telecentres is actually useful (such as a government service) and provides relevant content (Bhatnagar, 2003; Heeks, 2002). More recent telecentre initiatives are focussing on local content development in their plans and actively seeking partners who can contribute to this, such as local farmers' organisations, educational institutions and NGOs (Oestmann & Dymond, 2001). Social development is understood in terms of building social capital as an engine for creativity, networks and sustainable growth. Meddie (2006) defines social capital as the total sum of person-to-person or institutional interactions and mutual support. And the resilience of a community is measured by the amount of social capital at its disposal. Telecentres have been instrumental in increasing social capital in communities by providing free of charge services for selected activities (Meddie, 2006). Meddie (2006) further adds that telecentres largely depend on government subsidies and development partners and therefore financial and social sustainability of telecentres remain key challenges of digital inclusion programmes.

Institutional sustainability defines the relation of ICT for development projects with various public and private institutions. Various political actors are involved in the development and implementation of any such project (Kuriyan et al., 2006). Institutionalisation of such initiatives is necessary. This is because it provides legitimacy regardless of the evidence of its technical value (Avgerou, 2003). Leadership is another factor which affects telecentres' sustainability. Kumar and Best (2006) in their study of the SARI rural e-government project in India found that lack of effective public leadership and sustained commitment was one of the factors in its failure. They lay emphasis on the need to institutionalise the services provided through telecentres rather than allowing them to be dependent on individual initiatives.

Environmental sustainability relates to the environment friendlessness of various technological hardware components used in telecentres. It is the ability of various hardware components to be disposed off easily and in an environment friendly way (Kumar & Best, 2006).

Harris et al. (2003) have listed other sustainability parameters such as staff capability, community acceptance and service delivery in addition to financial sustainability. Staff sustainability refers to the continuous availability of skilled staff for projects that introduce new skills; it is the extent to which trained people, or their trained replacements, continue to work in the same area and that their capabilities are maintained and utilized. Adequate training of the telecentre staff is another sustainability factor (Kumar & Best, 2006). Staff should be comfortable in handling any hardware and software used in the telecentres. Community acceptance is important for the sustainability of centres and depends on how they cater to the needs of the community. Thus, sustaining community acceptance and social sustainability reflects a similar concept, the focus of which is providing services based on the needs of community. Sustaining service delivery relates to the continuous supply of information which communities find useful. It is also instrumental in sustaining the overall services of a telecentre in terms of adapting to evolving community needs, pro-actively seeking new sources of useful information and creating community awareness on the nature and value of information (Harris et al., 2003). Bailey's (2009) study points out four focus areas for achieving sustainability namely, the social context of the telecentre, participatory methods for needs assessment, knowledge sharing among stakeholders and the continued development of core capabilities of telecentres.

E-GOVERNMENT AND TELECENTRES IN INDIA

Telecentres have been implemented worldwide and India is also not left behind. Telecentres in India have become a common delivery channel of ICT for development services. Telecentre approach has been primarily associated with rural areas. In India, terms like village or rural knowledge centres, and information centres, information kiosks are used synonymously with telecentres. India has high numbers of telecentre-based initiatives being piloted, replicated and scaled up by various government and non-government agencies. There are two types of telecentres in India namely the profit oriented and the non-profit oriented. According to Conroy (2006), in Indian context, the majority of telecentres are profit-making, and the operators' purpose to serve the community is debatable. Non-profit centres are implemented by NGOs or local government and have some mechanism to cover operational costs, for example, through service delivery charges (Conroy, 2006).

The data on the exact number of telecentres in India is not available, but a rough estimate gives the figure of around 50,000 telecentres dotting various parts of rural areas (Mukerji, 2013). NEGP is an initiative of Governmnent of India (GOI) under a public private partnership (PPP) model to improve service delivery to citizens and businesses through 100,000 telecentres for 600,000 villages in India i.e. one CSC for every 6 villages. The government of India committed around 1billion dollars for setting up Common Service Centres (CSCs) under its National e-Governance Plan (Mukerji, 2008). According to the Government of India[5], by 2012, 99357 CSCs have been established in 33 states/union territories. GOI envisages CSCs as integrated front-end delivery points for the government, the private and the social sector services to the rural citizens of India. The nature of the PPP can be characterized as 'build-own operate' with the private sector responsible for setting up and running the centres (Prasad & Ray, 2012). The CSCs scheme uses a public private partnership model. According to the model, the CSCs scheme has a 3-tier structure consisting of the CSC operator (called Village Level Entrepreneur or VLE), the Service Centre Agency (SCA) that is responsible for covering a group of districts and a State Designated Agency (SDA) identified by the state government as responsible for managing the implementation over the entire State[6]. The main aim of the CSCs is to offer web-enabled e-governance services in rural areas, including application forms, certificates, and utility payments such as electricity, telephone and water bills [7]. A CSC in Mushedpur village of Gurgoan district of Haryana, India, provides various government-to-citizen (G2C) and business-to-consumer (B2C) services. The centre provides various government certificates like caste, domicile, income certificates. In addition, services such as 'nakal' (copies of various government documents), application collection and submission for subsidy on housing schemes, Laadli scheme for the girl child (Ladli referring to 'dear one') and Indira Gandhi Vivah Shagun Yojna ('Marriage gift scheme)' are provided through the centres. B2C services include computer education, mobile top-ups, railway/air ticket booking and Internet surfing (Malhotra & Krishnaswamy, 2011).

The telecentres under the CSC scheme are built on different business models taking into account the vision and competencies of the SCA under whose jurisdiction the telecentre lies, and the different backgrounds of the entrepreneurs. For financial sustainability the policy makers believe that the revenue from Government-to Consumer (G2C) services would be sufficient to cover the operator's cash flow requirements [8]. Monitoring of the project is done by a private organization called IL&FS (Indian Leasing and Financial Services). The monitoring is based on two metrics: the number of CSCs set up against the planned timeline, and the amount of uptime, i.e. connectivity to the internet, in each CSC [9].

Initial experiments with telecentres started with setting up of MS Swaminathan Research Foundation's (MSSRF) establishment of knowledge centres in 10 villages. In 1998, MS Swaminathan MSSRF, with funding from IDRC implemented Information Village Research Project in Pondicherry, India[10]. Other projects such as Warana Wired Village Project were piloted in 70 villages in Kohlapur and Sangli districts in the western Indian state of Maharashtra. India's telecentre movement has been diverse with respect to the kind of agency involved, the ownership of individual kiosks, the purpose and technology deployed, the services provided, goals, models, operating paradigms, and geographic distribution (Mukerji, 2008; Toyama et al., 2004). Several telecentre projects were piloted in different parts of the country. These include 'Gyandoot' in Madhya Pradesh, Sustainable Access in Rural India (SARI) in Tamil Nadu and Tarahaat in Bundelkhand, Dhristee in six states (Sirsa in Haryana, Jaipur in Rajasthan, Dewas in Madhya Pradesh, Trichy in Tamil Nadu, Sonitpur in Assam and Madhubani in Bihar), Dairy Information Services Kiosk (DISK) in Gujarat, Tarahaat in Bundelkhand district of Uttar Pradesh and Bhatinda in Punjab to name a few. Some telecentres initiatives like e-choupal, dristee, DISK were for making profit while initiatives like 'Gyandoot' and SARI were mainly not-for-profit initiatives. As evident from these examples every sector is involved, including big corporations (like the Indian Tobacco Corporation), entrepreneurs, government, and NGOs (like MSSRF).

Telecentres in India face the same sustainability issues as observed in other developing countries, given the diverse contexts and types of telecentres.

In India, enterprise or information kiosks approach has been used in urban and semi-urban areas whose purpose is about developing services for sale (Meddie, 2006). Internet cafes depict the enterprise approach in urban areas. But this approach is not suitable to rural areas because it has very low social capital development potential. Therefore, it is weak in terms of social sustainability. If it ever finds users with enough capacity to pay, users will be too few to sustain the model (Meddie, 2006). As evident in the above discussion, telecentres in rural areas have mostly been implemented for socio-economic development. Thus, focus is more on building socio-economic capital rather than generating income. Hence, rural telecentres in India face immense sustainability challenges. For example, sustainability has been related to the shift in power relationships in the delivery of services due to telecentres in rural areas of India. This is more applicable to e-government services through telecentres in rural areas where local government officers perceive a threat to their role, authority and influence in the community (Kumar & Best, 2006). This may lead to the weakening of support from local government officers which in turn may have an impact on telecentre sustainability. Political setup in state, district or at village level plays a dominant part in telecentre sustainability as observed by Kuriyan et al. (2006) in their study of 'Akshaya' project. They found that politics of the 'Akshaya' project between the Muslim League and Communist Party at the local level revealed conflicts between redistribution and financial sustainability of telecentres. For example, the League's involvement in the project generated opposition from the CPI (M) supporting population and Panchayat members in Malappuram. In another example, in Madhya Pradesh, 'Gyandoot' had the active support of the government head, Digvijay Singh, who belonged to Congress Party. In 2003, the Bharatiya Janata Party (BJP) took over political control, and showed less interest in the initiative (Conroy, 2006). Therefore, it is evident that sustainability forms the biggest challenge in the implementation of telecentres projects in India given the country's diversity of socio-economic and political context.

IMPACT OF TELECENTRES IN INDIA IN RELATION TO GOOD GOVERNANCE

There are examples of telecentre based projects which have met certain tenets of good governance. For example, initiatives like 'Gyandoot' and 'Dristee' have sought to increase the level of e-governance at the state level by negotiating with state governments to provide various services on the Internet. 'Mahiti Mitra' project, in Kutch district of Gujarat, provides another tenet of good governance i.e. empowerment of citizens. Mishra's (2013) study on 'Mahiti Mitra' project concluded that government welfare schemes application forms, information-based and right to information (RTI) services bring about human, political and social empowerment of telecentre users. Mishra (2013) also found that the centres which showed greater development impact lacked financial sustainability. In another study, Madon (2008) used development lens to investigate 'Akshaya' and 'FRIENDS' telecentre projects in Kerala. She found that the centres enhanced citizens' quality of life by providing citizens hassle free access to government services and information. The study also found that women visited centres due to the 'government' tag associated with centres; hence, these centres were perceived as 'safe' for women and therefore reflected greater use than traditional government departments. 'Bhoomi' (meaning land)[11] project in Karnataka, is another successful e-government project in rural areas. The aim of the project is on-line delivery and management of land records. There is a decrease in corruption related to land records as the project reduced the discretion of government officials by the introduction of an online request for the any change/update in land records (Bhatnagar & Singh, 2010). They also inferred that the quality of service delivery and quality of governance improved significantly with computerization of land records. Thus, from the above examples it can be inferred that telecentres have been helpful in meeting tenets of good governance like, quality of life, transparency, empowerment, increased access to government services and decrease in corruption. Therefore, telecentres may be used in rural areas to meet the tenets of good governance.

CONCLUSION

It can be concluded from the chapter that e-governance can achieve the tenets of good governance by making government accountable, responsive and accessible to citizens. E-governance has the potential to improve and enhance government-citizen relations. One of the main objectives of e-governance is to make governments more open in their interaction with citizens through information access pertaining to the political processes and services of governments. In urban areas, Internet is often used as a medium to deliver e-government services but in rural areas Internet is not a feasible option due to various reasons like illiteracy, lack of infrastructure etc. Telecentres have become an appropriate medium for the delivery of government services in rural areas where citizens can access services irrespective of educational qualification or economic or social status. Through telecentres, e-government services are more accessible to citizens than the conventional government departments and therefore telecentres promote good governance. Sustainability is a major issue associated with telecentres and therefore it may be a major constraint in the promotion of good governance in rural areas.

REFERENCES

Al-Tawil, M. K., & Sait, M. S. (2007). E-governance-Where We Stand. In *Pro-Poor Public Service Delivery with ICTs-Making local e-governance work towards achieving the Millennium Development Goals*. Retrieved February 2, 2013, from http://www.unapcict.org/ecohub/resources/apdip-e-note-6-2013-icts-for-povertyreduction/at_download/attachment1

Avgerou, C. (2003). *The link between ICT and economic growth in the discourse of development Organizational information systems in the context of globalization*. Springer. doi:10.1007/978-0-387-35695-2_23

Bailey, A. (2009). Issues affecting the social sustainability of telecentres in developing contexts: A field study of sixteen telecentres in Jamaica. *The Electronic Journal of Information Systems in Developing Countries, 36*.

Bailur, S., Ratan, A., Toyama, K., Veeraraghavan, R., Dhwani, A. N., Premji, A., & Roof, O. (2007). *Review of Research on Rural PC Kiosks*. Retrieved 22/09/2010, from http://groups.csail.mit.edu/cag/ict4dev/papers/Kiosks%20Research.pdf

Bertot, J. C., Jaeger, P. T., & Grimes, J. M. (2010). Using ICTs to create a culture of transparency: E-government and social media as openness and anti-corruption tools for societies. *Government Information Quarterly*, *27*(3), 264–271. doi:10.1016/j.giq.2010.03.001

Bhargava, V., Cutler, K., & Ritchie, D. (2011). *Stimulating the Demand for Good Governance*. Academic Press.

Bhatnagar, S. (2003). E-government and access to information. *Global Corruption Report*, 24-32.

Bhatnagar, S., & Singh, N. (2010). *Results from a study of impact of e-government projects in India*. Academic Press.

Brillantes, A. Jr, & Fernandez, M. T. (2013). Toward A Reform Framework for Good Governance: Focus On Anti-Corruption. *Philippine Journal of Public Administration*, *54*(1-2), 87–127.

Chandra, D. S., & Yokoyama, K. (2011). *The role of good governance in the knowledge-based economic growth of East Asia–A study on Japan, Newly Industrialized Economies*. Graduate School of Economics, Kyushu University.

Conroy, C. (2006). *Telecentre initiatives in rural India: Failed fad or the way forward? Natural resources institute*. University of Greenwich.

Fukuyama, F. (2013). What Is Governance? *Governance: An International Journal of Policy, Administration and Institutions*, *26*(3), 347–368. doi:10.1111/gove.12035

Gant, J. (2008). *Electronic Government for Developing Countries. International Telecommunication Union*. Geneva: ITU.

Geldof, M., & Unwin, T. (2005). *Becoming an information society: The role of new IT in development*. Paper presented at the Wilton Park Conference. New York, NY.

Godbole, M. (2001). *Report of the one man committee on good governance*. Academic Press.

Gopakumar, K. (2006). *E-governance services through Telecentres-Role of Human Intermediary and issues of Trust*. Paper presented at the Information and Communication Technologies and Development, 2006. New York, NY. doi:10.1109/ICTD.2006.301850

Grindle, M. (2004). Good enough governance: Poverty reduction and reform in developing countries. *Governance: An International Journal of Policy, Administration and Institutions*, *17*(4), 525–548. doi:10.1111/j.0952-1895.2004.00256.x

Grindle, M. (2011). Good enough governance revisited. *Development Policy Review*, *29*(s1), s199–s221. doi:10.1111/j.1467-7679.2011.00526.x

Grindle, M. (2012). Good governance: The inflation of an idea. *Planning Ideas That Matter: Livability, Territoriality, Governance, and Reflective Practice, 259.*

Haque, S., & Pathrannarakul, P. (2013). E-Government towards good governance: A global appraisal. *Journal of E-Governance*, *36*(1), 25–34.

Harris, R., Kumar, A., & Balaji, V. (2003). Sustainable telecentres? Two cases from India. *The Digital Challenge: Information Technology in the Development Context, 8*, 124-135.

Heeks, R. (2001). *Understanding e-governance for development*. Institute for Development Policy and Management Manchester.

Heeks, R. (2002). e-Government in Africa: Promise and practice. *Information Polity*, *7*(2), 97–114.

Hellström, J. (2011). *Mobile governance: Applications, challenges and scaling-up Mobile Technologies for Conflict Management*. Springer.

Hyden, G. (2001). *Governance and Development: Sorting Out the Basics*. World Governance Survey Working Paper, 1.

Keniston, K., & Kumar, D. (2003). The four digital divides. *Online Erişim, 21*, 2010.

Kumar, R., & Best, M. (2006). Impact and sustainability of e-government services in developing countries: Lessons learned from Tamil Nadu, India. *The Information Society*, *22*(1), 1–12. doi:10.1080/01972240500388149

Kuriyan, R., Toyama, K., & Ray, I. (2006). *Integrating social development and financial sustainability: The challenges of rural computer kiosks in Kerala*. Paper presented at the Information and Communication Technologies and Development, 2006. New York, NY.

Madon, S. (2008). Evaluating the developmental impact of e-governance initiatives: An exploratory framework. ICTs and Indian Social Change: Diffusion, Poverty. *Governance: An International Journal of Policy, Administration and Institutions*, 268.

Madon, S. (2009). *E-governance for development: A focus on rural India*. Palgrave Macmillan.

Malhotra, C., & Krishnaswamy, G. (2011). Citizens' Expectations from Rural Telecentres: A Case Study of Implementation of Common Service Centres in Mushedpur Village, Haryana, India. World Academy of Science, Engineering and Technology, 53.

Meddie, M. (2006). Rethinking telecentre sustainability: How to implement a social enterprise approach-Lessons from India and Africa. *Journal of Community Informatics*, *2*(3).

Miklian, J., & Carney, S. (2013). Corruption, Justice and Violence in Democratic India. *SAIS Review*, *33*(1), 37–49. doi:10.1353/sais.2013.0011

Mishra, G. (2013). *Role of telecenters in empowering citizens: A case study of 'Mahiti Mitra' project in Kutch district of Gujarat, India*. Paper presented at the Global Humanitarian Technology Conference: South Asia Satellite (GHTC-SAS). New York, NY.

Misra, A. (2013). *Empowerment of backward classes through reservation policy with reference to Dr. BR Ambedkar's vision and challenges in current socio-legal milieu*. Academic Press.

Misund, G., & Hoiberg, J. (2003). *Sustainable information technology for global sustainability*. Digital Earth. Paper presented at the Information Resources for Global Sustainability Symposium. New York, NY.

Moore, M. (2006). Good Government?. *IDS Bulletin*, *37*(4), 50–56. doi:10.1111/j.1759-5436.2006.tb00286.x

Mukerji, M. (2008). Telecentres in rural India: emergence and a typology. *The Electronic Journal of Information Systems in Developing Countries, 35*.

Mukerji, M. (2013). *ICTs and Development: A Study of Telecentres in Rural India*. Palgrave Macmillan.

Ndou, V. (2004). E–Government for developing countries: Opportunities and challenges. *EJISDC*, *18*(1), 1–24.

Oestmann, S., & Dymond, A. C. (2001). Telecentres—Experiences, lessons and trends. Perspectives on Distance Education. Telecentres: Case Studies and Key Issues. The Commonwealth of Learning.

Okot-Uma, R. W. (2000). *Electronic governance: re-inventing good governance*. London: Commonwealth Secretariat.

Ott, J. C. (2010). Good governance and happiness in nations: Technical quality precedes democracy and quality beats size. *Journal of Happiness Studies*, *11*(3), 353–368. doi:10.1007/s10902-009-9144-7

Prasad, R., & Ray, R. S. (2012). *Telecentres go where mobile phones fear to tread: Evidence from India*. Paper presented at the Regional International Telecommunications Society India Conference. New Delhi, India.

Rogers, E. M., & Shukla, P. (2001). The role of Telecenters in development communication and the digital divide. *The Journal of Development Communication*, *2*(12), 26–31.

Roman, R., & Colle, R. (2002). *Themes and issues in telecentre sustainability* (Vol. 10). Institute for Development Policy and Management, University of Manchester.

Schuppan, T. (2009). E-Government in developing countries: Experiences from sub-Saharan Africa. *Government Information Quarterly*, *26*(1), 118–127. doi:10.1016/j.giq.2008.01.006

Sharma, S. K. (2005). Good Governance in Ancient India. *Facets of Good Governance, 1*.

Singh, B. P. (2008). The Challenge of Good Governance in India: Need for Innovative Approaches. *Ash Institute for Democratic Governance and Innovation*. Available online: http://www.innovations.harvard.edu/cache/documents/1034/103461.pdf

Taqiuddin, M. (2011). Strengthening Open Government: India Country Paper. *Better Service Delivery through Open Government and Innovative Policies, 4*.

Toyama, K., Kiri, K., Ratan, M. L., Nileshwar, A., Vedashree, R., & MacGregor, R. F. (2004). *Rural kiosks in India*. MSR Techincal Report.

Venkatesh, V., Sykes, T. A., & Venkatraman, S. (2013). Understanding e-Government portal use in rural India: Role of demographic and personality characteristics. *Information Systems Journal*.

Weiss, T. G. (2000). Governance, good governance and global governance: Conceptual and actual challenges. *Third World Quarterly*, *21*(5), 795–814. doi:10.1080/713701075

Whyte, A. (1999). *Understanding the role of community telecentres in development: A proposed approach to evaluation*. Paper presented at Telecentre Evaluation: A Global Perspective. Quebec, Canada.

ADDITIONAL READING

Attwood, H., Diga, K., Braathen, E., & May, J. (2013). Telecentre functionality in South Africa: Re-enabling the community ICT access environment. *The Journal of Community Informatics*, *9*(4).

Avgerou, C. (2010). Discourses on ICT and Development. Information Technologies & International Development, 6(3).

Breitenbach, M. C. (2013). Telecentres for sustainable rural development: Review and case study of a South African rural telecentre. *Development Southern Africa*, *30*(2), 262–278. doi:10.1080/0376835X.2013.797229

Brown, I., & Marsden, C. T. (2013). *Regulating code: Good governance and better regulation in the information age*. MIT Press.

Charag, O., & Ahmad, S. M. (2013). Impact of e–Governance System Practices on Good Governance in India-An Empirical Study (Doctoral dissertation).

Foley, C. F., Goldsmith-Pinkham, P., Greenstein, J., & Zwick, E. (2014). *Opting out of good governance (No. w19953)*. National Bureau of Economic Research. doi:10.3386/w19953

Ghimire, A. R. (2013). Information, communication and social networks: The innovative role of telecentres in rural Nepal. *Innovation and Development*, *3*(1), 142–142. doi:10.1080/2157930X.2012.721530

Gimeno, J. D. (2012). Democracy as the Missing Link: Global Rankings of E-Governance in Southeast Asia.

Grindle, M. (2012). Good governance: The inflation of an idea. Planning Ideas That Matter: Livability, Territoriality, Governance, and Reflective Practice, 259.

Haque, M. S. (2002). E-governance in India: Its impacts on relations among citizens, politicians and public servants. *International Review of Administrative Sciences*, *68*(2), 231–250. doi:10.1177/0020852302682005

Haque, S., & Pathrannarakul, P. (2013). E-Government towards good governance: A global appraisal. *Journal of E-Governance*, *36*(1), 25–34.

Hayes, N., & Westrup, C. (2012). Context and the processes of ICT for development. *Information and Organization*, *22*(1), 23–36. doi:10.1016/j.infoandorg.2011.10.001

Hill, M. (2013). A Starting Point: Understanding Governance, Good Governance and Water Governance. In Climate Change and Water Governance (pp. 17-28). Springer Netherlands.

Hilty, L. M., & Hercheui, M. D. (2010). *ICT and sustainable development. InWhat Kind of Information Society? Governance, Virtuality, Surveillance, Sustainability, Resilience* (pp. 227–235). Springer Berlin Heidelberg. doi:10.1007/978-3-642-15479-9_22

Mazzarella, W. (2006). Internet X-ray: E-governance, Transparency, and the Politics of Immediation in India. *Public Culture*, *18*(3), 473–505. doi:10.1215/08992363-2006-016

McNeil, M., & Malena, C. (Eds.). (2010). *Demanding good governance: Lessons from social accountability initiatives in Africa*. World Bank Publications. doi:10.1596/978-0-8213-8380-3

Miller, P. (2013). From the Digital Divide to Digital Inclusion and Beyond: Update on Telecentres and Community Technology Centers (CTCs). Available at SSRN 2241167.

Mishra, S., & Kant, R. (2013). Social Inclusion through E-Governance: A Study of the Beneficiaries of Uttar Pradesh (UP). *Sumedha Journal Of Management*, *2*(2), 128–136.

Mukherjee, D., & Menon, G. (2013). 11 Technology and Its Role in Good Governance. *Governance, Development, and Social Work*, *36*, 201.

Muñoz, L. A., & Bolívar, M. P. R. (2014). Learning from the Experience. Systemic Thinking for e-Government Development in Developing Countries: A Question Unsolved. In New Perspectives in Information Systems and Technologies, Volume 1 (pp. 309-321). Springer International Publishing.

Ott, J. C. (2010). Good governance and happiness in nations: Technical quality precedes democracy and quality beats size. *Journal of Happiness Studies*, *11*(3), 353–368. doi:10.1007/s10902-009-9144-7

Parthasarathy, B. (2011). Shirin Madon: e-Governance for Development: A Focus on Rural India. Information Technologies & International Development,7(4), pp-81.

Paul, S. (2007). A case study of e-governance initiatives in India. *The International Information & Library Review*, *39*(3), 176–184. doi:10.1016/j.iilr.2007.06.003

Prabhu, C. S. R. (2013). *E-governance: Concepts and case studies*. PHI Learning Pvt. Ltd.

Samah, B. A., & Badsar, M. (2013). Factors Influencing Rural Community Empowerment to Achieve Telecentres' Ownership. *Social Sciences*, *8*(5), 461–465.

KEY TERMS AND DEFINITIONS

E-Government: It is use of ICT to deliver various government services for effectiveness and efficiency.

E-Participation: Use of ICT by citizens to participate in various democratic processes of a country.

E-Services: Delivery of government services through ICTs like the Internet, telecentres, etc.

ICT: Information and Communication Technology (ICT) include tools which help in data collection, storage, processing, information retrieval, and dissemination.

ICT4D: ICT is seen as a potential tool to enhance development in a region/ state /country.

Mediator: A person who helps people to use services of a telecentre. He interacts with ICT on behalf of a person who lacks IT skills.

Telecentre: A place where ICT (mainly computer) is used to deliver various government/non-government services. Usually a mediator acts as a link between technology and people with little or no IT skills.

ENDNOTES

1 It is an ancient epic of India which contains eighteen sections on number of topics on the Hindu way of life.

2 It contains the ancient system of political administration under the directing principle of dharma (rule of law). It is the compilation of the functions, duties, roles, and characteristics of a good, popular, and dutiful king.

3 The section mainly discusses life at the court of King Dhritrashtra.

4 The section discusses life of Pandavas during their twelve year of exile in the forest.

5 Please refer to Annual Report on Electronics and Information Technology, http://deity.gov.in/sites/upload_files/dit/files/Annual%20Report%202012-13.pdf, accessed on 28/04/2014.

6 Retrieved from http://www.ilfsindia.com/downloads/bus_concept/CSC_ILFS_website.pdf, accessed on 12/05/2013.

7 Retrieved from http://www.indg.in/e-governance/cscscheme/common-service-centres-scheme, accessed on 12/05/2013.

8 Retrieved from http://www.mit.gov.in/content/common-services-centers, accessed on 12/05/2013.

9 Retrieved from the Government CSC website http://www.csc-india.org/, accessed on 17/05/2013.

10 Taken from http://www.mission2007.in/iec-pub/pubfile/ICT4D_workshop%20book.pdf, accessed on 17/05/2013.

11 Retrieved from http://www.bhoomi.karnataka.gov.in/landrecordsonweb/, accessed on 04/04/2014.

Chapter 5
Ensuring Continued Usage of an E-Government Service in Malaysia:
The Role of Perceived Usefulness and User Satisfaction

Santhanamery Thominathan
Universiti Teknologi MARA, Malaysia

Thurasamy Ramayah
Universiti Sains Malaysia, Malaysia

ABSTRACT

This chapter highlights the importance of continuance usage intention of a technology. Continuance intention is defined as one's intention to continue using or long-term usage intention of a technology. Although initial acceptance is important in identifying the success of an information system, continued usage is even more significant in ensuring the long-term viability of technology innovations and in enhancing the financial and quality performance of an organization. Therefore, this chapter aims to examine the continuance usage intention of e-filing system by taxpayers in Malaysia. The data were collected from 153 taxpayers in the northern region of Malaysia using survey method. The result shows a significant relationship between perceived usefulness and continuance usage intention. Surprisingly, perceived usefulness was found to be insignificantly related to satisfaction and satisfaction towards continuance usage intention. Implication of these findings to the Inland Revenue Board of Malaysia is also elaborated.

INTRODUCTION

Successful diffusion of information communications technology (ICT) has technologies triggered the usage of Internet, e-commerce, and eventually in electronic government (e-government) (Khanh, 2014). Vathanophas, Krittayaphongphun and Klomsiri (2008) explains that the speedy growth in the use of internet and the emergence of e-commerce have put a growing pressure on the government to cater for citizens need electronically. E-government represents a fundamen-

DOI: 10.4018/978-1-4666-7266-6.ch005

tal change in the whole public sector structure, values, culture and the ways conducting business by utilizing the potential of ICT as a tool in the government agency (Alshehri, Drew &Alfarraj, 2012). E-government is being deployed not only to provide citizen services but for public sector efficiency purposes, improving transparency and accountability in government functions and allowing for cost savings in government administration. ICTs are changing the way the government does business for the people (UNPAN, 2008). The increasing power of ICT has also provided the governments with the flexibility of providing services and information to citizens through multi-channel. Citizens have diverse needs and demands for services; therefore it is no longer sustainable for governments to utilize one preferred way of service provision over the other. It is now ever more essential that governments exploit all possible delivery channels in order to reach out to as many people as possible, no matter how poor, illiterate or isolated (UNPAN, 2012).

Guided by Vision 2020, Malaysia has embarked on an ambitious plan by launching the Multimedia Super Corridor (MSC) in August 1996. MSC is a government designated zone, designed to leapfrog Malaysia into information and knowledge era (Boon, Ramayah, Ping & Lo, 2013). Seven specific flagship applications were identified as the pioneering MSC projects, which includes e-government as one of the flagships (Muhammad Rais&Nazariah, 2003). The Vision of e-government is to transform administrative process and service delivery through the use of ICT and multimedia (Lean, Zailani, Ramayah and Fernando, 2009). The projects under the e-Government flagship have been started since ten years ago aimed at building a more effective and efficient way to communicate and transact with the citizens and industries. One of the projects under e-government flagship is Online Tax System or e-Filing (Hussein, Mohamed, Ahlan, Mahmud &Aditiawarman (2010).

As such, the objective of this paper is to evaluate the role of perceived usefulness and user satisfaction in ensuring the continuance usage intention of e-government services in Malaysia focusing on e-filing system.

BACKGROUND

E-Filing system in Malaysia was introduced in 2006 by the Malaysian Inland Revenue Board (IRBM) to the Malaysian taxpayers. E-Filing system as a whole integrates tax preparation, tax filing and tax payment, which serves as a major advantage over traditional manual procedure (Ambali, 2009). Under the e-filing system, taxpayers need to fill their tax returns electronically via internet. The submission via e-filing has shown a tremendous increase since its launching in 2006 particularly for individual taxpayers. The number of submission grew from 186,271 (2006) to 873,095 (2007) (Annual Report IRBM, 2007) to 1,171,105 (2008) to 1,466,507 (2009) (Annual Report IRBM, 2009) to 1,666,134 (Annual Report IRBM, 2010). This shows that 33% of the total registered individual taxpayers (5,040,782) have filed their income taxes via e-filing in 2010 (Annual Report IRBM, 2010). The number of submission increases further to 1, 800,000 (2011) and 2,100,000 (2012) (New Straits Times, 2012) (refer to Figure 1). Various advantages are highlighted that can be provided by e-filing system such as the IRBM improves the efficiency of the tax assessment method, by increasing tax collection and reducing computation errors. Secondly, it saves taxpayers' time as tax returns are sent electronically to the IRBM. Thirdly, cost effective as it reduces cost on printing, imaging, postal and storage since it is paperless. Finally, the tax calculation is more accurate due to automatic calculation and detection of mathematical errors and incomplete fields by the system (Hasmah, 2009).

Figure 1. Submission via e-filing
(Adapted from: Annual Report IRBM, New Strait Times, 2012).

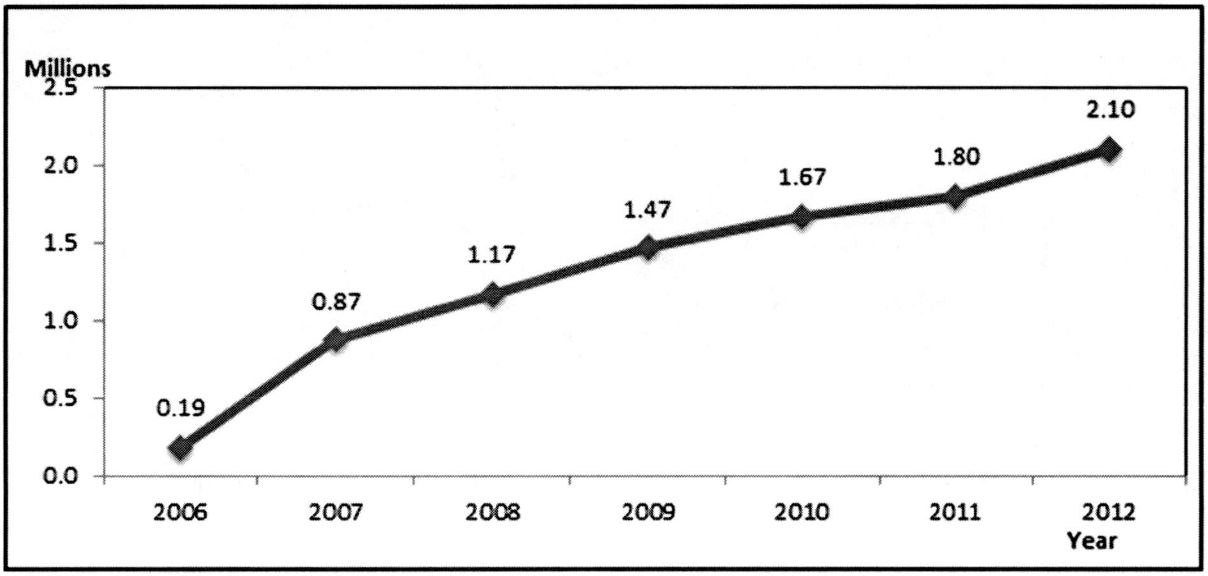

MAIN FOCUS OF THE CHAPTER

Theoretical Background and the Research Model

Based on the evaluation of the theoretical finding from previous literatures as well as the recommendations from previous researches, the research model as illustrated in Figure 2 were constructed to explore the relationship expected in this study. Basically the theoretical framework proposed that there exist a direct relationship between perceived usefulness and satisfaction towards e-filing continuance usage intention and also the indirect effect of perceived usefulness through satisfaction. Perceived Usefulness has been determined as the primary determinant of people's intention to use computer by Technology Acceptance Model (Davis, Bagozzi&Warshaw, 1989) whereas, satisfaction, on the other hand was posits as the most important determinant of users' continuance usage intention by Expectation Confirmation Model (ECM) (Liao, Palvia& Chen, 2009). The major area of this study is the continuance usage intention, whereby customers' repurchasing or loyalty is critical to the success and profitability of online stores (Chiu, Chang, Cheng & Fang, 2009). Significantly while there has been encouraging interest shown in determining continuance usage intention, however, very little effort is undertaken in determining the effect of perceived usefulness and satisfaction on the continuance usage intentions particularly in e-government perspectives.

In addition, a thorough review of the relevant literature on technology adoption shows that the majority of the research conducted in Malaysia has focused on the pre-adoption environment (intention to adopt a technology) while lacking in research on post adoption environment (continuance usage intention after initial adoption). Therefore, this study intends to fill the aforementioned gap. Figure 2 represents the theoretical model

Figure 2. Theoretical model

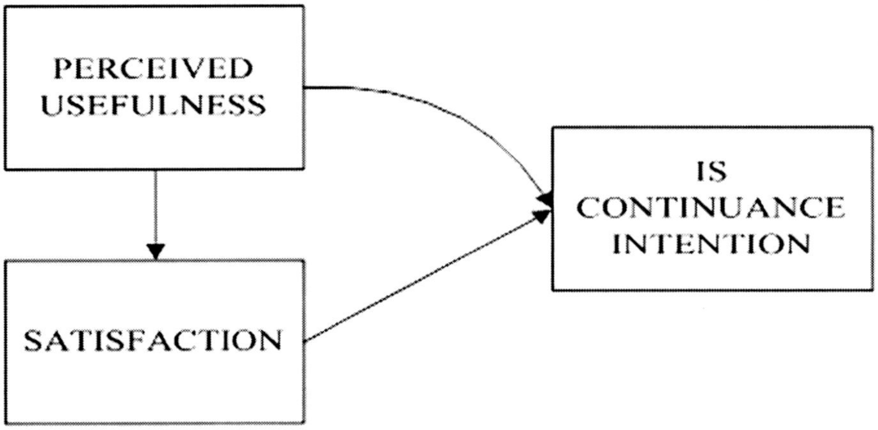

Theories and Models in Technology Acceptance

Individuals' decision to adopt a technology has always been the central point of IS research, various theoretical models have been designed and used to investigate technology acceptance in the information technology literature. Among them are:

Theory of Reasoned Action (TRA)

TRA is one of the primary and prominent theories of human behavior; however it is a general model with no specific belief for a particular behavior (Davis et al., 1989). According to this theory, behavioral intention to perform a behavior is determined by a person's attitude and subjective norm. A person's attitude towards a behavior is determined by the beliefs and evaluation about the consequences of performing the behavior, conversely subjective norm refers to the influence of the people surrounding the person about performing a particular behavior (Davis et al., 1989)

Technology Acceptance Model (TAM)

The purpose of TAM is to examine the impact of external factors on internal beliefs, attitudes and

Figure 3. Theory of Reasoned Action (TRA)

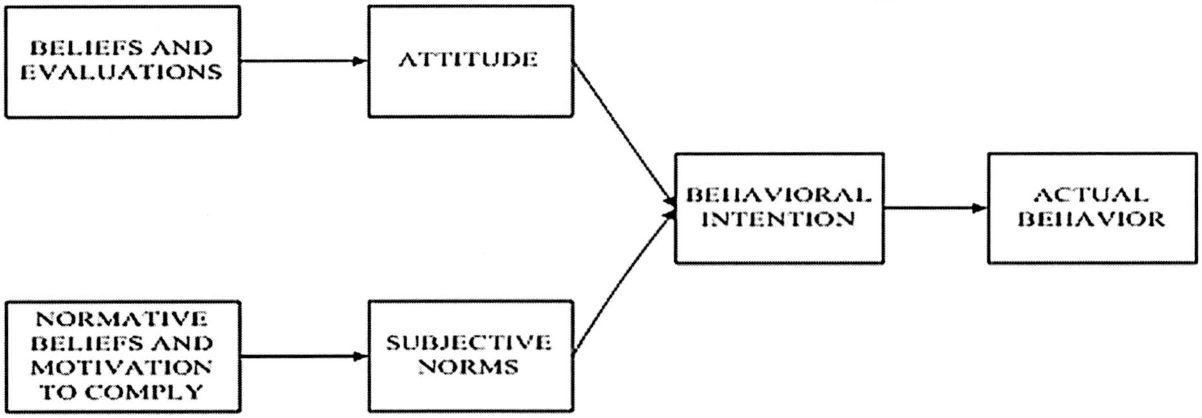

intentions. Basically there are two types of beliefs introduced by TAM; perceived usefulness (PU) and perceived ease of use (PEOU) that affects attitude and acceptance behavior. PU is defined as "the degree to which a person believes that using a particular system would enhance his or her job performance (Davis, 1989). Alternatively PEOU is defined as "the degree to which a person believes that using a particular system would be free of effort" (Davis, 1989). Perceived usefulness was stated as a primary determinant and perceived ease of use was a secondary determinant of people's intention to use computers (Davis et al., 1989)

So, based on TAM, behavioral intention in using a computer system is jointly determined by attitude and perceived usefulness and does not consider subjective norm as a direct influence towards behavioral intention.

Expectation Confirmation Model (ECM)

ECM was introduced by Bhattcherjee (2001), which describes the user's behavior in "continued to use" an information system. ECM was actually an adaptation of Expectation Confirmation Theory (ECT) which was introduced by Oliver

Figure 4. Technology Acceptance Model (TAM)

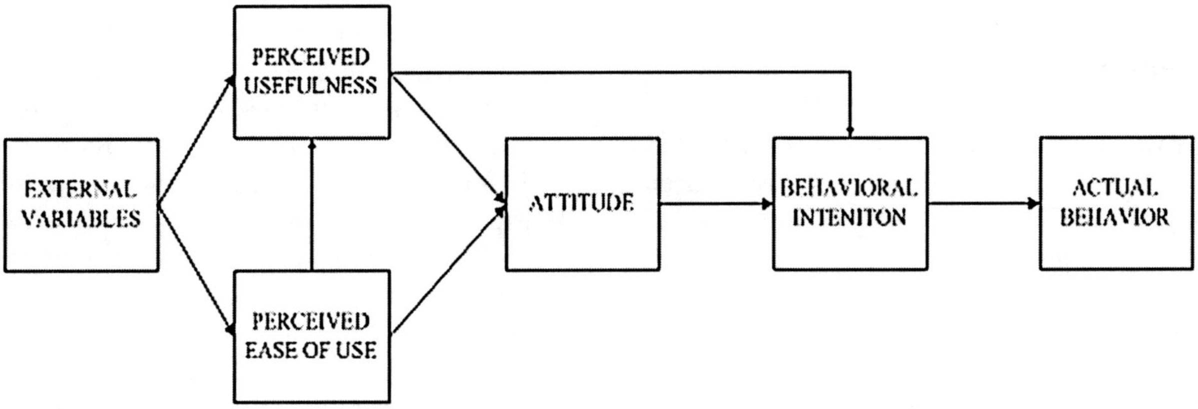

Figure 5. Expectation Confirmation Model (ECM)

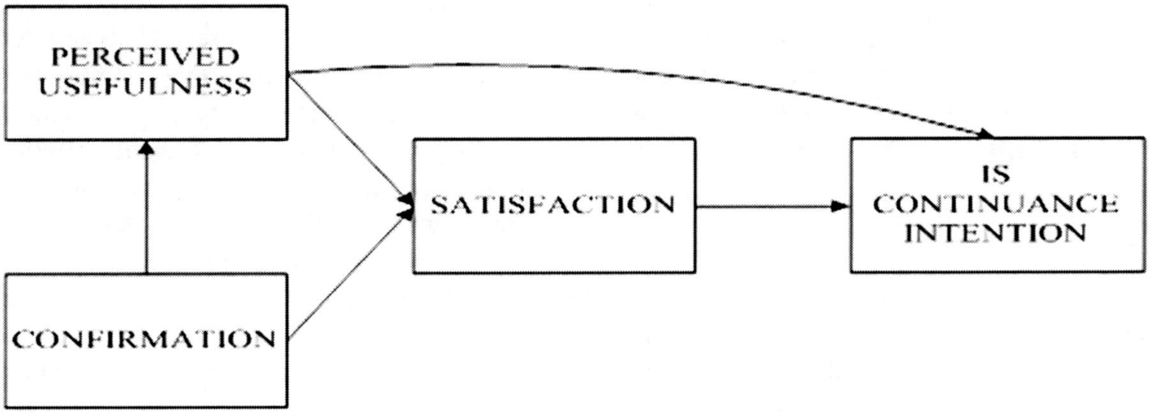

(1980). ECT is widely used in consumer behavior research to study consumer satisfaction, post purchase behavior and service marketing in general. ECM's major purpose is to evaluate an individual's continuance and loyalty intention towards a system use (Liao et al., 2009). It posits that individuals intention to continue IT usage is dependable on users' level of satisfaction, confirmation of expectation and post adoption expectation (perceived usefulness) (Lee, 2010). However ECM argues that the most important determinant of continuance intention is users' satisfaction and satisfaction on the other hand, is a function of expectation and confirmation of expectation (Liao et al. 2009). Confirmation is positively related to satisfaction and disconfirmation signifies failure to achieve expectation (Bhattarcherjee, 2001).

Continuance Intention

Continuance intention is defined as ones intention to continue using a service in the post acceptance stage it is similar to ones repurchase decision as both decisions are influenced by initial usage (Bhattacherjee, 2001). Research on continuance usage intention have been explored both at the organizational and individual level of analysis (Limayem, Hirt& Cheung, 2007), the individual level of analysis assumes that IS continuance behaviour is the continued usage of IS by adopters, which is follows an initial acceptance decision (Kim, Chan & Chan, 2007). However, unlike initial acceptance decision, IS continuance depends on various factors that affect the individuals' decision to continually using a particular system (Limayem, Hirt& Chin, 2001).

Perceived Usefulness

Perceived usefulness was defined "as the prospective user's subjective probability that using a specific application system will increase his or her job performance within an organizational context (Davis et al., 1989). It was found that perceived usefulness was correlated with all technology usage. Research by Hung, Chang and Hwang (2011), Al-maghrabi, Dennis and Halliday (2011), Wang, Oh, Wang and Zhang (2010), Bhattacherjee (2001), establish that perceived usefulness has a significant positive influence on continuance usage intention of a technology.

Satisfaction

Satisfaction is defined as the "pleasurable fulfillment response resulting from an evaluation with respective to how well the consumption of a product or service meets a need, desire, or goal" (Deng, Turner, Gehling& Prince, 2010). According to Expectation Confirmation Theory (ECT) (Bhattacherjee, 2001) and Expectancy Disconfirmation Theory (EDT) (Oliver, 1980) consumers intention to repurchase a product or continuously use a system is determined by the prior satisfaction with the product or services. Based on EDT, for a customer to reach their repurchase decision, it involves several stages: firstly, form a initial expectation for the product or services, secondly, form a perception of the performance of the product or services; thirdly, form a confirmation on their expectation and performance of the product or services; fourthly, form a satisfaction feeling towards the product or services and finally satisfaction leads to repurchase.

Prior study also found that perceived usefulness to be significantly influence satisfaction towards continuance intention to use self-service technologies. The study justifies that the more useful a self-service technology, the more satisfactory it will be, thus consumers will continually uses the services (Chen, Chen & Chen, 2009). Doong, Wang and Chen (2007) discovers that perceived usefulness which is the users perception of Online Reputation System's (ORS) benefit have a significant impact on satisfaction towards continuance intention to use the system. Indeed, Bhattacherjee (2001) also found that perceived usefulness has a significant positive impact on satisfaction towards continuance intention. Besides, Chen, Huang, Hsu, Tseng and Lee (2010); Limayem and Cheung (2008) and Roca, Chiu & Martinez (2006), also found a significant positive relationship between perceived usefulness and satisfaction towards continuance usage intention.

Research by Hung et al. (2011) found that perceived usefulness has a positive relationship in determining the continuance intention towards web based learning system. Similarly, Al-maghrabi et al. (2011) also revealed that perceived usefulness is the main determinant of continuance intention of e-shopping in Saudi Arabia. Correspondingly, Shiau, Huang and Shih (2011) examined the continuance intention of blog users' and reported that perceived usefulness of the blogs positively influence the blogger's intention to continually using blogs. Study on the citizen's continuance intention to use e-government websites found that perceived usefulness directly enhanced citizen's continuance intention to use e-government websites (Wangpipatwong, Chutimaskul&Papasratorn, 2008). Further, Eriksson and Nilsson (2007) investigated the determinants of continued use of internet banking and reveals that the Estonian consumers' internet banking continuance usage intention is positively affected by perceived usefulness.

Thus it is hypothesized that:

H1: Perceived usefulness has a direct positive relationship on satisfaction towards e-filing continuance usage intentions

H2: Perceived usefulness has a direct positive relationship towards continuance usage intention.

Literatures have also demonstrated that users' continuance intention is determined by their satisfaction with the information system usage (Lee, 2010; Roca et al., 2006). Ong and Day (2010) found that the outcome of user satisfaction with Social Media Service such as YouTube and Facebook is the continued usage of these services. Satisfaction also was found to be the strongest predictor of users' continuance intention of Enterprise Resource Planning system compared to individual differences such as personal innovativeness, computer anxiety and computer self-efficacy (Chou & Chen, 2009). Further, Deng et al. (2010) based on their study revealed a positive relationship between satisfaction and continued usage intention. The study concluded that the more satisfied a user, the more likely he/she will continue using the technology. Similarly, customer satisfaction has an important impact towards IS continuance usage intention because user who are more satisfied with their experience will have a higher level of continued use (Limayem& Cheung, 2008).

Based on the findings above, it can be surmised that:

H3: Satisfaction has a positive significant relationship towards e-filing continuance usage intention.

RESEARCH METHOD

Data Collection Method

Data was collected from 153 taxpayers in the northern region of Malaysia which consist of Penang and Perak using a structured questionnaire which was derived from the questionnaire. The questionnaire consists of 5 sections. The first section elicited the screening question, the second section collected the demographic data, the third measured the perceived usefulness, section fourth on the user satisfaction and last section measured continuance intention. The sample selected were taxpayers who had used the e-filing system at least once as the measures required them to express the perceived usefulness, satisfaction and continuance intention.

Measures

The measures were all adapted from the published literature. The measures for continuance intention were from Bhatterchejee (2001). Perceived Usefulness measures were adapted from Davis et al., (1989) whereas Measures for satisfaction were adapted from Spreng, Mackenzie &Olshavsky (1996).

Sample Profile

The demographic of the respondents tabulated in Table 1 were derived from descriptive analysis. The majority of the age group (21.6%) was in the category of 50-54 years old. Male (61.4%) outnumbered the females (38.6%). In terms of ethnicity the majority of the respondents are Malays (46.4%), followed by Chinese (28.8%) and Indians (24.8%) which somewhat reflects the ethnic group distribution in Malaysia. About 35.9% of the total respondents are highly educated with Bachelor degree and followed by Diploma/College Level. (30.1%) The majority of the respondents (32.7%) are earning within RM3000-RM3999 per month with majority (83%) are married respondents. Lastly about 75.8% and 45.1% of the respondents claimed to have experience in computer usage and internet usage approximately 10 years and above respectively.

DATA ANALYSIS

Smart PLS version 2.0, a variance based Structural Equation Modelling (SEM) was used to analyze the hypotheses generated. The reasons for using this technique are as follows:

- PLS is known for its ability to handle both reflective and formative measures.
- PLS places a minimal restriction on the sample size (Chin, 1998).

Table 1. Demographics of the respondents

Demographic Type	Frequency (N)	Percent
Age		
25-29 years	19	12.4
30-34 years	26	17.0
35-39 years	19	12.4
40-44 years	26	17.0
45-49 years	17	11.1
50-54 years	33	21.6
55 years and above	13	8.5
Gender		
Male	94	61.4
Female	59	38.6
Ethnicity		
Malay	71	46.4
Chinese	44	28.8
Indian	38	24.8
Education		
Diploma/ College Level	46	30.1
Bachelor Degree	55	35.9
Masters Degree	19	12.4
Doctoral Degree	1	0.7
Others	28	18.3
Income		
RM2000 - RM2999	34	22.2
RM3000 - RM3999	50	32.7
RM4000 - RM4999	31	20.3
RM5000 - RM5999	20	13.1
RM6000 - RM6999	10	6.5
RM7000 and above	7	4.6
Marital Status		
Single	26	17.0
Married	127	83.0
Computer Usage		
1-3 years	7	4.6
4-6 years	10	6.5
7-9 years	19	12.4
10 years and above	116	75.8
Internet Usage		
1-3 years	11	7.2

continued on following page

Table 1. Continued

Demographic Type	Frequency (N)	Percent
4-6 years	39	25.5
7-9 years	34	22.2
10 years and above	69	45.1

Note: Because of missing responses, N and percentage may not add up to 153 and 100, respectively.

The two step analytical procedure suggested by Anderson and Gerbing (1988) was adopted to analyze data whereby the measurement model was evaluated first and then followed by the structural model. Also following the suggestion of Chin (1998), the bootstrapping method (500 resample) was done to determine the significant level of loadings, weights and path coefficients. Figure 6 shows the Research Model.

Measurement Model

Convergent validity is the degree to which the items that are indicators of a specific construct should converge or share a high proportion of variance in common (Hair, Black, Babin& Anderson, 2010). According to Hair et al. (2010), factor loadings and average variance extracted (AVE) of more than 0.5 and composite reliability (CR) of 0.7 or above is deemed to be acceptable. As can be seen from Table 2, all loadings and AVE are above 0.5 and the composite reliability values are more than 0.7. Therefore, we can conclude that convergent validity has been established.

Next, we assessed the Discriminant validity which is the extent to which a construct is truly distinct from other constructs (Hair et al., 2010). This can be established by low correlations between all the measure of the interest and the measure of other constructs. To address discriminant validity the square root of the AVE is compared against the correlations of the other constructs, when the AVE extracted is greater than its correlations with all the other constructs then discriminant validity has been established (Fornell & Larcker, 1981) (refer Table 3).

Structural Model

The structural model represents the relationship between constructs or latent variables that were

Figure 6. Research model

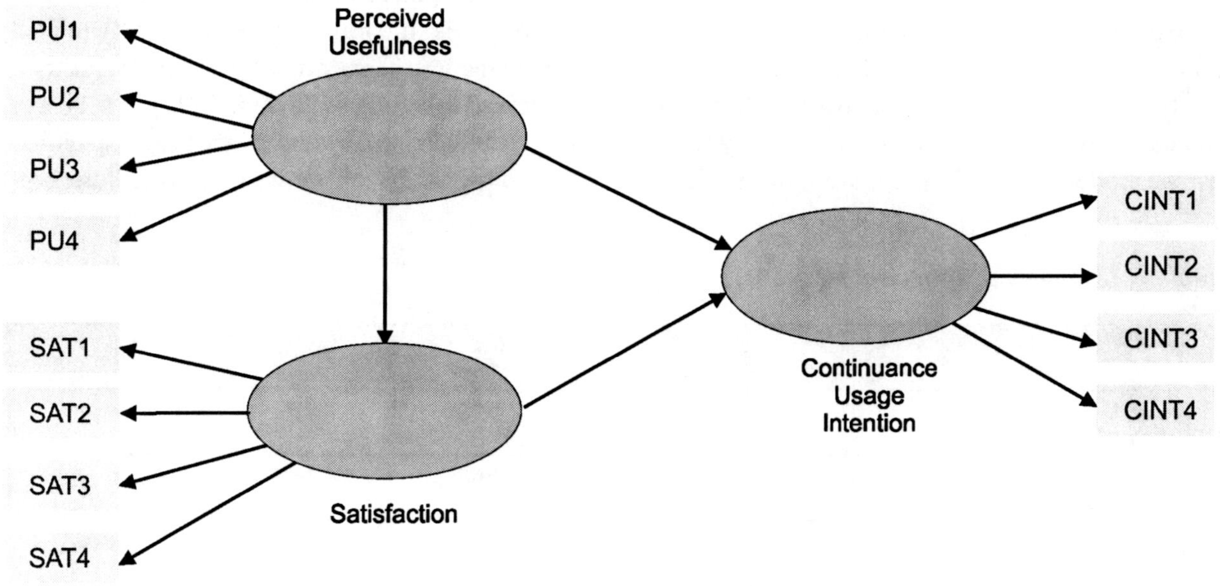

Table 2. Result of measurement model

Convergent Validity				
Construct	**Item**	**Factor Loading**	**AVE**	**Composite Reliability**
Perceived Usefulness	PU1	0.953	0.903	0.974
	PU2	0.952		
	PU3	0.945		
	PU4	0.952		
Satisfaction	SAT1	0.774	0.869	0.963
	SAT2	0.970		
	SAT3	0.984		
	SAT4	0.984		
Continuance	CINT1	0.938	0.897	0.972
Intention	CINT2	0.968		
	CINT3	0.942		
	CINT4	0.940		

Table 3. Discriminant validity of construct

Constructs	1	2	3	4
Continuance Intention	**0.947**			
Perceived usefulness	0.735	**0.950**		
Satisfaction	0.011	0.081	**0.932**	

hypothesized in the research model. The goodness of the theoretical model is established by the variance explained (R^2) of the endogenous constructs and the significance of all path estimates (Chin, 2010). Together the R^2 and the path coefficients indicate how well the data support the hypothesized model (Chin, 1998). Figure 7 and Table 4, show the results of the structural model from the PLS output. Perceived Usefulness ($\beta = 0.081$) was found in this study to be not significantly related to Satisfaction, hence not supporting H1. Further, Perceived Usefulness ($\beta = 0.739$, $p < 0.1$) was significantly related to continuance usage intention explaining 54.2% of the variance therefore sup-

Table 4. Summary of structural model

Path	Hypotheses	Path Coefficient	Standard Error	t-Value	Results
Perceived Usefulness -> Satisfaction	H1	0.081	0.079	1.027	Not Supported
Perceived Usefulness -> Continuance Intention	H2	0.739	0.050	14.850***	Supported
Satisfaction -> Continuance Intention	H3	-0.049	0.050	0.973	Not Supported

Note: *** p < 0.01, ** p < 0.05, * p < 0.1.

Figure 7. Structural model

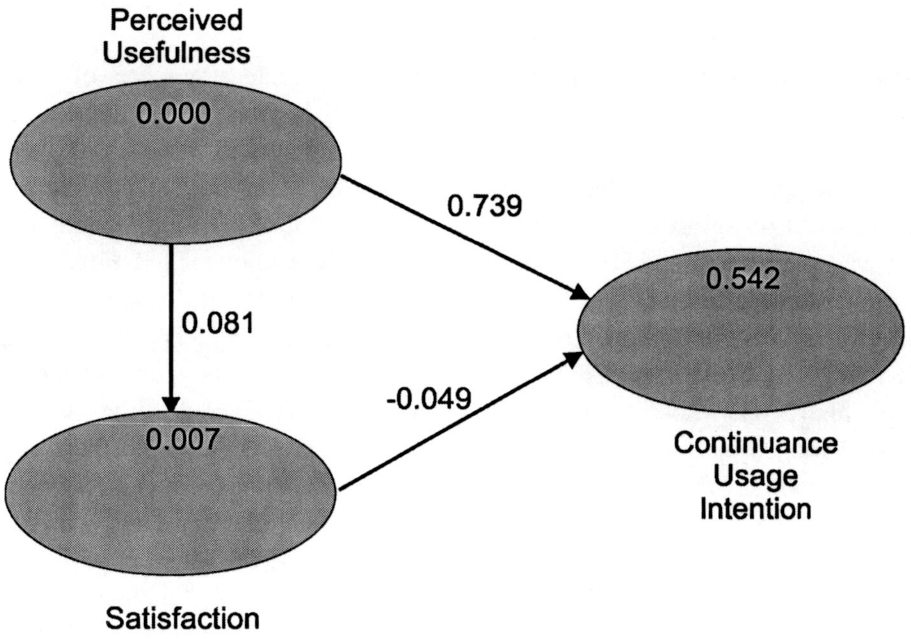

ports the H2. However Satisfaction (β = -0.049) was found to be inversely and not significantly related to continuance usage intention. Closer look on the findings reveals that perceived usefulness is the most important predictor of continuance usage intention.

Apart from that, "blindfolding" procedure was also performed to measure the predictive relevance (Q^2) of the model fit. The Q^2 "represents a measure of how well observed values are reconstructed by the model and its parameter estimates" (Chin, 1998). Models with Q^2 greater than zero imply that the model has predictive relevance. Table 5 shows the result of the blindfolding results. Omission distance of 7 was utilized as Chin (1998) indicates that values between 5 and 10 are feasible (refer to Table 5).

Table 5. Blindfolding result

Construct	CV Red	CV Comm
Satisfaction	0.004	0.833
Continuance Intention	0.482	0.801

DISCUSSION

The purpose of this study was to test the effect of perceived usefulness and satisfaction on the continuance usage intention of e-filing system among the taxpayers in the northern region of Malaysia. The result of the study is in line with the previous studies which found perceived usefulness is significantly related to e-filing continuance usage intention such as Li and Shi (2012), Islam (2012), Hung et al. (2011), Al-maghrabi et al. (2011), Wang et al. (2010), Lin and Ong (2010), Limayem and Cheung (2008), Wangpipatwong et al. (2008), Eriksson and Nilsson (2007), Lin, Wu & Tsai (2005) and Bhattacherjee (2001). This implies that a web portal has to provide all necessary and fundamental capabilities to avoid turning away users after their initial usage (Lin et al., 2005). A local study has indicated that any technological devices provided in enhancing the service boundary between the government and its citizen must be found to be useful. Thus, e-filing system must be seen as a better alternative by the taxpayers in submitting their income tax in terms of time, cost and convenience compared to manual submission; failure on this will lead the taxpayers to abandon the system in the long run (Ambali, 2009).

The result of this study on the insignificant relationship between perceived usefulness and satisfaction and satisfaction towards continuance usage intention was unexpected and contradicts with many previous studies, however it is in line with the study by Li and Shi (2012), Lin, Chen & Fang (2011), Kim (2010), Sorebo and Eikbrokk (2008) and Lin et al., (2005) whose studies also found a negative relationship between perceived usefulness and satisfaction. This may be due to the fact that since e-filing system is offered by the government of Malaysia, it may have been considered as a "mandatory usage" whereby the taxpayers perceived that sooner or later they have to familiarize themselves and adapt to the usage of the system. As such, since there is no real usage choice, the usefulness of the system will be the main concern of the taxpayers. Another possible explanation could be due to the fact that as indicated by Oliver (1980) that satisfaction is the main influence for the post purchase attitude which means that the higher the satisfaction the more positive attitude that a user will have towards a particular system. As such, satisfaction may not have a direct influence on continuance usage intention but an indirect effect towards attitude. This is proven by the findings of Kwak, McDaniel and Kim (2012) whose study reveals that satisfaction does not have a direct effect on loyalty but it has a significant effect in influencing the attitude in determining the continuance usage intention of users in a sports video gaming context. Similarly, in the context of e-filing system in Malaysia, satisfaction may not have a direct influence in determining the continuance usage of the e-filing system but may have a strong influence on attitude of the taxpayers in persuading them to continually use the system.

LIMITATION AND SUGGESTION FOR FUTURE RESEARCH

The study tested the effect of perceived usefulness, satisfaction and continuance usage intention of e-filing system among taxpayers in northern region of Malaysia. Despite the useful findings of this study, there are several limitations that need to be acknowledged. Firstly, due to time and resource constraint the sample size of the study is only limited to 153 respondents. Secondly, the findings cannot be generalized extensively in Malaysia as the scope of the study is only limited to the taxpayers in the northern region only. As such caution need to be taken when generalizing to the whole country. Lastly, this study only focus on testing the effect of perceived usefulness, satisfaction and continuance usage intention and does not incorporate the actual usage behavior in the proposed model.

Therefore, future research can expand this study by:

1. Expanding the study to other states in Malaysia,
2. Extending the model by incorporating the actual usage behavior or any other relevant variables based on the latest literatures suggestions, and
3. Including the construct of attitude in examining the relationship between satisfaction, attitude and continuance usage intention.

CONCLUSION

In this study, it was found that perceived usefulness is useful and significant predictor of continuance usage intention of e-filing system. Perceived usefulness was found to be the strongest predictor of continuance usage intention compared to satisfaction in this study. The findings provided by this study may enable the IRBM to think seriously on enhancing the perceived usefulness of the e-filing system to attract more taxpayers to utilize the system and to create strategies to further boost the awareness of the taxpayers. In short, further research is needed to improve the study better and to address its limitations. It is hoped that this study would give a basic understanding on the continuance usage intention of e-filing system among taxpayers in Malaysia.

REFERENCES

Al-maghrabi, T., Dennis, C., & Halliday, S. V. (2011). Understanding The Factors That Derive Continuance Intention Of E-Shopping In Saudi Arabia: Age Group Differences In Behaviour. *Journal of Enterprise Information Management*, *24*(1), 85–111. doi:10.1108/17410391111097447

Alshehri, M., Drew, S., & Alfarraj, O. (2012). A Comprehensive Analysis of E-Government services adoption in Saudi Arabia: Obstacles and Challenges. *International Journal of Advanced Computer Science and Applications*, *3*(2), 1–6. doi:10.14569/IJACSA.2012.030201

Ambali, A. R. (2009). E-government Policy: Ground Issues in E-Filing System. *European Journal of Soil Science*, *11*(2), 249–266.

Anderson, J. C., & Gerbing, D. W. (1988). Structural Equation Modeling in Practice: A Review and Recommended Two-Step Approach. *Psychological Bulletin*, *103*(3), 411–423. doi:10.1037/0033-2909.103.3.411

Annual Report Inland Revenue Board of Malaysia. (2007). Retrieved from http://www.hasil.gov.my/pdf/pdfam/AR2007_2.pdf

Annual Report Inland Revenue Board of Malaysia. (2009). Retrieved from http://www.hasil.gov.my/pdf/pdfam/AR2009_2.pdf

Annual Report Inland Revenue Board of Malaysia. (2010). Retrieved from http://www.hasil.org.my/pdf/pdfam/AR2010_2.pdf

Bhattacherjee, A. (2001). Understanding Information Systems Continuance: An Expectation-Confirmation Model. *Management Information Systems Quarterly*, *25*(3), 351–370. doi:10.2307/3250921

Boon, N. Y., Ramayah, T., Ping, T. A., & Lo, M. (2013). Intention to Use E-Government Websites among UniversitiSains Malaysia (USM) Students. In P. Ordóñez de Pablos, J. Lovelle, J. Gayo, & R. Tennyson (Eds.), *E-Procurement Management for Successful Electronic Government Systems* (pp. 169–180). Hershey, PA: Information Science Reference; doi:10.4018/978-1-4666-2119-0.ch011

Chen, S. C., Chen, H. H., & Chen, M. F. (2009). Determinants of Satisfaction and Continuance Intention Towards Self-Service Technologies. *Industrial Management & Data Systems*, *109*(9), 1248–1263. doi:10.1108/02635570911002306

Chen, Y. Y., Huang, H. L., Hsu, Y. C., Tseng, H. C., & Lee, Y. C. (2010). Confirmation of Expectations and Satisfaction with the Internet Shopping: The Role of Internet Self-efficacy. *Computer and Information Science*, *3*(3), 14–22. doi:10.5539/cis.v3n3p14

Chin, W. W. (1998). Commentary: Issues and Opinion on Structural Equation Modeling. *Management Information Systems Quarterly*, *22*(1), vii–xvi.

Chin, W. W. (2010). How to Write Up and Report PLS Analyses. In V. Esposito Vinzi et al. (Eds.), *Handbook of Partial Least Squares: Concepts, Methods and Applications* (pp. 655–689). Springer Handbooks of Computational Statistics, Springer-Verlag Berlin Heidelberg. doi:10.1007/978-3-540-32827-8_29

Chiu, C. M., Chang, C. C., Cheng, H. L., & Fang, Y. H. (2009). Determinants of Customer Repurchase Intention in Online Shopping. *Online Information Review*, *33*(4), 761–784. doi:10.1108/14684520910985710

Chou, S. W., & Chen, P. Y. (2009). The Influence of Individual Differences on Continuance Intentions of Enterprise Resource Planning (ERP). *International Journal of Human-Computer Studies*, *67*(6), 484–496. doi:10.1016/j.ijhcs.2009.01.001

Davis, F. D. (1989). Perceived Usefulness, Perceived Ease of Use and User Acceptance of Information Technology. *Management Information Systems Quarterly*, *13*(3), 319–340. doi:10.2307/249008

Davis, F. D., Bagozzi, R. P., & Warshaw, P. R. (1989). User Acceptance of Computer Technology: A Comparison of Two Theoretical Models. *Management Science*, *15*(8), 982–1003. doi:10.1287/mnsc.35.8.982

Deng, L., Turner, D. E., Gehling, R., & Prince, B. (2010). User Experience, Satisfaction, and Continual Usage Intention of IT. *European Journal of Information Systems*, *19*(1), 60–75. doi:10.1057/ejis.2009.50

Doong, H. S., Wang, H. C., & Chen, P. H. (2007). An Empirical Study of Online Reputation System Continuance. In *Proceedings of International Conference on Wireless Communications, Networking and Mobile Computing*, (pp. 3816-3819). Academic Press. doi:10.1109/WICOM.2007.944

Eriksson, K., & Nilsson, D. (2007). Determinants of the Continued Use of Self-Service Technology: The Case of Internet Banking. *Technovation*, *27*(4), 159–167. doi:10.1016/j.technovation.2006.11.001

Fang, Z. (2002). E-Government in Digital Era: Concept, Practice and Development. *International Journal of the Computer, the Internet and Management*, *10*(2), 1-22.

Fornell, C., & Larcker, D. F. (1981). Evaluating Structural Equation Models with Unobservable Variables and Measurement Error. *JMR, Journal of Marketing Research*, *18*(1), 39–50. doi:10.2307/3151312

Fu, J. R., Farn, C. K., & Chao, W. P. (2006). Acceptance of Electronic Tax Filing: A Study of Taxpayer Intentions. *Information & Management*, *43*(1), 109–126. doi:10.1016/j.im.2005.04.001

Hair, J. F., Jr., Black, W. C., Babin, B. J., & Anderson, R. E. (2010).Multivariate Data Analysis: A Global Perspective (7thed.). Pearson Prentice Hall.

Hasmah, A. (2009). *e-Filing Pays*. Retrieved from http://www.intanbk.intan.my/i-portal/nict/nict/day1/session3parallel1(session3a)/Dato_hasmah_e-filing_Pays.pdf/

Hung, M. C., Chang, I. C., & Hwang, H. G. (2011). Exploring Academic Teachers' Continuance Toward The Web-Based Learning System: The Role Of Causal Attributions. *Computers & Education*, *57*(2), 1530–1543. doi:10.1016/j.compedu.2011.02.001

Hussein, R., Mohamed, N., Ahlan, A. R., Mahmud, M., & Aditiawarman, U. (2010). An Integrated Model on Online Tax Adoption in Malaysia. In *Proceedings of European, Mediterranean & Middle Eastern Conference on Information Systems (EMCIS)*, (pp. 1-16). EMCIS.

Islam, A. K. M. N. (2012). The Role of Perceived System Quality as Educators' Motivation to Continue E-learning System Use. *AIS Transactions on Human-Computer Interaction*, *4*(1), 25–43.

Khanh, N. T. V. (2014). The Critical Factors Affecting E-Government Adoption: A Conceptual Framework in Vietnam. *Computers & Society*. Retrieved from http://arxiv.org/ftp/arxiv/papers/1401/1401.4876.pdf

Kim, B. (2010). An Empirical Investigation of Mobile Data Service Continuance: Incorporating the Theory of Planned Behavior Into The Expectation–Confirmation Model. *Expert Systems with Applications*, *37*(10), 7033–7039. doi:10.1016/j.eswa.2010.03.015

Kim, H. W., Chan, H. C., & Chan, Y. P. (2007). A Balanced Thinking-Feelings Model of Information Systems Continuance. *International Journal of Human-Computer Studies*, *65*(6), 511–525. doi:10.1016/j.ijhcs.2006.11.009

Kwak, D. H., McDaniel, S., & Kim, K. T. (2012). Revisiting the Satisfaction-Loyalty Relationship in the Sport Video Gaming Context: The Mediating Role of Consumer Expertise. *Journal of Sports Management*, *26*(1), 81–91.

Lean, O. K., Zailani, S., Ramayah, T., & Fernando, Y. (2009). Factors Influencing Intention to Use e-Government Services Among Citizens in Malaysia. *International Journal of Information Management*, *29*(6), 458–475. doi:10.1016/j.ijinfomgt.2009.03.012

Lee, M. C. (2010). Explaining and Predicting Users' Continuance Intention Toward e-Learning: An Extension of the Expectation-Confirmation Model. *Computers & Education*, *54*(2), 506–516. doi:10.1016/j.compedu.2009.09.002

Li, G., & Shi, X. (2012). The Determinants of Consumers' Purchase Intention to Online Group-Buying. *Advanced Materials Research*, *459*, 372–376.

Liao, C., Palvia, P., & Chen, J. L. (2009). Information Technology Adoption Behavior Life Cycle: Toward a Technology Continuance Theory (TCT). *International Journal of Information Management*, *29*(4), 309–320. doi:10.1016/j.ijinfomgt.2009.03.004

Limayem, M., & Cheung, C. M. K. (2008). Understanding Information System Continuance: The Case of Internet-Based Learning Technologies. *Information & Management*, *45*(4), 227–232. doi:10.1016/j.im.2008.02.005

Limayem, M., Hirt, S. G., & Cheung, C. M. K. (2007). How Habit Limits the Predictive Power of Intention: The Case of Information System Continuance. *Management Information Systems Quarterly*, *31*(4), 705–737.

Limayem, M., Hirt, S. G., & Chin, W. W. (2001). Intention Does Not Always Matter: The Contingent Role of Habit on IT Usage Behavior. In *Proceedings of the 9th European Conference on Information Systems*, (pp. 274-286). Academic Press.

Lin, C. S., Wu, S., & Tsai, R. J. (2005). Integrating Perceived Playfulness Into Expectation-Confirmation Model For Web Portal Context. *Information & Management*, *42*(5), 683–693. doi:10.1016/j.im.2004.04.003

Lin, K.M., Chen, N.S., & Fang, K. (2011). Understanding E-Learning Continuance Intention: A Negative Critical Incidents Perspectives. *Behaviour & Information Technology*, 1362 – 3001.

Lin, M. Y. C., & Ong, C. S. (2010).Understanding Information System Continuance Intention: A Five Factor Model of Personality Perspectives. In *Proceedings of the Pacific Asia Conference on Information System (PACIS)*, (pp. 366-376). PACIS.

Melville, A. (2005). *Taxation: Finance Act 2004* (10th ed.). Edinburgh, UK: Prentice Hall, Pearson Education Limited.

Muhammad Rais, A. K., & Nazariah, M. K. (2003). *E-Government in Malaysia. In Pelanduk Publications (M)*. Sdn Bhd.

New Straits Times (NST). (2012). *15 percent increase in e-Filing, says LHDN*. Retrieved on February 14th, 2013 from http://www.nst.com.my/latest/15-per-cent-increase-in-e-filing-says-lhdn-1.91623

Oliver, R. L. (1980). A Cognitive Model of the Antecedents and Consequences of Satisfaction Decisions. *JMR, Journal of Marketing Research*, *17*(4), 460–469. doi:10.2307/3150499

Ong, C. S., & Day, M. Y. (2010).An Integrated Evaluation Model of User Satisfaction with Social Media Services. In *Proceeding of the International Conference on Information Reuse and Integration (IRI)*, (pp. 195-200). IRI. doi:10.1109/IRI.2010.5558940

Raman, V. V. (2008). Examining the "e" in Government and Governance: A Case Study in Alternatives from Bangalore City India. *The Journal of Community Informatics*, *4*(2).

Roca, J. C., Chiu, C. M., & Martinez, F. J. (2006). Understanding e-Learning Continuance Intention: An Extension of the Technology Acceptance Model. *International Journal of Human-Computer Studies*, *64*(8), 683–696. doi:10.1016/j.ijhcs.2006.01.003

Shiau, W. L., Huang, L. C., & Shih, C. H. (2011). Understanding Continuance Intention of Blog Users: A Perspective of Flow and Expectation Confirmation Theory. *Journal of Convergence Information Technology*, *6*(4), 306–317. doi:10.4156/jcit.vol6.issue4.33

Sorebo, O., & Eikebrokk, T. R. (2008). Explaining IS Continuance in Environments where Usage is Mandatory. *Computers in Human Behavior*, *24*(5), 2357–2371. doi:10.1016/j.chb.2008.02.011

Spreng, R. A., MacKenzie, S. B., & Olshavsky, R. W. (1996). A Reexamination of the Determinants of Consumer Satisfaction. *Journal of Marketing*, *60*(3), 15–32. doi:10.2307/1251839

United Nations E-Government Readiness Survey (UNPAN). (2008). *From E-Government to Connected Governance*. Retrieved from http://unpan1.un.org/intradoc/groups/public/documents/un/unpan028607.pdf

United Nations E-Government Survey (UNPAN). (2012). *E-Government for the People*. Retrieved from http://unpan1.un.org/intradoc/groups/public/documents/un/unpan048065.pdf

Vathanophas, V., Krittayaphongphun, N., & Klomsiri, C. (2008). Technology Acceptance Toward e-Government Initiative in Royal Thai Navy. *Transforming Government: People, Process and Policy*, *2*(4), 256–282.

Wang, T., Oh, L. B., Wang, K., & Zhang, B. (2010).An Empirical Study of the Impact of Trial Experiences on the Continued Usage of Mobile Newspapers. In *Proceeding of the Pacific Asia Conference on Information Systems (PACIS)*, (pp. 1148-1159). PACIS.

Wangpipatwong, S., Chutimaskul, W., & Papasratorn, B. (2008). Understanding Citizen's Continuance Intention to Use e-Government Website: A Composite View of Technology Acceptance Model and Computer Self-Efficacy. *The Electronic. Journal of E-Government*, *6*(1), 55–64.

ADDITIONAL READING

Alalwan, J. A. (2013). Continuance Intention to Use Government 2.0 Services: The Impact of Citizens' Satisfaction and Involvement. *International Journal of Electronic Government Research*, *9*(3), 58–73. doi:10.4018/jegr.2013070104

Alawneh, A., Al-Refai, H., & Batiha, K. (2013). Measuring User Satisfaction from e-Government Services: Lessons from Jordan. *Government Information Quarterly*, *30*(3), 277–288. doi:10.1016/j.giq.2013.03.001

Alomari, M. K., Sandhu, K., & Woods, P. (2014). Exploring Citizen Perceptions Of Barriers To E-Government Adoption In A Developing Country. *Transforming Government: People. Process and Policy*, *8*(1), 131–150.

Alruwaie, M., El-Haddadeh, R., & Weerakkody, V. (2012).A Framework for Evaluating Citizens' Expectations and Satisfaction toward Continued Intention to Use E-Government Services.In Electronic Government (pp. 273-286).Springer Berlin Heidelberg.

Alryalat, M., Dwivedi, Y. K., & Williams, M. D. (2013).Examining Jordanian Citizens' Intention to Adopt Electronic Government.*Electronic Government, an International Journal, 10*(3), 324-342.

Antón, C., Camarero, C., & San José, R. (2013). Public Employee Acceptance of New Technological Processes: The Case of an Internal Call Centre. *Public Management Review*, (ahead-of-print), 1-24.

Beiglo, S. H. B., & Zare, R. (2011). A Survey on Factors Effecting Continuity the Use of Government'E-Services. *Australian Journal of Basic and Applied Sciences*, *5*(8), 209–220.

Jiang, X. (2011).Enhancing Users' Continuance Intention to E-Government Portals: An Empirical Study.*Proceeding of the International Conference on Management and Service Sciences (MASS)*, 1-4.

Jiang, X., & Ji, S. (2014). E-Government Web Portal Adoption: A Service Level and Service Quality Perspectives. *Proceedings of the 47th International Conference on System Science (HICSS) on IEEE*, 6-9 January, 2179-2188 doi:10.1109/HICSS.2014.275

Liang, S. W., & Lu, H. P. (2013). Adoption of E-Government Services: An Empirical Study of the Online Tax Filing System in Taiwan. *Online Information Review*, *37*(3), 6–6. doi:10.1108/OIR-01-2012-0004

Liu, Y. L., Wu, C. L., & Chang, P. Y. (2014). Examining Consumers Adoption and Continuance Intention of Online Group Buying from User Experience Perspectives.*Applied Mechanics and Materials*, *519*, 395–398.

Lu, C. T., & Ting, C. T. (2013). A Study Of Tax E-Filing Acceptance Model: A Structural Equation Modeling Approach. In *Computer and Information Science (ICIS), 12th International Conference onIEEE/ACIS*, 1-6. doi:10.1109/ICIS.2013.6607854

Magro, M. J. (2012). A Review of Social Media Use in E-Government. *American Scientist*, *2*, 148–161.

Rana, N. P., Dwivedi, Y. K., & Williams, M. D. (2013).Evaluating Alternative Theoretical Models for Examining Citizen Centric Adoption of e-Government.*Transforming Government: People. Process and Policy*, *7*(1), 27–49.

Wang, C. (2014). Antecedents and Consequences of perceived value in Mobile Government continuance use: An empirical research in China. *Computers in Human Behavior*, *34*, 140–147. doi:10.1016/j.chb.2014.01.034

Zhou, T. (2013). Understanding Continuance Usage of Mobile Sites. *Industrial Management & Data Systems*, *113*(9), 1286–1299. doi:10.1108/IMDS-01-2013-0001

KEY TERMS AND DEFINITIONS

Continuance Intention: Refers to ones intention to continue using or long term usage intention of a technology (Bhattacherjee, 2001).

E-Filing System: A system that allows taxpayers to submit their income tax details online and is considered as an alternative to the usual manual paper submission (Ambali, 2009).

Electronic Government: E-government refers to the use of information technology by government agencies, such as web-based Networks, the Internet, and mobile computing, that have the ability to transform relations with citizens, businesses, and other arms of government (Fang, 2002).

Information Communication Technologies (ICT): A broadly used term that can encompass many technologies used to produce, process, exchange, and manage information and knowledge (Raman, 2008).

Manual Filing: The traditional submission method "either by hand or typewriter. Taxpayers usually perform complex calculations using mental arithmetic or calculator, and then the return is delivered to the tax agency through the postal service or in person (Fu, Farn, & Chao, 2006).

Perceived Usefulness: Defined "as the prospective user's subjective probability that using a specific application system will increase his or her job performance within an organizational context (Davis, Bagozzi & Warshaw, 1989).

Satisfaction: Defined as the "pleasurable fulfillment response resulting from an evaluation with respective to how well the consumption of a product or service meets a need, desire, or goal" (Deng, Turner, Gehling& Prince, 2010).

Taxpayers: Individuals who are liable to pay income tax on all of his or her income for a tax year (Melville, 2005).

Section 2
Business Process Modeling for E-Government Services

Chapter 6
Raising Citizen-Government Communication with Business Process Models

Renata Araujo
Federal University of the State of Rio de Janeiro, Brazil

Claudia Cappelli
Federal University of the State of Rio de Janeiro, Brazil

Priscila Engiel
Pontifical Catholic University of Rio de Janeiro, Brazil

ABSTRACT

This chapter draws out the challenge of how to provide information to citizens with respect to organizational business processes, particularly public service processes. The aim is to discuss the issues concerning organizations' disclosure to citizens, particularly in describing how services are performed in these organizations. It relies on the idea that an urgent step to improve citizen participation in public matters, especially in public service delivery, is to provide citizens with ways to understand how and why internal processes must be conducted. The chapter reports on how business process models can be used for organizational communication and describes proposals to extend this communication to external actors. The conclusion presents remarks on challenges and future work.

INTRODUCTION

Organizations have been charged for their ability to provide transparency regarding their performance, management and outcomes. Such ability is deemed as a step ahead towards offering good quality services to their clients/citizens. Different laws and treaties have been signed demonstrating the intention both from the public and the private sectors to obtain transparency, like Sarbanes-Oxley, BASEL – Basel Committee on Banking Supervision, EITI – Extractive Industries Transparency Initiative, OGP – Open Government Partnership and FOIA – Freedom of Information Action. In different countries and especially in Brazil, the Transparency Law (Law 131, 2009) and the Ac-

DOI: 10.4018/978-1-4666-7266-6.ch006

cess Law (Law 12.527, 2011) have been enacted, guiding public organizations toward publishing information for citizen use through their web portals. Additionally, the Service Portfolio for Citizens (Statute nº 6932, 2011) has rendered mandatory for Brazilian public institutions providing services to the population, to present detailed information about each service provided.

One implication of this movement towards organizational transparency, is that it can be seen as an important step to widen democracy and citizen participation in public matters (Harrison et al., 2011) (Diirr, Araujo & Cappelli, 2009) (Fung, Graham, & Weil, 2007). Organizational transparency can be seen as the basis for democratic information access, social participation and dialogue between public organizations and citizens, giving ground to innovative approaches to support this dialogue (Niehaves & Malsch, 2009) (Candiello, Albarelli & Cortesi, 2010) (Harrison et al., 2011).

In order to improve efficiency and to better manage their processes, organizations have been interested in self-understanding. To address this challenge, they have invested in Business Process Management (BPM) approaches (Dumas et al., 2013). To implement BPM, organizations must build models representing their business process operations. These models are artifacts for defining, analyzing, implementing and managing organizational processes. Therefore, business process models comprise important instruments for communicating information about organizational processes among those responsible for process management and operation (managers and actors) as well as those who consume their outcomes (clients) (Melcher et al., 2009) (Ferreira, Araujo & Baião, 2010).

The main focus of this chapter is to show how business process models can be used to promote organizational transparency on public service processes. The chapter will present perspectives on the issues, controversies and problems of presenting business process models to citizens and their effectiveness for understanding service delivery activities, responsibilities, rules and outcomes.

The chapter starts in Section 2 with a literature review on the use of business process models as artifact for organizational internal communication and why and how these can be shifted to become an instrument for promoting transparency and communication between public organizations and their clients (citizens). Following this, Section 3 presents an approach for transforming public service process models obtained as an outcome of business process management initiatives into process models understandable by citizens (Engiel, 2012). Section 4 presents examples of public service process model transformation in a public organization within the educational domain. Recommendations are also outlined on the use of the catalogue by process analysts and findings about the level of understandability acquired by the generated models are discussed. The chapter closes with remarks on challenges and future work.

BUSINESS PROCESS MODELS AS COMMUNICATION ARTIFACTS

Business models are a set of views of distinct aspects of a business (Eriksson & Penker, 2000) (BPMN 2014). Combined, these views move towards broad understanding about the organization and its business. This can also be used as a basis for business improvement and innovation. From the main aspects that an organization must know about its business, business process models answer the question about *how* the work is performed in order to achieve the desired business goals. (Sharp et al., 2008)(Eriksson et al., 2000) (IDS Scheer, 2008). To answer this question, business process models usually describe the fundamental parts of a process, i.e. the information which comprises the '3Rs' of a process: Rules (why and how to perform the process), Routes (the flow of activities necessary to accomplish its goal) and Roles (who is responsible for each activity in the process).

There are different ways of describing a process, where each approach tries to capture distinct information about a process (Vergidis et al., 2008). Although a process can be described as a textual narrative, graphical languages are preferable. For instance, workflow diagrams focuses on the sequence of steps for accomplishing a process (Browining, 2009)(Stolfa & Vondrák, 2004) (BPMN, 2014) (eEPC, 2014) (Aguilar-Saven, 2004) (Eriksson & Penker, 2000). Dataflows aim at representing how information flows and is processed through process execution (Aguilar-Saven, 2004). Role interaction models depict communication among process actors (Phalp & Shepperd, 2000) (Aguilar-Saven, 2004) (Yu et al., 2006). Finally, processes can be described using formal logic (Barjis, 2008) (Van Der Aalst et al., 2009).

The main use of a business process model is to create common understanding of how a process and, consequently, an organization carries out its business. The process model is a communication artifact about how the organization works, which can be shared and used for mutual understanding, education, discussion and improvements (Becker et al., 2000) (Barjis, 2008) (Sharp et al., 2008) (Barjis et al., 2007)(Melcher et al., 2009)(Ferreira, et al., 2010).

Nevertheless, the choice of which presentation a business process model will have depends on the purpose of its use and its target audience (Aguilar-Saven, 2004). For example, dataflows are useful when the aim is to understand how information is generated and managed through process execution. Role interaction diagrams are useful when it is expected to observe collaboration intensity among different process actors. Workflows, in turn, allow for observing the execution steps through time and the rules to which they are submitted, for improvement and compliance verification.

Considering a process model as a communication artifact is reinforced by research work focused on how to improve process model legibility. They discuss and propose alternatives for improving process model understandability, especially concerning their use as internal communication artifacts (Ferreira, et al., 2010) (Chaitin, 2006) (Recker & Dreiling, 2007)(Mendling, et al., 2007) (Mendling & Strembeck, 2008).

Considering the business process management initiatives within public organizations, it is argued that organizations can use the process models obtained through these initiatives as a communication artifact for citizens on the manner how services are provided. However, just bringing process models to the external environment light would not be effective if we consider that process models may not be easily understood by citizens. Transparency is not only achieved just by providing information; also, the information must be easy to understand. (Fung et al., 2007) (Leite & Cappelli, 2008).

Rendering processes transparent is a step toward expanding democracy and citizen participation in public affairs (Diirr et al., 2009). Citizens will be willing to participate in process improvement if information about this process can be provided, especially on how the process is performed, what the rules restricting it are, what documentation and information is needed etc.

Organizing and making this information available is not an easy task and, very often, organizations limit themselves to describing to their clients a list of services provided and what citizens must do in order to have these services. Information about how the process is performed internally within the organization, its costs and complexity, its needs to follow specific regulations, is usually omitted. This information, although not directly mandatory for having a service provided, helps to educate and show process complexity to service users, opening up opportunities for dialogue.

Whenever a citizen is able to understand the details of *how* a service is provided, it is expected that he or she can become aware of the complexity and effort that the organization must cope with and the number of ungrounded complaints about the service, for instance, may decrease. Additionally, by understanding the process, citizens can be more knowledgeable and motivated to discuss improvements and changes to the process (Kokkinakos et. al. 2012) (Chaitin, 2006).

DESIGNING FOR PROCESS MODELS UNDERSTANDABILITY

At a first glance, business process models are difficult to be understood by citizens, due to their technical purpose and language (see Figure 3). Citizens may be not interested in technical details about the process, but rather in understanding its objectives, rules and information flow. The issue is, then, how to publish process model information to ensure citizens' understanding. Research work (Niehaves and Malsch, 2009) (Candiello et al., 2010) argues that new process management methods should be defined in order to cope with the dialogue between citizens and government. We add our contribution to this challenge by providing a way to design business process models for transparency and understandability. The intention is not to improve notations like BPMN, eEPC, UML and others with more elements, but rather transform existing elements into others more understandable to the audience.

To perform organizational process models transformation in order to generate models that can be understood by citizens, it is necessary to define the characteristics that make this model more intelligible, and, therefore, more transparent. Following an approach for defining quality attributes in the software engineering area (Cysneiros et al., 2003) (Chung et al., 2000) a *Catalog of Public Service Process Model Understandability* was defined, comprising the characteristics that must be included in a process model in order to make this more intelligible to citizens (Figure 1). This catalogue was defined starting from the concept of Organizational Transparency defined by Leite & Cappelli (2008), where a five-degree model for organizational transparency was structured (Cappelli et al., 2013), gathering a set of characteristics for organizational transparency.

Figure 1. Catalog of Public Services Process Models Understandability

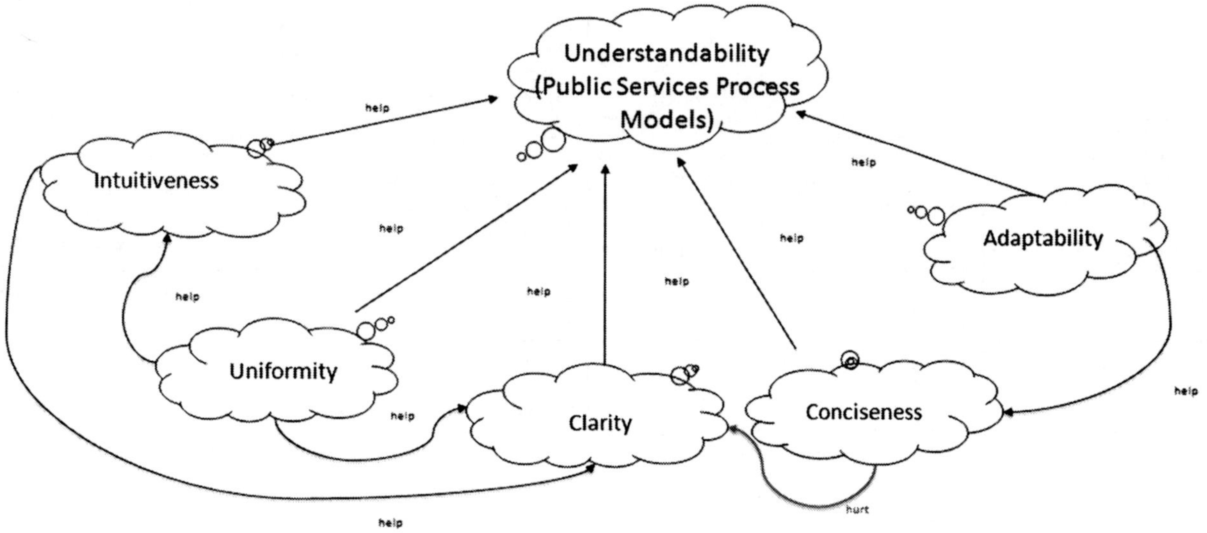

Considering understanding as one of the main targets of organizational transparency, a set of characteristics from the Organizational Transparency Catalog was selected to compose the Catalog of Public Service Process Model Understandability – Adaptability, Intuitiveness, Clarity, Conciseness and Uniformity (Figure 1). Public services may have different audience profiles, with distinct interests in different parts of the process. Organizations may need to have different views of the process for different target audiences. Different views may comprise distinct sets of process information as well as different representations of process elements. Adaptability is the characteristic which will allow changes in the process model to cope with different citizens' profiles, according to the organization transparency strategy. Public service clients usually have little or no knowledge of process notation and of its domain. Process model should use less technical language and make use of well-known metaphors/analogies to represent process elements. Intuitiveness is the ability to allow stakeholders to read process model representation without requiring previous knowledge of the domain and/or of the notation used to describe the process. Citizens access and read the process in order to easily find precise and clear information. Clarity is the ability to allow for the discrimination of a process object/element used in process representation avoiding ambiguity. Conciseness is the ability to summarize the content, helping citizens to find information faster. Conciseness may hurt clarity, since summarizing information may render it less clear. Finally, Uniformity will provide the ability to have a unique form of description and representation of each process element.

The catalogue also contains operationalizations and implementation mechanisms that a process analyst may use to implement each characteristic. The choice of which operationalizations and implementation mechanisms will be applied in the process model is a design decision by the process analyst, based on information about the context in which the process model will be used. Table 1 presents examples of operationalizations for the characteristics presented in the catalog (Figure 1).

Table 1. Examples of operationalizations and implementation mechanisms

Characteristic	Operationalization	Implementation Mechanisms
Adaptability	Define different views of the process model according to the target audience	1. Identify the target audience – who, in the external environment, is interested in information about the process; describing the profile of each audience group; 2. Associate which process elements/information (activity, flow, rules, actors etc) are relevant to each profile; and 3. Define ways by which each element will be identified (colour, size, etc) in the model, considering each profile.
	Explain the process model	1. Provide a textual description of the overall model
Clarity	Associate each activity to its actor/ responsible party	1. Use the same color to identify activities and the party responsible for their execution; or 2. Associate activities and their actor with arrows
	Associate each activity to its rules	1. Associate activities to their rules using an arrow; or 2. Create a table associating each activity with the rules which apply to them
Conciseness	Reduce process complexity	1. Present the process model with the minimum number of activities/flow required for its execution; or 2. Do not include subprocesses.
Intuitiveness	Build models independent of notations	1. Use known metaphors/icons to represent elements of the process
Uniformity	Standardize elements of the process model	1. Determine the shape, size, and color of each element of the process

One condition for using the catalogue is starting the design activity from a previous process model described using workflow representations (Aguilar-Saven, 2004), like the one shown in Figure 3. This is important because the catalogue organizes operationalizations and implementation mechanisms which take into account the existence of common elements in workflow representations: actors, activities, the flow among activities, activity inputs and outputs, resources (documents) and business rules.

The use of the catalog is performed as shown in Figure 2. In summary, the catalog will support the process analyst in his design decisions along the task of creating a new process model to be presented to citizens, starting from the public service process model already created in the organization. Initially, the process analyst needs to understand the process owner/manager's expectations about the target audience's understanding needs regarding the public service/process. These expectations help the designer in the next activity: choosing the characteristics in the catalogue relevant as design goals. For each characteristic, the analyst may also choose the operationalizations and the implementation mechanisms to fit the designed process into the target scenario. If none of the operationalizations or implementation mechanisms seem adequate, the designer can suggest and include a new one, contributing to the continuous evolution of catalog design knowledge.

DESIGNING PUBLIC SERVICE PROCESS MODELS FOR CITIZEN UNDERSTANDING

This section presents two examples of a public service process model transformation for citizen understanding. The first example is the process funding request for research activities at a public university in Brazil. The process is called the "PROAP process". The process had been modeled as a result of a business process management initiative inside the university using the eEPC notation (EPC, 2014). Figure 4 shows this process.

After a meeting with the process owner—the university head—the process main target audience

Figure 2. Process model design for citizen understandability

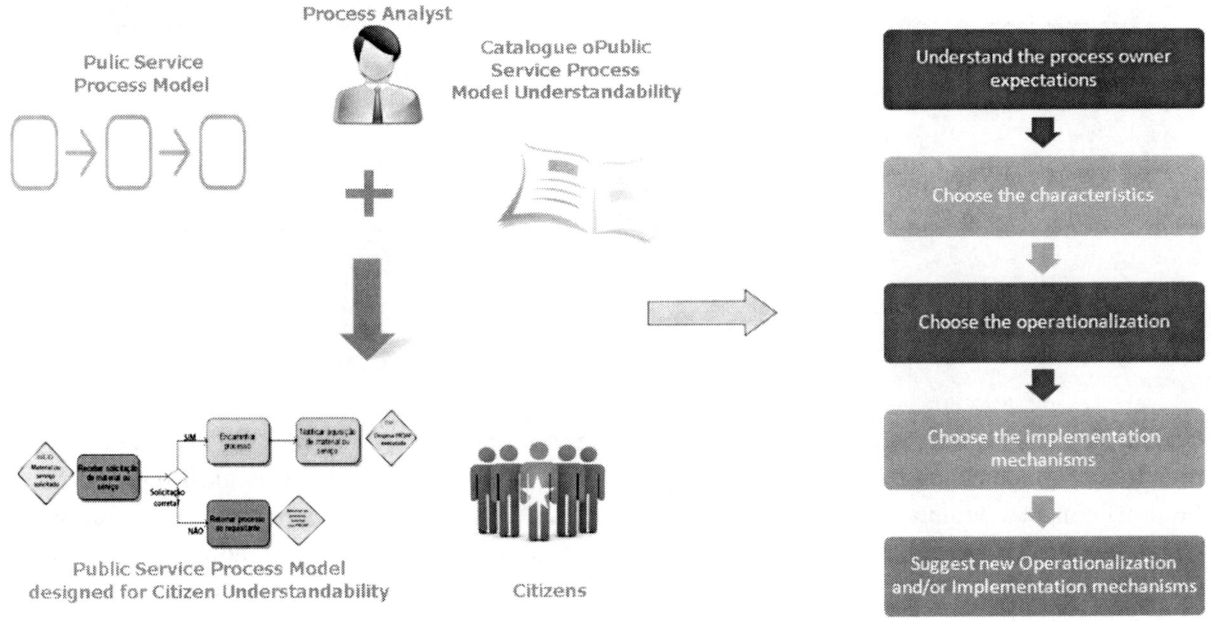

Figure 3. PROAP process model (eEPC notation)

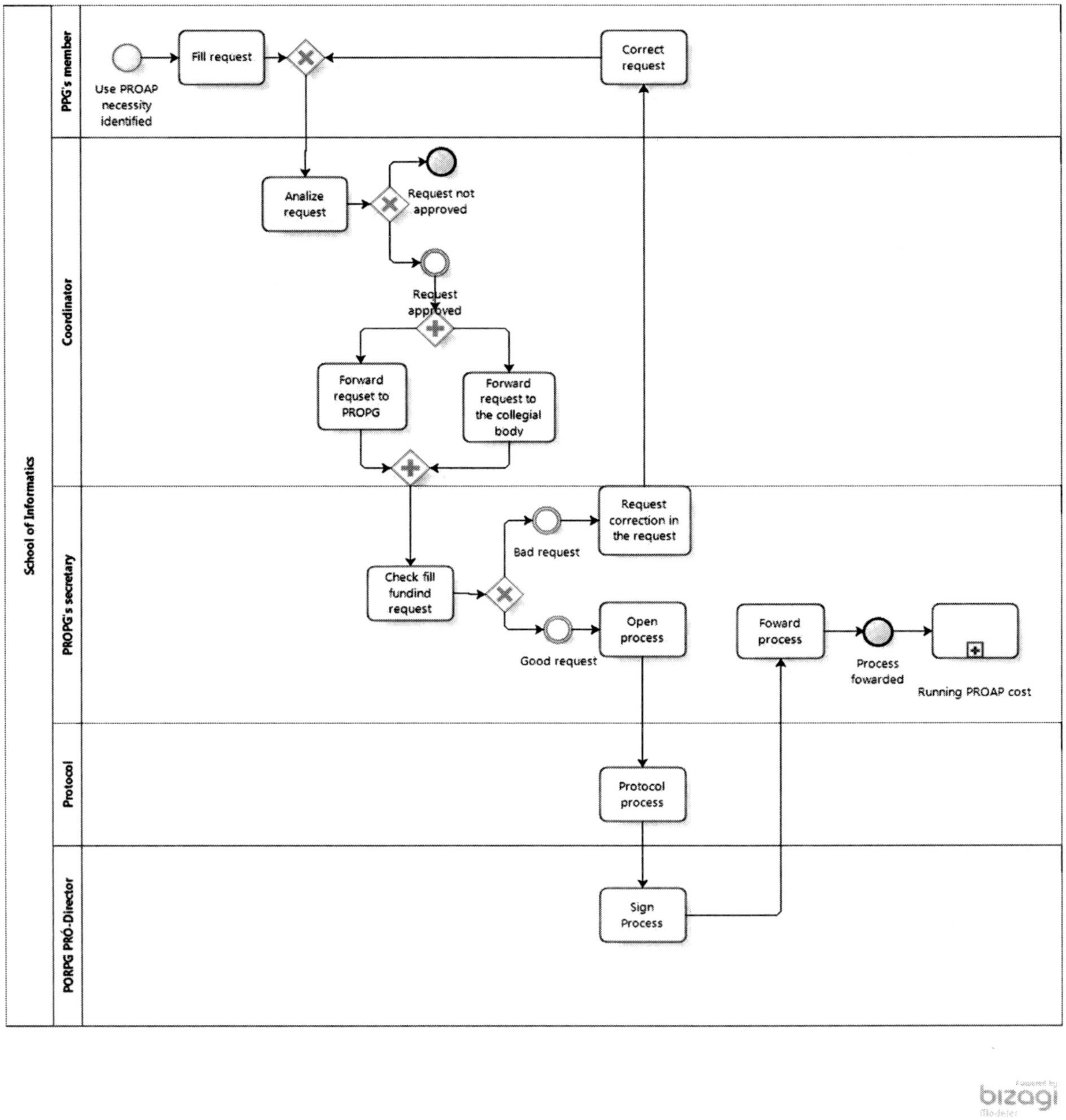

could be identified: students, researchers and coordinators of graduate courses at the university. The profile of this audience could be described as highly-educated people, where students and researchers aim at requesting for funding and following up these requests until their completion. Coordinators, in their turn, aim at following up all requests and understanding the process in

Figure 4. PROAP model designed for understandability

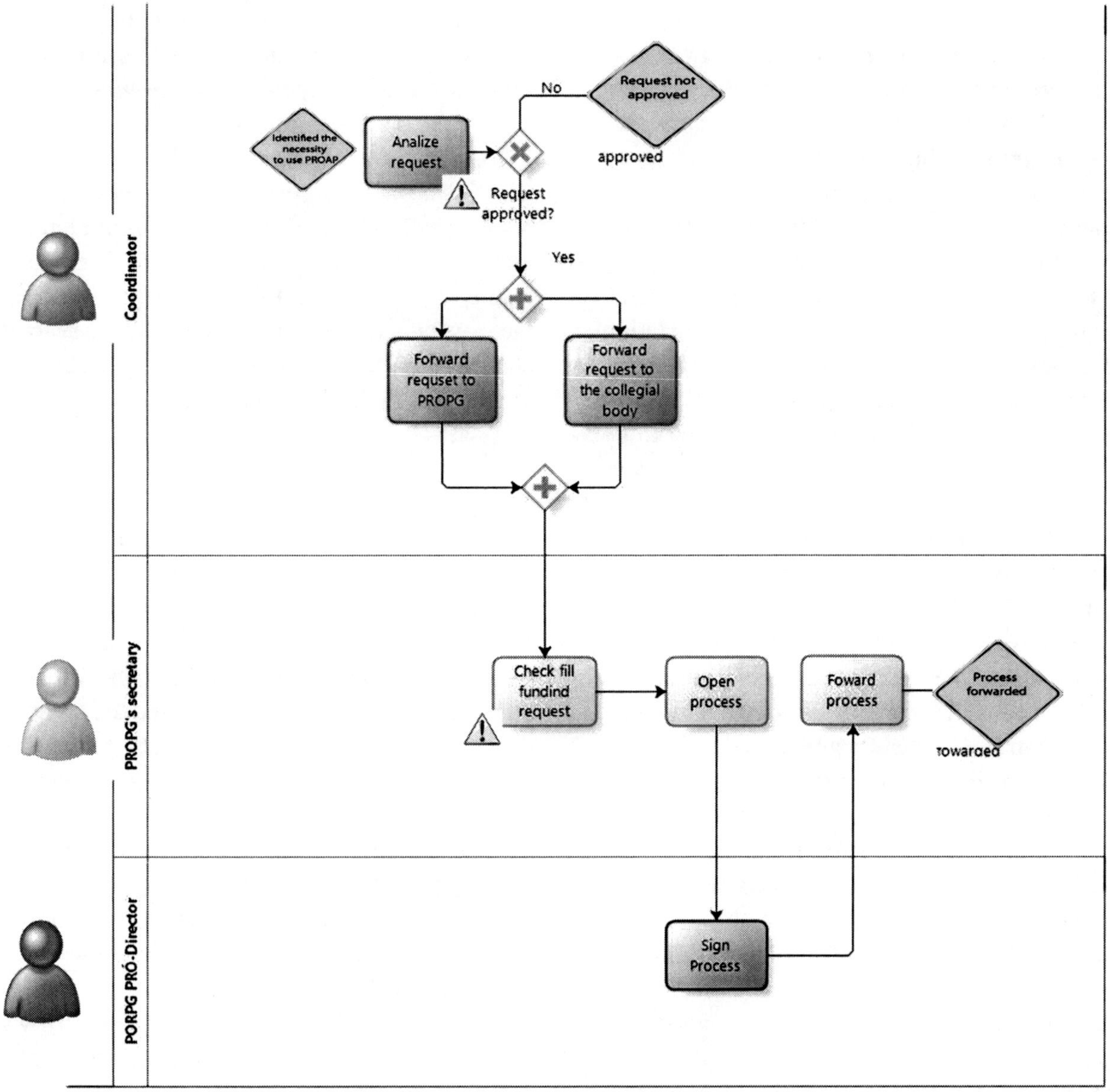

order to guide researchers on how to obtain and request funding. As described by the process manager, the focus for process understandability should be the students, since they represent the number of "clients" which make fewer funding service requests within a 4-year period being, therefore, less experienced with its process and rules. A secondary audience for this process could be any Brazilian citizen, if he/she finds interest in understanding how this organization deals with the funding requests. However, at this first attempt to publicize the process, design decisions focus on the internal audience.

The process manager expected that, by changing process presentation, it would be possible to establish greater commitment among process actors and more visibility on how the process flows among them, avoiding bottlenecks, and causing requests for information to be addressed to the right department. A more understandable description of the process could also improve participants' knowledge of its rules, avoiding communication problems and delays. The process manager also reported that, due to the high number of doubts perceived in the requests, the information to be prioritized for understanding the service was process rules, required documents and the overall workflow. Management information and accounting for the Brazilian Government could be omitted to the public at this stage.

Figure 4 shows the model designed by a process analyst, using the operationalizations suggested by the catalog. To achieve the adaptability goal, students and researchers were selected as the main 'clients' profile. The important changes of this diagram as to the original model in eEPC are: the use of icons to represent actors (intuitiveness); the reduced number of activities (conciseness), so as to focus on the activities relevant to the audience; and metaphors, such as traffic signs to represent events and exclamation points to represent associated rules (intuitiveness). The analyst also decided to describe in the decision points the specific questions/decisions to be taken in that point of the process (clarity).

The most remarkable aspect of this transformation is how the process could be summarized to be presented to the public. The flow of activities, decision points and the rules applied to them comprise the main information being presented, reflecting the need for understanding the sequence and flow of activities to be tracked after a request performed by this process client. Finally, distinct colors help the reader understand the main responsibilities for process activities. Overall, the publication of the designed public service process description in Figure 4 is a step ahead in providing transparency on how the organization deals internally with each request, opening opportunities for its understanding and further dialogue.

As another example, it might be interesting to describe how even a very simple process (in technical terms) could be designed to improve citizen understanding. The process shown in Figure 5 is also a process from a public university, describing the flow of activities for giving students a second chance to perform their exams, if their absence can be justified. The process is named 'second call'. This process was modeled using the BPMN notation (BPMN, 2014).

For this case, the process manager explained the expectations of the students and their complaints about this process. Students complained about the lack of understanding of their responsibilities in the process, not understanding the rules, the moment when they should act in the process, the role that other actors played in the process and the order of their activities. The process analyst chooses the characteristics best applied to this case, as well as mechanisms and operationalizations.

The designed model is presented in Figure 6. The process analyst chose implementation mechanisms such as: use the same colors for the activities and their actor; include business rules associated with each activity; number activities to indicate their sequence; use of green arrows to show main process flow. Although previously simple, it is expected that the designed process model be more adapted to its readers at this context. The process was reduced in size, becoming more concise, making it easier to find the information. It became more friendly and closer to the user – for instance using the "you" to determine the activities under the student's responsibility.

Initial evaluations showed the benefits of the designed model for users' understanding of the process and the service provided. An exploratory evaluation consisted of showing the models

Figure 5. "Second Call" process model

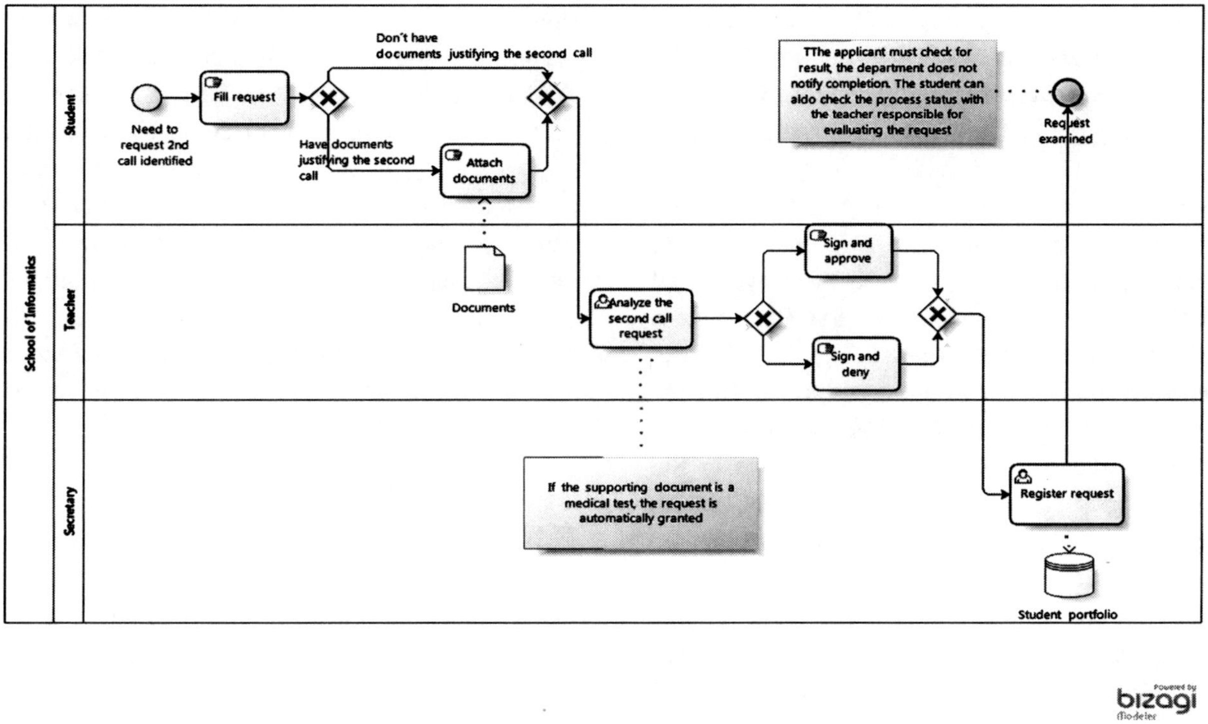

Figure 6. "Second Call" process model designed for understandability

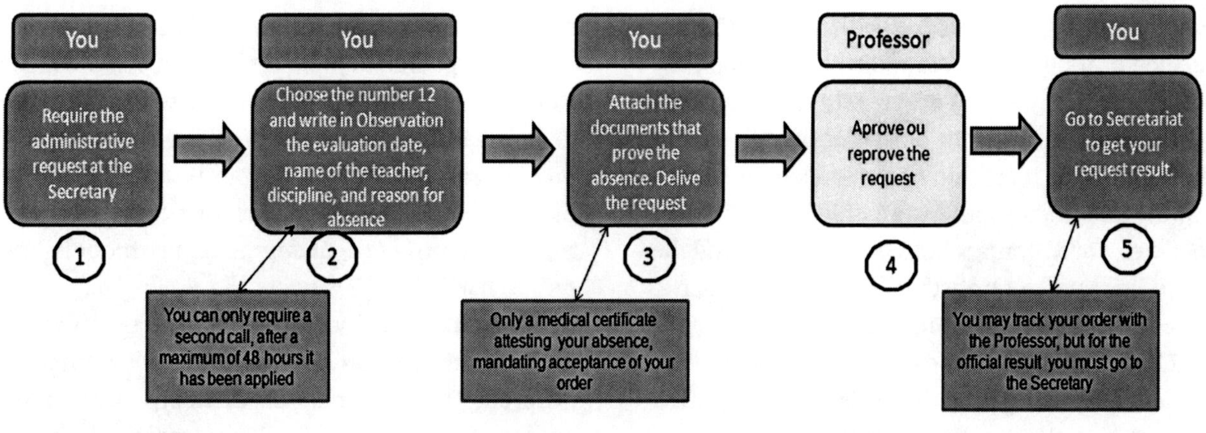

(BPMN and the designed model, Figures 5 and 6, respectively) to two different groups (2 participants each) of the organization under study. The processes were presented separately to participants of each group as well as a set of questions (8) about the process to check their understanding. Participants should write down the time spent to answer each question. All participants did not have any previous experience with the service modeled in the process, but they had some experience on process modeling, including BPMN.

As mentioned before, the proposal to design a new model was to improve the understanding about the users' responsibilities in the process, the rules affecting the process and the role of each actor in the process. Questions made to participants tried to capture their understanding about these issues. Although they are very simple process models, the differences on their understanding were significant. All participants answered all the questions correctly, but the time and richness of their answers were very different. About the user's responsibility in the process, participants using the designed model took half of the time to answer correctly what their role was in the service provision. About the other actors' role in the process (Secretary and Professor), participants using the designed model showed difficulties to answer what the Secretary's activities were, since this actor does not appear in the model. However, participants using the designed model took 1/5 of the time to answer about the professors' role in the process. Regarding rules, using the designed model, participants spent less time to answer the questions, the time difference being below 50%. Finally, some questions tried to determine whether service users were able to understand when they could interact with the organization and process participants in order to have information about their claim, or its result. Only participants reading the designed model were able to understand that they could contact both the Secretary and the Professor (and not only the Secretary) in order to have information about it.

Observations on this exploratory exercise may explain how using process models and designing them for understanding, can raise interaction among citizens and public institutions. The results showed us that the information about the designed processes can be obtained comprising both the flow of activities as well as an understanding of which parts of the process need user intervention and which parts are responsibility of the public institution. Users are also aware of the rules imposed to the process and the restriction applied both to him as well as to the public organization which can help them understand, for instance, that difficulties in having the service provided are due to too restrictive rules. Finally, understanding the process makes users aware of possibilities of interaction with different process actors bearing better understanding of who will be able to answer for the process at each point of its execution. This knowledge, associated with appropriate communication tools, could naturally lead to citizen-public administration direct communication, raising their proximity level.

FUTURE RESEARCH DIRECTIONS

Challenges and future work for providing transparency of business process models could be envisioned considering both organizational internal challenges and how to leverage citizens' understanding of these models. From the first perspective, coping with transparency requires organizations to develop efficient practices to structure and render internal information available and updated to public (Cappelli et al., 2013). Regarding business process models and their understandability, future research could encompass procedures and tools to design internal business process models—used for business process management—into understandable models for public use.

Research directions on how to leverage citizens' understanding of process models could comprise different ways for explaining distinct aspects of the process. Rules, for example, are a particular case. One of the most difficult aspects to be explained to citizens about a process entails the business rules which restrict its execution and impact service provision. The complexity of explaining business rules lies on the high number of rules governing public administration processes and on the difficulty to explain them, not in general terms, but in the process execution context. Ideas on how to explain business rules and process outcomes to citizens are very welcome.

Citizen profiling is a key aspect concerning public service process understandability. The use of approaches to identify and describe citizens' profile is important to refine the choice of characteristics and operationalizations for understandability design. Finally, transparency could be expected to be a starting point to establish or raise government and citizen's communication and dialogue (Araujo et al., 2013). As a consequence, approaches to supporting conversations or interaction among citizens and between citizens and public organizations based on the information made available, for instance, the process model, could be envisioned (Diir et al., 2011).

CONCLUSION

In this chapter, we introduce the idea of a systematic way for public organizations to provide citizens with transparency on how public services are expected to be internally performed so as to be delivered. The need for process transparency follows the current demands on public transparency, especially in the Brazilian context, where public organizations are currently obliged to describe to their clients detailed information on how to have services provided.

Business process models come out as a potential artifact to communicate to citizens how a service is organized and executed internally to organizations. The advantage is that business process models are already internal communication artifacts being largely constructed by public organizations searching for better management approaches and process effectiveness and efficiency. The challenge comprises how to translate this representation into a model which can be understood by citizens. A set of understandability goals to be achieved in this task was organized into a catalog from which process analysts could base their design decisions.

The examples presented in the chapter show that the catalog may lead to less complex process descriptions. They also illustrate that this transformation is possible. The resulting process models have characteristics that should facilitate communication between the organization and citizens, and that they can be customized to different target audience profiles.

Transparency—access, visibility and understanding—of a public service process is the first step to raise communication between public organizations and citizens. Process description and its specific elements (activities, actors, rules) turn out to be a reference to guide citizens' comments, complaints, suggestions, etc., about the process, and to help public organizations identify specific process aspects which need improvements. The extension of process transparency with tools which can progressively support interaction among organizations and citizens is an endeavor for innovative ways of citizen engagement and participation.

Challenges for this approach comprise the overall challenges related to transparency. To be transparent, an organization needs to be well structured to provide correct, real and relevant information. Transparency should also be supported by internal practices which render the activity of publishing information to the external environment easy and productive. Finally, transparency might bring, as a natural consequence, reactions and comments which need to be processed, managed and answered by government. Organizations need to be prepared to cope with this task, and citizens must be continuously educated on how to contribute and participate. At long last, transparency, communication and dialogue can be viewed as ways to educate – citizens and governments – for Democracy.

REFERENCES

Aguilar-Saven, R. S. (2004). Business process modeling: Review and framework. *International Journal of Production Economics*, *90*(2), 129–149. doi:10.1016/S0925-5273(03)00102-6

Araujo, R. M., Taher, Y., Heuvel, W. V. D., & Cappelli, C. (2013). Evolving Government-Citizen Ties in Public Service Design and Delivery. In *Proceedings of IFIP EGOV Conference*, (pp. 19-26). IFIP.

Barjis, J. (2008). The Importance of Business Process Modeling in Software Systems Design. *Journal of The Science of Computer Programming*, *71*(1), 73–87. doi:10.1016/j.scico.2008.01.002

Becker, J., Kugeler, M., & Rosenman, M. (2003). *Process Management*. Springer. doi:10.1007/978-3-540-24798-2

BPMN. (2014). Object Management Group. *Business Process Modeling Notation*. Retrieved February 03, 2014, from http://www.omg.org/spec/BPMN/2.0/

Browning, T. R. (2009). Towards a process architecture framework for product development processes. *Springer, 12*(1) pp. 1-90.

Candiello, A., Albarelli, A., & Cortesi, A. (2010). Three-layered QoS for eGovernment web services. In *Proceedings of DGO'2010*, (pp. 217-222). DGO.

Cappelli, C., Leite, J. C. S. P., Engiel, P., & Araujo, R. M. (2013). Managing Transparency Guided by a Maturity Model. In *Proceedings of 3rd Global Conference on Transparency Research*. Paris: Academic Press.

Chaitin, G. (2006). The Limits Of Reason. *Scientific American*, *294*(3), 74–81. doi:10.1038/scientificamerican0306-74 PMID:16502614

Chung, L., Nixon, B., Yu, E., & Mylopoulos, J. (2000). *Non-Functional Requirements in Software Engineering*. Kluwer Academic Publishers. doi:10.1007/978-1-4615-5269-7

Cysneiros, L. M., Yu, E., & Leite, J. C. S. P. (2003). Cataloguing Non Functional requirements as Softgoal Networks. In *Proceedings of 11th International Requirements Engineering Conference*, (pp. 13-20). Monterey, CA: Academic Press.

Diirr, B., Araujo, R., & Cappelli, C. (2009). An Approach for Defining Digital Democracy Support based on ICT. In *Proceedings of the 13th International Conference on Computer Supported Cooperative Work in Design*. Academic Press. doi:10.1109/CSCWD.2009.4968059

Diirr, B., Araujo, R. M., & Cappelli, C. (2011). Talking about Public Service Processes. In *Proceedings of International Conference on eParticipation*, (vol. 1, pp. 252-261). Academic Press.

Dumas, M., La Rosa, M., Mendling, J., & Reijers, H. (2013). *Fundamentals of Business Process Management*. Springer. doi:10.1007/978-3-642-33143-5

Engiel, P. (2012). *Designing public services business process models for understandability*. (MSc dissertation). Federal University of the State of Rio de Janeiro, Brazil. (in Portuguese)

EPC. (2014). *Event-Driven Process Chain*. Retrieved February 03, 2014, from http://en.wikipedia.org/wiki/Event-driven_process_chain

Eriksson, H. E., & Penker, M. (2000). *Business modeling with UML*. Chichester, UK: Wiley.

Ferreira, J. S. J., Araujo, R. M., & Baião, F. A. (2010) Identifying Ruptures In Business-It Communication Through Business Models. In *Proceedings of 12th International Conference on Enterprise Information Systems*. Academic Press.

Fung, A., Graham, M., & Weil, D. (2007). *Full Disclosure: The Perils and Promise of Transparency*. London: Cambridge University Press. doi:10.1017/CBO9780511510533

Harrison, T. M., Guerrero, S., Burke, G. B., Cook, M., Cresswell, A., & Helbig, N. et al. (2011). Open Government and E-Government: Democratic Challenges from a Public Value Perspective. In *Proceedings of the 12th Annual International Digital Government Research Conference* (pp. 1-9). doi:10.1145/2037556.2037597

IDS SCHEER. (2003). Aris method. Author.

Kokkinakos, P., Koussouris, K., Panopoulos, D., Askounis, D., Ramfos, A., Georgousopoulos, C., & Wittern, E. (2012). Citizens Collaboration and Co-Creation and Public Service Delivery: The COCKPIT Project. *International Journal of Electronic Government Research.*

Law 12.527. (2011). *Information Access Law - Regulation of access to information*. Retrieved October 15, 2013, from http://www.planalto.gov.br/ccivil_03/_Ato2011-2014/2011/Lei/L12527.htm

Law 131. (2009). *Transparency Law*. Retrieved October 15, 2013, from https://www.planalto.gov.br/ccivil_03/Leis/LCP/Lcp131.htm

Leite, J. C. S. P., & Cappelli, C. (2008). Exploring i* Characteristics that Support Software Transparency. In *Proceedings of the 3rd International i* Workshop*, (pp. 51-54). Academic Press.

Melcher, J., Mendling, J., Reijers, H. A., & Seese, D. (2009). On Measuring the Understandability of Process Models. In *Proceedings of 1st Workshop on Empirical Research in BPM*. Ulm, Germany: Academic Press.

Mendling, J., Reijers, H., & Cardoso, J. (2007). What makes process models understandable? Lecture Notes in Computer Science, 4714, 48-63.

Mendling, J., & Strembeck, M. (2008) Influence factors of understanding business process models. In *Proceedings of 11th International Conference on Business Information Systems*. Springer-Verlag. doi:10.1007/978-3-540-79396-0_13

Niehaves, B., & Malsch, R. (2009). Democratizing Process Innovation? On Citizen Involvement in Public Sector BPM. In *Proceedings of 8th International Conference Egov*. Linz, Austria: Egov. doi:10.1007/978-3-642-03516-6_21

Phalp, K. T., & Shepperd, M. (2000). Quantitative Analysis of Static Models of Processes. *Journal of Systems and Software*, *52*(2-3), 105–112. doi:10.1016/S0164-1212(99)00136-3

Recker, J., & Dreiling, A. (2007). Does it matter which process modelling language we teach or use? an experimental study on understanding process modeling languages without formal education. In *Proceedings of 18th Australasian Conference on Information Systems*, (pp. 356-366). Toowoomba, Australia: Academic Press.

Sharp, A., & Mcdermott, P. (2010). *Workflow Modeling: Tools For Process Improvement And Application Development*. Norwood, MA: Artech House.

Statute N° 6.932. (2009). *Provides a simplification of public service to citizens*. Retrieved October 15, 2013, from http://www.planalto.gov.br/ccivil_03/_Ato2007-2010/2009/Decreto/D6932.htm

Štolfa, S., & Vondrák, I. (2004). A description of business process modeling as a tool for definition of requirements specification. In Proceedings of System Integration (pp. 463-469). Academic Press.

Van Der Aalst, W. M. P., Pesic, M., & Schonenberg, H. (2009). Declarative workflows: Balancing between flexibility and support. *Computer Science Research for Development*, *23*(2), 99–113.

Vergidis, K., Tiwari, A., & Majeed, B. (2008). Business process analysis and optimization: beyond reengineering. *IEEE Transactions on* Systems, Man, and Cybernetics, Part C: Applications and Reviews, *38*(1), 69–82.

Yu, E., Strohmaier, M., & Deng, X. (2006). Exploring intentional modeling and analysis for enterprise architecture. In *Proceedings of Edoc 2006 Conference Workshop on Trends in Enterprise Architecture Research*. IEEE Computer Science Press. doi:10.1109/EDOCW.2006.36

Mendling, J., Reijers, H. A., & Cardos, J. (2007). What Makes Process Models Understandable? *IEEE Transactions on Systems, Man, and Cybernetics*, Part A, 41(2), pp. 449-462. *Proceedings of 5th International Conference, BPM 2007*, Pg. 24-28.

Reijers, H. A., & Mendling, J. (2011). A Study Into the Factors That Influence the Understandability of Business Process Models. *IEEE Transactions on Systems, Man, and Cybernetics. Part A*, *41*(3), 449–462.

ADDITIONAL READING

Becker, J., Algermissen, L., & Falk, T. (2012). *Modernizing Processes in Public Administrations. Process Management in the Age of e-Government and New Public Management*. Springer. doi:10.1007/978-3-642-21356-4

Edelmann, N., Höchtl, J., & Sachs, M. (2012). *Collaboration for Open Innovation Processes in Public Administrations* (pp. 21–37). Empowering Open and Collaborative Governance. doi:10.1007/978-3-642-27219-6_2

Gil-Garcia, J. R. (Ed.). (2013). *E-Government Success Factors and Measures – Theories, Concepts and Methodologies*. IGI Global. doi:10.4018/978-1-4666-4058-0

KEY TERMS AND DEFINITIONS

Business Process Management: An approach to aligning organization's business processes with the wants and needs of clients. A systematic approach to continuously improve business effectiveness and efficiency while striving for innovation, flexibility, and integration with technology.

Business Process Model: Artifact that represents the operational specifications of business processes.

Business Process Modeling: The activity of representing processes of an enterprise, so that the current process may be analyzed and improved.

Organizational Transparency: Ability of organizations of being transparent to their clients and/or society.

Understandability: Capability of being understood.

Chapter 7
Towards the Integration of E-Government Process in the University of Murcia: Business Process Strategy

Jesús D. Jiménez Re
Universidad de Murcia, Spain

M. Antonia Martínez-Carreras
Universidad de Murcia, Spain

ABSTRACT

Several countries are adopting e-government strategies for adapting the administrative procedures to automated process with the aim of obtaining efficient and agile processes. In this sense, the European Union has published some directives which indicate the need for European countries to adopt e-government in the public administration. Additionally, the Spanish government has published laws and documents for supporting the adoption of e-government in the different public administration. Concretely, the University of Murcia has developed a strategy for the adoption of e-government using a service-oriented platform. Indeed, this strategy has evolved for the adoption of BPM for its administrative processes. The aim of this chapter is explaining the strategy for the adoption of business processes in the University of Murcia.

INTRODUCTION

Several initiatives have been launched in many countries with the aim of modernizing the public services. In this sense different reports and documents have indicated the need for investing in technologies for offering better services to citizens and organizations (Department of Public Expenditure and Reform, 2011; United Nations, 2012) and thus reducing the burden for them. This trend is named electronic Government (e-Government) and it can be defined as the "the use of information technology to enable and improve the efficiency with which government services are provided to citizens, employees, businesses and agencies" (Carter & Belanger, 2005).

Although several countries have improved their services through the use of more sophisti-

DOI: 10.4018/978-1-4666-7266-6.ch007

cated web pages, according to the Department of Public Expenditure and Reform (2012) countries still need to introduce more technologies and automated processes with the aim of reducing the burden of processes currently needed for citizens and organizations. In several public processes the citizens and organization have to present physical documents which are delivered manually from one section to other section, producing sometimes delays in the delivery due to human causes such as illnesses, oversight or overwork of the public worker. By means of automated processes this documentation is immediately available to the next section or administration in the business process once the documentation has been analyzed and completed by the corresponding section or administration. In this sense public bodies have to ensure that the sharing of data between different public organizations provides a reduction of the number of times citizens or businesses have to ask for data.

Dealing with the objective of making faster the public processes needed for citizens, the inclusion of business processes technologies may allow to carry out some of these processes electronically avoiding the passing "paper" between several public workers. In this line Strykowski and Wojciechowski (2012) indicated the need of increasing the quality of public service execution by introducing a fundamental change in the way public administration works. Moreover they stated that "In the case of public administration, such procedures are primarily associated with information processing, which is perfectly suited to be taken over by computer systems".

Business Process Management (BPM) consists in the analysis, design, implementation and monitoring of business processes which allows the design of intra-organizational and cross-organizational processes. According to Muehlen and Indulska (2010), "business processes are logically ordered sets of activities that produce a result of value to the customer". Some BPM tools may help to public administration to model the internal processes as well as deployment them in a platform. These tools usually support a graphical notation and standards with the aim of designing the processes. Although several notations have appeared along these years, such as Business Model Language (BML) (Johannesson & Perjons, 2001), recent trends focus on the use of Business Process Model and Notation (BPMN) (BPMN link).

In order to model the processes of an organization it is needed the communication between several departments and sections. Moreover, this communication is quite crucial when processes involve different organizations. In addition, the people involved in these designs do not have to be aware of deep issues of the selected technology. Indeed easy graphic tools should be used for allowing all the responsible to be able to design the right process previous to the implementation. Therefore, the introduction of these technologies should be associated to an organizational methodology.

Among the most important open source tools we can find for modeling and developing business processes we can highlight the followings: Bonita BPM, Intalio BPMS and jBPM. The integration of these technologies involves in turn the use of Service Oriented Architecture (SOA), which implies also a change in the development of applications. As well as processes have to be designed, analysts have to design services to be reusable for the different processes. Thus, it is also an important step in the adoption of BPM.

The University of Murcia is a public administration which started the convergence to e-Government in 2005 when its master plan 'Towards e-Government' was created. Among the goals of this plan is the integration and redefinition of a number of existing administrative applications toward more streamlined operations.

Some challenges were initially found due to the legacy systems and the number of vertical applications for different departments of the University.

After a first analysis, procedures from different areas of the University were inconsistent, making it difficult for electronic office personnel to streamline procedures, and sometimes to support the varying procedures that strained the system.

These challenges influenced the motivation for developing a new architectural infrastructure based on Service Oriented Architecture (SOA) paradigm along previous years. Several of e-Government services have been implemented such as Digital Signature, Registry, Record Management, and Notification.

Currently, the University of Murcia has the software infrastructure ready to move forward with a new stage where business process management paradigm would be applied. However, the adoption of BPM is not just to choose a BPM Suite (BPMS) and applied it. It requires the adoption of a methodology which involves all process participants.

The aim of this chapter is to present a methodology for integrating e-Government business processes over the Software Oriented Architecture developed in the University of Murcia. Due to the open source strategy in the University of Murcia collected in its master plan, the software tools used for developing business processes have to be open source. Therefore we will also depict a comparison between the most important open source tools for BPM, indicated the one selected in the University of Murcia

This chapter is structured as follows. In the first section we will describe the introduction of the work. The second section will describe the background in business process and e-governance carried out in public administration. Thirdly, we analyze prior works related to the adoption of e-governance in Universities. Then, we will review the most important technologies for designing business processes dealing as well with a comparison with some existing tools, such as Bonita BPM and Intalio BPMS. The fifth section describes the methodology designed in the University of Murcia for dealing with the automation of some existing processes. After that, we comment the lessons learned of this methodology. Finally we will indicate the conclusion and future lines of this work.

BACKGROUND

The integration of e-Government in public administration involves crucial changes not only in the use of technologies but also in the culture of people (citizens, business, public workers, etc), influencing the collaboration between citizens and the public administration as well as the collaboration between several public administration (Weerakkody, Janssen, & Dwivedi, 2011). The adoption of e-Government in the countries has been promoted from different important organizations such as the United Nations and the European Union (EU).

Reviewing the literature we can find several works related to the research, results, guidelines for introducing e-Government, and evaluations of the current e-Government adoption in different countries (Chatfield, 2009; Collins, 2009; Tsai, Choi, & Perry, 2009; Rose & Grant, 2010; Weerakkody et al., 2011). The integration of e-Government has involved several previous changes in the law of several countries (Walser & Schaffroth, 2011; Concha, Astudillo, Porrúa & Pimenta, 2012; Estevez & Janowski, 2013) in questions such as the management of electronic documents, electronic signature or the validity of these signatures. In this sense, several countries have created laws and normative for supporting and dealing with these novelty issues, such the case of Spain (BOE, 2007).

Lastly, the EU Service directive is fostering the integration of BPM initiatives in the public administration (Department of Public Expenditure and Reform, 2012). Previously, it was indicated the use of Service Oriented Architecture (SOA) in the building of e-Government services (Directive 2006/123/EC). According to Arendsen, Peters, ter Hedde and van Dijk (2014), the main goal of the EU with the adoption of e-Government is the reduction of the burden of public administration. In this sense, the use of electronic documents, the definition of data formats for exchanging data as well as the use of business process automation may influence in the efficiency and the time response.

In spite of the big prominence of BPM, the research and the integration of it in organizations is still in its infancy (Škrinjar & Trkman, 2013). However, it is acquiring a big prominence in the practice and business process management has been the top business priority of chief information officers in every year between 2007 and 2010 (Škrinjar & Trkman, 2013).

Some of the works (Walser & Schaffroth, 2011; Gong & Janssen, 2012) indicate some of the difficulties of introducing BPM in public administration because of the large quantity of process in the public administrations, regulations concerns, and the problems of current BPM tools for fulfilling flexibility and agility. Zwicker, Fettke, & Loos (2010) offer e-Government models for obtaining more efficient processes, Nograšek and Vintar, (2014) provide a e-Government framework for adopting the transformation in organization and other works (Schooley & Horan, 2007; Weerakkody, Janssen & Dwivedi, 2011; Markus & Jacobson, 2010) deal with the need for sharing processes and exchange data with other public administrations.

More specifically, in Walser and Schaffroth (2012) is described the state of the integration of business process in Switzerland. In that work is stated that the adoption of BPM requires a deep collaboration between the different stakeholders as well as a change in culture. Additionally, the adoption of BPM and interoperability is part of the e-Government strategy implementation. Thus, for aligning a common strategy in the adoption of BPM, the Swiss government has created a collective reference framework defining shared concepts for any public administrations.

In Niehaves, Plattfaut and Becker (2013) is presented a work that analyzes the capabilities of adopting BPM in local government. Additionally, the works of Nograšek and Vintar (2014) and Zwicker et al. (2010) include some of these capabilities for providing a framework for transforming organization and for implementing a business process model for creating efficient processes respectively. More concretely the capabilities that should be considered in the adoption of BPM are the following:

- **Strategic Alignment:** Reflects the business process in the organization and the organizational priorities, with the aim of obtaining performance improvements.
- **Governance:** Refers to the capability of having a good definition of the roles and responsibilities for BPM.
- **Methods Chosen for the BPM Realization:** One of the most used is Business Process Management Notation (BPMN).
- **Information Technologies:** Artifacts or software needed for the full cycle of business processes.
- **People:** Determining who compose the staff involved in BPM and the training of them.
- **Culture:** Should foster the development of business process and BPM.

In the study of Niehaves et al. (2013) they founded that some of these capabilities, such as Strategic alignment and Governance, were not carried out in the analyzed local governments. Although the Methods and Information Technologies were adopted, in some cases the tools and the developments were quite poor. Even in some studies, the people did not have the right knowledge and thus the culture for accepting these new trends were quite negative.

With the aim of guiding the strategic alignment in the EU countries "the European Union service directive (directive 2006/123/EC), for instance, defines some special requirements for the European Union member states concerning the design of administrative processes and management. But state authorities can also determine some propositions for local administrations in certain fields" (Zwicker et al., 2010).

Similarly to Switzerland (Walser & Schaffroth, 2011), the Spanish government has published some documents and laws with the aim of maintaining a common strategic in their public administrations (Muñoz-Cañavate & Hípola, 2011) and regulates the adoption of e-Government.

In fact, the Royal Decree 4/2010 (BOE, 2010) regulates the National Interoperability Framework within the e-Government scope in Spain. This Royal Decree is based on the recommendation of the EU, elaborated by the community program IDABC (http://ec.europa.eu/idabc/en/document/2319/5644.html#IDArole). In this law it is divided interoperability in three dimensions: organizational, semantic and technical dimensions. Regarding the use of IT, the law indicates the independence of IT selected for carrying out the development of electronic services. It is also pointed that common services and information should be shared between the public administrations, with the aim of fulfilling the Spanish law as well as EU recommendations of sharing and collaboration.

Considering how the services are available for citizens or other organizations, the Spanish law stated that "Public Administrations will establish and publish the access and use conditions of the services, data, documents and records in electronic format which will be available for the rest of Administrations specifying the aims, the modalities of consumption, consulting or interaction, the requirements that must satisfy the potential users, user profiles involved in the use of the services, protocols and functional and technical criteria necessary to access to these services, the necessary mechanisms of government of the interoperable systems, as well as the applicable security conditions". Additionally, the law stated that for publishing the services available for other administration it should be used the SARA communication network (http://administracionelectronica.gob.es/ctt/verPestanaGeneral.htm?idIniciativa=207#.UufVehC0qUk), in this sense the collaboration and sharing between public administrations can be guaranteed.

Considering the three dimensions of interoperability indicated in the Spanish Royal Decree 4/2010, the articles 8 and 9 indicate the Organizational dimension of interoperability. More precisely they deal with the way Public Administrations have to publish their services, and the need of using inventories for maintaining the administrative process and services, respectively. The article 10 and 11 deal with the Semantic and Technical Interoperability dimensions respectively. These articles regulate the need of expose the data models needed for exchanging information as well as indicate the use of open standards and common infrastructures for communicating services.

Apart from this law, the Spanish Government has published several technical documents for supporting the development of the three dimensions of interoperability. Some of them were also regulated by means of norms. All the documents as well as the laws which regulate the e-Government initiatives are published in a Web Portal maintained for the National Government (http://administracionelectronica.gob.es/).

With regards to the Semantic and Technical Interoperability the Spanish Government has published documents indicating aspects such the kind of standards that local administration should select, protocols for communicating data (such as the use of XML and Web Services), the data models that have to be used for interoperability, digital signatures, etc (more information in http://administracionelectronica.gob.es/pae_Home/pae_Estrategias/pae_Interoperabilidad_Inicio/

pae_Normas_tecnicas_de_interoperabilidad.html#CATALOGOESTANDARES).

Considering the organizational dimension, in the article 8 and 9 of the Spanish Royal Decree 4/2010 it is indicated the use of inventories for registering and maintaining the processes and services developed for each public administration so as to be available to citizens or other administrations. For facilitating the management of inventories the Spanish Government has created and application named SIA (http://administracionelectronica.gob.es/ctt/verPestanaGeneral.htm?idIniciativa=215#.Uui1OhC0qUm) and has developed some documents proposing a common taxonomy for processes and services as well as the attributes needed for integrating processes or services in the SIA application.

In section Business Process Strategy in the University of Murcia we will deal with how the University of Murcia is dealing with this reference framework for the integration of BPM strategies.

RELATED WORK

The adoption of e-Government Information technologies (IT) in Universities is a new research field. Although there are some research studies related to the implementation of systems for e-Governance, few of them deal with the implementation phase. Dey and Sobhnan (2008) describe some important items and recommendations to bear in mind in the implementation of e-Governance in Universities. More concretely they indicate the following items: identifying challenges for e-Governance implementation and mitigate them; planning of necessary information systems and identifying suitable tools and Project management frameworks. The paper indicates some pre-requisites universities should fulfill for the introduction of e-governance but it does not describes any experience in the implementation of it.

In the same line, Bhanti, Lehri and Kumar (2012) describe the need of rethinking and re-engineering the structure of the systems of higher education in India according to its functions and processes. The paper also indicates that e-governance in higher education should improve key processes in universities like grants, the use of certificates, approval processes for some requests, etc, bearing in mind all the stakeholders of universities. In fact the paper describes elements that may be transformed in all the India Universities, dealing with similar data structure for exchanging information between the different universities.

Precisely, Suri and Kaur (2013) analyses the problems of the current systems in the Panjab University and it presents the results of the satisfaction of students and teachers about the web portal of the university and the learning systems.

The work of Kahcevi and Taskin (2013) describes the need of having quality processes in higher education and it stated that having good management of systems and information implies good quality. This work presents a framework based on three dimensions, strategic management, process management, and individual performance management. Moreover the implementation of it is structured in three phases: target determination process (determines the strategic goals and apply them in the process goals and analyze the individual ones), improvement planning phase (monitoring each dimension analyzing the necessary improvements according to the strategic plan), performance evaluation phase (by means of monitoring it can be determine the performance of each dimension).

Apart from the learning systems and web portals, universities have to deal with several administrative processes. In this sense, Tuček and Basl (2011) indicates that higher education institutions should give attention to the following areas: administration and management of institutions; finance; property; human resource and informatics. In fact, the work describes the use of BPM for supporting and developing effective management principles, especially supportive economic and administrative processes.

Other paper which describes the use of BPM in a research center is the one described in Sentanin, Almada Santos and Chiappetta Jabbour (2008). Indeed, it deals with the different stages for implementing BPM for carrying out processes for obtaining funds for research, which is also interesting in the scope of universities. As the other works, it does not deal with the real implementation of any process.

Considering the Spanish context regarding the adoption of e-governance and the use of IT for obtaining agile systems, in 2010 a group of universities started to have some meetings and even they analyses and described a model for obtaining efficient and good systems in the Spanish universities (Fernández Martínez & Llorens, 2011). This group consists of 8 universities, included the University of Murcia.

REVIEW OF BUSINESS PROCESS TECHNOLOGIES

Service Oriented Architecture (SOA) has been widely adopted in different countries, including Spain. SOA has changed the way of developing application in 2000s decade. Indeed, it changed the focus from an object oriented programming model to a service oriented vision, separating what a service could offer from how is implemented.

Currently, Business Process Management (BPM) is an established approach for managing and improving organizational processes in both the private and public sectors (Niehaves et al, 2013). The main aim of BPM is the creation of efficient and effective business processes. In the creation of processes one crucial issue is the business process modeling, which is the activity of representing processes of an enterprise (Chinosi & Trombetta, 2012). This task is usually carried out by business analysts and managers who are trying to improve process efficiency and quality.

Business processes should be described graphically focusing in processes and its relationship with participants (people), systems and software. This part is well-known as the business process modeling. The main effort in business process modeling is to obtain a common visual notation where business consultant, manager, clients and IT staff are all able to understand what the business processes are and how they should work in their organizations.

The Business Process Management Notation (BPMN) emerged with the aim of modeling business process and help in the design (or redesign) of them. BPMN 1.0 and 1.1 standards were a first attend to obtain a visual process notation understandable by all business users including the business analysts that create the initial drafts of the processes, the technical developers responsible for implementing the processes, and finally, the business people who will manage and monitor these processes. Business processes are described as a sequence of events, tasks, sub processes and gateways (BPMN link). Although it is supported by the majority of BPMS, the most significant problem of these early versions was that BPMN was only a graphical standard but it did not describe how serialize the business processes.

BPMN 2.0 was designed to overcome previous standard limitations. It standardizes how to serialize processes defining a XML Schema reference and the process execution conformance, allowing the BPMS to implement native BPMN engines. It defines new graphical improvements in order to offer a more powerful semantic language. Therefore, there are three different application domains for using this modeling language: pure description of processes, simulation and the execution of processes (Chinosi & Trombetta, 2012).

Latest BPMS products are able to implement a BPMN 2.0 native engine without the necessity of complex transformation.

Currently there is a wide range of BPM tools available for carrying out the full cycle of BPM (designing, simulation, execution and monitoring of processes), also named as BPM suite, and other tools which manage some part of cycle.

Among the kind of IT tools used for supporting BPM, Richardson and Miers (2013) divide them in two main groups, those allowing traditional BPM and Dynamic BPM. In the first group it is included those tools focused in the procedures, indeed the management of the processes and the workflow. In the second group, it is included those tools which allow as well the management of the processes but also includes collaborative features, more visibility and control to the workers, social collaboration, etc.

Other division of the BPMS are concerning to the license, having two kinds of systems: the open source BPMS and the commercial BPMS. As we can see in next paragraphs, the reviewed open source BPMS are included in the traditional BPMS and some of the commercial are included in the Dynamic BPM. Next paragraphs describe some of the most important tools in BPM:

- **jBPM:** An open BPM suite which manages the full cycle of the business processes allowing business activity monitoring and activity reports. Additionally, it supports the use of Business rules and event processing. This tool is included in the traditional BPM group. The last version jBPM 6 allows the execution of business processes using the BPMN 2.0 specification. (https://www.jboss.org/jbpm).
- **Adonis:** Offers two kinds of licenses a community edition tool which allows the modeling and simulation of business processes based on BPMN 2.0 and the commercial one which allows the same features and the obtainment of the BPMN xml for executing it. Moreover it offers a wide set of tools for helping in the documentation of processes. (http://www.adonis-community.com/).
- **ActiveVOS:** A commercial BPM suite which deals with the modeling, simulation and execution of business processes. ActiveVOS executes BPMN 2.0 models directly on a high-performance BPEL (OASIS, 2007) engine that runs on any standards-based Java Enterprise Edition server, including Oracle Web Logic Server, IBM WebSphere Application Server, JBoss Application Server or Apache Tomcat (http://www.activevos.com/). This suite provides monitoring, real-time dashboard for analyzing the executable processes and tools for reporting the complete process. This suite belongs to the traditional BPM group.
- **Appian BPM Suite:** A commercial BPM suite covering all the different applications domains of BPM. The design tool is based on BPMN 2.0. Additionally it provides features such as document management, social collaboration, mobile access and development, intelligent analysis, report and analysis SOA integrations, etc. This suite belongs to the Dynamic BPM group. (https://www.appian.com/bpm-software/bpm-suite.jsp).
- **BonitaSoft BPM:** An open solution which deals with modeling, simulation and execution of business process. Its design tool is based on BPMN 1.1, although the new version will be based on BPMN 2.0. This suite can manage previous process described in XPDL o jBPM. Like other suites it also provides support for monitoring and optimization. Although it includes some collaboration issues for modeling business process according to Richardson and Miers (2013) this suit is classified as a traditional BPM. The software is offered with four modalities, one with a community licences and others, including more features, as commercial. (http://www.bonitasoft.com/).

- **Intalio BPM Suite:** The first open source Business Process Management Suite. It offers a comprehensive enterprise-class platform to design, deploy, and manage the most complex business processes. Like the other suites, it also supports the BPMN 2.0 and SOA services. Additionally, it also offers dashboard for monitoring processes and key elements and it supports integration of Alfresco Document Management Systems and Liferay. This tool is included in the traditional BPM group. The software is offered in a community edition and fully featured enterprise edition. (http://www.intalio.com/products/bpms/overview/).
- **The Cubetto Toolset:** A tool for modeling only business processes in BPMN 2.0. (http://cubetto.semture.de/en/)
- **Oracle:** BPM is a commercial BPM suite for the full cycle of BPM, which also supports BPMN 2.0 for modeling processes, process analysis and reporting, intelligent task routing, collaborative spaces for workers, social collaboration, event-driven architecture, standard dashboard for analyzing key elements and the integration of business intelligence by means of Oracle Business Intelligence, among others features. This tool is considered a Dynamic BPM. (http://www.oracle.com/us/technologies/bpm/overview/index.html).
- **Tibco BPM:** A commercial BPM suite which manages the full cycle of BPM, the monitoring of processes, collaboration, intelligent operations, etc. It is classified as Dynamic BPM. (http://www.tibco.com.au/products/automation/business-process-management/default.jsp)

As seen in previous section, previous to the adoption of tools for designing processes is quite important to specify the strategic alignment and bearing in mind all the BPM capabilities in the organization.

BUSINESS PROCESS STRATEGY IN THE UNIVERSITY OF MURCIA

We may draw a parallel diagram between the University of Murcia and evolution of technologies. Prior to 2005 the University had a lot of database-centric applications which were based on heterogeneous technology environments. Until this moment, the application development was carried out 'on-demand', according to the user requirements and needs.

In 2005 was approved a master plan for the creation of a core framework based on SOA paradigm for offering the main services for the administrative applications, previous to the Spanish law 11/2007 and the directive Directive 2006/123/EC. This framework is named Electra (Electronic Administration platform) and it has implied a significant improvement in order to develop new applications since it centralizes all relevant e-Government services, and new applications are developed reusing some existent services and/or integrating new ones in this platform.

Figure 1 shows the current Electra platform and some of the services integrated in it. These services are invoked by some legacy client / server applications, web applications and, as we will describe later, by processes running in the BPMS server. As we can appreciate from this figure, most of the services are developed using Web services standards. Additionally, as indicated in the law 11/2007, the services created for the e-Government are included in National Spanish network SARA and the platform uses the Provider Security Certification (PSCs) for obtaining certificates and validating the signatures of the electronic documents.

The Electra platform has contributed to an advantageous progress to e-Government adoption in the University of Murcia. However, most of the administrative applications integrate these services mixed in their logic that is without any business process methodology.

Figure 1. Electra architecture

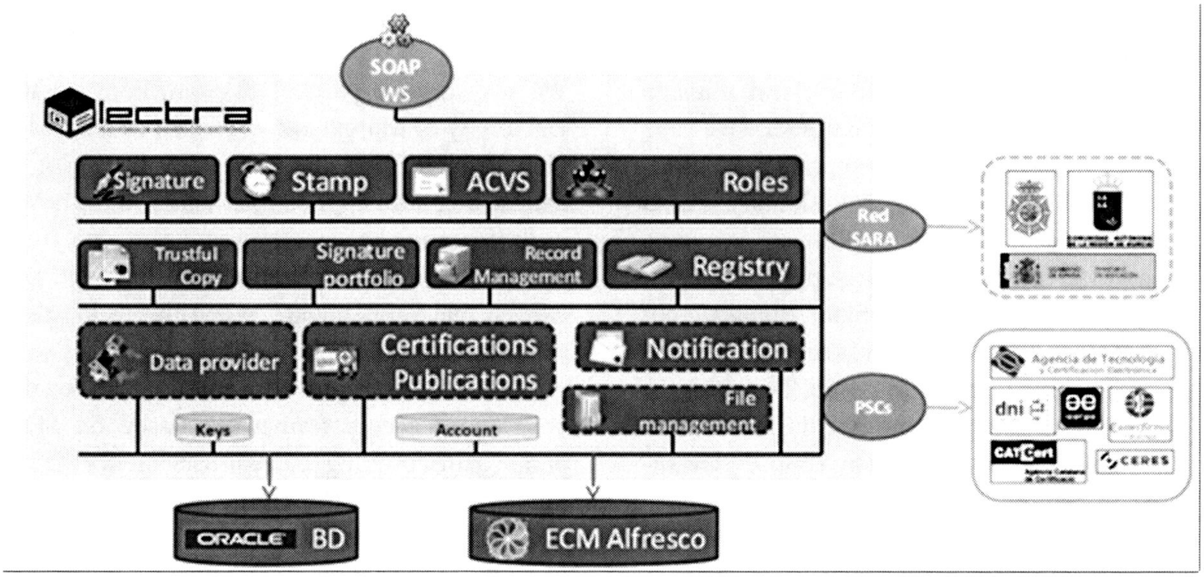

This framework was the ground for the creation of a strategy for integrating BPM in the University of Murcia. The BPM strategy emerged from the 'Methodologies, Standards and Software Quality' department (http://www.um.es/atica/mncs) in 2010. The first step in this strategy started finding out a typical business process in the administration and re-engineering it using BPM. Therefore, an administrative process from the human resources section was chosen. The selected process involves tasks of request, supervision and payment of social aids for workers of the University. Previous to the development of the automated process, workers had to complete a form, sign it manually and to register it in the Registry section of the University of Murcia for carrying out the request of this aid. The automation of this process imply less administrative burden to the staff in the Registry section as well as provide a more comfortable process to the worker, who can apply this aid from his/her PC using his/her digital signature.

Previous to dealing with the development of this administrative process, some technical staff analyzed several suites for adopting the BPM. Bearing in mind that part of the strategy of the University of Murcia is adopting open software and the fact that Intalio was totally SOA oriented, this suite was the most appropriate solution found in that moment. In order to acquire the enough level of knowledge for managing the tool and for the support in case of problems, the University of Murcia paid a subscription license, and part of staff was trained with Intalio official courses. Additionally, internal courses were carried out for distributing the knowledge of Intalio and BPM between the different IT development sections in the University of Murcia. Apart from the Intalio BPMS, the University has recently adopted the use of Adonis software, since it allows a more powerful analysis.

For developing the selected process the technical staff and the project manager had to meet with responsible staff of human resources section with the aim of analyzing it in detail. Through this analysis, other needed administrative processes were discovered. Some of them were part of the same objective and others were reusable process for others further administrative procedures. All of them was designed and implemented as well as new services which were added to Electra platform.

During the two years of the development of the social aid administrative process it was necessary the development of new services. This period has been useful for:

1. Testing Electra SOA platform in an intense and demanding condition such a BPMS requests.
2. Acquiring experience in business process analysis.
3. Checking the BPMS possibilities for a general purpose in the University of Murcia environment.

After the execution of this process, new changes emerged, some of them due to modification in norms and other due to the fact that some unnecessary tasks were discovered in the process. Moreover, the development of this business process fosters the creation of a BPM methodology for integrating the different administrative processes in a structured way.

The main objective of this methodology is to define a set of administrative procedures which allow managing the creation, modification and removal of administrative process in the Inventory and Catalogue of processes of the University of Murcia. The Inventory is the official and public website where all administrative processes are published, both electronic and non-electronic. The Catalogue is the official website which allows citizens to initiate an electronic administrative process in the University. In fact, the Catalogue consists of electronic processes, which may be implemented by a BPMS or other software. Apart from other roles, the methodology proposed the creation of a Business Process Management Unit (BPMU) in the University context, which is formed by different staff from diverse sections.

Figure 2 depicts the set of administrative procedures that form part of the BPM methodology. These procedures are classified in two groups: the Management Processes and the IT Processes. The first group includes the procedures started by the different Head of the sections, and the second group is technical procedures which help to carry out the procedures defined for the first group.

The following paragraphs describe all the procedures depicted in Figure 2:

- **Add Administrative Process to Inventory:** It contains all tasks involved from the request for inventorying an administrative process to adding it to the Inventory of the University of Murcia. The procedure starts when a new Inventory Request has been received in University management staff. It continues with a set of meeting where BPMU and the requester of the process find out the main metadata about the process and the related processes. The result of these meetings is a list of related processes which should be described together. For every of these processes, the 'Technical descriptive analysis' procedure is started. Note that this procedure has to be executed previous to request an electronic adaptation.
- **Technical Descriptive Analysis:** It is a technical procedure which is called by both 'Add administrative process to Inventory' and 'Modify administrative process in Inventory' procedures. The main task of this procedure is to find out the metadata information about the process, writing down this information in the Process Template. The metadata is stored in the process template as attributes. The number, name and type of the attributes have been adopted from the Spanish SIA proposal, which has been adapted to the University of Murcia context. These attributes have been grouped into different groups. For instance, there are set of attributes which reference to the administrative effort; there is a normative attribute group; technical detail attributes and metric attributes.

Figure 2. Administrative procedures for the BPM methodology

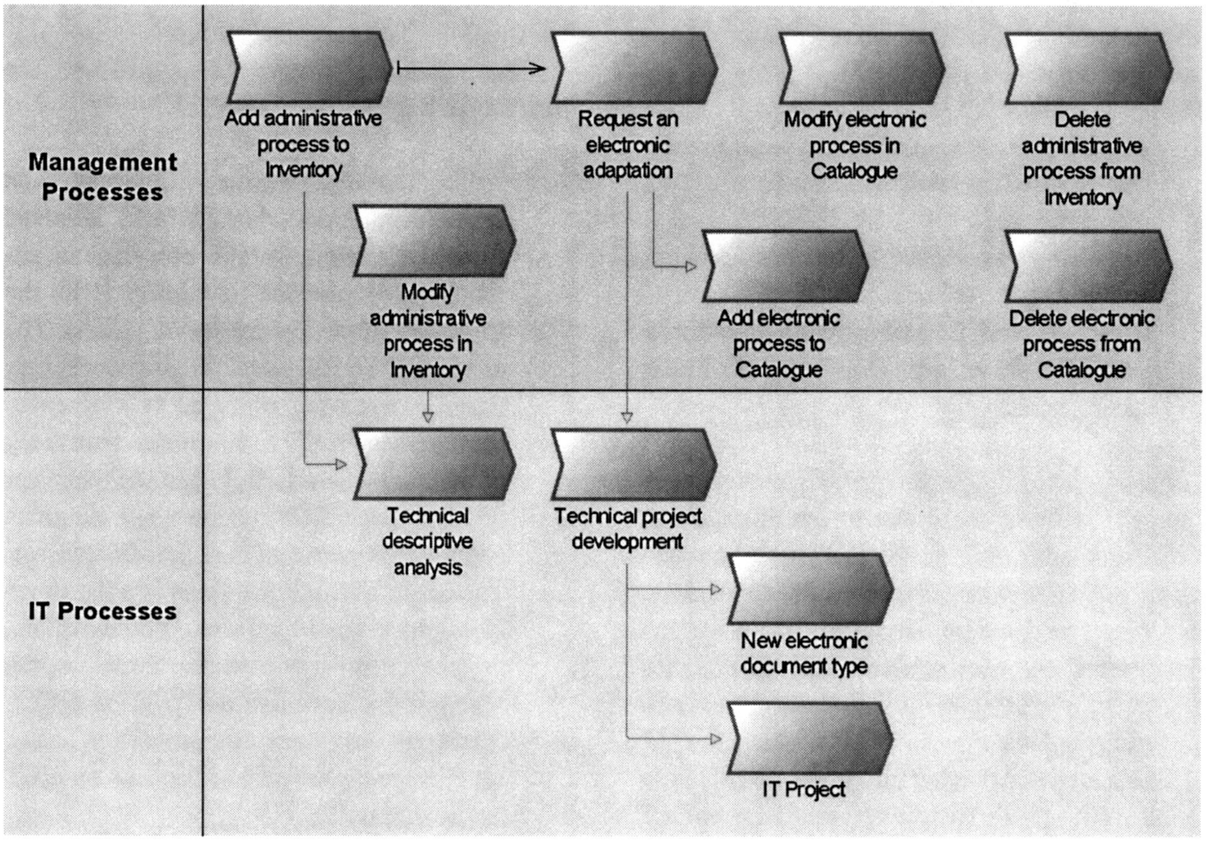

- **Modify Administrative Process in Inventory:** It defines the tasks to be executed when an administrative process modification request is received. The BPMU evaluate how the changes affect to the process. Depending on the impact of the changes, the procedure defines whether a new technical descriptive analysis or minor changes has to be carried out in the process template.
- **Request an Electronic Adaptation:** It represents the general tasks for adapting a non-electronic administrative process to an electronic process. This procedure involves preparing a viability study in a first phase. If the adaptation to an electronic process is viable, the procedure defines the tasks for a formal developing request to technical staff. Then the procedure starts the 'Technical project development' procedure and then, it starts the 'Add electronic process to Catalogue'.
- **Technical Project Development:** This technical procedure describes the required tasks to deal with the analysis and implementation of an administrative process. It provides the technical templates, guidelines, tools and software which have to be used for the analysis and implementation. Along the procedure lifecycle, it may start the 'New electronic document type' and 'IT project' procedures.
- **New Electronic Document Type:** Administrative procedures deal with lots of documents. Concerning electronic documents, they may be classified into different

types. The Electra platform and its Record management service support the concept of Document Type. In this sense, an administrative process is related with a list of document types. This procedure represents the tasks from the request of a new document type to the inclusion of the document type to be used by electronic processes. Apart from BPMU and the requester of the process, the Archive section, which is in charge of the revision and approval of these document types, takes part in this procedure.

- **Add Electronic Process to Catalogue:** It represents the tasks to publish the information about an electronic process in the official website of the University. Through this website, citizens may find out all relevant information about the process such as related norm, process requirements, requested documentation, description and phases of the process, and a link to start the electronic process.
- **Modify Electronic Process in Catalogue:** It defines the tasks to modify published information about a process in the official website.
- **Delete Administrative Process from Inventory:** It contains the tasks to be executed when the request for removing the administrative process is requested.
- **Delete Electronic Process from Catalogue:** It represents the tasks to remove an electronic process from the official website.

LESSONS LEARNED

The experience of the University of Murcia along these years has shown that the adoption of BPM for administrative processes should be supported by a strong methodology. This methodology will be the support for taking the decision of what processes are needed to implement.

As explained before, one of the problems found in the development of the social aid process was that some related business processes involved in a same process where unknown at the beginning of the design. Workers know how to carry out the administrative procedures, even managing the possible exceptions, however when the analysis of the social aid process was carried out, this information was discovered little by little by means of different meetings and tests of the process. Moreover, some of the staff responsible for this process was trained in the use of BPM tools for allowing them to model the processes and the different roles working on them.

For that reason, the University of Murcia decided to create this strategy, for allowing the description of processes even if they are not going to be automated. Therefore, the strategy should indicate the steps to integrate, classify, and remove administrative processes to the public administration. Though the strategy would be known by the entire process owners, it is important to emphasize the presence of the BPMU which provides an adequate support to the rest of the departments.

Another reason for the creation of this methodology is offering the possibility of defining and documenting the administrative processes in the University, despite the fact that several of them are not going to be implemented so far, maybe for the difficulties of the process or maybe for the lack of funds.

The current technology for implementation BPM processes is based on Service Oriented Architecture (SOA) which allows to implement processes through services orchestration. The key point for describing the process is to discover what the granularity and quantity of these services are. The University of Murcia Electra SOA platform has demonstrated to provide a good base for this purpose, although the emergence of new laws and requirements obliges to review and create services frequently.

CONCLUSION AND FUTURE WORK

As we have seen along this chapter, the adoption of e-Government implies redesign the complete way of working of public administrations. In fact, the emergence of web services and SOA framework has been the ground for creating more efficient and agile services to citizens. The laws and documents offered from the National Government for regulating the way of dealing with these technologies have been a big advance in Spanish administrations.

Although public administrations are advancing in the adoption of new technologies for transforming the public administration, further steps should be carry out. In that sense we have seen that EU try to impulse the use of BPM for automating part of the administrative procedures with the purpose of obtaining agile and efficient administrations.

However, the adoption of BPM in public sector involves several steps and implies to fulfill several capabilities dealing with well-defined strategies, well-structured administrations, analyzing standards and methods as well as analyzing IT software and changing the culture of people. Dealing with all these elements is not easy since they imply several changes in the structure and the way of working. Moreover, the quantity of norms and laws which regulate these organizations make more difficult the building of these processes.

Additionally, the inclusion of e-Governance in higher education is a field quite unexplored. Although there are some works analyzing this topic, very few deal with the implementation of them.

In this chapter we have described the current state of the e-Government strategy at the University of Murcia. We have depicted several of the prior steps needed previous to the adoption of BPM strategy. As commented in the chapter, one of the first steps was the creation of a services platform (ELECTRA) for maintaining the services created. With the adoption of an initial BPM strategy, an administrative process was modeled and created with the Intalio BPMS.

The creation of this process has helped to the University to bear in mind the difficulties involved in the building of BPM, such as changes in the norms and even the need of analyst for structuring processes in the correct way.

After this first development, the University of Murcia detected the need of the creation of a strategy for registering and analyzing some of the current administrative processes carried out in the University. In this strategy, the creation of a Business Process Management Unit (BPMU) is proposed. The strategy defines how the University has to structure the administrative processes and consider the difficulties that can appear in the building of them. Additionally, this strategy describes how to convert the process in electronic way.

As described in the chapter, the University of Murcia has carried out the BPM capabilities adopting strategies and methodologies, creating or re-organizing responsible workers for the analysis and design of BPM, adopting methodologies and standards such as BPMN for describing the processes, using IT software such Intalio BPMS and Adonis tools and obtaining formed staff in the modeling and development of business process through courses training.

These last years, the University of Murcia has been mainly defining the foundations for a SOA and BPM infrastructure and culture, but only a few administrative processes have been classified and automated. The challenge next years will be incorporate more and more processes to the Inventory and Catalogue progressively, analyzing and documenting them. This challenge must be leaded by the University head staff and the BPMU, and it will be possible to achieve success if entire University staff is involved.

REFERENCES

Arendsen, R., Peters, O., ter Hedde, M., & van Dijk, J. (2014). Does e-government reduce the administrative burden of businesses? An assessment of business-to-government systems usage in the Netherlands. *Government Information Quarterly*.

Bhanti, P., Lehri, S., & Kumar, N. (2012). E-Governance: An Approach towards the integration of higher Education System in India. *International Journal of Emerging Technology and Advanced Engineering*, *2* (8), 225-229.

BOE. (2007). *LAW 11/2007, of 22 June, on electronic access to Public Services for members of the public*. Available from http://administracionelectronica.gob.es/pae_Home/dms/pae_Home/documentos/Documentacion/pae_BIBLIOTECA_NORMATIVA_ESTATAL_Leyes/LAW_11-2007_22Jun2007_eGov_Spain_NIPO_000-10-075-0.pdf

BOE. (2010). *Spanish National Interoperability Framework*. Royal Decree 4/2010, of January 8th, which regulates the National Interoperability Framework within the e-government scope. Available from http://administracionelectronica.gob.es/ctt/resources/c5df845d-a98c-4854-90c1-4973408b500f?idIniciativa=145&idElemento=71

Carter, L., & Belanger, F. (2005). The utilization of e-government services: Citizien trust, innovation and acceptance factors. *Information Systems Journal*, *15*(1), 5–25. doi:10.1111/j.1365-2575.2005.00183.x

Chatfield, A. T. (2009). Public Service Reform through e-Government: A Case Study of 'e-Tax' in Japan. *Electronic. Journal of E-Government*, *7*(2), 135–146.

Chinosi, M., & Trombetta, A. (2012). BPMN: An introduction to the standard. *Computer Standards & Interfaces*, *34*(1), 124–134. doi:10.1016/j.csi.2011.06.002

Collins, T. (2009). From Ottawa to Lausanne: Much Done but More to Do? *Electronic. Journal of E-Government*, *7*(2), 147–154.

Concha, G., Astudillo, H., Porrúa, M., & Pimenta, C. (2012). E-Government procurement observatory, maturity model and early measurements. *Government Information Quarterly*, *29*(1), 43–50. doi:10.1016/j.giq.2011.08.005

Department of Public Expenditure and Reform. (2011). *Public Service Reform Plan*. Retrieved from http://reformplan.per.gov.ie/files/2012/01/Public-Service-Reform-28112011.pdf

Department of Public Expenditure and Reform. (2012). *Supporting public service reform e-government 2012-2015*. Retrieved from http://per.gov.ie/wp-content/uploads/eGovernment-2012-2015.pdf

Dey, S. K., & Sobhan, A. (2008). Conceptual Framework for Introducing e-Governance in University Administration. In *Proceedings of Conference International Conference on Theory and Practice of Electronic Governance*. doi:10.1145/1509096.1509186

Directive 2006/123/EC. (2006). *European Parliament and of the Council of 12 December 2006 on services in the internal market*. Retrieved from http://eur-lex.europa.eu/LexUriServ/LexUriServ.do?uri=OJ:L:2006:376:0036:0068:en:pdf

Estevez, E., & Janowski, T. (2013). Electronic Governance for Sustainable Development — Conceptual framework and state of research. *Government Information Quarterly*, *30*(1), 94–109. doi:10.1016/j.giq.2012.11.001

Fernández Martínez, A., & Llorens, L. (2011). Gobierno de la TI para las Universidades. *CRUE*. Retrieved from http://www.crue.org/Publicaciones/Documents/Gobierno%20TI/gobierno_de_las_TI_para_universidades.pdf

Gong, Y., & Janssen, M. (2012). From policy implementation to business process management: Principles for creating flexibility and agility. *Government Information Quarterly*, *29*(1), 61–71. doi:10.1016/j.giq.2011.08.004

Johannesson, P., & Perjons, E. (2001). Design principles for process modelling in enterprise application integration. *Information Systems*, *26*(1), 165–184. doi:10.1016/S0306-4379(01)00015-1

Kahcevi, T. C., & Taskin, H. (2013). Integrated enterprise management system for higher education institutions based on strategic and process management: The case study of Sakarya University. *Procedia: Social and Behavioral Sciences*, *106*, 1505–1513. doi:10.1016/j.sbspro.2013.12.170

Lönn, C., & Uppström, E. (2013). Process Management Challenges in Swedish Public Sector: A Bottom Up Initiative. EGOV 2013. *LNCS*, *8074*, 212–223.

Markus, M. L., & Jacobson, D. D. (2010). Business Process Governance. In J. vom Brocke & M. Rosemann (Eds.), Handbook on Business Process Management 2, (pp. 201-222). Academic Press.

Muehlen, M., & Indulska, M. (2010). Modeling languages for business processes and business rules: A representational Analysis. *Information Systems*, *35*(4), 379–390. doi:10.1016/j.is.2009.02.006

Muñoz-Cañavate, A., & Hípola, P. (2011). Electronic administration in Spain: From its beginnings to the present. *Government Information Quarterly*, *28*(1), 74–90. doi:10.1016/j.giq.2010.05.008

Niehaves, B., Plattfaut, R., & Becker, J. (2013). Business process management capabilities in local governments: A multi-method study. *Government Information Quarterly*, *30*(3), 217–225. doi:10.1016/j.giq.2013.03.002

Nograšek, J. & Vintar, M. (2014). E-government and organisational transformation of government: Black box revisited? *Government Information Quarterly*.

OASIS. (2007). *Business process execution language* (WS-BPEL 2.0). Retrieved from http://docs.oasis-open.org/wsbpel/2.0/wsbpel-v2.0.html

Richardson, C., & Miers, D. (2013). *The Forrester Wave™: BPM Suites, Q1*. Academic Press.

Rose, W. R., & Grant, G. G. (2010). Critical issues pertaining to the planning and implementation of E-Government initiatives. *Government Information Quarterly*, *27*(1), 26–33. doi:10.1016/j.giq.2009.06.002

Schooley, B. L., & Horan, T. A. (2007). Towards end-to-end government performance management: Case study of interorganizational information integration in emergency medical services (EMS). *Government Information Quarterly*, *24*(4), 755–784. doi:10.1016/j.giq.2007.04.001

Sentanin, O. F., Almada Santos, F. C., & Chiappetta Jabbour, C. J. (2008). Business process management in a Brazilian public research centre. *Business Process Management*, *14*(4), 483–496. doi:10.1108/14637150810888037

Škrinjar, R., & Trkman, P. (2013). Increasing process orientation with business process management: Critical practices. *International Journal of Information Management*, *33*(1), 48–60. doi:10.1016/j.ijinfomgt.2012.05.011

Strykowski, S. & Wojciechowski, R. (2012). Composable Modeling and Execution of Administrative Procedures. In *Advancing Democracy, Government and Governance* (LNCS), (vol. 52-66). Berlin: Springer.

Suri, G., & Kaur, S. (2013). A study on e-Governance initiatives in Panjab University. In *Proceedings of Conference 7th International Conference on Education, Management and Technology*. Academic Press.

Tsai, N., Choi, B., & Perry, M. (2009). Improving the process of E-Government initiative: An in-depth case study of web-based GIS implementation. *Government Information Quarterly*, *26*(2), 368–376. doi:10.1016/j.giq.2008.11.007

Tuček, D., & Basl, J. (2011). Using BPM Principles to increase efficiency of processes in Higher education in the CR. In *Proceedings of International Conference on Education and Education technologies* (WORLD –EDU ´11). Academic Press.

United Nations. (2012). *E-Government Survey 2012: E-Government for the people*. Retrieved from http://unpan1.un.org/intradoc/groups/public/documents/un/unpan048065.pdf

Vukšić, V. B., Bach, M. P., & Popovič, A. (2013). Supporting performance management with business process management and business intelligence: A case analysis of integration and orchestration. *International Journal of Information Management*, *33*(4), 613–619. doi:10.1016/j.ijinfomgt.2013.03.008

Walser, K., & Schaffroth, M. (2011). BPM and BPMN as Integrating Concepts in eGovernment. *The Swiss eGovernment BPM Ecosystem S-BPM ONE*, 106–120.

Weerakkody, V., Janssen, M., & Dwivedi, Y. K. (2011). Transformational change and business process reengineering (BPR): Lessons from the British and Dutch public sector. *Government Information Quarterly*, *28*(3), 320–328. doi:10.1016/j.giq.2010.07.010

XPDL. (n.d.). *WfMC, XML process definition language* (XPDL 2.2). Retrieved from http://www.xpdl.org/index.html

Zwicker, J., Fettke, P., & Loos, P. (2010). Business process maturity in public administrations. In J. vom Brocke & M. Rosemann (Eds.), Handbook on business process management, (vol. 2, pp. 369–400). Academic Press.

KEY TERMS AND DEFINITIONS

Administrative Procedure: Regulated process which describes the tasks involved in public procedure.

BPM: Business process management is a paradigm that focuses on aligning all organizational elements to improve operational performance in the definition of business processes.

BPM Strategy: The BPM strategy indicates what are the business processes in the organization and the priorities in implementing it.

BPM Technologies: Standards and tools for helping in the BPM cycle, bearing in mind the design, modeling and execution of a business process.

Catalogue of Procedures: The official and public website which allows citizens to initiate an electronic administrative process in a public Administration. It only contains electronic processes.

e-Government: The administration of government by means of information technology. In general, it means the transformation of work routines and processes through the application of information and communication technologies within and between state institutions as well as between the government and citizens or businesses.

Inventory of Procedures: The official and public website of a public Administration where the entire administrative processes are published, both electronic and non-electronic.

SOA: Service Oriented Architecture is an architectural style that supports service-orientation. Service-orientation is a way of modeling applications in terms of services. Finally, a service is a logical representation of a repeatable business activity that has a specified outcome.

Section 3

Harnessing the Citizen and E-Government Collective Intelligence

Chapter 8
Collective Intelligence in a Computer-Mediated Environment

Luigi Lancieri
University of Lille1, France

ABSTRACT

The role of the computer in the emergence of collective intelligence is most of the time underestimated. Outside the fact that it allows the collaboration between individuals, it modifies the interactions and memorizes the traces of the activity. These specific features lead to computer services becoming full actors of the interaction with their own influence like individuals. The resulting symbiosis effect boosts significantly the outcome of the human collaboration. Thus, the objective of this chapter is to deepen our understanding of these mechanisms in order to improve the management of collective intelligence.

INTRODUCTION

Collective intelligence is far from being a new concept. More than two thousand years ago, Aristotle (350 B.C.E) already states that:

The principle that the multitude ought to be supreme rather than the few best is one that is maintained......For the many, of whom each individual is but an ordinary person, when they meet together may very likely be better than the few good...For each individual among the many has a share of virtue and prudence, and when they meet together, they become in a manner one man, who has many feet, and hands, and senses; that is a figure of their mind and disposition.

Actually, not only collective intelligence is not new, but it is evoked in a wide variety of fields ranging from theoretical issues to applied domains. Thus, why adding a new chapter to the huge amount of literature available? From our point-of-view, there are two major answers to this question.

DOI: 10.4018/978-1-4666-7266-6.ch008

First, because even if this topic has been widely evoked, we still know very little about this emerging phenomenon. Looking at the behavior of social animals (bees, ants, ..) or human collectivities we have, for a long time, observed the leverage effect of the group commonly described as providing more than the sum of individual contributions. This observation set apart, we don't know the precise conditions of this emergence and why a small cause can, sometimes, generates mass consequences. What are the factors that increase the group cooperation and is it possible to artificially enhance or forecast these conditions? We may also ask why a collective behavior can provide positive outcomes (knowledge, mutual assistance,..) or suddenly leads to uncontrollable results such as herd effect. Even if social sciences give valuable enlightenments to these issues, we think that the intake of computer sciences has to be reconsidered in a new perspective. Not only can it give complementary answers, at the image of what is being done in other scientific fields such as in biology (genome research) or in physics, but also because the role and the influence of computer devices in human interactions are now almost unavoidable. But, what is this role more precisely?

The answer to this question is actually the main topic of this chapter and constitutes a change of point of view in front of a purely human-centered scientific posture. In our investigation, the computer is not seen as a passive device, but as an actor to full-fledged of the collective activity.

If it is obvious that the spreading of interconnected computer environments offers new opportunities for the cooperation between individuals, the understanding of the underlaying cooperation mechanisms is still limited. This contribution can seem evident when having in mind initiatives such as open projects like *Wikipedia.org*. We can also cite the popularity of opinion polls on a large scale such as those operated by *Change.org*. The surveys launched by an individual or a small group aspire to mobilize large numbers of citizens lobbying for a wide range of causes. In some cases, such initiatives may even influence governments policy. These results of the collective intelligence are favorable to the decision-making and generate structured knowledge or high value software. But here, the computer is seen as a service support, outside this added value, its own influence is not addressed.

Actually, another role sometime underestimated is that computer environments modify the interactions features and consequently their potential outcomes. A basic example of such changes appears if we remember that the non verbal interaction is often lost in computer communications such as in e-mail. It was shown that this loss of information can have unexpected consequences in human relations. Let's imagine that a small joke can be misinterpreted and can be felt as an affront without a smile or the adequate voice tone. Another example is that of the interactions delays reduction favored by the computers. It is no more necessary to move or to wait, a lot of things can be done from a smart-phone. The drawback is that such "time compression" gives more weight to impulsive behaviors, sometimes irreversible compared to those in the "real life". These phenomena are particularly sensitive to certain forms of mediated interactions such as those observed in on-line share trading. Given that collective phenomena can be sensitive to small variations, as amplified by snowball effect (see chaos theory), it seems necessary to seek to deepen the role of the computer in human interactions.

A third role, that we can evoke, starts from the observation that the interconnected computer environments such as Internet are actually a huge memory that keeps the traces of users activities and interactions. In theory, this large amount of data as well as in the general field of experimental sciences, can provide clues explaining complex emerging phenomena. In this way, traces analysis can be a useful addition to psychosocial assessment in the understanding of collective intelligence. For example, we will see in this chapter that the coherence of the group structure, measured from interaction traces can be a useful indicator for monitoring the group dynamics. However, traces analysis is not a trivial exercise. Beyond scientific difficulties related to the data interpretation, also appears the technical problem of data collection. Another challenge is the use of these indicators to make adaptable services based on a feedback loop such as collaborative filtering or recommendation systems. With these services, the group directly benefits from the collaboration of its members, through a reduced cognitive load.

Thus, as we will see, the computer offers new keys for exploring and enhancing collective intelligence with considerable challenges for social organization and governance. It is also important to evoke ethical and legal issues. Indeed, the recent debates concerning the individual right to control personal data seems to oppose itself to the use of traces. But ultimately, may be that the most important issue of our society is to offer the best compromise between the preservation of human rights and the technological contribution.

BACKGROUND

In short, the concept of collective intelligence often carries two main ideas, the leverage effect of the group action and the delegation of the individual control capacity. The leverage effect is sometimes expressed saying that the action of a group is more efficient than that of the sum of the individual's actions. The delegation effect involves that a group acquires a form of autonomy by the inheritance of a part of the power of its members. This means that somewhere, the group becomes an identity and that his action escapes, more or less, to the will of its members. An example of such unconscious delegation process can be observed in herd phenomena such as panic effects in the financial crachs. Evidently and contrary to the common idea, the collective intelligence does not always have positive consequences. Thus, most of the thinkers of the nineteen century had a poor idea of the collective action like Nietzsche (1886) who said that madness is rare in individuals, but in groups, parties or nations it is the rule.

The expression "collective intelligence" appears in a wide series of scientific fields even if the understanding of the background concept is far from being shared by all. It probably began being mentioned after having been observed in the nature. The organized behavior of social animals such as ants or bees has been extensively studied. For Bonabeau et al (1999) who studied what is called swarm intelligence, the collective intelligence allows to solve problems that cannot be solved by individuals acting separately. This basic definition is interesting because it links together the group action and the most shared view of the intelligence that involves adaptation and problems solving capacity. But for some researchers, collective intelligence can be developed only by humans, to build and share high level constructions such as artifacts or culture (Levy, 1999). Thus, definitions for human collective intelligence often put ahead, emotions, opinions or creativity. These two extreme views involving either a low or a high level of individual cognitive capacity have also been simulated in computer science with artificial agents. Finally, we can sum up the different views saying that collective intelligence involves interactions between individuals, collective consequences and a form of coordination between the local and the global level.

Regarding the fundamentals at the basics of this functioning, the debates in computer sciences reflect those in philosophy and psychology between the cognitivism and the models that focus on interaction (connexionism, constructivism, ..). In his book J.B. Smith (1994) evoked a series of formal models showing how individual and collective cognition can be used in computers. In short, formal models aim at describing how a computer has to perform tasks depending on rules. This strategy has been applied historically in artificial intelligence. Our posture is different in the sense that we do not seek to replace the human by the computer. We try to describe the natural interactions between humans and computers and use the corresponding descriptors in order to enhance the collaboration between individuals. In this sense, we are more inspired by socio-constructionist theories than by cognitivist models.

In what follows, we situate ourselves, as an observer of real contexts where humans interact in more or less structured organizations. The governance of these organizations largely depends on the stream of influences between individuals and the group.

FROM INDIVIDUAL INTERACTIONS TO COLLECTIVE BEHAVIORS

The form of collaboration between individuals may largely differ, but we may split it in two modes depending on that the collaboration is explicit or not. In explicit collaboration all individuals are aware participating to a common task. At a limited scale, this can be a brainstorming group in a factory, to a worldwide project such as the open initiatives (e.g. *Linux*, *Sourceforge.net* or the *Wikipedia* project). In all cases, the motivation or the degree of contribution of individuals may vary, but all are conscious to collaborate to a common goal. Conversely, the implicit cooperation implies that actors are not always mindful of cooperating or do not realize the extent or the ultimate goal of their cooperation. A basic example of this kind of process is the page-rank algorithm that is used in recent search engines. This process, that puts ahead the best popular research results on the basis of the indirect cooperation, is very similar to which operates in opinion polls. In implicit collaboration, individuals are first of all motivated by a personal strategy, but their actions can finally result, more or less unwittingly, in a collective performance (Lancieri, 2004). They watch films or give their opinion on the web because they want to do so. Their first motivation is not to provide data that will be used for statistics or to enhance a search engine. Anyway, such collective opinion is more and more used to forecast events such as in financial markets, elections or sports.

Johnson (1999) used the same principle, with artificial agents, to explore the underlaying mechanisms of these collective performances. In his experiment, the agents are programmed to act individually in order to find the shortest path in a maze. Then, Johnson looks at all the individual paths and for each node of the maze, computes the decision took by the majority of the agents. For all the steps, he obtains the collective solution which appears to be the shortest possible path. This experience shows several conditions to exploit the capacity of the group. The first one is the need of equilibrium between the diversity and the homogeneity of individual contributions. Indeed, if each agent takes the same path, the added value of the group is useless. The diversity of opinions allows the minimizing of the possible individual errors and bringing new opportunities or ideas. To paraphrase the words of Bateson (1972) we must remember that knowledge arises from the difference. But conversely, if all the agents' paths are different, here again, no group solution (consensus) is possible. So, the key is the equilibrium in the various dimensions of the solving process. Even if most of the time the diversity is understood in term of variety of domain of expertise, but curiously the variety of capacity seems also to be a good thing. Several works show that even individuals with few social interconnections or with a low personal capacity are necessary to enhance the group ability (Granovetter, 1983; Page, 2008). The emotional diversity is also fundamental as was evidenced by Woolley et *al* (2010) who showed the role of womens in the performance of a group. With his colleagues, she used a general collective intelligence factor (c-factor), comparable to the individual IQ that explains a group's performance. We may imagine that, for educational reasons, "intelligent" people tend to have a similar way of thinking that reduces the diversity of the group. In a certain way, the collective intelligence is not always compatible with the "intelligence" of all individuals of the group.

This equilibrium lack can come from exogenous conditions or from the influence of the group itself. Organizational pressures can occur, as in a factory where the manager wants to setup a brainstorming group with the best experts of a domain. This seems to be a wise decision but in some situations, the added value of such association can be limited in comparison with a multidisciplinary group. The individual influences that lead to a lack of diversity are also often linked to the trend to mimic others. This phenomenon occurs in a context of uncertainty and is particularly sensitive to initial conditions. The same mechanisms appear in social norms or in fashions. In such situations, the imitation behavior limits the cognitive load of individuals and makes easy the taking of usual decisions. In this case, the weight of the first idea, even if it is under optimal, is followed sequentially and reinforces itself as a snow ball in what the economists call information cascades (Bikhchandani, Hirshleifer, & Welch, 1992; Hung & Plot, 2001). Then, the choice of the majority appears as reassuring, which helps to reinforce its credibility. At the end, the majority has accepted a possible wrong option without remembering why.

Fortunately, it appears that the cost of the decision perceived by individuals may limit the effect of information cascades (Boyd & Richerson, 2005). This cost is not the same for someone who can undergo the direct consequence of his decision such as an entrepreneur compared to a civil servant for whom the risks of a bad decision are more limited. The cost-gain equation can also be evoked considering the selfishness of individuals who in some occasions, keep and hide the information instead of cooperate, in order to gain power over others. But, strangely, the common wealth can start with a form of selfishness. In the everyday life, one can cite many chains of complex activities that requires coordination between actors that first take care to their own advantages before to participate to a collective profit (e.g. agriculture which feeds distributive trades which feeds restaurants,..). The games theory contains a large quantity of examples showing the influence of personal interests on the motivation to collaborate. The well known prisoner's dilemma has allowed to study the equilibrium between the selfishness and the generosity in groups.

RELATION BETWEEN THE LOCAL AND THE GLOBAL LEVEL

The group behavior can be operated in two extreme modes of organization either purely centralized or decentralized. Both paradigms have been studied and even used in some real large scale situations. The centralized governance, by definition, is few favorable to collective intelligence. As in the caricature of the army model, individuals' initiatives are not allowed. In order to make the collective behavior controllable and foreseeable, all individuals should obey to a unique source of directives. This model seeks more the collective power (addition of individual forces) than the collective intelligence. In the decentralized model, the governance is delegated to individuals who have the freedom of action and of interactions with other individuals. The collective intelligence is more likely to emerge in such context.

Some authors have pointed out that, in decentralized organizations, the phenomena of emergence are marked by a paradox between differentiation and standardization. For example, in the emergence of fashions, that we have previously evoked, the motivation to follow the tendency starts from a will to be different. However, the final result is the standardization because the mass finally tends to follow the tendency. Wamier and Lecocq (2004) speak about a phenomenon of "identical differentiation". This process is characteristic of relations between collectives and individualities. Indeed, when a fashion evolves to the point where it is shared by all, another fashion emerges, making it possible for individuals to be different again. These more or less slow and interdependent mechanisms are difficult to forecast in the short term, but are clearly visible on long-term cycles. The well known dilemma of the El Farol bar, based on a real story, is a model showing such cycles of influences in a group (Arthur, 1994). It begin from the observation that people are not motivated to come in a bar when it is empty or crowded, but progressively in an increasing and decreasing way depending on its level of attendance. Whether at large or at more limited scale, we can observe two mechanisms linking the local and the global level: the informational aggregation and the feedback loop capacity.

Due to the informational aggregation effect, individuals make their decisions from a synthesis of what they perceive of the group behavior. In other words, each individual computes a kind of global trend instead of looking at the behavior of each other individuals. In relative terms, this process was also observed in the experiment of Johnson when he computes the group solution from the choice of the majority. Aggregation is a centralized process, sometimes mechanical, with no judgment or pressure. It collects, synthesizes and dispatches local information among the group. In a session of face-to-face brainstorming, the mechanism of aggregation is operated by the animator and with a device (white-board). The animator has not a directive role, but rather makes a smooth coordination that ensures a cool and equitable participation. The white-board as a media is essential; it ensures the mechanisms of memorization and forgetting that allow the most essential parts of the discussion to emerge. The remarkable point here is that the aggregation process involves a loss of information comparable to the forgetting effect in the human memory.

Secondly, the informational feedback loop provides to each individual the collective aggregated perception. But, by the way, from where does this perception come? In front of a bar, the situation or the ambiance is perceived by the view and ear and the decision to come in or not is taken immediately. But, for a long term process such as a fashion, things go differently. The modern speed of the emergence or the change of fashions cannot be explained by the direct perception of the real world. Only the relay of media (magazines, television, Internet) can provide enough memory for this, at more long term, aggregation process. We will see that the control of this loop is a necessary step to manage collective intelligence.

The relative simplicity of this process is a fundamental opportunity for intelligent service automation if we compare it to the difficulty to substitute the human intelligence for the computers. From the era when was born the artificial intelligence with its hopes and disillusions, the future probably tends towards the automated management of the synergy between the human intelligences. This new form of governance is implicit, but it doesn't exclude, rather complements, the formal delegation of power to a management team. In all cases, the media is changing the mode of management of groups or of organizations.

THE MEDIA AND THE ENVIRONMENT: MORE THAN BASIC MEDIATORS

Depending on contexts, the term "media" may have different definitions. In a strict sense, it refers to impersonal means of information dissemination, used to communicate and normally, without the possibility of customization. In a more open vision, this word has the meaning of an intermediate and correspond to components (hardware, software, content) used for the interaction between individuals. The tools associated with the Internet such as email or web servers are media and as such, are naturally involved in a complex and mutual influence within the interaction between individuals.

Indeed, first, the media influence the interaction insofar they alter the perception of the reality and change the individual behavior. Actually, the media create a new equilibrium adding, but also removing functionalities. The communication becomes, almost independent from the time and space and has the capacity of memorization data for future use. This leads to the situation in which tools like short messages systems, forums or even the basic e-mail have changed the use of writing at the expense of the use of snail mail. But, the media also remove some elements of the communication. A basic example is the non verbal communication such as the smile or the gesture that are missing with the telephone or the mail. This loss of information about the intentions allied with the spontaneity offered by the media leads to unexpected consequences. Sociologists have shown, for example, that the lower the loss of information induced by the media is limited, the more relationships of trust settle and contribute positively to resolve conflicts. This was observed comparing chat and phone with face-to-face communications (Doise, 2003).

On the other hand, and even if it seems less obvious at first glance, the reciprocal relationship is also true insofar the interaction has an influence on the functionality and the performance of the media. This is particularly observable in file-sharing networks that use a peer-to-peer technology where the popularity of a film increases de-facto the amount of sources and consequently the file download speed. Thus, the popularity of a content leads to more comfort of use. Similarly, this effect is also observable in some forums where users can gain the status of expert from the community. A rank of expertise then appears as a star mark automatically added in the user interface when a new post comes in the forum. Thus, the group behavior tends to modify the user interface which in return will modify the behavior or the choices of the group. Sometimes, this causality loop induces not wished effects. In such forums, sometime simply because of lack of time, the users tend to read only the posts from the designed experts which consequently tend to exclude new contributors.

The media are thus potentially context-sensitive in the sense that they are influenced by their use at a given time, in a given place and with a given intention. Pushing this logic to its limits, the environment becomes a full part of the media. In pervasive computing that supports ambient intelligence, the processing, storage and communication capabilities are scattered and distributed to the extreme (clothing, connected objects, infrastructure). The environment allows the continuity in the activity even in movement, and inherits of the features and the behavior of the media. This vision is also consistent with the theory of activity that gives to the media an extended role in the interactions (Engeström, 1999). To clarify ideas, let us consider a user on vacation who could receive spontaneously on his smart-phone a message stating that the monument he has in front of him has a story out of the ordinary. The time and place of the transmission of this information make sense. In this case, not only the context framework is extended integrating the time, space and the memory of the activity, but also it is supported by functions merged into the environment. These functions are for example, the wireless network that enables mobile communication and can deliver geo-localization capacities among others. This illustration is not futuristic. One example is the museum of the city of Strasbourg (France) where the visitor uses a device that allows to receive throughout his visit an audio explanation directly and precisely in relation with the area of the museum where he is located (see also Apple IBeacon device). Beyond confined places, today's technology allows these services to be extended to large areas such as in future smart cities.

With its new status of media, the environment also inherits of its properties and in particular that linked to the mutual influence. In this sense, the mediated environment amplifies and accelerates what already exists in face-to-face relations. Initially, individuals choose locations and times of activity depending on their inner characteristics (proximity, pleasant, functional, ...) and because other people have made the same choice. It is what happens when we go at 10 o clock to the meeting room because all the members of our team are available for a working session. These choices affect the constraints and the functionality of the environment which retro-act on the choices of individuals. Because the meeting room appears to be convenient, it was decided to enhance its features with video-conference capacities. As a consequence, the room becomes less available and often needs an early booking. Through this game of continue mutual influences, media and environments become adaptable, active and play a symbiotic role with individuals.

If we try to isolate the both sides of this symbiotic relation, we can put ahead a model of generalized media that results from the merge of various basic elements that are the time, the space of exchanges and the structure of interactions. The time corresponds, not only, to the interaction duration, but also to the level of its synchronization or the reaction time between the cause and the consequence of an exchange. The spontaneity or the frequency at which take place an interaction can lead to a great difference in the final results. Axelrod (1984) shows, for example, that the trust or the behavior in a relation comes after repeated interactions because of the anticipation that the relation will last. The space of exchange represents the framework of the interaction. This structuring element which is the extent or the degree of inking in the physical world will allow the deployment of a capacity of memorization that will be a fertile ground for the emergence of collective properties. The depth of the shared memory, the level of visibility of individuals activities, the level of fusion between physical space and informational space are constituent elements of this property. Finally, the structure of interactions is an organizational measure extending what we can observe in well known media such as forum boards (many to many) or as web-site (one too many). This measure will be described with more details in the next section.

Even if, of course, the comparison between the human and the media has its limits, several common features lead us to consider it as a full actor of the interaction. Probably the most important is it capacity to anticipate. We will see that, in the same way the individual activity is socially and culturally influenced, proportionately speaking, a recommendation system, for example, gives advices on the basis of other users' activity. This model is dynamic and reflexive in that each contributors in the interaction, whether a human or a machine including the environment has a vision of the interaction (a feedback link) and has the ability to adapt itself to it. This collective symbiosis through computers is largely dependent from traces of activity.

ANALYSIS OF TRACES, THE MEANING FROM DATA

We saw that media are important to be considered for three reasons. First, because it can efficiently support the collective activity, secondly it modifies the interactions between individuals and finally, because it stores traces that are as much of memory pieces witnessing the activity and interactions. In a broad view, the concept of trace can cover any form of information generated subsequently to the activity of individuals. Thus, a basic web server log file as well as the content of an email are among others, examples of traces that can contain thematic, chronological, or even geographical clues, describing the activity. These data can be used to compute purely quantitative indicators such as the number of users accessing to a resource, but also to analyze words of documents and other elements related to the semantic of the interaction. Incidentally, even quantitative data can be interpreted from a qualitative point-of-view and can describe difficultly observable or hidden behaviors. Not only these indicators can help us to better understand the functioning of groups, but they also can be used to build adaptable services that enhance the collective performances as by a form of self-management.

The Measure Problem

The research in this domain could be divided into two main categories, according to whether the phenomena are observed or simulated. Observation can be done directly or by the mean of surveys either experimentally or in operational situations. The major problem of the observation strategy is the incapacity to perceive all the aspects of a complex behavior. The variation of influences or of consensus among a large number of actors produces emergent properties that, sometimes, appear after a delay difficult to forecast, or on a short duration (percolation effect) and thus are difficultly observable. Even at a small scale, the experiments are hard to setup and thus, they introduce a distance that can be temporal or contextual with the reality. Another problem is the observation bias where the observed situation is influenced by the observer. Nowadays, observing social phenomena can be compared with the situation of the chemistry or the biology 200 years ago, before the invention of the microscope. Global effects can be observed, but it was difficult to understand underlying mechanisms. An important step appears with the evolution of computers allowing the simulation of collective behaviors. The difficulty is that the simulation requires a prior programmable model of the individual behavior as well as a model of interaction between agents (Smith, 1994). These models are far from being known due to the human complexity. The strategy is then to make hypothesis on basics models and to verify if the simulated behavior corresponds to what is known from the reality. Even if the simulation is essential to the test of hypothesis, it has limits inherent to the necessity to have accurate models. A new path is then to find the way to collect and analyze data in the current of the real activity in order to understand the behaviors.

The Individual

Let us first consider the case of the user's thematic profile, a set of data describing the user's topics of interest frequently used for personalization purposes. With the proliferation of the on-line information and services, personalization and adaptability become a real challenge. The keywords contained in the profile are either provided directly by the user through an on-line form or collected from his traces, for example, from the consulted web pages. Due to its contextual and temporal variability, building an accurate user's profile is far from being obvious. Yet, despite this complexity, methodologies of profiles validation are rarely addressed by the researchers. But the good news is that although simplistic, the implementation of metrics applicable to intangible items such as the user's profile is possible with reasonable results in term of probability. Thus, in an experiment, we show that the similarity between two users' profiles composed of several hundreds of words corresponds to a similarity of their activity of 70% (Lancieri, 2005). Outside the words contained in a web document, its structure of hyper-links is also very informative and can be used to build a statistical indicator of the user level of expertise. This measurement starts from the observation that statistically, the complex web documents that are highly technical and somewhat popularized like the European constitution have few hyper-links. Conversely, a summarized or a vulgarized web page will tend to have more hyper-links, allowing the website to deepen the main content. Thus, following this theory, a scientist, for example, will consult more probably a higher fraction of web documents with few links compared to an average user. Beyond describing the individual activity, this philosophy can be applied to better understand the collective behavior.

The Collective

The main drawback of the user profile is its static nature since, like a picture, it represents a view of an individual at a given time. But, the web documents can also be analyzed in a dynamic perspective and, in relation with an adaptable period of time including the future activity of users (Davison, 2002). Thus, we observe that 47% of pages visited by an average user correspond to links contained in one of the two previously visited pages. In observing things differently, we see that pages already visited has 25% of probability to be accessed again. If now, instead of considering the activity of an individual, we observe a group, this value grows to 50%. One might wonder about the meaning of this figure and on its evolution factors. A group, of course, consults more pages than an isolated user but, the rate of redundancy of activity being based itself on the total number of pages viewed, one might expect that this ratio remains stable, whatever the number of users considered. In reality, the fact that a group creates more redundancy of consultation comes from the effect of sharing and synergy own to groups. That is to say that the more there are individuals, the more increases the likelihood that one of them would be interested in others reading, hence increasing the redundancy of consultations. This observation led us to propose the redundancy of activity, easy to compute, as a measure of group consistency. This refers to the diversity within groups that we mentioned at the beginning of our discussion. A group of people with a large variety of interests is likely to have a low level of redundancy rate compared to a group where people are interested in a narrowest range of topics. This relationship, relatively intuitive, has been experimentally verified (Lancieri, 2005). Another interest of this approach is that it allows the evaluation of the synergy of a group before to form it, which can be considered as a management method.

In a comparable way, Kapur et *al* (2006) studied the mechanisms of convergences in newsgroups oriented to problems solving. They developed a measurement of the group activity convergence by computing the number of interactions going in the same direction (Np) and against (Nn) the objective laid down for the group. The convergence ratio (Cr=Np-Nn)/(Np+Nn)) was computed at each stage of a problem resolution. The authors observed that phenomena of emergence appeared very early, in the first 30 to 40% of the time of the group discussion. In addition, statistical tests showed that the convergence ratio, easy to compute, was a very good guide to the level of performance of the group (see also IQ from Woolley *et al,* 2010).

These examples show how to compute indicators that synthesize the group conduct, but it could be instructive to evaluate the individual behavior in comparison of that of the group, during a period of time. This gives a view of extreme or conformist attitudes. Starting from the profile vector of each user, the idea is to replace each vectors by a single numerical value representing at each time slot (e.g one week) the euclidean distance between the vector of an individual and the aggregated vectors of the group (comparable to the gravity center). Thus, in Figure 1, the succession of the Ei values (E1, E2, ..) represents the evolution of one user behavior (symbolized by the upper dotted plot) compared to that of the group (symbolized by the lower dotted plot).

Let us note that the inertia of the group profile is very high because it combines and smoothes the individual behaviors variations. Compared to the group inertia that appears as a benchmark for its stability, a user profile will vary more significantly. By analogy to physic, this approach is similar to the measure of difference of potentials. The chronological plot of the Ei values can be

Figure 1. Compared evolution of users behaviors

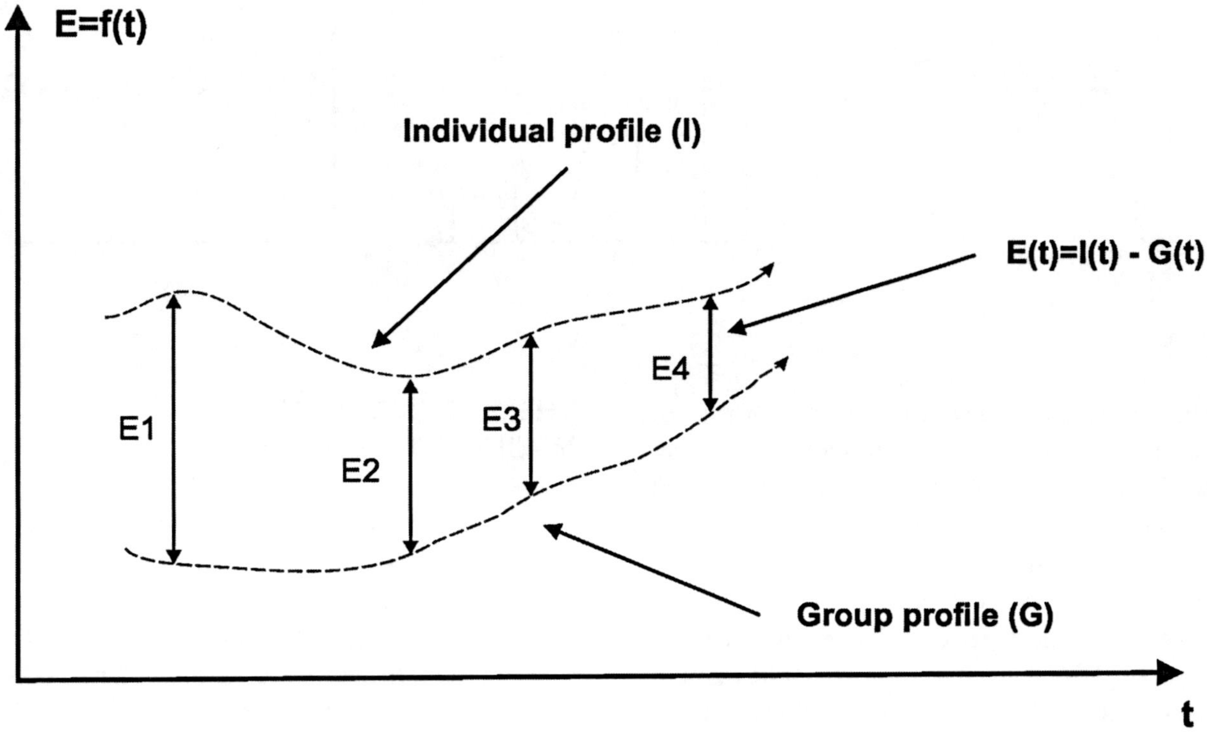

automatically computed and used for monitoring purposes. In order to show an example of use of such method, let us imagine a fictive situation with one hundred people. Each one has a more or less independent work that requires surfing the web for collecting information. In this case, it is possible to monitor the evolution of users' thematic profile and form a brainstorming group depending on criteria of thematic homogeneity. The goal could be to put together individuals with different topics of interest (i.e. Ei values plot far from the zero level).

The Structure

A convenient model of group interactions is that of the network that can be analyzed through the graph theory. One can refer to the article of Barabási (2007) that provides an extended state of the art in this domain. What is interesting with the network model is that it allows the describing properties of the whole group starting from local characteristics more "easy" to obtain. Moreover, such model is generalizable in wide variety of domains and forms of interactions. In the following example, we present a way to measure the structure of interactions in the physical world involving users' moves in a research lab building (Benayoune & Lancieri, 2005). The localization data were obtained through traces of users' crossovers between 17 WIFI hot-spots distributed over the site. These data are commonly available on most wireless routers and allow a statistical view of the activity of each of these hot-spots. A synthesis is shown in Figure 2 where the thickness of the lines (Figure 2a) represent a path between the hot-spots more or less traveled by users. This intensity is reported in the histogram of the Figure 2b where the bars correspond to the level of hot-spots activity ordered in a decreasing order. A hot-spot with a large activity means that the corresponding area is often crossed by users.

Figure 2. Modeling of the structure of spaces occupancy

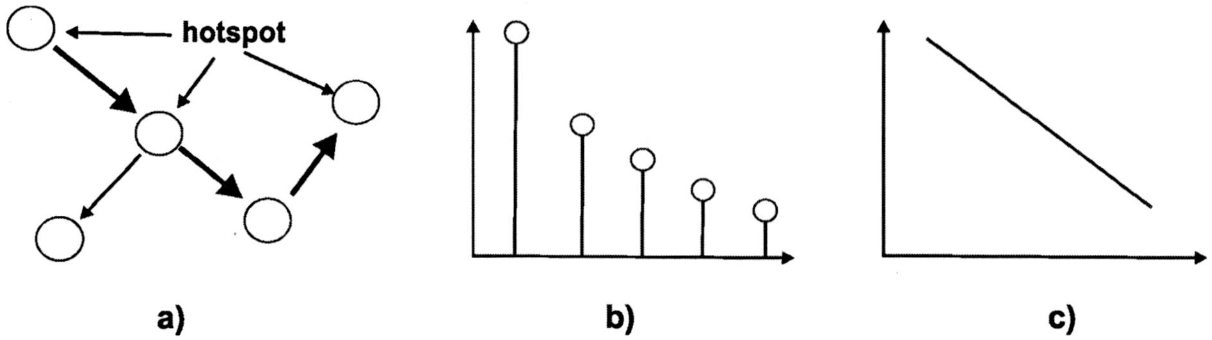

The logarithmic transformation on both axes of this histogram provides a straight line (Figure 2c). This linearity refers to the concept of internal similarity (Long tail, fractal, ..) own to power law distributions (eg Pareto, Zipf law, ...). It is interesting to note that the slope of this curve is a synthetic indicator of the structure of spaces occupancy. A more horizontal slope implies a more homogeneous dispersion of the occupancy in all areas. Conversely, a slope that tends toward the vertical would be the sign of over-occupation of some places compared to others (for more details, see Lancieri, 2007).

The same strategy has been applied to model interactions in social networks. We showed that on-line forums on open source technologies have a characteristic slope more horizontal than those linked to corporations' products (Lancieri, 2000). This finally appears quite logical since the distribution of the contribution (posts) is expected to be more equitable in open-source compared to the industry world where the communication is canalized and maintained by a minority of the company representatives.

Whether in on-line contexts or in the physical word, these methods can be used to provide contextualized mediated services. We can imagine a situation where once identified the main areas of activity, these spaces can be enhanced with public services or commerces adapted to the moment of the day (more or less attendance).

THE STRENGTH OF MEDIATED SERVICES

It may seem obvious that a shared memory is mandatory when it comes of collective intelligence. Even in the more basic situation of a face-to-face discussion, the common view is shared in the memory of each interlocutor. In most of the mediated services such as wiki, forums or the web itself, the shared memory is present. A common view is extracted thanks to the informational aggregation process previously evoked. In addition, the indicators or other form of knowledge extracted from the users activity, whatever its accuracy, can be used to provide value-added services based on the necessity of a shared knowledge or a consensus. This need appears especially in recommendation services that help decision making in a context of information overload by extracting the main choices from a critical mass of people. First, let us say that the trust that a user may have in recommendations may vary depending on the way a recommendation is done. A Nielsen (2009) survey shows that 70% of the consumers tend to trust the opinion of other consumers posted online, but only 24% trust in advertising received on their mobile phone. In comparison, 90% trust the advices coming from known people, 62% from TV, and 37% from on-line banners among others.

In some occasions, the user makes directly his own opinion on a product after having browsed the evaluations made by other buyers. Plenty of web sites contains such evaluation (*epinion.com, booking .com*, …). In this case, the web site provides a part of the information aggregation in the sense that all opinions are visible and that a consensus rating is computed. In an extended approach, such strategies have been used as automatic polls in order to forecast the result of elections or sport competitions. A more automated process is that of collaborative filtering systems such as that used by *Amazon.com*. This merchant advises a book to a customer because its recommendation system has observed the similarity between his browsing history and that of other users. This forecasting service can be found for any kind of items such as films and represents a high commercial challenge. As evidence, in 2009, the Netflix competition has awarded a prize of US$1,000,000 to the winner of the best collaborative filtering algorithm. In this case, the user has almost nothing to do, the advices are automatically aggregated starting from the activity of other users and spontaneously provided through a personalization of the user interface. Here, the trust in the advice largely depends in the trust the user has on the merchant. According to Swearingen, users tend to buy 20% of the items recommended by Amazon (Swearingen & Sinha, 2002).

A last example showing how a decision can be made more easy thanks to the mediated collaboration is that of the on-line brainstorming (Lancieri, Lavallard & Mason, 2005; Veilleroy, Eurin, Hoogstoel & Lancieri, 2013). The Qlim platform was designed to support the on-line group creativity, on the basis of a feedback mechanism, as it occurs in a brainstorming session (see also Delphi method). In short, the process starts as an on-line questionnaire with few questions and answer choices. Participants are invited by e-mail to answer these questions, add new questions and new answer choices. The user interface allows these changes in "one click". Then, users are automatically notified by e-mail for all new contributions occurred during the day. They can go back to modify their answers at any time or make new propositions for questions or answers choices, and so on. This system was tested with a dozen of asynchronous brainstorming sessions, each involving an average of 20 students. As for face-to-face sessions, Qlim allows to take benefit from the collective thinking, but with several enhancements. First, the mode of expression based on questions allows participants not only to give ideas, but also to partly solve the problem. Indeed, as said Charles Kettering, a problem well stated is a problem half solved. Second, the participations can be made from any place, at any time, asynchronously and anonymously without the pressure of the group look. Third, it integrates a graphic monitoring the consensus evolution and the interactions. It enables, for example, to make a link between the changes of opinions and the leadership in groups.

The influence of the group on individual decisions has been evoked by social sciences, but it is difficult to observe. In web recommendation systems, traces allow a better evaluation of such influence, but this remains approximative. With Qlim, this process of influence can be studied more accurately with all traced interactions because the process converge pretty rapidly. In all these examples, we saw that the media offer a key functionality that is the aggregation capacity of all the individual interactions in a collective intelligence (decision, consensus, advice, ..). First, it provides the computer framework necessary to support the collaboration (often through the web), keeps the traces of interactions, synthesizes the trends, computes the results. The aggregation capacity provided by the media combined to the human intelligence finally gives its real power to the collective intelligence. But even if the potential is substantial, it is not out of risks coming from the reuse of personal data.

ON THE ETHICAL AND LEGAL ASPECTS OF THE USE OF TRACES

By nature, the use of traces of activities is problematic from an ethical and a legal point-of-view. Indeed, each individual has the right to preserve his privacy and not to disclose the portion of his activity that he considers as personal. In legal terms, the laws of most democratic countries govern the practices as the "Data Protection Directive" in the European Union. The basic principle is ultimately quite logical in the sense that the user must be informed and accept for the use of his personal data. That said, the legislation may be inconsistent and the willingness of some countries may also be limited when the economic and political interests are at stake. Many examples have shown that traces have been used unbeknownst to users, sometimes with painful consequences. Without going into philosophical debates, we can make several observations on these issues.

Different Types of Risks

On the technology side, and before all other considerations, it is important to observe that most media have a natural ability to record the activity. At the origin, for checking the proper functioning of computer systems, these capabilities have also been used to make statistics and extended to CRM (Customer Relationship Management). In some cases, the ignorance of the media functioning can also cause some misuses leading to any indiscretions with unexpected consequences. The newspapers cited a lot of examples of individuals that have been dismissed for having put on their blog some criticisms against their company or sometimes simply for having a philosophy of life judged out of the norm.

Outside personal indiscretions, the problem may come from the imprudence of others. Indeed, several social networks platforms exploit the ability to integrate directly contacts address books (e.g. from Gmail). Except if we not use email, each of us may one day find his address on bad sites and be "watered" by spam simply because of some careless friends. The traces can also be used by pressure groups to orient the information, organize over-classification of certain links in the search engines or make abusive redirections. The case of "Google bombing" is typical of this risk that made headlines during the 2007 presidential campaign in France. On this occasion, any user making a search on the candidate name "Nicolas Sarkozy" saw himself redirected to a web site related to "Iznogood". Using a weakness in the page-rank technique, this method is very simple and virtually unstoppable. It was enough that was made a sufficient number of links between the name of the candidate and the address of the website Iznogood-the-film. As can be expected, other political figures, with more or less humor, have been targeted by this kind of manipulation. In the other side, the recent news concerning the mass hidden monitoring operated by the NSA have woken up the fears of big brother, as in the novel of Georges Orwell (1949). Even if all countries monitor a part of their populations for security reasons, the motivations are sometimes less clear. (Rusbridger, 2013)

But, at short term, the most important risk is probably related to malicious softwares. We should be conscious of our increasing dependence to computers systems ranging from banking services to energy power management. In such context a wide spread of computer viruses can cause real damages having an impact on the whole economy (loss of jobs) and cause society disorganization. Without going so far, the spyware is one of the most common and the most current of these softwares associated with the risk of traces operation. Having said, this concept is blurred in the minds of individuals and is often mixed with a popular form of psychosis which distorts or multiplies the risk perception. An example of a real risk associated with Trojan spyware is that of keylogers that makes a distant capture of passwords or credit card numbers in order to misuse the user identity (e.g Chewbacca). The keyloger can take various forms, but usually a firewall, an anti-virus up to date and a little common sense allows the reduction of the risk significantly. Moreover, introducing such processes on a user's machine is an offense clearly identified. These examples show that even if the risk associated with the use of traces exists and should not be underestimated, it is not always seen in its reality, sometimes overvalued or underestimated and not necessarily focused on the good actors.

Evolution of the Risk Perception

Historically, we can see that regarding the mediated activity, the vision of the borders of privacy have evolved over the time. At the beginning of the use of the phone, for example, users considered as an intrusion of having to pick up the handset. They perceived as a risk to have a caller with whom they not wanted to talk. So it was customary that a servant plays the role of mediator (Flichy, 2006). More recently, the example of British in term of sensitivity to individual freedoms has also evolved. First, the simple fact of having to present their identity card was considered as an infringement of their freedom, they accept now widely the security cameras scattered in English cities as in all modern countries (Porter, 2004).

The reasons for these changes of opinions come without doubt from the habituation and from a new equilibrium between the perceived benefits in terms of security compared to the risks in terms of loss of freedom. This reminds us what we said above in relation with the establishment of trust (see above Axelrod statement). The regular usage of the technology has definitely changed the perceived nature of the problem, revealing that negative expectations may be overvalued. Regarding traces of on-line activities, the question may also be partially addressed in this way. The regular arrests of terrorists or of pedophiles by tracking their on-line traces are also likely to change public opinion. The evolution of the perception of the balance between risks and benefits could also be measured remembering that the use of credit cards in e-commerce was not built in a day, even with a lot of guaranties. It gained the trust after a long era of suspicions and fears. With the practice and the awareness that the risk was small compared to the benefits, the acceptance has evolved gradually.

Under another perspective, a decade ago, some users have seen a resurgence of the hegemonic will of Microsoft when it proposed a control software with the new versions of Windows operating system. Over the course of time, even if these fears are not completely allayed, we see that this software also enables to protect, relatively reliably, the computers by automatically installing updates that secure the system significantly. The question of the perception of the balance between risks and benefits is the same here. Even if we can not underestimate the commercial ulterior motives of Microsoft (which may seem normal for an industrial), is this risk higher than the benefit of avoiding security holes in our computer? A recent enlightenment to this question was given by the results of the 2014 Cisco security report that states that 99% of all mobile malwares in 2013 was aimed at Android, which is an open-source operating system!

Beyond the individual perception, the influence of the group is also a factor since many individuals are determined by what does or feels the majority. The perception of risk is also affected by these phenomena. The ethologists show, for example, that the organization of animal groups (school of fish) is partly motivated by the fact that the perception of the risk of being the victim of a predator is lower in a group. This fact can be observed in the case of illegal downloading (peer to peer) where the argument of the mass is more or less consciously seen as a protection. Anyway, as we consider the individual or the group, issues of acceptability are essential when we are trying to implement a tool or a service. This situation therefore also arises regarding the use of traces.

CONCLUSION

At the moment where the compression of time and space allowed by computers tends to expand our vision of knowledge, the use of media is at the heart of a lot of debates and research works. Apart from methodological issues, we can put forward several points in relation with governance that we believe worth to investigate.

First, let us cite the need for governments to obtain a feedback from the population. The relationship between the public opinion and the wealth of the democracy has often been evoked (Fishkin, 1992). At the beginning, this question was largely ignored since governments, often totalitarian, did not saw the necessity to consult the people under their administration. After several revolutions, every one (should) understand that a good governance requires rules approved by the majority. Thus, it is not rare to observe the organization of polls in order to see if the public opinion is mature for some sensitive decisions. For some politicians, having this feedback is only necessary to avoid the risk of people dissatisfaction but for others, the collective opinion is a real added value for governance. For example, the theory of public choice (Nobel price JM Buchanan) tries to adapt the collective insight of the market laws to the politic administration. In such view, the motivation of individuals in front of the collective benefits is a key issue.

In some countries, official public "votations" are frequently organized on the direct push of citizens. This is the case in Switzerland where the law dictates that any petition garnering 100,000 signatures must be put to a nationwide vote. Recently, the majority in favor of immigration restriction make the buzz. This trend to vote from public initiatives is accelerated with media such as tweeter where the public opinion can be evaluated immediately on almost every topic. Researchers have designed automatic systems that compute the opinion ratio that can be interpreted as an indirect vote. The methods we evoked in this chapter are possibly usable at large scale, but also in local context as in factory as we seen with the e-brainstorming Qlim tool.

Another contribution of such "social monitoring" is to better understand the trend of the society. We can observe that the media capacity allows a new form of direct organization between people. This is a clue showing that central institutions related to education or commerces lose a part of their power. Indeed, it is not rare to note people acting together when they want to buy something or if they want to defend their rights more effectively (class action). Other initiatives such as micro business or crowd-funding already functioning show this trend to people empowerment. In the educational context the development of MOOCs (Massive On-line Open Courses) is also a clear sign of this tendency. In some case, the diploma, the age limit, the location or the inscription fees is no more an issue. Whatever the topic, courses can be found freely on the web for all people who are ready to make efforts.

Of course, this presentation should not make forget the side effects. The lack of control and of guaranty can be a real drawback but in the other side, the fall in the Orwell word is also a risk. Furthermore, whereas the diversity is positive regarding the emergence of collective intelligence, the overload of information is rather a break. Thus, the major concern could be to identify the right mode of control in order to take the better profit of the collective intelligence. The actual answers are still basic. By making an analogy with the wind, which can be used only when it appears, since, if the phenomenon is well known, it is not possible to control it. It is a little bit the same with collective intelligence; the possibility of control seems still a dream. Yet, as we have seen, in a certain way, such management is possible. Human driven adaptable services such as recommendations systems could be the key to reach the equilibrium between constraints and benefits. But what are the conditions, the benefits and the limit of such strategy? Even if we gave some partial answers to these questions it remains a lot of works to do. In this sense, this still emerging field of research is a real challenge.

REFERENCES

Aristotle. (350 B.C.E). *Aristotle, Politics Book 3 part 11.*

Arthur, W. B. (1994). Inductive reasoning and bounded rationality. *The American Economic Review*, *84*(2), 406–411.

Axelrod, R. (1984). *The Evolution of Cooperation*. Basic Books.

Barabási, A. L. (2007). The architecture of complexity. *IEEE Control Systems Magazine*, *27*(4), 33–42. doi:10.1109/MCS.2007.384127

Bateson, G. (1972). *Steps to an Ecology of Mind: Collected Essays in Anthropology, Psychiatry, Evolution, and Epistemology*. University of Chicago Press.

Benayoune, F., & Lancieri, L. (2005). Toward a modelization of mobile learners behavior for the design and the evaluation of advanced training systems. *IADIS International Journal on WWW/Internet*, *3*(2), 45-58.

Bikhchandani, S., Hirshleifer, D., & Welch, I. (1992). A theory of fads, fashion, custom, and cultural change as informational cascades. *Journal of Political Economy*, *100*(5), 992–1026. doi:10.1086/261849

Bonabeau, E., Theraulaz, G., & Dorigo, M. (1999). *Swarm Intelligence: From Natural to Artificial Systems*. Santa Fe Institute Studies in the Sciences of Complexity.

Boyd, R., & Richerson, P. J. (2005). *The Origin and Evolution of Cultures (Evolution and Cognition)*. Oxford University Press.

Davison, B. D. (2002) Predicting Web Actions from HTML Content. In *Proceedings of Thirteenth ACM Conference on Hypertext and Hypermedia (HT'02)*. ACM. doi:10.1145/513338.513380

Doise, W. (2003). Les relations entre groups. In Psychologie social. Puf edit (in French).

Engeström, Y. (1999). Activity theory and individual and social transformation. In Y. Engeström, R. Miettinen, & R.-L. Punamäki (Eds.), Perspectives on Activity Theory, (pp. 19-38). Cambridge University Press. doi:10.1017/CBO9780511812774.003

Flichy, P. (2006). Une histoire de la communication moderne, vie publique, vie privée, ed la découverte. Academic Press. (French)

George, O. (1949). Nineteen Eighty-Four (1984). London: Secker and Warburg.

Granovetter, M. (1983). The strength of weak ties: A network theory revisited. *Sociological Theory*, *1*(1), 201–233. doi:10.2307/202051

Hung, A. A., & Plott, C. R. (2001). Information cascades: Replication and an extension to majority rule and conformity-rewarding institutions. *The American Economic Review*, *91*(5), 1508–1520. doi:10.1257/aer.91.5.1508

Johnson, N. L. (1999). Diversity in decentralized systems: Enabling self-organizing solutions. In *Proceedings of Decentralization II Conference*. UCLA.

Kapur, M., Voiklis, J., Kinzer, C.K., & Black, J. (2006). Insights into the emergence of convergence in group discussions. In *Proceedings of the 7th International Conference on Learning Sciences*. Academic Press.

Lancieri, L. (2000). A connectionist approach for evaluating the complexity of interactions in the World Wide Web: The case of News Groups. In *Proceedings of IEEE International Joint Conference on Neural Network IJCNN 2000*. IEEE.

Lancieri, L. (2004). Reusing Implicit Cooperation: A novel approach to knowledge management. *TripleC*, *2*(1), 28-46.

Lancieri, L. (2005) Semantic organization of data networks. In *Proceedings of IEEE International Conference on Computational Intelligence for Modelling Control and Automation, (CIMCA'2005)*. IEEE.

Lancieri, L. (2007). Modelling collective behaviour using traces of individual activity. In *Proceedings of 19th International Conference on Systems Research, Informatics and Cybernetics (InterSymp2007)*. Academic Press.

Lancieri, L., Lavallard, A., & Manson, P. (2005). E-brainstorming: Optimization of collaborative learning thanks to online questionnaires. In *Proceedings of IADIS International Conference Cognition and Exploratory Learning in Digital Age (CELDA 2005)*. IADIS.

Lévy, P. (1999). *Collective Intelligence: Mankind's Emerging World in Cyberspace*. Perseus Books.

Nielsen. (2009). *Nielsen Global Online Consumer Survey April 2009*. Retrieved from http://www.nielsen.com/content/dam/corporate/us/en/newswire/uploads/2009/07/pr_global-study_07709.pdf

Nietzsche, F. (1886). Beyond Good and Evil. Penguin Classics.

Page, S. E. (2008). *The Difference: How the Power of Diversity Creates Better Groups, Firms, Schools, and Societies*. Princeton University Press.

Porter, H. (2004). If you value your freedom, reject this sinister ID card: We should be afraid of future governments, whose nature we can't predict. *The Guardian*. Retrieved from http://www.guardian.co.uk/comment/story/0,1375584,00.html

Rusbridger. (2013). *NSA surveillance goes beyond Orwell's imagination*. Retrieved from http://www.theguardian.com/world/2013/sep/23/orwell-nsa-surveillance-alan-rusbridger

Smith, J. B. (1994). *Collective Intelligence in Computer-based Collaboration*. Lawrence Erlbaum Associates.

Swearingen, K., & Sinha, R. (2002). Interaction Design for Recommender Systems. In *Proceedings of Designing Interactive Systems*. DIS.

Veilleroy, Y., Eurin, G., Hoogstoel, & Lancieri, L. (2013). Exploring Collective Intelligence in Online Brainstorming. In *Proceedings of the Third International Conference on Advanced Collaborative Networks, Systems and Applications (Colla2013)*. Academic Press.

Warnier, V., & Lecocq, X. (2004). L'émergence de la mode dans un secteur: Une stratégie collective. In *Le cas du Prêt-à-Porter: Actes de l'atelier Stratégies collectives*. Academic Press (In French).

Woolley, A. W., Chabris, C. F., Pentland, A., Hashmi, N., & Malone, T. W. (2010). Evidence for a Collective Intelligence Factor in the Performance of Human Groups. *Science*, *330*(6004), 686–688. doi:10.1126/science.1193147 PMID:20929725

ADDITIONAL READING

Ball, P. (2006). *Critical Mass: How One Thing Leads to Another*. Macmillan.

Ekpe, B. (2009). *The United Nations and the Rationale for Collective Intelligence*. Cambria press.

Nielsen, M. (2011). *Reinventing Discovery: The New Era of Networked Science*. Princeton University Press.

Surowiecki, J. (2005). *The Wisdom of Crowds,* New York Times.

Tovey, M. (Ed.). (2008) *Collective Intelligence: Creating a Prosperous World at Peace*, Earth Intelligence Network (EIN), under the Creative Commons Licence, also available at http://www.scip.org/files/resources/tovey-collective-intelligence.pdf

Zara, O. (2008), *Le management de l'intelligence collective: vers une nouvelle gouvernance*, M21 Editions, also availlable in English, Translated by Julie E. Johnson at http://www.axiopole.com/pdf/Managing_collective_intelligence.pdf

KEY TERMS AND DEFINITIONS

Context: Circumstances and conditions surrounding an event or set of interactions.

Emergence: An emergent phenomenon appears as the consequence of interactions between a set of elements in a system. This result is different and irreducible to the causes that gave it birth.

Interactions: Reciprocal action or influence it established between several elements. Here, the object of the interaction is mainly information or knowledge but in some cases it may be a question of energy, goods or services (eg Economics).

Mediated Services: Computer supported services that facilitate the interactions between individuals. In most of the cases mediated services tend to replicate existing human supported services (e-mail-snail mail).

Recommendation System: A specific form of information filtering to present elements (objects or information) in a contextual manner.

Symbiosis: (from the Greek sun "with" and BIOO "live") is an intimate and lasting association between several content (symbionts) of different kind. In the animal kingdom we observe this phenomenon, which results in a mutual support between different species.

Chapter 9
Open Social Innovation

Teresa Cristina Monteiro Martins
Universidade Federal de Lavras, Brazil

Paulo Henrique de Souza Bermejo
Universidade Federal de Lavras, Brazil

ABSTRACT

Social innovation and open innovation are two concepts that have gained prominence in the last decade. Small social innovations have the potential to change the global system, expanding through a collaborative process. Furthermore, the collaborative process is the main characteristic of open innovation. Social and open innovations are relevant and emerging; their relationship with each other has been neglected in the literature. Based on the study of social innovation and open innovation, this chapter proposes a framework about the "open social innovation" and demonstrates how it can be implemented through examples in Brazil and the US. Based on the literature review and these examples, it is evident that "open social innovation" is already a reality in many regions and is a combination of the two original concepts converging in collaborative process.

INTRODUCTION

In the global context, the concept of innovation has been considered highly important in economic development. Initially linked to the economic field and related to new technologies, in the last decade, innovation has gained prominence in new formats. These include social innovation in order to meet social needs or cause changes in social practices, and open innovation, to achieve efficiency and effectiveness.

Studies on social innovation are relevant to the current context in which theories on social management, localism (Schaffers et al., 2011), the expansion of the public sphere, citizen participation, and social movements have emerged in public administration. Studies on open innovation have accompanied the global demand for efficient methods to generate effective innovations.

At the governmental level, both have been discussed as means to stimulate new democratic practices, such as the use of open innovation to promote social innovation by the Obama administration (Parvanta, Roth, & Keller, 2013); social innovation and the optimization of localism (Schaffers et al., 2011); and various initiatives like the European Commission's Social Innovation Europe and Innovation Union programs (Wobbe,

DOI: 10.4018/978-1-4666-7266-6.ch009

2012). Governments have realized that it is necessary to innovate socially in order to confront crises in the public sector, public budget cuts, and poor policy performance (Murray, Caulier-Grice, & Mulgan, 2010; the application of the PrizeIdea Platform of the government innovation).

The themes of social and open innovation are present in practical cases in which there is collaboration between public and private actors in the pursuit of meeting the social needs of communities. However, the relationship between the two concepts is still neglected in the literature, as there are few articles related to the topics. Further studies on the applicability of open innovation methodologies in various contexts are necessary (Huizingh, 2011); on the other hand, the study of social innovation is also necessary in order to determine what effectively generates innovation in social practices as well as the current mechanisms for the resolution of social problems (Paulini, Murty, & Maher, 2013).

Recently, Chalmers (2013) introduced the two concepts together, proposing that open innovation can reduce barriers to social innovation; the author proposes the "Open Social Innovation" concept, but this remains open for future discussion. Examples are necessary for its consolidation and the research problem persists: how can open innovation contribute to social innovation?

Aiming to fill the gaps left by Chalmers (2013), this exploratory qualitative study (Collis & Hussey, 2005) proposes to explore the "Open Social Innovation" concept as a junction between social and open innovation. To this end, we present a literature review on innovation, social innovation, and open innovation. Following is an "Open Social Innovation" section, which synthesizes these concepts in a comparative framework to explain the concept while uniting the characteristics of these two types of innovation. Examples of "Open Social Innovation" concept techniques will be presented. In the next section, the concept of "Open Social Innovation" will be discussed, as related to other work in the field. Finally, conclusions are presented, including research limitations and several assumptions to be tested in further studies.

INNOVATION

The ability to innovate is an intrinsic characteristic of human beings (Simms, 2006). The concept of innovation was initially linked to the economy, especially in the work of Schumpeter (1961). The author defines innovation as "the commercial or industrial application of something new – a new product, process, or method of production; a new market or source of supply; a new form of commercial, business, or financial organization" (Schumpeter (1961), p. xix). This definition shows the close link between innovation and the ability of firms to develop processes that are appropriate for the capitalist context.

The ability to innovate has also been considered in several other important fields, including the technological and managerial fields. In 1996, the European Commission, in the Green Paper on innovation, showed that innovation is more than an economic mechanism or a technical process; it is also a social phenomenon, in which the individual needs are combined with them creativity for generate innovations. (Commission, 1996). In the Green Paper, the innovation is" synonym for the successful production, assimilation and exploitation of novelty in the economic and social spheres. It offers new solutions to problems and thus makes it possible to meet the needs of both the individual and society" (Commission, 1996).

Thus, the innovation aims of meeting needs and, according to Schumpeter (1961) the innovation is:

1. A new or improved product or process, and
2. A commercial or industrial application of that product or process.

Based on (Commission, 1996), it is possible to divide the second category into the following two subcategories:

2.1. The broadcast application of novelty in the economic area, which corresponds to technical innovation, and
2.2. The diffusion of the novelty in the social area, which corresponds to social innovation.

The distinction between technological and social innovation will be clarified when the characteristics of social innovation are presented in the next section.

SOCIAL INNOVATION

Social innovation as a field of study is a relatively new development; however, as a phenomenon, social innovation has historically determined the evolution of societies (Mulgan, 2006). Simms (2006) differentiates technical innovations from social innovations. Technical innovations range from the stone ax up through instant communication, while social innovations include spiritual belief systems, nations, and globalization. Furthermore, technical innovations are crucial for the generation of social innovation, while social innovations are determinants for generating innovative techniques. Social innovations can also take tangible form as a technology, since it meant the welfare of communities and the public good (Cloutier, 2003).

According to Cloutier (2003), the "innovative" aspect of social innovation can be identified as part of a context in which the individual seeks to change the perceptions toward an unsatisfactory situation, i.e., a social need or a problem that compromises wellbeing and community. These problems are triggersfor society to act to intentionally remedy this situation and achieve the desired result (Cajaiba-Santana, 2013; Murray et al., 2010).

Who promote this kind of intentional action can be one person that change the way to see the world and develop different ways of solving problems (Cloutier, 2003). This promoter of social innovations is named a social entrepreneur. A social entrepreneur is someone who develops activities not only for personal gain, but to achieve social objectives as well (Lettice & Parekh, 2010). The social entrepreneur is one who based on social values insert an innovation in the context of the market, but not for profit. The entrepreneurship social can culminate in a social innovation, if it lead to systemic change in social practices (Michele-Lee Moore, 2012).

There are a variety of actors capable of promoting social innovation, including the following: policy makers, through the creation of legal conditions for the promotion of innovation; foundations, entrepreneurs, and philanthropists, through funding or supporting innovation; and social organizations, through their efforts to find innovative solutions to meet social needs (Murray et al., 2010). The government also can improve its performance in society and support social improvements that come from within society (Pol & Ville, 2009). And the social organizations are an important device to social innovation process because they can play an important mediating role between 'sticky' context-specific user knowledge, and complex forms of technological knowledge (Chalmers, 2013). Despite these social organizations are within the market context.

There are still problems with the performance of governments in stimulating innovation and the social mobilization of society (Baldwin & Von Hippel, 2010; Chalmers, 2013; Neumeier, 2012; Pol & Ville, 2009), but the examples in this chapter shown initiatives from some governments and communities work together to produce solutions to social needs, through new technologies. However, it is also important for changes to occur in the culture and values, i.e., putting the company first, developing a democratic voice, and prioritizing the individual and relationships over systems and structures (Murray et al., 2010). Thus, social innovations do not start from a specific actor, but can be made by individuals, communities, social groups, organizations or groups motivated by governments.

The "social" aspect of social innovation can be identified in its socially constructed process undertaken by the social groups affected by a social need. The social innovations are distinguished by alliances between creative individuals with ideas and energy, on the one hand, and institutions with power and money to make those changes a reality on the other.

Authors like Cajaiba-Santana (2013), Brown and Wyatt (2010), and Murray et al. (2010) proposed conceptual models that assist in understanding how this process occurs. Through detailing the social innovation process proposed by these authors, it is possible to assign characteristics that are more tangible to what occurs within the structure of society, from the time a problem occurs until the time when a social change occurs or a new product is created to solve the problem.

Brown and Wyatt (2010) and Murray et al. (2010) have a more focused view regarding the changes required to address a social need. Murray et al.'s model (2010) is divided into the following (not necessarily sequential) six steps:

1. Identification of the problem;
2. Generation of proposals and ideas regarding how to solve the problem, which may involve formal methods to attract ideas and experiences from various sources;
3. Prototyping ideas and testing them in practice;
4. Support, which happens during the everyday implementation of that idea;
5. Scaling and diffusion stage in which various strategies are used to promote innovation; and
6. Systemic change, which is the end objective of social innovation and new models involving or composed of several smaller innovation architectures.

Considering that the aim of social innovation is to meet a social need, the model presented by Brown and Wyatt (2010) should also be considered because it is based on the methodology of designer thinking, which aims to incorporate consumer insights for prototyping effective products that meet consumer needs. According to the authors, the processes of technological innovations should be guided by the needs of the people who will consume the product. Thus, the process of social innovation must seek a way to consider the culture and needs of all people living in a given community.

Another author explains how the Social Innovation occurs is Cajaiba-Santana (2013), which. Unlike Brown and Wyatt (2010), and Murray et al. (2010), who believes that social innovation can be observed from an institutional perspective? As a result of the exchange of knowledge and resources among the mobilized actors, social innovation can also be observed from the point of view of structure, or as a social process in which individuals collectively engage in intentional actions and reflexively monitor the results of their actions.

In any of these models, it is important that there is exchange of ideas and values among the public, private, and nonprofit sectors regarding investments in socially responsible projects; changes in roles and relationships between companies, government, and nonprofit organizations; and the mixing of principles and mechanisms based on market innovations that have public and philanthropic support support (Murray et al., 2010; Neumeier, 2012; Phills, Deiglmeier, & Miller, 2008) And seems that this collaborative approach will continue to grow in this century due to the success of recent innovations like Wikipedia, the Open University, microcredit, and consumer cooperatives, all of which are examples of social innovations that feature innovative forms of collaboration between individuals. However, it is also clear divergence on the authors about the headline target of social innovation.

As for the results, the authors expected them to fall under two perspectives: structural, for changing social structures through new social practices, and instrumental, for generating an instrument that meets a social need. The first perspective originates from Chombart de Lauwe (1976), as presented by Cloutier (2003). "Social Innovation is an action aimed at creating new social structures, new social relations, new forms of decision." As well, Taylor (1970) argues, "Social innovations are new ways of doing things with the explicit purpose of responding to social needs."

In this chapter, a structural perspective is considered that has a fundamental characteristic the changes in social practices (attitudes, behaviors or perceptions) that enable the improvement of any service, process, or social necessity (Cajaiba-Santana, 2013). This action can result in meeting a social need, but this is a result of the construction of additional changes in the attitudes, behaviors, or perceptions of a group of people who gather in a network of aligned interests to seek new and better ways to act collaboratively inside and outside that group (Cajaiba-Santana, 2013). Thus, social innovations manifest as changes in attitudes, perceptions, or behaviors, resulting in new social practices created collectively and intentionally targeted to a desired social objective, causing social change (Cajaiba-Santana, 2013; Neumeier, 2012).

Considered from a structural perspective, social innovations are not material; instead, they focus on building action (Howaldt, Schwarz, Henning, & Hees, 2010; Neumeier, 2012). While technical innovation occurs when a product or service is broadcast by a commercial or industrial application, social innovation occurs when a change is socially accepted, widely diffused throughout society or in certain sub-areas of society, and institutionalized as a new social practice (Howaldt et al., 2010)

Thus, from a structural perspective, social needs are met through social change, which is the key feature of social innovation. From an instrumental perspective, it is noted that social innovation can also occur through technical artifacts—new products, processes, or services—provided they meet a social need and are geared toward the public good.

Taylor (1970) pioneered the term social innovation in the sense of new ways of doing things with the explicit purpose of responding to social needs. Among these needs, we can quote new ways to combat poverty and crime, and we can consider those leading to obtaining a product, process, or program that profoundly alters basic routines, resources, authority flows, or beliefs in any system social (Westley, 2008).

The results of social innovation, from this perspective, may be process metrics, models, and methods used as forms of the social economy (Murray et al., 2010). From this perspective, social innovations may be materials, activities, or services generated to meet a social need; but they differ from innovation businesses by engaging institutions dedicated to social services and not for profit (Pol & Ville, 2009).

This concept can be observed in practice in institutions that promote social innovation, including the Young Foundation, created in 2005 in the UK, or the Social Innovation Europe Initiative, which adopts the concept of Murray et al. (2010) to seek resolutions to problems and create new social relations. As well, the creation of the Social Innovation Fund (SIF) by the U.S. Office of Social Innovation and Civil Participation stimulates community solutions to solve social problems, which is social innovation.

According to Pol and Ville (2009), social innovation has several overlapping definitions involving institutional change, social purposes, and the public good. In a broad sense, is has been suggested that social innovation can be defined as new ideas with the potential to improve quality of life. Using social innovation and new ideas that generate social gains to change the direction of society improves quality of life. According to Phills et al. (2008), social innovation is any innovative and useful solution to achieve a social good, to meet a need, or solve a problem in a more effective, efficient, or sustainable way than existing approaches from which benefits are generated for society as a whole. This may be in the form of a new product, process, or methodology, as well as an idea, a law, a social movement, or an intervention.

Thus, based on the authors cited above, main features of social innovation are considered:

1. It is a novelty;
2. It is not motivated by profit;
3. It is motivated by an unsatisfactory social situation;
4. It is initiated by an intentional action, aiming for a specific result;
5. It is socially constructed by those affected by social needs;
6. It is not directly linked to a specific sector of society;
7. It generates changes in society or new products that enable us to meet a social need and generate benefits to social structures.

OPEN INNOVATION

Henry Chesbrough's definition of the term "open innovation" is probably the most widely used definition (Dahlander & Gann, 2010): "open innovation means that valuable ideas can come from inside or outside the company and can go to market from inside or outside the company as well" (H. W. Chesbrough, 2003, p. 43). The author also provides a definition of closed innovation, referring to it as the old paradigm in which companies create their ideas and then develop, build, market, distribute, and use them for their own benefit and profit. As opposed to open innovation, closed innovation does not allow the use or marketing of ideas from outside the company.

Although it is a concept that originates in the business strategy and innovation literature (Seltzer & Mahmoudi, 2013), open innovation cannot be classified as technical or social innovation. Unlike these two types of innovation, open innovation is not differentiated by its results, but rather by its construction process; that is, open innovation is differentiated by a company's conscious efforts to share ideas with other companies and incorporate ideas from outside the company into its innovation processes (Seltzer & Mahmoudi, 2013).

Open innovation is mainly used in the context of private companies in the following industries: electronics, food, financial services, automotive, and biotechnology. It is also used in other contexts characterized by globalization and the intensification and diffusion of technologies and new business models (Huizingh, 2011). However, some open innovation methodologies have been applied in the field of public administration as a way to integrate government and society. Examples include initiatives using 1) crowdsourcing methods in which a challenge is posted online and a prize is offered for the best response to the challenge, and 2) crowdstorming methods that are used to gather the largest number of ideas about a topic. These methodologies are found in initiatives such as the Office of social innovation and Civic Participation, in USA (The-White-House, 2014); and in Brazil, the platform PrizeIdea (PrêmioIdeia, in Portuguese)[1], which is linked to Facebook ("PremioIdeia," 2014).

Dahlander and Gann (2010) argue that innovations must not only be categorized as open or closed, but as part of a continuum, ranging from fully closed to fully open. Dahlander and Gann (2010) categorize open innovation into four stages of this continuum (according to the Table 1).

Beyond these categories, the open innovation can be categorized by its processes, according to Enkel, Gassmann, and Chesbrough (2009), the following processes may occur:

1. **From the Outside In:** The innovation process occurs with the entry of external knowledge, obtained mainly from business customers.
2. **From the Inside Out:** The process of innovation is a source of profit for the company in which some ideas are transferred to other companies and advantages are obtained to gain profit by licensing the idea as opposed to developing the idea.
3. **Coupled Process:** The process of innovation is developed jointly between companies and consists of a mixture of the first two types of processes.

Open innovation excels particularly in the area of public administration. One example of open innovation is crowdsourcing, which is a technique used to seek outside contributions for solutions to problems, offering rewards to participants (Seltzer & Mahmoudi, 2013). As well, crowdstorming uses the Internet to encourage people to brainstorm online and provide ideas to resolve a problem (Abrahamson, Ryder, & Unterberg, 2013). These methodologies encourage citizens to engage in finding solutions to a problem and to promote the construction of knowledge between governments and societies (Abrahamson et al., 2013; Seltzer & Mahmoudi, 2013)

Common feature of all methodologies Open Innovation is presented to encouraging collaboration. According Baldwin and Von Hippel (2010), a model of open and collaborative innovation must include a process that allows user engagement innovation and ensures that those who share the work of generating the project can openly show the results of their individual and collective efforts. Thus, while open innovation is a set of practices adopted by companies aiming to profit from innovation, it is also a cognitive model for the creation, interpretation, and research of new practices (H. Chesbrough, Vanhaverbeke, & West, 2008).

The results of using open innovation include the socially innovative way organizations distribute and assimilate knowledge from multiple sources (Chalmers, 2013), which impacts the effectiveness of the innovation since the organizations interact to form networks of innovation and provide collective knowledge.

In the field of public administration, the hope is that Open Innovation results in the construction of more porous organizational structures capable of absorbing the knowledge and the demands of the various stakeholders in the process of Social Innovation (Chalmers, 2013). Thus, the distributed knowledge from various sources can be assimilated and used in other processes of innovation.

Table 1. Types of social innovation according to Dahlander and Gann (2010)

	Pecuniary	Non-Pecuniary
Output (internal to the external environment)	Companies market their inventions and technologies through licensing or sale. " Selling"	Companies reveal internal resources without financial rewards, instead seeking indirect benefits. " Revealing"
Input (the external environment to internal)	Companies acquire foreign expertise as sources of innovation. " Acquiring"	Companies use ideas available in the external environment as sources of innovation. " Sourcing"

'OPEN SOCIAL INNOVATION'

Despite the relevance of the two themes, social innovation and open innovation are two distinct concepts (Chalmers, 2013). However, there is already a move towards adopting more open practices in relation to solving social problems by society (Chalmers, 2013), exemplified by government initiatives mentioned in section 2. Table 2 shows characteristics of Open Innovation and Social Innovation, as its actors, objectives, processes, and expected outcomes, to then relate the concepts.

With respect to the actors, Table 2 shows that both concepts focus on the individuals affected by innovation or those who have some interest in generating innovation. Social innovation involves the interests of society as it works toward fulfilling needs through the formation of new social practices or by creating new products, services, processes, or structures. In addition, acting governments seek legitimacy for political actions by focusing on the citizen; and yet, public and private institutions and social organizations support the resolution of social problems that affect their institutional objectives (Seltzer & Mahmoudi, 2013). As originally proposed, open innovation with economic purposes involves the interest of users that assist companies in the production of articles that meet their needs more effectively, on the one hand (Baldwin & Von Hippel, 2010). On the other hand, it involves the interest of companies that pursue the effectiveness of their innovations, thus maximizing profit. In both cases, there is no quest for legitimacy. In the private sector, the legitimacy of a product guarantees profit; in the public sector, legitimacy is sought by governments for the welfare of society and for political interests, such as reelection (Seltzer & Mahmoudi, 2013).

Regarding the objectives, the concept of social innovation is also divided among the authors who consider it an instrument (product, process, or service) that is generated to meet a social need, such as the approach initiated by Taylor (1970). Other authors who follow Chombart deLauwe (1976) argue that the main feature of social innovation

Table 2. Characteristics of social innovation and open innovation

	Social Innovation	Open Innovation
Actors	Individuals (Lettice & Parekh, 2010), policymakers, foundations, entrepreneurs, philanthropists, social organizations (Murray et al., 2010), and governments (Pol & Ville, 2009); civil society organisations, local communities and puclic servants (Europen-Commission, 2013).	Mainly private companies (Huizingh, 2011), involving users of innovations (Baldwin & Von Hippel, 2010).
Objectives	Structural objectives: social change (Cajaiba-Santana, 2013).	Products, services, systems, and models aimed at the users' demand (Baldwin & Von Hippel, 2010).
	Instrumental: create technical articles that meet a social need (Taylor, 1970).	
Process	Process: collective action (Neumeier, 2012) and intentional innovation by stakeholders (Cajaiba-Santana, 2013).	Collaborative, using some methodology (Costumer partner, Crowdsourcing, Crowstorming, etc.) (Loren, 2011)
Expected results	Results are expected to provide benefits to society through products, processes or services that meet a social need (Taylor, 1970), or social changes that institutionalize a new social practice (Howaldt et al., 2010).	New products, services, systems, and more effective models are developed in the context of more porous organizational structures that feature greater absorption capacity and involvement of various stakeholders in the innovation process (Chalmers, 2013).

is the structural changes in society and meeting social needs. In both cases, social welfare is the primary target.

According to its original objective, open innovation is market-oriented and aimed at improving the innovation process with profit as the main objective. However, literature issues exist regarding its applicability to new contexts (Huizingh, 2011), that achieve innovations beyond the boundaries of the private sphere and even assist in overcoming barriers in the development of other types of innovation, such as social innovation (Chalmers, 2013). Thus, open innovation focuses on technical innovation aims of profit; social innovation is aimed at meeting social needs.

When answering the particular social need of collective action, rather than top-down decisions or individually generated solutions, social and open innovation converge around the collaborative process, which is focused on the user. Social innovation must occur in a process of exchanging ideas and values between the actors in society, the public and private sectors, and non-profit organizations (Phills et al., 2008). In addition, the main feature of the collaborative open innovation process between organizations that engage in different types of partnerships is acquiring ideas and resources from the external environment (H. W. Chesbrough, 2003).

In the public sector, it has been proposed that public institutions—by assuming the characteristics of open innovation as a more sensitive view of societal structures—allow social communities to overcome the barriers that prevent them from innovating from the bottom up. Thus, when public institutions are open, they provide means for greater social involvement in finding solutions then wellbeing and localism. Opening organizations responsible for public good allows society to solve problems on its own, generating social innovations.

Collaboration is an inherent characteristic of open innovation; organizations need to be open to various internal and external actors participating in the process of innovation, as it is believed to be impossible for an organization to have a team of the best people in several areas (H. W. Chesbrough, 2003). Similar to open innovation, the participation of various actors is desirable in social innovation, as the citizens who live in society best perceive social needs; therefore, public participation is critical to finding solutions to these problems ((Neumeier, 2012).

Aiming to achieve this collaborative process, several methods of open innovation are being proposed with strategies for establishing partnerships between organizations, involving consumers in the production of innovations, or bringing together various actors around the same issue (Loren, 2011). Thus, open innovation works by providing mechanisms that users of services and public policies are able to create for themselves; innovations are aimed at community welfare through new practices and social mobilization to solve problems.

From the analysis of the characteristics of social and open innovation, it has been proposed that open innovation is more than a means to achieve social innovation. The two concepts converge in the characteristic of "collaboration between the actors" and form "Open Social Innovation." Social innovation meets open innovation when using a methodology that promotes collaboration among diverse stakeholders in the development of innovation agents. In addition, open innovation meets social innovation, as demonstrated by non-profits that change the structure of society or meet a social need.

Thus, this article proposes that "Open Social Innovation" occurs:

1. Through collaborative processes of open innovation. The types of non-pecuniary open innovation (Dahlander & Gann, 2010) are used to generate benefits for the collective good, as represented by new solutions to social problems or changes in social practices.

Figure 1. Conceptual model of the relationship between open innovation and social innovation

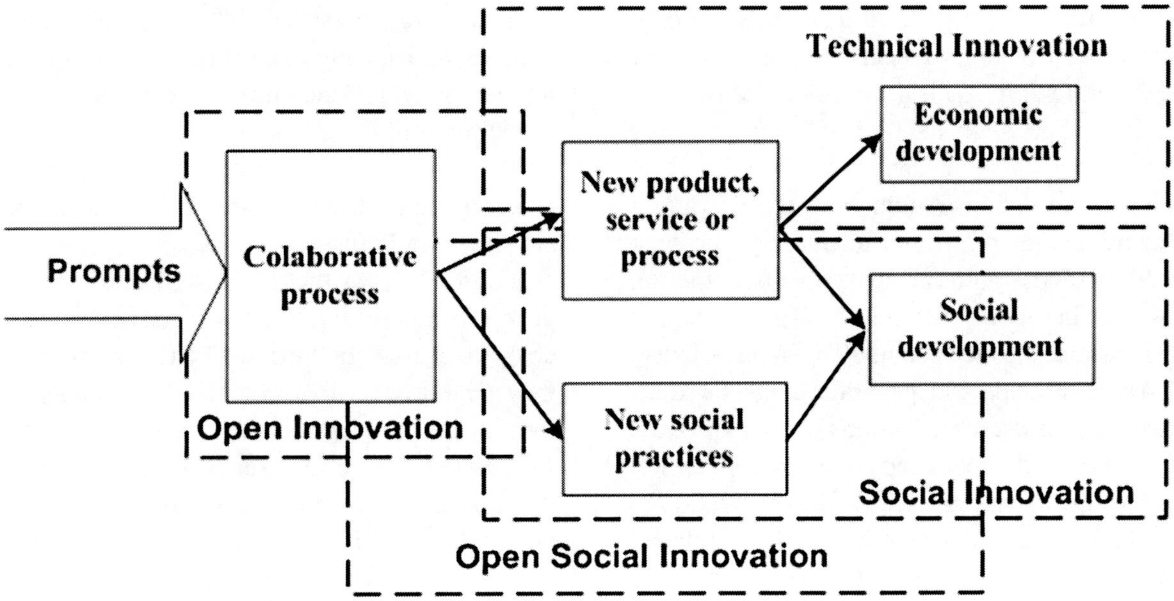

2. As public institutions become more permeable to absorbing citizen demands, structures are sought to enable the self-organization of society in the search of viable solutions to their problems.
3. When open innovation aims to create instruments that cause changes in the social structure or to collective social needs.
4. When open innovation promotes the spread of new social practices or the replication of new instruments without costs in other contexts; through the formation of collaborative networks, it is possible to provide innovative social ideas to be improved by the exchange of knowledge and ideas of individuals in other contexts and locations.

The next section illustrates the theory that was presented in the previous section; it shows practical examples of what this article considers "Open Social Innovation." The following examples show the use of a methodology for open innovation in order to contribute to the emergence of social innovations.

SOCIAL CHALLENGE IDEAS: 'OPEN' SOCIAL INNOVATION IN BRAZIL AND USA

This literature shows that open innovation methodologies can aid in the collaborative construction of technical innovations as social innovations. The examples below show the use of two open innovation methodologies: crowdsourcing and crowdstorming, which are used to promote social challenges to ideas, generating social innovation through public engagement. In the context of these challenges, social innovation can be characterized by new social practices, new policies, new social organizations, and new services generated through citizen participation in the challenge. In addition, open innovation is characterized by encouraging the exchange of ideas among citizens, governments, and private institutions as well as the dissemination of these ideas in order to facilitate the diffusion of innovation.

A social ideas challenge is an online challenge or inquiry into a social problem, such as, "what can be done to improve the sanitation of the city?" The challenge is directed to a group on the Internet, persons residing in the same city, persons who belong to a certain community, or the general public. This group should post ideas to solve the problem and discuss the ideas of the other participants. Challenges can be created by various types of institutions and with different motivations: governmental institutions can seek social partnerships to encourage the participation of society in solving complex social problems and add legitimacy to their actions (The-White-House, 2014); politicians can generate ideas for their policy proposals; organizations can seek private solutions aimed at increased project sustainability; and the community can seek self-organization to meet their demands (Mindmixer, 2014). Aimed at achieving greater engagement, whoever promotes the challenge offers a prize to the participants. The awards are generally given to the individual with the most participation or the best idea.

Social challenges result in multiple ideas that represent the demands of the community's vision of its own members, and they are usually intended for agents and public bodies to inspire new public policies and improve services. The ideas can be exploited by private and public organizations, generating benefits for the authors of ideas and innovative organizations. These benefits are in addition to inspiring ideas that promote community action and social entrepreneurship from the participants of the challenge.

In short, the characteristics that classify challenges to social ideas as "Open Social Innovations" are shown in Figure 2.

Figure 2 shows that citizens, institutions, and governments are motivated by social issues and the desire to change. In the case of citizens for prizes, they are motivated to join social ideas challenges, forming interactive online communities. One of the founders of the Mindmixer software application that houses these online communities, Bowden, argues the objective of these challenges is to bring together "a lot of people who want to get involved in politics or decision making in their communities" (Casserly, 2013). Any organization—though mainly public institutions and governments—can hire these software platforms to launch challenges that aim to solve social problems, initiate public consultations, and formulate questions that allow citizens to participate in public management and find solutions to address a public problem. Beginning this challenge on the platform, proposed

Figure 2. ''Open social innovation'' in social challenges ideas

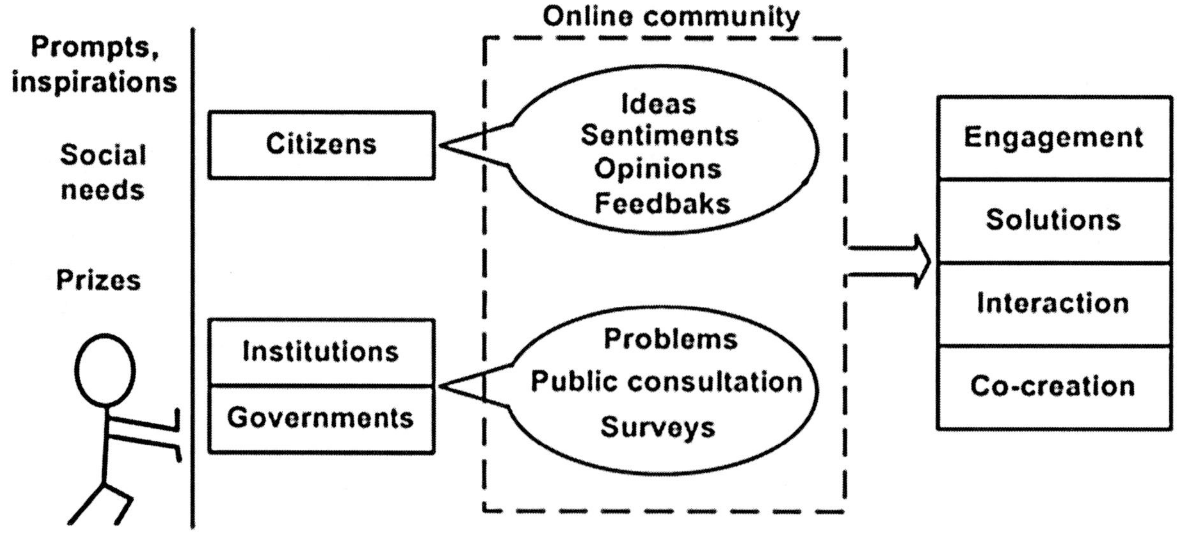

citizens submit ideas, after which they are evaluated and opined. The other participants express their opinions and perceptions regarding what was proposed.

To illustrate the application of the concepts associated with the implementation of "Open Social Innovation," two software application examples that promote social ideas challenges will be presented.

The first example is the Mindmixer platform, available to citizens in the USA and parts of Canada. The platform implements the methodology of crowdsourcing open innovation. The builder of the community creates a video introduction to draw the attention of a group of participants. People using Mindmixer via social networks like Facebook, LinkedIn, or Google+ propose ideas and collaborate by voting for or complementing the ideas of other participants. The objective of Mindmixer is to harness the power of the Internet and social media through online engagement tools that connect public organizations and community members who might not be involved (Mindmixer, 2014).

Another innovative initiative using these concepts is available in Brazil. Using the software program PrizeIdeia, governments and third-sector companies have submitted population questions in search of ideas for innovation and social development. Behind these interactions, PrizeIdeia puts into practice the concepts of open innovation with crowdstorming and social innovation. The PrizeIdeia software also uses the concept of gamification, which incorporates greater societal involvement in the proposition, discussion, and evaluation of innovative ideas for questions presented by governments and corporations. The users who engage most in the challenge of ideas and earn the most points by the end of the consultation period are given awards.

The following are some examples of online communities using these two software platforms. The communities are described as well as the characteristics that identify them as "Open Social Innovations."

Example A: Park City, Utah, USA

Park City is a city in the state of Utah in the U.S. Public officials in the city created an online community using the Mindmixer platform, since February 4, 2013 (http://www.letstalkparkcity.com/activity). According to the platform information, online communities are created as virtual town halls, where community discussions around reforms being carried out in the city could be stimulated. Using the platform, prefecture agents and community leaders pose questions about citizen perceptions of city projects. This way, citizens generate the best ideas for the development of the project. As well, they discuss and evaluate the ideas proposed by other participants, finding solutions collectively. The ideas submitted make up a report that is sent to community leaders who consider the decisions regarding the community and assign the ideas a status or either not feasible, being revised, in progress, or implemented. This status demonstrates how close the idea is to fruition. The mayor and other agents that make up the public administration of a city participate in the platform as listeners, taking suggestions for consideration at city hall and exploring the problems with new questions. Citizen participation is encouraged through a rewards program. With every participation, citizens accumulate a number of points that can be redeemed for rewards in a small shop. As a result, residents responding to promoting economic development, quality of life, and city sustainability proposed several ideas. Among these ideas, one that stood out was in corporating the use of composting containers to reduce the amount of waste. According to Bauters (2013), the idea received support from the community and it was passed on to the manager of municipal environmental sustainability for consideration.

Example B: Military Policy of the State of Minas Gerais, Brazil

The Military Policy of the State of Minas Gerais has developed challenges of ideas represented by its 8th Battalion located at the southeast of the State of Minas Gerais. These challenges have been realized evolving citizens of one city. These challenges have used the PrêmioIdeia platform and aimed to encourage citizens to participate in generating ideas to solve a specific problem. The challenges proposed by this public safety institution are grouped in an online community called the Safe City Project. Its first challenge, in question, was released on September 23, 2013 and is justified by a growth in the quantity of property crimes between the years 2012-2013. Bidders Challenge is an institution of the State of Minas Gerais that offers a prize throughout the challenge to the participants that best contribute to the resolution of the problem by sharing ideas as well as commenting on and evaluating the ideas of other participants. With Mindmixer, participants accumulate points; however, points are not redeemable for rewards but are added together to determine the winner of the challenge. The results of two months of online competition are 336 ideas, which focus on initiatives that can be adopted by the police, city hall, prosecutors, and citizens to fight against property crime. These initiatives make up a report on citizen perceptions regarding this issue, which will support studies on the strategic planning of local police. More than innovative ideas, the police search community approaches and the legitimacy of projects. With the Safe City Project, several ideas have emerged in order to create networks of communication between the community and police to fight against property crimes ("PremioIdeia," 2014). These ideas ratify a project launched by the police shortly after the completion of the challenge, in which the Battalion launched the "Network of Protected Republics," which, according to local media, is a unique project in Brazil. This project, already implemented, connects college students and police through technologies such as WhatsApp and Facebook, seeking cooperation of all in monitoring sites and actions to curb property crimes. The results of the application of this platform was presented by Martins and Bermejo (2014). These authors showed the government innovations generated by the PrizeIdea Platform.

Thus, in order to be collaborative, social challenges to open innovation ideas seek solutions to problems and improve these solutions by interacting with participating agents. In addition, other people should be allowed to access and use ideas

Table 3. Characteristics of "open social innovation" found in Examples A and B

	Example A: Mindmixer	Example B: PrizeIdeia	Open Social Innovation
Actors	Actors Community Leaders, Mayor, public officials and citizens interested in improving the public policy of the city.	Public officials and citizens affected by crimes against property.	Focus in particular affected by social necessity and supported by institutions interested and motivated individual for an unsatisfactory situation.
Objectives	Receive suggestions on actions to be implemented to improve the community.	Find solutions on how to tackle a specific problem that are crimes against property.	Meeting a social need or change in the practices of society
Process	Use of process technologies and open innovation as tools for generating ideas outside the town hall, to improve public management.	Use of technologies and open innovation as tools for discussion between public officials and citizens on solving a specific problem.	Collaborative with the participation of those affected by social need.
Outcomes	Displaying Virtual Town Hall with several ideas posted and a channel of communication between society, community leaders and city hall.	Opening a traditional institution of the State, for community participation and co-production of solutions to a problem.	New products, services, processes, or changes in social practices that generate social benefits.

that apply to their communities. As the examples demonstrate, new participatory practices spread around the world and may constitute innovation in the form of civic participation by bringing together people in a virtual way. This is because, according to Chong (2013), innovation promotes online forums where communities come together to discuss problems and solutions.

Thus, the main social innovation generated by both platforms is a new model to generate audience engagement, cooperation, and the exchange of knowledge among citizens and officials in solving social problems. In both examples, the community is invited to interact with public officials and share information about the local situation as well as prospective improvements to social welfare. Social innovation occurs through the new participatory practices of citizens, as made possible by technical innovations, such as the Internet; software applications that implement methodologies; crowdsourcing; and crowdstorming.

The platforms have characteristics that relate to "Open Social Innovation," including: the aim of generating new ideas to solve social problems; actions that are geared toward the desired result, which is the resolution of this problem; issues raised in challenges aimed at meeting a social need, not profit for the group; solutions that emerge from collaborations between different actors involved in innovation; and results that translate into changes, leading to community improvements.

DISCUSSION AND PROPOSITIONS

This article introduced "Open Social Innovation," proposed by Chalmers (2013), as a social innovation collectively constructed through interactions between socially innovative organizations and local communities. A social innovation with a collaborative approach—in which it is believed that the opening of public institutions, governments, and nonprofit organizations for citizen participation adds greater effectiveness to innovations—has the methodologies of open innovation to encourage effectiveness in different areas of knowledge.

As demonstrated in the article, collaboration is a characteristic of "Open Social Innovation," which, as cited by Cajaiba-Santana (2013), differentiates from social innovation with agent-centric perspectives, i.e., "Open Social Innovation" is not created through actions taken by specific individuals; it differs from social innovation approaches promoted by social entrepreneurs, as presented by Lettice and Parekh (2010).

As several authors posit, social innovation is a complex concept and viewed from various perspectives. Most applicants in the works surveyed in this literature review are either structural or instrumental prospects. This work does not intend to create a new concept; rather, it proposes a discussion on opening up the social innovation process. Some authors attribute 'social' innovation to meeting a social need, and others link the 'social' to changes in social practices. This article aims to highlight the 'social' in relation to the opening of public institutions to society to generate participation and innovation in public services, public policy planning, structural discussions, and public administration in general. Beyond the context of the public sector, openness refers to the establishment of broad channels of communication. This is characteristic of open innovation, which aims to exchange knowledge between communities to generate useful solutions to local social problems. These solutions are disseminated and adapted within other contexts; social practices are innovated, bringing benefits to other communities.

The concept of open public institutions grew in the last decade, especially with open government initiatives as strengthened by the advancement of technology in the public sector. These initiatives, called government-to-citizen (Linders, 2012), make available public information to citizens and attach greater openness to government practices. However, to innovate openly, initiatives are needed that also allow a flow of knowledge to citizen governments and citizen-to-citizen initiatives for self-organization to solve social problems and bring about change in their communities.

The examples can be studied long term to indicate the contributions of open innovation in meeting the demands of communities, ensuring that innovation was opened by the participating institutions, discussing ideas with citizens, and using these ideas to strategically plan. Nevertheless, more than the results of open innovation use in the long term, the examples demonstrate innovative strategic planning of these proponents. Through online communities, institutions now have a view of society processes and innovations in the form of a participative society.

CONCLUSION AND FUTURE RESEARCH DIRECTIONS

It has been concluded that that open innovation can contribute to social innovation through collaborative processes that encourage interaction between different actors, the internal and external public, and private organizations. When open innovation is used to meet a social need or change community practices, innovation is also social. Similarly, social innovation is also open innovation when a collaborative process is employed in which organizations are open to capturing societal knowledge regarding the best courses of action to solve their problems. Therefore, the common feature is collaboration, since open innovation can contribute to social innovation.

The examples illustrate how open innovation can contribute to society participation in solving problems and communicating between citizens, public officials, and representatives of public and private institutions. However, an in-depth study of the cases cited is still needed. In this sense, the characteristics of "Open Social Innovation" are shown in this chapter. Some assumptions can be tested through the in-depth analysis of the social challenges of ideas and other open innovations aimed at finding effective collaboration processes for social innovation.

The first proposition is that open innovation can create better solutions for social needs. As Chalmers (2013) demonstrates, increasing the number of users in the generation of social innovation through open innovation mitigates the risks of introducing innovations because they are generated from a wide range of expertise that complement each other. To evaluate this proposition, social challenge ideas or other cases of open innovation could be investigated with respect to their impact in a specific area.

The second proposition is that the collaborative process characteristic of open innovation can be considered a means to generate social innovations. According to the principles of open innovation, an organization does not innovate in isolation, but rather by engaging with different types of partners and acquiring ideas and resources from the external environment (H. W. Chesbrough, 2003). As in open innovation, those hoping to innovate socially should seek mechanisms for interaction between the various stakeholders involved. Factors that determined certain social innovation and check to see if any of these factors are related to open innovation can be investigated.

The third proposition is that the network structure formed by the mechanisms of open innovation contributes to the replication of innovations in different social contexts. The long-term outcomes of social challenge ideas in different cities can be compared and the results can be presented in future research. As was previously discussed, the usage of open innovation methodologies and the generation of social innovation spread in the collaborative network in which it was created. This resonates with Pol and Ville (2009) suggestion that when an innovation is successful, other people and communities can benefit from this new idea; thus, the marginal cost of one more person making use of the new idea is zero.

A fourth and final proposition is that the use of open innovation methodologies by governments is a means of capturing knowledge for public management. As Neumeier (2012) observes, the problems of a region and the necessary actions to address them are better perceived by the citizens of this region. The implementation of strategies based on such local perceptions is beginning to attract more attention from public administration officials. In the case of the social challenge ideas, an analysis of what can be extracted from the suggested ideas and how the government uses this information may indicate how the knowledge captured in a network can be used in collaboration with public management.

This work contributes to the areas of social and open innovation; "Open Social Innovation" is presented as a junction of the concepts of social and open innovation and presents assumptions to be tested to question the concepts presented. Next, examples were found of the open innovation methodologies that contribute to social innovation. The limitation of this study is a lack of present empirical evidence of the long-term results of the application of "Open Social Innovation" or the effective use of open innovation methodologies to stimulate social innovation. Future work may explore these assumptions or investigate other examples that use other techniques of open innovation and have generated changes in social practices to benefit a social group. Case studies that explore the considerations presented here can help to fill the main shortcomings of the research, such as the need for an empirical validation of the suggested relationships. The role of governments should also be explored in order to produce more participatory public management through techniques of open innovation.

REFERENCES

Abrahamson, S., Ryder, P., & Unterberg, B. (2013). *Crowdstorm: The Future of Innovation, Ideas, and Problem Solving*. John Wiley & Sons.

Baldwin, C., & Von Hippel, E. (2010). Modeling a paradigm shift: From producer innovation to user and open collaborative innovation. *Harvard Business School Finance Working Paper,* (10-038), 4764-4709.

Brown, T., & Wyatt, J. (2010). Design thinking for social innovation. *Stanford Social Innovation Review*, *8*(1), 30–35.

Cajaiba-Santana, G. (2013). Social innovation: Moving the field forward. A conceptual framework. *Technological Forecasting and Social Change*.

Casserly, M. (2013). MindMixer Acquires VoterTide, Bets Social Tech Can Save Democratic Process. *Entrepreneurship*. Retrieved 31-01-2014, 2014, from http://www.forbes.com/sites/meghancasserly/2013/03/26/mindmixer-acquires-votertide-bets-social-tech-can-save-democratic-process/

Chalmers, D. (2013). Social innovation: An exploration of the barriers faced by innovating organizations in the social economy. *Local Economy*, *28*(1), 17–34. doi:10.1177/0269094212463677

Chesbrough, H., Vanhaverbeke, W., & West, J. (2008). *Open Innovation: Researching a New Paradigm: Researching a New Paradigm*. Oxford University Press.

Chesbrough, H. W. (2003). *Open innovation: The new imperative for creating and profiting from technology*. Harvard Business Press.

Cloutier, J. (2003). *Qu'est-ce que l'innovation sociale?* Crises.

Collis, J., & Hussey, R. (2005). Pesquisa em administração: Um guia prático para alunos de graduação e pós-graduação. *The Bookman.*

European Commission. (1996). The Green Book on Innovation. Luxembourg: European Commission.

Dahlander, L., & Gann, D. M. (2010). How open is innovation? *Research Policy, 39*(6), 699–709. doi:10.1016/j.respol.2010.01.013

Enkel, E., Gassmann, O., & Chesbrough, H. (2009). Open R&D and open innovation: Exploring the phenomenon. *Research Management, 39*(4), 311–316.

Howaldt, J., Schwarz, M., Henning, K., & Hees, F. (2010). *Social innovation: Concepts, research fields and international trends*. IMA/ZLW.

Huizingh, E. K. (2011). Open innovation: State of the art and future perspectives. *Technovation, 31*(1), 2–9. doi:10.1016/j.technovation.2010.10.002

Lettice, F., & Parekh, M. (2010). The social innovation process: Themes, challenges and implications for practice. *International Journal of Technology Management, 51*(1), 139–158. doi:10.1504/IJTM.2010.033133

Linders, D. (2012). From e-government to we-government: Defining a typology for citizen coproduction in the age of social media. *Government Information Quarterly, 29*(4), 446–454. doi:10.1016/j.giq.2012.06.003

Loren, J. D. (2011). What is Open Innovation? In A guide to Open Innovation and Crowdsourcing (Vol. 1). Kogan Page.

Martins and Bermejo. (2014). Open social innovation based on Idea Crowdsourcing. 11th European, Mediterranean and Middle Eastern Conference on Information Systems 2014.

Michele-Lee Moore, F. R. W., Tjornbo, O., & Holroyd, C. (2012). The loop, the lens, and the lesson: Using resilience theory to examine public policy and social innovation. In A. M. Nicholls (Ed.), Social Innovation Blurring Boundaries to Reconfigure Markets (Vol. 1, pp. 114-136). London: Academic Press.

Mindmixer. (2014). *About Mindmixer*. Retrieved 15-01, 2014, from http://www.mindmixer.com/#how

Mulgan, G. (2006). The process of social innovation. *Innovations, 1*(2), 145-162.

Murray, R., Caulier-Grice, J., & Mulgan, G. (2010). *The open book of social innovation*. National Endowment for Science, Technology and the Art.

Neumeier, S. (2012). Why do Social Innovations in Rural Development Matter and Should They be Considered More Seriously in Rural Development Research?–Proposal for a Stronger Focus on Social Innovations in Rural Development Research. *Sociologia Ruralis, 52*(1), 48–69. doi:10.1111/j.1467-9523.2011.00553.x

Parvanta, C., Roth, Y., & Keller, H. (2013). Crowdsourcing 101 A Few Basics to Make You the Leader of the Pack. *Health Promotion Practice, 14*(2), 163–167. doi:10.1177/1524839912470654 PMID:23299912

Paulini, M., Murty, P., & Maher, M. L. (2013). Design processes in collective innovation communities: A study of communication. *CoDesign, 9*(2), 90–112. doi:10.1080/15710882.2012.716850

Phills, J. A., Deiglmeier, K., & Miller, D. T. (2008). Rediscovering social innovation. *Stanford Social Innovation Review, 6*(4), 34–43.

Pol, E., & Ville, S. (2009). Social innovation: Buzz word or enduring term? *Journal of Socio-Economics*, *38*(6), 878–885. doi:10.1016/j.socec.2009.02.011

PrêmioIdeia. (2014). *PrizeIdea - A plataform for open social innovation*. Retrieved 22-05, 2014, from http://www.premioideia.com

Schaffers, H., Komninos, N., Pallot, M., Trousse, B., Nilsson, M., & Oliveira, A. (2011). *Smart cities and the future internet: towards cooperation frameworks for open innovation. In The future internet* (pp. 431–446). Springer. doi:10.1007/978-3-642-20898-0_31

Schumpeter, J. A. (1961). *The theory of economic development: An inquiry into profits, capital, credit, interest, and the business cycle* (Vol. 55). Transaction Books.

Seltzer, E., & Mahmoudi, D. (2013). Citizen Participation, Open Innovation, and Crowdsourcing: Challenges and Opportunities for Planning. *Journal of Planning Literature*, *28*(1), 3–18. doi:10.1177/0885412212469112

Simms, J. R. (2006). Technical and social innovation determinants of behaviour. *Systems Research and Behavioral Science*, *23*(3), 383–393. doi:10.1002/sres.734

Taylor, J. B. (1970). Introducing social innovation. *The Journal of Applied Behavioral Science*, *6*(1), 69–77. doi:10.1177/002188637000600104

White House. (2014). *About SICP - The Community Solutions Agenda*. Retrieved 18-01, 2014, from http://www.whitehouse.gov/administration/eop/sicp/about

Wobbe, W. (2012). Measuring social innovation and monitoring progress of EU polices. In H.-W. F. J. Howaldt (Ed.), *Challenge Social Innovation: Potentials for Business, Social Entrepreneurship, Welfare and Civil Society*. Berlin: Springer. doi:10.1007/978-3-642-32879-4_19

ADDITIONAL READING

Adams, S. A. (2011). Sourcing the crowd for health services improvement: The reflexive patient and "share-your-experience" websites. *Social Science & Medicine*, *72*(7), 1069–1076. doi:10.1016/j.socscimed.2011.02.001 PMID:21414701

Alcock, P. (2010). Building the Big Society: a new policy environment for the third sector in England. Voluntary sector review, 1(3), 379-389.

Allen, K. (2008). Developing trends and challenges for the information industry examined in the context of the Online Information Conference. *Business Information Review*, *25*(2), 81–85. doi:10.1177/0266382108090809

Andersen, K. N., Medaglia, R., & Henriksen, H. Z. (2012). Social media in public health care: Impact domain propositions. *Government Information Quarterly*, *29*(4), 462–469. doi:10.1016/j.giq.2012.07.004

Bahir, E., & Peled, A. (2013). Identifying and Tracking Major Events Using Geo-Social Networks. *Social Science Computer Review*, *31*(4), 458–470. doi:10.1177/0894439313483689

Bauwens, M. (2009). Class and capital in peer production. *Capital and Class*, *33*(1), 121–141. doi:10.1177/030981680909700107

Bertot, J. C., Jaeger, P. T., & Grimes, J. M. (2010). Using ICTs to create a culture of transparency: E-government and social media as openness and anti-corruption tools for societies. *Government Information Quarterly*, *27*(3), 264–271. doi:10.1016/j.giq.2010.03.001

Bertot, J. C., Jaeger, P. T., & Hansen, D. (2012). The impact of polices on government social media usage: Issues, challenges, and recommendations. *Government Information Quarterly*, *29*(1), 30–40. doi:10.1016/j.giq.2011.04.004

Bonabeau, E. Decisions 2.0: The Power of Collective Intelligence.

Brabham, D. C. (2009). Crowdsourcing the Public Participation Process for Planning Projects. *Planning Theory, 8*(3), 242–262. doi:10.1177/1473095209104824

Brabham, D. C. (2010). Moving the Crowd at Threadless. *Information Communication and Society, 13*(8), 1122–1145. doi:10.1080/13691181003624090

Chalmers, D. M., & Balan-Vnuk, E. (2013). Innovating not-for-profit social ventures: Exploring the microfoundations of internal and external absorptive capacity routines. *International Small Business Journal, 31*(7), 785–810. doi:10.1177/0266242612465630

Chun, S. A., & Luna Reyes, L. F. (2012). Social media in government. *Government Information Quarterly, 29*(4), 441–445. doi:10.1016/j.giq.2012.07.003

Djellal, F., Gallouj, F., & Miles, I. (2013). Two decades of research on innovation in services: Which place for public services? *Structural Change and Economic Dynamics, 27*(0), 98–117. doi:10.1016/j.strueco.2013.06.005

Gerami, N. (2013). Attracting a crowd: What societal verification means for arms control: The US response. *The Bulletin of the Atomic Scientists, 69*(3), 14–18. doi:10.1177/0096340213485943

Kelly, M., Ferranto, S., Lei, S., Ueda, K.-i., & Huntsinger, L. (2012). Expanding the table: The web as a tool for participatory adaptive management in California forests. *Journal of Environmental Management, 109*(0), 1–11. doi:10.1016/j.jenvman.2012.04.035 PMID:22659644

Lee, G., & Kwak, Y. H. (2012). An Open Government Maturity Model for social media-based public engagement. *Government Information Quarterly, 29*(4), 492–503. doi:10.1016/j.giq.2012.06.001

Lee, J. J., Ceyhan, P., Jordan-Cooley, W., & Sung, W. (2013). GREENIFY: A Real-World Action Game for Climate Change Education. *Simulation & Gaming, 44*(2-3), 349–365. doi:10.1177/1046878112470539

Lorenzi, D., Vaidya, J., Chun, S., Shafiq, B., & Atluri, V. (2014). Enhancing the government service experience through QR codes on mobile platforms. *Government Information Quarterly, 31*(1), 6–16. doi:10.1016/j.giq.2013.05.025

Luna-Reyes, L. F., Bertot, J. C., & Mellouli, S. (2014). Open Government, Open Data and Digital Government. *Government Information Quarterly, 31*(1), 4–5. doi:10.1016/j.giq.2013.09.001

Mergel, I. (2013). Social media adoption and resulting tactics in the US federal government. *Government Information Quarterly, 30*(2), 123–130. doi:10.1016/j.giq.2012.12.004

Michele-Lee Moore, F. R. W. Ola Tjornbo, Carin Holroyd. (2012). The loop, the lens, and the lesson: using resilience theory to examine public policy and social innovation. In A. M. Alex Nicholls (Ed.), Social Innovation Blurring Boundaries to Reconfigure Markets (Vol. 1, pp. 114-136). London.

Nograšek, J., & Vintar, M. (2014). E-government and organisational transformation of government: Black box revisited? *Government Information Quarterly, 31*(1), 108–118. doi:10.1016/j.giq.2013.07.006

Shaw, E., & de Bruin, A. (2013). Reconsidering capitalism: The promise of social innovation and social entrepreneurship? *International Small Business Journal, 31*(7), 737–746. doi:10.1177/0266242613497494

Silva, J. (2014). The dynamic internet: How technology, users, and business are transforming the network, Christopher Yoo. AEI Press, Washington, D.C. (2012), ISBN: 978-0844772271. *Government Information Quarterly*, *31*(1), 210. doi:10.1016/j.giq.2013.07.001

Sutherlin, G. (2013). A voice in the crowd: Broader implications for crowdsourcing translation during crisis. *Journal of Information Science*, *39*(3), 397–409. doi:10.1177/0165551512471593

Westley, F. (2008). The social innovation dynamic. Frances Westley, SiG@ Waterloo.

Wilson, S. C. (2014). e-Government legislation: Implementation issues for programs for low-income people. *Government Information Quarterly*, *31*(1), 42–49. doi:10.1016/j.giq.2013.04.002

Zuiderwijk, A., & Janssen, M. (2014). Open data policies, their implementation and impact: A framework for comparison. *Government Information Quarterly*, *31*(1), 17–29. doi:10.1016/j.giq.2013.04.003

KEY TERMS AND DEFINITIONS

Crowdsourcing: "The act of taking a job traditionally performed by a designated agent (usually an employee) and outsourcing it to undefined generally large group of people in the form of open call" (Howe, 2006).

Crowdstorming: The ability to absorb ideas from different sources, mainly external, conducting a brainstorming through the Internet.

Open Innovation: "Means that valuable ideas can come from inside or outside the company and can go to market from inside or outside the company as well" (H. W. Chesbrough, 2003, p. 43).

'Open Social Innovation': When social innovation is seen from a collaborative point of view, organizations become more porous structures that make it possible to overcome the barriers that prevent communities from innovating from the bottom up.

Social Challenge Ideas: A challenge online to encouraging participants to submit ideas in order to solve a specific problem, which may be useful to government and society. Citizens submit ideas and a prize is offered for the best response to the challenge.

Social Innovation: "An initiative aimed at creating new social structures, new social relations, new forms of decision" (Chombart de Lauwe (1976) cited from the Cloutier (2003)).

ENDNOTE

1 See www.premioideia.com.

Chapter 10
E-Government Documents and Data Clustering

Goran Šimić
University of Defense, Serbia

ABSTRACT

This chapter is about documents and data clustering as a process of preparing the information resources stored in the e-government systems for advanced search. These resources are mainly represented as textual data stored as field values in the databases or located as documents in file repositories. Due to their growth in number, search for some specific information takes more time. Different techniques are used for this purpose. Most of them include information retrieval based on a variety of text similarity measures. The cost of such processing depends on preparation of resources for searching. Clustering represents the most commonly used technique for such a purpose, and this fact is the basic motive for this chapter.

INTRODUCTION

According to complexity of contemporary life, the governments try to establish close relations with citizens as much as possible in order to better understand their needs and problems, to offer them different kind of help and to satisfy their expectations. In such a situation the institutions offer the variety of Web services named e-government, or open government to make the information their systems already hold accessible to the people regardless of time and location. The information retrieval (IR) from big data collections stored in e-government information systems (IS) represents the important part of the solution. The data in such collections are heterogeneously structured and presented. Therefore, they can be hardly categorized depending on information they contain. The clustering represents the way for grouping the data based on their mutual similarity and without satisfactory descriptions provided by metadata self-contained in the documents and other content used.

Clustering can be performed on every kind of data: textual, visual and audio data as well as combination of these three. It is used especially for huge amount of data that are not well structured, or that are not structured at all. If it is not the case, some filtering and sorting are enough for preparing the data for information retrieval. Unfortunately, actual information systems are congested with different kind of content due to

DOI: 10.4018/978-1-4666-7266-6.ch010

long time of data accumulation, their distributed nature, demands to exchange the data with the other systems, different types of data and various formats that the data are stored in. Therefore, the software developers faced a complex problem how to integrate the same system functions to be applicable on such heterogeneous content. One of the most important pieces in the solution of this problem is clustering.

Basically, clustering represents a process of grouping data by using some algorithm or mathematical function. In both cases the calculating of similarity between data represents the main principle.

The considerations in the chapter are mainly related to clustering of textual content. In e-government IS the data are commonly stored in databases while the documents can be held in both the databases (DB) and repositories. Generally, DB provides easier way for grouping data and retrieving the information. There are eight parts in chapter. After the background briefly presented, the basic concepts used in clustering are described. Further, the common measures such as text frequency and inverse document frequency commonly used in clustering are described there. Moreover, some modifications of them as well as their combination are explained. The third section is about the clustering taxonomies. Many of them could be found in the research papers and the most common approach is followed—hierarchical and partition clustering represents the basic classification. Another one is also important: 'hard' (discrete) and 'soft' (fuzzy) clustering. For clarity the considerations are richly illustrated with the examples. In the fourth section the clustering techniques and algorithms are described. Two important techniques are presented: K-means and Fuzzy C-means. The fifth section is about different formats and structures used for representing text content. The case study about clustering in ADVANSE system is presented after. Finally, the future plans and conclusions are presented in the last two sections.

Background

In contemporary e-government IS the clustering represents one of the techniques for improving advanced search and information retrieval, providing of high quality of citizen services as a final goal. Further, such a goal cannot be achieved without clustering due to rapid growth of content in amount and number. On the other hand there are more citizens' demands in form of questions and searching queries due to expansion of computer literacy and awareness of existence of E-Government services on the Internet (Fang, 2002). Therefore, the institutions need to improve their services in way to reduce the responding time and to provide higher quality of response.

The clustering exists more than 50 years (Krippendorff, 1980) but its development is strongly related with the progress in IT. Firstly it is used in anthropology (Driver & Kroeber, 1932) and psychology (Zubin, 1938) for building typologies of cultures and individuals by using empirical data. Since the early '60 its usage has been spread out from the human researches to biology, geography, astronomy, finance and so far. From the 'just for researching' analysis it has been developed to extraordinary useful set of techniques and algorithms that are implemented as modules of software products or as separate tools designed for business purposes. When the first book about clustering was published (Sneath & Sokal, 1973) there were numbers of applications as well as techniques and algorithms already built. Common for all of them is that from the beginning, clustering or cluster analysis has been dedicated to generation of descriptive data models through extraction of classes from concrete data objects. All of the other background considerations are put in the next 3 sections of this chapter.

BASIC CONCEPTS

For dealing with clusters and clustering, there are some concepts to be assumed. Basically, the clusters are usually considered as the data sets formed through the clustering process. This way the text clustering represents a process of grouping text items (e.g. *Word* documents, *PDF* files, Web pages, e-mails, etc.) into clusters based on similarity of their content. Than the clustering can be formally described as a problem by the next assumptions:

If there are *M* text items, *N* clusters, and an item is represented with *T* while a cluster is represented with *C*, thenthe set of all text items can be represented as $TS = \{T_1, T_2, T_3, ..., T_m\}$ andthe clustered structure can be represented as a set $CS = \{C_1, C_2, C_3, ..., C_n\}$;

This way each cluster represents the sub-set of text items $Ci = \{T_p, ..., T_q\} \mid 1 \leq \{p,q\} \leq M, 1 \leq i \leq N$ that are similar to each other and different from text items that belong to other clusters;

Finally, particular text item can be universally referenced as T_{ij} where *i* indicates belonging to particular cluster while *j* is index of text item in *TS*.

In accordance with conventions mentioned above, next is a graphical representation (Figure 1) of 3 clusters (*N=3*) with 14 text items (*M=14*). The similarity between items is expressed by their mutual distance. The shorter distance the greater similarity.

Representation of text items as dots in 2D plane are very often in documents about clustering. They can be represented in different ways depending on which approach is used in particular case: 'Dots in 2D plane' is usual in considerations about partition clustering, while the linked three structures are the usual representation in hierarchical clustering. Both of cases mentioned do not represent the real nature of text content.

Text Content Representation

While in the data clustering the data could be processed in their original form, in text clustering the original representation of text items is not appropriate. There are several reasons that may cause the problems:

Figure 1. Clusters' graphical representation

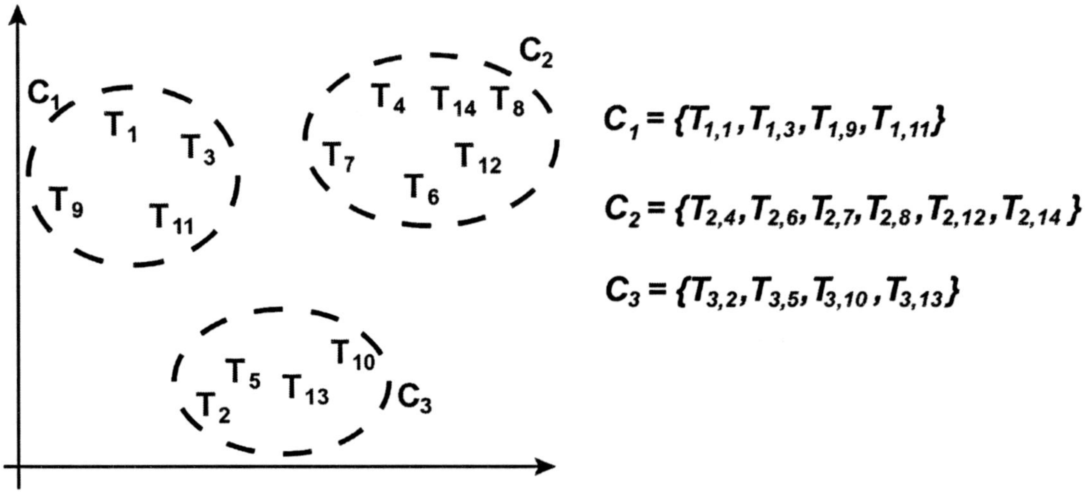

- Text items differ in length; it is much easier to process short text of one or few sentences that represents a compact unit of information than such item as whole document that can consist of number of pages;
- Text items consist of:
  - Words that do not contain any information at all or information relevant for clustering;
  - Special characters such as periods, scores, brackets, quotes, hyphens, and many others with the purpose to provide sentence constructions to be readable for the human users;
  - Numbers that can hold important information and therefore, they need to be considered together with the other parts of text;
  - Words that contain interesting information could be in forms that are different from basic one; for instance, they could be in: singular/plural, active/passive, different tenses, with prefixes and/or suffixes, etc.

Due to reasons mentioned, the information relevant for clustering needs to be extracted from the text items. Originally, text item can be represented as an ordered set of 'text chunks' of different type and importance. The unimportant chunks would be removed and rest of them would be examined. The next example illustrates this process:

- Let's get the sentence "Thus, Facebook has positioned itself to acquire pieces of the users' profiles that are likely unavailable to other data aggregators." (Example is retrieved from http://www.bbc.co.uk/news/technology-25584286) as text item T.
  - Its set based original representation is: *T = {'Thus', ',', 'Facebook', 'has', 'positioned', 'itself', 'to', ..., 'aggregators.'}*;
  - Since there are words and characters that do not carry any information (such as *'thus', ',', 'has', 'itself', 'of', 'the', 'are'*, etc.) they are eliminated;
  - Further, rest of words need to be normalized in their basic form (*stemming* process) and just after that the appropriate representation of text item is made;
  - Finally, the terms this representation consists of need to be weighted and as a result of overall process explained, the original sentence as a particular text item is represented by set of ordered pairs of terms and weights: $T = \{(t_1, w_1),(t_2, w_2),(t_3, w_3),..,(t_k, w_k)\}$, or simpler, assuming that the terms are given in ordered list, as a vector of term weights: $\overline{T} = < w_1, w_2, ..., w_k >$.

Such a representation of the text content (word, sentence, section, or whole document) is used in vector space model (VCM) where each word represents the particular dimension and they are mutually independent – orthogonal to each other. Due to its simplicity, VCM model is frequently used for representing the text in the clustering process. The main disadvantage of VCM is that it does not support the collocations – ordered sequences of words that, appearing together, have the specific meaning different from particular words they consist of. If there are *M* text items and *K* terms than they form the matrix of term weights (Figure 2) that is often used in considerations about the text items clustering. Text items are denoted

Figure 2. Matrix of term weights

$$
\begin{array}{c} \\ t_1 \\ t_2 \\ \vdots \\ t_M \end{array}
\begin{array}{c} \begin{array}{cccc} T_1 & T_2 & \cdots & T_N \end{array} \\ \begin{bmatrix} 0 & 0.4 & \cdots & w_{1N} \\ 0.02 & 0.13 & \cdots & w_{2N} \\ \vdots & \vdots & & \vdots \\ w_{M1} & w_{M2} & \cdots & w_{MN} \end{bmatrix} \end{array}
$$

by T_i, terms by t_j while weights are denoted by w_{ij}. This way each row in matrix represents one vector of term weights.

Weights can be calculated in different ways. There are some characteristic measures used for weighting of text content.

Term Frequency

Term frequency (*TF*) represents the number of occurrences of term in particular text item (Salton & Buckley, 1988). Let's consider the next example sentence as a text item:

Since the subject of clustering *is vast, and we can't cover it in its entirety, we offer an overview of* clustering *algorithms according to* cluster *structure,* cluster *data type, and data size.*

Then, for 'cluster' term frequency is *TF=4,* for 'algorithm' *TF=1* and for 'data' *TF=2*. It is obvious that in the whole document about clustering will be much more appearances of term 'cluster' than in the one sentence just as an example above. On the other hand, number of occurrences is not proper measure of text item significance. Such problems are solved in different ways; one of them is normalization of *TF* by maximum term weight in text item:

$$NTF_t = a + (1 - a) * \frac{TF_t}{TF_{\max}}, \tag{1}$$

where TF_{max} represents *TF* of term which has maximum number of occurrences. Corrective value *a* (smoothing term) is added to the expression for controlling the influence of TF_{max} on *NTF* value. Next chart shows the effects of different values of *a* (Figure 3).

Another smoothing technique is by using logarithmic instead linear function:

$$LTF_t = \log(TF_t) + 1, \tag{2}$$

where *LTF* is logarithmic representation of real TF (TF>0) (Figure 4).

This way, the growth of LTF is higher for few than for numerous occurrences of term. Owing to non-linear representation of *TF* the undesired behavior (for example: the text which has 10 occurrences of term has 10 times more significance than one which has just one occurrence) is eliminated.

Inverse Document Frequency

Defining of term relevance is important for clustering. The more items that contain the term the less relevance the term has. Therefore, the new criteria had to be included - *IDF* (inverse document frequency) (Church & Gale, 1999). *IDF* is expressed by non-linear logarithmic function for a given set of *N* text items:

$$IDF_t = \log\left(\frac{N}{df_t}\right), \tag{3}$$

Figure 3. Normalized term frequency with different values of smoothing factor

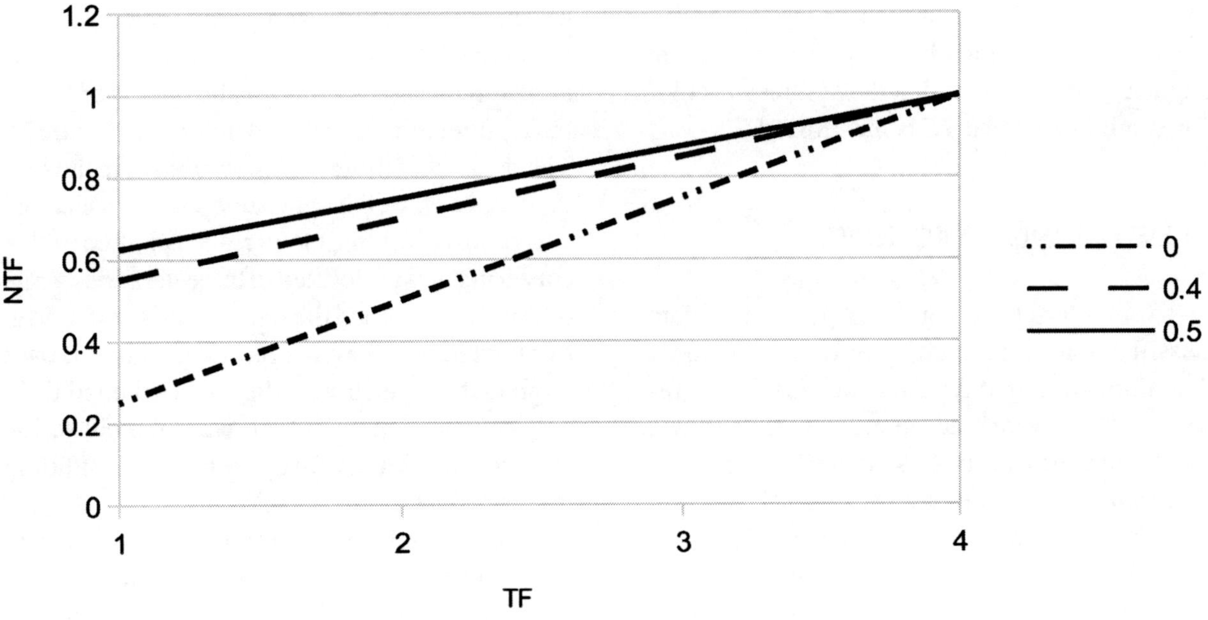

Figure 4. Behavior of LTF depending on TF value

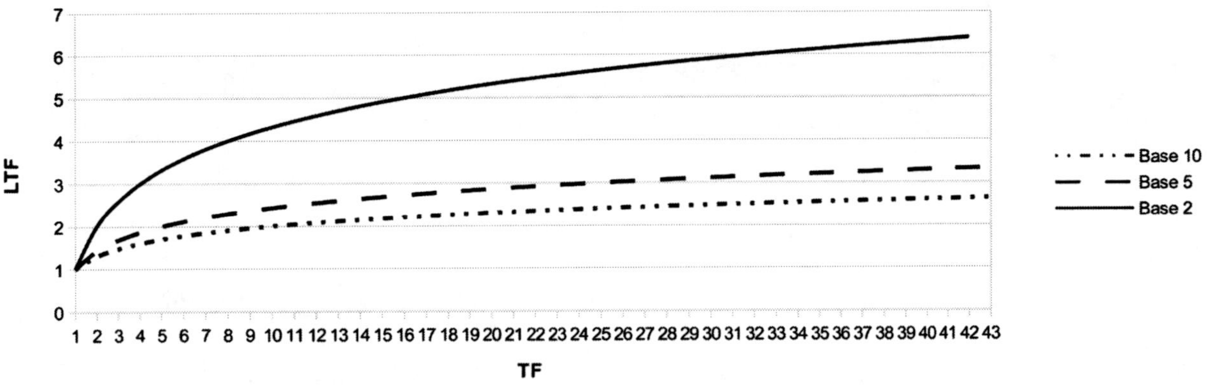

where *df* (document frequency) is number of text items that contain term *t*. IDF value is defined for each term in particular text item and it is declining as the number of text items containing *t* in the set growing up.

TFIDF: Combination of Previous Two

Due to different purposes of TF and IDF and opposite effects they produce, the text items can be better qualified by using both of them in the same time. Therefore, the new measure is used for term weighting and it is labeled as *TFIDF* (Yang & Chute, 1994). It is calculated as a scalar product of *TF* and *IDF*:

$$TFIDF = TF * IDF\ , \tag{4}$$

Term weight has a zero value for either *TF* or *IDF*. Instead of *TF*, the values of *NTF* or *LTF* can be used. Next two charts (Figure 6) show dependence of *TFIDF* regarding to applied *TF* function (linear / logarithm TF) and document frequency. It is obvious that the best results are if *DF* is minimized and *TF* is maximized.

CLUSTERING TAXONOMIES

Motivation for clustering lies in problem of data classification without sufficient knowledge about the information that the data contains. Many research efforts were made in order to solve such a problem and provide better searching capabilities, data mining or pattern recognition. All of them describe one of numerous approaches used. For better understanding of such complex subject matter the clustering taxonomy represents the start point of more detailed considerations. The most completed one is in (Jain, Murty & Flynn, 1999) in which hierarchical and partitioned clustering represent the two basic approaches. The process of hierarchical clustering can be presented by the binary tree structure called dendogram (Figure 5). The same set of the text items is used as in illustration above as well as the same way in which the clustering performed on. In case of agglomerative clustering, it is performed in three iterations while by divisive clustering the same effect is produced in two iterations in the example. Generally, it is hard to predict in which way the satisfied conditions will be met sooner. In both ways the clustering is performed iteratively by merging of / splitting into two clusters per iteration.

The hierarchical clustering is mentioned in almost all of literature and research papers due to its obviousness that in such approach the clusters are linked and they form tree structure in two ways:

Figure 5. Hierarchical clustering

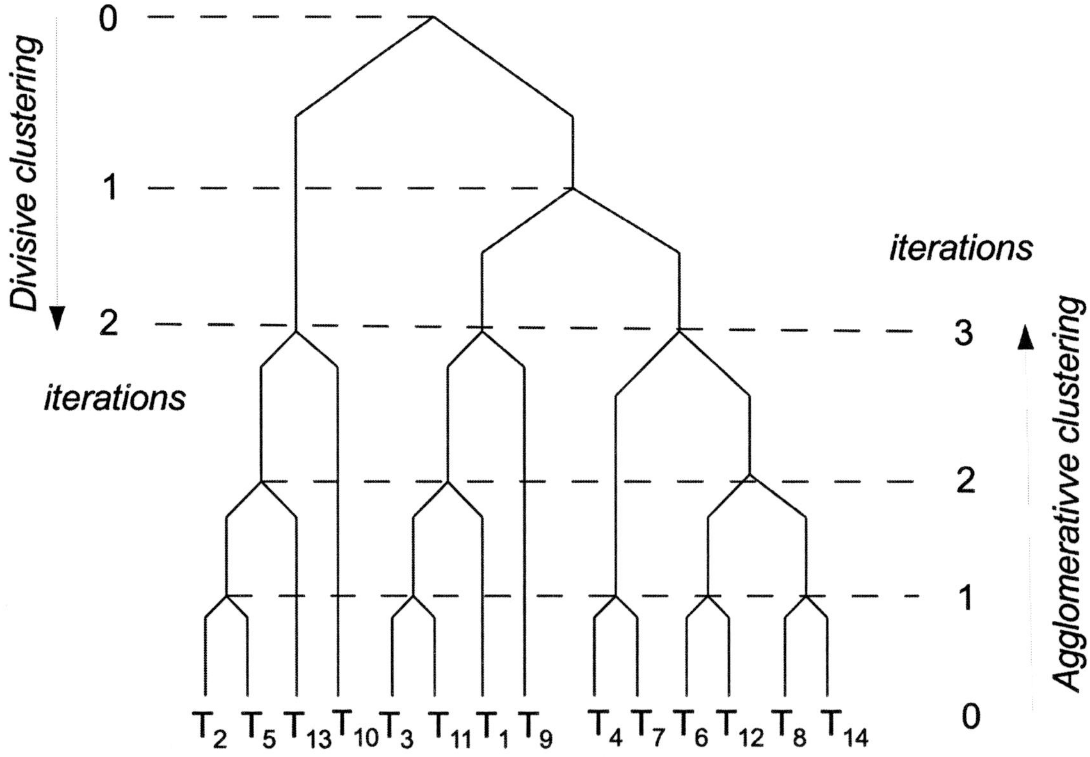

Figure 6. Bottom up hierarchical clustering

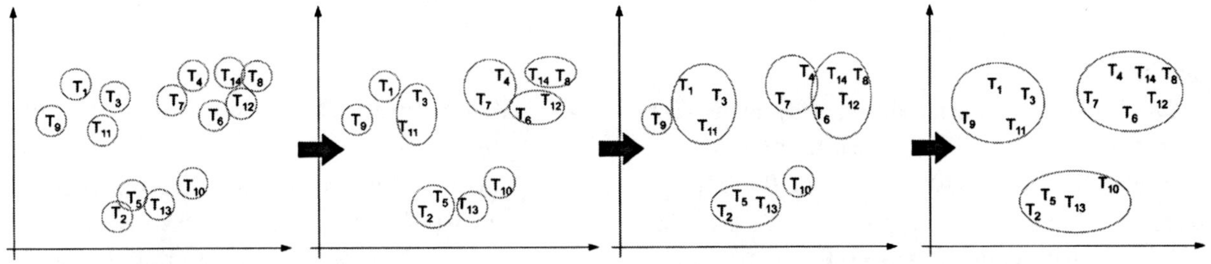

- Agglomerative clustering, and
- Divisive clustering.

Agglomerative Hierarchical Clustering

Agglomerative hierarchical 'Bottom up' clustering (Figure 6) represents repeating process in which the new cluster is formed by linking of two or more others. The new one replaces previous ones. The merging process repeatedly continues until finishing criteria is satisfied and the tree structure is formed as its result.

There are several types of agglomerative clustering:

- **Single Link Clustering:** Depends on similarity criteria: the most similar clusters ('nearest neighbors') are linked to each other.
- **Complete Link Clustering:** Based on the longest distance (dissimilarity) between clusters to be merged.
- **Average Link Clustering:** Includes all of the distances between items of clusters for calculating of average value and two clusters whose average distance is minimal will be merged.

Divisive Hierarchical Clustering

Divisive hierarchical clustering, or so called 'top down' approach in which the whole data set is considered as one cluster; following the criteria the new clusters are produced by 'splitting' the previous one(s), the process repeatedly continues but in the opposite direction than in 'bottom up' approach—the result is the same in structure and it lasts until finishing criteria is satisfied. There are two types of divisive clustering (Rijsbergen, 1979):

- **Monothetic Divisive Clustering:** Iterative splitting items into new pairs of clusters based on the 'same' values of criteria. As a final outcome, the clusters are represented as conjunctions of criteria.
- **Polythetic Divisive Clustering:** Includes all criteria in the splitting process simultaneously: there are more so called cut levels in.

Partition Clustering

While hierarchical clustering is based on connectivity between entities to be clustered (single / complete / average links), iterative process of splitting (divisive) or merging (agglomerative) clusters until specified conditions are satisfied, the partition clustering is based on predefined number of clusters in which the items are to be clustered in. Also there are no links formed between clusters. There are neither merging nor splitting of them. They (clusters) are formed ad-hoc by using one of the measures of central tendency. The name 'partition' is due to the clusters acts as partitions in the 2D space (flat) model that changes their shape and their mutual boundaries but their number remains the same (Figure 7). Therefore, in some research documents partition clustering is called flat clustering.

The common representation is by using 2D space. Partition clustering also has iterative nature. Basically, the centroids (crosses in the Figure 16) are used in partitioning process. The process includes both objective functions for determining the cluster boundaries and recalculation of centroids until the clusters' boundaries are stabilized. Partition clustering is suitable for large document collections due to their low computational requirements regarding to hierarchical clustering.

Clustering Based on Text Representation

For the text clustering there is another taxonomy based on how the text is represented and processed (Zheng, Cheng, Huang, & Man, 2006). This way there are three levels of text representation and clustering:

- **Word Based Clustering:** This is the simplest one depending on text segmentation into particular words for determination of key words and statistical processing after; this type of clustering is appropriate for automatically text processing.
- **Knowledge Based Clustering:** Predefined domain ontology is needed; with this knowledge the text can be processed and clustered efficiently; there are some disadvantages such as narrow specialization and dependence of quality of domain model (ontology).
- **Information Based Clustering:** Extracting of information from the text content to be clustered; for this purpose

Figure 7. Partition clustering

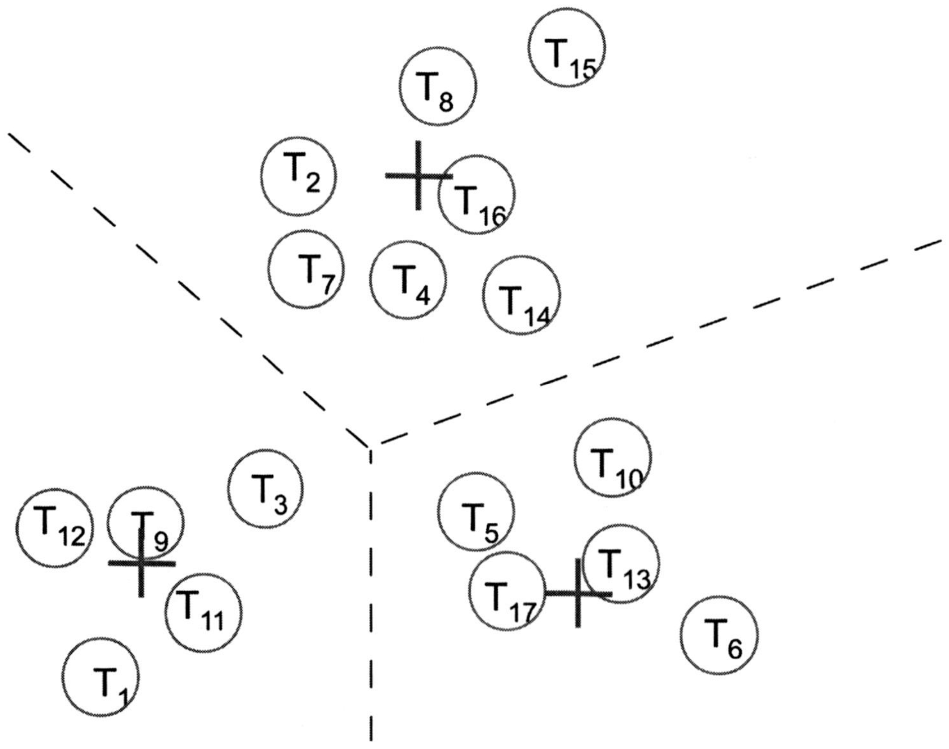

the system performs the semantic analysis of text segments and phrases and makes the conclusions about the information that are hold.

In a context of automatic taxonomy construction and depending on how the information can be derived from the whole set of text items there is another classification of clustering (Cimiano, Hotho & Staab, 2013):

- Clustering based on similarity measurement, and
- Clustering based on set theory.

Clustering Based on Set Theory

All classifications mentioned above imply the use of different similarity measures for clustering. However, the next classification which depends on set theory is different. It has become interesting owing to growing use of fuzzy clustering. Such classification depends on membership function which expresses the degree of belonging of particular text item to some cluster. This way the membership function is used as clustering criteria (Conrad, Al-Kofahi, Zhao & Karypis, 2005). There are two approaches, basically:

- 'Hard' clustering, and
- 'Soft' clustering.

Hard clustering represents conventional approach based on 'traditional' set theory. It means that an entity can belong to only one cluster; Clustering is performed in discrete manner. Both hierarchical agglomerative and divisive clustering belong to hard clustering class. Partition clustering could belong to either hard or soft clustering class. All of the examples previously presented are 'hard' clustered due to discrete values which are used as clustering criteria. Regardless of changing the boundaries of partitions during the clustering process, 'partition hard clustering' exactly means that items to be clustered belong to single cluster.

In the matrix in Figure 8, 'hard' clustering is expressed by membership function. If an item belongs to the cluster its value is 1, otherwise is 0. There are 8 items (T1-T8) and 5 clusters (c1 - c5). In presented example it is obvious that the items would be clustered as: c1={T4, T6}, c2={T5}, c3={T2,T7}, c4={T3} and c5={T1,T8}.

Soft clustering represents approach in which the clusters can be mutually overlapped. Other words an item can belong to more than one cluster. For instance, such flexibility could be useful for document bases where one document covers (belongs to) several topics or categories. Soft clustering is based on fuzzy set theory for 'soft' clusters act as fuzzy sets. Owing to concept of membership function it is possible for each item to express the degree of membership to every particular cluster. The next example illustrates the soft clustering of 8 items into 5 clusters (Figure 9). The values in the cells of matrix represent the membership function values. For instance, item T1 belongs to c1 with degree 0.15 and to c5 with 0.85 while T4 belongs to almost all clusters in some degree: c1 with 0.64, c2 with 0.31, c4 with 0.05 and c5 with

Figure 8. Hard clustering

		Clusters				
		c1	c2	c3	c4	c5
Items	T1	0	0	0	0	1
	T2	0	0	1	0	0
	T3	0	0	0	1	0
	T4	1	0	0	0	0
	T5	0	1	0	0	0
	T6	1	0	0	0	0
	T7	0	0	1	0	0
	T8	0	0	0	0	1

Figure 9. Soft clustering

		Clusters				
		c1	c2	c3	c4	c5
Items	T1	0.15	0	0	0	0.85
	T2	0	0.1	0.9	0	0
	T3	0	0	0.2	0.8	0
	T4	0.6	0.3	0	0.05	0.05
	T5	0	0.9	0	0	0.1
	T6	0.85	0.15	0	0	0
	T7	0	0.13	0.71	0.16	0
	T8	0	0	0.11	0.42	0.47

0.05. It is obvious that membership values can be considered as weights and this way each item can be presented by term weights vector: T1={0.15, 0, 0, 0, 0.85} or T1={(c1,0.15),(c5,0.85)}.

Based on considerations in this section and previous one it could be concluded that the hard clustering represented special case of soft clustering regarding to the values of membership function. Its value varies in range [0,1]. In hard clustering only the limit values are used (0,1).

TEXT CLUSTERING ALGORITHMS

Two representative clustering algorithms are presented in this section. They depend on the basic concepts used for content representation and can be used for different clustering needs. This way K-means clustering is designed for 'hard' clustering while fuzzy c-mean is appropriate for 'soft' clustering. Throughout this section the similarity measures, measures of central tendencies are in focus.

K-Means

K-means is used in partition clustering that means the number of clusters is predefined and it is labeled with K. In other words, there is K sets in which the items are clustered to. Also there are K dimensions considered during the clustering process. K-means technique is based on distances between data points and referent point of cluster. The cluster centroids (geometrical centers of 2D regions) are commonly used for this purpose. Their positions are changeable during the iterations in order to minimize the sum of squares within the clusters. If there are K clusters and *N* items, the sum of squares (SS) can be calculated by the next equation:

$$SS = \sum_{i=1}^{K}\sum_{j=1}^{N}\left(w_j - \overline{w_i}\right)^2, \qquad (5)$$

where:

- w_j represents the weight of the *j*-th item in the *i*-th cluster, and
- w_i represents the mean (centroid of the *i*-th cluster).

Centroid represents the geometric center of the region (cluster) and if there is finite set of points (items in the cluster), in accordance with the expression above, it is calculated as arithmetic mean value:

$$\overline{w_i} = \frac{1}{n}\sum_{j=1}^{N} w_j, \qquad (6)$$

where *N* is the number of items in the cluster and each item is represented by its weight w_j. The results calculated by equations 5 and 6 are used for SS minimization. It means that SS represents an objective function that is recalculated through iterations until the goal is not satisfied (e.g. until the centroid value is the same in two consecutive iterations. If there are K clusters, for the first iteration K items (seed) are declared as centroids randomly or by some rule (pseudo-randomly). There are two methods for creating *K* means seed mentioned in literature – Random (Hamerly &

Elkan, 2002) and Forgy (Garijo, Riquelme & Toro, 2002) partition. This initialization influences on a final form of clusters. Forgy partition randomly declares K items and it tries to spread the centroids out of the items. Random partition declares K fictive centers and assigns the items to them. Then the real centroids of initial clusters are calculated. This method tries to make the centroids closer to each one (make them convergent).

Both of Random and Forgy partition, regardless of different initialization effects are not optimized (Elkan, 2004). Therefore, there are other initialization methods developed. One of them is Furthest First (FF) (Hochbaum & Shmoys, 1985). The basic description is: the first centroid is randomly defined and the next one is the point of furthest distance of the first, the third one is the furthest point of both and this process repeats until the K centroids are determined.

After the initialization the clusters are formed for the first time and they are empty. The first iteration starts by calculating the distances of each item from all of the centroids. This is performed iteratively and after that the item will belong to the cluster whose centroid is the closest to. This way the clusters are filled with the items and the next is the correction of initial centroids depending on the values of the items that belong to cluster.

It is performed by recalculation of the centroids for each cluster (Equation 6). As a result of this processing the new centroids are determined due to the items assigned to the initial clusters. The next iteration can start by repeating of the first step - the recalculation of the distances of each item from all of the new formed centroids (Equation 5) and their assignment to the closest ones (clusters).

Practically, this is a process of alternative assignment (items to centroids) and update (centroids) steps which represent the algorithm called same as method - K-means algorithm. It lasts until both of two conditions are satisfied:

- There are changes of centroids' positions, and
- Maximum number of iterations is not reached.

The second condition is the safety one; it protects the system in the case of small K number and huge number of items in which it is likely to be many iterations and lot of calculations.

Fuzzy C-Mean

Fuzzy C-mean (FCM) is a 'soft' version of K-means algorithm. Although there are several techniques and algorithms based on fuzzy logic and fuzzy set theory is the very popular one (Bezdek, 1981 & Dunn, 1973). In FCM the membership function plays the main role enabling the one item can belong to more than one cluster with some degree. For instance, if there are 3 clusters that the particular item belongs to, than there are 3 values associated to the item that represent the degree of membership to the clusters. Their sum is 1 due to membership values in range [0, 1]. This way K-means hard clustering represents the special case of the soft clustering based on fuzzy set theory. Further, expressions used in K-means are modified for more general approach:

$$FCM = \sum_{i=1}^{K} \sum_{j=1}^{N} m_{ij} \left(w_j - \overline{w_i} \right)^2 , \tag{7}$$

where m_{ij} represents membership function that puts in the relation between the item *j* and cluster *i*. In hard clustering $m_{ij} \in \{0,1\}$. Otherwise the membership value is $m_{ij} \in R, 0 \le m_{ij} \le 1$. In the visual representation the items that belong to more than one cluster belong to their intersections (Figure 10).

For instance, in the illustration above both of items T_3, and T_{11} belong to both of clusters C_1 and

Figure 10. Soft clustering set representation

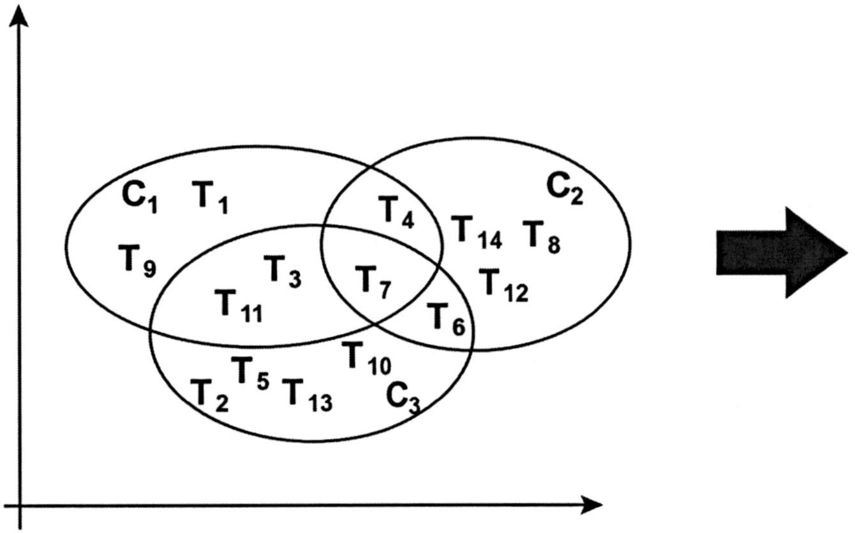

Items	Clusters c1	c2	c3
T1	1	0	0
T2	0	0	1
T3	0.8	0	0.2
T4	0.64	0.36	0
T5	0	0	1
T6	0	0.72	0.28
T7	0.21	0.17	0.62
T8	0	1	0
T9	1	0	0
T10	0	0	1
T11	0.34	0	0.66
T12	0	1	0
T13	0	0	1
T14	0	1	0

C_3 while item T_7 belongs to C_1, C_2 and C_3, and so on. The degrees of membership for particular items ($T_1 - T_{14}$) to the clusters ($C_1 - C_3$) are given as cell values in the matrix on the right hand side. Membership function can be calculated in different ways. One of the most mentioned approaches taken from (Babu & Murt, 1994) and adapted to chapter content is:

$$m_{ij} = \frac{1}{\sum_{k=1}^{K} \left(\frac{dist\left(w_j, \overline{w_i}\right)}{dist\left(w_j, \overline{w_k}\right)} \right)^{\frac{1}{m-1}}}, \qquad (8)$$

where, like in the previous expressions m_{ij} represents membership function of item j for cluster i, w_i is weight of item i, K is number of clusters, while w_i and w_k represent centroids of considered cluster i and cluster k. Finally, there is fuzzy modifier m with purpose to change the fuzziness behavior. The relations between distances (*dist*) represent the basic principle of the equation (8). More precisely, the distance between item j and centroid of cluster i is divided with distance of the same item with the centroids of other clusters. The reciprocal value of sum of these fractions represents the membership function. Regardless of more general approach, by its introducing the complexity of clustering is increased.

STRUCTURED NATURE OF THE CONTENT

From the global prospective, there are several document formats publicly used for representing e-Government content. Depending on the official data collected from the different countries' regulations, the most accepted one is the *Open Document* format (ODF, ISO/IEC 26300). This standard is developed by Organization for the Advancement of Structured Information Standards (OASIS). ODF formatted document is XML structured. It could be in form of archive document (*odt* file extension) or of flat document (*fodt* file extension). Prefix open means that the standard is fully transparent. It helps everyone who wants to build applications for manipulating the documents in any way. Next is a part of official document which represents the 'Law of Labor' and which is *fodt* formatted—as a flat open document (Figure 11).

Figure 11. Part of 'Law of Labor' ODF formatted document

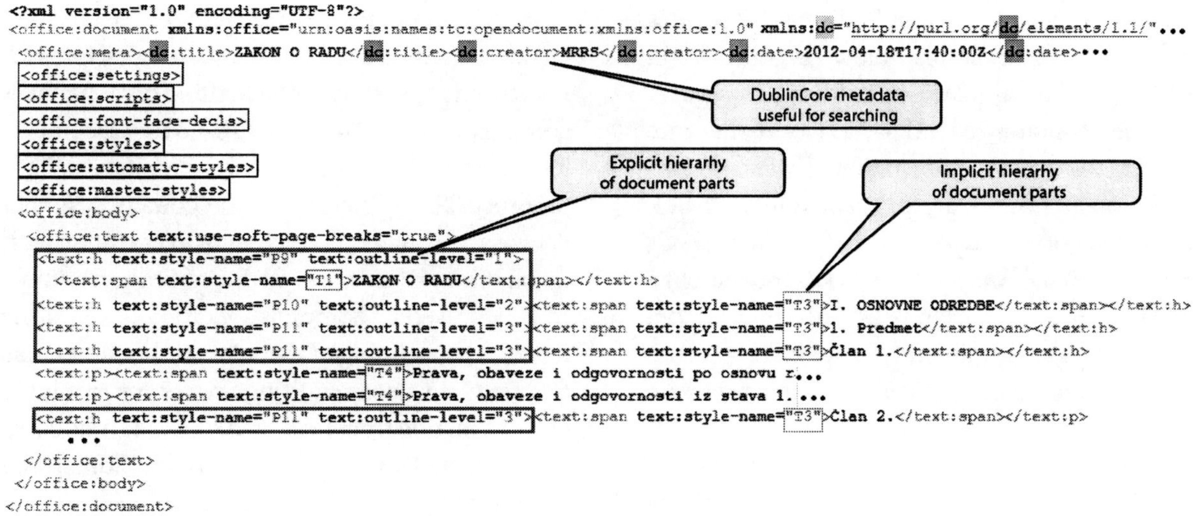

It is obvious that the file has *office:document* as a root XML element. Metadata are stored in *office:meta* element. ODF includes different ways to store metadata. Commonly accepted Dublin Core (*dc* namespace) specification is partially used: *Title, Creator, Description, Subject, Date* and *Language* are found to be relevant in *odt* and *fodt* documents (more details about *dc* could be found further in this section).

Whole content of the document is stored in *office:body* element. The law documents are usually consisted of pure textual content and therefore *office:text* element is only used. In the presented example, content is separated into the text paragraphs regardless of the content type: title, subtitles and sections. These parts are different only in formatting (text style). This way the document title has T1 style, section title – T2, article number – T3 and article content – T4. These are the only data for structure based on differentiating of the content parts. Therefore, such document organization is characterized as 'flat' one – in the hierarchy all of them are at the same level in XML document tree. Contemporary text processors that support ODF put in the document metadata information useful for searching and clustering. Dublin Core specification is commonly used for this purpose. In the 3rd row of the example above, there are several tags with the *dc* prefix – the Dublin Core namespace. This general purpose framework is designed for describing the resources and providing their better searching capabilities. Dublin Core schema (DCM, ISO 15836:2009) is a set of metadata consisting of 15 elements – fields: *Title, Creator, Subject, Description, Publisher, Contributor, Date, Type, Format, Identifier, Source, Language, Relation, Coverage* and *Rights*. This international standard has been wide accepted since 2000. Although, the most of the e-Government systems develop their own standards (more or less based on, or similar to DCM), still there is no specification for describing e-Government documents.

Apart from metadata, the ODF content is well-structured into headings of different levels (*text:h* tags) and paragraphs (*text:p* tags). Headings hold titles and their subtitles and paragraphs of content. Such document organization enables text analysis considering the titles and subtitles as parts of domain structure as well as descriptions of related content.

Another format commonly used is Office Open XML (OOXML, ISO/IEC 29500) developed by Microsoft. This format is similar to previous one and for comparing purposes, the same document ('Law of Labor') formatted in Open XML, is presented in the example below (Figure 12). In OOXML the document is considered as a package which contains several parts. Two of them are shown in the example: document (*document.xml*) which consists of document's text content (titles, subtitles, sections and paragraphs) and document's properties (*core.xml*) which holds document's metadata. Similar to the usage of Dublin Core standard (tags with dc prefixes) which provides the document searching and indexing based on metadata in the ODF.

Owing to well-structured content (*Title, Subtitle, Emphasis* and simple content) the text analysis can be performed in the same way as in ODF documents. Unfortunately, in OOXML documents the different formatting models (schemas) are used in order to provide export of specific MS Office formatted documents into the open formats. It resulted in overload of formatting data. It makes comparing of ODF and OOXML documents based on their structure more complex and the preprocessing (filtering) of the content becomes necessary. Using only metadata in considering is not at the satisfactory level due to limited number of fields used in common specification (Dublin Core). The mapping of metadata fields, other than Dublin Core, needs additional work for providing transformation from ODF and OOXML into some common and more general format. Sometimes such efforts produce loss of information important for analysis due to moving the process to more abstract level.

Figure 12. Part of 'Law of Labor' OOXML formatted document

```
<?xml version="1.0" encoding="UTF-8" standalone="yes"?>
<?mso-application progid="Word.Document"?>
<pkg:package xmlns:pkg="http://schemas.microsoft.com/office/2006/xmlPackage">
    <pkg:part>
    <pkg:part>
    <pkg:part pkg:name="/word/document.xml" pkg:contentType="application/vnd.openxmlfor
        <pkg:xmlData>
            <w:document mc:Ignorable="w14 wp14" xmlns:wpc="http://schemas.micr
                <w:body>
                    <w:p w:rsidR="007C4376" w:rsidRPr="007C4376" w:rsidRD     ="007C43'
                        <w:pPr><w:pStyle w:val="Title"/></w:pPr>
                        <w:r w:rsidRPr="007C4376"> <w:t>ZAKON O   DU</w:t> </w:r>
                    </w:p>
                    <w:p w:rsidR="007C4376" w:rsidRPr="007C4376" w:rsidRDefault="007C4376" w:rsidP="00E26338">
                        <w:pPr><w:pStyle w:val="Subtitle"/></w:pPr>
                        <w:r w:rsidRPr="007C4376"><w:t>I. OSNOVNE ODREDBE</w:t></w:r>
                    </w:p>
                    <w:p w:rsidR="007C4376" w:rsidRPr="00E26338" w:rsidRDefault="007C4376" w:rsidP="007C4376">
                        <w:pPr> <w:rPr><w:rStyle w:val="Emphasis"/></w:rPr></w:pPr>
                        <w:r w:rsidRPr="00E26338"> <w:t>1. Predmet</w:t></w:r>
                    </w:p>
                    ...
    <pkg:part pkg:name="/docProps/core.xml" pkg:contentType="application/vnd.openxmlformats-package.cc
        <pkg:xmlData>
            <cp:coreProperties xmlns:cp="http://schemas.openxmlformats.org/package/2006/metadata/core-
                <dc:title>ZAKON O RADU</dc:title>
                <dc:creator>MRRS</dc:creator>
                <cp:lastModifiedBy>MRRS</cp:lastModifiedBy>
                <cp:revision>2</cp:revision>
                <dcterms:created xsi:type="dcterms:W3CDTF">2012-04-18T22:42:00Z</dcterms:created>
                <dcterms:modified xsi:type="dcterms:W3CDTF">2012-04-18T22:42:00Z</dcterms:modified>
            </cp:coreProperties>
        </pkg:xmlData>
    </pkg:part>
```

Explicit hierarhy of document parts

DublinCore metadata useful for searching

One more commonly used format is extension of Portable Document Format designed for preservation of e-documents (PDF/A, ISO 19005). This self-contained format inhered lot of advanced characteristics of PDF specification. Regardless of its complexity, PDF/A document represent the structure split into head, body, cross reference table and ending trailer. The content useful for searching is comprised as a hierarchy of objects in a body part. The root element is document's catalog. Basically, it is dictionary which contains key value pairs that describe the document structure. The most of the objects in document hierarchy are dictionaries. For instance, each page of document is represented by page object – dictionary which contains references to all of the page content as well as its annotations. The parent node to each page object is page tree – node which represents document's sub-tree object (Figure 13).

Page object has child nodes such as content streams and annotations. Outline hierarchy clarifies the structure of the document's content. It can be automatically extracted in creation time by using bookmarks – sections' tags formed by navigating key values (e.g. previous, next, parent, first, last, count, destination, etc.). PDF document can contain the hyperlinks – references to the other PDF documents. Named destinations objects are used for this purpose.

Apart from descriptions made by using dictionaries, PDF/A document as well as its parts can be described by metadata (since PDF version 1.4). For searching purposes PDF document should be described with so – called metadata streams. Metadata streams are built in descriptions of the PDF document. They can describe both document as a whole and its parts (objects it consists of). Metadata streams are usually positioned in the last part of the document before the trailer. They represent the separate objects in the document and they are recognizable due to dictionary they have with the two additional entries *Type*: *Metadata* and *Subtype: XML*. The example below shows the metadata stream object with id = 48 0 which describes the 'Law of Labor' document (Figure 14).

The information content of PDF documents is fragmented and represented by byte streams regardless its nature (pure textual content or illus-

Figure 13. PDF document structure

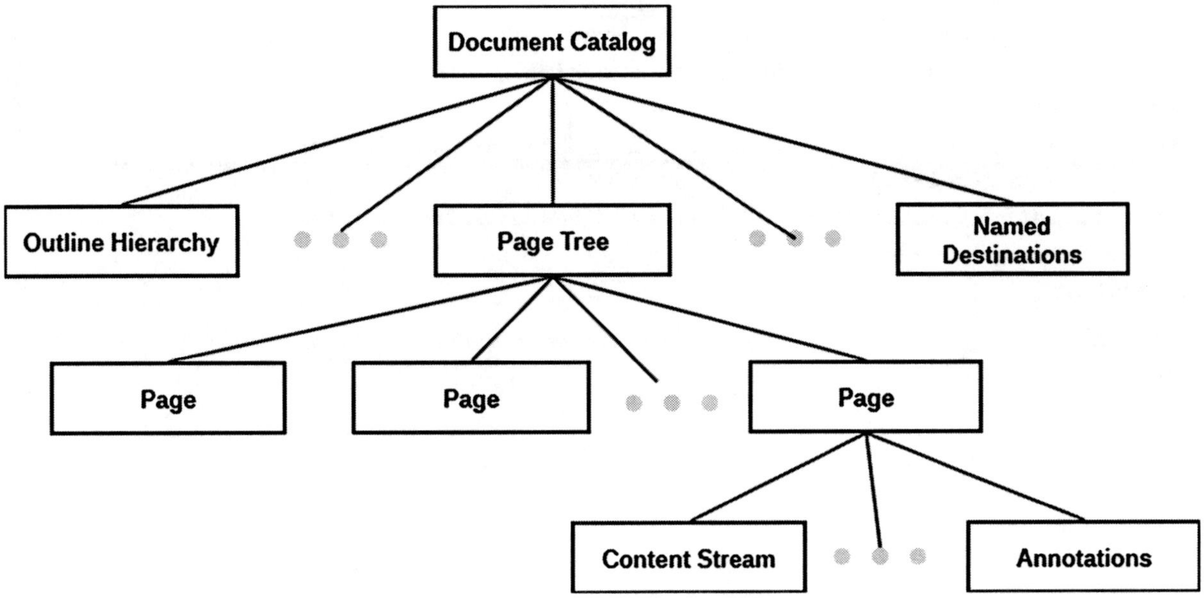

Figure 14. Metadata stream of PDF document

```
48 0 obj
<</Type/Metadata/Subtype/XML/Length 3395>>
stream
<?xpacket begin="???" id="W5M0MpCehiHzreSzNTczkc9d"?>
<x:xmpmeta xmlns:x="adobe:ns:meta/">
 <rdf:RDF xmlns:rdf="http://www.w3.org/1999/02/22-rdf-syntax-ns#">
  <rdf:Description xmlns:pdfaid="http://www.aiim.org/pdfa/ns/id/">
   <pdfaid:part>1</pdfaid:part>
   <pdfaid:conformance>A</pdfaid:conformance>
  </rdf:Description>
  <rdf:Description xmlns:dc="http://purl.org/dc/elements/1.1/">
   <dc:title>
    <rdf:Alt>
     <rdf:li xml:lang="x-default">Zakon o radu</rdf:li>
    </rdf:Alt>
   </dc:title>
   <dc:creator>
    <rdf:Seq>
     <rdf:li>MRRS</rdf:li>
    </rdf:Seq>
   </dc:creator>
   <dc:description>
    <rdf:Alt>
     <rdf:li xml:lang="x-default">Zakon o pravima i obavezama radnika</rdf:li>
    </rdf:Alt>
   </dc:description>
  </rdf:Description>
  <rdf:Description xmlns:pdf="http://ns.adobe.com/pdf/1.3/">
   <pdf:Producer>LibreOffice 4.0</pdf:Producer>
   <pdf:Keywords>zakon o radu, zakon o mobingu, ustav</pdf:Keywords>
  </rdf:Description>
  <rdf:Description xmlns:xmp="http://ns.adobe.com/xap/1.0/">
   <xmp:CreatorTool>Writer</xmp:CreatorTool>
   <xmp:CreateDate>2014-04-28T20:37:53+02:00</xmp:CreateDate>
  </rdf:Description>
 </rdf:RDF>
</x:xmpmeta>
<?xpacket end="w"?>
endstream
endobj
```

tration). Therefore, in order to improve searching capabilities, metadata streams are used. They are stored in separate XML formatted part of document and they are readable even for applications that cannot parse the rest of PDF formatted content. In the example above, the scripts marked with red rectangles enclose the descriptions useful for searching. As in ODF and OOXML documents, Dublin Core specification is used (the first rectangle). Other metadata standards are also applicable. For instance, key words entry is made by using PDF specification. Metadata are machine interpretable due to namespace specified for each format used in document.

The clustering is always much easier if the content is well-described. The amount of data to be processed is less incomparable than in the case of analyzing the whole document content. Regardless of prevailing formatting data in ODF and especially in OOXML documents, it is much easier to process the content by using XML parsers, extracting the data useful for clustering than to consider the plain text in order to find similarity between documents based on different statistical measures. On the other hand, PDF/A is often dominant format used for creating e-Government documents due to its protection of document credibility and authenticity. Moreover, PDF/A is designed to obtain long time durability due to its platform independence provided by self-contained resources (font specification, referencing, etc.).

Beside the published formal documents, contemporary e-government portals provide the services that enable the citizens to explain the problem they have or information they are interested in. These services are offered in form of forums and social blogs where the information exchange is performed through instant messaging or as a simple mail service in which the citizens' requests and institutional responses are sent by e-mails. Due to Web availability, especially through the mobile platforms (tablets and smart phones), the number of users grows fast and data exchanged form big data collections stored commonly in database tables. They can be reused for the future interaction due to lots of similar content. Unfortunately, this content is almost flat: selecting the category usually represents the only way in which the citizen can better describe its request. Citizens often select the wrong category, request can belong to more than one category, or even more, they cannot decide which category their requests belong to. For these reasons, the clustering represents the part of solution for improving the quality of e-government services. In the next illustration (Figure 15) the database table designed for storing messages in an e-government service is shown.

The candidate fields that can be useful for searching and clustering are topic id, subject and message body. The fragment represents the interaction between two users in where one of them is asking for information about the documents he should have for school enrolment and other one responds by information based on his experience. It is obvious that the field values for topic id and subject are the same. Therefore, except general categorization, these fields are not relevant for extracting detailed information from the content. Only body field is useful for this purpose. Moreover there are similar contents that can be

Figure 15. Example of the message thread in an e-government service

ID_MSG	ID_TOPIC	posterTime	ID_MEMBER	subject	posterName	posterEmail	posterIP	body
896	4	1181851962	64	Odg: Diskusije na temu upisa	Diamond	diamond....	194.10...	[quote author=boka link=topic=4.msg894#msg894
897	4	1181852128	49	Odg: Diskusije na temu upisa	boka	bokadin_...	77.46....	hvala na savetu,ali gde da nadjem?
898	4	1181852180	49	Odg: Diskusije na temu upisa	boka	bokadin_...	77.46....	nisam imao istoriju,tehnicki 2 godine,ali realno 4!pa
899	4	1181852306	64	Odg: Diskusije na temu upisa	Diamond	diamond....	194.10...	Ima┼í http://www.kpa.edu.yu/diskusije/index.php
900	4	1181852394	49	Odg: Diskusije na temu upisa	boka	bokadin_...	77.46....	zato sto geografiju nisam imao uopste... zavrsio sam
901	4	1181852479	64	Odg: Diskusije na temu upisa	Diamond	diamond....	194.10...	Napisala sam ti onda gde da se obrati┼í! :m

grouped regardless of topics and subjects used. Therefore, the clustering represents appropriate approach for it. The formatting data found in body field represent additional problem. The content should be cleared of these extra data that could produce the 'information noise' during the clustering process. The presented example points out the common structure frequently used for holding both instant messages and e-mails.

In the most of the formats presented above, XML is used for representing structured content. There are lots of tools providing fast and easy parsing of XML structured data and obtaining efficiently navigation and inspecting the content inside as well as related content. Regardless of the structured nature of documents and other content used, due to lack of appropriate metadata, or improper composing of the documents, it is often necessary to transform the content for measuring the similarity and clustering data in order to provide higher quality of e-Government services. It is common that, according to approving procedures, the government institutions are publishing the documents periodically. The result is that in the same edition (publication) there are contents for different purposes and moreover, that belong to very different domains. This way in the same document can be found promotion decrees, law amendments, rule books, tax ranges and amounts. Therefore, the content should be preprocessed: separated, filtered and described by measured statistical values and only in this way clustering may obtain grouping related to information the content consist of.

In case of clustering of well described documents, it is possible to define the fields in which the content has to be sorted to. Fields are the parts of structured content such as title, abstract, author, keywords, sections, sub-sections, paragraphs, references and indexes. All of them are included into the clustering process and their influence on its result can be adapted by using additional (boosting) factors. This way the fields are not of the same importance for making decision about which cluster the content belongs to.

CLUSTERING IN ADVANSE: CASE STUDY

To clarify what exactly clustering means for information retrieval, in this section is presented ADVANSE (*ADVanced ANSwering Engine*) framework (Simic, Jeremic, Kajan, Randjelovic & Presnall, 2014) developed for improving e-Government services with the goal to reduce the time for answering the citizen's questions and to reduce the engagement of subject matter experts in this process. Apart from providing the transparency of their activities, publishing of documents and announcements, it is expected that e-Government services are capable for communication with the citizens. The interaction scenario which has been the most interested for research consists of the following:

- Citizen makes a request for specific information elaborating his specific case through the appropriate Web form,
- Official receives the request, examines citizen's request trying to discover the nature of the problem and sends it to specific domain expert, and
- Subject matter expert (SME) tries to make answer and respond in time.

Such features of e-government portals are not at appropriate level. Officials have difficulties in defining which category the request belongs to and in delivering it to the appropriate SME. Sometimes the request has to be decomposed due to more than one category included in. In this case request should be delivered to more than one SME. Citizens are often disappointed by the long responding time and / or inappropriate response. On the other hand, by the time, lots of citizens – e-Government communication data have been stored in the CMS. There are citizens' questions, comments, complaints and SME responses. They are stored in the same way as in the example described in previous section. Analyzing these data it is discovered that there is a lot of redundancy depending on domain (e.g. the most redundant are domains: education, tax regulations; the least ones are domains such as health care and law). Nevertheless, the average redundancy as well as weaknesses mentioned, gave us the motives for developing the ADVANCE framework.

Preparing Content for Clustering

There are various types of content useful for responding on citizens' requests. Generally, there are documents stored as files at the repository and messages saved in the databases. As mentioned, in both cases the content is hold within CMS and the main efforts are focused on providing the better searching capabilities for the citizens. It is easy to define general categories of the content (e.g. law, finance, health care, etc.) but hard to granulate it in specific subcategories. If there are lots of categories offered to the citizens, they are more confused which category their issues belong to. It implies possibility that the request could be wrongly addressed. On the other hand, without some sort of indexing and grouping, the searching capabilities descending during a time due to growing number of files and other data stored in the CMS. Therefore the clustering is used and the content had to be prepared for this process.

The clustering needs the content to be presented in the flat text due to analysis and measurement of the text parameters important for grouping (Section 2). Such processes need to eliminate all of the non-information content. It means that for instance, the PDF, XLS, DOC, DOCX, ODT and similar file formats need to be transformed in the pure text format. Contemporary CMS provide to the users the rich text formatting tools to compose messages by putting the tables, pictures and other multimedia content in them. Therefore, the same processing has to be performed on the database data. Fortunately, there are specialized software products designed for such a kind of text filtering. One of them is Tika framework (Mattmann & Zitting, 2012). Different operations on different document formats can be performed.

Word and PDF documents, Excel spreadsheets, HTML pages and other content based on XML formatting structure represent some of the formats that are supported. Framework is able to recognize the format due to reach media (MIME) types library built in distribution. Language detection and code pages used can also be automatically detected. Apart from filtering the pure text content, Tika is also used for extracting the metadata from the content (Figure 16). As a result there is also flat text content which consists of key – value pairs. There is support for Dublin Core specification, PDF metadata, RDF and many others. This way, various clustering approaches can be implemented. For instant, with messages and e-mails there is no need for such text extraction due to well-defined structure of tables that these data are stored in.

As mentioned, human readable text content consists of words that do not contain information relevant for clustering (articles, conjunctions, pronouns, etc.) commonly entitled stop words. Also there are characters such as periods, scores, brackets, quotes, hyphens and many others that are used in constructing of sentences. Such non–information content should also be removed before further analyzing. Furthermore, there are interesting words and phrases often presented in the form which is not appropriate for clustering. Therefore, they should be transformed into normalized form which implies singular, infinitive, present tense form with, or without suffixes and prefixes depending on meaning they hold. This complex processing is performed in analyzing phase. In the presented solution the *Lucene* framework is used for it (Hatcher, Gospodnetic

Figure 16. Text extraction

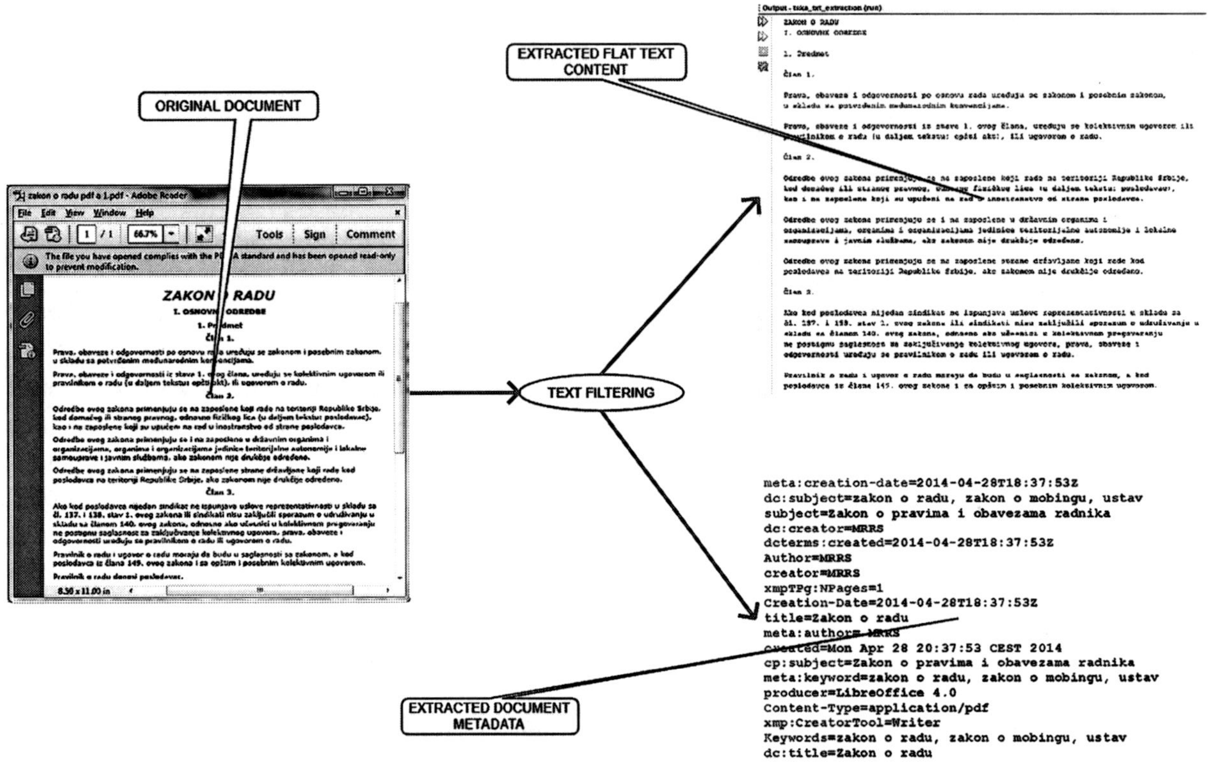

& McCandless, 2009), due to numerous analyzers and tokenizers that support different languages and alphabets which are already built. Moreover the new ones, adapted for Serbian language were developed. During analysis, the inverted indexing is performed for providing statistical data that describe the extracted text content for clustering purposes (Figure 17). That includes text normalization, creating the term vectors and term frequency measurement. Such information as term frequencies and term positions, necessary for creating Vector Space Model are collected.

The term vectors represent the outcomes of the analyzing process (*tvf* file in the *index* directory) which is appropriate as input format for clustering. Besides the frequencies, they hold references to the documents they belong to. This way, TF-IDF statistical values are calculated. The term positions are also included in the vector for analyzing common occurrences of two or more terms in the considered content (collocations). Beside the morphological transformation of the particular words in analyzed content, the *Lucene* framework provides recognizing of synonyms, abbreviations and aliases (steaming). As mentioned, the metadata are also extracted and separated from the rest of content. Although they can be analyzed in the same way as a regular content, more useful approach is to provide their transformation into common format ready for similarity measuring during the clustering process.

Content Clustering

The clustering represents one of the key processes in ADVANSE system. It improves advanced searching on huge data and document collections which implies that it improves the quality of e-government services. During extraction and analyzing phases, the term vectors are formed by

Figure 17. Basic concepts in analyzing phase

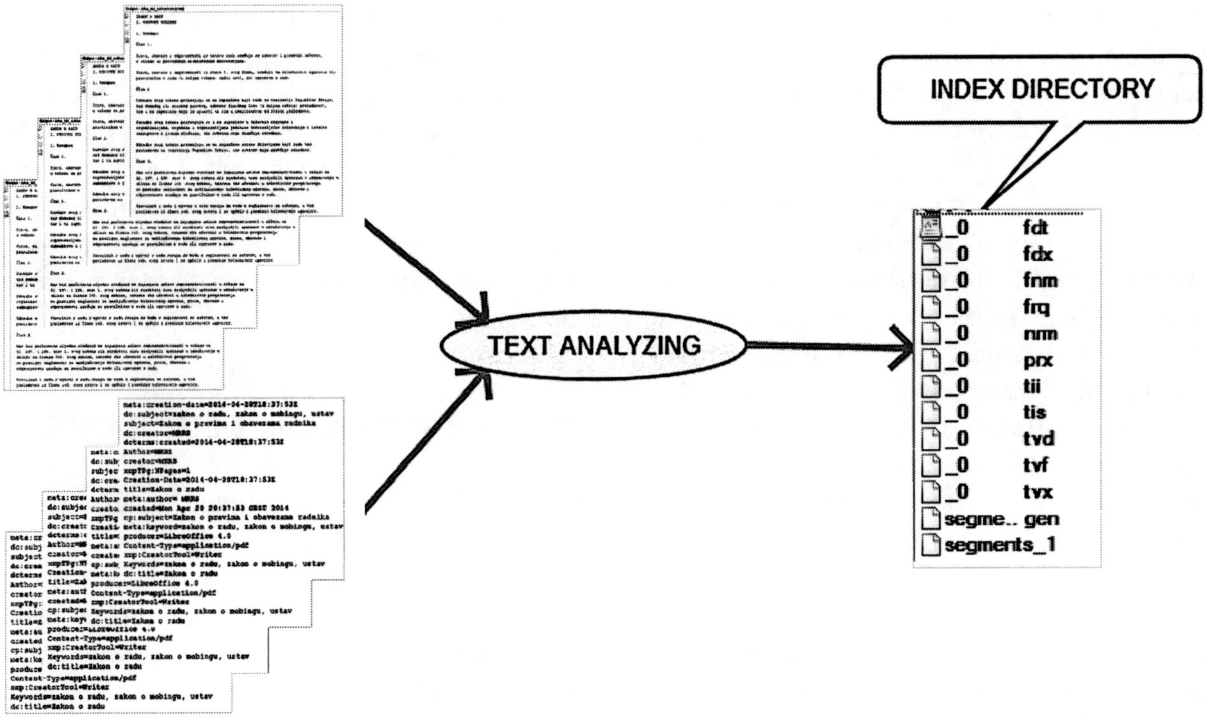

content of data and documents needed to be clustered. As described, there are many clustering techniques and algorithms. Finding appropriate one for clustering e-government data and documents represents big challenge due to great heterogeneity of formats used, different domains included and ways the content is combined (Section 5). There is need to provide the same resource that could be retrieved for different citizens' requests; moreover for questions about different domains. For providing better resolution and flexibility in responding to the citizens, modified Fuzzy C-mean algorithm (FCM) is used. Fuzzy approach means that the clusters are considered as fuzzy sets and the values can belong to more than one fuzzy set (cluster) in degree determined by membership function. FCM clustering function (Zou, Wang & Hu, 2008) is modified in ADVANSE (Equation 15) only by including the membership function m_{ij} of particular item x_i (document or data) as a measure of its belonging to the particular cluster *ij*.

$$f_{fcm} = \sum_{i=1}^{N} \sum_{j=1}^{K} m_{ij}(x_i), \quad (15)$$

where *N* is number of items to be clustered and *K* is number of clusters. This way, each item has *K* values of membership function and clustering can be presented as a *NxK* matrix. Determining the degree of membership of each item to each cluster represents the key point of fuzzy clustering process. This value is calculated in ADVANSE by next equation (Equation 16)

$$m_{t,q} = k \cdot tf_{t,q} \cdot idf_{t,c} = k \cdot \log(f_{t,q} + 1) \cdot \log \frac{N_{q,c}}{N_{q,t,c}}, \quad (16)$$

where *t* represents clusters' key term and *q* represents the item to be clustered. The value is obtained by using both term frequency ($tf_{t,q}$) and inverse document frequency ($idf_{t,q}$), while *k* represents additional coefficient – correction factor which provides the better dispersion of the values of $m_{t,q}$ in the range. This coefficient is calculated as reciprocal of TF-IDF function maximum. Term and inverse document frequencies are obtained during the analyzing process. As a result of the clustering the values of membership function are stored in separate table (clusters table) ready to be used in information retrieval. In the presented example (Figure 18) this is left hand side table. It consists of only three fields: text item id, cluster id and value of membership function. This value varies between 0 and 1. The item belongs to cluster as more as membership value is higher. Zero value means that item does not belong to cluster at all.

One row in table with text items (right hand side table) relates to as many rows in the clusters table as many clusters are in the system. The clusters table acts as a map that relates the text items that are similar to each other. This way whole process is encircled. It started from the row data – table that holds text items. In the next phase, the data and metadata content is extracted from different representation formats. Further, the extracted content is analyzed for obtaining the statistical data necessary for clustering and finally, as a result of clustering process the new table is populated with text items' and clusters' ids as well as membership function values. Their fields again, are referenced from rows in the text items table. In processing the citizen's request, ADVANSE performs its analyzing and determining the clusters it could belong to. After this pre-filtering process the detailed searching is performed but only the items from selected clusters are involved. This way better searching resolution and shorter response time is provided.

FUTURE RESEARCH DIRECTIONS

Regardless of the focus on textual content which has predominant part in E-government data and documents, described clustering techniques are also applicable on other types of content. The algorithms are almost the same but the criteria are created in accordance with the nature of the data to be clustered. Such measures as term frequency and inverse document frequency cannot be used, but, for instance, self-organized maps are found useful in clustering textual data as well as pictures, especially in combination with some other criteria (e.g. picture histograms).

Figure 18. Clustering results and source data

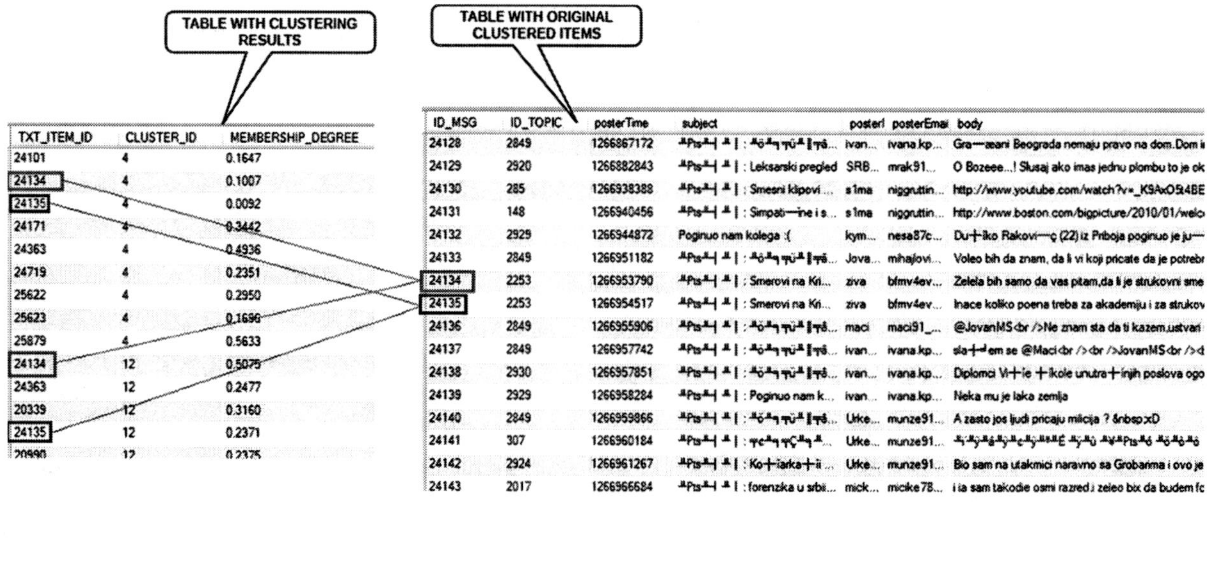

It is obvious that the integration of different approaches is one of the main objectives for the clustering development in the future due to heterogenic sources, formats and types of data to be clustered. The system should respond to demands for clustering in such circumstances by grouping content in more qualitative way.

Further, there is a lot of space for researching better methods for processing of text content due to multinational (multilingual) contexts which the contemporary e-government IS currently facing. The commonly applied solution for overcoming such a problem is the 'bag of words' representation of text content as well as using quantitative similarity measures instead of semantic analysis of the sentences. Therefore, the future improvements are expected. In all of the techniques and algorithms mentioned the common characteristic is that only one criteria and method is used. The improvements are made by including the modifications in mathematical models used by adding and / or changing some of the factors, coefficients as well as using logarithmic instead of linear functions.

Hybrid approaches by using multi-criteria decision making analysis and adding self-controlled (loop back) mechanisms in algorithm is suggested instead. Such approach needs more processing time and it may become critical factor due to large number of data or documents to be clustered. Therefore, creating representative sample of the content which is followed by 'probe' clustering of this should be helpful in hybrid solution. There are already existing techniques for creating such samples: random sampling, data condensations, density based approaches, grid based approaches, 'divide and conquer', incremental learning (Xu & Wuncsh, 2008). The 'probe' clustering by using different criteria can be evaluated by using some of internal evaluation technique (e.g. Davies-Bouldin or Dunn indexes). The technique and algorithm with the best performance should represent the decision which would be applied on whole set of content to be clustered.

Advanced content analysis performed in the preparing phase represents the other direction in which the future clustering could be developed. Latent semantic analysis offers sets of measures that could be applied on the content to be processed in preparing phase. Moreover there are different functions for multi-lingual support. On the other hand, 'bag of words' is still common representation of text items. Therefore, recognizing of language and domain context, than applying of lemmatization, n-gram analysis and other lexical computing techniques should be used in semantically preparing of content before advanced clustering.

CONCLUSION

Clustering represents important phase in preparing the content for information retrieval, especially if there are numerous documents and huge amount of data in the storage. Moreover, clustering could be applied to different kinds of content regarding their structure, format and domain. The considerations in this chapter are focused on textual content due to its importance for e-government services. This way, the knowledge about language the textual content is written on is of great importance. Missing the implementation of appropriate language rules can produce unexpected and unwanted clustering results. Therefore the content preparation before clustering is necessary due to lot of specific things that make one language different from another: alphabet, writing rules, dictionary, grammar, stop words, collocations and many others. Textual content has to be normalized while non-informative content has to be removed before clustering. After extraction the content can be considered as 'bag of words' where each word represents a term relevant for clustering. Since processing data have to be of quantitative nature, the content is transformed in vector space model which consists of particular term vectors. For describing the term vectors, the most common values used are the term frequency (TF) and inverse document frequency (IDF) combined in TF-IDF parameter.

On the other hand, clustering represents only one solution for unsupervised grouping of content. In this case, the clustering criteria are provided either during the preprocessing immediately before clustering (e.g. in partition clustering) or as one of the iterative steps of clustering algorithm (e.g. in hierarchical clustering). It means that content can be grouped without knowledge about the information it holds. In this case, one of the problems is to define how many clusters should be created. The extreme values ('too many' and 'not enough') are not recommended because the results will be useless for IR. It is desirable if the content domain can be recognized for using related dictionary in defining the number of clusters and initial centroids. If it is not possible, the number can be selected from some range by chance.

Regardless of approach the clustering algorithms are designed to be applied on a huge content. By eliminating both the 'stop words' and the text formatting characters, by transforming the rest of words in their basic form, describing them by quantitative values and representing by term vectors, the complexity is gradually reduced before real clustering is performed. Moreover, it happens before system starts to receive searching queries. Therefore the only challenge is to find appropriate clustering algorithm.

Also, there is opportunity that well-structured content described by metadata can be clustered regarding to more than one criterion. Contemporary clustering engines enable the parts of content to be analyzed separately; the importance of particular parts can be changed by using different weights and finally, they can be considered together again in making decisions.

In one of sections different clustering taxonomies are presented. Basically there are two main categorizations. The first one depends on how the clusters are considered - either as the hierarchical structures or as the space models. Other one is based on the set theory. This way the hierarchical agglomerative and divisive clustering are described first and 'hard' and 'soft' approaches are considered after. It is pointed out in the chapter that the most clustering techniques belong to the 'hard' clustering due to the items to be clustered belong to only one cluster. The specific 'soft' clustering approach is explained with more details with the accent on the fact that the item can belong to more than one cluster, according to the set theory intersection concept. Moreover, in the presented case study it is evident that the boundaries between clusters are not relevant anymore due to introducing of degree of membership as only clustering criteria. Therefore such approaches are so called 'soft' clustering. There are techniques that are not presented in the chapter because they need more detailed considerations. Such are latent semantic indexing and log likelihood ratio used for finding the collocations – constructions of two or more words (n-grams) that produce the new meaning different from their particular ones. Actual clustering frameworks provide the basic functions for dealing with collocations. The main disadvantage of such approaches is that their complexity exponentially grows regarding the number of words in n-grams. Therefore the bi-grams are commonly used.

REFERENCES

Babu, P., & Murt, N. (1994). Clustering With Evolution Strategies. *Journal of Pattern Recognition*, *27*(2), 321–329. doi:10.1016/0031-3203(94)90063-9

Bezdek, J. C. (1981). *Pattern Recognition with Fuzzy Objective Function Algoritms*. New York: Plenum Press. doi:10.1007/978-1-4757-0450-1

Church, K., & Gale, W. (1999). Inverse Document Frequency (IDF): A Measure of Deviations from Poisson. In S. Armstrong (Ed.), *Natural Language Processing Using Very Large Corpora* (pp. 283–295). Kower Academic Publishers, Springer. doi:10.1007/978-94-017-2390-9_18

Cimiano, P., Hotho, A., & Staab, S. (2013). *Comparing Conceptual, Divisive and Agglomerative Clustering for Learning Taxonomies from Text.* Bielefeld University. Retrieved October 14, 2013, from http://pub.uni-bielefeld.de/luur

Conrad, J., Al-Kofahi, K., Zhao, Y., & Karypis, G. (2005). Effective Document Clustering for Large Heterogeneous Law Firm Collections. In *Proceedings of the Tenth International Conference on Artificial Intelligence and Law* (pp. 177 – 187), Bologna, Italy: ACM. doi:10.1145/1165485.1165513

Driver, E., & Kroeber, L. (1932). Quantitative expression of cultural relationships. *University of Caltfornia Publications in American Archeology and Ethnology*, *31*, 211–256.

Dunn, J. C. (1973). A fuzzy relative of the ISO-DATA process and its use in detecting compact well-separated clusters. *Journal of Cybernetics*, *3*(3), 32–57. doi:10.1080/01969727308546046

Elkan, C. (2004). *Clustering with k-means: faster, smarter, cheaper.* Paper presented at the Workshop on Clustering High-Dimensional Data, SIAM International Conference on Data Mining (SDM 2004). Lake Buena Vista, FL.

Fang, Z. (2002). E-Government in Digital Era: Concept, Practice, and Development. *International Journal of the Computer, the Internet and Management*, *10*(2), 1–22.

Garijo, F., Riquelme, J., & Toro, M. (2002). A GRASP algorithm for Clustering. In *Proceedings of IBERAMIA 2002 (LNAI), (vol. 2527,* pp. 214 – 223). Seville, Spain: University of Seville.

Hamerly, G., & Elkan, C. (2002). Alternatives to the k-means algorithm that find better clusterings. In *Proceedings of the Eleventh International Conference on Information and Knowledge Management (CIKM)* (pp. 600-607). ACM. doi:10.1145/584887.584890

Hatcher, E., Gospodnetic, O., & McCandless, M. (2009). *Lucene in Action*. Greenwich, CT: Manning Publications.

Hochbaum, D., & Shmoys, D. (1985). A best possible heuristic for the k-center problem. *Mathematics of Operations Research, 10*(2), 180–184. doi:10.1287/moor.10.2.180

Jain, A., Murty, M., & Flynn, P. (1999). Data Clustering: A Review. *ACM Computing Surveys*, *31*(3), 255–322. doi:10.1145/331499.331504

Khan, S., & Kant, S. (2007). Computation of Initial Modes for K-modes Clustering Algorithm using Evidence Accumulation. In *Proceedings of The Twentieth International Joint Conference on Artificial Intelligence IJCAI-07* (pp 2784-2789). Hyderabad, India: IJCAI.

Krippendorff, K. (1980). Clustering. In J. Cappella & P. Monge (Eds.), *Multivariate techniques in human communication research* (pp. 259–307). New York: Academic Press Inc.

Mattmann, C., & Zitting, J. (2012). *Tika in Action*. Greenwich, CT: Manning Publications.

Rijsbergen, K. (1979). *Information Retrieval* (2nd ed.). London: Butterworth-Heinemann.

Salton, G., & Buckley, C. (1988). Term-weighting approaches in automatic text retrieval. *Information Processing & Management, 24*(5), 513–523. doi:10.1016/0306-4573(88)90021-0

Simic, G., Jeremic, Z., Kajan, E., Randjelovic, D., & Presnall, A. (2014). A Framework for Delivering e-Government Support. *Acta Polytechnica Hungarica, 11*(1), 79–96.

Sokal, R., & Sneath, A. (1963). *Principles of numerical taxonomy*. San Francisco, CA: Freeman.

Xu, R., & Wuncsh, D. (2008). *Clustering*. Wiley-IEEE Press. doi:10.1002/9780470382776

Yang, Y., & Chute, C. G. (1994). An Example-Based Mapping Method for Text Categorization and Retrieval. *ACM Transactions on Information Systems, 12*(3), 252–277. doi:10.1145/183422.183424

Zheng, Y., Cheng, X., Huang, R., & Man, Y. (2006). A Comparative Study on Text Clustering Methods. In X. Li, O. R. Zaiane, & Z. Li (Eds.), *ADMA 2006, (LNAI), (vol. 4093,* pp. 644–651). Berlin: Springer-Verlag. doi:10.1007/11811305_71

Zou, K., Wang, Z., & Hu, M. (2008). An new initialization method for fuzzy c-means algorithm. *Journal of Fuzzy Optimization and Decision Making, 7*(4), 409–416. doi:10.1007/s10700-008-9048-8

Zubin, A. (1938). A technique for measuring likemindedness. *Journal of Abnormal and Social Psychology, 33*(4), 508–516. doi:10.1037/h0055441

ADDITIONAL READING

Aggarwal, C., & Reddy, C. (Eds.). (2014). *Data Clustering: Algorithms and Applications*. Boca Raton, USA: Taylor & Francis Group.

Baeza-Yates, R. A., Fuhr, N., & Andmaarek, Y. S. (2006). Special issue on XML retrieval. *ACM Transactions on Information Systems, 24*(4), 4. doi:10.1145/1185877.1185878

Berry, M., & Castellanos, M. (2008). *Survey of Text Mining II: Clustering, Classification, and Retrieval*. New York, USA: Springer. doi:10.1007/978-1-84800-046-9

Ingersoll, G., Morton, T., & Farris, A. (2013). *Taming Text - How To Find, Organize, And Manipulate It*. Greenwich, USA: Manning Publications.

Manning, C., Raghavan, P., & Schütze, H. (2009). *An Introduction to Information Retrieval*. Cambridge, England: Cambridge University Press.

Marmanis, H., & Babenko, D. (2009). *Algorithms of the Intelligent Web*. Greenwich, USA: Manning Publications.

Miner, G., Elder, J., Hill, T., Nisbet, R., Delen, D., & Fast, A. (2012). *Practical Text Mining and Statistical Analysis for Non-structured Text Data Applications*. New York, USA: Elsevier.

Owen, S., Anil, R., Dunning, T., & Friedman, E. (2012). *Mahout in Action*. Greenwich, USA: Manning Publications.

Russell, A. (2013). *Mining the Social Web* (2nd ed.). Sebastopol, USA: O'Reilly Media.

Srivastava, A., & Sahami, M. (Eds.). (2009). *Text Mining: Classification, Clustering, and Applications*. Boca Raton, USA: Taylor & Francis Group. doi:10.1201/9781420059458

Tagarelli, A. & Greco, S. (2010). Semantic Clustering of XML Documents, *ACM Transactions on Information Systems, 28*(1), Article 3

Weiss, S., Indurkhya, N., Zhang, T., & Damerau, F. (2005). *Text Mining: Predictive Methods for Analyzing Unstructured Information*. New York, USA: Springer. doi:10.1007/978-0-387-34555-0

Witten, I., & Frank, E. (2005). *Data Mining: Practical Machine Learning Tools and Techniques* (2nd ed.). New York, USA: Elsevier.

Witten, I., Frank, E., & Hall, M. (2011). *Data Mining: Practical Machine Learning Tools and Techniques* (3rd ed.). Burlington, USA: Elsevier.

KEY TERMS AND DEFINITIONS

Clustering: Unsupervised grouping of data.

Hierarchical Clustering: During the iterative process the clusters are formed either by splitting one into two new clusters or by merging two clusters into new one.

Inverse Document Frequency (IDF): Measure used in text content clustering.

Partition Clustering: Based on predefined number the clusters are initially formed as 2D regions which change their shape during iterations based on using some of measures of central tendencies.

Soft Clustering: The item can belong to more than one cluster.

SOM Clustering: Clustering based on Neural Networks principles by changing weights of connections between input and output nodes.

Term Frequency (TF): One of the basic measures used in text content clustering.

TFIDF: The most used measure–combination of TF and IDF.

Chapter 11
Semantic Framework for an Efficient Information Retrieval in the E-Government Repositories

Antonio Martín
Universidad de Sevilla, Spain

Carlos León
Universidad de Sevilla, Spain

ABSTRACT

An enormous quantity of heterogeneous and distributed information is stored in e-government repositories. Access to these collections poses a serious challenge, however, because present search techniques based on manually annotated metadata and linear replay of material selected by the user do not scale effectively or efficiently to large collections. The artificial intelligence and Semantic Web provide a common framework that allows knowledge to be shared and reused in an efficient way. This chapter proposes a comprehensive approach for discovering information objects in large digital collections based on analysis of recorded semantic metadata in those objects and the application of expert system technologies. The authors suggest a conceptual architecture for a semantic search engine. They use case-based reasoning methodology to develop a prototype. OntoloGov is a collaborative effort that proposes a new form of interaction between citizens and e-government repositories, where the latter are adapted to users and their surroundings.

INTRODUCTION

E-Government is the use of information and communication technologies to improve the activities of public sector organizations. Repositories enable citizens to interact effectively with information distributed across a network: publications, forms, guides, policies, legislation, etc. These network information systems support search and display of items from organized collections. In the historical evolution of digital archives, repositories, and public web sites, the mechanisms for retrieval of official documents and public knowledge have been particularly important. In the traditional search engines the information is treated as an ordinary database that manages the contents and positions.

DOI: 10.4018/978-1-4666-7266-6.ch011

The result generated by the current search engines is a list of Web addresses that contain or treat the pattern. The useful information buried under the useless information cannot be discovered. It is disconcerting for the end user and sometimes it takes a long time to search for needed information. Despite large investments and efforts have been made, there are still a lot of unsolved problems. Thus, it is necessary to develop new intelligent and semantic models that offer more possibilities.

There are researchers and works in related fields which include ontology retrieval methods such as (Jimeno-Yepes, Berlanga-Llavori, & Rebholz-Schuhmann, 2010) who present a system which uses an ontology query model to analyse the usefulness of ontologies in effectively performing document searches and proposes an algorithm to refine ontologies for information retrieval tasks with preliminary positive results. (Diaz-Galiano, Martin-Valdivia, & Urena-Lopez, 2009) uses a medical ontology to improve a Multimodal Information Retrieval System by expanding the user's query with medical terms. This study (Chen, 2008) combines swarm intelligence and Web Services to transform a conventional library system into an intelligent library system with high integrity, usability, correctness, and reliability software for readers. The research (Cho & Hyun, 2006) proposes meta-concepts with which the ontology developers describe the domain concepts of parts libraries. The meta-concepts have explicit ontological semantics, so that they help to identify domain concepts consistently and structure them systematically. This study (Sasaki & Kiyoki, 2005) presents a formulation and case studies of the conditions for patenting content-based retrieval processes in digital libraries, especially in image libraries. This paper (Bainbridge, Dewsnip, & Witten, 2005) focuses on methods for evaluating different symbolic music matching strategies, and describes a series of experiments that compare and contrast results obtained using three dominant paradigms. This research (Toledo, Ale, Chiotti, & Galli, 2011) proposes organizational memory architecture, and annotation and retrieval information strategies based on domain ontologies that take in account complex words to retrieve information through natural language queries.

There are a lot of researches on applying these new technologies into current information retrieval systems, but no research addresses Artificial Intelligence (AI) and semantic issues from the whole life cycle and architecture point of view (Govedarova, Stoyanov, & Popchev, 2008). Although search engines have developed increasingly effective, information overload obstructs precise searches. Our work differs from related projects in that we build ontology-based contextual profiles and we introduce an approaches used metadata-based in ontology search and expert system technologies (Warren, 2005). We study improving the efficiency methods to search a distributed data space like E-Government storehouses. We presented an intelligent approach for optimize a search engine in a specific domain. The objective has focused on creating technologically complex environments E-Government domain. It incorporates Semantic Web and AI technologies to enable not only precise location of public resources but also the automatic or semi-automatic learning (Stuckenschmidt and Harmelen, 2001). We focus our discussion on case indexing and retrieval strategies and provide a perception of the technical aspects of the application. For this reason we are improving representation by incorporating more metadata from within the information.

Our approach for realizing content-based search and retrieval information implies the application of the Case-Based Reasoning (CBR) technology (Toussaint and Cheng, 2006). Our objective here is thus to contribute to a better knowledge retrieval in the E-Government field. This paper describes semantic interoperability problems and presents an intelligent architecture to address them, called OntoloGov. Obviously, our system is a prototype but, nevertheless, it gives a good picture of the on-going activities in this new and important field. We concentrate on the critical issue of metadata/ontology-based search and expert system technologies. More specifically the objective is investigated from a search perspective possible intelligent infrastructures form constructing decentralized public repositories where no global schema exists.

The contributions are divided into next sections. In the first section, short descriptions of important aspects in E-Government domain and semantic interoperability, the research problems and current work in it are reported. The second section focuses on the ontology design process and provides a general overview about our prototype architecture. Then we summarize its main components and describe how can interact AI and Semantic Web to enhancement a search engine. Next we study the CBR framework and its features for implementing the reasoning process over ontologies (GAIA, 2012). Finally we present the results of our ongoing work on the adaptation of the framework and we outline the future works.

MOTIVATION AND REQUIREMENTS

In the historical evolution of E-Government repositories, the mechanisms for retrieval information and knowledge have been particularly important. These network information systems support search and display of items from organized collections. Reuse this knowledge is an important area in this domain. The Semantic Web provides a common framework that allows knowledge to be shared and reused across community citizens (Sure & Studer, 2005).

Repositories and digital archives are privileged area for the application of innovative, knowledge intensive services that provide a flexible and efficient method for searching information and guarantee the user with a set of results actually related to his/her interest. Sevilla University institutional repository is dedicated to the production, maintenance, delivery, and preservation of a wide range of high-quality networked resources for citizens, scholars, and students at University and elsewhere. This repository includes services to effectively share their materials and provide greater access to digital content (Witten & Bainbridge, 2003)

Our objective here is thus to contribute to a better knowledge retrieval in the institutional repositories field. This scheme is based on the next principles: knowledge items are abstracted to a characterization by metadata description witch is used for further processing. This characterization is based on a vocabulary/ontology that is shared to case the access to the relevant information sources. This begets new challenges to docent community and motivates researchers to look for intelligent information retrieval approach and ontologies that search and/or filter information automatically based on some higher level of understanding are required. We make an effort in this direction by investigating techniques that attempt to utilize ontologies to improve effectiveness in information retrieval. Thus, ontologies are seen as key enablers for the Semantic Web. We have proposed a method to efficiently search for the target information on a digital repository network with multiple independent information sources (Ding, 2004). The use of AI and ontologies as a knowledge representation formalism offers many advantages in information retrieval (Guha, McCool, & Miller, 2003). In our work we analysed the relationship between both factors ontologies and expert systems.

We focus our discussion on case indexing and retrieval strategies and provide a perception of the technical aspects of the application. For this reason we are improving representation by incorporating more metadata within the information representation. (Luger, 2002). We discuss an opportunity and challenge in this domain with a specific view of intelligent information processing that takes into account the semantics of the knowledge items. In this paper we study architecture of the search layer in this particular dominium, a web-based catalogue for the University of Seville. The hypothesis is that with a case-based reasoning expert system and by incorporating limited semantic knowledge, it is possible to improve the effectiveness of an information retrieval system (Sun and Finnie, 2004). More specifically, the objectives are decomposed into:

- Explore and understand the requirements for rendering semantic search in an institutional repository.
- Investigate from a search perspective possible intelligent infrastructures form constructing decentralized digital repositories where no global schema exists.
- Investigate how semantic technologies can be used to provide additional semantic properties from existing resources.
- Analyse the implementation results, and evaluate the viability of our approaches in enabling search in intelligent-based digital repositories.

To reach these goals we need to consider information interoperability. In other words the capacity of different information systems, applications and services to communicate, share and interchange data, information and knowledge in an effective and precise way, as well as to integrate with other systems, applications and services in order to deliver new electronic products and services. E-Government initiatives, such as interoperability between public services, require establishing collaborative semantic repositories among public and private sector organizations. Particularly we require Semantic Interoperability, which is one of the key elements of the programme to support the set-up of the European E-Government services.

INTEROPERABILITY REQUIREMENTS

In June 2002, European heads of state adopted the Europe Action Plan 2005 at the Seville summit. It calls on the European Commission to issue an agreed interoperability framework to support the delivery of European E-Government services to citizens and enterprises. This recommends technical policies and specifications for joining up public administration information systems across the EU. This research is based on open standards and the use of open source software. These aspects are the pillars to support the European delivery of E-Government services of the recently adopted European Interoperability Framework (EIF) (SEC, 2003) and its Spanish equivalent (MAP, 2014). This document is reference for interoperability of the new Interoperable Delivery of Pan-European E-Government Services to Public Administrations, Business and Citizens programme (IDAbc). European Institutions and Agencies should use the European interoperability framework for their operations with each other and with citizens, enterprises and administrations in the respective EU Member States (EIF, 2014). Member States Administrations must use the guidance provided by the EIF to supplement their national E-Government Interoperability Frameworks with a pan-European dimension and thus enable pan-European interoperability

In this context interoperability is the ability of information and communication technology systems and of the business processes they support to exchange data and to enable sharing of information and knowledge. The ISO/IEC 2382 Information Technology Vocabulary defines interoperability as the capability to communicate, execute programs, or transfer data among various functional units in a manner that requires the user to have little or no knowledge of the unique characteristics of those units. An interoperability framework can be described as a set of standards and guidelines, which describe the way in which organisations have agreed, or should agree, to interact with each other.

Interoperability can be considered on very different abstraction levels, and the distinctions to be made in this respect cut across all the other matrix dimensions. Within a continuum ranging from a very concrete to a very abstract perspective it is possible to distinguish three layers as shown in Figure 1.

The aspects of interoperability as a general concept or approach cover technical, semantic, and organisational issues, usually referenced as interoperability layers. Interoperability is conceived on different main abstraction levels:

- **Organisational Interoperability Level:** Processes, defined as workflow sequences of tasks, integrated in a service-oriented environment.
- **Technical Interoperability Level:** Signals, low-level services and data transfer protocols.
- **Semantic Interoperability Level:** Information in various shared knowledge representation structures such as taxonomies, ontologies, or topic maps. Semantic interoperability is not just with about the packaging of data (data format), but mostly focuses into simultaneous transmission of their meaning (semantics). The meaning of the data is transmitted with the data itself, in an "information package" independent of any information system. Semantic interoperability shared vocabulary, and its associated links to an ontology, which provides the basis for machine interpretation and understanding of the logic of the message. This is success by adding metadata (information used to describe other data) and linking each data element to a shared vocabulary.

Two or more entities achieve interoperability when they are capable of communicating and exchanging data, which concerns to specified data formats and communication protocols. Exchanging normalized data is a prerequisite for semantic interoperability and refers to the packaging and transmission mechanisms for data. In the semantic interoperability there are concepts and methods available, but which are not yet standardized. However for organizational interoperability it is by far less obvious what has to be standardized, who could develop and establish appropriate standards, and what is necessary for their operation and maintenance.

Figure 1. Abstraction layers interoperability

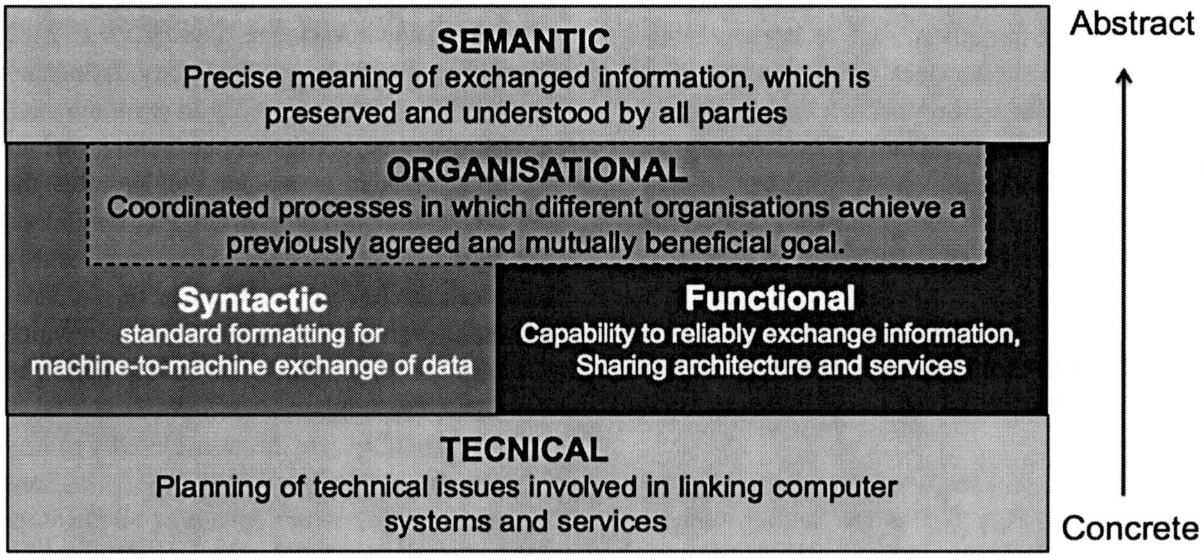

In this chapter we have focused our work in semantic interoperability analysis. For this purpose we use ontologies and semantic approach. This area implies the collaboration of many actors, such as local repositories, information workers and suppliers, which is why we can quote the following reasons for the need to develop/define a central ontology:

- Providing a semantic typing for the data distributed all over the repositories in order to facilitate the information request by citizens through efficient search engines. Entities can be assumed to be the institutions offering digital services, digital repositories, public platforms or simply Web services.
- Sharing common understanding of the structure of information among intelligent agents, facilitating the extraction of information and processing of documents. Objects of interaction, the entities that actually need to be processed in semantic interoperability scenarios. Choices range from the full content of digital information objects to mere representations of such objects, which in turn are often conceived as metadata attribute sets.
- Enabling reuse of existing domain knowledge and its further extension, providing a contextual framework enabling unambiguous communication of complex and detailed concepts.

However, semantic interoperability problems emerge as these organizations may differ in the terms and meanings they use to communicate, express their needs and describe resources they make available to each other. Moreover, interoperability can be considered on different abstraction levels, and the distinctions to be made in this respect cut across all the other matrix dimensions. Within a continuum ranging from a very concrete to a very abstract perspective it is possible to distinguish the four layers of technical, syntactic, functional and semantic interoperability. We must bear in mind that interoperability framework is, therefore, not a static document and may have to be adapted over time as technologies, standards and administrative requirements change. In the next sections we establish the base of all these aspects in our platform OntoloGov.

THE ONTOLOGOV ARCHITECTURE

In order to support semantic retrieval knowledge in Sevilla institutional repositories we develop a prototype named OntoloGov based on ontologies and expert system technologies. The proposed architecture is based on our approach to information retrieval in an efficient way by means of metadata characterizations and domain ontology inclusion. It implies to use ontology as vocabulary to define complex, multi-relational case structures to support the CBR processes. Our system works comparing objects that can be retrieved across heterogeneous repositories and capturing a semantic view of the world independent of data representation. The architecture of our system is shown in Figure 2, which mainly includes three parts: intelligent user interface, ontology knowledge base, and the search engine.

The framework presented in the next sections is built on established and widely accepted standards for data transfer and exchange (XML), web services (WSDL, SA-WSDL) and process models (BPMN, BPEL). The main focus of this paper is on semantic interoperability; however, other levels are addressed as well, their corresponding characteristics and functions are studied in the following paragraph. Use of technological standards enables different kinds of interoperability constitute a major dimension with more traditional approaches geared towards librarian metadata interoperability such as Z39.50 / SRU+SRW or the harvesting methods based on OAI-PMH or again web service based approaches (SOAP/UDDI) and

Figure 2. System architecture of OntoloGov

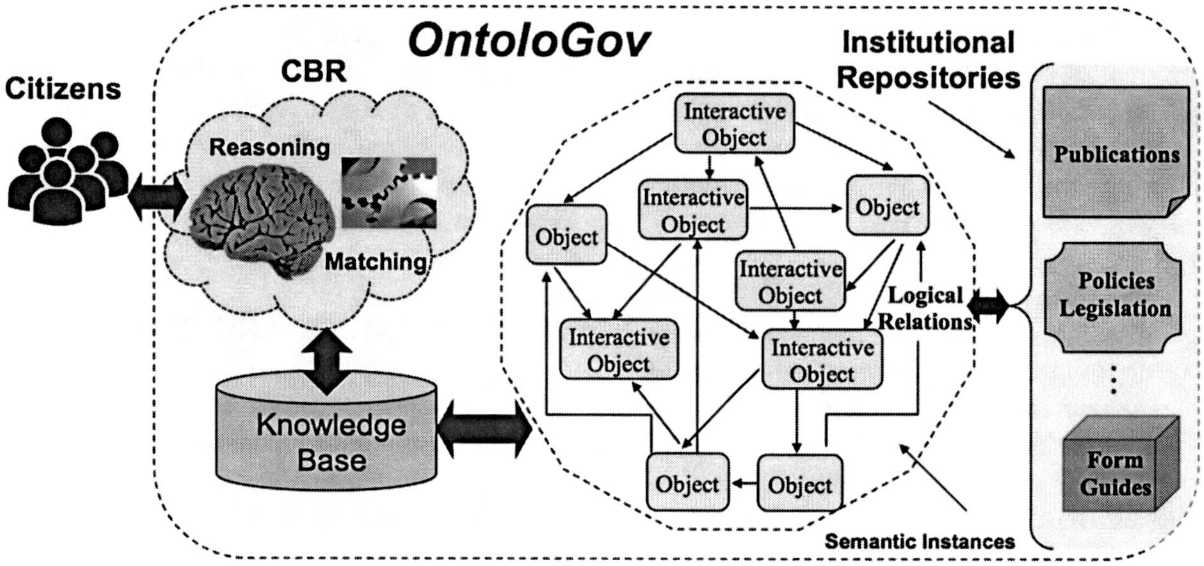

the Java based API defined in JCR (JSR 170/283) as well as GRID based platforms such as iRods.

OntoloGov system uses its internal knowledge bases and inference mechanisms to process information about the electronic resources in Seville University repositories. At this stage we consider to use ontology as vocabulary for defining the case structure like attribute-value pairs. Ontology knowledge base is the kernel part for semantic retrieval information. Ontology is a knowledge structure, which identify the concepts, property of concept, resources, and relationships among them to enable share and reuse of knowledge that are needed to acquire knowledge in a specific search domain. The metadata descriptions of the resources and repository objects (cases) are abstracted from the details of their physical representation and are stored in the Case Base. Ontology provides information about resources and services where concepts are types, or classes, individuals are allowed values, or objects and relations are the attributes describing the objects (Staab and Studer, 2005).

Inference Engine contains a CBR component that automatically searches for similar queries-answer pairs based on the knowledge that the system extracted from the questions text (Bridge, G¨oker, McGinty, & Smyth, 2006). Case Base has a memory organization interface that assumes that whole case-base can be read into memory for the CBR to work with it. Also we have implemented a new interface, which allows retrieving cases enough to satisfy a SQL query. We used a CBR shell, software that can be used to develop several applications that require cased-based reasoning methodology. In this work we analysed the CBR object-oriented framework development environments JColibri (Díaz-Agudo, Gonzâlez-Calero, Recio-García, & Sânchez-Ruiz, 2007). This framework work as open software development environment and facilitate the reuse of their design as well as implementations. The CBR engine uses an evaluation function to calculate the new case ranking, and the answered question updates the query and the rankings in the displays. The questions are ranked according to their potential for retrieval and matching.

The acceptability of a system depends to a great extent on the quality of this user interface component (Quan and Karger, 2004). Advanced conversational user interface interacts with users to solve a query, defined as the set of questions selected and answered by the user during conversation. Interface is designed and developed to improve communication between humans and the platform. Interfaces are provided for browsing, searching and facilitating Web contents and services. Interface enhances the flexibility, usability, and power of human-computer interaction for all users. In realizing the user interface we have exploited knowledge of users, tasks, tools, and content, as well as devices for supporting interaction within different contexts of use. During each search the user selects one item from two displays: ranked questions and ordered cases. In our system the user interacts with the system to fill in the gaps to retrieve the right cases.

CASE-BASED REASONING

CBR is widely discussed in the literature as a technology for building information systems to support knowledge management, where metadata descriptions for characterizing knowledge items are used. As mentioned in the previous sections, for the realization of the intelligent search we chose the framework jColibri a java-based configuration that supports the development of knowledge intensive CBR applications and help in the integration of ontology in them. In this section we describe in more detail how JColibri supports rapid prototyping of CBR applications. This includes the generation of case representations, the definition of similarity measures, the testing of retrieval and use of explanation functionality, and finally the implementation of stand-alone applications.

In our CBR application, problems are described by metadata concerning desired characteristics of an institutional resource, and the solution to the problem is a pointer to a resource described by metadata (Gomez-Perez, Corcho, & Fernandez-Lopez, 2003). These characterizations are called cases and are stored in a Case Base. CBR case data could be considered as a portion of the knowledge (metadata) about an OntoloGov object (Zhaohao and Gavin, 2005). Every case contains both index with the association terms of the ontology and the relation documents residing on the repository network:

- **Description of the Category Terms:** Keywords are mapped to ontology entities, namely individuals, data values, concepts, data ranges, as well as object and data properties. These indexes are formally described in terms of framework domain taxonomy and they are used for indexing cases.
- **Solution:** Search request comprises one or more search terms of ontology, the derived solution to the search and the additional information that justifies these retrieval documents.

The development of a quite simple Case-Based Reasoning application already involves a number of steps, such as collecting case and background knowledge, modelling a suitable case representation, defining an accurate similarity measure, implementing retrieval functionality, and implementing user interfaces. Compared with other AI approaches, CBR allows to reduce the effort required for knowledge acquisition and representation significantly, which is certainly one of the major reasons for the commercial success of CBR applications. Nevertheless, implementing a CBR application from scratch remains a time-consuming software engineering process and requires a lot of specific experience beyond pure programming skills.

Previous work has shown that CBR provides a number of advantages over alternative approaches:

- CBR doesn't require extensive analysis of domain knowledge. CBR permits problem solving even if domain knowledge is incomplete. The most important thing is to know how to compare two cases.

- CBR allows shortcuts in reasoning. If a suitable case is found, a solution can be proposed quickly.
- CBR can lead to improved explanation capability in situations where the most comprehensible explanations are those that involve specific instances.
- CBR can help in avoiding errors made before and learn from the errors and success. In CBR, the system keeps a record of each situation that occurred for future reference.

Case-Based Reasoning is a problem solving paradigm that solves a new problem, in our case a new search, by remembering a previous similar situation and by reusing information and knowledge of that situation. A new problem is solved by retrieving one or more previously experienced cases, reusing the case, revising, and retaining. In our system when a description of the current problem is input to the system the reasoning cycle may be described by the processes in Figure 3.

- **Retrieval:** The system retrieves the closest-matching cases stored in a case base. Main focus of methods in this category is to find similarity between cases. Similarity function can be parameterized through system configuration.
- **Reuse:** A complete design where case-based and slot-based adaptation can be

Figure 3. Case Based Reasoning Cycle in OntoloGov system

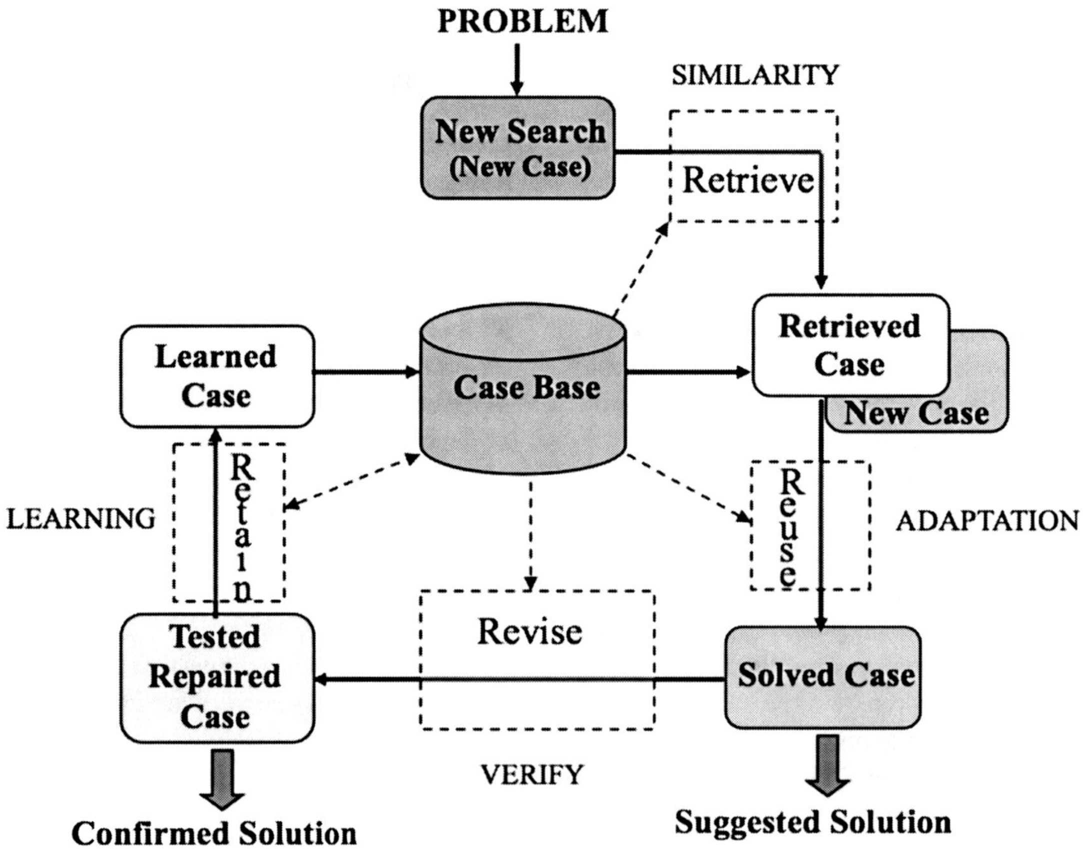

hooked is provided. If appropriate, the validated solution is added to the case for use in future problem solving.

- **Revise the Proposed Solution if Necessary:** Since the proposed result could be inadequate, this process can correct the first proposed solution. The system uses the current problem and closest-matching cases to generate a solution to the current problem. It should be noted that the differences in adaptation power depend on how well the domain is understood.
- **Retain the New Solution as a Part of a New Case:** The solution is validated through feedback from the user or the environment. This process enables CBR to learn and create a new solution that should be added to the knowledge base.

Although CBR claims to reduce the effort required for developing knowledge-based systems substantially compared with more traditional AI approaches, the implementation of a CBR application from scratch is still a time consuming task. By providing easy to use model CBR generation, data import, similarity modelling, explanation, and testing functionality together with comfortable graphical user interfaces, the tool enables even CBR novices to rapidly create their first CBR applications. Nevertheless, at the same time it ensures enough flexibility to enable expert users to implement advanced CBR applications.

CBR claims to reduce the effort required for developing knowledge-based systems substantially compared with more traditional AI technologies, the implementation of a CBR application from scratch is still a time consuming task. The development of a quite simple CBR application already involves a number of steps, such as collecting case and background knowledge, modelling a suitable case representation, defining an accurate similarity measure, implementing retrieval functionality, and implementing user interfaces. Compared with other AI approaches, CBR allows to reduce the effort required for knowledge acquisition and representation significantly, which is certainly one of the major reasons for the commercial success of CBR applications. Nevertheless, implementing a CBR application from scratch remains a time-consuming software engineering process and requires a lot of specific experience beyond pure programming skills.

For these purposes, more easily available and less complex CBR tools are required. The key idea of the system is to combine software reuse with the more general AI paradigm of separating the reasoning algorithms from the domain model. In this chapter we present a novel, freely available tool for rapid prototyping of CBR applications that focuses on the similarity-based retrieval step, like for example case-based product recommender systems. The Open Source JColibri1 system provides a framework for building CBR systems based on state-of-the-art Software Engineering techniques. Our motivation for choosing jColibri framework is based on a comparative analysis between it and other frameworks, designed to facilitate the development of CBR applications. jColibri enhances the other CBR shells: CATCBR, CBR*Tools, IUCBRF, Orenge, in several aspects:

- **Availability:** Open source framework.
- **Implementation:** The Java implementation is one of our main requirements with respect to the easy integration in the OntoloGov system, which is implemented in J2EE environment.

Another decision criterion for our choice is connected with the fact that jColibri affords the opportunity to incorporate ontology in the CBR application to use it for case representation and content-based reasoning methods to assess the similarity between them. By providing easy to use model generation, data import, similarity modelling, explanation, and testing functionality together with comfortable graphical user interfaces, the tool enables even CBR novices to rapidly create their first CBR applications. Nevertheless, at the same time it ensures enough flexibility to enable expert users to implement advanced CBR applications.

Standard cases are composed by several attributes with different simple data types (Integer, String). We use the concept data type supported by the jColibri framework to indicate that an attribute is going to represent a concept of the ontology. The values of this attribute are going to be the corresponding instances of the linked concept. Except from the concept type, the architecture takes advantage, as well, of another feature of jColibri framework – the two-layer organization of the case base. The metadata descriptions of the resources and library objects (cases) are abstracted from the details of their physical representation in the Electronic Catalogue and are stored in the case base. This way the same methods can operate over different types of information repositories. The mapping (the process is described in the following) between the two layers is realized by connectors read the values of the data base columns and ontology and return them to the application, i.e. assign them to the attributes of the case. Basing on the same idea, the case base implements a common interface for the similarity methods to assess the cases. This way the organization and indexation of case base will not affect the implementation of the reasoning methods.

ONTOLOGY DESIGN AND DEVELOPMENT

The main objective of our system is to improve the modelling of a semantic coherence for allowing the interoperability of different modules of environments dedicated to E-Government. We have proposed to use ontology together with CBR in the acquisition of an expert knowledge in the specific domain. The primary information managed in the OntoloGov domain is metadata about institutional resources, such as guides, publications, forms, digital services, etc. We need a vocabulary of concepts, resources and services for our information system described in the scenario requires definitions about the relationships between objects of discourse and their attributes (Taniar and Rahayu, 2006). OntoloGov project contains a collection of codes, visualization tools, computing resources, and data sets distributed across the grids, for which we have developed a well-defined ontology using RDF language. RDF is used to define the structure of the metadata describing SUR resources. Our ontology can be regarded as quaternion OntoSearch:={profile, collection, source, relation) where profiles represent the user kinds, collection contains all the services and resources of the institutional repository and matter cover the different information sources: electronic services, official web pages, publications, guides, etc., and relation is a set of relationships intended primarily for standardization across ontologies.

We integrated three essential sources to the system: electronic resources, catalogue of documents, and personal Data Base. The W3C defines standards that can be used to design an ontology (W3C, 2014). We wrote the description of these classes and the properties in RDF semantic markup language. We choose Protégé as our ontology editor, which supports knowledge acquisition and knowledge base development (Protégé, 2013). It is a powerful development and knowledge-modelling tool with an open architecture. Protégé uses OWL and RDF as ontology language to establish semantic relations (Heflin, 2004).

Protégé provides an environment for the creation and development of underlying semantic knowledge structures-ontologies and semantically annotated web services that may be organised into a dynamic process workflow. For the construction of the ontology of our system, we followed steps detailed below.

- **Determine the Domain and Scope of the Ontology:** This should provide the location of different on-line resources.

These are included from different sources: Publications Catalogue, Web Sites, Electronic Resources, etc. Also ontology must be adapted to needs of user kinds.

- **Enumerate Important Terms in the Ontology:** It is useful to write down a list of all terms we would like either to make statements about or to explain to a user. Initially, it is important to get a comprehensive list of terms without worrying about overlap between concepts they represent, relations among the terms, or any properties that the concepts may have, or whether the concepts are classes or slots.
- **Define the Classes and the Class Hierarchy:** When designing the ontology, we firs need to group together related resources of the institutional repositories. There are three major groups of resources: users, services, and resources. In order to realize ontology-based intelligent retrieval, we need to build case base of knowledge with inheritance structure. The ontology and its sub-classes are established according to the taxonomies profile. A detailed picture of our effort in designing this ontology is available in the Figure 4. This shows the high level classification of classes to group together OntoloGov resources as well as things that are related with these resources. Profile ontology includes several attributes like Electronic_Resources, Digital_Collections, Publication Catalogue, Public Services, etc.
- **Define the Properties of Classes and Define the Facets of the Slots:** The classes alone will not provide enough information to answer the semantic searches. Once we have defined some of the classes, we must describe the internal structure of concepts. In order to relate ontology classes to each other, we defined our own meaningful properties for the ontology and we defined a class hierarchy associated with meaningful properties. Slots can have different facets describing the value type, allowed values, the number of the values (cardinality), and other features of the values the slot can take. In the following we give a short RDF description that defined the concept of the user teacher that is a subclass of Member_Community_University.

Figure 4. Class hierarchy for the OntoloGov ontology

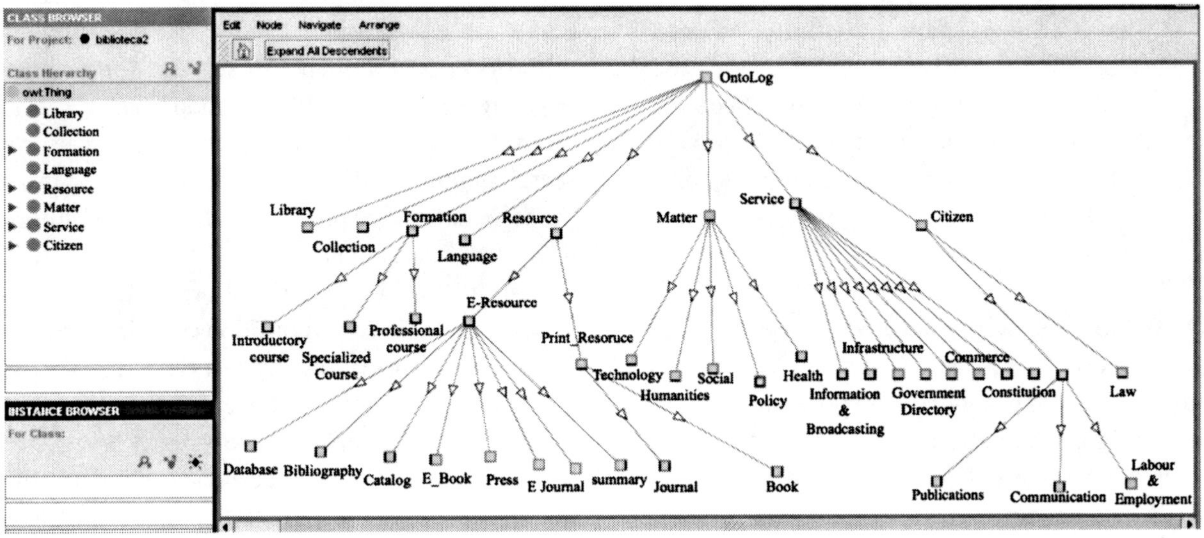

```
<rdf:Description
rdf:about="#Teacher">
<rdfs:comment rdf:datatype=
"http://www.w3.org/2001/
XMLSchema#string">
Teacher profile for affiliated col-
leges
</rdfs:comment>
  <rdfs:subClassOf rdf:resource=
"#Members of the University commu-
nity"/>
<rdf:type rdf:resource=
"http://www.w3.org/2002/07/
owl#Class"/>
</rdf:Description>
```

- **Generating the Ontology Instances with SW Languages:** The last step is creating individual instances of classes in the hierarchy. Defining an individual instance of a class requires choosing a class, creating an individual instance of that class, and filling in the slot values. After designing the ontology, we wrote the description of these classes and the properties in RDF semantic markup language. To provide a conversational CBR system to retrieve the requested metadata satisfying a user query we need to add enough initial instances and item instances to knowledge base. For this purpose we have followed next steps. First we choose a certain item, and create a blank instance for item. Then the domain expert, in this case administrative staff fills blank units of instance according the domain knowledge (Horridge and Knublauch, 2004).

10.000 cases were collected for user profiles and their different resources and services. This is sufficient for our proof-of-concept demonstration, but would not be sufficiently efficient to access large resource sets. Each case contains a set of attributes concerning both metadata and knowledge. However, our prototype is currently being extended to enable efficient retrieval directly from a database, which will enable its use for large-scale sets of resources. As a plus, domain specific rules defined by domain experts (manually or by tools) can infer more complex high-level semantic descriptions, for example, by combining low-level features in local repositories. On one hand, the rules can be used to facilitate the task of resource annotation by deriving additional metadata from existing ones.

Keeping in mind that our final goal is to reformulate queries in the ontology to queries in another with least loss of semantics, we come to a process for addressing complex relations between two ontologies. As mentioned in previous sections, relations among ontologies can be composed as a form of declarative rules, which can be further, handled in inference engines. In our approach, we choose to use the Semantic Web Rule Language (SWRL), which is based on a combination of OWL DL and OWL Lite with the Case-Based reasoning sublanguages, to compose declarative search rules (Bechhofer, Harmelen, Hendler, Horrocks, McGuinness, Patel-Schneider, & Stein, 2004).

CONVERSATION INTERFACE

As we have seen in previous sections our system has a graphical user interface for determining initial user requirements in search. Rather than building static user profiles, contextual systems try to adapt to the user's current search. The user's search is monitored by capturing information from the different citizen profiles. OntoloGov monitors user's tasks, anticipates search-based information needs, and proactively provide users with relevant information. This configuration contains the user requirements most typically described the relative needs, tasks, and goals of the user for an individual search. For this a statistical analysis has been done to determine the importance values and establishing specified user requirements. This statistical analysis even can in fact lay the foundation for searches in a particular user profile.

A technical administrator will have a view very different from an end user providing content as an author. Different conceptions, again, will emerge from the perspectives of a digital content aggregator, a 'meta user' or a policy maker. It consists of one user profile, consumer search agent components and bring together a variety of necessary information from different user's resources. The objective of profile intelligence has focused on creating of user profiles: Staff, Administrator, and Visitor. The user interface helps to user to build a particular profile that contains his interest search areas in the University Repositories domain. Interoperability concepts differ substantially from those of a content consuming end user. In an intelligence profile setting, people are surrounded by intelligent interfaces merged, thus creating a computing-capable environment with intelligent communication and processing available to the user by means of a simple, natural, and effortless human-system interaction. The user enters query commands and the system asks questions during the inference process. Besides, the user will be able to solve new searches for which he has not been instructed, because the user profiles what he has learnt during the previous searchers.

The client-side CBR engine is used to collect information with users and interact with the server-side application. Based on input from users, it retrieves the most appropriate case and shows the solution. A schematic of the architecture is shown in Figure 5.

The easiest to implement interfaces communicate with the user through a scrolling dialog. The advantage of CBR is that users need only input text partially describing the problem and then the system can assist in further complete the problem description in an interactive conversation style. The following guidelines for CBR design were proposed: reuse questions, order context questions before detail questions, eliminate questions that do not distinguish cases, ask for only one thing in a question, and use a similar, short number of questions per case. The user begins the search devising the starting query. Suppose the user is looking for some resource about "Computer Science electronic resource" in the institutional digital repositories in the domain of Seville University. The user inputs the keywords in the user profile interface. The required resources should contain some knowledge about "Computer Science" and related issues. After searching, some resources are returned as results, which are shown in Figure 6. The results include a list of web pages with titles, a link to the page, and a short description showing where the keywords have matched content within the page.

Retrieval of Similar Cases Process

CBR systems typically apply retrieval and matching algorithms to a case base of past problem-solution pairs. CBR is based on the intuition that new searches are often similar to previously encountered searches, and therefore, that past results may be reused directly or through adaptation in the current situation. The main purpose of establishing intelligent retrieval ontology is to provide consistent and explicit metadata in the process of knowledge retrieval. Retrieval processes get back information from the case library a set of potentially useful cases, all of which partially match the new situation. Many applications have demonstrated that an induced decision tree is a good approach to case retrieval in CBR systems. In this chapter, the decision tree induction algorithm described in (Breslow & Aha, 1997) was used to build a decision tree, and the inductive retrieval technique was used to retrieve cases. Our system provides multilayer retrieval methods:

1. **Intelligent Profiles Interface:** Low-level selection of query profile options, which mainly include the four kinds of user:

Figure 5. User profiles, Graphical User interface

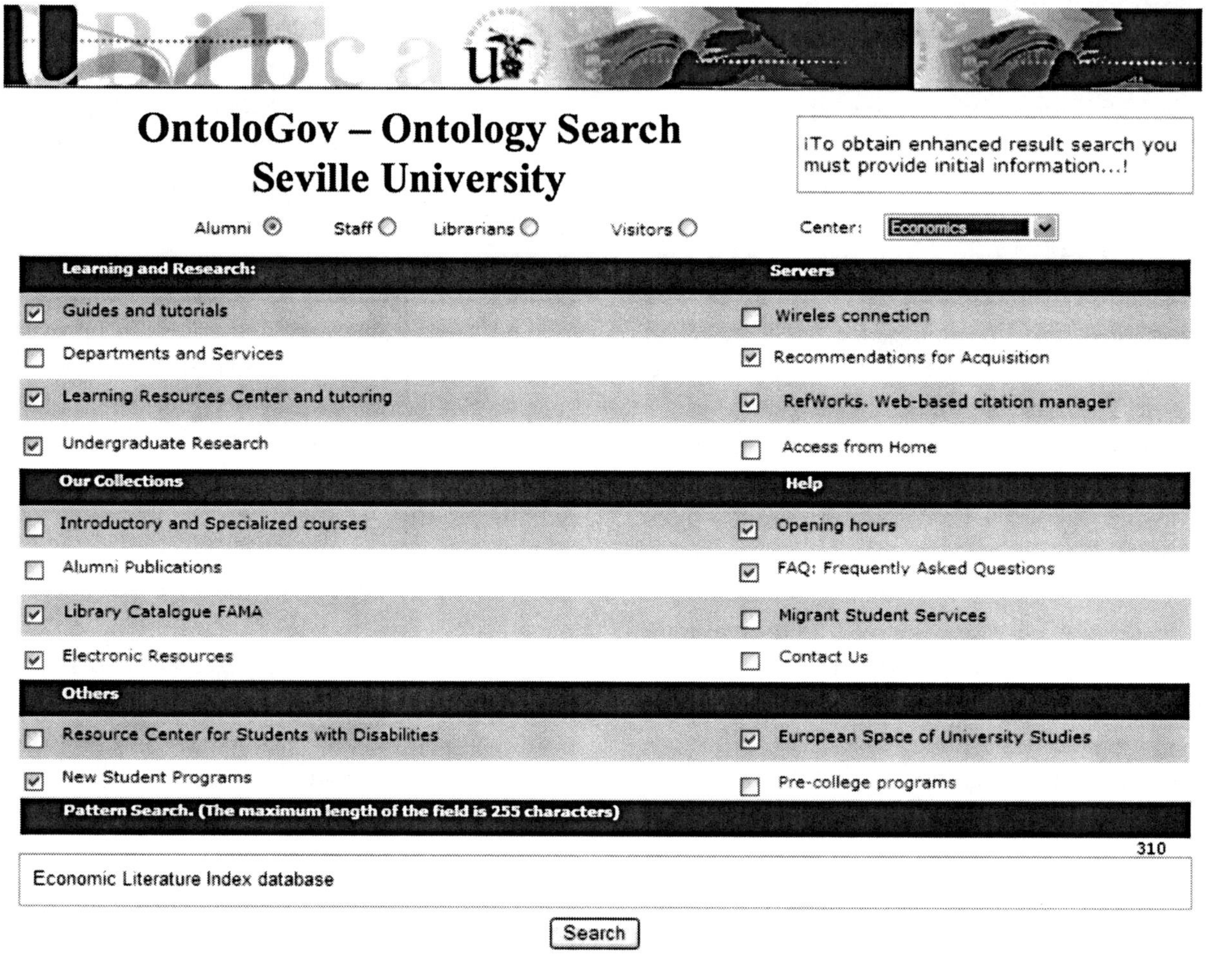

Teachers, staff, students and visitors. The users can specify certain initial items, i.e. the characteristics and conditions for a search.

2. Ontology semantic search can query on classes, subclasses or attributes of knowledge base, and matched cases are called back.
3. The retrieval process identifies the features of the case with the most similar query. Our Inference Engine contains the CBR component that automatically searches for similar queries-answer pairs based on the knowledge that the system extracted from the questions text. The system uses similarity metrics to find the best matching case. Similarity retrieval expands the original query conditions, and generates extended query conditions, which can be directly used in knowledge retrieval. Similarity measures used in CBR are of critical importance during the retrieval of knowledge items for a new query. Unlike in early CBR approaches, the recent view is that similarity is usually not just an arbitrary distance measure, but function that approximately measure utility, as in Figure 7.

We used a computational based retrieval where numerical similarity functions are used to assess and order the cases regarding the query. The retrieval strategy used in our system is nearest-

Figure 6. Search engine results page

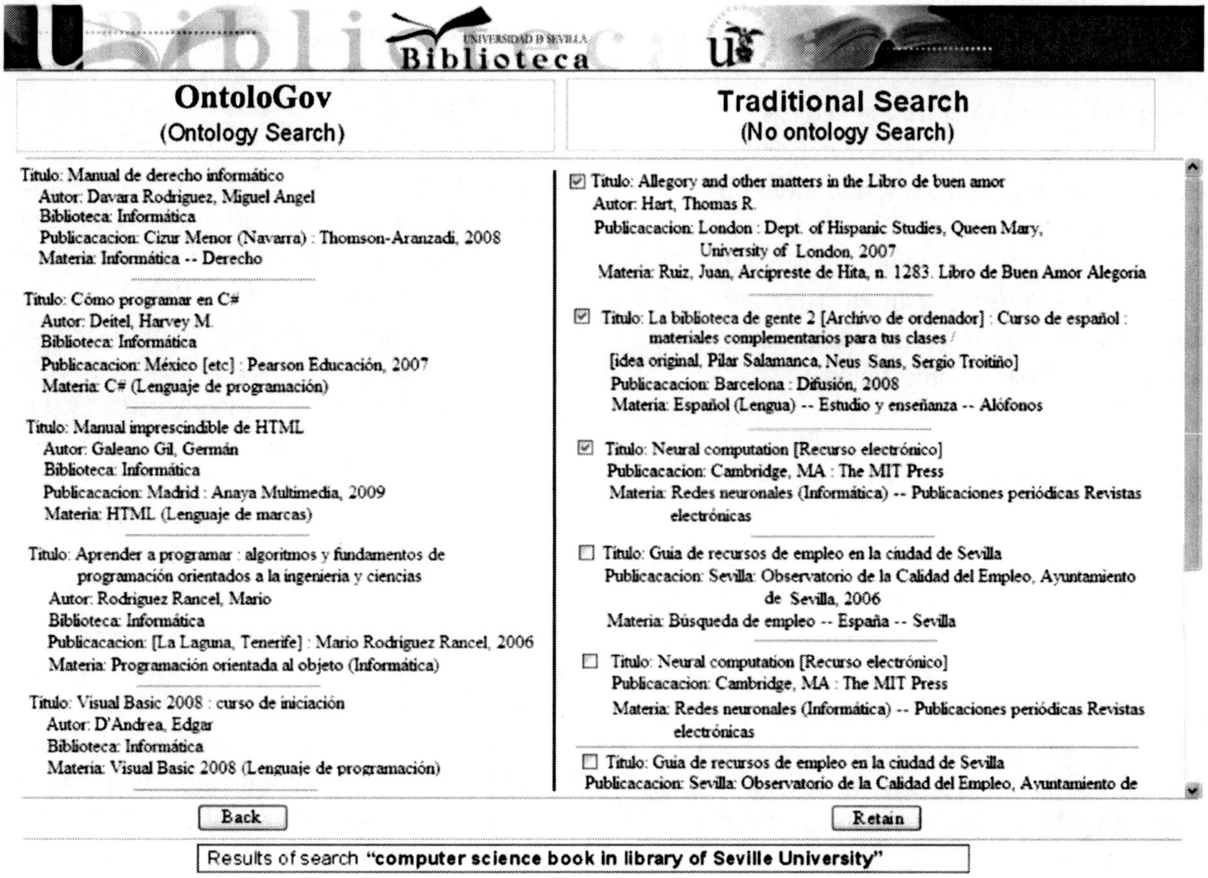

Figure 7. Retrieval cases process

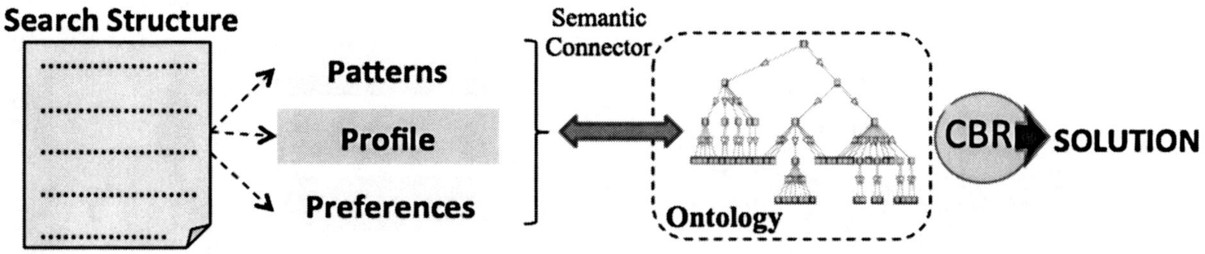

neighbour approach (Finnie and Sun, 2002). This approach involves the assessment of similarity between stored cases and the new input case, based on matching a weighted sum of features. A typical algorithm for calculating nearest neighbour matching is next:

$$similarity(Case_I, Case_R) = \frac{\sum_{i=1}^{n} w_i^{\times sim(f_i^I, f_i^R)}}{\sum_{i=1}^{n} w_i}$$

where w_i is the importance weighting of a feature (or slot), *sim* is the similarity function of features, and f_i^I and f_i^R are the values for feature *i* in the input and retrieved cases respectively. An important advantage of similarity-cased retrieval is that if there is no case that exactly matches the user's requirements, this can show the cases that are most similar to her query. The use of structured representations of cases requires approaches for similarity assessment that allow to compares two differently structured objects, in particular, objects belonging to different object classes.

EXPERIMENTAL EVALUATION

Experiments have been carried out in order to test the efficiency of AI and Ontologies in retrieval information in the University repository. These are conducted to evaluate the effectiveness of run-time ontology mapping. The main goal has been to check if the mechanism of query formulation, assisted by an agent, gives a suitable tool for augmenting the number of significant documents, extracted from the Sevilla University institutional repository, to be stored in the CBR.

For our experiments we considered 100 users with different profiles. So that we could establish a context for the users, they were asked to at least start their essay before issuing any queries to system. They were also asked to look through all the results returned by OntoloGov before clicking on any result. We compared the top 10 search results of each keyword phrase per search engine. Our application recorded which results on which they clicked, which we used as a form of implicit user relevance in our analysis. We must consider that retrieved documents relevance is subjective. That is different people can assign distinct values of relevance to a same document. In our study we have agreed different values to measure the quality of retrieved documents, excellent, good, acceptable and poor.

After the data was collected, we had a log of queries averaging five queries per user. Of these queries, some of them had to be removed, either because there were multiple results clicked, no results clicked, or there was no information available for that particular query. The remaining queries were analysed and evaluated, shown in Figure 8.

In each experiment we report the average rank of the user-clicked result for our baseline system,

Figure 8. Comparison of valid pages percentage

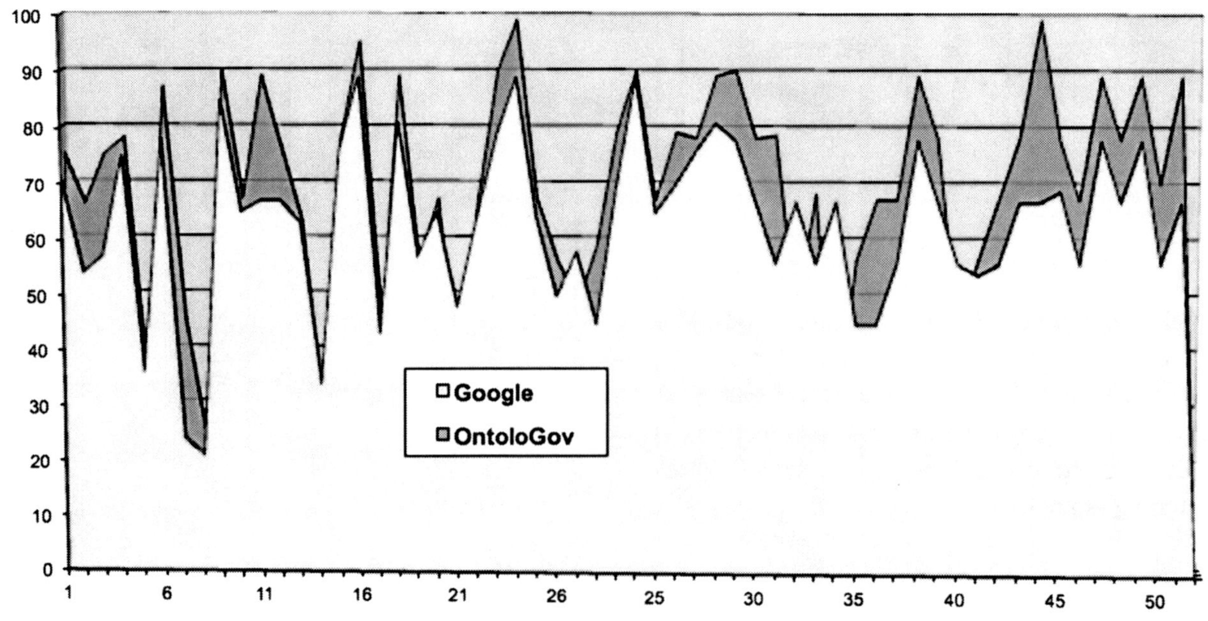

Google and for our search engine OntoloGov. Then we calculated the rank for each retrieval document by combining the various values and comparing the total number of extracted documents and documents consulted by the user (Table 1).

In our study domain we can observe the best final ranking was obtained for our prototype OntoloGov and an interesting improvement over the performance of Google. Test of significance is the analysis of the number of searches that have been resolved satisfactory by OntoloGov. As noted in Table 1, our system performs satisfactorily with about a 94.6% rate of success in real cases.

Another important aspect of the design and implementation of an intelligent system is determination of the degree of speed in the answer that the system provides. During the experimentation, heuristics and measures that are commonly adopted in information retrieval have been used. While the users were performing these searches, an application was continually running in the background on the server, and capturing the content of queries typed and the results of the searches. Statistical analysis has been done to determine the importance values in the results.

Figure 9 shows a sample plot of these parameters that was collected as a part of the experiment. We can establish that speed in our system improves the proceeding time and the average of the traditional search engine. The results for OntoloGov are 15.1% better than proceeding time and 19.5% better than executing time searches/sec in the traditional search engines.

Table 1. Analysis of retrieved documents relevance for select queries

	Excellent	Good	Acceptable	Poor
OntoloGov	5.5%	39.3%	40.6%	14.4%
Google	2.7%	31%	44.8%	21.3%

CONCLUSION AND FUTURE WORK

We have investigated how the semantic technologies can be used to provide additional semantics from existing resources in institutional repositories. For this purpose we presented a system based on ontology and AI architecture for knowledge management in the Seville repositories. We described an effort to design and develop a prototype for management the resources in a repository such as OntoloGov project, and to exploit them to aid users as they select resources. Our study addresses the main aspects of a Semantic Web information retrieval system architecture trying to answer the requirements of the next-generation Semantic Web user. This scheme is based on the next principle: knowledge items are abstracted to a characterization by metadata description witch is used for further processing.

Semantic interoperability is the heart of European digital repository vision. As a consequence, interoperability we achieve different properties: federating objects from distributed sources, joining knowledge from heterogeneous sources with different community background. To put our aims into practice we should first of all develop the domain ontology and study how the content-based similarity between the concepts typed attributes could be assessed in CBR system. A dedicated inference mechanism is used to answer queries conforming to the logic formalism and terms defined in our ontology. We have been working on the design of entirely ontology-based structure of the case and the development of our own reasoning methods in jColibri to operate with it. It introduced a prototype web-based CBR retrieval system, which operates on an RDF file store. This system combines RDF representation and CBR recommendation methodology to do code selection for the resources codes; thus it applies a CBR approach with RDF data model. Furthermore an

Figure 9. OntoloGov search analysis report

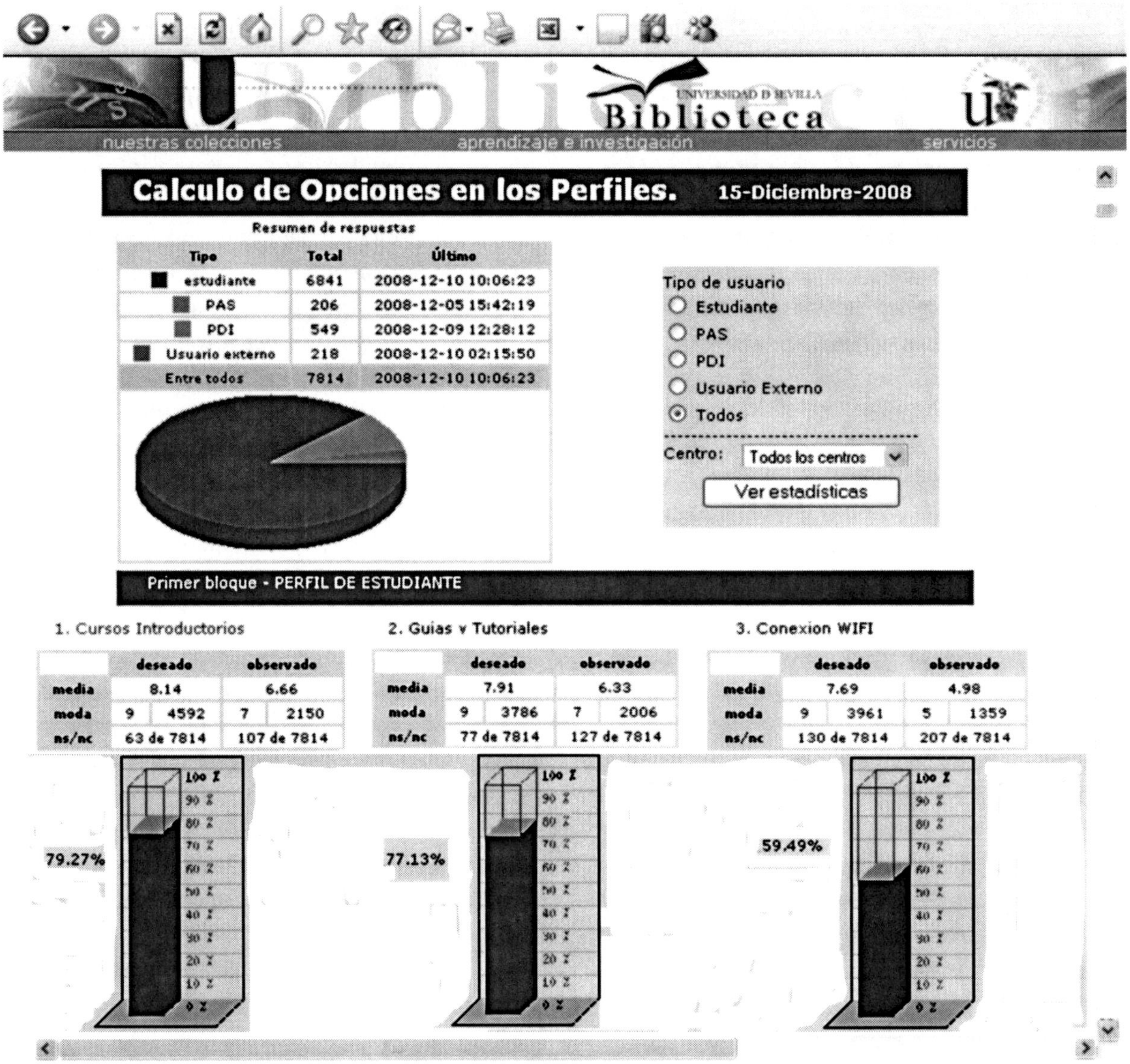

intelligent agent was illustrated for assisting the user by suggesting improved ways to query the system on the ground of the resources in Sevilla University Repositories according to his own preferences, which come to represent his interests.

Finally the study analyses the implementation results, and evaluates the viability of our approaches in enabling search in intelligent-based digital repositories. OntoloGov can be part of a bigger framework of interacting global information networks including e. g. other digital libraries, scientific repositories and commercial providers, and relies as much as possible on standards and existing building blocks as well as be based on web standards.

The results demonstrate that by improving representation by incorporating more metadata from within the information and the ontology into the retrieval process, the effectiveness of the information retrieval is enhanced. Future work will concern the exploitation of information coming from others institutional repositories and digital services and further refine the suggested queries, to extend the system to provide another type of support, as well as to refine and evaluate the system through user testing. It is also necessary the development of an authoring tool for user authentication, efficient ontology parsing and real-life applications.

REFERENCES

Bainbridge, D., Dewsnip, M., & Witten, I. H. (2005). Searching digital music libraries. *Information Processing & amp. Management*, *4*(1), 41–56.

Bechhofer, S., Harmelen, F.V., Hendler, J., Horrocks, I., McGuinness, D.L, Patel-Schneider, P.F, & Stein, L.A. (2004). OWL web ontology language reference. *W3C Recommendation, 10*.

Breslow, L. A., & Aha, D.W. (1997). Simplifying decision trees: A survey. *The Knowledge Engineering Review Archive*, *12*(1), 1-40.

Bridge, M., G¨oker, H., McGinty, L., & Smyth, B. (2006). Case-based recommender systems. *The Knowledge Engineering Review*.

Chen, L. (2008). Design and implementation of intelligent library system. *Library Collections, Acquisitions & Technical Services*, *32*(3–4), 127–141. doi:10.1016/j.lcats.2008.09.001

Cho, J. S., & Hyun, K. H. (2006). Meta-ontology for automated information integration of parts libraries. *Computer Aided Design*, *38*(7), 713–725. doi:10.1016/j.cad.2006.03.002

Díaz-Agudo, B., González-Calero, P.A., Recio-García, J., & Sánchez-Ruiz, A. (2007). Building CBR systems with jColibri. *Journal of Science of Computer Programming*.

Diaz-Galiano, M. C., Martin-Valdivia, M. T., & Urena-Lopez, L. A. (2009). Query expansion with a medical ontology to improve a multimodal information retrieval system. *Computers in Biology and Medicine*, *39*(4), 396–403. doi:10.1016/j.compbiomed.2009.01.012 PMID:19268924

Ding, H. (2004). Towards the metadata integration issues in peer-to-peer based digital libraries. In GCC (LNCS), (Vol. 3251). Berlin, Germany: Springer.

EIF. (2014, April 21). *European Interoperability Framework Version 2*. Retrieved from http://ec.europa.eu/isa/strategy/doc/annex_ii_eif_en.pdf

Finnie, G., & Sun, Z. (2002). Similarity and metrics in case-based reasoning. *International Journal of Intelligent Systems*, *17*(3), 273–287. doi:10.1002/int.10021

GAIA - Group for Artificial Intelligence Applications. (2012). *jCOLIBRI project - Distribution of the development environment with LGPL*. Complutense University of Madrid. Retrieved May 18, 2014, from http://gaia.fdi.ucm.es/grupo/projects/

Gomez-Perez, A., Corcho, A. O., & Fernandez-Lopez, M. (2003). *Ontological Engineering*. Berlin: Springer.

Govedarova, D., Stoyanov, S., & Popchev, I. (2008). An Ontology Based CBR Architecture for Knowledge Management in BULCHINO Catalogue. In *Proceedings of International Conference on Computer Systems and Technologies*. Academic Press. doi:10.1145/1500879.1500953

Guha, R., McCool, R., & Miller, E. (2003). Semantic search. In *Proceedings of WWW2003*. WWW.

Heflin, J. (2004). OWL Web Ontology Language Use Cases and Requirements. *W3C Recommendation*.

Horridge, M., & Knublauch, H. (2004). *A Practical Guide To Building OWL Ontologies Using The Protégé-OWL Plugin and CO-ODE Tools*. The University of Manchester.

Jimeno-Yepes, A., Berlanga-Llavori, R., & Rebholz-Schuhmann, D. (2010). Ontology refinement for improved information retrieval. *Information Processing & Management*, *46*(4), 426–435. doi:10.1016/j.ipm.2009.05.008

Luger, G. F. (2002). Artificial Intelligence, Structures and Strategies for Complex Problem Solving (4th ed.). Pearson Education Limited.

MAP. (2014). *Aplicaciones utilizadas para el ejercicio de potestades: Criterios de Seguridad, Normalización y Conservación*. Ministerio de Administraciones Públicas. Retrieved from http://www.csi.map.es/csi/criterios/index.html

PROTÉGÉ. (2013, December 16). *The Protégé Ontology Editor and Knowledge Acquisition System*. Retrieved from http://protege.stanford.edu/

Quan, D., & Karger, D. R. (2004). How to make a semantic web browser. In *Proceedings of WWW2004*. WWW. doi:10.1145/988672.988707

Sasaki, H., & Kiyoki, Y. (2005). A formulation for patenting content-based retrieval processes in digital libraries, *Information Processing &amp. Management*, *41*(1), 57–74.

SEC. (2003). *Commission Staff Workking Paper: Linking up Europe, the importance of interoperability for egovernment services*. Retrieved from http://europa.eu.int/ISPO/ida/export/files/en/1523.pdf

Staab, S., & Studer, R. (2005). *Handbook on Ontologies*. Berlin: Springer.

Stuckenschmidt, H., & Harmelen, F. V. (2001). *Ontology-based metadata generation from semi-structured information. In Proceedings of K-CAP* (pp. 163–170). ACM.

Sun, Z., & Finnie, G. (2004). *Intelligent Techniques in E-Commerce: A Case-based Reasoning Perspective*. Heidelberg, Germany: Springer-Verlag. doi:10.1007/978-3-540-40003-5

Sure, Y., & Studer, R. (2005). Semantic Web technologies for digital libraries. Library Management Journal, 26.

Taniar, D., & Rahayu, J. W. (2006). *Web semantics and ontology*. Hershey, PA: Idea Group. doi:10.4018/978-1-59140-905-2

Toledo, C. M., Ale, M. A., Chiotti, O., & Galli, M. R. (2011). An Ontology-driven Document Retrieval Strategy for Organizational Knowledge Management Systems. *Electronic Notes in Theoretical Computer Science*, *281*, 21–34. doi:10.1016/j.entcs.2011.11.023

Toussaint, J., & Cheng, K. (2006). Web-based CBR (case-based reasoning) as a tool with the application to tooling selection. *International Journal of Advanced Manufacturing Technology*, *29*(1-2), 24–34. doi:10.1007/s00170-004-2501-0

W3C. (2014). *RDF Vocabulary Description Language 1.0: RDF Schema*. Retrieved from http://www.w3.org/TR/rdf-schema/

Warren, P. (2005). *Applying semantic technologies to a digital library: a case study. Library Management Journal*.

Witten, I. H., & Bainbridge, D. (2003). *How to Build a Digital Libary*. Morgan Kaufmann.

Zhaohao, S., & Gavin, F. (2005). A Unified Logical Model for CBR-based E-commerce Systems. *International Journal of Intelligent Systems*, *20*(1), 29–46. doi:10.1002/int.20052

KEY TERMS AND DEFINITIONS

Case-Based Reasoning: A technique for problem/search solving which looks for previous examples, which are similar to the current problem/search.

Digital Library: Provides electronic documents and resources to select, structure, offer intellectual access to, interpret, distribute, preserve the integrity of, and ensure the persistence of collections of digital works so that they are readily and available for use by a defined community or set of communities.

Knowledge Management: The management of cycle for optimal performance across all aspects of search information in the Semantic Web domain.

Ontology: A set of concepts such as things, events, and relations, which are specified in a representative way in order to create an agreed-upon vocabulary for exchanging information. Ontology is the specification of conceptualizations, working model of entities, and interactions used to help programs and humans share knowledge in a specific domain such as electronic commerce, planning activity, etc.

Retrieval Information: Finding material usually documents of a structure or unstructured nature usually text that satisfies an information need from within large collections and repositories.

Semantic Web: Extension of the current Web that provides an efficient way to find, share, reuse and combine knowledge. The Semantic Web provides common formats for the interchange of data, which is based on machine readable information and builds on XML technology's capability to define customized tagging schemes and RDF's (Resource Description Framework) flexible approach to representing data.

Chapter 12
The German Electronic Identity Card:
Lessons Learned

Christoph Sorge
CISPA and Institute of Legal Informatics, Saarland University, Germany

ABSTRACT

Authentication is an important aspect of e-government applications, as in many cases the identity of a citizen has to be established before provision of a service. Germany is among the countries that have established an electronic identification and authentication infrastructure, based on an electronic identity card. The card enables both local and remote authentication to service providers and authorities. While privacy-enhancing technologies have been used to a large extent in its design and there are no known attacks on its security protocols, the eID card has been harshly criticized. Less than a third of the citizens requesting an identity card choose to activate the eID function. Using the example of Germany, this chapter discusses whether the establishment of an electronic authentication infrastructure makes sense and presents possible reasons for the German eID card's lack of success. In addition, the author considers electronic signatures and their integration in an electronic authentication infrastructure.

INTRODUCTION

In many countries, the provision of identity cards, enabling citizens to prove their identities to authorities or private companies (like banks), is considered as a task of the state. Smartcard technology allows integrating additional features, like storage of biometric data, in such identity cards. Given the growing importance of e-business and e-government transactions, some countries have also decided to support remote authentication to the respective service providers. Both developments can be combined (i.e., remote authentication can be performed by a chip on an identity card), but this is not strictly a necessity. For example, Malaysia's MyKad (Loo, Yeow, & Chong, 2009) uses a multi-application smartcard that can, in principle, be used locally and remotely. The Austrian Bürgerkarte for remote authentication, on the other hand, is not bound to a national iden-

DOI: 10.4018/978-1-4666-7266-6.ch012

tity card scheme. There is a multitude of design options for identity card schemes and electronic authentication; for an (incomplete) overview of existing schemes in Europe, see (Zefferer, 2010).

In this chapter, we focus on Germany, where a new identity card was introduced in November, 2010. Besides changing the dimensions of the identity card and improving the protection against forgery, the main innovation lies in the addition of a contactless smartcard. Like existing electronic passports, the smartcard can be used at border controls and during other inspections of the identity card by authorities; this way, the authenticity of the data contained on the card can be confirmed, and (optionally) stored fingerprints can be used for biometric verification of the card holder's identity. Like in case of the (older) electronic passport, data stored on the smartcard can be digitally signed, thus making it very difficult (if not impossible) to forge any information.

In addition, the smartcard can also be used for (remote) authentication to service providers, e.g. online retailers, banks or e-government services (so-called eID function). This feature requires the user to purchase a smartcard reader; the service provider needs a certificate confirming his authorization to use specific information from the identity card, and server software implementing the protocols used by the card. For each service provider, a different identifier is used; the creation of user profiles across service providers is therefore not possible based on those identifiers.

Finally, the electronic identity card is a secure signature creation device, as specified by the European Signature Directive; thus, it can potentially be used to sign documents in a legally binding manner. However, the certificates used in the signature creation process are issued by private companies.

The remainder of this chapter is structured as follows: First, we give a short overview on smartcards, and describe the technology and the infrastructure used for the German eID card. We then comment on the current adoption of the electronic authentication infrastructure based on the eID card. Next, based on the example of Germany, we discuss whether the introduction of such an infrastructure makes sense, and describe related benefits. The chapter concludes with an outlook on possible future research directions.

BACKGROUND

In this section, we first provide some general background about smartcards, before looking at the Geman eID card in more detail.

Smartcards

Though the idea of smartcards has been around since 1968, the first major successful rollout was not until the 1990s (Shelfer & Procaccino, 2002). Among the earliest applications was the replacement of banking cards with magnetic stripes: smartcards have the advantage of a greater memory capacity. In this chapter, we focus on smartcards that come with a processor, instead of pure storage cards; in fact, some authors consider only such processor cards as smartcards.

Such a processor can enforce access control restrictions, and in addition, it can perform (cryptographic) computations. For example, cryptographic keys can be stored on the card, and the processor makes sure that these keys are only used after the card holder has been authenticated using a secret PIN. The keys never have to leave the card. As a consequence, some operations that have to be performed by a trustworthy component (e.g. the computation of an electronic wallet's current balance) can be performed on the card, while previously (using magnetic stripes), a trusted server had to be contacted.

Among the most common smart cars are bank cards and subscriber identity modules (SIM cards) used for the authentication of mobile phones to GSM, UMTS or LTE networks. In addition, Shelfer & Procaccino (2002) point out that "just about anything found in a person's wallet has the potential to be stored on a smart card".

The ISO 7816 standard, consisting of 15 parts, specifies the most relevant aspects of smartcards, including physical dimensions, electrical and electronic aspects, and communication protocols. For a more detailed introduction, refer to Shelfer & Procaccino, 2002.

Identity Cards in Germany

All Germans who are at least 16 years old, and who spend most of their time in Germany, are required to possess an identity card.[1] The identity card can be replaced by a passport; however, as the identity card is smaller, cheaper, and also valid as a travel document in most European countries, most citizens request one instead of, or in addition to, a passport.

Until October, 2010, the identity card was designed for visual/optical inspection (including by electronic readers) only, and used the ID-2 format. The newly introduced identity card uses the ID-1 format (credit card format), and contains a smartcard with a wireless interface.

In the remainder of this chapter, we will focus on the features of this smartcard and ignore the features of the identity card designed for visual inspection.

Security Protocols

The German electronic identity card implements a number of security protocols, specified by the German Federal Office for Information Security (Bundesamt für Sicherheit in der Informationstechnik, 2012):

- **The PACE Protocol (Password-Authenticated Connection Establishment):** Establishes a secure connection between the smartcard reader and the identity card, authenticated by a password. In case of local inspection by police or other authorities entitled to verify citizens' identities, a number printed on the eID card, the Card Access Number (CAN), is used as the password for this protocol. However, this authentication requires the subsequent terminal authentication to be performed with a certificate specifically issued for that purpose. If the user intends to authenticate towards a service provider, a secret six-digit PIN is used instead. The PACE protocol has been proven secure against offline password-guessing, so eavesdropping is not an issue despite the wireless communication channel. Brute-force attacks on the PIN are prevented as the card is locked after three unsuccessful authentication attempts. It can be unlocked using the CAN or, if the new attempt also fails, using a long PIN Unblocking Key (PUK). During the PACE protocol, the communication partners also agree on key material, which is used for authentication and encryption of the subsequent communication.
- **The Extended Access Control (EAC) Protocol, Version 2:** It consists of terminal authentication and chip authentication. The terminal authentication protocol is executed between the eID card and the terminal, i.e. the actual intended communication partner to which the user would like to authenticate. For example, the terminal can be run by an e-government service or a company to which service provision is outsourced. Terminal authentication is based on a certificate, which contains information about the service provider and attributes that provider has access to.
- **Chip Authentication:** Executed between the same two parties, is based on Diffie-Hellman, where the eID card's key pair is

static, and the public Diffie-Hellman value is signed by the eID card's issuer ("passive authentication").

- **The Restricted Identification Protocol:** Once an eID card has been recognized as authentic, the Restricted Identification protocol is used to generate an identifier which is unique for the tuple (eID card, service provider), with the service provider's identity taken from the certificate used during terminal authentication. Tracking the usage of one eID card across several service providers is not possible, as the respective identifiers cannot be linked to each other. In essence, the Restricted Identification protocol can be thought of as generating a hash value of (secret stored by eID card || service provider identity). The actual protocol is based on the Diffie-Hellman principle, thereby achieving additional functionality: The identifier used by a specific eID card for a specific service provider can be reconstructed by two cooperating authorities to enable revocation. To prevent abuse of the revocation feature, a single authority cannot do the same.

Figure 1 illustrates the relation between the PACE, terminal authentication, and chip authentication protocols. Restricted identification is performed over the secure channel established after the aforementioned protocols have been executed.

In addition to the security protocols in a narrower sense, two more features are worth mentioning: The eID card can do more than just transmit previously stored, authenticated data. For the age verification feature, the terminal transmits a date to the eID card. The card answers whether or not its owner was born before that date. This way, transmission of the precise date of birth is avoided when it is not required. Note that age verification can only be performed once per execution of the terminal authentication and PACE protocols (thus, once per PIN entry). As a

Figure 1. Relation between PACE, terminal, and chip authentication performed during use of the eID card. PACE requires the user to enter his PIN code; in addition, the user may select (restrict) the data fields to be transmitted to a service provider. This user interaction is omitted in the figure.

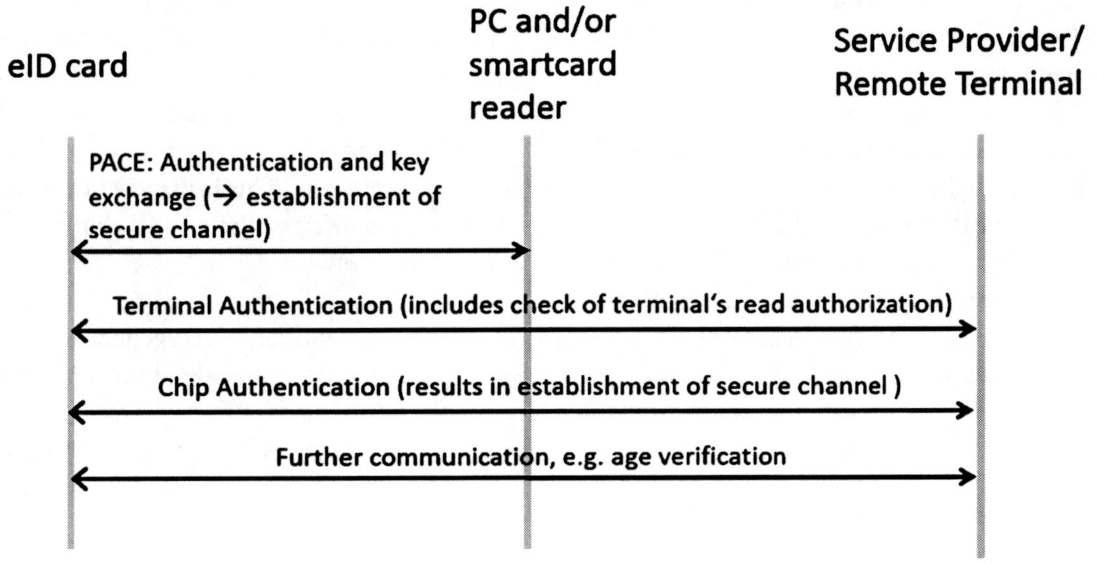

result, the service provider cannot determine the date of birth more precisely by querying the eID card several times (Bundesamt für Sicherheit in der Informationstechnik, 2013).

Community ID verification was also designed with the goal to transmit as coarse-grained information as possible. Each German municipality has a unique identifier, the municipality key. It consists of identifiers for the country, state, administrative region, county and municipality. The municipality key for the eID card holder's place of residence is stored on the card. Depending on the required granularity, a service provider can read parts of the municipality key (e.g., only the state, or the state and the administrative region within that state). Use of this feature makes sense if services are supposed to be available only for inhabitants of a certain region, e.g. all citizens residing in a certain state (Bundesamt für Sicherheit in der Informationstechnik, 2011).

Public-Key Infrastructure

The eID card heavily relies on public-key cryptography. Therefore, a public key infrastructure (PKI) must be in place to ensure authenticity of public keys. More specifically, there are two separate infrastructures. One PKI has been established for signing data stored on eID cards: The root certification authority, called the Country Signer Certificate Authority (CSCA) signs the Document Signer (DS) certificates of identity card manufacturers, which sign the data on the cards.

The second PKI is defined for granting access to the cards. The certificates of this PKI are used during the terminal authentication protocol. There are three separate certification trees: One is for official inspection of the identity card, e.g. by police and other authorities that are entitled to verify citizens' identities. If a terminal has such a certificate, the Card Access Number is used instead of the user's PIN during the PACE protocol. As the CAN is only printed on, but not stored outside the card, this is supposed to make sure that such an inspection is only performed locally.

The second certification tree is for the eID function, i.e. for electronic authentication both to private companies and to e-government services. Service providers can request certificates authorizing access to eID cards. Access can be restricted, e.g. to age verification only; when requesting a certificate, a service provider must state reasons why it needs the specific data it requests access to. There is a fee for certificate issuing, but it is negligible in comparison to the operating cost of an eID server.

Finally, the last certification tree is required for the electronic signature function. Owners of an eID card who want to use it to electronically sign documents need access to the card in the first place, i.e. their smartcard readers require a certificate, just like a service provider.

Security Assessment

There are no known attacks on the security protocols used, and the eID card appears to be a well-engineered system reaching the goals it was designed for. The PACE protocol has been proven secure (Bender, Fischlin, & Kügler, 2009); other protocols used rely on widely accepted principles and assumptions. There have, however, been claims of security breaches, which were discussed in the general press. This is not a contradiction to the stated security of the system, but illustrates mismatches between:

- The expectations of the general public and the actual design goals of the eID card and its environment, and
- The security achieved by cryptographic protocols on the one hand and the security

achieved by actual implementations and by embedding the eID card system in an insecure environment on the other hand.

Remaining security issues with the eID card are as follows:

- The eID card does not know the current date or time, so it may accept an expired certificate during the terminal authentication protocol. However, during terminal authentication, the eID card stores the date when the presented terminal certificate was issued. During future executions of the terminal authentication protocol, certificates that have expired before that date will no longer be accepted.
- Security of the authentication depends on a secure PIN entry method. The eID card can be used with secure smartcard readers, which have their own PIN pad and their own display. While it is not completely impossible to compromise these smartcard readers, they achieve a much higher security level than the users' PCs: Due to their specialization, their smaller code base, and their limited interface, there are fewer possibilities of attack. However, the eID card can also be used in conjunction with simple smartcard readers, in which case the PIN is entered on the user's PC. In that case, malware on the PC can read the PIN. Afterwards, the eID card can thus be used by the malware to authenticate to arbitrary service providers, as long as the card is in proximity to the reader.
- The software written to support the eID card could also introduce security issues, as the security of complex software cannot be guaranteed given the current state of the art. This concerns both the server-side and the client-side software. However, the client-side software has been particularly criticized. It uses plug-ins for communication with web browsers. At the time of this writing, the application supports (only) Internet Explorer, Firefox, and iceweasel. In case of Firefox, only the so-called "Extended Support Release" of version 24 is supported, while version 29 is current. Versions of the application for different operating systems have download sizes between about 60 and about 90 megabytes, despite limited functionality and a simplistic user interface. The first major vulnerability of the application was discovered less than a day after its initial publication (Kossel, 2010).
- The eID card provides secure authentication, electronic signatures, and age and address verification. It does not go beyond that; in particular, after an authentication has taken place, communication sessions between the user and the service provider could, for example, be taken over by an attacker who has installed malware on the user's PC. This is obvious to computer scientists, but not necessarily to the general public.

There is another aspect of the electronic identity card that may be considered as a less-than-elegant design decision: Chip authentication is based on a traditional public-key cryptographic scheme. If applied in a straightforward manner, this would render the Restricted Identification protocol useless: Service providers could track their customers (and exchange information about them with other service providers) based on the public key[2] presented during chip authentication. There are cryptographic protocols with which an entity can prove that it belongs to a certain group (in case of the eID card, the group would be the entirety of all valid eID cards), without revealing any additional information (like a specific public key). Both anonymous credential schemes and the related group signature schemes (Bellare, Micciancio, & Warinschi, 2003) would be suited for that purpose. However, implementation of these schemes on (contactless) smartcards is still a challenge, so it was not an option for eID cards introduced in 2010. Instead, all eID cards of one batch share a common key pair for chip authentication to private sector terminals. If an attacker manages to extract the private key from one eID card, this implies that the corresponding public key for more than a million eID cards must be revoked. However, chances for a successful attack on a state-of-the-art smartcard are considered slim.

The privacy features of the German eID card, such as the Restricted Identification protocol and the age verification scheme, are unique, at least for such a large-scale and general-purpose electronic authentication infrastructure. There are currently no known attacks on these features.

Adoption

To become useful, an electronic authentication must be accepted by service providers and used by the respective users. At the time of this writing, the German Ministry of the Interior's website (Federal Ministry of the Interior, 2013) lists:

- Eight insurance companies,
- Six finance-related service providers, and
- Seven other service providers

accepting the eID card (in addition to e-government services, which we will discuss separately). While most of these service providers allow the eID card to be used for the login to each session, a few of them only use the card for a one-off registration – relying on traditional means of authentication for later application sessions. In particular, there is no bank among the finance-related service providers that allows the eID card to be used for frequent tasks in online banking (like checking the account balance or performing money transfers). There is, however, a bank running an automated teller machine that accepts the eID card.

Due to the low number of services, and due to their nature, it is unlikely that any citizens frequently use the eID card for private sector services.

The adoption of the eID card for e-government services is more difficult to judge. There are a few federal agencies supporting the eID card for specific applications. In addition, all federal states allow (one-off) registration for an electronic filing of tax declarations with authentication based on the eID card. 9 out of 16 states offer additional services, sometimes limited to a few cities per state (Federal Ministry of the Interior, 2013).

The limited number of services corresponds to a lack of user acceptance. According to a report from November, 2013 (three years after introduction of the eID card), 21 million eID cards, plus 2.2 million eID cards for foreigners (electronic resident permit), having the same electronic functionality, had been issued by that time (Borchers, 2013). However, only 28% of the users decided to activate the eID function (which is free if chosen when the card is first issued).

GOVERNMENT-OPERATED ELECTRONIC AUTHENTICATION INFRASTRUCTURES: HELPFUL OR USELESS?

In this section, we discuss if the establishment of electronic identification and authentication infrastructures (we will omit the identification aspect for brevity) makes sense. We deal with the question whether such infrastructures should be run by governments, and try to identify reasons for their lack of acceptance. The section concludes with remarks on electronic signatures, which may also benefit from the availability of an electronic authentication infrastructure.

Costs and Benefits of Electronic Authentication Infrastructures

From an economic perspective, answering the question whether the establishment of an electronic authentication infrastructure makes sense seems simple only at first glance: If – and only if – the benefit (for the economy of the whole) outweighs the costs, then such an infrastructure should be introduced.

Determining the costs to be borne by the operator is relatively simple, though a lot of factors (like the establishment of new business processes, training measures, and cost of hardware including guarantees for long-term availability) have to be taken into account. Moreover, the question is which part of the costs is to be considered: in the German example, one motivation for the introduction of the new eID card was to improve the identity card's protection against forgery, as the chip stores data which can be electronically signed. In other words, one has to consider only the additional costs of establishing an electronic authentication infrastructure (beyond the components needed for border controls and inspection by the police).

For various reasons, the benefit is almost impossible to be measured beforehand.

Firstly, the benefit of the infrastructure depends on its acceptance by service providers and end users. In case of Germany, despite all theoretic advantages, the eID card and its infrastructure have little benefit because they are hardly used. Alternative means of authentication must still be available to be able to serve all users. In addition to the many German citizens who do not want to use the eID card, and the citizens who wait for the expiration of their old ID card until requesting the eID card, there is a huge group who is not entitled to get one: Foreigners cannot get the normal eID card (which is reserved for Germans). While there is a specific eID card for foreigners, it is only available to non-EU foreigners. Citizens of European Union member states cannot get either of the cards.

Secondly, the main benefit of an authentication infrastructure is to reduce the damage (and/or costs) caused by the drawbacks of existing authentication mechanisms. The costs of existing authentication mechanisms could be:

- *Caused by a lower reliability of these alternative mechanisms.* The problem of identity theft, for example, can be attributed to the use of weak authentication schemes. Unfortunately, getting reliable numbers concerning the magnitude of identity theft is difficult. The U.S. Department of Justice reports that 7% of all U.S. citizens aged 16 or above were victims of identity theft in 2012, resulting in direct and indirect losses of 24.7 billion US$ (Harrell & Langton, 2013). Yet, this number is not an indication for the severity of the problem in other countries, as the susceptibility to identity theft is influenced by a lot of factors. Consumers' attitudes, the prevalence of electronic payment schemes, and the availability of a (non-electronic) identification/authentication infrastructure may play a role.
- *Even if the total damage caused by identity theft is known, a closer investigation is required to find out how much of the damage was related to electronic authentication,* and was caused by usage of a weak authentication scheme (i.e. could have been avoided by a better one).
- *Direct costs related to the alternative mechanisms.* For example, the identity of a person may be verified by sending a letter to the person's address, and verifying that this letter actually arrives. Besides the postage, direct costs include expenses for paper, printing, and processing of replies. To achieve a higher security level, additional services are available. For example, Deutsche Post offers a service called "Postident", which involves check-

ing the consumer's identity card or passport. Prices are dependent on the number of identity checks performed, but Deutsche Post's website states a maximum price of EUR 6.61, plus VAT and return postage (Deutsche Post, 2014); obviously, variable costs for an electronic authentication infrastructure can be lower. Whether this outweighs the fixed costs of establishing an electronic authentication scheme is unclear; among others, this depends on the number of authentications actually required.

- *Caused by a lower user acceptance for the alternative mechanisms.* This seems plausible in case of media discontinuities (if use of an electronic service requires the user to authenticate using non-electronic means, and possibly to wait to the next business day for this authentication to take place). Given the current adoption of the German eID card, however, it seems the user acceptance of alternative mechanisms is not lower at all.

To summarize, there is no general answer to the question whether an electronic authentication infrastructure makes sense, as the answer depends on country-specific circumstances. The current lack of user acceptance for the German solution does not mean that electronic authentication infrastructures are a bad idea in general, but could also be attributed to specific mistakes made by German authorities.

OPERATION BY THE GOVERNMENT?

Assuming it does make sense to introduce such an infrastructure, the next question is by whom it can – and should – be operated, and whether the state is the appropriate entity.

Independent of the technology used, a major cost factor of electronic authentication is the verification of the users' identities. A number of industries have access to data that can be used for identity verification (or at least address verification), e.g. utilities, banks, or postal services. The Austrian electronic authentication concept, the Bürgerkarte, allows eID cards to be issued by banks or other service providers. The same concept could have been applied in Germany. However, the use of state-issued identity cards enables a higher coverage, and is also very reliable: Banks and other companies that require secure authentication use the government-issued identity card for that purpose, so they cannot achieve a higher reliability than provided by that card itself.

In addition to being reliable, a requirement for an electronic authentication infrastructure is for it to be trusted. There has been little research to assess whether involvement of the government is helpful to achieve this trust. A qualitative assessment has been provided by researchers investigating the acceptance of the German eID card using the focus group method (Harbach, Fahl, Rieger, & Smith, 2013): Apparently, there are users for whom government involvement is a deterrent, and others who trust the government more than private companies. The authors get to the result that on the whole, the government was considered more trustworthy with respect to the gathering of personal data than companies. Due to the limited number of persons involved in the study, this result cannot simply be transferred to the German population as a whole, let alone other countries.

Even if we assume that a government should run an electronic authentication infrastructure, and is best-suited to establish the identity of citizens, the question remains whether the infrastructure should be directly coupled with existing identification schemes. More precisely, is the German solution of combining the eID card with the national identity card reasonable?

Once again, there is the cost argument. As becomes visible when looking at the electronic passport – which was introduced long before the eID card – the addition of a smartcard to identity documents has been considered advantageous even without the benefits of a generally available electronic authentication infrastructure. On the long run, adding some functionality – part of which uses cryptographic algorithms anyway implemented – seems to be the more efficient option in comparison to the roll-out of separate cards. In addition, a single card is easier to store, and more convenient to handle, than if several separate cards were used.

Interestingly, Harbach et al. (2013) point out that the official nature of the identity card may even deter people from using it for internet-based services; one of their participants pointed out that the identity card was a "very personal document" and might therefore not be suited for "playing around on the Internet". In addition, they observe that the use of an identity card with a photo can be perceived to contradict the pseudonymous authentication feature provided by the card. Both aspects are related to the fact that the eID card is government-issued, but are reinforced by the combination with the mandatory national identity card.

Usefulness for E-Government Services

A lot of electronic government services are currently offered that do not use strong authentication, or even do not use any authentication at all. To judge the usefulness of an electronic authentication infrastructure, the question is whether existing e-government services would still benefit from a more secure authentication, and whether additional services could be offered with such an infrastructure.

A benefit can only be expected from an electronic authentication infrastructure for services which do not require the physical presence of the citizen.

According to American literature (Cook, 2000), citizens commonly wish for services like renewal of driver's licenses, voter registration and the filing of (state) taxes. These services can benefit from an electronic authentication infrastructure, as they require secure authentication. In contrast to the U.S., however, voters do not need to register in Germany; moreover, the need for renewing driver's licenses was only introduced so recently that no German driver's license has expired yet. On the other hand, German residents have to report their place of residence when moving – this service, too, could be offered electronically and requires authentication of the citizen.

Cook (2000) also lists voting on the Internet – which is currently out of the question, as even the use of computers as voting machines within a polling station is not legal in Germany due to the requirement for verifiability of the election process (Bundesverfassungsgericht/Federal Constitutional Court, 2009). Requesting hunting and fishing licenses, and ordering birth, death, and marriage certificates (as also listed by Cook), on the other hand, would make sense in Germany as well. The latter is already possible in some municipalities, even without using eID-based authentication;[3] introducing an authentication requirement would further reduce the risk of abuse, but given the limited information available on these certificates, it seems that authentication is not currently considered necessary.

Further services listed by Cook (2000) are state park information and reservations (which do not require strong authentication), access to "one-stop shopping" (with authentication only required for transactional services, which we have already listed separately), and accessing medical information from the National Institute of Health (which is a research institute, so this service is not about individuals' medical records and does not require strong authentication either).

To summarize, while the services that can benefit from an electronic authentication infrastructure may differ between countries, there are services for which such an infrastructure (as offered in Germany on the basis of the eID card) makes sense. Whether the number of such services justifies the effort invested into that infrastructure is a different issue – therefore, allowing private-sector service providers to benefit from the infrastructure appears to be a good move of German authorities.

Beyond Authentication: Electronic Signatures

Closely related to electronic authentication infrastructures are electronic and digital signatures.

Digital signature schemes are public-key cryptographic schemes that ensure integrity and authenticity of the document, and which also achieve non-repudiation: Only the owner of a private cryptographic key can generate a signature, which can be verified by anyone with access to the corresponding public key.

Digital signatures are a common technique to achieve authentication. A simple authentication protocol may consist of a random number sent as challenge, and a digital signature of that random number sent in response as a proof of identity. Still, an infrastructure for electronic authentication is not equivalent to an infrastructure for signatures. There is an important difference concerning regulation: For so-called electronic signatures, a legal framework has been established by the European Union (European Signature Directive, 1999). It defines electronic signatures as "data in electronic form which are attached to or logically associated with other electronic data and which serve as a method of authentication". There are different categories of electronic signatures: (Simple) electronic signatures as defined above, advanced electronic signatures (which require the use of cryptographic digital signature scheme), and qualified electronic signatures (a term not used in the directive itself, which calls them "advanced electronic signatures which are based on a qualified certificate and which are created by a secure-signature-creation device")[4]. The latter are of particular interest, as there are legal consequences attached to them. For example, qualified electronic signatures are considered as equivalent to handwritten signatures for most purposes. In some cases, they are already used for e-government services – in Germany, one example is the electronic request for a court order for payment (*Mahnbescheid*).

Unfortunately, while purely software-based solutions (which can even be obtained for free) are sufficient for the generation of advanced electronic signatures, the two additional requirements for qualified electronic signature are not as easy to fulfill. A qualified certificate requires the involvement of a certification authority, which must adhere to certain regulations, and can be held liable for mistakes made during the certification process. Operation of such certification authorities is not limited to governments. Instead, the legislator has chosen to allow competition between private companies, as long as the companies fulfill the requirement set forth in the directive and national laws.

A secure signature creation device must guarantee security of the private key; typically, secure signature creation devices are implemented as smartcards.

Both requirements are not necessarily met in an electronic authentication infrastructure. However, if that infrastructure is sufficiently reliable, it can enable a simpler and cheaper authentication of customers towards the certification authority, so a certificate can be issued purely based on the electronic authentication. The German eID card supports both; given that secure key storage and implementation of cryptographic algorithms were anyway required, the main functionality of a secure signature creation device was already available. When the eID card was introduced, it was decided not to ship the card with a pre-installed certificate, but to keep the concept of private-sector certification authorities. Once authentication to a certification authority (using the eID card) is successful, a qualified certificate can be loaded onto the card, and it can be used to sign documents. However, it took more than two years after introduction of the eID card for the first certification authority to support this process.

Lessons Learned

While a quantification of individual influence factors seems difficult, a number of possible reasons for the limited adoption of the German eID card solution have been identified, and could be addressed by the government:

- **Usability Could be Improved:** In particular, the necessity for users to install an application that supports only a limited set of browser versions is problematic.
- **Security of the Overall System Could be Improved:** This includes an audit of the above-mentioned client application, but also the promotion of secure smartcard readers (with their own display and PIN pad). Unfortunately, this contradicts the cost efficiency of the system. On the other hand, authentication based on the eID card is more secure than purely password-based authentication, even if insecure readers are used (a fact that has not been communicated very well).
- **Trust in the System Requires Information:** For example, the study by Harbach et al. (2013) considers insufficient information as a major obstacle for the system's adoption. Official information about the eID card is available on the Internet and from the Federal Ministry of the Interior, but Harbach et al. report difficulties in getting that information on a local level.
- **The Number of Services Could be Increased:** Partly, this can be achieved by the (federal and state) governments themselves by providing additional e-government services. In addition, the costs for private sector service providers can be influenced, for example by providing the required server software for free.

The German example does not provide clear insights for other countries, as the local circumstances may have a major influence on eID solutions. However, in addition to the issues listed above, an important consideration for the introduction of an eID scheme is the desired security level: Which services are to be supported, and do they allow making a tradeoff between security and usability – both on the service provider and on the user side? For example, alternative solutions to the German one could enable some limited features without authorization certificates, or could omit PIN entry in case of low security requirements. Obviously, such a decision requires a detailed analysis of the individual services, and the security and privacy implications of the chosen tradeoff.

FUTURE RESEARCH DIRECTIONS

There are still lots of open research issues in the field of electronic authentication infrastructures. Some of them are technological questions. Looking at the German eID card, an obvious issue is the chip authentication towards service providers with a key pair shared by a large number of cards: Replacing that concept with an anonymous credential or group signature scheme would be more elegant, but additional research is required to achieve a practical implementation for contactless smartcards – though major steps in this direction have already been taken; for example, there is an implementation for java cards that takes a few seconds for the execution of an anonymous credential protocol (Bichsel, Camenisch, Groß, & Shoup, 2009).

To achieve a breakthrough for the usage of an eID infrastructure, however, more relevant issues concern the integration into a larger context: Business processes of companies and government agencies have to be adapted, the legal framework has to be in place, and people have to perceive a benefit before using the eID card. To better understand the impediments of eID adoption, an interdisciplinary effort is required, involving not just computer scientists, but also taking social sciences' perspective into account.

CONCLUSION

This chapter has introduced the core concepts of the German electronic identity card. The electronic authentication infrastructure built around the card is well-designed, and there are no known attacks on the security protocols employed, or affecting the privacy of users of the eID card. Mistakes have still been made – including the provision of a client application for the eID card whose first major vulnerability was discovered within a day of its publication. Less than a third of the citizens requesting a new identity card also opt for the eID feature, though its activation is free. The number of private sector services taking advantage of the card is still very low, and not all states offer e-government services (beyond tax filing) which support eID-based authentication.

The combination of a national identity card, an electronic authentication infrastructure and an infrastructure for electronic signatures could still prove useful, but requires more investments, and in particular the provision of services that actually benefit from its use.

REFERENCES

Bellare, M., Micciancio, D., & Warinschi, B. (2003). Foundations of Group Signatures: Formal Definitions, Simplified Requirements, and a Construction Based on General Assumptions. In E. Biham (Ed.), *Advances in Cryptology — EUROCRYPT 2003: International Conference on the Theory and Applications of Cryptographic Techniques* (LNCS), (*vol. 2656*, pp. 614-629). Berlin: Springer. doi:10.1007/3-540-39200-9_38

Bender, J., Fischlin, M., & Kügler, D. (2009). Security Analysis of the PACE Key-Agreement Protocol. In P. Samarati, M. Yung, F. Martinelli, & C. Ardagna (Eds.), *Information Security: 12th International Conference, ISC 2009,* (LNCS), (vol. 5735, pp. 33-48). Berlin: Springer. doi:10.1007/978-3-642-04474-8_3

Bichsel, P., Camenisch, J., Groß, T., & Shoup, V. (2009). Anonymous credentials on a standard java card. In *Proceedings of the 16th ACM Conference on Computer and Communications Security (CCS '09)* (pp. 600-610). New York: ACM. doi:10.1145/1653662.1653734

Borchers, D. (2013, November 1). *Der ePerso hat Geburtstag: Drei Jahre neuer Personalausweis.* Retrieved from Heise Online: http://heise.de/-2037387

Bundesamt für Sicherheit in der Informationstechnik. (2011, March 10). *Technical Guideline TR-03127: Architecture electronic Identity Card and electronic Resident Permit.* Retrieved January 20, 2014, from https://www.bsi.bund.de/SharedDocs/Downloads/DE/BSI/Publikationen/TechnischeRichtlinien/TR03127/BSI-TR-03127_en_pdf.pdf?__blob=publicationFile

Bundesamt für Sicherheit in der Informationstechnik. (2012, March). *Technical Guideline TR-03110-1, Version 2.10: Advanced Security Mechanisms for Machine Readable Travel Documents Part 1*. Retrieved from https://www.bsi.bund.de/SharedDocs/Downloads/EN/BSI/Publications/TechGuidelines/TR03110/TR-03110_v2.1_P1pdf.pdf?__blob=publicationFile

Bundesamt für Sicherheit in der Informationstechnik. (2012, March). *Technical Guideline TR-03110-2, Version 2.10: Advanced Security Mechanisms for Machine Readable Travel Documents Part 2*. Retrieved from https://www.bsi.bund.de/SharedDocs/Downloads/EN/BSI/Publications/TechGuidelines/TR03110/TR-03110_v2.1_P2pdf.pdf?__blob=publicationFile

Bundesamt für Sicherheit in der Informationstechnik. (2013, July). *Technical Guideline TR-03110-3, Version 2.11: Advanced Security Mechanisms for Machine Readable Travel Documents Part 3*. Retrieved from https://www.bsi.bund.de/SharedDocs/Downloads/EN/BSI/Publications/TechGuidelines/TR03110/TR-03110_v2_11_P3pdf.pdf?__blob=publicationFile Bundesverfassungsgericht/Federal

Constitutional Court. (2009, March 3). *Judgment of the Second Senate of 3 March 2009 on the basis of the oral hearing of 28 October 2008*. Retrieved January 20, 2014, from https://www.bundesverfassungsgericht.de/entscheidungen/rs20090303_2bvc000307en.html

Cook, M. E. (2000, October). *What Citizens Want From E-Government: Current Practce Research*. Retrieved January 20, 2014, from http://www.netcaucus.info/books/egov2001/pdf/citizen.pdf

Deutsche Post. (2014). *Postident*. Retrieved January 20, 2014, from https://www.deutschepost.de/dpag?tab=1&skin=hi&check=yes&lang=de_EN&xmlFile=link1017202_1009859 Directive 1999/93/EC

Federal Ministry of the Interior. (2013). *German National Identity Card*. Retrieved January 20, 2014, from http://www.personalausweisportal.de/EN/Citizens/Applications/applications_node.html

Harbach, M., Fahl, S., Rieger, M., & Smith, M. (2013). On the Acceptance of Privacy-Preserving Authentication Technology: The Curious Case of National Identity Cards. In E. De Cristofaro & M. Wright (Eds.), *Privacy Enhancing Technologies: 13th International Symposium, PETS 2013* (LNCS), (*vol. 7981*, pp. 245-264). Berlin: Springer. doi:10.1007/978-3-642-39077-7_13

Harrell, E., & Langton, L. (2013, December). *Victims of Identity Theft, 2012*. Retrieved January 20, 2014, from U.S. Department of Justice, Bureau of Justice Statistics: http://www.bjs.gov/content/pub/pdf/vit12.pdf

Kossel, A. (2010, November 9). *Neuer Personalausweis: AusweisApp mit Lücken*. Retrieved January 20, 2014, from Heise Online: http://heise.de/-1133376

Loo, W., Yeow, P., & Chong, S. (2009, April). User acceptance of Malaysian government multipurpose smartcard applications. *Government Information Quarterly*, *26*(2), 358–367. doi:10.1016/j.giq.2008.07.004

Shelfer, K., & Procaccino, J. (2002, July). Smart Card Evolution. *Communications of the ACM*, *45*(7), 83–88. doi:10.1145/514236.514239

Yeow, P., & Loo, W. (2011). Acceptability of ATM and Transit Applications Embedded in Multipurpose Smart Identity Card: An Exploratory Study in Malaysia. In *Applied Technology Integration in Governmental Organizations* (pp. 118–137). New E-Government Research.

Zefferer, T. (2010). *STORK Work Item 3.3.5: Smartcard eID comparison.* Retrieved from STORK Project: https://www.eid-stork.eu/index.php?option=com_processes&Itemid=&act=streamDocument&did=1384

ADDITIONAL READING

Aichholzer, G., & Strauss, S. (2009). The Citizen's Role in National Electronic Identity Management - A Case-study on Austria. In *The Second International Conference on Advances in Human-oriented and Personalized Mechanisms, Technologies, and Services, 2009. CENTRIC '09* (pp. 45-50). Washington, D.C.: IEEE Computer Society. doi:10.1109/CENTRIC.2009.13

Arcieri, F., Ciclosi, M., Fioravanti, F., Nardelli, E., & Talamo, M. (2004). The Italian electronic identity card: a short introduction. In *Proceedings of the 2004 annual national conference on Digital government research* (Vol. 262 of the ACM International Conference Proceeding Series). Digital Government Society of North America.

Arora, S. (2008, May). National e-ID card schemes: A European overview. *Information Security Technical Report*, *13*(2), 46–53. doi:10.1016/j.istr.2008.08.002

Bramhall, P., Hansen, M., Rannenberg, K., & Roessler, T. (2007, July-August). User-Centric Identity Management: New Trends in Standardization and Regulation. *IEEE Security and Privacy*, *5*(4), 84–87. doi:10.1109/MSP.2007.99

El Maliki, T., & Seigneur, J.-M. (2007). A Survey of User-centric Identity Management Technologies. In PeñalverL.DiniO.MulhollandJ.Nieto-TaladrizO. (Eds.), *The International Conference on Emerging Security Information, Systems, and Technologies, 2007. SecureWare 2007.* (pp. 12-17). Washington, D.C.: IEEE Computer Society. doi:10.1109/SECUREWARE.2007.4385303

Grönlund, Å. (2010, July). Electronic identity management in Sweden: Governance of a market approach. *Identity in the Information Society*, *3*(1), 195–211. doi:10.1007/s12394-010-0043-1

Hammershøj, A., Sapuppo, A., Iqbal, Z., Elahi, N., Chowdhury, M., Heikkinen, S., et al. (2009, May). *User Profiles, Personalization and Privacy: WWRF Outlook Jointly Prepared by WG1, WG2 and WG7.* Retrieved January 20, 2014, from Wireless World Research Forum: http://wwrf.ch/files/wwrf/content/files/publications/outlook/Outlook3.pdf

Hansen, M., Schwartz, A., & Cooper, A. (2008, March-April). Privacy and Identity Management. *IEEE Security and Privacy*, *6*(2), 38–45. doi:10.1109/MSP.2008.41

Martens, T. (2010, July). Electronic identity management in Estonia between market and state governance. *Identity in the Information Society*, *3*(1), 213–233. doi:10.1007/s12394-010-0044-0

Mason, S. (2012). *Electronic Signatures in Law* (3rd ed.). Cambridge, UK: Cambridge University Press. doi:10.1017/CBO9780511998058

McKenzie, R., Crompton, M., & Wallis, C. (2008, March-April). Use cases for identity management in e-government. *IEEE Security and Privacy*, *6*(2), 51–57. doi:10.1109/MSP.2008.51

Naumann, I., & Hogben, G. (2008, August). Privacy features of European eID card specifications. *Network Security*, *2008*(8), 9–13. doi:10.1016/S1353-4858(08)70097-7

Noack, T., & Kubicek, H. (2010, July). The introduction of online authentication as part of the new electronic national identity card in Germany. *Identity in the Information Society*, *3*(1), 87–110. doi:10.1007/s12394-010-0051-1

Rissanen, T. (2010, July). Electronic identity in Finland: ID cards vs. bank IDs. *Identity in the Information Society*, *3*(1), 175–194. doi:10.1007/s12394-010-0049-8

Sorge, C., & Westhoff, D. (2008). eIDs und Identitätsmanagement. *Datenschutz und Datensicherheit*, *32*(5), 337–341. doi:10.1007/s11623-008-0080-1

Stallings, W. (2013). *Cryptography and Network Security: Principles and Practice* (6th ed.). Harlow, England: Pearson Education.

Wolf, C., Preneel, B., & De Cock, D. (2006). The Belgian Electronic Identity Card (Overview). In J. Dittmann (Ed.), Sicherheit 2006: Sicherheit - Schutz und Zuverlässigkeit, Beiträge der 3. Jahrestagung des Fachbereichs Sicherheit der Gesellschaft für Informatik e.v. (GI), 20.-22. Februar 2006 in Magdeburg (Vol. 77 of the series Lecture Notes in Informatics (LNI), pp. 298-301). Bonn: Bonner Köllen Verlag.

Zwingelberg, H. (2011). Necessary Processing of Personal Data: The Need-to-Know Principle and Processing Data from the New German Identity Card. In S. Fischer-Hübner, P. Duquenoy, M. Hansen, R. Leenes, & G. Zhang (Eds.), *Privacy and Identity Management for Life: 6th IFIP WG 9.2, 9.6/11.7, 11.4, 11.6/PrimeLife International Summer School, Helsingborg, Sweden, August 2-6, 2010, Revised Selected Papers* (Vol. 352 of the series IFIP Advances in Information and Communication Technology, pp. 151-163). Berlin/Heidelberg: Springer.

KEY TERMS AND DEFINITIONS

Digital Signature: Public-key cryptographic scheme that ensures authenticity and integrity of a document, and which also reaches the goal of non-repudiation (i.e. the holder of a private key cannot deny having signed a document if verification with the corresponding public key is successful).

eID card: Smartcard that implements protocols used for the authentication of a user towards a service provider over an electronic communication channel.

Electronic Signature: Legal term, describing data attached to other data (e.g., a document) and that serve the purpose of authentication.

Extended Access Control (EAC): Protocol, consisting of terminal authentication and chip authentication, that enables mutual authentication and establishment of a secure communication channel between a smartcard (eID card) and a terminal.

Password Authenticated Connection Establishment (PACE): Protocol used for authentication of a smartcard reader towards the German eID card, and for establishment of a secure channel between the card and the reader.

Public Key Infrastructure (PKI): Infrastructure for the authentication of public keys used in digital signature schemes and/or for the encryption of data. Public keys are usually authenticated by trusted certification authorities, which use digital signature schemes to confirm the mapping between a public key and the identity of its owner.

Restricted Identification (RI): Protocol that allows generation of an identifier which is specific for one combination of an eID card and a service provider.

ENDNOTES

1 Identity Card Act (Personalausweisgesetz) of 2009, section 1, subsection 1. There are exceptions to the general rule, which are omitted in this chapter for clarity.

2 More precisely: The public Diffie-Hellman value.

3 The author encountered this as an electronic service in the e-government portal of one state, and was given the choice to either use eID-based authentication, or to just supply his address with no authentication at all.

4 The presentation of electronic signature legislation in this chapter is simplified. For a more detailed discussion of the different categories of electronic signatures, see the specialized literature.

Chapter 13
Sentiment Analysis, Social Media, and Public Administration

Daniel José Silva Oliveira
Universidade Federal de Lavras (UFLA), Brazil

Paulo Henrique de Souza Bermejo
Universidade Federal de Lavras (UFLA), Brazil

Pamela Aparecida dos Santos
Universidade Federal de Lavras (UFLA), Brazil

ABSTRACT

This chapter describes how sentiment analysis, based on texts taken from social media, can be an instrument for measuring popular opinion about government services and can contribute to evaluating and developing public administration. This is an applied, interdisciplinary, qualitative, exploratory, and technological study. Throughout the chapter, the main theoretical and conceptual formulations about the subject are reviewed, and practical demonstrations are made using opinion-mining tools that provide high accuracy in data processing. For demonstration purposes, topics that triggered the popular protests of June 2013 in Brazil were selected, involving million people across the country. A total of 51,857 messages posted on social media about these topics were collected, processed, and analyzed. Through that analysis, it can be observed that even after six months, the factors that motivated the protests continued generating citizen dissatisfaction.

INTRODUCTION

The large volume of data posted on the Internet through social media is producing important changes in people's communication, knowledge sharing, and sentiments that influence social, political, and economic behaviors worldwide (Montoyo, Martínez-Barco, & Balahur, 2012).

Mostafa (2013) points out that opinions expressed on social media are vital in influencing government behavior in many areas. For example, in political and public management areas, these

DOI: 10.4018/978-1-4666-7266-6.ch013

media have the power to disseminate opinions that may result in both improved public services and protests motivated by citizen dissatisfaction with government (O'Callaghan et al., 2014; Papacharissi & Oliveira, 2012).

The popularity of these tools is considerable, making them a significant information source that can also be used to improve public services. Therefore, in addition to direct channels where citizens can send their opinions by e-mail, through online portals, and other complaint mechanisms, social media tools (blogs, microblogs, social networking sites, among others) can be used to promote participatory and citizen-oriented public services (Sobaci & Karkin, 2013). However, the sheer volume of information circulating on the Internet requires technologies enabling its analysis (Bonson, Torres, Royo, & Flowers, 2012).

Sentiment analysis, or opinion mining, is an automated knowledge discovery technique that aims to find hidden patterns in a large amount of textual information, including social media (Mostafa, 2013). The goal of sentiment analysis is to create a knowledge base in a structured, explicit manner containing reviews (positive, negative, and neutral) that express sentiments, evaluations, and perceptions about any subject (Fortuny, Smedt, Martens, & Daelemans, 2012; Sobkowicz, Kaschesky, & Bouchard, 2012).

In this context, this study aims to propose a technique of sentiment analysis as a tool to allow public administrators to use information circulating on social media for strategic purposes. In other words, this study describes how sentiment analysis can be used as an instrument for measuring public opinion about public services and identifying citizens' main dissatisfactions with government, so that government can reset its priorities and avoid unpopularity or even conflict.

This work is justified because it is necessary to understand the social media applications' use as acceptable channels for interaction between the government and its stakeholders, which can potentially make a difference in the perceptions and sentiments of citizens in relation to the government (Mergel, 2013a). Moreover, "despite the growing attention to analyzing user-generated content from social media, most [...] researchers have little knowledge about how to apply content-mining methods" (Yoon, Elhadad, & Bakken, 2013, p. 122) and lack appropriate metrics to identify the impacts of the government's actions on social media (Hofmann, Beverungen, Räckers, & Becker, 2013; Mergel, 2012). In addition, this study presents relevant theoretical and empirical contributions showing how to apply sentiment analysis to identify widespread social media opinions on politics and public management.

Thus, this chapter explores the sentiment analysis of data mining on social media about important topics in public administration, demonstrating its potential and capacity to identify citizens' views.

The next section of this chapter presents the theoretical background. The third section introduces social media as data sources. The fourth section explores recent literature about sentiment analysis of social media, describing the main issues, advantages, and limitations of the technique, and further presenting works related to the topic. The fifth section demonstrates the application of sentiment analysis to public administration by means of a practical example. Finally, the chapter concludes with information about future trends regarding the use of sentiment analysis of social media as a form of establishing a dialogue between government and citizens aiming to achieve a more democratic public management.

Background

Increasingly, citizens are using social media to communicate with families, friends, coworkers, companies, and even government (Kavanaugh et al., 2012). In addition, social media include a set of technologies that allow collaborative communication between stakeholders and government (Oliveira & Welch, 2013).

We can see on social media an increasing number of users interested in many aspects of politics (Sobkowicz et al., 2012). They cover the whole spectrum of stakeholders, from ordinary citizens who express their opinions about everyday life, to politicians who use the media to communicate their ideas, journalists who criticize their government, and governments sharing their actions (Tsytsarau & Palpanas, 2012). Opinions expressed on social media play an important role in influencing everything from the products people buy to the presidential candidates they support (Eirinaki, Pisal, & Singh, 2012). In many instances, analysts and other users are interested in tracking sentiment changes about a product, political candidate, business, or the next big thing (Pang & Lee, 2008).

Adoption of innovative techniques for analyzing social media is creating expectations about future innovation opportunities, and the appearance of tools is allowing public administrations to use social media as a source of knowledge (Criado, Sandoval-Almazan, & Gil-Garcia, 2013). One of these tools is sentiment analysis, also known as opinion mining (Sobkowicz et al., 2012).

Sentiment analysis is a very useful technique for monitoring social media because it automatically characterizes the general feelings of its users in relation to a specific brand or organization, defining whether it is viewed positively or negatively (Sobaci & Karkin, 2013). Sentiment analysis can be applied to various types of texts, online and offline, but this study focuses on analyzing texts extracted from social media because they represent a powerful tool for interaction between governments and citizens (Khan, Yoon, Kim, & Park, 2014). In addition, social media as a data source has the potential to contribute to improvements in public service delivery, making the relationship between citizens and public institutions more democratic (Sobaci & Karkin, 2013).

Even in non-democratic regimes, the inhabitants of cyberspace gathers degrees of freedom to express their opinions, making social media an environment propitious to the spread of favorable or contrary opinions about government actions (Galindo Cáceres, 2011). Recent studies show that social media have been used in several countries for articulation of popular protests, such as the Arab Spring, which was marked by protests and conflicts in the Middle East and North Africa in response to conflicts that had occurred in Egypt (Chen, 2011; Glass & Colbaugh, 2012; Lewiński & Mohammed, 2012; Lim, 2012; Papacharissi & Oliveira, 2012) and Syria (O'Callaghan et al., 2014). More recently, in June 2013, a series of popular protests was organized through social media in Brazil. According to data from the Instituto Brasileiro de Opinião Pública e Estatística (Brazilian Institute of Public Opinion and Statistics) (Ibope, 2013a), 62% of protesters knew about the event through Facebook, and 75% of those urged others to join the movement through Facebook and Twitter. This example demonstrates the power of social media to spread information and influence public opinion.

Many organizations, especially large corporations, have realized the importance of opinions expressed on social media and use sentiment analysis as a gauge of public opinion toward their brands (Cambria, Schuller, Yunqing, & Havasi, 2013). In public administration, sentiment analysis is less used, and most studies are focused on elections, for example, in the U.S.A (Choy, Cheong, Laik, & Shung, 2012; Mostafa, 2013; Zappavigna, 2011), Germany (Mostafa, 2013; Tumasjan, Sprenger, Sandner, & Welpe, 2011), Singapore (Sreekumar & Vadrevu, 2013), and Sweden (Larsson & Moe, 2011; Mostafa, 2013). On the other hand, public management is a field that is far more dynamic in cyberspace (Galindo Cáceres, 2011). Hofmann, et al. (2013) found that the benefits obtained from social media information are not limited to private sector organizations, but also extend to governments. According to Sobkowicz et al.

(2012), until recently, policymakers had few indicators about citizen's opinions, and what most people felt and thought about government actions was inaccessible. Currently, some governments are using social media to promote transparency, citizen participation, and collaboration, and social media have become an information source that contributes to decision making (Bertot, Jaeger, & Hansen, 2012; Chun & Luna Reyes, 2012; Criado et al., 2013; Meijer & Thaens, 2013; Mergel, 2012, 2013a, 2013b; Mossberger, Wu, & Crawford, 2013; Snead, 2013).

This chapter proposes that sentiment analysis of text extracted from social media can be used to reveal trends in public opinion and to identify whether citizens are satisfied with public services, helping governments to address popular concerns and, thus, reducing the risk of conflict.

To know the potential of social media as a data source capable of revealing citizens' opinions about politics and public management, it is necessary to understand how public authorities can use sentiment analysis strategically.

SOCIAL MEDIA AS DATA SOURCES

The Internet has dramatically changed the way that individuals express their views and opinions because now, they can do about almost any topic, relevant or not, through social media (Liu, 2010). The social media are applications based on the Internet designed to promote social interaction, collaboration, learning set and the fast propagation of information society. (Bonsón et al., 2012; Kavanaugh et al., 2012).

User-generated content on social media represents new, measurable sources of information with many practical applications (Moreo, Romero, Castro, & Zurita, 2012). Unmistakably, social media have become an extremely popular communication platform on which people can learn others' opinions and express their own (C. Zhang, Zeng, Li, Wang, & Zuo, 2009). Now, the Internet is available to many people, because less-expensive hardware has caused a cultural revolution, since people worldwide are now able to interact with one another; they can enjoy freedom of expression and easily access all kinds of information (Moreo et al., 2012). Through social media, people can be updated about any political or social issue in their district, state, country, or the world (Eirinaki et al., 2012). According to Bonsón, Torres, Royo, and Flores (2012, p. 125), "these platforms can be considered the next generation of the official website, incorporating in the same site the community, their opinions, the content and the most sophisticated tools for the distribution and analysis of all this information."

Social media are changing people's way of life and how they seek information and communicate (Oliveira & Welch, 2013). It is understood that the media panorama has changed dramatically in recent years, because traditional media (for example, newspapers, magazines, and TV) now are complemented or replaced by online social communication. In contrast to the content provided by traditional media sources, social media content tends to be more human oriented (Yu et al., 2013).

Now, newspapers and other news channels are updating their online content and refreshing their sites often, allowing people to track news almost in real time (Fortuny et al., 2012). Some studies, such as those of Nunomura (2013) and Yu et al. (2013), emphasize the importance of social media and its power against traditional media. On the other hand, traditional media are often described as uni-directional influences, but this situation is changing because, as users are increasingly selective in their choice of information sources, media managers have sought to adjust their programming to meet the preferences of the target audience (Sobkowicz et al., 2012).

According to Fortuny et al. (2012), in an imperfect scenario, biased media could disseminate information to the public and influence preference, for example, for one or another political party or candidate, thus creating a political reality. However, the knowledge obtained from social media is extremely valuable because millions of opinions are expressed about a particular topic, so it is highly unlikely that a majority of this information is biased (Mostafa, 2013). As stated by Nunomura (2013), if on one hand, we still need more studies of social media as a barometer of public opinion; on the other hand, we already see that social media amplify this concept and, in some cases, occupy a very important role beyond mere repeaters of news originated by traditional media.

Thus, social media have become sources of data, capable of measuring popular opinion about any subject, including politics and public management (Sobkowicz et al., 2012). Consequently, in recent years the amount of academic and corporate research exploring these data sources has increased (Yu et al., 2013). In contrast to earlier times, when finding sources of information was the main problem for organizations and individuals, today the information society challenges them to develop and implement mechanisms to mine and retrieve relevant data from the huge amount of information available, transforming them into knowledge that can contribute to the decision-making process (Montoyo et al., 2012).

SENTIMENT ANALISYS IN SOCIAL MEDIA

Although there are many highly accurate methods to analyze and extract relevant knowledge from structured data (for example, tables or databases), the task of extracting useful information from unstructured data (for example, text or speech) like social media is a major challenge (Montoyo et al., 2012). The solution to this question has been sought by many researchers in a subfield of Natural Language Processing (NLP) and called sentiment analysis (Fortuny et al., 2012).

According to Montoyo et al. (2012), NLP is a discipline of Artificial Intelligence (AI) that deals with the automatic processing of natural language in text or speech, and it is largely employed in search engines like Google and Bing. Sentiment analysis is a technique also known as opinion mining, attitude analysis, subjective analysis, favorability analysis, and extracting users' opinions from texts (Di Caro & Grella, 2013; Kontopoulos, Berberidis, Dergiades, & Bassiliades, 2013; Lane, Clarke, & Hender, 2012; Montoyo et al., 2012; Mouthami et al., 2013; Pang & Lee, 2008). Sentiment analysis is a technique for identifying, extracting, classifying, and analyzing subjective information, such as opinions and feelings on various topics, from texts (Fortuny et al., 2012; Yoon et al., 2013).

Mostafa (2013) points out that sentiment analysis is a technique for automated knowledge discovery that aims to find hidden patterns in large amounts of textual data, such as comments submitted on social media. The goal of sentiment analysis is to identify people's views on specific topics, not only in the data structure case (Di Caro & Grella, 2013). Similarly, Santos, Esmin, Zambalde, and Nobre (2011) explain that sentiment analysis is concerned with classifying texts not by topic but by sentiment or opinion contained in a particular document. Its purpose is to create a knowledge base containing opinions in a more organized, explicit way (Sobkowicz et al., 2012).

Although opinion is a very broad concept, sentiment analysis primarily focuses on positive and negative sentiment (Moreo et al., 2012). It is used to extract opinions, feelings, and subjectivity in unstructured text to identify whether the expressions indicate a positive (favorable) or negative (unfavorable) opinion for the subject (Pang & Lee, 2008). Thus, sentiment analysis can be interpreted as a classification task in which each category (positive or negative) is a sentiment (Prabowo & Thelwall, 2009). Bae and Lee (2012) and Abbasi et al. (2008) agree that sentiment analysis typically deals with identifying polarity, that is, determine whether a text is objective or subjective and if a subjective text contains positive or negative sentiment rather than distinct emotions (for example, joy or sadness). Kontopoulos et al. (2013) and Mostafa (2013) also consider neutral opinion within the polarity and agree that sentiment analysis is a process that aims to determine if the polarity of a textual corpus (document, sentence, paragraph, etc.) tends to be positive, negative, or neutral.

Many sentiment analysis approaches use language resources or machine learning to classify text (Kontopoulos et al., 2013; Yu et al., 2013). The languages resources approach compares text to lists of positive and negative words, and automated identification of textual polarity depends on the frequency with which these words appear in the document (Yu et al., 2013). The learning machine approach prepares a sentiment classifier from a training set to distinguish positive, negative, and neutral sentiment in texts (Kontopoulos et al., 2013). Prabowo and Thelwall (2009) argue that use of multiple classifiers in a hybrid approach may improve the efficacy of sentiment analysis.

This study describes how sentiment analysis can be used to reveal trends in public opinion about government actions. Therefore, it is not our goal to discover new means to mine opinion. Many tools exist that can be used to mine and analyze data on social media. One of these tools will be shown later, because firstly, it is necessary to consider the advantages and disadvantages of this technique.

Technique Advantages and Limitations

A primary advantage of sentiment analysis of social media is that the information generated by data mining is free of the noise that may be introduced by the interviewees in the case of personal interviews (Mostafa, 2013). Formal or informal opinion, depending on where it is posted, is extremely important, because it reflects the sentiment of the uncensored user. Through a direct interview, a person might feel intimidated and not respond frankly, in contrast to what is usually found in opinions posted on the Web (Santos et al., 2011). Moreover, in this case, sentiment analysis is an option to overcome the lack of civic engagement by citizens (Mergel 2012, 2013a, 2013b; Mossberger, Wu, & Crawford, 2013).

Currently, sentiment analysis is receiving much attention because of its wide range of direct applications, such as analysis of products, services, public profiles, and political trends, among others (Di Caro & Grella, 2013). Even issues of interest to public safety or the general quality of life (for example, traffic and air quality) can be discovered, monitored, and mitigated by information flows of social media detecting meaningful patterns and trends (Kavanaugh et al., 2012).

The fact that so many people express themselves on social media about all subjects makes opinions less biased and, therefore, more reliable (Montoyo et al., 2012). Galindo Cáceres (2011) corroborates this position, stating that inhabitants of cyberspace, the "new citizens," have much to say and teach and can propose many changes. Due to these reasons, the opinions expressed on the Web are increasingly considered as a basis for decision making or obtaining an unbiased feedback (Montoyo et al., 2012). Additionally, working with information extracted from social media does not always need large investments by the organization (Oliveira & Welch, 2013). Traditional research based on interviews generates significant costs that can limit or disable their application, especially considering the small budget and shrinking of the government at all levels (Kavanaugh et al., 2012).

Some limitations of sentiment analysis based on data extracted from social media should also be observed. The first important problem that still needs to be solved is the lack of substantial resources for languages besides English (Colbaugh & Glass, 2012; Montoyo et al., 2012; Yang & Yu, 2013; P. Zhang & He, 2013). Such resources should be adapted to the types of text to be analyzed and each language involved (Montoyo et al., 2012). There are also other language issues to be considered, such as the presence of noise in communication and informal language, including slang and unofficial abbreviations (Montoyo et al., 2012; Moreo et al., 2012; Yang & Yu, 2013).

Another limitation is the possible change of the individual in relation to social perception, feeling pressured to go against the majority opinion or any formal or informal group (Ceron, Curini, Iacus, & Porro, 2013; Yu et al., 2013).

Related Works

In public administration, there are few studies about sentiment analysis and opinion mining. The following is a summary of some studies identified in this step of this research.

Fortuny et al.'s (2012) paper entitled "Media coverage in times of political crisis: A text mining approach" approaches traditional media's coverage of political issues in Belgium during a period of political crisis at the end of 2011. The study measures the social sentiments of citizens in relation to the country's political parties, extracting data news from online versions of major newspapers over a ten-month period. Through research, the authors find a bias in the coverage of traditional media in political texts.

In their article, "Opinion mining in social media: Modeling, simulating, and forecasting political opinions in the web," Sobkowicz et al. (2012) investigate whether online content can be explored to inform decision makers about individual opinions, emerging trends, and potential impacts of policy initiatives. The authors apply some real life examples that divide opinions involving politics and public policy management.

Park, Lim, Sams, Nam, and Park (2010), in their article entitled "Networked politics on Cyworld: The text and sentiment of Korean political profiles," identify Korean citizens' opinions expressed on a social media site called Cyworld. The authors analyze the most common topics in the political scenario of Korea and the opinions of electors faced with the political parties. The authors show, in the case studied, that citizens' views tend to be positive when referring to opposition parties and negative for the party in power.

From these studies, it can be understood that sentiment analysis based on data collected on social media is undoubtedly a source of knowledge about the government. According to Prabowo and Thelwall (2009), with this knowledge, government officials may analyze public opinion about public services and policy issues. The next section will use a practical example to examine whether this is possible.

SENTIMENT ANALYSIS IN PRACTICE

To demonstrate how sentiment analysis can be used as a barometer of public opinion on government actions, we take as an example the popular protests in Brazil in June 2013. Six months after the events occurred, we identified opinions of Brazilian citizens about the factors that had motivated them. According to the Ibope survey (2013b), the protests in Brazil were motivated by citizens' dissatisfaction about various public issues. Another survey conducted by Ibope (2013a) reveals that social media was the channel most used by citizens to promote and organize protests and to comment on them. Our intention in using this example is to verify whether sentiment analysis of social media, performed six months after the protests, reveals that citizens remain dissatisfied about those issues or whether they feel there has been improvement.

Procedures

Sentiment analysis requires researchers to collect, code, and process data. The existing literature does not define a single model for these steps, since sentiment analysis studies use diverse methods and techniques (e.g., Li & Liu, 2012; Liu, 2010; Robaldo & Di Caro, 2013; Sobkowicz et al., 2012;

Yoon et al., 2013; P. Hang & He, 2013). This study used steps based on Tsytsarau and Palpanas (2012) that included:

1. Select topics for analysis;
2. Define search terms;
3. Choose data source;
4. Select opinion mining application;
5. Collect data;
6. Prepare data;
7. Delimit training corpus;
8. Perform automated sentiment analysis;
9. Validate results.

The topics (step 1) were chosen from the main factors that motivated the demonstrations in Brazil, as identified by Ibope (2013b) and the Causa Brasil platform (http://www.causabrasil.com.br/). The factors most cited as the cause of the events and chosen as topics for this study were public transport, combating corruption, health, education, spending on the 2014 FIFA World Cup, and Federal Government.

The search terms (step 2) were selected from a set of terms used on the social media monitoring platform *Causa Brasil* during the demonstrations. The criterion used was to choose three Portuguese terms related to each topic. These terms should be as neutral as possible so as not to influence results, and at the same time practicable to implement the technique. The selected terms are shown in Table 1.

The selected data sources (step 3) were the social media most used by Brazilian citizens during demonstrations in June 2013. According to Ibope (2013a), at one of the largest demonstrations that occurred in the country, 62% of the protesters learned about the event through Facebook, and 75% of those called on others to join via Facebook and Twitter. Thus, both of them represent the data sources for this work.

Selecting the application (step 4) for opinion mining was based on some requirements. First, the system should allow data processing in Portuguese and be able to extract data from Facebook and Twitter using the search terms previously identified. It was also necessary for the system to collect data for a specific amount of time. From these requirements, an online text analysis application called DiscoverText was adopted (http://www.discovertext.com). DiscoverText is used for analyzing cloud-based data, which is able to capture, filter, search, sort, and analyze large volumes of structured and unstructured data texts. Through this application, it is possible to

Table 1. Search terms used in data mining

Topics	Terms	Topics (Portuguese)	Terms (Portuguese)
Public transport	Public transport, free pass, ticket prices.	Transporte público	Transporte público, passe livre, preço das passagens.
Combating corruption	Combating corruption, PCI (Parliamentary Commission of Inquiry), mensalão trial.	Combate à corrupção	Combate à corrupção, CPI, julgamento mensalão.
Education	Education, teacher salaries, public school.	Educação	Educação, salário professor, escola pública.
Health	Health, public hospitals, health centers.	Saúde	Saúde, hospitais públicos, posto de saúde.
Spending on the World Cup	Spending on the World Cup, works of the Cup, spending on stadiums.	Gastos com a Copa do Mundo	Gastos com a Copa, obras da Copa, gastos com estádios.
Federal Government	Federal Government, Dilma Rousseff, President Dilma.	Governo Federal	Governo Federal, Dilma Rousseff, Presidenta Dilma.

customize and reuse classifiers based on machine learning, allowing the combined use of algorithms and human coding, which increases the accuracy of the results.

Data collection (step 5) was performed by DiscoverText in December 2013, using all the search terms identified in Table 1. The data extraction was followed by the data preparation (6), excluding noise (duplicate data, links, etc.) and applying some filters to ensure that the database was composed only of the mentions made by Brazilian citizens.

The training corpus or training set (step 7) was delimited from a stratified random sample (Cochran, 2007). The first step was to extract a sample of 100 mentions on each topic, forming a base of test data containing a total of 700 entries. For every 70 mentions manually classified, equivalent to 10% of the total, an automated classification of the entire test base was made and the hits were recorded, until a satisfactory accuracy was obtained. Precision was calculated by dividing the number of correct classifications by the total mentions (Eirinaki et al., 2012). After manually classifying 30% of the mentions, the automated classification achieved 81% accuracy. In the literature, a tool that generates 80% accuracy on average is already considered satisfactory (Mostafa, 2013; Yoon et al., 2013; Yu et al., 2013). Thus, the training corpus considered for this study was 30% of the mentions collected for each topic, as shown in Table 2.

The data listed in Table 2 presents a large reduction in numbers from raw data to processed data. This is due to the applied filters during the preparation of the data that eliminated the noise of the raw data and deleted mentions made on Twitter and Facebook by news agencies (traditional media). Thus, the data set on each topic consisted only of mentions by Brazilian citizens related to the search terms previously identified. The processed data from the training corpus was calculated for each topic in a 30% proportion, and the data which was randomly collected from each data set was classified manually.

After defining the training corpus and manually classifying the sample, all data sets were automatically classified (step 8) and the sentiments (positive, neutral, and negative) were generated for each topic, as shown in Figure 1.

Besides knowing the sentiments of citizens about each topic and what may have influenced their opinions, it is crucial to validate (step 9) these results by calculating reliability. Accuracy was calculated from new, stratified random sample (Cochran, 2007) data that have been processed automatically. The sample size was 30% of the analyzed data, while maintaining the same proportion of tests performed on the training set. Thus, the calculation precision of the automated analysis is based on Eirinaki et al. (2012), and should be as close as possible to the value found in that test, or 81%.

The arithmetic mean of the accuracy of all topics was 76.33%. Therefore, there was a loss of 4.66% accuracy, compared with the result obtained in the first test set (81%). This happened because the accuracy of opinion mining may fluctuate according to the subject studied and the data quality.

Table 2. Training corpus calculation

Topics	Raw Data	Processed Data (Dataset)	Training Corpus
Public transport	7,874	795	239
Combating corruption	8,595	1,892	568
Education	9,996	1,419	426
Health	5,178	814	245
Spending on the World Cup	6,606	1,737	522
Federal Government	13,608	2,642	793
TOTAL	51,857	9,299	2,793

Table 3. Accuracy of sentiment analysis

Topic	Accuracy
Public transport	76%
Combating corruption	74%
Education	80%
Health	82%
Spending on the World Cup	77%
Federal Government	69%

ANALYSIS OF RESULTS

After the automated classification of topics that motivated the popular demonstrations in June 2013 in Brazil, it was observed that even after six months, the factors that triggered the protests continued causing dissatisfaction among Brazilian citizens, as shown in Figure 1.

The sentiment analysis with data extracted from Twitter and Facebook revealed a predominance of negative opinions on all the topics identified.

Figure 1. Sentiment analysis of Brazilians posts six months after the popular protests of June 2013

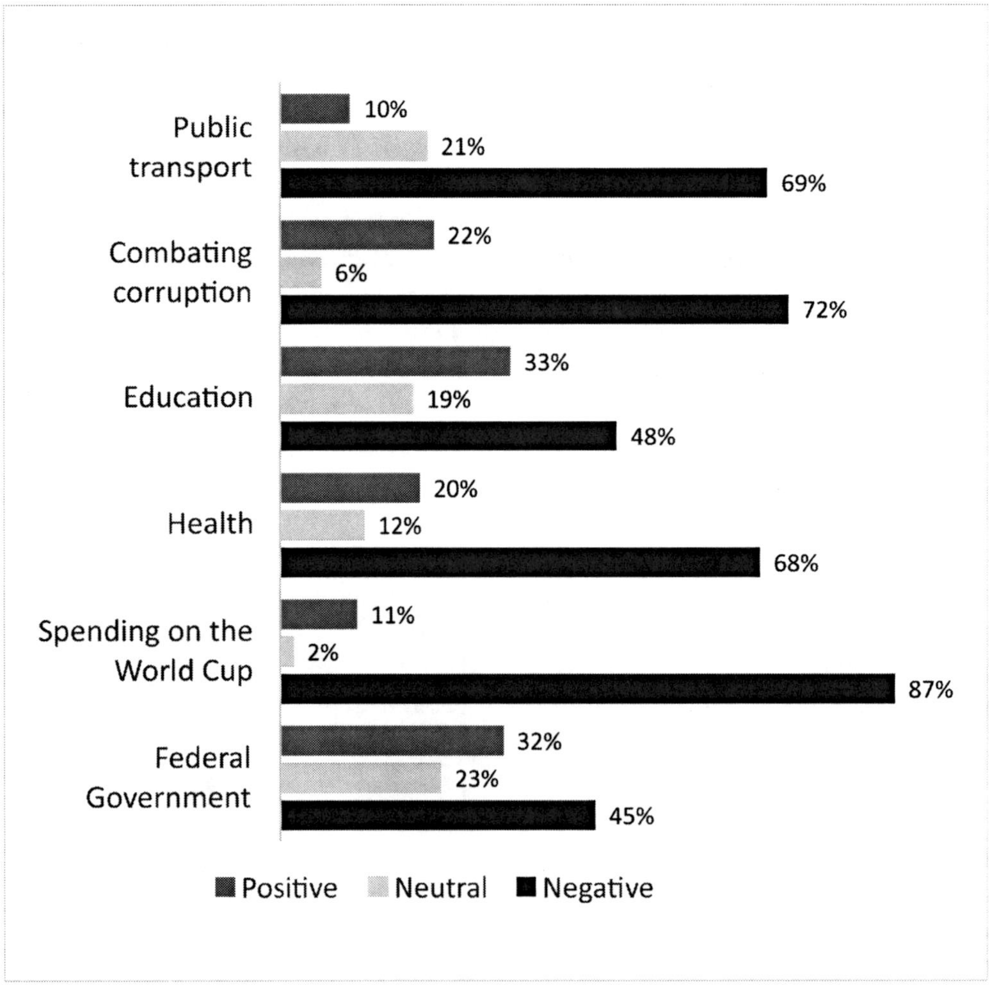

Among them, spending on the World Cup generated the highest number of negative mentions (87%). By reading some of these comments, one can easily understand the negative trend. Citizens expressed themselves on social media with strong opposition against the level of public spending on the preparations for the 2014 FIFA World Cup: "10 billion spent on building stadiums. And the people without education, health, and security. And no future" (User A, Twitter, December 19, 2013). (Original comment in Portuguese: "10 bilhões gastos na construção de estádios de futebol. E o povo sem educação, saúde e segurança. E sem futuro").

The topic with the second highest number of negative mentions was combating corruption (72%). Reading these particular comments reveals the hopelessness of Brazilians in the fight against corruption, for example: "The corrupt to be deposed? Never will happen! Well-informed citizens? Never will happen! Well-equipped hospitals? Never will happen! Never will happen!! Never will happen!!" (User B, Twitter, December 22, 2013). ("Os corruptos cassados? Nunca serão! Cidadãos bem informados? Nunca serão! Hospitais bem equipados? Nunca serão! Nunca serão!! Nunca serão!!").

Next in the negative mentions with nearly equal percentages were the public transport (69%) and health (68%) topics, driven by expressions such as: "I am very angry about public health. How can the city of Tupã not have a neonatal ICU??? My daughter had to be rushed to another city... What is happening, mayor?? Oh yeah, I just remembered, all funds they receive would only make squares, concerts, carnival..." (User C, Facebook, December 16, 2013). ("Estou muito revoltada com a saúde Pública. Como pode na cidade de Tupã não ter uma UTI Neonatal????? Minha filha teve que ser levada às pressas para outra cidade.... O que acontece prefeito??? Ah sim, acabei de me lembrar; toda verba que recebem seria somente para fazer praças, shows, carnaval....") and "This DF public transport is in chaos today due to overcrowding of the bus, had a discussion among passengers due to lack of space" (User D, Twitter, December 15, 2013). ("Este transporte público do DF está um caos, hoje devido a superlotação do ônibus, teve uma discussão entre passageiros por falta de espaço").

The topics with more positive mentions were education (33%) and Federal Government (32%). A more detailed analysis of the mentions relating to these two topics perceived that these results were driven by opinions that revealed government investments in infrastructure, for example: "Dilma Rousseff comes to Montes Claros to deliver affordable housing (User E, Twitter, December 9, 2013). ("Dilma vem a Montes Claros entregar casas populares"). The Federal Government was also the topic with the highest number of neutral terms. These mentions were marked by comments that did not clearly express a positive or negative position about the topic, such as: "President Dilma Rousseff has just arrived in Porto Alegre" (User F, Twitter, December 19, 2013). ("Presidente Dilma Rousseff acaba de chegar em Porto Alegre").

Figure 1 outlines a predominantly negative scenario on the topics studied. In none of the topics did positive or neutral mentions overcome the negative, demonstrating the dissatisfaction of most citizens. However, one should exercise caution and consideration in interpreting these results, because even using tools with high accuracy does not eliminate the margin of error. Moreover, citizens' views can be influenced to a greater or lesser degree by supporters and opponents of the current government, as well as traditional media.

In this context, according to the results shown in Table 3, the topic which was less accurate after all data has been classified was the Federal Government. A careful analysis of the mentions classified incorrectly indicates that the tool's accuracy has been affected by false positives and mentions with a high level of irony, for example: "Dilma realize, you do not escape nor from elderly!:)" (User G, Twitter, December 29, 2013) and "Dilma Rousseff is the theme of the latest carnival marching" (User H, Facebook, December 18, 2013). (Original comments in Portuguese: "Ta vendo Dilma você não escapa nem dos idosos!:)" and "Dilma Rousseff é o tema da mais recente marchinha carnavalesca").

Among the six topics, health showed the highest accuracy in automated opinion mining. Analyzing the collected references to this topic, we find a reasonable number of phrases expressing clear and objective opinions, for example: "The public hospitals in Brazil are horrible, government enters and exits, government remains the same..." (User I, Twitter, December 14, 2013). ("Os hospitais públicos do Brasil são horríveis, entra governo e sai governo, continua a mesma coisa..."). Thus, data sets that have good textual coherence and objective sentences can increase the accuracy of automated classification. On the other hand, a data set composed of phrases that contain irony, slang, and misspellings can considerably reduce the reliability of the results. In this case, it is recommended that researchers increase the sample size of the training corpus to achieve greater precision or even perform a more detailed analysis of these data.

FUTURE RESEARCH DIRECTIONS

Information and communication technologies are rapidly changing the ways that government services have been delivered to citizens over the past few years. The large volume of data generated in the communications among the state, market, and society results in a valuable data source that have not been taken advantage of in its totality. The main challenges are related to lack of mechanisms that have high precision in processing unstructured data, mainly due to semantic problems and scarce resources in dealing with multilingual data.

There are basically two main areas for future research about sentiment analysis in public administration. The first is about more accurate development of tools that are also flexible in processing data in languages other than English (Colbaugh & Glass, 2012. Montoyo et al., 2012; Yang & Yu, 2013; Yoon et al., 2013; P. Zhang & He, 2013). The second field consists of discovering new methods to apply sentiment analysis in real cases that do not focus only elections, but seek new solutions to strategic problems of public administration. One promising avenue is to evaluate how much sentiment analysis can help promote a more participatory management, establishing a dialogical relationship between government and society.

Sentiment analysis should be applied to allow governments to consider citizens' opinions when making decisions, thus contributing to more democratic public management.

CONCLUSION

This chapter has introduced social media as an active channel through which users express their opinions about various topics, including their satisfaction or dissatisfaction with the government's actions. In contrast to closed channels, for example, telephone and email, the information posted on social media can be disseminated quickly, consolidating public opinion with possibilities, in some cases, considerable repercussions. However, the challenge has been in applying a processing method and analyzing unstructured data with satisfactory precision. The proposal presented as a means to overcome this challenge is sentiment analysis.

This theoretical review of social media and sentiment analysis have demonstrated the possibility of using views expressed on social media to measure public opinion about topics defined. To exemplify the application of sentiment analysis in politics, especially public management, a practical case has been presented, taking current views of citizens about the issues that motivated popular protests in Brazil in June 2013. Results show that even six months after those events, many Brazilian citizens remain dissatisfied with their government's actions, especially those related to public spending on the 2014 FIFA World Cup, combating corruption, public transport, and health. These issues generated more than 68% of the negative opinions. Lack of government positions that meet the population's aspirations can generate unpopularity.

In view of this challenge, sentiment analysis can help public managers and elected representatives monitor public opinion on government and public services and identify issues on which there is great demand for improvement. Then, government can set priorities, devise strategies to intervene in problems, and act to meet the public interest. These actions can generate a higher level of satisfaction among citizens, which can contribute to maintenance of order. This scenario is especially plausible when the "spotlight" will be on the country during the FIFA 2014 World Cup, the 2014 presidential elections, and preparations for the 2016 Olympic Games, all of which provide the perfect stage for popular demonstrations.

Although results of this study show the reasonable accuracy of automated data analysis, some limitations should be noted. First, these results reveal the opinions of citizens who are users of social media and who were investigated according to the topics and terms defined in this study. Thus, it is inappropriate to generalize the numbers presented here to a larger population. Still, the findings are important because they point out trends in public opinion about the topics defined.

REFERENCES

Abbasi, A., Chen, H., Salem, A., Abbasi, A., Chen, H., & Salem, A. (2008). Sentiment analysis in multiple languages: Feature selection for opinion classification in Web forums. *ACM Transactions on Information Systems*, *26*(3), 1–34. doi:10.1145/1361684.1361685

Bae, Y., & Lee, H. (2012). Sentiment analysis of twitter audiences: Measuring the positive or negative influence of popular twitterers. *Journal of the American Society for Information Science and Technology*, *63*(12), 2521–2535. doi:10.1002/asi.22768

Bertot, J. C., Jaeger, P. T., & Hansen, D. (2012). The impact of polices on government social media usage: Issues, challenges, and recommendations. *Government Information Quarterly*, *29*(1), 30–40. doi:10.1016/j.giq.2011.04.004

Bonsón, E., Torres, L., Royo, S., & Flores, F. (2012). Local e-government 2.0: Social media and corporate transparency in municipalities. *Government Information Quarterly*, *29*(2), 123–132. doi:10.1016/j.giq.2011.10.001

Cambria, E., Schuller, B., Yunqing, X., & Havasi, C. (2013). New Avenues in Opinion Mining and Sentiment Analysis. *IEEE Intelligent Systems*, *28*(2), 15–21. doi:10.1109/MIS.2013.30

Ceron, A., Curini, L., Iacus, S. M., & Porro, G. (2013). Every tweet counts? How sentiment analysis of social media can improve our knowledge of citizens' political preferences with an application to Italy and France. *New Media & Society*, *16*(2), 340–358. doi:10.1177/1461444813480466

Chen, T. M. (2011). How networks changed the world. *IEEE Network*, *25*(6), 2–3. doi:10.1109/MNET.2011.6085635

Choy, M., Cheong, M. L. F., Laik, M. N., & Shung, K. P. (2012). US Presidential Election 2012 Prediction using Census Corrected Twitter Model. *CoRR, abs/1211.0938.*

Chun, S. A., & Luna Reyes, L. F. (2012). Social media in government. *Government Information Quarterly*, *29*(4), 441–445. doi:10.1016/j.giq.2012.07.003

Cochran, W. G. (2007). *Sampling techniques*. John Wiley & Sons.

Criado, J. I., Sandoval-Almazan, R., & Gil-Garcia, J. R. (2013). Government innovation through social media. *Government Information Quarterly*, *30*(4), 319–326. doi:10.1016/j.giq.2013.10.003

Di Caro, L., & Grella, M. (2013). Sentiment analysis via dependency parsing. *Computer Standards & Interfaces*, *35*(5), 442–453. doi:10.1016/j.csi.2012.10.005

Eirinaki, M., Pisal, S., & Singh, J. (2012). Feature-based opinion mining and ranking. *Journal of Computer and System Sciences*, *78*(4), 1175–1184. doi:10.1016/j.jcss.2011.10.007

Fortuny, E. J., Smedt, T. D., Martens, D., & Daelemans, W. (2012). Media coverage in times of political crisis: A text mining approach. *Expert Systems with Applications*, *39*(14), 11616–11622. doi:10.1016/j.eswa.2012.04.013

Galindo Cáceres, J. (2011). Las nuevas tecnologías de información y comunicación y las políticas culturales en México: Ingeniería en Comunicación Social del servicio de redes sociales Facebook. *Intercom: Revista Brasileira de Ciências da Comunicação*, *34*, 175–196.

Glass, K., & Colbaugh, R. (2012). Estimating the sentiment of social media content for security informatics applications. *Security Informatics*, *1*(1), 1–16. doi:10.1186/2190-8532-1-3

Hofmann, S., Beverungen, D., Räckers, M., & Becker, J. (2013). What makes local governments' online communications successful? Insights from a multi-method analysis of Facebook. *Government Information Quarterly*, *30*(4), 387–396. doi:10.1016/j.giq.2013.05.013

Ibope. (2013a). *89% dos manifestantes não se sentem representados por partidos*. Retrieved October 29, 2013, from http://www.ibope.com.br/pt-br/noticias/Paginas/89-dos-manifestantes-nao-se-sentem-representados-por-partidos.aspx

Ibope. (2013b). *Veja pesquisa completa do Ibope sobre os manifestantes*. Retrieved November 12, 2013, from http://g1.globo.com/brasil/noticia/2013/06/veja-integra-da-pesquisa-do-ibope-sobre-os-manifestantes.html

Kavanaugh, A. L., Fox, E. A., Sheetz, S. D., Yang, S., Li, L. T., & Shoemaker, D. J. et al. (2012). Social media use by government: From the routine to the critical. *Government Information Quarterly*, *29*(4), 480–491. doi:10.1016/j.giq.2012.06.002

Kontopoulos, E., Berberidis, C., Dergiades, T., & Bassiliades, N. (2013). Ontology-based sentiment analysis of twitter posts. *Expert Systems with Applications*, *40*(10), 4065–4074. doi:10.1016/j.eswa.2013.01.001

Lane, P. C. R., Clarke, D., & Hender, P. (2012). On developing robust models for favourability analysis: Model choice, feature sets and imbalanced data. *Decision Support Systems*, *53*(4), 712–718. doi:10.1016/j.dss.2012.05.028

Larsson, A. O., & Moe, H. (2011). Studying political microblogging: Twitter users in the 2010 Swedish election campaign. *New Media & Society*, *14*(5), 729–747. doi:10.1177/1461444811422894

Lewiński, M., & Mohammed, D. (2012). Deliberate design or unintended consequences: The argumentative uses of Facebook during the Arab spring. *Journal of Public Deliberation*, *8*(1), 11.

Li, G., & Liu, F. (2012). Application of a clustering method on sentiment analysis. *Journal of Information Science*, *38*(2), 127–139. doi:10.1177/0165551511432670

Lim, M. (2012). Clicks, Cabs, and Coffee Houses: Social Media and Oppositional Movements in Egypt, 2004–2011. *Journal of Communication*, *62*(2), 231–248. doi:10.1111/j.1460-2466.2012.01628.x

Liu, B. (2010). Sentiment Analysis and Subjectivity. Handbook of Natural Language Processing, 2, 627-666.

Meijer, A., & Thaens, M. (2013). Social media strategies: Understanding the differences between North American police departments. *Government Information Quarterly, 30*(4), 343–350. doi:10.1016/j.giq.2013.05.023

Mergel, I. (2012). The social media innovation challenge in the public sector. [Article]. *Information Polity: The International Journal of Government & Democracy in the Information Age, 17*(3/4), 281–292.

Mergel, I. (2013a). A framework for interpreting social media interactions in the public sector. *Government Information Quarterly, 30*(4), 327–334. doi:10.1016/j.giq.2013.05.015

Mergel, I. (2013b). Social media adoption and resulting tactics in the U.S. federal government. *Government Information Quarterly, 30*(2), 123–130. doi:10.1016/j.giq.2012.12.004

Montoyo, A., Martínez-Barco, P., & Balahur, A. (2012). Subjectivity and sentiment analysis: An overview of the current state of the area and envisaged developments. *Decision Support Systems, 53*(4), 675–679. doi:10.1016/j.dss.2012.05.022

Moreo, A., Romero, M., Castro, J. L., & Zurita, J. M. (2012). Lexicon-based Comments-oriented News Sentiment Analyzer system. *Expert Systems with Applications, 39*(10), 9166–9180. doi:10.1016/j.eswa.2012.02.057

Mossberger, K., Wu, Y., & Crawford, J. (2013). Connecting citizens and local governments? Social media and interactivity in major U.S. cities. *Government Information Quarterly, 30*(4), 351–358. doi:10.1016/j.giq.2013.05.016

Mostafa, M. M. (2013). More than words: Social networks' text mining for consumer brand sentiments. *Expert Systems with Applications, 40*(10), 4241–4251. doi:10.1016/j.eswa.2013.01.019

Mouthami, K., Devi, K. N., & Bhaskaran, V. M. (2013). *Sentiment analysis and classification based on textual reviews.* Paper presented at the Information Communication and Embedded Systems (ICICES). New York, NY. doi:10.1109/ICICES.2013.6508366

Nunomura, E. (2013). A imprensa, o Twitter e as eleições de 2010 no Brasil. *Intercom: Revista Brasileira de Ciências da Comunicação, 36*, 103–126.

O'Callaghan, D., Prucha, N., Greene, D., Conway, M., Carthy, J., & Cunningham, P. (2014). Online Social Media in the Syria Conflict: Encompassing the Extremes and the In-Betweens. *arXiv preprint arXiv:1401.7535.*

Oliveira, G. H. M., & Welch, E. W. (2013). Social media use in local government: Linkage of technology, task, and organizational context. *Government Information Quarterly, 30*(4), 397–405. doi:10.1016/j.giq.2013.05.019

Pang, B., & Lee, L. (2008). Opinion mining and sentiment analysis. *Foundations and Trends in Information Retrieval, 2*(1-2), 1–135. doi:10.1561/1500000011

Papacharissi, Z., & Oliveira, M. F. (2012). Affective News and Networked Publics: The Rhythms of News Storytelling on #Egypt. *Journal of Communication, 62*(2), 266–282. doi:10.1111/j.1460-2466.2012.01630.x

Park, S. J., Lim, Y. S., Sams, S., Nam, S. M., & Park, H. W. (2010). Networked Politics on Cyworld: The Text and Sentiment of Korean Political Profiles. *Social Science Computer Review*, *29*(3), 288–299. doi:10.1177/0894439310382509

Prabowo, R., & Thelwall, M. (2009). Sentiment analysis: A combined approach. *Journal of Informetrics*, *3*(2), 143–157. doi:10.1016/j.joi.2009.01.003

Robaldo, L., & Di Caro, L. (2013). OpinionMining-ML. *Computer Standards & Interfaces*, *35*(5), 454–469. doi:10.1016/j.csi.2012.10.004

Santos, L. M., Esmin, A. A. A., Zambalde, A. L., & Nobre, F. M. (2011). Twitter, análise de sentimento e desenvolvimento de produtos: Quanto os usuários estão expressando suas opiniões? *Prisma.Com,* (13).

Snead, J. T. (2013). Social media use in the U.S. Executive branch. *Government Information Quarterly*, *30*(1), 56–63. doi:10.1016/j.giq.2012.09.001

Sobaci, M. Z., & Karkin, N. (2013). The use of twitter by mayors in Turkey: Tweets for better public services? *Government Information Quarterly*, *30*(4), 417–425. doi:10.1016/j.giq.2013.05.014

Sobkowicz, P., Kaschesky, M., & Bouchard, G. (2012). Opinion mining in social media: Modeling, simulating, and forecasting political opinions in the web. *Government Information Quarterly*, *29*(4), 470–479. doi:10.1016/j.giq.2012.06.005

Sreekumar, T. T., & Vadrevu, S. (2013). Subpolitics and Democracy: The Role of New Media in the 2011 General Elections in Singapore. *Science, Technology & Society*, *18*(2), 231–249. doi:10.1177/0971721813489458

Tsytsarau, M., & Palpanas, T. (2012). Survey on mining subjective data on the web. *Data Mining and Knowledge Discovery*, *24*(3), 478–514. doi:10.1007/s10618-011-0238-6

Tumasjan, A., Sprenger, T. O., Sandner, P. G., & Welpe, I. M. (2011). Election Forecasts With Twitter: How 140 Characters Reflect the Political Landscape. *Social Science Computer Review*, *29*(4), 402–418. doi:10.1177/0894439310386557

Yang, D.-H., & Yu, G. (2013). A method of feature selection and sentiment similarity for Chinese micro-blogs. *Journal of Information Science*, *39*(4), 429–441. doi:10.1177/0165551513480308

Yoon, S., Elhadad, N., & Bakken, S. (2013). A Practical Approach for Content Mining of Tweets. *American Journal of Preventive Medicine*, *45*(1), 122–129. doi:10.1016/j.amepre.2013.02.025 PMID:23790998

Yu, Y., Duan, W., & Cao, Q. (2013). The impact of social and conventional media on firm equity value: A sentiment analysis approach. *Decision Support Systems*, *55*(4), 919–926. doi:10.1016/j.dss.2012.12.028

Zappavigna, M. (2011). Ambient affiliation: A linguistic perspective on Twitter. *New Media & Society*, *13*(5), 788–806. doi:10.1177/1461444810385097

Zhang, C., Zeng, D., Li, J., Wang, F.-Y., & Zuo, W. (2009). Sentiment analysis of Chinese documents: From sentence to document level. *Journal of the American Society for Information Science and Technology*, *60*(12), 2474–2487. doi:10.1002/asi.21206

Zhang, P., & He, Z. (2013). A weakly supervised approach to Chinese sentiment classification using partitioned self-training. *Journal of Information Science*, *39*(6), 815–831. doi:10.1177/0165551513480330

ADDITIONAL READING

Abdelsalam, H. M., Reddick, C. G., Gamal, S., & Al-shaar, A. (2013). Social media in Egyptian government websites: Presence, usage, and effectiveness. *Government Information Quarterly*, *30*(4), 406–416. doi:10.1016/j.giq.2013.05.020

Ackland, R. (2009). Social Network Services as Data Sources and Platforms for e-Researching Social Networks. *Social Science Computer Review*, *27*(4), 481–492. doi:10.1177/0894439309332291

Bai, X. (2011). Predicting consumer sentiments from online text. *Decision Support Systems*, *50*(4), 732–742. doi:10.1016/j.dss.2010.08.024

Bekkers, V., Edwards, A., & de Kool, D. (2013). Social media monitoring: Responsive governance in the shadow of surveillance? *Government Information Quarterly*, *30*(4), 335–342. doi:10.1016/j.giq.2013.05.024

Bertot, J. C., Jaeger, P. T., & Grimes, J. M. (2012). Promoting transparency and accountability through ICTs, social media, and collaborative e-government. *Transforming Government: People. Process and Policy*, *6*(1), 78–91.

Chadwick, A. (2012). Web 2.0: New Challenges for the Study of E-Democracy in an Era of Informational Exuberance. In S. Coleman & P. M. Shane (Eds.), *Connecting Democracy: Online Consultation and the Flow of Political Communication* (pp. 45–74). MIT Press.

Ferro, E., Loukis, E. N., Charalabidis, Y., & Osella, M. (2013). Policy making 2.0: From theory to practice. *Government Information Quarterly*, *30*(4), 359–368. doi:10.1016/j.giq.2013.05.018

Gopal, R., Marsden, J. R., & Vanthienen, J. (2011). Information mining — Reflections on recent advancements and the road ahead in data, text, and media mining. *Decision Support Systems*, *51*(4), 727–731. doi:10.1016/j.dss.2011.01.008

Gustafsson, N. (2012). The subtle nature of Facebook politics: Swedish social network site users and political participation. *New Media & Society*, *14*(7), 1111–1127. doi:10.1177/1461444812439551

He, W., Zha, S., & Li, L. (2013). Social media competitive analysis and text mining: A case study in the pizza industry. *International Journal of Information Management*, *33*(3), 464–472. doi:10.1016/j.ijinfomgt.2013.01.001

Joseph, R. C. (2013). A structured analysis of e-government studies: Trends and opportunities. *Government Information Quarterly*, *30*(4), 435–440. doi:10.1016/j.giq.2013.05.006

Khoo, C. S. G., Nourbakhsh, A., & Na, J. C. (2012). Sentiment analysis of online news text: A case study of appraisal theory. *Online Information Review*, *36*(6), 858–878. doi:10.1108/14684521211287936

Leong, C. K., Lee, Y. H., & Mak, W. K. (2012). Mining sentiments in SMS texts for teaching evaluation. *Expert Systems with Applications*, *39*(3), 2584–2589. doi:10.1016/j.eswa.2011.08.113

Li, N., & Wu, D. D. (2010). Using text mining and sentiment analysis for online forums hotspot detection and forecast. *Decision Support Systems*, *48*(2), 354–368. doi:10.1016/j.dss.2009.09.003

Linders, D. (2012). From e-government to we-government: Defining a typology for citizen coproduction in the age of social media. *Government Information Quarterly*, *29*(4), 446–454. doi:10.1016/j.giq.2012.06.003

Malouf, R., & Mullen, T. (2008). Taking sides: User classification for informal online political discourse. *Internet Research*, *18*(2), 177–190. doi:10.1108/10662240810862239

Meijer, A., & Thaens, M. (2013). Social media strategies: Understanding the differences between North American police departments. *Government Information Quarterly*, *30*(4), 343–350. doi:10.1016/j.giq.2013.05.023

Movafaghi, S., & Bullock, J. (2011). Sentiment Web Mining. *Social and Behavioral Sciences*, *26*(0), 191–197.

Pang, B., Lee, L., & Vaithyanathan, S. (2002, July). Thumbs up?: sentiment classification using machine learning techniques. In *Proceedings of the ACL-02 conference on Empirical methods in natural language processing-Volume 10* (pp. 79-86). Association for Computational Linguistics. doi:10.3115/1118693.1118704

Picazo-Vela, S., Gutiérrez-Martínez, I., & Luna-Reyes, L. F. (2012). Understanding risks, benefits, and strategic alternatives of social media applications in the public sector. *Government Information Quarterly*, *29*(4), 504–511. doi:10.1016/j.giq.2012.07.002

Snead, J. T. (2013). Social media use in the U.S. Executive branch. *Government Information Quarterly*, *30*(1), 56–63. doi:10.1016/j.giq.2012.09.001

Taboada, M., Brooke, J., Tofiloski, M., Voll, K., & Stede, M. (2011). Lexicon-Based Methods for Sentiment Analysis. *Computational Linguistics*, *37*(2), 267–307. doi:10.1162/COLI_a_00049

Tang, H., Tan, S., & Cheng, X. (2009). A survey on sentiment detection of reviews. *Expert Systems with Applications*, *36*(7), 10760–10773. doi:10.1016/j.eswa.2009.02.063

Zagal, J. P., Tomuro, N., & Shepitsen, A. (2011). Natural Language Processing in Game Studies Research: An Overview. *Simulation & Gaming*.

Zheng, L. (2013). Social media in Chinese government: Drivers, challenges and capabilities. *Government Information Quarterly*, *30*(4), 369–376. doi:10.1016/j.giq.2013.05.017

KEY TERMS AND DEFINITIONS

Causa Brasil Platform: This is an online platform that scans social media (Facebook, Twitter, and others) with monitoring tools, search for terms most commented on social media related to protests in Brazil.

DiscoverText: Commercial application that performs analysis of cloud-based text, which allows users to customize and reuse classifiers, based on machine learning with the combined use of algorithms and human coding. This application is able to capture, filter, search, sort, and analyze large volumes of structured and unstructured data.

Facebook: Social network that allows users to share texts, pictures, news, links, files, among others. It also provides the creation of thematic groups and the installation of various applications.

Machine Learning: It is a subfield of artificial intelligence often used in data mining that identifies rules and patterns of large data sets (NLP), based on the use of algorithms and application training through a training corpus.

Natural Language Processing (NLP): Automatic processing of text that identifies patterns and allows the classification and/or coding of the data.

Popular Demonstrations in Brazil: Demonstrations that happened in Brazil in June 2013, which began with the increase in public transport fares and then focused on protests against public spending on large sporting events, the poor quality of public services, corruption, and impunity. These demonstrations have turned into a mobilization of large proportions with their rapid spread and coverage by social media.

Sentiment Analysis: Also known as opinion mining, it is a technique that allows classification and analysis of a large amount of texts to identify opinions and/or sentiments in an automated form.

Social Media: These are platforms that allow interactions among people through sharing content such as texts, images, videos, audios, and others. Examples: Twitter, Facebook, YouTube, Flickr.

Twitter: Microblog that allows users to share texts (tweets) and links of up to 140 characters with their followers.

Section 4
E-Health: Issues and Solutions

Chapter 14
Privacy-Friendly Management of Electronic Health Records in the eHealth Context

Milica Milutinovic
KU Leuven, Belgium

Bart De Decker
KU Leuven, Belgium

ABSTRACT

Electronic Health Records (EHRs) are becoming the ubiquitous technology for managing patients' records in many countries. They allow for easier transfer and analysis of patient data on a large scale. However, privacy concerns linked to this technology are emerging. Namely, patients rarely fully understand how EHRs are managed. Additionally, the records are not necessarily stored within the organization where the patient is receiving her healthcare. This service may be delegated to a remote provider, and it is not always clear which health-provisioning entities have access to this data. Therefore, in this chapter the authors propose an alternative where users can keep and manage their records in their existing eHealth systems. The approach is user-centric and enables the patients to have better control over their data while still allowing for special measures to be taken in case of emergency situations with the goal of providing the required care to the patient.

INTRODUCTION

Electronic health records (EHRs) are becoming the core part of the official healthcare reforms in many western countries. They represent collections of health-related information of patients that are stored in an electronic form. The driving force for their implementation is cost savings. They alleviate the problem of redundancy and the related increase in expenses, as tests and procedures do not need to be repeated, since the information can be accessible to multiple healthcare providers. Compared to the traditional approach of storing the patients' data, the benefits of EHRs are also easier transfer and analysis of health data on a large scale. Additionally, they allow for merging the data across different healthcare domains. This reform in health-related information manage-

DOI: 10.4018/978-1-4666-7266-6.ch014

ment is therefore expected to ensure better care provisioning and reductions in healthcare costs. However, the EHR are also raising certain concerns of the patients. Due to the electronic nature and non-transparent handling of EHR records, the patients are increasingly worried about the privacy of their data. Consequentially, one of the main obstacles to EHR adoption are the privacy and security concerns of the users (Hiller, McMullen, Chumney, & Baumer, 2011).

In the current system design, the users are not in control over their medical records. In most systems, the retrieval of the electronic records from a central database does not need to be authorised by the user at the time of retrieval and for each medical person accessing it. Moreover, the access can also be carried out without the user's knowledge. While the facilitation of the exchange of health information about a patient between various sources is considered to be a major benefit of the EHR systems, this inter-domain exchange of data is yet another reason why patients are distrustful about the offered privacy protection.

In order to address the aforementioned issues, this work provides a novel system model that grants the users augmented control over their data. To the best of our knowledge, this is the first approach that considers integration of EHRs into the eHealth assistance systems. The resulting system implements the preferences of users with regards to their data management, while ensuring appropriate care in emergency situations.

Background

With the technological advances in the areas of sensor monitoring and communication technologies, the eHealth systems have become an important area of research. They are seen as a cost-effective solution for provisioning continuous care to a person's home, especially in remote areas. Initial approaches were focusing on the integration of sensor technologies for health parameters measurement, while the later research broadens the services that these systems are able to offer.

A large body of research focuses on extending the monitoring of the patient. The monitoring equipment is deployed as a body area network (Jovanov, Milenkovic, Otto, & de Groen, 2005; Otto, Milenkovic, Sanders, & Jovanov, 2006;Kim, Jarochowski, & Ryu, 2006) or is integrated in a single device (Sum, Zheng, & Mak, 2005). There are initiatives to capture detected falls using accelerometers(Tabar,Keshavarz, & Aghajan, 2006), automatically analyse patient posture via video (Lo, Wang, & Yang, 2005), or to utilise a GPS system for keeping track of the patient's location(Boulos et al., 2007).

The importance of the eHealth systems is also illustrated in a number of European initiatives, such as the ongoing GiraffPlus project, epSOS (2008-2013), MobiHealth (2002-2004) and AMON (2001-2002) projects. Currently, this type of systems is developed to manage only the data that is collected by the home equipment, i.e. the body and environmental sensors. The caregivers are accessing this data for assessment and determining whether the patient requires assistance. In a similar manner, the home base station can also hold the electronic health records (EHRs) of the patient. This would not only allow for a more complete overview of the patient's status, but would also enable patients to have a better control over their data.

The EHRs are a part of the healthcare reforms in many countries. In 1998 the UK started a makeover of its healthcare system. The key component of the change is the NHS Care Records Service, which is supposed to provide EHR technology to all patients in the UK. However, their initiative to create a database of merged records is raising privacy concerns (Terry& Francis, 2007).Other surveys have also shown that it is necessary to balance privacy with the EHR deployment

(Luchenski et al., 2012). Work of Dhopeshwarkar et al. (Dhopeshwarkar, Kern, O'Donnell, Edwards, & Kaushal, 2012) investigates the preferences of healthcare consumers around their health information exchange. Most of the participants in this survey stated that they would want a permission to be requested before any party could access their information. Most of the participants would additionally want mechanisms for stopping the information viewing by an external party, if that is requested by the owner. They also prefer to select which parts of their data can be shared. Another important finding of the survey showed that the biggest part of the users would be comfortable with data storage on an editable, readable portable device they would hold. As the users of eHealth systems already have appropriate equipment deployed in their home, this means that it can be used for the storage of these records as well. The privacy concerns are also not limited to the older generations. The studies done in the UK suggest that young generations, as well as adults have concerns about the usage of EHRs for medical research purposes (Ipsos, 2007; Paterson, 2010). In order to support the deployment of electronic health records, security and privacy concerns need to be tackled. They are currently one of the biggest impediments for adoption of EHRs (Hiller et al., 2011).

Another goal of the electronic health records is to make the entire EHR available for patients and clinicians beyond one domain. This is compatible to the approach described in this work, as patient's data will be collected across healthcare domains. Therefore, patients with a long history or those that utilize care services offered by multiple providers would be able to benefit from the approach of merging their health-related data. Moreover, the patients would be able to review their records and refer back to the given instructions, which is an important benefit (Ross, 2009).

As the eHealth systems have an increasing presence and are envisioned to bring cost-effective care to the patient, the trend that is expected will beto extend the range of the services they are able to offer. We therefore observe the electronic health records utilisation and management in the eHealth systems. We analyse the accompanying privacy concerns of EHR systems and aim to mitigate them by granting the users more control over their data.

EHR MANAGEMENT IN EHEALTH SYSTEMS

This section focuses on the eHealth systems and presents a system architecture for which the electronic health records management scheme is developed. The requirements for allowing EHR management in the eHealth systems are also listed and the proposed solutions are driven with these requirements. Finally, an overview of the protocols for managing the EHR records of a patient through her eHealth system is given.

System Requirements

This section outlines the requirements regarding security and privacy of user records that need to be fulfilled by the system:

1. **Records Should Only Be Accessed by Authorised Personnel:** This is a requirement posed by the legislation (HIPAA, 1996; MPA 2013). In order to achieve it, strict access control is required in the system. The patient should be able to limit the availability of her information and to explicitly assign access authorisations to her caregivers. Furthermore, legislation in some countries imposes the rule that non-medical personnel cannot access medical data of a patient. This should also be ensured by the system.
2. **Patient's Approval Is Needed for Inclusion in the Network of Caregivers:** The patient herself has control over the creation and extension of the network of her caregivers.

It should not be possible for unauthorised parties to infiltrate into the network and subsequently make requests for accessing the records of the patient.

3. **The Caregivers of a Patient Should Be Anonymous towards the System and Observers:** As the information on the types of caregivers that are involved in the treatment of the patient can disclose details about the patient's health, the network of caregivers should not be visible to all the actors in the system. In other words, the commercial entities of the eHealth system and external parties should not be able to see details about patients' networks, such as the identities of the caregivers or their medical training. Additionally, even members of a patient's network need special authorisation in order to be able to learn information about the other members.
4. **All Access to the Patient's Records Should Be Logged for Possible Auditing:** Any request and access to patients' records needs to be recorded by the system. This includes the authentication of the requestor, in order to identify the actors at auditing time. In case of a misuse attempt, such as an unauthorised party trying to gain access to patient's records, the system should be able to detect it and provide the transcript information to designated authorities for identifying and sanctioning the perpetrator.
5. **Enabling Emergency Procedures:** This means that in case the user is not able to allow access to the records that are immediately needed for help in emergency situations, mechanisms should be in place to allow break-the-glass access.

Underlying System Architecture

The system architecture that is considered for extension to handle the electronic health records of a patient is described in the following text. It is comprised of four levels. The periphery of the system consists of sensors, used for monitoring the patients' health parameters (such as heart rate or blood pressure), environmental parameters (such as temperature or humidity) and other indoor equipment used for communication purposes. The health monitoring sensors range from simple devices that only record the measured parameters, to more complex devices able to assess the measurements. The end users are also equipped with devices used for communication with other entities; those can be a hand-held device with buttons, a microphone, a speaker and a fall detector, or a video camera and a screen.

All this equipment is then connected to a central indoor element denoted as a base station. The base station is gathering all the measurements that the sensors record and represents a gateway to the rest of the system. The tasks of the base station are recording and assessing the sensor measurements according to predefined criteria, maintaining the network of patient's caregivers, managing communication with them and performing access control to patient's data. It also manages the tasks that are requested by the patient and raises alerts in emergency situations.

The main commercially-run part of the system is a dispatching centre. It is connected to the base stations of all the patients and relays the communication with their caregivers, as illustrated in Figure 1. It also provides technical support and is in charge of initial system installation at the patients' homes. However, due to the commercial nature of the dispatching centre, it does not have access to any sensitive data of the patients, such as their health parameters' measurements and in addition cannot learn to which caregivers they are connected.

All the administrative tasks are handled by a separate entity, the administration centre. It handles registration of patients and their caregivers and issues credentials to both the patients and their caregivers who wish to use the system. It also handles tasks such as payments.

Figure 1. The connections of patients and their caregivers are maintained by the dispatching centre

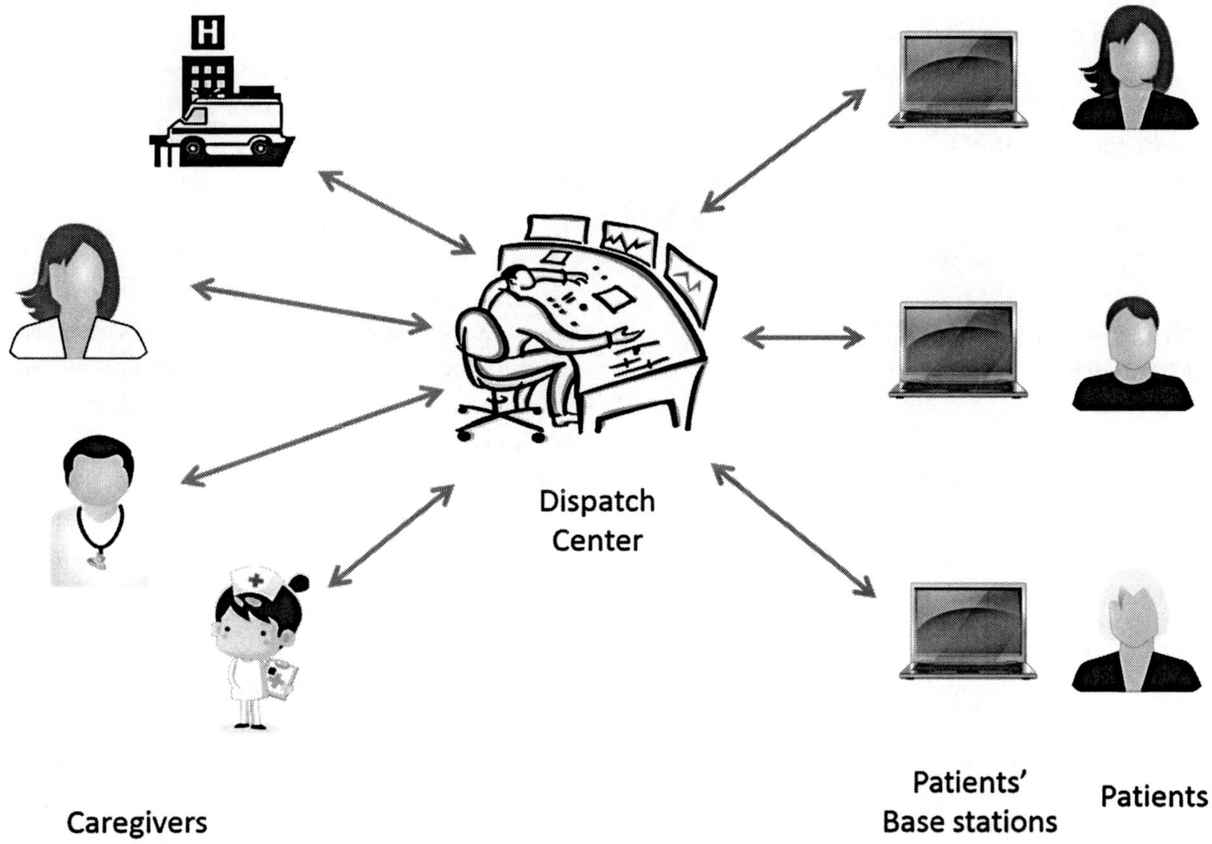

For details on the functioning of the described system, we refer the reader to the work of Milutinovic and De Decker (Milutinovic& De Decker, 2013).

Preliminaries

For taking part in the described system, all caregivers must be issued with an anonymous credential. Both patients and their caregivers contact a trusted credential authority and are issued with a credential that records their data. For patients, this data can be personal information, such as name and address or contact details, and is recoded on a smart card, while for caregivers this data also includes their area of expertise and level of medical training and is recorded in an anonymous credential. Anonymous credential technology is used to ensure privacy-friendly functioning of the system, as this type of credentials allows holders to show only selected attributes of the credential and prove their validity. Furthermore, all the entities hold public-private key pairs certified in trusted certificates, which can be used to encrypt the communication between two parties and ensure secrecy of the exchanged data.

System Functioning

An important aspect of the system is that every patient has a care network associated with her. The network includes her regular caregivers, such as family members, as well as medical professionals and organizations, such as GPs, specialists or hospitals. This network is created and changes to it are controlled by the patient side of the system.

The base station, which is the core element of the indoor equipment, handles the information about the caregivers and their authorisations. In order to specify the assigned authorisations, the caregivers are assigned with roles, which are used as a first level of access control, and more details on their authorisations can then be specified by the patient herself or her principal caregiver, if the patient is not in a position to do so.

Patient's Care Networks Management

The information about the patient's caregivers is kept in the form of a network. The central node of the network is the patient, who is then connected to all her caregivers, as illustrated in Figure 2. The information about these networks is kept both in the dispatching centre and in the base station. The dispatching centre only sees the pseudonyms of the network nodes, while the base station of a patient can hold details, such as identities or qualifications of caregivers. As the base station is patient's proprietary equipment, there are no privacy issues with having it maintain this type of information.

Patient-Caregiver Connection

In order for a caregiver to join a patient's network, he would need an invitation from the patient and would need to authenticate when establishing the connection. The invitation is an electronic token and is obtained through a channel such as email. It is encrypted with the public key of the caregiver in order to protect it from disclosure to unauthorised recipients. Even when the invitation is obtained, the caregiver would establish

Figure 2. Patient's care network; all the entities are associated with a pseudonym, while the identities are hidden from the dispatching centre.

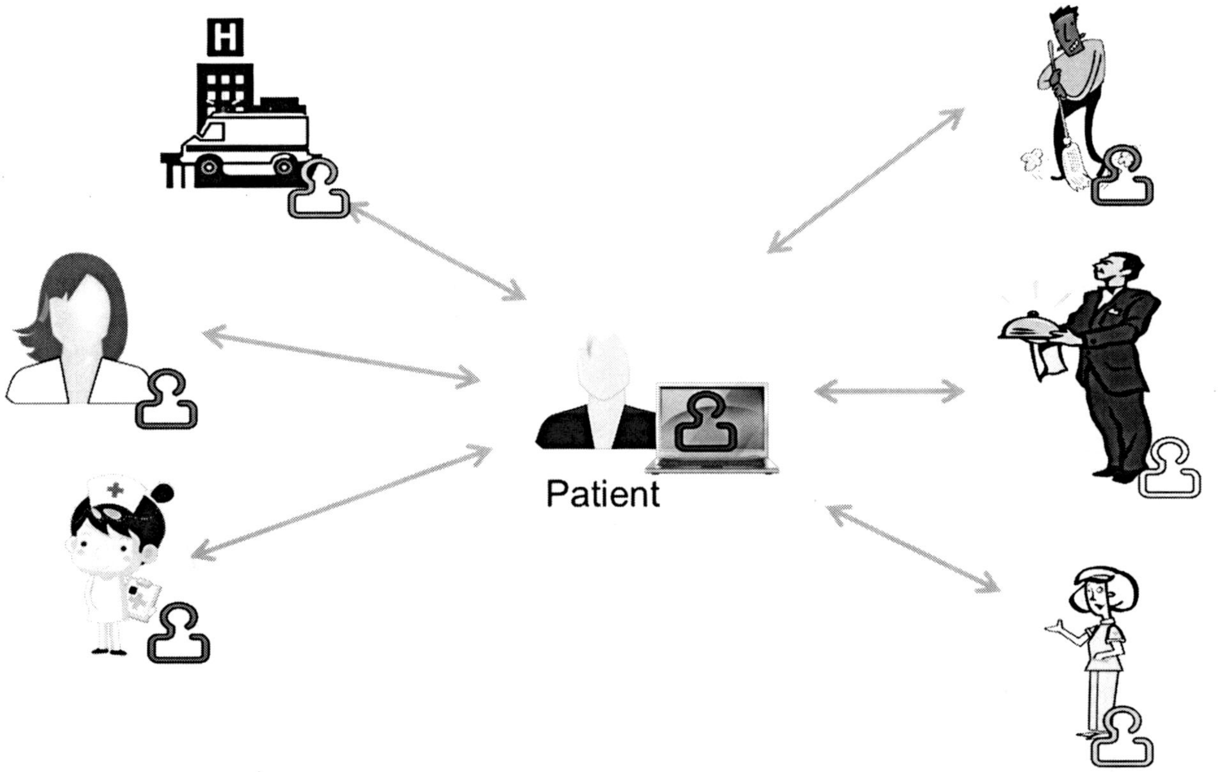

a connection with the base station of the patient and authenticate in order to prove his identity. When the caregiver is accepted, he is issued with an additional credential specifying his role and authorisations and the patient's pseudonym. The caregiver then establishes a pseudonymous communication with the dispatching centre in order to join a patient's network. The pseudonym is derived from a secret attribute contained in the anonymous credential and allows the caregiver to prove that he is the owner of the credential used to produce the pseudonym. Furthermore, when making a request to access data in the patient's base station, the caregiver can authenticate anonymously with the dispatching centre, only proving that he is a part of the patient's network. Other parties that do not belong to a patient's network would not be able to impersonate a member, as they do not possess the appropriate anonymous credential which records the patient's pseudonym.

Requesting Access to Patient's Data

When a caregiver wishes to access sensor data in a patient's base stations, e.g. in order to assess the status of the patient and perform a remote check-up, he will send an appropriate request to the patient through the dispatching centre. The dispatching centre is expected to perform the first level of access control and only transfer verified requests to the base station.

When making a request the caregiver initially authenticates towards the dispatching centre. For this purpose he does not disclose his identity, but uses the anonymous credential that certifies his authorisations and role. The credential is utilised to provide the following proofs to the dispatching centre:

1. That the caregiver is connected to the patient in question, i.e. that the pseudonym of the patient is recorded in his credential; and
2. The high-level description of the role he has and medical training.

The caregiver also sends a high-level description of the request he is making. This allows the dispatching centre to make a decision whether the request can be relayed to the base station. Next to these proofs, the caregiver sends an encryption of the detailed request and his proof of identity, which are encrypted with the patient's public key. This way, the dispatching centre can only see the high-level request and make the access control decision based on that, while the patient sees the complete data. If the role specification does not authorise the caregiver to make the specified request, access is denied. Otherwise, the request is relayed to the base station, which performs the final level of access control based on the identity of the caregiver.

Patient-Centric Approach to EHRs

The described system for home assistance can be extended to encompass patient electronic health records management. The base station of the patient has the resources to store/maintain the patient records and enforce the appropriate access control, similarly as for the other patient data that needs to be accessed remotely. This section describes the benefits of this approach and details the protocols that can be employed for allowing the EHR management in an eHealth system.

Flexible User Policies

With the proposed system, the user is able to specify desired access control policies. They are intended for governing the access control to the records and thus give the patients more control over their data. It is assumed that the access to the records needs to be allowed to the designated caregivers of a patient, which need to have a complete overview of the patient's status. However, for other entities, such as nurses or caregivers in specialised areas that do not require an overview of all the records, the patient policies may be applied.

Statistical Analysis of Anonymised Records

Furthermore, there are initiatives to gather anonymised patient records in order to perform large scale medical data analysis. However, recent examples indicate that the anonymisation process may not be sufficient to prevent revealing identifying information and patients tend to be distrustful towards these measures. This is also the reason why so many patients tend to withdraw from these options. An added value of the approach proposed in this work is allowing the patient to choose the level of anonymity under which the records are disclosed for statistical analysis. This is also a way to ensure involvement of a larger number of patients.

Access Control in Emergency Situations

The system can be extended with break-the-glass procedures (Brucker 2009; Ferreira 2006). That would allow extending the access control policies to allow emergency access to the data by authorised entities, while the user does not need to grant an explicit approval at the time of emergency situation.

Privacy-Preserving Protocols

Gathering Patient Records

The base station of a patient should collect all the records of the patient. An important benefit of this approach is that the patient would be able to review the records made by medical personnel and be reminded of the actions needed to be performed, by checking for instance the prescribed dosages of medications.

After the patient's visit to the doctor or after a caregiver has accessed the sensor measurements remotely, a new record would be created. In order to deliver the newly created electronic health record, the caregiver would establish a connection with the base station. The request to connect is relayed via the dispatching centre, in a similar way as the request to access sensor measurements, as explained in the previous sections. The session is established between the caregiver and the base station to allow the base station to retrieve the record. The communication is encrypted and the authenticity of the communicating party would be provided through public key certificates. The records that are obtained are additionally signed by the creator. This allows verifying that they have indeed originated from a specific entity. After reception of the record, the base station would send back a signed confirmation to the caregiver, which would allow him to prove that the record was delivered to the patient, and no misuse was attempted.

Caregiver's Access to Patient Records

When a caregiver wishes to access the records in the patient's base station, the procedure is similar as for accessing the sensor measurements (Figure 3). When making the request, the caregiver proves that he is connected to the patient, by proving that his anonymous credential contains the patient's pseudonym. Additionally, he proves that he is a medical caregiver, but does not disclose the details, such as the field of expertise or the level of medical training. This way, the information the dispatching centre learns is kept to a minimum, while it is still able to exercise a coarse grained access control. When the proof is created, the dispatching centre is presented with a high-level overview of the request and the role of the caregiver. It can then verify whether the role enables the caregiver to make the request.

While the dispatching centre sees only a high level request, the detailed request is signed and encrypted for the patient, as it is considered to reveal sensitive information about the patient's care requirements. If the access is granted by the dispatching centre, the request is relayed to the

Figure 3. Caregiver's request to access patient's records in her base station; the communication is relayed through the dispatching centre, which cannot see any identifying or medical data.

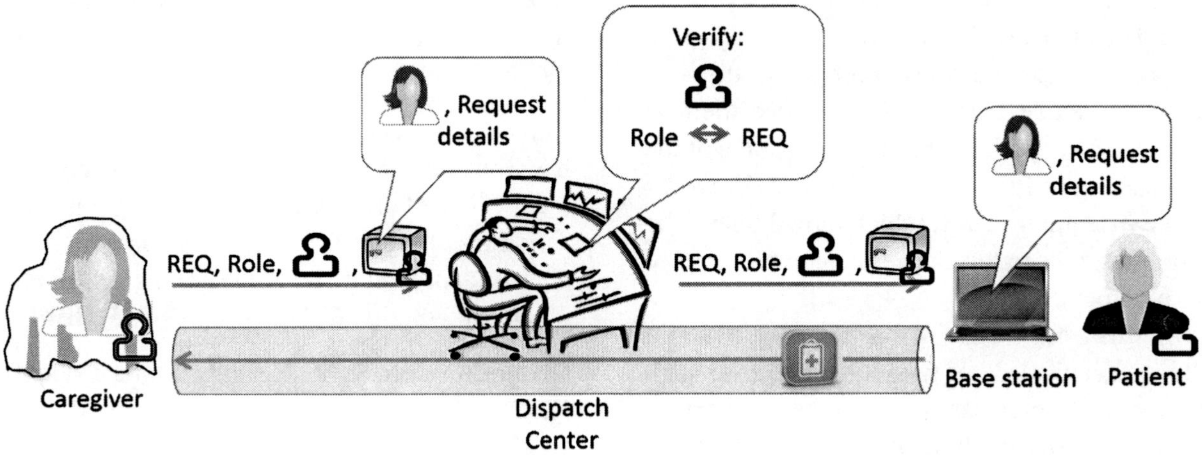

patient's base station. The base station is then able to see the identity of the caregiver and verify the authenticity of the request. The signature is used to prove that the request did not originate from an external party and links it to the caregiver. Based on detailed authorisations kept in the base station, it is decided whether the access is to be granted or not. In case the caregiver is allowed to review the records, he establishes a tunnelled communication with the base station, i.e. communication that is end-to-end encrypted, disallowing other parties from seeing any exchanged information.

Secure Logging of the Accesses

After the access to the records is granted to a caregiver, the base station makes a record of this access. This record contains the signed request and the authentication transcript. This proves that the request has originated from a specific caregiver and which records were accessed by him. In case a problem is detected, it is possible to prove with the logged transcripts which parties had access to which records. Consequently, this can be used to identify a misuser.

FUTURE RESEARCH DIRECTIONS

In our future work, we will investigate extended scenarios of the records management in order to achieve the highest level of user privacy. Furthermore, backup and recovery of patients' records is a serious concern. We will therefore focus on this issue in order to design the appropriate measurements that would provide security of the patients' records.

CONCLUSION

The EHR records are a prevailing direction in the development of healthcare systems. Many countries are aiming for widening their application and include them as part of their national healthcare planning. As the privacy of users is of utmost importance in the healthcare domain, the issue of health records management is considered a crucial one. The NHS on the United Kingdom recently had to delay its official plans for the anonymised records sharing scheme by six months due to privacy concerns. This example shows that the EHR management needs to provide strict assurance to the users that their data will be handled in an appropriate manner and that their privacy will not be endangered. Studies also show, as discussed in the previous text, that a large portion of patients is willing to handle their records, i.e. collect them on their personal device. Therefore, we find that the approach of shifting the electronic health records to the eHealth systems, which already have the resources to keep this data, is a natural course of development.

In this work we have described protocols that allow eHealth systems to exchange records with the medical organisations and other authorised healthcare provisioning entities. The proposal also enables the patients to define their access control policies and can be extended with break-the-glass mechanisms. Finally, secure logs of transactions' transcripts enable the user to see who has accessed her data and how often and possibly identify a misuser.

REFERENCES

Anliker, U., Ward, J. A., Lukowicz, P., Troster, G., Dolveck, F., & Baer, M. et al. (2004). AMON: A wearable multiparameter medical monitoring and alert system. *IEEE Transactions on* Information Technology in Biomedicine, *8*(4), 415–427.

Blumenthal, D., & Tavenner, M. (2010). The "meaningful use" regulation for electronic health records. *The New England Journal of Medicine*, *363*(6), 501–504. doi:10.1056/NEJMp1006114 PMID:20647183

Boulos, M., Rocha, A., Martins, A., Vicente, M., Bolz, A., Feld, R., … Kinirons, M. (2007). CAALYX: A new generation of location-based services in healthcare. *International Journal of Health Geographics*, *6*(1), 9.

Brucker, A. D., & Petritsch, H. (2009, June). Extending access control models with break-glass. In *Proceedings of the 14th ACM symposium on Access control models and technologies* (pp. 197-206). ACM. doi:10.1145/1542207.1542239

Coradeschi, S., Cesta, A., Cortellessa, G., Coraci, L., Gonzalez, J., Karlsson, L., … Otslund, B. (2013, June). Giraffplus: Combining social interaction and long term monitoring for promoting independent living. In *Proceedings of Human System Interaction (HSI),* (pp. 578-585). IEEE.

Dhopeshwarkar, R. V., Kern, L. M., O'Donnell, H. C., Edwards, A. M., & Kaushal, R. (2012). Health care consumers' preferences around health information exchange. *Annals of Family Medicine*, *10*(5), 428–434. doi:10.1370/afm.1396 PMID:22966106

Ferreira, A., Cruz-Correia, R., Antunes, L., Farinha, P., Oliveira-Palhares, E., Chadwick, D. W., & Costa-Pereira, A. (2006, June). How to break access control in a controlled manner. In *Proceedings of Computer-Based Medical Systems, 2006. CBMS 2006. 19th IEEE International Symposium on* (pp. 847-854). IEEE.

Hiller, J., McMullen, M. S., Chumney, W. M., & Baumer, D. L. (2011). Privacy and security in the implementation of health information technology (electronic health records): US and EU compared. *BUJ Sci. & Tech. L.*, *17*, 1.

HIPAA. (1996). *Health information privacy.* Retrieved from http://www.hhs.gov/ocr/privacy/index.html

Ipsos, M. O. R. I. (2007). *The use of personal health information in medical research: general public consultation*. London: Medical Research Council.

Jones, V., van Halteren, A., Dokovsky, N., Koprinkov, G., Bults, R., Konstantas, D., & Herzog, R. (2006). Mobihealth: Mobile health services based on body area networks. Springer US.

Jovanov, E., Milenkovic, A., Otto, C. & de Groen, P. (2005). A wireless body area network of intelligent motion sensors for computer assisted physical rehabilitation. *Journal of NeuroEngineering and Rehabilitation, 2*(1), 6.

Kim, H., Jarochowski, B., & Ryu, D. (2006). A proposal for a home-based health monitoring system for the elderly or disabled. In *Computers Helping People with Special Needs* (pp. 473–479). Springer Berlin Heidelberg. doi:10.1007/11788713_71

Lindén, F. (2009). epSOS, smart open services for European patients from strategies to services—eHealth as the enabler for cross-border healthcare. *Infrastructures for Health Care, 23.*

Lo, B., Wang, J., & Yang, G. (2005). From imaging networks to behavior profiling: Ubiquitous sensing for managed homecare of the elderly. In *Proceedings of the 3rd International Conference on Pervasive Computing.* Academic Press.

Luchenski, S., Balasanthiran, A., Marston, C., Sasaki, K., Majeed, A., Bell, D., & Reed, J. E. (2012). Survey of patient and public perceptions of electronic health records for healthcare, policy and research: Study protocol. *BMC Medical Informatics and Decision Making, 12*(1), 40. doi:10.1186/1472-6947-12-40 PMID:22621621

Milutinovic, M., & De Decker, B. (2013). Comprehensive eHealth system design for privacy protection. Technical Report (CW Reports), CW643. Department of Computer Science, KU Leuven.

MPA. (2013). *Access to health records.* Retrieved from http://www.medicalprotection.org/uk/england-factsheets/access-to-health-records

Otto, C., Milenkovic, A., Sanders, C., & Jovanov, E. (2006). System architecture of a wireless body area sensor network for ubiquitous health monitoring. *Journal of Mobile Multimedia, 1*(4), 307–326.

Paterson, L. (2010). *Privacy and Prejudice: Young People's Views on the Development and Use of Electronic Patient Records.* Royal Academy of Engineering.

Ross, J. (2009). Electronic medical records: The promises and challenges. *Journal of Perianesthesia Nursing, 24*(5), 327–329. doi:10.1016/j.jopan.2009.08.002 PMID:19853820

Sum, K. W., Zheng, Y. P., & Mak, A. F. T. (2005). Vital sign monitoring for elderly at home: Development of a compound sensor for pulse rate and motion. *Studies in Health Technology and Informatics, 117,* 43. PMID:16282652

Tabar, A., Keshavarz, A., & Aghajan, H. (2006). Smart home care network using sensor fusion and distributed vision-based reasoning. In *Proceedings of the 4th ACM International Workshop on Video Surveillance and Sensor Networks (VSSN'06),* (pp. 145 – 154). New York, NY: ACM. doi:10.1145/1178782.1178804

Terry, N. P., & Francis, L. P. (2007). Ensuring the privacy and confidentiality of electronic health records. *U. Ill. L. Rev.*, 681.

ADDITIONAL READING

Bajo, J., Fraile, J. A., Pérez-Lancho, B., & Corchado, J. (2010). The THOMAS architecture in home care scenarios: A case study. *Expert Systems with Applications, 37*(5), 3986–3999. doi:10.1016/j.eswa.2009.11.017

Bergmann, J., Bott, O. J., Pretschner, D. P., & Hau, R. (2007). An e-consent-based shared EHR system architecture for integrated healthcare networks. *International Journal of Medical Informatics*, *76*(2-3), 130–136. doi:10.1016/j.ijmedinf.2006.07.013 PMID:16971171

Black, A. D., Car, J., Pagliari, C., Anandan, C., Cresswell, K., & Bokun, T. et al. (2011). The impact of eHealth on the quality and safety of health care: A systematic overview. *PLoS Medicine*, *8*(1), e1000387. doi:10.1371/journal.pmed.1000387 PMID:21267058

Brands, S. (2002). A technical overview of digital credentials.

Canale, S., Delli Priscoli, F., Mignanti, S., Oddi, G., Sassano, A., Macone, D., et al. (2013, February). The Bravehealth Software Architecture for the Monitoring of Patients Affected by CVD. In *eTELEMED 2013, The Fifth International Conference on eHealth, Telemedicine, and Social Medicine* (pp. 29-34).

Demuynck, L., & De Decker, B. (2005, January). Privacy-preserving electronic health records. In *Communications and Multimedia Security* (pp. 150–159). Springer Berlin Heidelberg. doi:10.1007/11552055_15

Deng, M., De Cock, D., & Preneel, B. (2009). An interoperable cross-context architecture to manage distributed personal e-Health information. In M. M. Cunha, R. Simoes, & A. Tavares (Eds.), *Handbook of Research on Developments in e- Health and Telemedicine: Technological and Social Perspectives* (pp. 576–602). Hershey, PA, USA: IGI Global. doi:10.4018/978-1-61520-670-4.ch027

Dhukaram, A. V., Baber, C., Elloumi, L., van Beijnum, B. J., & De Stefanis, P. (2011, May). End-user perception towards pervasive cardiac healthcare services: Benefits, acceptance, adoption, risks, security, privacy and trust. In *Pervasive Computing Technologies for Healthcare (PervasiveHealth), 2011 5th International Conference on* (pp. 478-484). IEEE.

Durresi, A., Merkoci, A., Durresi, M., & Barolli, L. (2007). Integrated biomedical system for ubiquitous health monitoring. In T. Enokido, L. Barolli & M. Takizawa (Eds), *Proceedings of the 1st Network-Based Information Systems, LNCS, Vol. 4658*(pp. 397-405). Berlin/Heidelberg: Springer doi:10.1007/978-3-540-74573-0_41

Ekeland, A. G., Bowes, A., & Flottorp, S. (2010). Effectiveness of telemedicine: A systematic review of reviews. *International Journal of Medical Informatics*, *79*(11), 736–771. doi:10.1016/j.ijmedinf.2010.08.006 PMID:20884286

ERA. (2005-2007). eHealth ERA - A European Union Coordination Action. Retrieved from http://www.ehealth-era.org

Fan, L., Buchanan, W., Thummler, C., Lo, O., Khedim, A., Uthmani, O., et al. (2011). DACAR platform for eHealth services cloud. *IEEE 4th International Conference on Cloud Computing (CLOUD)*(pp. 219-226). IEEE.

Field, M. J., & Grigsby, J. (2002). Telemedicine and remote patient monitoring. *Journal of the American Medical Association*, *288*(4), 423–425. doi:10.1001/jama.288.4.423 PMID:12132953

Gao, T., Pesto, C., Selavo, L., Chen, Y., Ko, J., Lim, J. H., et al. (2008, May). Wireless medical sensor networks in emergency response: Implementation and pilot results. In *Technologies for Homeland Security, 2008 IEEE Conference on* (pp. 187-192). IEEE.

Gatzoulis, L., & Iakovidis, I. (2007). Wearable and portable eHealth systems. [IEEE.]. *Engineering in Medicine and Biology Magazine, IEEE, 26*(5), 51–56. doi:10.1109/EMB.2007.901787 PMID:17941323

Johnston, B., Weeler, L., Deuser, J., & Sousa, K. H. (2000). Outcomes of the Kaiser Permanente tele-home health research project. *Archives of Family Medicine, 9*(1), 40–45. doi:10.1001/archfami.9.1.40 PMID:10664641

Joint NEMA/COCIR/JIRA Security and Privacy Committee (SPC). (2004). Break-glass—An approach to granting emergency access to healthcare systems (White paper), 6 pages. Retrieved from http://www.medicalimaging.org/wp-content/uploads/2011/02/Break-Glass_-_Emergency_Access_to_Healthcare_Systems.pdf

Jurik, A. D., & Weaver, A. C. (2008). Remote medical monitoring. *IEEE Computer, 41*(4), 96–99. doi:10.1109/MC.2008.133

Kara, A. (2001). Protecting privacy in remote-patient monitoring. *Computer, 34*(5), 24–27. doi:10.1109/2.920607

Lee, M., & Gatton, T. M. (2010). Wireless health data exchange for home healthcare monitoring systems. *Sensors (Basel, Switzerland), 4*(4), 3243–3260. doi:10.3390/s100403243 PMID:22319296

Lymberis, A. (2003). Smart wearables for remote health monitoring, from prevention to rehabilitation: current R&D, future challenges. In *Proceedings of the 4th International IEEE EMBS Special Topic Conference on Information Technology Applications in Biomedicine*, 272–275. doi:10.1109/ITAB.2003.1222530

Mitchell, J. (2000). Increasing the cost-effectiveness of telemedicine by embracing e-health. *Journal of Telemedicine and Telecare, 6*(suppl 1), 16–19. doi:10.1258/1357633001934500 PMID:10793960

Otto, C., Milenkoviç, A., Sanders, C. & Jovanov. E. (2005). © Rinton Press System architecture of a wireless body area sensor network for ubiquitous health monitoring. *Journal of Mobile Multimedia.*

Rhee, S., Yang, B. H., Chang, K., & Asada, H. H. (1998, October). The ring sensor: a new ambulatory wearable sensor for twenty-four hour patient monitoring. In *Engineering in Medicine and Biology Society, 1998. Proceedings of the 20th Annual International Conference of the IEEE* (Vol. 4), (pp. 1906-1909). IEEE.

Rodríguez-Molinero, A., Catalá, A., Díaz, M., Rodríguez, J., Fernández de la Puente, E., & Tabuenca, A. et al. (2008).CAALYX: Evidence-based selection of health sensors for elderly telemonitoring. In *Proceedings of the 6th Conference of the International Society for Gerontechnology.* doi:10.4017/gt.2008.07.02.135.00

Sun, J., Fang, Y., & Zhu, X. (2010). Privacy and emergency response in e-healthcare leveraging wireless body sensor networks. *Wireless Communications, IEEE, 17*(1), 66–73. doi:10.1109/MWC.2010.5416352

Varshney, U. (2007). Pervasive healthcare and wireless health monitoring. *Mobile Networks and Applications, 12*(2-3), 113–127. doi:10.1007/s11036-007-0017-1

KEY TERMS AND DEFINITIONS

Anonymisation: Extracting all information from a set of data liked to one user that would allow identifying the data owner.

Anonymous Credential: This credential technology allows the holder of the credential to disclose a chosen part of the certified data and still prove that it has been signed by the trusted issuer. This selective disclosure is useful for ensuring privacy in systems where authentications and accountability is also required.

Break-the-Glass: This procedure allows for quick access to some resources in case of emergency situations. In case of healthcare, this means that the patients' health information required for appropriate care provisioning can be accessed without regular permits.

Credential Pseudonym: The pseudonym that is created from information recorded in an anonymous credential, which allows only the credential holder to authenticate under that pseudonym.

Digital Signature: A scheme for demonstrating the authenticity of a digital message.

Electronic Health Records: These records represent a collection of health information about a patient, recorded in an electronic form. Due to the digital nature of these records, the sharing is eased and analysis of patient data is enabled on a large scale.

Misuser: A party which attempts to misuse a system.

Network of Caregivers: The set of caregiver of a patient that is taking part and provides care to the patient through the eHealth system.

Pseudonym: A name that is created to be used in a certain context, typically utilised to hide the identity of an individual.

Pseudonymous Relationship: Relationship between parties where one or more parties are known solely by their pseudonym.

Chapter 15
Early Warning System and Adaptation Advice to Reduce Human Health Consequences of Extreme Weather Conditions and Air Pollution

Dragan Bogdanović
State University of Novi Pazar, Serbia

Konstansa Lazarević
State University of Novi Pazar, Serbia

ABSTRACT

The authors developed a multi-site Internet service to provide the public with real time information about local weather and air quality, how they may affect health, and how general population and different sensitive population groups can protect their health during periods of extreme weather conditions or increased air pollution levels. The information service is based on data obtained from the Republic Hydrometeorological Service of Serbia and Serbian Environment Protection Agency. Health warnings and recommendations are given separately for each AIQ and heat index or wind chill index value, for each sensitive population group, as well as for the general population. The project is currently implemented on the website of the Institute of Occupational Health Niš and will be offered to other healthcare institutions in Serbia. Evaluation of the system should enable redefinition of heat and wind chill indices and air pollution threshold values if necessary. This chapter explores the service.

INTRODUCTION

Exposure to adverse weather conditions or high concentrations of air pollutants is associated with a wide range of acute and chronic health effects, especially in children, the elderly, and in patients with chronic diseases. Pyramid of the health effects of adverse weather conditions and air pollution starts from subclinical effects, continued with deterioration of organ functions, the appearance of new or worsening of existing symptoms, increased use of drugs, activity reduction, an increased number

DOI: 10.4018/978-1-4666-7266-6.ch015

of physician visits, increased use of emergency medical services, increased number of admissions to hospital treatment, and ends with the increased number of deaths.

The growing problems of climate change and air pollution have caused the development of a system for monitoring health risks and issuing warnings in many countries. In the U.S., the National Weather Service was developed, using the National Weather Hazards application to monitor, alert, and provide advice on risk due to the effects of many meteorological factors: snow, wind, floods, extreme heat and cold over the Internet (http://www.nws.noaa.gov). United States Environmental Protection Agency - EPA calculates and displays the Air Quality Index (http://www.airnow.gov) and issues warnings for increased concentration of pollutants in the air. In the UK, the website of the National Weather Service (http://www.metoffice.gov.uk) gives an overview of the current meteorological conditions and air quality index. Warnings are issued when the values of these factors are sufficient to pose a threat to human health and the presentation contains a number of recommendations regarding appropriate behavior and preparations for risk mitigation due to the effects of extreme weather conditions. Similar systems exist in other countries: Canada (http://www.ec.gc.ca), Australia (http://www.bom.gov.au), France (http://france.meteofrance.com), Germany (http://www.umweltbundesamt.de), as well as other countries.

Internet applications for weather and air pollution monitoring, as well as for providing health advice and issuing warnings have been developed, not only on national level, but also for regions of large countries (USA, Canada, China, Australia), as well as in many cities in the world.

Within the "New information technologies for analytical decision-making based on the organization of experiments and observations, and their application in biological, economic and social systems" project, funded by the Ministry of Education, Science and Technological Development of the Republic of Serbia, the first system for early warning and providing recommendations for reducing the adverse health consequences of air pollution and meteorological conditions is under development in Serbia. The system is interfaced with using a web application and is intended for use by the general population and vulnerable population groups in the cities of Serbia. At this stage, the system has been implemented on the website of the Institute of Occupational Medicine in Nis, and will be offered in other towns in Serbia.

BACKGROUND

Air Pollution

The earliest recorded problems with outdoor air pollution occurred due to burning fossil fuels in large cities (Brimblecombe, 1987). Industrialization and transport have led to an increase in the concentration of pollutants in the air. By the mid- twentieth century, there have been a few short-lived episodes in which exceptionally high levels of air pollution have influenced the occurrence of excessive mortality and morbidity. The most dramatic three episodes took place in the Meuse Valley in Belgium in 1930. (Nemery et al., 2001), Donora, Pennsylvania in 1948. (Davis, 2002) and in London in 1952 (Bell & Davis, 2001; UK Ministry of Health, 1954) These episodes prompted the authorities in many countries to start the research on the impact of air pollution on human health and to enact legislation that would improve air quality. These measures and activities have greatly contributed to alleviating the problem in the developed countries, but air pollution remains a serious, now global, worldwide problem, with intense negative effects on public health (Ezzati et al., 2002) In many areas of the world, the levels of air pollution are still extremely high, as is the case in large cities of China and India (WHO, 2001)

While the impact of the extremely high concentration of pollutants was clearly visible during the above excess situations, contemporary studies of air pollution in developed countries give attention to the impact of much lower concentrations of pollutants.

Pollutants in the Outside Air

Particles

Many pollutants can, alone or in combination with others, affect the health of people, but over the last two decades particles (particulate matter - PM) are becoming the main subject of research (Brunekreef & Holgate, 2002). They represent a heterogeneous mixture of solid and liquid substances suspended in the air, which vary in size and chemical composition in space and time.

Natural and artificial sources of particles are: internal combustion engines, dust from roads, industry, metal processing operations, agricultural and construction activities, firing, clay dust, pollen, molds, forest fires and the burning of agricultural waste, volcanic emissions and sea spray.

There are thousands of elements and compounds that were detected in the particles at various locations, but the most common ones are: nitrates, sulfates, organic and elemental carbon, organic compounds (e.g., polycyclic aromatic hydrocarbons), biological substances (endotoxin, cell components), and metals (iron, copper, nickel, zinc and vanadium).

Due to the complex nature of the particles, their measurement, classification and regulation are based mainly on the defined size ranges. They are most commonly classified as the total suspended solids or TSP, particles that easily penetrate the tracheobronchial tree or PM_{10} (aerodynamic diameter of less than 10 μm) and the fine particles that can reach alveoli or $PM_{2.5}$ (aerodynamic diameter of less than 2.5 μm). More recently, the attention of researchers is focusing on ultrafine particles or UFP, with a diameter of less than 0.1 μm, which originate from combustion processes (Daigle et al., 2003).

Sulfur Dioxide

Sulfur dioxide (SO_2) is very irritating, colorless, soluble gas with an intense smell and taste. In contact with water, it produces sulfuric acid, which is responsible for its strong irritating effect on the eyes, mucous membranes and skin (Lipset, 2001). It can also cause narrowing of the airways and lead to an exacerbation of chronic lung disease symptoms and increased frequency of attacks in asthmatic patients.

The main source of this pollutant in the air is the burning of fuels containing sulfur, especially in power plants and diesel engines (the primary reason for the change in the composition of diesel fuel) and smelting of metal ores that contain sulfur. Sulfur dioxide oxidizes to sulfur trioxide, which, due to the strong affinity to water quickly turns into sulfuric acid (WHO, 1987).

Nitrogen Oxides

Nitrogen oxides are reactive compounds which include NO, NO_2, NO_3, N_2O_4, and N_2O_5. These compounds are commonly labeled with NO_X because a mixture of these compounds is usually present in the air. Nitric acid in the gaseous state (HNO_3) is a major source of particulate nitrates and is produced when nitrogen dioxide reacts with hydroxyl radicals during the day, or when the nitrogen pentoxide reacts with water vapor during the night (U.S. EPA, 1993).

A large number of toxicological and epidemiological researches have focused on nitrogen dioxide, due to the fact that the creation of tropospheric ozone and other photochemical oxidants starts with the photolysis of nitrogen dioxide.

The main artificial source of nitrogen oxides in the air is the combustion of fossil fuels in motor vehicles and industrial processes. The high combustion temperature leads to the oxidation of atmospheric nitrogen, first to nitrogen monoxide, then to nitrogen dioxide. A typical daily pattern of nitrogen oxide concentration movement indicates a low base concentration with morning and afternoon spikes, due to the traffic rush hour.

Nitrogen dioxide and nitric oxide are naturally produced as a product of metabolism of bacteria, and in far lesser extent as a result of volcanic activity.

Carbon Monoxide

Carbon monoxide (CO) is a gas without color, smell and taste that links to hemoglobin with the affinity 250 times more potent than oxygen and is therefore affecting the reduction of systemic delivery of oxygen to tissues. Carbon monoxide also binds to cytochrome oxidase, which further adds to cell hypoxia, and is associated with the other extravascular proteins such as myoglobin, cytochrome P-450, catalase and peroxidase (Seger & Welch, 2001). On exposure to high concentrations, which usually occurs indoors, it leads to loss of consciousness, and high concentrations can lead to death. At lower levels of concentration, reduced oxygen transport may increase the risk of cardiovascular disorders and mental dysfunction.

Carbon monoxide is the product of partial oxidation of carbon. External sources include motor vehicles, motor boats, lawn mowers, chain saws and other equipment running on fossil fuels, and using fuel for heating purposes. According to the study on the measured concentrations of this pollutant, it is more often used as an indicator of air pollution resulting from the burning than it actually causes adverse health effects. However, under certain conditions, for example in poorly ventilated public garages, carbon monoxide can reach concentrations that lead to a significant increase of carboxyhemoglobin in patients with atherosclerosis or other diseases of the cardiovascular system.

Ozone

Ozone (O_3) is a highly reactive, colorless gas with a characteristic odor. Exposure to low concentrations is inevitable because ozone is formed in natural processes and during human activities. The negative effects of short-term exposure to high concentrations of this pollutant are the inflammatory response of the airways and increased sensitivity to allergens, such as pollen, resulting in reduced pulmonary function.

In the troposphere ozone is caused by the action of solar UV radiation on nitric oxides and reactive hydrocarbons, emitted by motor vehicles and many industrial sources (U.S. EPA, 1996).

Ozone concentrations are increased during hot, sunny days. Typical concentration profile in cities is characterized by a broad peak which lasts from late morning to late afternoon and early evening.

Biological Mechanisms of Action of Air Pollution

Estimated biological mechanisms of air pollution influence on cardiovascular and respiratory systems include direct effects on the cardiovascular system, blood, lung receptors and indirect effects expressed through pulmonary oxidative stress and inflammatory responses. Direct effects may arise from the action of agents that can easily pass through the pulmonary epithelium into the blood circulation, such as gases and possibly ultra fine particles - UFP (Nemmar et al., 2002a) together with the soluble components from $PM_{2.5}$. The activation of pulmonary neural reflexes due to the interaction of particles with lung receptors can also play an important role. Direct effects, under appropriate conditions, can contribute to instability of vascular plaques, or initiate a cardiac arrhythmia. These effects of air pollution are the likely explanation for the occurrence of rapid (within a few hours) cardiovascular responses such as increase in the number of acute myocardial infarction.

Less acute (up to several days) and chronic indirect effects may occur due to oxidative stress or pulmonary inflammation induced by inhaled pollutants. This, consequently, can contribute to a systemic inflammatory condition, which can, in reverse direction, activate hemostasis mechanisms and accelerate atherosclerosis.

Pulmonary and Systemic Oxidative Stress and Inflammation

Inhalation of air pollutants causes pulmonary oxidative stress and inflammation (Kelly, 2003). Lung exposure to high particle concentrations and ozone causes an inflammatory response as evidenced by the in vivo animal models (Godleski et al., 2002) as well as in vitro cell models (Li et al., 1996). The presence of $PM_{2.5}$-associated-metals is associated with acute changes in cardiovascular and respiratory physiology (Cakmak et al., 2014), and soluble metals in the particles contributes to the inflammatory process by increased oxidative stress (Ghio & Devlin, 2001). In addition, lung inflammation can occur by direct effects of ultrafine particles, which are independent of the transition metals or soluble components (Brown et al., 2000). Similarly, ozone provokes pulmonary inflammatory response through oxidative stress and deterioration of lung function (Samet et al., 2001).

In the studies it was established that the oxidative stress occurs after exposure to ultra-fine particles of coal and exhaust gases of diesel engines (Shukla et al., 2000) as well as $PM_{2.5}$ (Sorensen et al., 2003). In vivo experiments on rats with the use of in situ hemiluminescence methods showed a rapid occurrence of oxidative stress in the lung tissue, but also in the cardiac muscle (Gurgueira et al., 2002). This can occur as a response to the presence of transition metals or of free radicals, which are known to exist in $PM_{2.5}$ as a result of the atmospheric chemical reactions. Exposure to increased concentrations of $PM_{2.5}$ is also associated with increased levels of markers of lipid and protein oxidation in the human blood. Free radicals also contribute to the development of pulmonary inflammation.

Oxidative stress triggers specific transcription factors, including nucleus factor B and the protein-1 activator that regulate the expression of genes producing cytokines, chemokines and other proinflammatory mediators.

The exhaust gases of diesel engines or their organic extracts may, through oxidative effects on mitochondria, induce apoptosis or necrosis of macrophages and cells of the respiratory epithelium, which may impair the ability to defend against infection and to increase the reactivity of the air passages (Li et al., 2003).

Larger particles, rather than fine, affect the release of endotoxin in a yet unsolved way, which also induces proinflammatory cytokines (Monn & Becker, 1999), increases the pulmonary inflammation and airway reactivity, increases the number of systemic immune cells, and reduces lung function.

Intrapulmonary responses stimulated by particles can also affect neurogenic inflammation. Sensitive neurons in contact with the irritating particles within the air passages can be stimulated to release neuropeptides (for example, substance P, a peptide that affects the calcitonin gene and neurokinin A), which initiate inflammation that involves the release of cytokines, secretion of mucus and vasodilation.

Neuropeptides act on various types of cells in the lungs, such as the epithelial and smooth muscle cells, which results in the modulation of inflammation, and increased air passage sensitivity. They also affect immune cells (polymorphonuclear leukocytes, lymphocytes, eosinophils, and others), which enhances the inflammatory response. In vitro experiments indicate that the receptors for specific irritants (vanilloid or capsaicin) in neurons are mediators of neurogenic inflammation associated with particles (Veronesi et al., 2000).

Several controlled exposition studies showed that the inhalation of particles (Nightingale et al.,

2000), and ozone (Aris et al., 1993) causes both pulmonary and systemic inflammatory response in humans. One hour of exposure to very high concentrations of exhaust gases from diesel engines has caused an inflammatory reaction in the lungs of healthy adults. This response included an increased number of polymorphonuclears, T and B lymphocytes, mast cells and increased level of mediators of inflammation (Salvi et al., 1999).

Diesel engine exhaust gases enhance mRNA transcription of interleukin-8 (IL-8, the protein which draws polymorphonuclears onto the damaged location), and increased IL-8 and growth-regulatory oncogene amplify the airway inflammation (Salvi et al., 2000).

All of these controlled exposure studies indicate that particles can cause moderate pulmonary inflammatory response in healthy individuals, and increase the level of blood factors affecting coagulation, even without any damage to the lungs.

Some studies suggest the existence of a systemic inflammatory response after exposure to air pollution. In humans, exposure to the forest fire smoke (as measured PM_{10} and SO_2), at concentrations that did not cause changes in pulmonary function, have led to the stimulation of bone marrow to release immature polymorphonucleates into circulation (Tan et al., 2000). In an experiment on animals, in rabbits who intrapharyngeally received 5 mg of PM_{10} twice a week for 3 weeks, the production of polymorphonucleates in the bone marrow increased and they were released into the circulation (Mukae et al., 2001). PM_{10} exposure caused a diffuse inflammation in the lungs, with particles present in the alveolar macrophages, lung epithelial cells, and the walls of the air passages.

The Effects of Inflammation, Oxidative Stress, and the Increase of the Blood Factor

Exposure to air pollution can cause changes in the composition of blood, with possible serious consequences in patients with cardiovascular diseases. Seaton et al (1995) gave the general hypothesis that exposure to the particles causes alveolar inflammation, exacerbation of pre-existing lung disease, increases coagulation and with it the risk of adverse cardiovascular events. As already mentioned, a number of studies with the controlled exposure to particles showed an increase in cellular and biochemical markers of pulmonary and systemic inflammation.

Particles affect the increase of fibrinogen level (Ghio et al., 2003), key component of the coagulation and platelet thrombosis and major determinant of blood viscosity. Blood viscosity affects the severity of cardiovascular disease (Junker et al., 1998) and its increase depends on the increased levels of dissolved SO_2 and particles (Peters et al., 1997). Fibrinogen is also important as an independent risk factor for myocardial infarction.

Epidemiological data indicate possible effects of air pollution with particles on blood coagulation (Seaton et al., 1999). In contrast, Stark et al. (2013) have, in the semi experimental study conducted in adult healthy volunteers, found that the ex vivo creation of thrombin is associated with exposure to NO_2, nitrates and sulphates, but not with suspended particles and oxidative potential of inhaled ambient air.

Of note is the fact that the prediction of death and heart stroke in middle-aged men according to the level of fibrinogen in the plasma may be influenced by the presence of other, inflammation-sensitive proteins (Peters et al., 2000a), which suggests that inflammation plays an important role in determining cardiovascular risk. In addition, platelet aggregation may further enhance the development of acute thrombotic formation after exposure to the exhaust fumes (Nemmar et al., 2003) from a diesel engine, and fine particles (Nemmar et al., 2002b). The mechanism responsible for the activation of platelets and fibrinogen increase is not fully understood. These findings still support the contention that air pollution can acutely increase the risk of thrombosis, which may further result in ischemic disorders.

Increased concentrations of IL -6 are associated with increased risk of cardiovascular events (Ridker et al., 2000) and mortality (Volpato et al., 2001). The levels of serum IL-6, IL-1 and stimulating factor of granulocyte macrophage colons grow in healthy male subjects after exposure to air pollution from forest fires, and also grow in in vitro with exposure of macrophages from human lung to PM_{10} originating from urban areas (Van Eeden et al. 2001). IL-6 is directly involved in the regulation of the C-reactive protein synthesis in the liver. This protein is a sensitive indicator of infection, injury and inflammation, and is associated with an increased risk of cardiovascular disease (Ridker, 2001). The concentration of C-reactive protein is directly related with the exposure to the total suspended particulate matter and PM_{10} (Peters et al., 2001a). The mechanisms by which C-reactive protein increases the risk of cardiovascular events have been the subject of intensive research. One possibility is that it weakens the endothelial vasoreactivity in patients with already diseased coronary artery (Fichtlscherer et al., 2000). In addition, the C-reactive protein can directly contribute to the development and progression of atherosclerosis by a number of mechanisms which include changes in the formation of foam cells, the entry of monocytes into the arterial walls, the stimulation of prothrombin tissue factors and expression of adhesion molecules (Bhatt & Topol, 2002).

Inflammation (proinflammatory cytokines, C-reactive protein, and components of innate immunity) plays a significant role in the development of atherosclerosis and plaque instability (Libby, Ridker, & Maseri, 2002). It is possible that air pollution affects the systemic inflammation, causing atherosclerosis progression during a prolonged period of time (Suwa, et al., 2002) as well as activating acute plaque instability and sudden cardiovascular events in short time intervals.

In rabbits with hyperlipidaemia which have been exposed to the particles, progression of coronary atherosclerosis and increased extracellular lipid depot creation occured after 4 weeks (Libby, Ridker, & Maseri, 2002). Degree of the plaque formation correlates with the number of alveolar macrophages which conduct particle phagocytosis. These effects seem to be influenced by age, hypertension, hyperlipidemia, diabetes and other conditions associated with inflammation.

Changes in the blood vessels due to exposure to air pollution have also been proven. Inhalation of particles and ozone for 2 hours has resulted in a moderate vasoconstriction in healthy adult subjects (Brook et al., 2002). Similarly, in rats, the small pulmonary arteries reacted by constricting to short-term exposure to high concentrations of particles (Batalha et al., 2002). It is assumed that acute systemic inflammation and oxidative stress act as the trigger for endothelial dysfunction which can lead to vasoconstriction (Bonetti et al., 2003).

For now, the mechanisms that lead to changes in the state of blood vessels are not clear. However, several studies point to the fact that air pollution affects the cardiovascular hemodynamics (Bouthillier et al., 1998).

Literature data indicate that the external air pollution increases the blood pressure in coronary rehabilitation patients (Zanobetti et al., 2002) and also in adults with pulmonary diseases (Linn et al., 1999). Arterial vasoconstriction is the probable explanation for the findings of the ULTRA study (The Exposure and Risk Assessment for Fine and Ultrafine Particles in Ambient Air) (Pekkanen et al., 2002). The levels of particles in the air for two days prior to physical stress testing were significantly related to the increase of ST-segment depression during testing. This finding suggests the hypothesis that air pollution has an effect on myocardial ischemia, which was confirmed in an experimental study on dogs exposed to high concentrations of pollutants in the air (Wellenius et al., 2003). The results also provide a possible explanation of the theory of the impact of airborne particles on the dynamics of acute myocardial infarction. The research has identified a significant association between onset of symptoms and acute (levels within 2 hours before symptoms) and subacute (mean concentration during the previous day) exposure to $PM_{2.5}$ particles. Sudden arterial vasoconstriction (and / or possible endothelial dysfunction) can probably accelerate the emergence of acute coronary syndromes by initiating plaque instability or impairing myocardial nutrition in patients with existing atherosclerosis.

Cardiac Autonomic Nervous System

The impact of air pollution on mortality may be partially explained by its action on the autonomic nervous system. The ability to change heart rate (heart rate variability - HRV), a period of heart rate rest and blood pressure are regulated by the balance between the two parts of the autonomic nervous system: sympathetic and parasympathetic. Reducing the ability to change rhythm increases the risk of cardiovascular morbidity and mortality in the elderly, and in people with severe heart disease (Task Force of the European Society of Cardiology and the North American Society of Pacing and Electrophysiology, 1996). This conclusion was reached by analysis of heart rate by determining the standard deviation of the periods between normal R-R intervals, and the low frequency / high frequency relationship, measured with an electrocardiograph over a 24-hour period. Exposure to ambient particles reduces the ability to change rhythm (Magari et al., 2001). Reducing the parasympathetic influence on the heart may be an important mechanism of cardiovascular mortality increase due to tachyarrhythmias. Experimental studies of controlled exposure to air pollution confirmed the assumption that particles can impair the ability to change rhythm (Devlin et al., 2003; Pope et al., 1999). It has been found that the reduction of the ability to change rhythm occurs rapidly and in inverse proportion to the increase of the particle concentration.

It is not sufficiently clarified whether the observed short-term changes of the ability to alter the rhythm are in relation to the deterioration of cardiovascular outcomes and the initiation of serious arrhythmias in the long run. It is possible that for certain people, bradyarrhythmias caused by air pollution may affect sudden death.

Some evidence indicates that exposure to particulate matter causes clinically significant changes in the electrophysiology of the heart. The incidence of cardiac arrhythmias is associated with the $PM_{2.5}$ exposure in high-risk individuals (e.g., individuals with a artificial cardiac pacemaker). In a study on 100 patients who were observed for 3 years, it has been determined that the concentrations of nitrogen dioxide and carbon monoxide present in the air have been strongly linked with the artificial cardiac pacemaker malfunctions, and the soot exhibited somewhat lower effect (Peters et al., 2000b). Although this study was limited by a small number of high-risk patients and the lack of data on the device malfunctions, it points to the existence of possible adverse effects of particulate and gaseous pollutants on the balance of cardiac autonomic nervous system.

The study that used time series analysis to monitor the impact of particles on mortality (Hoek et al., 2001) supports this finding. It was proven that the risk of death from arrhythmia increases with the increase of the seven-day average concentrations of soot and particles.

The results of this study coincide with the result of a number of experimental studies on animals which indicate the induction of cardiac arrhythmia in the previously diseased animals (e.g., with pulmonary and systemic hypertension) that have been exposed to particles. In dogs exposed to particles for 6 hours for three consecutive days, an increase in the frequency of low and high heart rate frequencies occurred, as well as increased values of low frequency / high frequency relation (Godleski et al., 2000). Exposure to ashes produced by burning oil (component particles) led to tachyarrhythmias in rats (Wellenius et al., 2002). Such findings support the contention that air pollution may alter the balance of the autonomic nervous system in the direction of causing serious tachyarrhythmias.

The mechanism of action remains unclear, but it is assumed that involves activation of pulmonary neural reflex arc, the direct effects of pollutants on ion channels of cardiac cells, or the consequences of systemic inflammatory status.

RESULTS OF PREVIOUS EXAMINATIONS OF AIR POLLUTION INFLUENCE ON MORBIDITY AND MORTALITY

Increased concentrations of pollutants in the air usually exert their negative impact on the health by worsening the symptoms of pre-existing cardiovascular and respiratory diseases. (Samet et al., 2000). The increase in relative risk for morbidity and mortality due to air pollution is relatively low compared to the confirmed risk factors such as hypertension, increased cholesterol levels, infections or smoking. Nevertheless, this is a serious health problem if the number of exposed and length of exposure (the whole human life) is taken into account.

In recent years a number of studies that suggest an association between air pollution and cardiorespiratory disease increases significantly (Pope et al., 2000; Vanos, Hebbern, & Cakmak, 2014; Franchini & Mannucci, 2009). The studies are mainly based on the study of the impact of short-term and long-term exposure to air pollution on health. Observations relating to the adverse effects of short exposure are more numerous. In these studies, widespread short-term resultant occurrences in the population (mortality, incidence of symptoms, hospitalizations and doctor visits for health care) are associated with short-term variations in the concentration of pollutants in the outside air, usually through the use of population-based time series analysis.

Fewer studies have focused on the study of the adverse health effects of long-term exposure. These studies include analysis of data (eg, total mortality and in some cases cardiovascular events) from large cohorts from different geographic locations that differ in composition and concentrations of pollutants in the outside air.

EFFECTS OF LONG-TERM EXPOSURE TO AIR POLLUTION

The first large, prospective cohort study that confirmed the negative health impact of prolonged exposure to increased concentrations of pollutants in the air was the Harvard Six Cities study conducted by Dockery et al. (1993). It has been shown that chronic exposure to air pollutants has an impact on cardiovascular mortality. In a cohort of 8111 adults over 14 to 16 years of observation, overall mortality ratio in the most polluted and least polluted city was 1,26:1,00. Additional analysis adjustments in relation to the selected individual risk factors: gender, educational level, occupational exposure, BMI, smoking, hypertension and diabetes did not significantly modify this relationship. Of all the pollutants, the increase of concentration of particulate matter (PM) and sulfates showed the strongest association with the disease.

Tracking the cohort by Pope and associates (1995), organized by the American Cancer Society (ACS) is the largest study of long-term effects of air pollution. In about 500 000 adult residents from all 50 states from the USA, chronic exposure to a mixture of pollutants in the air is associated with mortality statistics for a period of 16 years. ACS study has increased the level of control for associated factors by introducing new ones, such as diet and gaseous pollutants. The results showed that any increase in annual mean $PM_{2.5}$ concentration of 10 μg/m^3 was accompanied by an increase in overall mortality by 4%, mortality from cardiopulmonary disease by 6%, and lung cancer mortality by 8%. Mortality was mostly associated with particles ($PM_{2.5}$), sulfate particles and sulfur dioxide. There was also an established dependence of cardiopulmonary mortality on average ozone concentrations for the 1982-1998 period. Educational level was a significant modifier in assessing the impact of particles on human health. People with low to medium education had increased risk of death and morbidity compared to those with higher education.

Hoek et al (2002) confirmed the importance of housing location within the city as the factor that can affect mortality from air pollution. In a cohort of 5000 adult patients observed for 8 years, exposure to pollutants originating from traffic caused the increase in mortality in the population of the city center in relation to the residents who live in less polluted urban areas. Of all the risk factors, living near busy roads was most strongly associated with cardiopulmonary mortality in this cohort (relative risk - RR: 1.95 and 95% IP: 1.09 to 3.52). This study also suggests that individual exposure to toxic components of air pollution can vary significantly among residents of a city.

Until recently, the specific causes of increased cardiovascular mortality due to long-term exposure to air pollution were vague. In the analysis of the ACS study, investigators point out the impact of particles on the specific causes of death (Pope et al., 2004). A statistically significant association between particulate matter ($PM_{2.5}$) and total cardiovascular mortality was confirmed by an increase in the concentration of $PM_{2.5}$ in 10 $\mu g/m^3$ (RR: 1.12, 95% IP: 1.08 to 1.15) during long-term exposure. The highest risk was found for ischemic heart disease (RR: 1.18, 95% IP: 1.14 to 1.23), which also represents the most common cause of death. The risk of death from arrhythmia, heart failure and cardiac arrest has also increased (RR: 1.13, 95% IP: 1.05 to 1.21). No evidence for increased mortality from other causes was found (e.g., aortic aneurysm, diabetes, hypertensive heart diseases or any respiratory diseases). These results indicate that the pollutants in the air deteriorate both non-ischemic and ischemic cardiovascular diseases.

Data on the impact of long-term exposure to air pollution on mortality is largely derived from the United States. A research in England has followed 835,607 patients in the 2003-2007 period, and the concentration of particulate matter, nitrogen dioxide, ozone, and sulfur dioxide. The obtained results suggest that exposure to the above pollutants, except ozone, increases the risk of all-cause mortality. A stronger association was found with respiratory disease mortality, which is not in accordance with the results of studies in the U.S., where the relationship was stronger between pollutants and mortality from cardiovascular disease (Carey et al., 2013).

In addition to the impact of the deterioration of the existing cardiopulmonary diseases, air pollution can also lead to an increase in the number of congenital heart defects. The biological mechanism of action of pollutants in their formation has not been clarified. Data from Eastern Europe, from areas that for many years have had high concentrations of pollutants originating from the industry, point to the possibility that high air pollution can affect an increase of the number of congenital heart defects (Smrcka & Leznarova, 1998). A recent study of birth registrations in Los Angeles found that the risk for ventricular septal defect increases by the dose-response principle with increasing exposure to carbon monoxide. Thus, the approximate relative risk (odds ratio - OR) for the second quartile compared to the first was 1.62 (95%IP: 1.05 to 2.48) for the third quartile 2.09 (95% IP: 1.19 to 3.67), and in the fourth quartile a whole 2.95 (95% IP: 1.44 to 6.05) (Ritz et al., 2002). A connection between valve defects, aortia and truncus and the levels of ozone was also noted. Particles and other pollutants measured did not show this correlation.

EFFECTS OF SHORT-TERM EXPOSURE TO AIR POLLUTION

The two largest studies so far to have analyzed the acute effects of air pollution are the National

Morbidity Mortality and Air Pollution Study (NMMAPS) in the United States (Dominici et al., 2003) and Air Pollution and Health: a European Approach-2- APHEA-2 project (Katsouyanni et al., 2001).

The NMMAPS study followed the health outcomes for 50 million people in the 20 largest U.S. cities. Any increase in PM_{10} concentration of 10 μg/m^3, was followed by increase of daily rate of general mortality of 0.21±0.06%, and mortality rate from cardiovascular disease of 0.31±0.09%.

APHEA-2 showed a slightly stronger association between adverse health outcomes and air pollution. With 43 million people in 29 European cities, the increase in daily mortality was 0.6% (95% IP: 0.4% to 0.8%) for any increase in PM_{10} concentration of 10 μg/m^3. Mortality from cardiovascular disease was higher by 0.69% (95% IP: 0.31% to 1.08%) (Zanobetti et al., 2003).

Both studies have confirmed the differences in their findings in relation to the geographical region. In Europe, cities with warmer climates have shown a greater degree of influence of air pollution on mortality. On the other hand, NMMAPS study confirmed the greater impact in the northern than in the southern areas. Perhaps such differences between these studies were caused by different habits of residents: time spent outdoors, use of leisure time, as well as various ambient conditions, and differences in the composition of mixtures of pollutants (Smith et al., 2001).

Hundreds of small, short-term studies on the effects of acute exposure to air pollution have been published in the last decades, as presented by Brunekreef and Holgate (2002) as well as Pope (2000) Most frequently, the daily mortality rate, the number of hospital admissions (Linn et al., 2000) health care visits (Delfino et al., 1997), and worsening of symptoms (Schwartz et al., 1994) show an increase in line with the increased levels of air pollution. Observations in North America (Burnett et al., 1999) and Europe indicate a higher rate of hospitalization for all cardiopulmonary diseases. Number of hospital admissions due to heart failure and ischemic heart disease rose by 0.8% and 0.7% for every increase of PM_{10} of 10 μg/m^3 (Morris, 2001).

More focused studies have shown an increased risk for acute myocardial infarction (Peters et al., 2001b), installation of artificial cardiac pacemakers (Peters et al., 2000b) and the finding of myocardial ischemia during stress tests (Pekkanen et al., 2002).

The extreme increase in air pollution has affected the increase in blood pressure during episodes of extended stagnation of air due to temperature inversions in Europe (Ibald - Mulli et al., 2001).

Bronchoconstrictory effects of sulfur dioxide are manifested mostly in people already suffering from asthma and chronic bronchitis. APHEA authors found a significant effect of this compound on the increase in mortality from respiratory diseases in almost all the cities of Western Europe (Katsouyanni et al., 2001).

The study of time series that examined the impact of air pollution on daily mortality in Austrian cities Graz and Linz has determined a correlation between nitrogen oxides and suspended particulate matter and daily mortality, including during summer when the concentrations of pollutants had lower values (Nurberg et al., 2013).

Studies in Seoul (Hong et al., 2002) and Taiwan (Tsai et al., 2003) indicated an increase of ischemic stroke incidence, which is directly related to the concentration of particles in the air.

The studies in Serbia have also shown that air pollution significantly affects the increase of the number of hospital admissions (Stankovic et al., 2012; Milosevic et al., 2010; Nikic et al., 2008) and mortality (Bogdanovic et al., 2006; Nikic et al., 2009) from cardiovascular and respiratory diseases.

THE INFLUENCE OF METEOROLOGICAL FACTORS

Air Temperature

The role of the center for body temperature regulation, which is located in the hypothalamus, is to maintain the temperature within an optimal range. At idle state, it is around 37° C, while during physical activity body temperature can rise to 38-39° C without any harmful effects on health. For the temperature to be within the physiological range, a balance between the creation and loss of body heat is necessary. The main source of body heat is metabolic activity, and there are other sources, such as solar radiation or various heaters. The means of body heat loss are convection-heat transmission to the surrounding air, conduction in contact with hard objects (e.g. floor), respiration, radiation and evaporation of sweat. Several mechanisms are involved in the regulation of body temperature, and the most important for heat loss are sweating and expansion of peripheral blood vessels, while muscle tremors and constriction of peripheral blood vessels are used to increase the temperature. To make the body temperature stable, the heat loss must be equal to the heat produced (Havenith, 2002).

Increased temperature can cause rash and redness of the skin, weakness, syncope and collapse. The basic mechanism of this phenomenon is the expansion of peripheral blood vessels and blood pressure decrease. In the absence of physical activity, the drop in blood pressure is greater because of the absence of muscle pump and the reduced flow of venous blood into the heart. Conversely, with increased muscle activity, blood pressure is maintained longer within the range of normal values, which creates the possibility of a further increase in body temperature, and when it reaches 40.5°C it can result in a heat shock, which involves cellular structure damage and dysfunction of the center for thermoregulation with a high risk for the occurrence of death. Heat stroke usually occurs in young and healthy people who are exposed to great physical strain at high temperature, for example at sporting events. The occurrence is sudden, and there are very severe complications such as respiratory distress, kidney and liver failure and disseminated intravascular coagulation (Donoghue, 1997).

In addition to increased physical activity, the most important predisposing factors for the occurrence of adverse health effects of increased temperature were older age, lack of acclimatization, dehydration, use of drugs that affect the thermoregulatory center (phenothiazines, barbiturates), obesity, poor physical condition and wearing protective clothing to prevent evaporation.

Elderly people are more sensitive to high temperatures due to physiological changes in the thermoregulation center, associated cardiovascular diseases, poor physical fitness and decreased ability to create sweat (Basu & Samet, 2002; Havenith, 2001).

The process of short-term acclimation to increased temperature takes 3 to 12 days, and full acclimatization is achieved only in a few years. Short-term acclimation physiologically involves an efficient sweating mechanism (earlier onset, higher quantity and wider distribution) and increased peripheral circulation, and it takes a few weeks after stopping high temperature. Long-term acclimation involves reducing basal body temperature, heart rate and metabolic rate, and these adaptive changes are retained for years after cessation of exposure to high temperature (Havenith, 2002).

At increased air temperatures, a greater amounts of liquid intake is necessary. Dehydration or hypohidration rarely occur in young healthy people if they are able to drink sufficient amounts of water and other liquids. In the elderly the presence of chronic diseases (dementia, incontinence), restricted mobility and decreased functional capacity have caused chronic hypohidration to becomes almost a physiological condition. Therefore, older persons are susceptible to the action of very small meteorological and pathological stress influences (Mentes & Culp, 2003; Hodgkinson, Evans, & Wood, 2003).

Good physical condition is a protective factor against the occurrence of adverse events, both from increased and decreased air temperatures. It contributes to an increased cardiovascular reserve, ie the possibility of the cardiovascular system to enhance the blood supply of the target tissue as needed, which is a prerequisite for efficient thermoregulation. In the elderly, the decline in fitness leads to avoidance of physical activity, and that in turn causes an even worse physical condition. Additionally, elderly people avoid exposure to low and high temperatures, which diminishes the ability of acclimation to such conditions (Anderson, 1999).

Obesity is another factor that increases the risk of adverse effects of increased temperatures on health and often correlates with a poor physical condition. Adipose tissue conducts heat poorly so the subcutaneous tissue in obese patients acts as a thermal insulator between the body and the external environment. In obese people is less metabolic activity per unit body weight leads to a higher degree of heating of the body, and when the temperature of the body increases in obese patients, more blood must be diverted to the peripheral blood vessels, which leads to a greater heart frequency and its stress. However, when the outside air temperature exceeds the temperature of the skin in obese people less heat is absorbed from the environment, which has a protective effect (Chan et al., 2001).

Low air temperatures affect the health of the people through a number of physiological processes. Stimulation of the skin thermoreceptors by increased sympathetic activity results in increased levels of catecholamines in plasma, peripheral vasoconstriction, tachycardia and increase in blood pressure. In addition, exposure to cold causes an increase in blood viscosity due to the increase in the number of red blood cells and platelets, as well as increased levels of cholesterol and fibrinogen in the plasma (Keatinge & Donaldson, 1995), and haemoconcentration yields occurrence or deterioration or existing thrombotic changes (Donaldson, 1997). Sudden death occurs as a result of rupture of atheromatous plaques due to hypertension and cold-induced coronary spasm (Donaldson & Keatinge, 1997). Because of bronchoconstriction caused by inhalation of cold air the risk of respiratory disease increases, and decline of cellular and humoral immunity was also demonstrated (Schaanning et al., 1996).

The air temperature has a major impact on morbidity and mortality. Studies that examine the effect of this factor on health are many and varied (Kovats & Koppe, 1994). Some of them are estimating "excess deaths" occurred under the influence of heat waves. Excess mortality is calculated as the difference between the increased and "expected" mortality, or one that can be predicted for a particular period in a particular area, based on data from previous years. Heatwaves constitute a great health risk and they are associated with significant excess morbidity and mortality. Cardiovascular and respiratory diseases were reported as the most common causes mortality (Bogdanovic et al., 2013). Risk factors for heat- related death include older age, pre-existing diseases, living alone, living on the top floor, lack of air- conditioning, and being overweight (Semenza et al., 2008). Populations in regions where extremely hot weather is relatively infrequent are most vulnerable to heat waves owing to a lack of behavioral adaptations (Piranda et al., 2005). Heat waves could reveal or aggravate several adverse drug reactions in elderly (Sommet et al., 2012). During the heat wave the greatest increase in mortality rates is related to diabetes mellitus, chronic kidney disease and diseases of the respiratory, nervous and digestive systems. Malignant neoplasms and cardiovascular mortality accounted to the highest absolute numbers of excess deaths (Basagaña et al., 2011).

People with diabetes are particularly vulnerable to heat because their bodies are less capable of adjusting to increases in temperature due to impairment of their autonomic control and endothelial function (Schwartz, 2005). Persons with kidney disease have a reduced ability to retain fluids and electrolytes. This can make dehydration and overheating happen more quickly. Moreover, when the body gets warm, it moves more blood to the skin in an attempt to reduce body temperature. This reduces both the blood flow and pressure in the kidneys making them more prone to overheating and less able to function (Hansen et al., 2008a). The mechanisms underlying the higher heat- mortality risk among those with nervous system diseases include impaired self -care, inadequate medical care and physiologic vulnerability (Hansen et al., 2008b). Heat stress can lead to down- regulation of epithelial growth -factor signaling, intestinal epithelial injury, impairment of the intestinal epithelial barrier function and increased mortality due to gastrointestinal hemorrhage (Liu et al., 2009). Cardiovascular and respiratory deaths can be triggered by heat when the thermoregulatory mechanisms of the body, such as increased respiratory and heart rate, increased blood circulation and surface sweat, put an additional stress on already ill heart and lungs (Schifano et al., 2009).

Study of time series is an effective way to evaluate the effect of temperature and other climatic factors on mortality in long periods of time. The regression lines obtained in this study show higher mortality rates when the measured temperature values are above and below optimum, that is, they possess an approximately U-shape. The values of the optimum temperature suggest the best adaptation of populations to local weather conditions and vary from city to city (Keating et al., 2000). Thus, the average daily air temperature during whitch there is the lowest number of fatalities, that is, when the inhabitants are acclimated the most, is 24°C in Valencia (Ballester, 1997), and 10°C in Oslo (Skrondal, & Bjertness, 2001).

Literature shows that temperature has an effect on increasing mortality rates from cardiovascular and respiratory diseases as a stress factor associated with the body, which is already burdened with a chronic illness. In France, a heat wave from 1 to 20 June 2003 caused the greatest increase in mortality in persons older than 75 years (National Institute of Public Health Surveillance, 2003). In children and infants the risk of dying due to the effects of high temperature also increased. In the U.S., approximately 4% of deaths associated with the effects of high temperature related to children aged up to 4 years (Centers for Disease Control and Prevention, 2002) People of lower socioeconomic status may be a more vulnerable group because of poor living conditions and lack of air conditioning (Smoyer, 1998).

The study of mortality data from 14 EU countries shows that the mortality rates in winter are significantly higher compared to the annual average (Healy, 2003). In Portugal, the increase in mortality in winter was 28%, followed by Ireland and Spain with an increase of 21%. The lowest variability was observed in Finland (10%), while the average increase in mortality in winter in all 14 countries was 16%. The occurence of a large increase in winter mortality in countries with warmer climates is called the "paradox of winter mortality." The most likely factor to explain this phenomenon is the method of construction of the residential buildings. In countries with higher average annual temperatures there is insufficient attention paid to heat insulation of households and they are therefore more difficult to heat in the winter when the temperature drops. In contrast, in countries with harshly cold climates, as is the case with Scandinavia, high-quality insulation is a construction standard, so that the temperature in the living space is easily maintained at the desired level (Clinch & Healy, 2000).

A study in England showed that mortality in persons older than 75 years during the winter months increases by 17% compared to the annual average, and that 8% of deaths in the elderly during winter is associated with low temperatures (Wilkinson et al., 2004). The mortality rate due to the effect of cold was 11% higher in women and by 20% in people whose medical history included chronic respiratory diseases, while the socioeconomic status did not show a significant influence.

The relationship between the mean daily temperature from June to August and mortality, particularly mortality from respiratory disease and mortality in the elderly was determined by examining the impact of the maximum daily temperature on mortality in 15 European cities (Baccini et al., 2008).

A study conducted in China in four different climatic zones has identified the connection between the high and low temperatures and an increased risk of cerebrovascular mortality in all climatic zones, but this relationship was significant only for low temperatures. It was also found that people who live in colder climate areas are more susceptible to the effects of high temperatures, and the ones from warmer climate areas are more susceptible to the effects of low temperature (Zhang et al., 2014).

Research in Serbia showed that Roma population had significantly higher excess winter mortality - EWM rate per 10,000 (129.2 vs. 76.6) for all causes, all respiratory diseases (26.5 vs. 8.0), and chronic lower respiratory diseases (23.0 vs. 5.2) in comparison to non - Roma population. Influenza and pneumonia related deaths Represented a small proportion of EWM in both populations. Cardiovascular EWM rate was slightly higher among non - Roma population. Regression analysis demonstrates that Roma ethnicity was associated with significant increase of respiratory rate EWM (regression coefficient (B) = 1:49, 95% CI: 0:45 to 2:54). There was no relationship between ethnicity and cardiovascular and all causes EWM rates (Blagojevic et al., 2012).

In addition to the impact on mortality, temperature changes also influence the increase of the number of hospital admissions and other indicators of morbidity. The project "Assessment and prevention of acute health effects of weather conditions in Europe" (PHEWE) was conducted in 16 major European cities with a variety of climate conditions, in which over 30 million people live (Michelozzi et al., 2007). The study included data on mortality and inpatient receptions in the 1990-2000 period. Each year is divided into winter (October to March) and summer (April to September) season. On average, the rate of overall mortality in the winter season was higher than in the summer season by 16%. The difference between the rates was lowest in Helsinki (10%), and highest in Valencia (22%) and Milan (21%). The rate of death from cardiovascular disease in the winter season was, on average, increased by 21% in Helsinki, by 7%, and in Milan for 34%. Death from respiratory disease in the winter season was on average 36% more frequent, 21% in Athens and in Zurich as much as 68%. The number of hospital admissions for cardiovascular disease in the winter season was higher by 11%, in London and Dublin by 5%, and in Paris by 16%. Hospital admissions for respiratory disease in winter season were 42% more frequent, 22% in Ljubljana and 57% in Valencia.

Atmospheric Pressure

Atmospheric pressure is a direct result of the weight of air (Martin, 1999). At sea level and 0°C temperature the atmospheric pressure is 760 mmHg (101.3 kilopascals, or 1 atmosphere). Atmospheric pressure decreases with increasing altitude, but it also decreases with increase in the temperature and humidity so its value varies according to the changes in these parameters. On the other hand, atmospheric pressure value is directly correlated with the value of the partial atmospheric pressure of oxygen (PO_2), which amounts to 160 mm Hg absolute pressure of 1 atmosphere. Decrease of the atmospheric pressure value causes less oxygen in the inhaled air and lower blood oxygen saturation, or tissue and organ hypoxia. The optimal values of PO_2 range from 120 mmHg to 460 mmHg. PO_2 values below 120 mmHg represent the dangerous hypoxic zone and a further decline seriously endangers human life functions, leading to a sudden loss of consciousness when the PO_2 value drops below 76 mmHg, and death if PO_2 value drops below 50 mmHg. Hypoxia causes cells of the central nervous system and the myocardium to suffer the fastest. PO_2 values above 460 mmHg to 1500 mmHg is the zone of hyperoxia which the body tolerates well over a longer period of time (from a few tens of minutes to a few hours). PO_2 values greater than 1500 mmHg relatively quickly lead to the manifestation of the toxic effects of oxygen.

Mountaineers, people in aircrafts and caisson workers may be exposed to extreme changes in atmospheric pressure, and health effects of exposure to these changes are the focus of analysis of a number of studies. The studies of health effects of pressure changes as meteorological factors- the changes that commonly occur in the environment- are rare.

Epidemiological studies suggest that possible mechanisms for the influence of air pollution on health are reduced blood oxygenation and heart rate changes. In a study conducted in Utah (USA) (Dockery et al., 1993) it was found that exposure to particulate pollutants leads to a significant increase of heart rate, while decreased hemoglobin oxygen saturation was statistically significantly correlated with the concentrations of pollutants in males over 80 years of age. The same study demonstrated that value oscillations of the atmospheric pressure lead to small, but statistically significant changes in hemoglobin oxygen saturation, as well as heart rate changes. Any drop in pressure of 25 mmHg caused a drop in the measured level of saturation of 0.6 to 0.7%, while the frequency of the heart rate increased by 1.5 beats per minute.

A controlled experiment was conducted in Ukraine on 12 healthy volunteers who were exposed to mild fluctuations in atmospheric pressure, which otherwise often occur in nature (Delyukov & Didyk, 1999). Oscillation amplitudes of 30 to 50 Pascals were applied, and pressure frequency changes ranged from 0,011 to 0,170 Hz. Exposing subjects to such pressure oscillations lasting 15 to 30 minutes caused a significant change in concentration and short-term memory, breathing became deeper and slower, and the heart rate frequency was also reduced.

An investigation of the possible effects of variations in atmospheric pressure on mortality, in which the control of the influence of other atmospheric parameters was performed, was carried out in Madrid (Gonzalez et al., 2001). Time-series analysis confirmed a significant correlation between anticyclone trend (high-pressure field from which spiraling winds originate) and mortality from circulatory and respiratory diseases.

The World Health Organization conducted the MONICA Project (MONitoring trends and determinants In CArdiovascular disease) in Lille (Danet et al., 1999), a city with moist ocean climate, and confirmed the existence of significant influence of atmospheric pressure- both decrease and increase- on the incidence and mortality of myocardial infarction.

Research in Serbia showed that the increased average daily values of atmospheric pressure for 1 mBar on the day when the event took place before and 7 days, were associated ($p < 0.05$) with the increase of the total risk of the occurrence of lower idiopathic extremity deep vein thrombosis (DVT) for 5.1% (0.7 to 9.8%) (Damnjanovic et al., 2012).

Air Humidity

Absolute air humidity is the amount of water vapor in a given volume of air and is expressed in g/m^3. Relative air humidity is the ratio of the amount of water vapor in the air sample at a certain temperature and the maximum amount of water vapor that can be contained in the same sample at the same temperature, and is expressed as a percentage. Warm air has a greater water vapor binding potential than cold air.

People are very sensitive to changes in humidity because it affects the process of evaporation of sweat. When the relative humidity reaches 100%, that is, when the air is fully saturated with water vapor, the process of evaporation is completely interrupted. As a result of this interaction, high humidity makes it difficult for the body to cool in the summer. The human body is best adapted for relative humidity of 40-60%.

The effects of low humidity are also significant in the winter. The cold dry air that passes through the respiratory system also heats within it. This heating increases the potential of air to absorb water vapor, which leads to the extraction of moisture from the upper airways and the dehydration of the epithelium of the nose, pharynx, larynx and trachea. Increasing the of the epithelial mucus viscosity reduces its defensive capability and influences the increased risk of viral and bacterial respiratory diseases.

In a study conducted in 12 U.S. cities, a significant correlation between relative humidity and the number of deaths from cardiovascular disease in general, acute myocardial infarction, obstructive lung disease and pneumonia (Braga, Zanobetti, & Schwartz, 2002) as well as the number of hospital admissions for cardiovascular disease (Schwartz, Samet, & Patz, 2004) has not been confirmed. Similar results were found in a study in Birmingham, where the temperature, pressure and humidity did not significantly influence the assessment of the impact of soot and sulfur dioxide on the number of hospital admissions for respiratory diseases (Walters et al., 1994). In contrast, examination of the influence of climatic factors on mortality from myocardial infarction on the territory of Athens showed that the average monthly value of relative humidity significantly affects the number of deaths from this disease (Dilaveris et al., 2006). On the territory of Athens, a significant correlation was established between the humidity and the number of emergency hospital admissions for acute coronary syndrome (Panagiotakos et al., 2004). A statistically significant correlation was confirmed only between the average monthly values of relative humidity and morbidity. A conclusion can be made that this weather factor takes longer to exert its effect on the cardiovascular system, in relation to changes in temperature and air pressure.

Other Meteorological Factors

In addition to the atmospheric pressure, temperature, and humidity, while assessing the acute impacts of air pollution on the health, some studies performed control of the effects of winds, clouds and precipitation.

The human body heats air molecules that surround it, transferring heat away from the skin. Under the conditions without air flow, a layer of warm molecules is held against the body and provides protection from colder air molecules. Wind removes this layer of warm air and in proportion to its speed body is cooling faster (Office of Climate, Water and Weather Services, 2001).

Stronger winds occur when large air masses are moving, and can affect health because they bring changes in weather conditions within very short intervals. Rapid changes in temperature affect the pH of the blood, blood pressure, diuresis and tissue permeability (Persinger, 1980). A study by the Climatological center of Canada has confirmed the increase of the rate of migraine attacks in the days when strong winds are blowing, barometric pressure drops, humidity rises and there are rapid variations of temperature (Cull, 1981). Rosen (1989) found that rapid changes in barometric pressure during the days with high winds are causing increased mortality from cardiovascular disease. On the other hand, the wind velocity influences the ventilation of housing, wherein due to smoking, firing, and cooking, the concentration of particles can be higher than the outside air.

The reduction of solar radiation caused by cloudiness may also cause adverse effects on human health. Increase of light levels leads to increased mental activity through stimulation of the autonomic nervous system and causes a general feeling of satisfaction. The sun's rays cause changes in neurotransmittory hormone synthesis, and increased production of epinephrine leads to physical and mental stimulation. In contrast, low light intensity leads to fatigue and sleepiness (Wolfe, 1981).

The largest number of previous studies on the health impacts of precipitation relates to the effects of snow. It was found that extensive snowfalls significantly impact the increase of death rates, as well as an increase in the number of hospitalizations due to cerebrovascular stroke and myocardial infarction (Faiche & Rose, 1979). The majority of negative health effects occurs three to eight days after the cessation of precipitation. The supposed mechanism of effect is the increased physical activity that snow requires (removal of snow, difficulty with walking, etc.). In men, the risk is higher than in women, probably because they are exposed to greater physical activities related to snow.

Rainfall has a limited impact on human health. Kalkstein proved that the overall mortality rate declines one day after a summer rain, and the supposed mechanism of effect is the indirect effect of lowering of high summer temperatures (Kalkstein & Valimont, 1986).

Precipitation and temperature also affect the shortening of the time spent outdoors, and the length of exposure to the outside air pollution.

OBSERVATIONS AND RESPONSES TO CLIMATE CHANGES

Growing concerns about air pollution and climate changing issues have introduced partnerships between weather services, civil protection agencies, and public health authorities in many communities to inform their residents about and protect them from the dangers of air pollution and weather to health. Major components of these systems are announcing advisories and implementing emergency measures when air pollution levels and forecast weather is expected to adversely affect the health of residents of a city or region.

We developed the first such system in Serbia, which issues information on meteorological conditions and air pollution, on the health risks due to the effect of these factors, and provides advice on reducing risk to both the general population, and particularly vulnerable population groups. At the same time, a database is being formed on the health consequences of unfavorable meteorological factors and air pollution, and the use of the system itself, which will allow the monitoring of the effectiveness of solutions and possible correction of limits of meteorological factors and air pollution for certain classes of health risks.

The system is a Web service that is used in the prevention of the consequences of the effects of adverse meteorological conditions and air pollution on health.

Our solution uses meteorological data that is retrieved via a direct link from the website of the Republic Hydrometeorological Service of Serbia (http://www.hidmet.gov.rs) and data on air pollution that are downloaded via a link from the website of the Agency for Environmental Protection of the Republic of Serbia - SEPA (http://www.sepa.gov.rs).

Meteorological data include temperature, air pressure, wind speed, and humidity. Based on the temperature values (T) expressed in degrees Celsius, and humidity (H) expressed in percents, the heat index (Hi) is calculated according to the formula:

$$Hi=T+5/9\times((6{,}112\times 10^{(7{,}5\times T/(237{,}7+T))})\times H/100-10)$$

Heat index values are, in relation to the level of health risk, divided into five classes: no risk (up to 26°C), caution (27 to 32°C), increased caution (33 to 41°C), danger (42 to 54°C) and extreme danger (over 54°C).

When the temperature is below 5°C, instead of the heat index, the wind chill index (WCi) is calculated, based on the temperature value (T) expressed in degrees Celsius, and wind speed (W) expressed in kilometers per hour:

$$WCi=13,12+0,6215\times T-11,37\times W^{0,16}+0,3965\times T\times W^{0,16}$$

This formula is used when the wind speed is greater than 2.5 kilometers per hour, and when it is lower, the wind chill index value is equal to the air temperature.

Wind chill index values in relation to the degree of health risk are divided into five classes: no risk (above 4°C), low risk (4 to 6°C), moderate risk (-7 to -17°C), high risk (-18 to -28°C), and very high risk (below -28°C).

The average 24-hour values of sulfur dioxide (SO_2), nitrogen dioxide (NO_2), particulate matter up to 10 micrometers in diameter (PM_{10}), carbon monoxide (CO) and ozone (O_3), expressed in micrograms per cubic meter (μg/m³) are classified in five classes of air quality index (AQI) in accordance to the limits defined by SEPA.

For the final classification of air quality index, the concentration of the least favorable pollutant is used. When the concentrations of pollutants are measured at a number of measuring points, highest measured values are used for classifying the air quality index.

The technical solution is a web application that is integrated into the existing website of the Institute of Occupational Health Niš. Application is managed by an administrator. Users access the application by clicking on the "Environment and Health" field. On first accessing the application, users are required to register and create a username and password which they use for all subsequent access. On first access, the users are presented with a survey that includes information on general socio-demographic characteristics (age, sex, weight, height, smoking habits), and health status (chronic diseases, medication use, health services use, hospitalization).

Users are presented with the same survey every subsequent month of application use.

At the bottom of the survey is the "Forward" command for data recording. By entering this command the user is granted access to the application.

The application includes five web pages.

"Home" includes the application name, a brief description of the purpose of the application, and a warning that users must not modify their continuing therapy based only on the information and recommendations from this website without previously consulting their doctor. The "About" page gives information about the project name and participants.

At the top of the "Data" page are the values of meteorological factors and the concentration of pollutants in the air sorted by date, time and

Table 1. Air quality classification

Air Quality Index					
Pollutant	Excellent	Good	Acceptable	Contaminated	Extremely Contaminated
SO_2	do 50,0	50,1-75,0	75,1-125,0	125,1-187,5	above 187,5
NO_2	do 42,5	42,6-60,0	60,1-85,0	85,1-125,0	above 125,0
PM_{10}	do 25,0	25,1-35,0	35,1-50,0	50,1-75,0	above 75,0
CO	do 2500	2501-3500	3501-5000	5001-10000	above 10000
O_3	do 60,0	60,1-85,0	85,1-120,0	120,1-180,0	above 180,0

measuring points. Below these values are tables with the air quality index classes and the indices of heat or wind chill.

Below the tables is the information about how these three factors can affect the health, what their class values in relation to the level of health risk are, as well as information on specifically vulnerable population groups. Next are recommendations on ways to reduce or eliminate health risks.

THE IMPACT OF AIR POLLUTION AND ADVERSE WEATHER CONDITIONS ON HEALTH

Air pollution and adverse weather conditions usually exert their negative impact on the health by worsening symptoms of pre-existing disease.

The biological mechanisms of air pollution effects include direct effects on the cardiovascular system, blood, lung receptors and indirect effects expressed through pulmonary oxidative stress and inflammatory responses. Direct effects may arise from the action of agents that can easily pass through the pulmonary epithelium into the circulation, such as gases, and the ultra-fine particles. Direct effects may contribute to the instability of vascular plaques, or initiate a cardiac arrhythmia. These effects of air pollution are the likely explanation for the occurrence of rapid (within hours) cardiovascular responses such as the increase in the number of acute myocardial infarction. Less acute (up to several days) and chronic indirect effects may occur due to oxidative stress or lung inflammation, which are caused by inhaled pollutants.

While at rest, the body temperature is around 37°C, and during physical exertion it can rise to 38-39°C without any harmful effects on health. In order to maintain the temperature within the physiological range it is necessary to create a balance between the heat generation and loss. Several mechanisms are involved in the regulation of body temperature, and the most important for heat loss

Figure 1. "Data" page

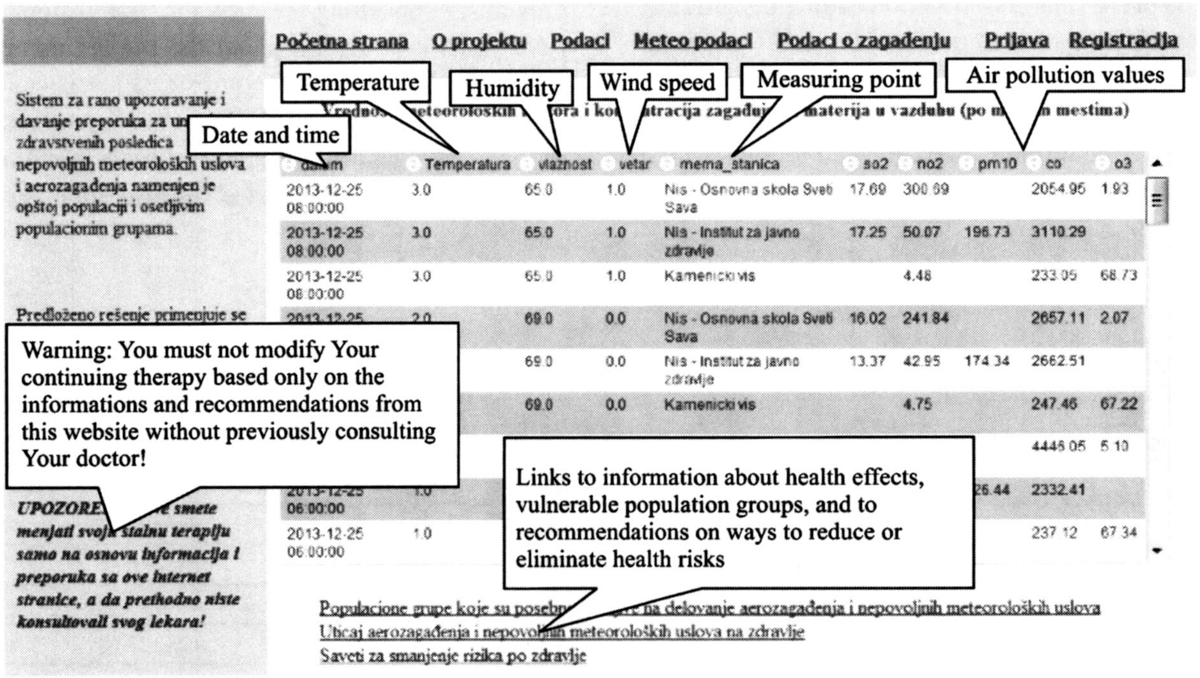

are sweating and expansion of peripheral blood vessels, while the most important mechanisms for temperature increase are muscle tremors and the constriction of peripheral blood vessels. Both excessively increased and decreased temperatures act as stress factors for the organism, especially in individuals who already suffer from chronic diseases.

Population Groups that are Particularly Vulnerable to the Effect of Air Pollution and Adverse Weather Conditions

Population groups that are particularly vulnerable to the effect of air pollution are children, people over 65 years of age, people with chronic diseases of the cardiovascular or respiratory systems- especially asthma, emphysema, chronic bronchitis, heart insufficiency and coronary artery disease, as well as people of all ages who train or perform heavy physical labor in the environment (Faustini et al., 2012; Calderón-Garcidueñas et al., 2007; Curtis et al., 2006).

Population groups that are particularly sensitive to the action of excessive heat are: people over 65 years of age, people living alone, obese people, people with diabetes, people with chronic kidney disease, lung, cardiovascular, nervous and digestive system disease, as well as persons in therapy with diuretics, antipsychotics, antiparkinsonian drugs, antiepileptic drugs, and beta blockers (Kravchenko et al., 2013; Baccini et al., 2008).

Population groups that are particularly sensitive to the action of excessive cold are: children, people over 65 years of age, people with mental health problems, people with health disorders that affect thermoregulation (decreased thyroid function, malnutrition, stroke, severe arthritis, Parkinson's disease, trauma, spinal cord injuries, burns), diabetics, and people in therapy using antidepressants, antipsychotics and/or sedatives.

Tips for Reducing Health Risks

If the concentrations of air pollutants are elevated:

- Reduce or limit your outdoor activities, especially those that require physical effort.
- Avoid staying in locations that you know to contain sources of air pollution, such as heavy traffic roads.
- Take your therapy on a regular basis.
- Stop smoking tobacco.
- Heat:
    - Avoid exposure to sunlight or heat sources.
    - If possible, stay in an air-conditioned space.
    - If you do not have air conditioning during the hottest part of the day, dim your apartment, close the blinds and draw the curtains, and ensure good ventilation during the night.
    - Avoid strenuous physical activity outdoors.
    - Edit your schedule of sports training.
    - If possible, conduct business activities in air-conditioned space, and if it is not possible, take frequent breaks at work.
    - Drink plenty of water and natural fruit juices (avoid alcohol, coffee and soft drinks).
    - Wear loose clothing that permits the evaporation of sweat.
    - Wear a hat and use sunscreen (spf of at least 15).
    - Never leave children or pets unattended in a car.
    - Rest as much as possible.
    - Call or visit friends and neighbors who belong to the group of people who are particularly sensitive to the action of excessive heat.

- In cold weather:
  - Put on warm, multi-layered clothing.
  - If you go outside, put on a hat, gloves and scarf, clothing should be resistant to wind.
  - Keep your apartment/house warm, 21°c in the living room and the kids' rooms, 18°c in other rooms.
  - Be physically active.
  - Take plenty of hot food and drinks.
  - When the value of the wind chill index is lower than -18°c, shorten your outdoor activities or stop them completely.
  - Have yourself vaccinated against the flu on time.
  - Provide a small stash of drugs that you constantly use.

The "Weather Data" page contains the values of meteorological data per hour for the current day, obtained from the Hydrometeorological Institute, the heat or wind chill index values, depending on the air temperature, and the level of health risk.

The "Information on pollution" page contains concentrations of pollutants in the air, sorted by the place and time of measurement, as well as the value of air quality index. If any of the pollutants in a particular time and a particular place is not measured, the field remains blank.

Early warning systems for adverse health effects due to air pollution are the most developed in the United States, Canada, and Europe. There are few successful cases in Asia (Taiwan, China, Hong Kong, Korea, Japan and Thailand), and several in Latin America (Argentina, Brazil, and Mexico City), and only one in Africa (Cape Town, South Africa). Most existing systems focus on monitoring the concentration of pollutants in real time at the surface. Information on air quality is usually communicated via web services. The EPA provides e-mail alerts (EPA), but this service is available only in the United States. E-mail alerts are also provided by the Ministry of Environ-

Figure 2. "Weather data" page

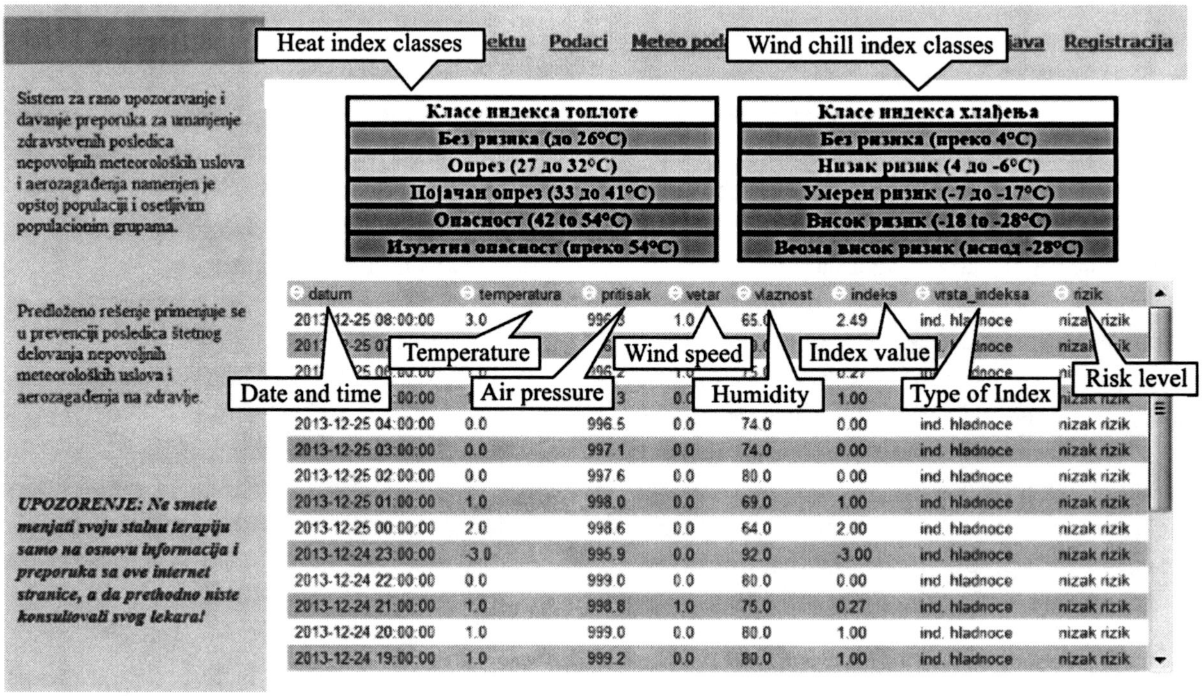

Figure 3. "Information on pollution" page

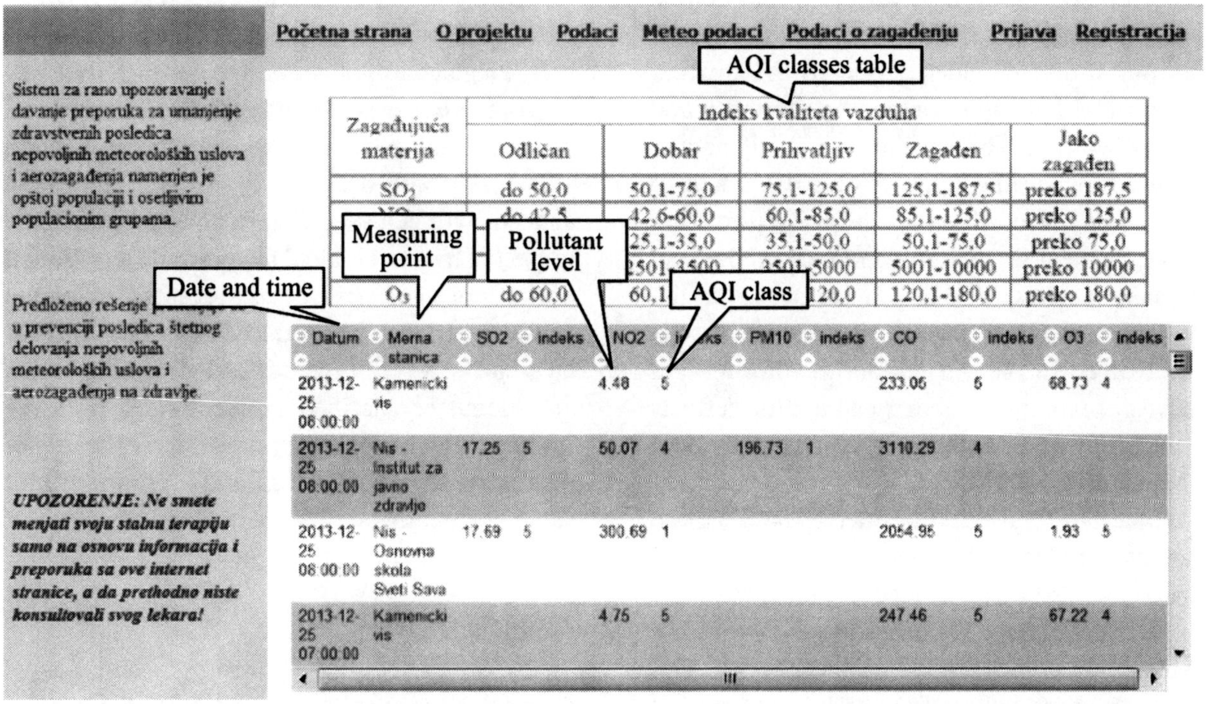

ment, Ontario, Canada. The EPA information service provides information on air quality to its subscribers via e-mail, cell phone or pager, in real time, allowing them to take steps to protect their health in emergency situations. Forecasting is an essential component of the early warning system, and agencies such as the Agency for Environmental Protection of the USA, Belgium, Germany, and Canada provide forecasts, which are fundamental for early warning. (Grasso & Singh, 2011). The aim of these notifications is to help people adapt their behavior in situations of increased concentrations of some pollutants (eg, "do not go out", "increase the use of medication in consultation with your doctor", etc.) (Kelly et al., 2012)

Even if climatic factors are studied separately, they are mutually dependently connected, taking into account that many pollutants such as carbon dioxide are greenhouse gases and their increase leads to global warming and climate change (von Schneidemesser & Monks, 2013). Since the 2003 heat wave in France (National Institute of Public Health Surveillance, 2003) caused a significant increase in mortality of persons older than 75 years, a number of European countries has, as part of its public health policy, introduced plans, systems and guidelines for the purposes of prevention of adverse health effects caused by the heat waves. The European Commision has funded the EUROHEAT project, which aims to give guidance in public health actions in the event of adverse weather conditions, especially heat waves (Matthies & Menne, 2009)

The Government of Quebec has introduced a real-time integrated system for monitoring and tracking of extreme heat events as part of its Action Plan on Climate Change (2006-2012). That system is a component of a broader approach that will also monitor the public health impact of all types of extreme weather events. After conducting a detailed needs analysis, the National Institute of Public Health of Quebec has developed and implemented an integrated web application, at first applied only for heat waves. The system is available to health professionals through a secure web portal and provides access to the weather forecast and indicators (including mortality and hospitalization). The system was implemented and used during the summer of 2010, where it served as an important tool in decision-making during the heat wave in the province of Quebec. The next steps will be to provide access to the application to other groups of professionals who are involved in the prevention, monitoring and analysis of extreme weather events and their effects on the health of the community and the individual (Cheban et al., 2013).

A question is raised on the effectiveness of these systems in reducing heat wave related mortality. Toloo et al. (2013) have cited 15 studies that examined the efficiency of heat wave early warning systems. Six studies found that fewer people died during the heat waves after the implementation of the warning system, and there was less use of health care. One study also estimates that the costs of running the heat wave early warning system will cost the U.S. $210,000, and that 117 lives were saved thanks to the system. The remaining eight studies examined the behavior of the population in relation to the warning systems. Evidence suggests that the warning systems were efficient in reducing mortality and morbidity, but other factors that affect morbidity and mortality during heat waves must also be considered.

FUTURE RESEARCH DIRECTIONS

A database is formed from all the data from the questionnaires filled in by users, as well as data on meteorological factors and air pollution which, in addition to the user characteristics and the number of adverse health events also includes the value of the concentration of pollutants in the air, and the values of meteorological factors, which will be used to evaluate the effectiveness of the application and its further development. The number of physician visits, use of emergency medical services, as well as the number of hospitalizations before using the application and during its use will be compared. It is expected that the number of adverse health events during use of the application will significantly decrease. In addition, regression analysis will be used to examine how great is the impact of meteorological factors and air pollution on the number of adverse health events. Regression analysis will also be used to check if the class of heat and wind chill indices and air quality index are adequately defined in accordance with the findings which will be acquired during the implementation of the application, and appropriate limit value corrections will be performed.

CONCLUSION

Use of this system provides citizens with information about weather conditions and air pollution, how they can affect the health and how the general population and various vulnerable population groups can protect their health during periods of adverse weather conditions or increased levels of air pollution. Also, this system provides formation of a database on concentrations of pollutants in the air, the values of meteorological factors, as well as changes in the number of adverse health consequences of air pollution and meteorological factors in application users. This will allow the tracking of the solution efficiency, as well as a possible correction of limit values of meteorological factors and air pollution for certain classes of health risks.

REFERENCES

Anderson, G. S. (1999). Human morphology and temperature regulation. *International Journal of Biometeorology*, *43*(3), 99–109. doi:10.1007/s004840050123 PMID:10639901

Aris, R. M., Christian, D., Hearne, P. Q., Kerr, K., Finkbeiner, W. E., & Balmes, J. R. (1993). Ozone-induced airway inflammation in human subjects as determined by airway lavage and biopsy. *The American Review of Respiratory Disease, 148*(5), 1363–1372. doi:10.1164/ajrccm/148.5.1363 PMID:8239177

Baccini, M., Biggeri, A., Accetta, G., Kosatsky, T., Katsouyanni, K., & Analitis, A. et al. (2008). Heat effects on mortality in 15 European cities. *Epidemiology (Cambridge, Mass.), 19*(5), 711–719. doi:10.1097/EDE.0b013e318176bfcd PMID:18520615

Ballester, F., Corella, D., Pérez-Hoyos, S., Sáez, M., & Hervás, A. (1997). Mortality as a function of temperature. A study in Valencia, Spain, 1991-1993. *International Journal of Epidemiology, 26*(3), 551–561. doi:10.1093/ije/26.3.551 PMID:9222780

Basagana, X., Sartini, C., Barrera-Gómez, J., Dadvand, P., Cunillera, J., & Ostro, B. et al. (2011). Heat waves and cause-specific mortality at all ages. *Epidemiology (Cambridge, Mass.), 22*(6), 765–772. doi:10.1097/EDE.0b013e31823031c5 PMID:21968768

Basu, R., & Samet, J. M. (2002). An exposure assessment study of ambient heat exposure in an elderly population in Baltimore, Maryland. *Environmental Health Perspectives, 110*(12), 1219–1224. doi:10.1289/ehp.021101219 PMID:12460801

Batalha, J. R., Saldiva, P. H., Clarke, R. W., Coull, B. A., Stearns, R. C., & Lawrence, J. et al. (2002). Concentrated ambient air particles induce vasoconstriction of small pulmonary arteries in rats. *Environmental Health Perspectives, 110*(12), 1191–1197. doi:10.1289/ehp.021101191 PMID:12460797

Bell, M. L., & Davis, D. L. (2001). Reassessment of the lethal London fog of 1952: Novel indicators of acute and chronic consequences of acute exposure to air pollution. *Environmental Health Perspectives, 109*(s3Suppl 3), 389–394. doi:10.1289/ehp.01109s3389 PMID:11427388

Bhatt, D. L., & Topol, E. J. (2002). Need to test the arterial inflammation hypothesis. *Circulation, 106*(1), 136–140. doi:10.1161/01.CIR.0000021112.29409.A2 PMID:12093783

Blagojevic, L. M., Bogdanovic, D. C., Jovic, S. J., Milosevic, Z. G., & Doličanin, Z. C. (2012). Excess winter mortality of Roma population in Serbia, 1992-2007. *Central European Journal of Public Health, 20*(2), 135–138. PMID:22966739

Bogdanovic, D. C., Milosevic, Z. G., Lazarevic, K. K., Doličanin, Z. C., Randelovic, D. M., & Bogdanovic, S. D. (2013). The impact of the July 2007 heat wave on daily mortality in Belgrade, Serbia. *Central European Journal of Public Health, 21*(3), 140–145. PMID:24344537

Bogdanovic, D. C., Nikic, D. S., Milosevic, Z. G., & Stankovic, A. M. (2006). Black smoke air pollution and daily non-accidental mortality in Nis, Serbia. *Central European Journal of Medicine, 1*(3), 292–297. doi:10.2478/s11536-006-0021-z

Bonetti, P. O., Lerman, L. O., & Lerman, A. (2003). Endothelial dysfunction: A marker of atherosclerotic risk. *Arteriosclerosis, Thrombosis, and Vascular Biology, 23*(2), 168–175. doi:10.1161/01.ATV.0000051384.43104.FC PMID:12588755

Bouthillier, L., Vincent, R., Goegan, P., Adamson, I. Y., Bjarnason, S., & Stewart, M. et al. (1998). Acute effects of inhaled urban particles and ozone: Lung morphology, macrophage activity, and plasma endothelin-1. *American Journal of Pathology, 153*(6), 1873–1884. doi:10.1016/S0002-9440(10)65701-X PMID:9846977

Braga, A. L., Zanobetti, A., & Schwartz, J. (2002). The effect of weather on respiratory and cardiovascular deaths in 12 US cities. *Environmental Health Perspectives*, *110*(9), 859–863. doi:10.1289/ehp.02110859 PMID:12204818

Brimblecombe, P. (1987). *The Big Smoke: A History of Air Pollution in London since Medieval Times Methuen*. London, UK.

Brook, R. D., Brook, J. R., Urch, B., Vincent, R., Rajagopalan, S., & Silverman, F. (2002). Inhalation of fine particulate air pollution and ozone causes acute arterial vasoconstriction in healthy adults. *Circulation*, *105*(13), 1534–1536. doi:10.1161/01.CIR.0000013838.94747.64 PMID:11927516

Brown, D. M., Stone, V., Findlay, P., MacNee, W., & Donaldson, K. (2000). Increased inflammation and intracellular calcium caused by ultrafine carbon black is independent of transition metals or other soluble components. *Occupational and Environmental Medicine*, *57*(10), 685–691. doi:10.1136/oem.57.10.685 PMID:10984341

Brunekreef, B., & Holgate, S. T. (2002). Air pollution and health. *Lancet*, *360*(9341), 1233–1242. doi:10.1016/S0140-6736(02)11274-8 PMID:12401268

Burnett, R. T., Smith-Doiron, M., Stieb, D., Cakmak, S., & Brook, J. R. (1999). Effects of particulate and gaseous air pollution on cardiorespiratory hospitalizations. *Archives of Environmental Health: An International Journal*, *54*(2), 130–139. doi:10.1080/00039899909602248 PMID:10094292

Cakmak, S., Dales, R., Kauri, L. M., Mahmud, M., Van Ryswyk, K., & Vanos, J. et al. (2014). Metal composition of fine particulate air pollution and acute changes in cardiorespiratory physiology. *Environmental Pollution*, *189*, 208–214. doi:10.1016/j.envpol.2014.03.004 PMID:24682071

Calderón-Garcidueñas, L., Franco-Lira, M., Torres-Jardón, R., Henriquez-Roldán, C., Barragán-Mejía, G., & Valencia-Salazar, G. et al. (2007). Pediatric respiratory and systemic effects of chronic air pollution exposure: Nose, lung, heart, and brain pathology. *Toxicologic Pathology*, *35*(1), 154–162. doi:10.1080/01926230601059985 PMID:17325984

Carey, I. M., Atkinson, R. W., Kent, A. J., van Staa, T., Cook, D. G., & Anderson, H. R. (2013). Mortality Associations with Long-Term Exposure to Outdoor Air Pollution in a National English Cohort. *American Journal of Respiratory and Critical Care Medicine*, *187*(11), 1226–1233. doi:10.1164/rccm.201210-1758OC PMID:23590261

Centers for Disease Control and Prevention. (2002). Heat related deaths – four states, July–August 2001 and United States, 1979–1999. *MMWR Mortality and Morbidity Weekly Report*, *51*, 528–531.

Chan, N. Y., Stacey, M. T., Smith, A. E., Ebi, K. L., & Wilson, T. F. (2001). An empirical mechanistic framework for heat-related illness. *Climate Research*, *16*(2), 133–143. doi:10.3354/cr016133

Chebana, F., Martel, B., Gosselin, P., Giroux, J. X., & Ouarda, T. B. (2013). A general and flexible methodology to define thresholds for heat health watch and warning systems, applied to the province of Québec (Canada). *International Journal of Biometeorology*, *57*(4), 631–644. doi:10.1007/s00484-012-0590-2 PMID:23100100

Clinch, J. P., & Healy, J. D. (2000). Housing standards and excess winter mortality. *Journal of Epidemiology and Community Health*, *54*(9), 719–720. doi:10.1136/jech.54.9.719 PMID:10942456

Cull, R. E. (1981). Barometric pressure and other factors in migraine. *Headache: The Journal of Head and Face Pain*, *21*(3), 102–104. doi:10.1111/j.1526-4610.1981.hed2103102.x PMID:7263217

Curtis, L., Rea, W., Smith-Willis, P., Fenyves, E., & Pan, Y. (2006). Adverse health effects of outdoor air pollutants. *Environment International*, *32*(6), 815–830. doi:10.1016/j.envint.2006.03.012 PMID:16730796

Daigle, C. C., Chalupa, D. C., Gibb, F. R., Morrow, P. E., Oberdörster, G., Utell, M. J., & Frampton, M. W. (2003). Ultrafine particle deposition in humans during rest and exercise. *Inhalation Toxicology*, *15*(6), 539–552. doi:10.1080/08958370304468 PMID:12692730

Damnjanovic, Z., Jovanovic, M. M., Bogdanovic, D. C., Smiljkovic, I. D., Ilic, N., & Damnjanovic, I. (2012). Relationship between the Incidence of Idiopathic Lower Extremity Deep Vein Thrombosis and the Location of the Thrombus depending on the Changes in Atmospheric Pressure. *Chirurgia*, *107*(4), 483–487. PMID:23025115

Danet, S., Richard, F., Montaye, M., Beauchant, S., Lemaire, B., & Graux, C. et al. (1999). Unhealthy Effects of Atmospheric Temperature and Pressure on the Occurrence of Myocardial Infarction and Coronary Deaths A 10-Year Survey: The Lille-World Health Organization MONICA Project (Monitoring Trends and Determinants in Cardiovascular Disease). *Circulation*, *100*(1), e1–e7. doi:10.1161/01.CIR.100.1.e1 PMID:10393689

Davis, D. L. (2003). *When smoke ran like water: Tales of environmental deception and the battle against pollution*. Basic Books.

Delfino, R. J., Murphy-Moulton, A. M., Burnett, R. T., Brook, J. R., & Becklake, M. R. (1997). Effects of air pollution on emergency room visits for respiratory illnesses in Montreal, Quebec. *American Journal of Respiratory and Critical Care Medicine*, *155*(2), 568–576. doi:10.1164/ajrccm.155.2.9032196 PMID:9032196

Delyukov, A. A., & Didyk, L. (1999). The effects of extra-low-frequency atmospheric pressure oscillations on human mental activity. *International Journal of Biometeorology*, *43*(1), 31–37. doi:10.1007/s004840050113 PMID:10466018

Devlin, R. B., Ghio, A. J., Kehrl, H., Sanders, G., & Cascio, W. (2003). Elderly humans exposed to concentrated air pollution particles have decreased heart rate variability. *The European Respiratory Journal*, *21*(suppl 40), 76–80. doi:10.1183/09031936.03.00402403 PMID:12762579

Dilaveris, P., Synetos, A., Giannopoulos, G., Gialafos, E., Pantazis, A., & Stefanadis, C. (2006). CLimate Impacts on Myocardial infarction deaths in the Athens TErritory: The CLIMATE study. *Heart (British Cardiac Society)*, *92*(12), 1747–1751. doi:10.1136/hrt.2006.091884 PMID:16840509

Dockery, D. W., Pope, C. A. III, Kanner, R. E., Villegas, M., & Schwartz, J. (1999). Daily changes in oxygen saturation and pulse rate associated with particulate air pollution and barometric pressure. *Research Report (Health Effects Institute)*, (83): 1–19. PMID:10192116

Dockery, D. W., Pope, C. A. III, Xu, X., Spengler, J. D., Ware, J. H., & Fay, M. E. et al. (1993). An asso.ciation between air pollution and mortality in six US cities. *The New England Journal of Medicine*, *329*(24), 1753–1759. doi:10.1056/NEJM199312093292401 PMID:8179653

Dominici, F., McDermott, A., Daniels, M., Zeger, S., & Samet, J. (2002). *A report to the health effects institute: reanalyses of the NMMAPS database*. Baltimore, MD: Department of Biostatisics and Epidemiology, Bloomberg School of Public Health, Johns Hopkins University.

Donaldson, G. (1997). Cold exposure and winter mortality from ischaemic heart disease, cerebrovascular disease, respiratory disease, and all causes in warm and cold regions of Europe. The Eurowinter Group. *Lancet*, *349*(9062), 1341–1346. doi:10.1016/S0140-6736(96)12338-2 PMID:9149695

Donaldson, G. C., & Keatinge, W. R. (1997). Early increases in ischaemic heart disease mortality dissociated from and later changes associated with respiratory mortality after cold weather in south east England. *Journal of Epidemiology and Community Health*, *51*(6), 643–648. doi:10.1136/jech.51.6.643 PMID:9519127

Donoghue, E. R., Graham, M. A., Jentzen, J. M., Lifschultz, B. D., Luke, J. L., & Mirchandani, H. G. (1997). Criteria for the diagnosis of heat-related deaths: National Association of Medical Examiners: position paper. *The American Journal of Forensic Medicine and Pathology*, *18*(1), 11–14. doi:10.1097/00000433-199703000-00002 PMID:9095294

Ezzati, M., Lopez, A. D., Rodgers, A., Vander Hoorn, S., & Murray, C. J. (2002). Selected major risk factors and global and regional burden of disease. *Lancet*, *360*(9343), 1347–1360. doi:10.1016/S0140-6736(02)11403-6 PMID:12423980

Faich, G., & Rose, R. (1979). Blizzard morbidity and mortality: Rhode Island, 1978. *American Journal of Public Health*, *69*(10), 1050–1052. doi:10.2105/AJPH.69.10.1050 PMID:484759

Faustini, A., Stafoggia, M., Cappai, G., & Forastiere, F. (2012). Short-term effects of air pollution in a cohort of patients with chronic obstructive pulmonary disease. *Epidemiology (Cambridge, Mass.)*, *23*(6), 861–879. doi:10.1097/EDE.0b013e31826767c2 PMID:23018970

Fichtlscherer, S., Rosenberger, G., Walter, D. H., Breuer, S., Dimmeler, S., & Zeiher, A. M. (2000). Elevated C-reactive protein levels and impaired endothelial vasoreactivity in patients with coronary artery disease. *Circulation*, *102*(9), 1000–1006. doi:10.1161/01.CIR.102.9.1000 PMID:10961964

Franchini, M., & Mannucci, P. M. (2009). Particulate air pollution and cardiovascular risk: Short-term and long-term effects. *Seminars in Thrombosis and Hemostasis*, *35*(7), 665–670. doi:10.1055/s-0029-1242720 PMID:20013533

Ghio, A. J., & Devlin, R. B. (2001). Inflammatory lung injury after bronchial instillation of air pollution particles. *American Journal of Respiratory and Critical Care Medicine*, *164*(4), 704–708. doi:10.1164/ajrccm.164.4.2011089 PMID:11520740

Ghio, A. J., Hall, A., Bassett, M. A., Cascio, W. E., & Devlin, R. B. (2003). Exposure to concentrated ambient particles alters hematologic indices in humans. *Inhalation Toxicology*, *15*(14), 1465–1478. doi:10.1080/08958370390249111 PMID:14648359

Godleski, J. J., Clarke, R. W., Coull, B. A., Saldiva, P. H., Jiang, N. F., Lawrence, J., & Koutrakis, P. (2002). Composition of inhaled urban air particles determines acute pulmonary responses. *The Annals of Occupational Hygiene*, *46*(suppl 1), 419–424. doi:10.1093/annhyg/46.suppl_1.419

Godleski, J. J., Verrier, R. L., Koutrakis, P., Catalano, P., Coull, B., & Reinisch, U. et al. (2000). Mechanisms of morbidity and mortality from exposure to ambient air particles. *Research Report (Health Effects Institute)*, *91*, 5–88. PMID:10817681

González, S., Díaz, J., Pajares, M. S., Alberdi, J. C., Otero, A., & López, C. (2001). Relationship between atmospheric pressure and mortality in the Madrid Autonomous Region: A time-series study. *International Journal of Biometeorology*, *45*(1), 34–40. doi:10.1007/s004840000076 PMID:11411413

Grasso, V. F., & Singh, A. (2011). *Early warning systems: State-of-art analysis and future directions. Draft report.* UNEP.

Gurgueira, S. A., Lawrence, J., Coull, B., Murthy, G. G., & González-Flecha, B. (2002). Rapid increases in the steady-state concentration of reactive oxygen species in the lungs and heart after particulate air pollution inhalation. *Environmental Health Perspectives*, *110*(8), 749–755. doi:10.1289/ehp.02110749 PMID:12153754

Hansen, A., Bi, P., Nitschke, M., Ryan, P., Pisaniello, D., & Tucker, G. (2008b). The effect of heat waves on mental health in a temperate Australian city. *Environmental Health Perspectives*, *116*(10), 1369–1375. doi:10.1289/ehp.11339 PMID:18941580

Hansen, A. L., Bi, P., Ryan, P., Nitschke, M., Pisaniello, D., & Tucker, G. (2008a). The effect of heat waves on hospital admissions for renal disease in a temperate city of Australia. *International Journal of Epidemiology*, *37*(6), 1359–1365. doi:10.1093/ije/dyn165 PMID:18710886

Havenith, G. (2001). Individualized model of human thermoregulation for the simulation of heat stress response. *Journal of Applied Physiology*, *90*(5), 1943–1954. PMID:11299289

Havenith, G. (2003). Interaction of clothing and thermoregulation. *Exogenous Dermatology*, *1*(5), 221–230. doi:10.1159/000068802

Healy, J. D. (2003). Excess winter mortality in Europe: A cross country analysis identifying key risk factors. *Journal of Epidemiology and Community Health*, *57*(10), 784–789. doi:10.1136/jech.57.10.784 PMID:14573581

Hodgkinson, B., Evans, D., & Wood, J. (2003). Maintaining oral hydration in older adults: A systematic review. *International Journal of Nursing Practice*, *9*(3), S19–S28. doi:10.1046/j.1440-172X.2003.00425.x PMID:12801253

Hoek, G., Brunekreef, B., Fischer, P., & van Wijnen, J. (2001). The association between air pollution and heart failure, arrhythmia, embolism, thrombosis, and other cardiovascular causes of death in a time series study. *Epidemiology (Cambridge, Mass.)*, *12*(3), 355–357. doi:10.1097/00001648-200105000-00017 PMID:11337606

Hoek, G., Brunekreef, B., Goldbohm, S., Fischer, P., & van den Brandt, P. A. (2002). Association between mortality and indicators of traffic-related air pollution in the Netherlands: A cohort study. *Lancet*, *360*(9341), 1203–1209. doi:10.1016/S0140-6736(02)11280-3 PMID:12401246

Hong, Y. C., Lee, J. T., Kim, H., & Kwon, H. J. (2002). Air pollution a new risk factor in ischemic stroke mortality. *Stroke*, *33*(9), 2165–2169. doi:10.1161/01.STR.0000026865.52610.5B PMID:12215581

Ibald-Mulli, A., Stieber, J., Wichmann, H. E., Koenig, W., & Peters, A. (2001). Effects of air pollution on blood pressure: A population-based approach. *American Journal of Public Health*, *91*(4), 571–577. doi:10.2105/AJPH.91.4.571 PMID:11291368

Junker, R., Heinrich, J., Ulbrich, H., Schulte, H., Schönfeld, R., Köhler, E., & Assmann, G. (1998). Relationship between plasma viscosity and the severity of coronary heart disease. *Arteriosclerosis, Thrombosis, and Vascular Biology*, *18*(6), 870–875. doi:10.1161/01.ATV.18.6.870 PMID:9633925

Kalkstein, L. S., & Valimont, K. M. (1986). An evaluation of summer discomfort in the United State using a relative climatological index. *Bulletin of the American Meteorological Society*, *67*(7), 842–848. doi:10.1175/1520-0477(1986)067<0842:AEOSDI>2.0.CO;2

Katsouyanni, K., Touloumi, G., Samoli, E., Gryparis, A., Le Tertre, A., & Monopolis, Y. et al. (2001). Confounding and effect modification in the short-term effects of ambient particles on total mortality: Results from 29 European cities within the APHEA2 project. *Epidemiology (Cambridge, Mass.)*, *12*(5), 521–531. doi:10.1097/00001648-200109000-00011 PMID:11505171

Keatinge, W. R., & Donaldson, G. C. (1995). Cardiovascular mortality in winter. *Arctic Medical Research*, *54*, 16–18. PMID:8900826

Keatinge, W. R., Donaldson, G. C., Cordioli, E., Martinelli, M., Kunst, A. E., & Mackenbach, J. P. et al. (2000). Heat related mortality in warm and cold regions of Europe: Observational study. *BMJ: British Medical Journal*, *321*(7262), 670–673. doi:10.1136/bmj.321.7262.670 PMID:10987770

Kelly, F. J. (2003). Oxidative stress: Its role in air pollution and adverse health effects. *Occupational and Environmental Medicine*, *60*(8), 612–616. doi:10.1136/oem.60.8.612 PMID:12883027

Kelly, F. J., Fuller, G. W., Walton, H. A., & Fussell, J. C. (2012). Monitoring air pollution: Use of early warning systems for public health. *Respirology (Carlton, Vic.)*, *17*(1), 7–19. doi:10.1111/j.1440-1843.2011.02065.x PMID:21942967

Kovats, R. S., & Koppe, C. (2005). Heatwaves: past and future impacts on health. In *Integration of public health with adaptation to climate change: Lessons learned and new directions*, (pp. 136-160). Academic Press.

Kravchenko, J., Abernethy, A. P., Fawzy, M., & Lyerly, H. K. (2013). Minimization of heatwave morbidity and mortality. *American Journal of Preventive Medicine*, *44*(3), 274–282. doi:10.1016/j.amepre.2012.11.015 PMID:23415125

Li, N., Sioutas, C., Cho, A., Schmitz, D., Misra, C., & Sempf, J. et al. (2003). U.ltrafin.e particulate pollutants induce oxidative stress and mitochondrial damage. *Environmental Health Perspectives*, *111*(4), 455–460. doi:10.1289/ehp.6000

Li, X. Y., Gilmour, P. S., Donaldson, K., & MacNee, W. (1996). Free radical activity and pro-inflammatory effects of particulate air pollution (PM10) in vivo and in vitro. *Thorax*, *51*(12), 1216–1222. doi:10.1136/thx.51.12.1216 PMID:8994518

Libby, P., Ridker, P. M., & Maseri, A. (2002). Inflammation and atherosclerosis. *Circulation*, *105*(9), 1135–1143. doi:10.1161/hc0902.104353 PMID:11877368

Linn, W.S., Gong, H. Jr., Clark, K.W., & Anderson, K.R. (1999). Day-to-day particulate exposures and health changes in Los Angeles area residents with severe lung disease. *Journal of the Air & Waste Management Association*, *49* (9), 108–115.

Linn, W. S., Szlachcic, Y., Gong, H. Jr, Kinney, P. L., & Berhane, K. T. (2000). Air pollution and daily hospital admissions in metropolitan Los Angeles. *Environmental Health Perspectives*, *108*(5), 427–434. doi:10.1289/ehp.00108427 PMID:10811569

Lipsett, M. J. (2001). Ozone. In J. B. Sullivan & G. R. Krieger (Eds.), *Clinical environmental health and toxic exposure* (2nd ed., pp. 806–818). Philadelphia, PA: Lippincott Williams & Wilkins.

Liu, F., Yin, J., Du, M., Yan, P., Xu, J., Zhu, X., & Yu, J. (2009). Heat-stress-induced damage to porcine small intestinal epithelium associated with downregulation of epithelial growth factor signaling. *Journal of Animal Science*, *87*(6), 1941–1949. doi:10.2527/jas.2008-1624 PMID:19213704

Magari, S. R., Hauser, R., Schwartz, J., Williams, P. L., Smith, T. J., & Christiani, D. C. (2001). Association of heart rate variability with occupational and environmental exposure to particulate air pollution. *Circulation*, *104*(9), 986–991. doi:10.1161/hc3401.095038 PMID:11524390

Martin, L. (1999). *All you really need to know to interpret arterial blood gases*. Wolters Kluwer Health.

Matthies, F., & Menne, B. (2009). Prevention and management of health hazards related to heatwaves. *International Journal of Circumpolar Health*, *68*(1). doi:10.3402/ijch.v68i1.18293 PMID:19331238

Mentes, J. C., & Culp, K. (2003). Reducing hydration-linked events in nursing home residents. *Clinical Nursing Research*, *12*(3), 210–225. doi:10.1177/1054773803252996 PMID:12918647

Michelozzi, P., Kirchmayer, U., Katsouyanni, K., Biggeri, A., McGregor, G., & Menne, B. et al. (2007). Assessment and prevention of acute health effects of weather conditions in Europe, the PHEWE project: Background, objectives, design. *Environmental Health*, *6*(1), 12–21. doi:10.1186/1476-069X-6-12 PMID:17456236

Milosević, Z., Bogdanović, D., Jović, S., Stanković, A., Milutinović, S., & Rancić, N. (2010). Influence of air pollution on hospital admissions for cardiovascular and respiratory diseases in Nis, Serbia]. *Vojnosanitetski Pregled. Military-Medical and Pharmaceutical Review*, *67*(6), 473–479. doi:10.2298/VSP1006473M PMID:20629426

Monn, C., & Becker, S. (1999). Cytotoxicity and induction of proinflammatory cytokines from human monocytes exposed to fine (PM2.5) and coarse particles (PM10-2.5) in outdoor and indoor air. *Toxicology and Applied Pharmacology*, *155*(3), 245–252. doi:10.1006/taap.1998.8591 PMID:10079210

Morris, R. D. (2001). Airborne particulates and hospital admissions for cardiovascular disease: A quantitative review of the evidence. *Environmental Health Perspectives*, *109*(s4Suppl 4), 495–500. doi:10.1289/ehp.01109s4495 PMID:11544153

Mukae, H., Vincent, R., Quinlan, K., English, D., Hards, J., Hogg, J. C., & van Eeden, S. F. (2001). The effect of repeated exposure to particulate air pollution (PM10) on the bone marrow. *American Journal of Respiratory and Critical Care Medicine*, *163*(1), 201–209. doi:10.1164/ajrccm.163.1.2002039 PMID:11208647

Nafstad, P., Skrondal, A., & Bjertness, E. (2001). Mortality and temperature in Oslo, Norway, 1990–1995. *European Journal of Epidemiology*, *17*(7), 621–627. doi:10.1023/A:1015547012242 PMID:12086075

National Institute of Public Health Surveillance. (2003). *Impact sanitaire de la vague de chaleur en France survenue en août 2003. Rapport d'étape – 29 août 2003*. Saint Maurice, France: National Institute of Public Health Surveillance.

Nemery, B., Hoet, P. H., & Nemmar, A. (2001). The Meuse Valley fog of 1930: An air pollution disaster. *Lancet*, *357*(9257), 704–708. doi:10.1016/S0140-6736(00)04135-0 PMID:11247570

Nemmar, A., Hoet, P. M., Vanquickenborne, B., Dinsdale, D., Thomeer, M., & Hoylaerts, M. F. et al. (2002a). Passage of inhaled particles into the blood circulation in humans. *Circulation*, *105*(4), 411–414. doi:10.1161/hc0402.104118 PMID:11815420

Nemmar, A., Hoylaerts, M. F., Hoet, P. H., Dinsdale, D., Smith, T., & Xu, H. et al. (2002b). Ultrafi. ne particles affect experimental thrombosis in an in vivo hamster model. *American Journal of Respiratory and Critical Care Medicine*, *166*(7), 998–1004. doi:10.1164/rccm.200110-026OC PMID:12359661

Neuberger, M., Moshammer, H., & Rabczenko, D. (2013). Acute and Subacute Effects of Urban Air Pollution on Cardiopulmonary Emergencies and Mortality: Time Series Studies in Austrian Cities. *International Journal of Environmental Research and Public Health*, *10*(10), 4728–4751. doi:10.3390/ijerph10104728 PMID:24157504

Nightingale, J. A., Maggs, R., Cullinan, P., Donnelly, L. E., Rogers, D. F., & Kinnersley, R. et al. (2000). Airway. inflammation after controlled exposure to diesel exhaust particulates. *American Journal of Respiratory and Critical Care Medicine*, *162*(1), 161–166. doi:10.1164/ajrccm.162.1.9908092 PMID:10903236

Nikic, D., Bogdanovic, D., Nikolic, M., Stankovic, A., Zivkovic, N., & Djordjevic, A. (2009). Air quality monitoring in NIS (SERBIA) and health impact assessment. *Environmental Monitoring and Assessment*, *158*(1-4), 499–506. doi:10.1007/s10661-008-0599-5 PMID:18951135

Nikić, D., Bogdanović, D., Stanković, A., Nikolić, M., & Milošević, Z. (2008). Impact of air pollution on the rate of hospital admission of children with respiratory diseases. *Vojnosanitetski Pregled. Military-Medical and Pharmaceutical Review*, *65*(11), 814–819. doi:10.2298/VSP0811814N PMID:19069711

Office of Climate, Water and Weather Services. (2001). *New wind chill temperature Index*. Washington, DC: Author.

Panagiotakos, D. B., Chrysohoou, C., Pitsavos, C., Nastos, P., Anadiotis, A., & Tentolouris, C. et al. (2004). Climatological variations in daily hospital admissions for acute coronary syndromes. *International Journal of Cardiology*, *94*(2), 229–233. doi:10.1016/j.ijcard.2003.04.050 PMID:15093986

Pekkanen, J., Peters, A., Hoek, G., Tiittanen, P., Brunekreef, B., & de Hartog, J. et al. (2002). Particulate Air Pollution and Risk of ST-Segment Depression During Repeated Submaximal Exercise Tests Among Subjects With Coronary Heart Disease The Exposure and Risk Assessment for Fine and Ultrafine Particles in Ambient Air (ULTRA) Study. *Circulation*, *106*(8), 933–938. doi:10.1161/01.CIR.0000027561.41736.3C PMID:12186796

Persinger, M. A. (1980). *The weather matrix and human behavior*. New York: Praeger.

Peters, A., Dockery, D. W., Muller, J. E., & Mittleman, M. A. (2001b). Increased particulate air pollution and the triggering of myocardial infarction. *Circulation*, *103*(23), 2810–2815. doi:10.1161/01.CIR.103.23.2810 PMID:11401937

Peters, A., Döring, A., Wichmann, H. E., & Koenig, W. (1997). Increased plasma viscosity during an air pollution episode: A link to mortality? *Lancet*, *349*(9065), 1582–1587. doi:10.1016/S0140-6736(97)01211-7 PMID:9174559

Peters, A., Fröhlich, M., Döring, A., Immervoll, T., Wichmann, H. E., & Hutchinson, W. L. et al. (2001a). Particulate air pollution is associated with an acute phase response in men: Results from the MONICA-Augsburg study. *European Heart Journal*, *22*(14), 1198–1204. doi:10.1053/euhj.2000.2483 PMID:11440492

Peters, A., Liu, E., Verrier, R. L., Schwartz, J., Gold, D. R., & Mittleman, M. et al. (2000b). Air pollution and incidence of cardiac arrhythmia. *Epidemiology (Cambridge, Mass.)*, *11*(1), 11–17. doi:10.1097/00001648-200001000-00005 PMID:10615837

Peters, A., Perz, S., Döring, A., Stieber, J., Koenig, W., & Wichmann, H.-E. (2000a). Activation of the autonomic nervous system and blood coagulation in association with an air pollution episode. *Inhalation Toxicology*, *12*, 51–61a. doi:10.1080/08958370050029770

Pirard, P., Vandentorren, S., Pascal, M., Laaidi, K., Le Tertre, A., Cassadou, S., & Ledrans, M. (2005). Summary of the mortality impact assessment of the 2003 heat wave in France. *European Communicable Disease Bulletin*, *10*(7), 153-156.

Pope, C. A. (2000). Epidemiology of fine particulate air pollution and human health: Biologic mechanisms and who's at risk? *Environmental Health Perspectives*, *108*, 713–723. doi:10.2307/3454408 PMID:10931790

Pope, C. A. III, Burnett, R. T., Thurston, G. D., Thun, M. J., Calle, E. E., Krewski, D., & Godleski, J. J. (2004). Cardiovascular mortality and long-term exposure to particulate air pollution: Epidemiological evidence of general pathophysiological pathways of disease. *Circulation*, *109*(1), 71–77. doi:10.1161/01.CIR.0000108927.80044.7F PMID:14676145

Pope, C. A. III, Thun, M. J., Namboodiri, M. M., Dockery, D. W., & Evans, J. S. et al. (1995). Particulate air pollution as a predictor of mortality in a prospective study of US adults. *American Journal of Respiratory and Critical Care Medicine*, *151*(pt1), 669–674. PMID:7881654

Pope, C. A. III, Verrierm, R. L., Lovett, E. G., Larson, A. C., Raizenne, M. E., & Kanner, R. E. et al. (1999). Heart rate variability associated with particulate air pollution. *American Heart Journal*, *138*(pt 1), 890–899. doi:10.1016/S0002-8703(99)70014-1 PMID:10539820

Ridker, P. M. (2001). High-sensitivity C-reactive protein: Potential adjunct for global risk assessment in the primary prevention of cardiovascular disease. *Circulation*, *103*(13), 1813–1818. doi:10.1161/01.CIR.103.13.1813 PMID:11282915

Ridker, P. M., Rifai, N., Stampfer, M. J., & Hennekens, C. H. (2000). Plasma concentration of interleukin-6 and the risk of future myocardial infarction among apparently healthy men. *Circulation*, *101*(15), 1767–1772. doi:10.1161/01.CIR.101.15.1767 PMID:10769275

Ritz, B., Yu, F., Fruin, S., Chapa, G., Shaw, G. M., & Harris, J. A. (2002). Ambient air pollution and risk of birth defects in Southern California. *American Journal of Epidemiology*, *155*(1), 17–25. doi:10.1093/aje/155.1.17 PMID:11772780

Rosen, S. (1989). *Weathering*. New York: Evans and Co Inc.

Salvi, S., Blomberg, A., Rudell, B., Kelly, F., Sandström, T., Holgate, S. T., & Frew, A. (1999). Acute inflammatory responses in the airways and peripheral blood after short-term exposure to diesel exhaust in healthy human volunteers. *American Journal of Respiratory and Critical Care Medicine*, *159*(3), 702–709. doi:10.1164/ajrccm.159.3.9709083 PMID:10051240

Salvi, S. S., Nordenhall, C., Blomberg, A., Rudell, B., Pourazar, J., & Kelly, F. J. et al. (2000). Acute e.xposure to diesel exhaust increases IL-8 and GRO-alpha production in healthy human airways. *American Journal of Respiratory and Critical Care Medicine*, *161*(pt 1), 550–557. doi:10.1164/ajrccm.161.2.9905052 PMID:10673199

Samet, J. M., Dominici, F., Curriero, F. C., Coursac, I., & Zeger, S. L. (2000). Fine particulate air pollution and mortality in 20 U.S. cities, 1987–1994. *The New England Journal of Medicine*, *343*(24), 1742–1749. doi:10.1056/NEJM200012143432401 PMID:11114312

Samet, J. M., Hatch, G. E., Horstman, D., Steck-Scott, S., Arab, L., & Bromberg, P. A. et al. (2001). Effect of antioxidant supplementation on ozone-induced lung injury in human subjects. *American Journal of Respiratory and Critical Care Medicine*, *164*(5), 819–825. doi:10.1164/ajrccm.164.5.2008003 PMID:11549539

Schaanning, J., Finsen, H., Lereim, I., & Saeterhaug, A. (1986). Effects of cold air inhalation combined with prolonged submaximal exercise on airway function in healthy young males. *European Journal ofRespiratory Diseases. Supplement*, *143*, 74–77. PMID:3462020

Schifano, P., Cappai, G., De Sario, M., Michelozzi, P., Marino, C., Bargagli, A. M., & Perucci, C. A. (2009). Susceptibility to heat wave-related mortality: A follow-up study of a cohort of elderly in Rome. *Environmental Health*, *8*(1), 50. doi:10.1186/1476-069X-8-50 PMID:19909505

Schwartz, J. (2005). Who is sensitive to extremes of temperature?: A case-only analysis. *Epidemiology (Cambridge, Mass.)*, *16*(1), 67–72. doi:10.1097/01.ede.0000147114.25957.71 PMID:15613947

Schwartz, J., Dockery, D. W., Neas, L. M., Wypij, D., Ware, J. H., & Spengler, J. D. et al. (1994). Acute effects of summer air pollution on respiratory symptom reporting in children. *American Journal of Respiratory and Critical Care Medicine*, *150*(5), 1234–1242. doi:10.1164/ajrccm.150.5.7952546 PMID:7952546

Schwartz, J., Samet, J. M., & Patz, J. A. (2004). Hospital admissions for heart disease: The effects of temperature and humidity. *Epidemiology (Cambridge, Mass.)*, *15*(6), 755–761. doi:10.1097/01.ede.0000134875.15919.0f PMID:15475726

Seaton, A., MacNee, W., Donaldson, K., & Godden, D. (1995). Particulate air pollution and acute health effects. *Lancet*, *345*(8943), 176–178. doi:10.1016/S0140-6736(95)90173-6 PMID:7741860

Seaton, A., Soutar, A., Crawford, V., Elton, R., McNerlan, S., & Cherrie, J. et al. (1999). Particulate air pollution and the blood. *Thorax*, *54*(11), 1027–1032. doi:10.1136/thx.54.11.1027 PMID:10525563

Seger, D. L., & Welch, L. W. (2001). Carbon monoxide. In J. B. Sullivan & G. R. Krieger (Eds.), *Clinical Environmental Health and Toxic Exposures* (2nd ed., pp. 722–727). Philadelphia, PA: Lippincott Williams & Wilkins.

Semenza, J. C., Wilson, D. J., Parra, J., Bontempo, B. D., Hart, M., Sailor, D. J., & George, L. A. (2008). Public perception and behavior change in relationship to hot weather and air pollution. *Environmental Research*, *107*(3), 401–411. doi:10.1016/j.envres.2008.03.005 PMID:18466894

Shukla, A., Timblin, C., BeruBe, K., Gordon, T., McKinney, W., & Driscoll, K. et al. (2000). Inhaled particulate matter causes expression of nuclear factor (NF)-kappaB–related genes and oxidant-dependent NF-kappaB activation in vitro. *American Journal of Respiratory Cell and Molecular Biology*, *23*(2), 182–187. doi:10.1165/ajrcmb.23.2.4035 PMID:10919984

Smith, R., Guttorp, P., Sheppard, L., Lumley, T., & Ishikawa, N. (2001). *Comments on the Criteria Document for Particulate Matter Air Pollution. NRCSE-TRS No. 066.* Seattle, WA: University of Washington, National Research Center for Statistics and the Environment.

Smoyer, K. E. (1998). A comparative analysis of heat waves and associated mortality in St. Louis, Missouri–1980 and 1995. *International Journal of Biometeorology*, *42*(1), 44–50. doi:10.1007/s004840050082 PMID:9780845

Smrcka, V., & Leznarova, D. (1998). Environmental pollution and occurrence of congenital defects in a 15-year period in a south Moravian district. *Acta Chirurgiae Plasticae*, *40*, 112–114. PMID:9949547

Sommet, A., Durrieu, G., Lapeyre-Mestre, M., & Montastruc, J. L. (2012). A comparative study of adverse drug reactions during two heat waves that occurred in France in 2003 and 2006. *Pharmacoepidemiology and Drug Safety*, *21*(3), 285–288. doi:10.1002/pds.2307 PMID:22162094

Sørensen, M., Daneshvar, B., Hansen, M., Dragsted, L. O., Hertel, O., Knudsen, L., & Loft, S. (2003). Personal PM2. 5 exposure and markers of oxidative stress in blood. *Environmental Health Perspectives*, *111*(2), 161–166. doi:10.1289/ehp.5646 PMID:12573899

Stankovic, A., Nikolic, M., & Bogdanovic, D. (2012). Short-term effects of black smoke on cardiovascular hospitalization in elderly in Niš, Serbia. *Chemical Industry and Chemical Engineering Quarterly, 18*(4-2), 661-665.

Strak, M., Hoek, G., Steenhof, M., Kilinc, E., Godri, K. J., & Gosens, I. et al. (2013). Components of ambient air pollution affect thrombin generation in healthy humans: The RAPTES project. *Occupational and Environmental Medicine*, *70*(5), 332–340. doi:10.1136/oemed-2012-100992 PMID:23378445

Suwa, T., Hogg, J. C., Quinlan, K. B., Ohgami, A., Vincent, R., & van Eeden, S. F. (2002). Particulate air pollution induces progression of atherosclerosis. *Journal of the American College of Cardiology*, *39*(6), 935–942. doi:10.1016/S0735-1097(02)01715-1 PMID:11897432

Tan, W. C., Qiu, D., Liam, B. L., Ng, T. P., Lee, S. H., & van EEDEN, S. F. et al. (2000). The human bone marrow response to acute air pollution caused by forest fires. *American Journal of Respiratory and Critical Care Medicine*, *161*(4), 1213–1217. doi:10.1164/ajrccm.161.4.9904084 PMID:10764314

Task Force of the European Society of Cardiology and the North American Society of Pacing and Electrophysiology. (1996). Heart rate variability: Standards of measurement, physiological interpretation, and clinical use. *Circulation*, *93*(5), 1043–1065. doi:10.1161/01.CIR.93.5.1043 PMID:8598068

Toloo, G., FitzGerald, G., Aitken, P., Verrall, K., & Tong, S. (2013). Evaluating the effectiveness of heat warning systems: Systematic review of epidemiological evidence. *International Journal of Public Health*, *58*(5), 667–681. doi:10.1007/s00038-013-0465-2 PMID:23564031

Tsai, S. S., Goggins, W. B., Chiu, H. F., & Yang, C. Y. (2003). Evidence for an association between air pollution and daily stroke admissions in Kaohsiung, Taiwan. *Stroke*, *34*(11), 2612–2616. doi:10.1161/01.STR.0000095564.33543.64 PMID:14551399

U.K. Ministry of Health. (1954). *Mortality and morbidity during the London Fog of December 1952. Reports on Public Health and Medical Subjects; No 95*. London: U.K. Ministry of Health.

US Environmental Protection Agency. (1993). Air Quality Criteria for Oxides of Nitrogen (Vol. 1). Research Triangle Park, NC: US Environmental Protection Agency.

US Environmental Protection Agency, Office of Research and Development, National Center for Environmental Assessment. (1996). Air Quality Criteria for Ozone and Related Photochemical Oxidants. Washington, DC: US Environmental Protection Agency.

van Eeden, S. F., Tan, W. C., Suwa, T., Mukae, H., Terashima, T., & Fujii, T. et al. (2001). Cytokines involved in the systemic inflammatory response induced by exposure to particulate matter air pollutants (PM10). *American Journal of Respiratory and Critical Care Medicine*, *164*(5), 826–830. doi:10.1164/ajrccm.164.5.2010160 PMID:11549540

Vanos, J. K., Hebbern, C., & Cakmak, S. (2014). Risk assessment for cardiovascular and respiratory mortality due to air pollution and synoptic meteorology in 10 Canadian cities. *Environmental Pollution*, *185*, 322–332. doi:10.1016/j.envpol.2013.11.007 PMID:24355413

Veronesi, B., Oortgiesen, M., Roy, J., Carter, J. D., Simon, S. A., & Gavett, S. H. (2000). Vanilloid (capsaicin) receptors influence inflammatory sensitivity in response to particulate matter. *Toxicology and Applied Pharmacology*, *169*(1), 66–76. doi:10.1006/taap.2000.9040 PMID:11076698

Volpato, S., Guralnik, J. M., Ferrucci, L., Balfour, J., Chaves, P., Fried, L. P., & Harris, T. B. (2001). Cardiovascular disease, interleukin-6, and risk of mortality in older women: The Women's Health and Aging Study. *Circulation*, *103*(7), 947–953. doi:10.1161/01.CIR.103.7.947 PMID:11181468

von Schneidemesser, E., & Monks, P. S. (2013). Air quality and climate–synergies and trade-offs. *Environmental Science: Processes & Impacts*, *15*(7), 1315–1325. PMID:23743609

Walters, S., Griffiths, R. K., & Ayres, J. G. (1994). Temporal association between hospital admissions for asthma in Birmingham and ambient levels of sulphur dioxide and smoke. *Thorax*, *49*(2), 133–140. doi:10.1136/thx.49.2.133 PMID:8128402

Wellenius, G. A., Coull, B. A., Godleski, J. J., Koutrakis, P., Okabe, K., & Savage, S. T. et al. (2003). Inhalation of concentrated ambient air particles exacerbates myocardial ischemia in conscious dogs. *Environmental Health Perspectives*, *111*(4), 402–408. doi:10.1289/ehp.5775 PMID:12676590

Wellenius, G. A., Saldiva, P. H., Batalha, J. R., Krishna Murthy, G. G., Coull, B. A., Verrier, R. L., & Godleski, J. J. (2002). Electrocardiographic changes during exposure to residual oil fly ash (ROFA) particles in a rat model of myocardial infarction. *Toxicological Sciences*, *66*(2), 327–335. doi:10.1093/toxsci/66.2.327 PMID:11896300

WHO. (1987). Air Quality Guidelines for Europe. Copenhagen: WHO Regional Publications.

WHO. (2001). *Air Quality and Health Air Management Information System AMIS 3.0*. Geneva, Switzerland: WHO.

Wilkinson, P., Pattenden, S., Armstrong, B., Fletcher, A., Kovats, R. S., Mangtani, P., & McMichael, A. J. (2004). Vulnerability to winter mortality in elderly people in Britain: Population based study. *BMJ (Clinical Research Ed.)*, *329*(7467), 647–652. doi:10.1136/bmj.38167.589907.55 PMID:15315961

Wolfe, C. P. (1981). Social impact assessment. *Impact Assessment Bulletin*, *1*(1), 9–19. doi:10.1080/07349165.1982.9725924

Zanobetti, A., Schwartz, J., Samoli, E., Gryparis, A., Touloumi, G., & Peacock, J. et al. (2003). The temporal pattern of respiratory and heart disease mortality in response to air pollution. *Environmental Health Perspectives*, *111*(9), 1188–1193. doi:10.1289/ehp.5712 PMID:12842772

Zanobetti, A., Schwartz, J., Sher, D., Eagan Bengston, E., Gates, K. A., Bar, M., … Gold, D. (2002). *Blood pressure and heart rate associated with PM2.5 in a cardiac rehabilitation study*. Paper presented at American Thoracic Society 98th Annual Conference. Atlanta, GA.

Zhang, Y., Li, S., Pan, X., Tong, S., Jaakkola, J. J., & Gasparrini, A. et al. (2014). The effects of ambient temperature on cerebrovascular mortality: An epidemiologic study in four climatic zones in China. *Environmental Health*, *13*(1), 24. doi:10.1186/1476-069X-13-24 PMID:24690204

KEY TERMS AND DEFINITIONS

Air Pollution: Air pollution is contamination of the indoor or outdoor environment by any chemical, physical or biological agent that modifies the natural characteristics of the atmosphere.

Early Warning System: Early warning system is any series of steps established to spot potential problems, and reduce their adverse effects.

Health: Health is a state of complete physical, mental and social well-being.

Heat Index: Heat index is a measurement of the air temperature in relation to the relative humidity, used as an indicator of the perceived temperature.

Wind Chill Index: Wind chill index is the perceived decrease in air temperature on exposed skin due to the flow of air. When the air temperature is below 5°C, the wind chill index is used as an indicator of the perceived temperature instead of the heat index.

Chapter 16
E-Health:
Current Status and Future Trends

Virginie Felizardo
University of Beira Interior, Covilhã, Portugal

Celina Alexandre
University of Beira Interior, Covilhã, Portugal

Paula Sousa
University of Beira Interior, Covilhã, Portugal

Rafael Couto
University of Beira Interior, Covilhã, Portugal

Daniel Sabugueiro
University of Beira Interior, Covilhã, Portugal

Nuno Garcia
University of Beira Interior, Covilhã, Portugal & Universidade Lusófona de Humanidades e Tecnologias, Lisbon, Portugal

Ivan Pires
University of Beira Interior, Covilhã, Portugal

ABSTRACT

Due to higher life expectancy, the number of older people continues to increase, and with it the number of cases of chronic diseases. Estimates indicate that the percentage of people with at least one chronic disease living in modern societies can reach as much as 40%, making chronic diseases one of the major challenges for modern healthcare systems. In order to reduce healthcare costs, solutions based on information and communication technologies have emerged. The expansion of e-Health solutions is associated with the increased demand for flexible, comprehensive, and cost-effective chronic care models, and continues expanding, putting together a very comprehensive set of knowledge. This chapter presents an inclusive and widespread current state of the art of e-health solutions for chronic diseases, proposing a number of predictable future trends and scenarios.

1. INTRODUCTION

The growing cost of healthcare and the aging of population have created many challenges for governments, healthcare providers and healthcare industry that they try to overcome using E-Health technologies, being one emerging area that has potential to improve healthcare service delivery, diagnostic monitoring, disease-tracking and related medical procedures. The use of wireless technologies to remotely monitor patients in an unobtrusive manner attracts great interest since it

DOI: 10.4018/978-1-4666-7266-6.ch016

can be done in a reliable and cost effective manner, offering personalized sustainable services to patients (Ragesh & Baskaran, 2012).

Thus, eHealth solutions are particularly identified by several characteristics, such as context aware, personalized, anticipatory, adaptive, ubiquity, transparency, performance, security, privacy (Acampora *et al.*, 2013).

From the point of view of functionality, these systems can be useful in different areas, including diagnosis, prognosis, screening, behavior discovery, therapy, decision support, hospital management, prediction of effectiveness of surgical procedures, continuous monitoring, medication, discovery of relationships among clinical and diagnosis data (Acampora *et al.*, 2013; Abdel-Aal, 2004, 2005).

In addition to these characteristics and tasks, also low cost and user-friendly interface help to improve comfort and life quality to users.

The remainder of this chapter is as follows: section 2 addresses the relevance and challenges of the e-Health; section 3 covers some available technologies and solution in e-Health divided in wearable multi-sensors platforms and support to care givers and care organizations; section 4 describes the issues of security and privacy of health data; and finishing, section 5 covers open research issues and future perspectives in e-Health.

2. RELEVANCE AND CHALLENGES

Health is something of common concern for everyone, as society live minded and wanting to live well as long as possible. With that in mind the delivery of high quality e-Health products is currently the main priority of each company that develops such products. Advances in e-Health solutions have shown that it is possible to get the most out of the existing technology by investing on it and creating newer and better technologies for this field. Newer and better technologies don't just refer to new products that do things a little bit better, or redefined products, but in fact, solutions that may profoundly improve the quality of treatment and broaden access to medical care.

These technologies aim to increase efficiency in health care treatments, improve quality of life, increase commitment to evidence-based medicine, empowerment of patients and consumers, and the development of new and more intimate relationships between patients and health care professionals. From a more abstract point-of-view, e-Health can be used to spread, share and relate health information through both patients and health professionals.

Nowadays there is an increasing consciousness about the importance and challenges e-Health and e-Health systems represent, being these challenges are as distinct as:

- An aging population, which demands for a longer-term care, consecutively demanding more elaborated and more available healthcare solutions, on which the Information Technologies (IT) may provide a solution like, for example, autonomous monitoring platforms that may synchronize patient vital data with a physician in real-time, and sound an alarm at the nearest healthcare facility if anything goes wrong with the patient;
- The rising expectations of patients from their healthcare professionals due to their access to the Internet that allows them to be better informed about their health issues by consulting and participating in health counselling forums;
- Pressure from the governments to reduce healthcare budgets by adopting IT solutions that automate manual procedures leading to cost reductions;
- A population that demands for better equipment conditions when hospitalized, like for example, newborn trackers, vital alarm systems, non-intrusive monitoring solutions, etc.

That consciousness and even enthusiasm about the potential that IT offers to healthcare has resulted in massive investments into IT companies and into the IT departments at Universities worldwide. The information technologies may be used, as said before, to record, process and share information on patients (*e.g.* electronic health records). These technologies may also be used as "electronic autonomous guiders" for procedural treatments (*e.g.* mobile apps) and even in solutions that may facilitate care, diagnosing and even perform surgeries from distance. Designing effective e-Health systems and services requires the enforcement of expertise from diverse fields and will surely benefit from interdisciplinary collaboration. In scope of that multidisciplinary team, there are already many working groups that may include health professionals, IT teams, and professionals from other related areas that work together. Not only those teams work inside companies, but with Universities as well, since university environments are usually more favorable to the design and development of new entrepreneurial concepts that eventually may result in future solutions for e-Health.

The return of this massive investment resulted in new solutions that are presented every single day, from wearable technologies, like smart clothing that monitors Electromyography (EMG), Electrocardiography (ECG) and Electroencephalography (EEG), or smart shoe soles that monitor the performance of athletes, to home solutions that are connected via Internet to a service health provider, and aim, for example, to monitor and/or diagnose patients with chronic illnesses. There is paraphernalia of new solutions being presented every day, and thus it can be said that IT has already gained an extremely important role in the Health research and business, and we all will certainly benefit from this current investment.

3. TELEMONITORING AND SELF-MANAGEMENT OF CHRONICDISEASES

According to World Health Organization, aging population is becoming a significant problem at the same time that sedentary lifestyle is causing millions of people to suffer from obesity or chronic diseases (Alwan *et al.*, 2011). Thus it is expected that this circumstance will contribute to a continued decline in the quality of services provided by an already overloaded healthcare system (Chen *et al.*, 2011). Several applications and solutions will benefit from the advanced integration of sensors and emerging wireless technologies, such as support to care givers and care organizations architectures or wearable multi-sensors platforms.

a. Support to Care Givers and Care Organizations

Information systems, such as electronic health records (EHRs), mobile phones and handheld computers (all of these components of m-health solutions), can be very valuable in providing health care in several settings (Blaya, Fraser & Holt, 2010).They can give support to people suffering from chronic conditions, such as Parkinson's disease or Alzheimer, allowing them to live independently in their own homes for as long as possible, and also support the care givers and care providers.

The projects presented in this section are a part of The Ambient Assisted Living (AAL) Joint Programme that aims to enhance the quality of life of older people and strengthen the industrial base in Europe through the use of Information and Communication Technologies (ICT). Most of these projects are focused on people with chronic conditions and their caregivers. Additionally,

Acampora *et al.* (2013) provides an overview on several aspects related to ambient intelligence in health care, and gives examples of other finished and on-going projects.

AGNES: User-Sensitive Home-Based Systems for Successful Ageing in a Networked Society

The *AGNES* project addresses chronic conditions, such as mild cognitive impairment and dementia. The main aim is to prevent, delay and help manage these conditions, emphasizing the role of the home as the care environment in which chronic conditions are largely self-managed.

The project applies ICT in innovative ways to support a personalized and person-centric care process, aimed at the needs of the individual elderly person, as well as formal and informal care givers. The objectives are to enhance mental and physical wellbeing by encouraging the older person to respond to physical, social and cognitive stimulation from outside, thus maintaining and even improving selective attention, memory span and prospective memory. The *AGNES* approach is to incorporate new healthcare technologies to keep the elderly mentally and socially stimulated and in contact with others by combining state detection and social network technologies, contributing significantly to supporting the elderly and their care givers (Waterworth, Ballesteros & Peter, 2009).

For this purpose, the *AGNES* project integrates several different technologies and devices, including (Waterworth, Ballesteros & Peter, 2009):

- Ambient devices for the display of information and events and for easy interaction with the home-based system and connected others;
- Web-cams and mobile phones for the unobtrusive detection of user states and activities;
- A social networking technology platform specifically designed to meet the needs of, and be usable by, the elderly person, and providing the communications channel through which people and applications will communicate;
- Diverse applications specifically aimed at the needs of the older person, to help deal with, or even prevent, the mild cognitive impairment that tends to be a chronic and worsening feature of this user population;
- Features that also support the needs of carers, both formal and informal, for information about the older person, their activities and current state.

The system consists of an ICT platform to create and maintain an easy-to-use web-based social network for individual persons. This platform is used to pass information between the social network and the elderly person. The technology in the in-home system supports the evaluation of the subjective and objective states of the elderly. The AGNES platform provides an information and communication channel between the elderly and the network, *i.e.* timely information about the activities and subjective states of the elderly person (*e.g.* presence, state of wellness) is passed to the network and information on the network (news, updates on activities of close persons, reminders of things "to do", etc.) is available for the elderly. Other functionalities include monitoring physical activities, which assists the elderly and the carers to plan and perform exercises, and to keep an appropriate diet (Waterworth, Ballesteros & Peter, 2009).

The system has two aspects regarding caregivers. Formal carers are assisted to manage their work load and improve communication and services as a result of better comprehension of the elderly needs. Informal carers have greater access to information about the person, and those at a distance will be enabled to keep in touch and share activities with their elderly family member or friend, and to know their current condition (Waterworth, Ballesteros & Peter, 2009).

ALADDIN: A Technology Platform for the Assisted Living of Dementia Elderly Individuals and Their Carers

The *ALADDIN* project addresses mild to moderate dementia chronic conditions, and aims to provide an integrated online clinical, educational and social support network for sufferers and their carers in the everyday management of the disease at home (Haritou *et al.*, 2012).

ALADDIN is a platform that provides planning, management and monitoring of the health status. This technology prevents emergency situations due to worsening symptoms, cognitive function, behavioral aspects, in the reduction of stress and burden in the home care situation, and maintaining the patient's and carer's quality of life (Cuno *et al.*, 2011).

The architecture of *ALADDIN*-platform consists of three main parts (Cuno *et al.*, 2011):

- **Carer's Client Application:** An application used by carers and patients to access the services of the platform. With this application, carers can answer the questionnaires about the patient's mental health condition, as well as their own. The information about the physiological measurements of the patient can be submitted by the caregiver using the application. The submitted data is analyzed by clinicians on a regular basis. Additionally, the application enables a caregiver to send a warning message to request the clinician to contact the caregiver in the near future;
- **Server Application:** The core of the platform. It implements the basic functionalities of the platform, provides secure communication with client applications, stores information about patients and carers, allows the exchange of information with external Hospital Information Systems (HIS) and provides a web based graphical user interface for clinicians and platform administrators to interact with the system;
- **External Services:** Provided by external web portals. There are two types of services involved: cognitive games and a social network. The integration of these services in the platform is achieved by integrating a web browser component in the Carer's Client Application, which opens a web page with the selected external service directly in the client application.

The system helps to ensure that the individual remains as long as possible in its familiar environment. The *ALADDIN*-platform is designed to stand out by its user-friendliness and simplicity, and it is expected that carer and patient should perceive the technology as a relief (Cuno *et al.*, 2011).

eCAALYX: Enhanced Complete Ambient Assisted Living Experience

eCAALYX builds on the strengths of the infrastructure and functionality already developed in the original *CAALYX* project (Boulos *et al.*, 2007).

eCAALYX offers a complete solution for improving the quality of life of elderly patients, to monitor their state of health, assess their health risk, promptly detecting and controlling any decompensation episodes, and providing them education focused on a healthy lifestyle, so that their independent life at home can be extended and their hospitalization or admission in nursing homes avoided for longer periods (Boulos *et al.*, 2009).

The *eCAALYX* system is composed of three main subsystems (Boulos *et al.*, 2009):

- **The Home Subsystem:** Includes Customer Premises Equipment (CPE), Set-top-box (STB)/interactive TV (to deliver health education and other functions), Tricorder and home sensors (those sensors that are stationary and not continuously worn on the body), all of them located at home;

- **The Mobile Subsystem:** Includes a smart garment, with all sensors integrated into a wireless BAN – Wearable Body Sensors (WBS), and a mobile phone;
- **The Caretaker Site:** Includes the Caretaker Server and the Auto-configuration Server.

The *eCAALYX*project also presents the *eCAALYX* Mobile Application which aims at building a remote monitoring system targeting older people with multiple chronic diseases. The *eCAALYX* Mobile Platform is a connection between the wearable health sensors used by the older person and the health professionals' Internet site, and reports the latter alerts and measurements obtained from sensors and the geographic location of the user. Additionally, the mobile platform is also able to reason with the raw sensor data to identify higher level information, including easy-to-detect anomalies such as tachycardia and signs of respiratory infections, based on established medical knowledge. A user interface is also provided, which allows the user to evaluate the most recent medical details obtained from sensors, perform new measurements, and communicate with the caretakers (Boulos *et al.*, 2011).

H@H: Health at Home

The Health at Home (*H@H*) project aims at solving societal problems related to the provision of healthcare services for Chronic Heart Failure (CHF) diagnosed elderly patients.

The model allows planning, controlling, and monitoring the activities carried out by patient, caregivers, social and sanitary professionals, enabling the medical staff to distantly monitor situations and take action in case of necessity. This will decrease the acting time in cases of destabilization of CHF patients and will reduce avoidable hospital re-admissions, resulting in an improved quality of life for the patient and in costs reduction (Sánchez-Tato *et al.*, 2010).

The system consists of a home monitoring and an alarm system for monitoring pathophysiological parameters, a control and communication system to allow interaction between the home system, and the Hospital Information System (HIS) (Sánchez-Tato *et al.*, 2010).

The *H@H* system has the typical client/server architecture. The communication between the two main parts is through the Internet. The patient is monitored by a set of Bluetooth sensing devices for measuring the main vital parameters and a home gateway that centralizes all needed computation and communication resources. The home gateway receives data from sensors and processes them to detect critical alterations. Then all data are forwarded to the remote server, using one of the transmission channels, to be further analyzed and made available in the existing HIS. In an alarm situation, caregivers or relatives are contacted via Short Message Service (SMS) and all pending data are sent to the server. In this way the clinician is enabled to monitor patients' situation at distance, taking actions in case of necessity (Saponara *et al.*, 2012).

The home gateway also provides an intuitive graphical user interface with reminder messages, images and animations in order to guide the patient in performing the scheduled activities. Furthermore, it allows the manual submission of perceived symptoms. The role of the remote server application is to receive data coming from gateways. Vital sign observations, raised alarms and other data are used to update the patients' record in the HIS. It also permits the management of all information related to the patient: browse historical data, plot data trends and revise his Operating Protocol (Saponara *et al.*, 2012).

HELP: Home-Based Empowered Living for Parkinson's Disease Patients

Current Parkinson's disease treatments improve symptoms but lead patients to develop a tolerance to the drug. But as the disease progresses it becomes more difficult to determine the exact drug dosage.

The *HELP* project aims to improve Parkinson's disease symptoms, by the development of a subcutaneous pump, which injects a gradual and constant flow of apomorphine (*i.e.* liquid drug for treating Parkinson's) throughout the day, improving the control of symptoms. However, this control method is not sufficient because the pump administers a constant dose, and the appropriate dose is variable and is a consequence of the patient's symptoms that fluctuate throughout the day.

This project has designed a "Parkinson's" sensor which sends relevant information to the platform and automatically establishes the optimal level of drug administration, depending on the state of each patient. At the same time, a constant level of drug is administered by another sub-system developed through the *HELP* project, consisting of an intraoral device embedded in the patient's mouth in the form of a tooth. This aims to achieve continuous dopaminergic stimulation, improving symptomatic benefits and minimizing concerns about complications resulting from intermittent dosage of medication (AAL, 2012).

The solution proposed by *HELP* is also highlighted by Telefónica (http://www.tid.es/en/): Telefónica has announced the results of a recently finished pilot that used mobile technology to remotely monitor and treat patients with Parkinson's disease, as the operator and its partners decide on future research and how to commercialize the technology (Handford *et al.*, 2013).

IS-ACTIVE: Inertial Sensing Systems for Advanced Chronic Condition Monitoring and Risk Prevention

IS-ACTIVE aimed the creation of person-centric healthcare solutions, based on recent advances in wireless inertial sensing systems, for patients with chronic conditions. This project highlights the role of the home as care environment, by providing real-time support to patients to monitor, self-manage and improve their physical condition according to their specific situation (IS-ACTIVE Project, 2010).

The sensor-based system proposed by *IS-ACTIVE* provides the patients an effective sensing system for daily use, which analyzes in real-time their physical activity and condition, and an easy-to-use interface and a natural feedback, in order to sensitize them to the importance of preventing and managing their chronic conditions; and provides the caregivers an effective remote monitoring tool, through which they investigate the success of the physical therapy and adapt it with minimal effort.

Figure 1 presents the main architectural components of *IS-ACTIVE*. The main important building blocks are:

- **Wireless Sensors Networks (WSNs):** The core technology of *IS-ACTIVE*, creating a pervasive environment around the user:
    - **Body Sensor Network (BSN):** *I.e.* on-body sensors, such as inertial sensors and physiological sensors;
    - **Infrastructure Sensors:** Such as environmental sensors (used for signaling possible adverse environmental conditions with respect to the user specific condition).
- **Technology-Aided Objects (TAOs):** Technology-enhanced daily objects that contribute to monitoring and assessing the physical training performance of patients at home and outdoors. Together, the on-body sensors and TAOs form the Extended Body Sensor Network (BSN+).
- **Feedback Devices:** Covering all user interaction aspects, providing the information sensed and processed by the WSN to the user.

Figure 1. Block diagram of IS-ACTIVE system architecture (IS-ACTIVE, 2010).

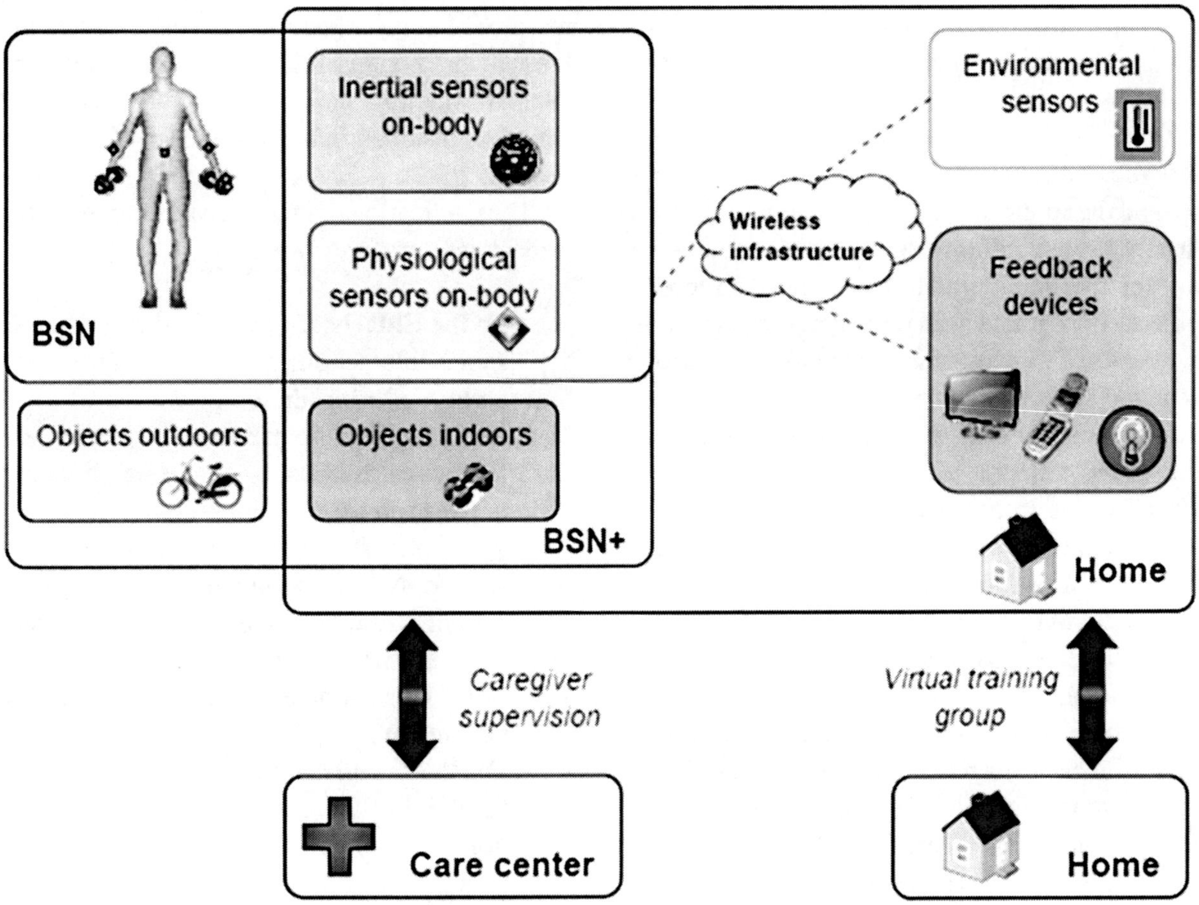

- **Home-Based Infrastructure:** The wireless communication infrastructure (hardware and software) interconnecting the above components (WSNs, technology-aided objects and feedback devices) in a seamless way.
- **Multiple Users/Patients:** Providing multiple patients with the possibility of exercising and using together the *IS-ACTIVE* system.
- **Communication with the Caregiver:** That allows him/her to assess the progress of the patient, as well as to give proper advice adapted to the current status and evolution of the disease.

PAMAP: Physical Activity Monitoring for Aging People

The *PAMAP* project allows monitoring the physical activity both in a clinical setting and in the subject's home environment. The goal is to provide physicians with the means to encourage people to a healthy activity level, and also to diagnose problems at an early stage (Hendeby *et al.*, 2010). It is designed to support physical rehabilitation and physical activitymonitoring services. The system can be used in a clinical environment, as well as, in daily life, thus providing health professionals with important information to diagnose problems at an early stage (Hendeby *et al.*, 2010).

The system has two separate conceptual parts: the information management and the underlying information acquisition system (the sensor network and associated information extraction technology) (Hendeby *et al.*, 2010).

From the information management point of view, the *PAMAP* system consists of the infrastructure and the applications used to monitor physical activity, present information, and provide an easy way for the main system users (the monitored subject, family and friends and the clinicians) to interact. From the data acquisition point of view, the *PAMAP* system consists of the sensor network and a control unit that links the sensors and several different I/O devices. An interactive TV (i-TV) interface is used to enable patients to gain access to their health record and the details of the rehabilitation plan to be followed.

The *PAMAP* system is a technical support system that can be used both preventive and to make rehabilitation more efficient. Moreover, the system allows for a more independent elderly life style, since it can be managed by the elderly themselves in their homes. This way, *PAMAP* encourages the elderly to keep an as active, independent, and normal life as possible (Hendeby *et al.*, 2010).

REMOTE: Remote Health and Social Care for Independent Living of Isolated Elderly with Chronic Conditions

REMOTE is a project concerned with the needs of elderly and individuals with chronic conditions, especially those living in isolation (geographical or social), and whose independent life is at risk with chronic conditions or lifestyle factors.

The *REMOTE* project provides support for an independent life at home with the aid of Ambient Intelligence (AmI) and tele-healthcare. The elderly's personal environment is enhanced with various kinds of monitoring and automation abilities for tracing activity and health condition, as well as detecting risks or critical situations. For this purpose the project uses and scales-up existing research prototypes and new systems for collecting human- and context-related data (including sensors attached to a person's body, or sensors and actuators installed in houses or cars) (REMOTE Project, 2012).

The applications and services developed in the project are three-part oriented:

- **To the Elderly:** To enhance their self-care, social interaction, and skills maintenance ability, offering the comfort, security and safety required: to maintain links with their family and friends, to go out for shopping or vacation etc.;
- **To Health Professionals:** To be provided with tools for continuous monitoring of a patient's situation (*e.g.* real time data and records of the patient's condition, activity, and life environment changes) and history patient data;
- **To Health and Care Insurance Providers:** Facilitating the development and integration of new services and new delivery platforms; this will meet their requirements concerning cost reduction, interoperability, and standardization of services.

ROSETTA: Guidance and Awareness Services for Independent Living

The *ROSETTA* project has developed an innovative, integrated system aiming at preventing and managing the problems that can occur as a result of chronic progressive diseases, such as dementia, Parkinson's disease and Alzheimer. The target group of *ROSETTA* includes elderly people, living in their own houses or in small-scale living communities, and their formal and/or informal caregivers.

The *ROSETTA* system functionalities are as follows:

- The system monitors the activities of the resident by means of multiple and different sensors;
- It generates an alarm in case of deviant activity/inactivity or wandering, which is forwarded to the caregiver (the AAPS part);
- The system generates a warning in case of long-term variations in the patterns of daily living, which is forwarded to the caregiver (EDS Lifestyle monitoring part);
- It supports the resident directly in carrying out his or her daily activities (EDN Elderly Day Navigator part).

The *ROSETTA* system is composed of three main parts: Unattended Autonomous Surveillance (UAS-AAPS), Early Detection System (EDS), Early Day Navigator (EDN) (ROSETTA Project, 2012).

The UAS-AAPS is for surveillance for emergencies, including those as a result of falling and straying, for persons with advanced dementia or persons with a combination of memory problems/mild dementia and Parkinson's disease. The possible emergencies are detected by sensors and a camera and reported to a mobile care team.

The EDS is the lifestyle monitoring system. Sensors in the home monitor the daily life pattern of persons living alone. These daily life patterns are available to care providers as well as informal carers via a computer programme.

The EDN part offers memory support for people with memory problems, through the development of a touch screen and an adapted Smartphone.

At the end of the project, the UAS-AAPS surveillance was almost market ready and therefore it was selected to be launch as first to the market in The Netherlands in 2013. The EDS Lifestyle monitoring is expected to be launched in The Netherlands and Germany in 2014.

To implement the market launch for the AAPS part of the ROSETTA system, early in 2013, the Institute for Technology Development, the Netherlands (TNO) has created a spin-off company called "Dutch Domotics" (http://www.dutchdomotics.com).

SOFTCARE: Unobtrusive Plug and Play Kit for Chronic Condition Monitoring Based on Customized Behavior Recognition from Wireless Localization and Remote Sensoring

Many older people who live at home may have or be at risk of developing a chronic condition. By monitoring their daily activity levels it is possible to warn carers about falls or other abnormal behaviors which might signal the beginning of a problem with the person's health.

The *SOFTCARE* project addresses the need to improve upon existing home care technology for the elderly by developing an easy-to-deploy and non-intrusive indoor wireless home monitoring system for the independent elderly that proactively monitors anomalies in behavior that may point to the onset of a chronic condition or indicate risk to physical wellbeing (CRIC, 2012), and at the same time allow carers and users to get real-time alarms in dangerous or potentially dangerous situations.

The system is composed by a small bracelet, with a 3D accelerometer and a mobile communication device, worn by the user, and static nodes placed in each room of the user's home.

As a result of the *SOFTCARE* project, the most relevant outcomes are:

- A prototype system composed by a bracelet, static nodes, gateways and a server side software application, that provides activity recognition and fall detection features;
- A set of algorithms for fall detection and activity recognition based on the information gathered by the bracelet.

The project consortium is currently negotiating with potential commercial partners to integrate *SOFTCARE* bracelet and algorithms (for fall detection and activity recognition) in an existing commercial product (AAL, 2012).

b. Wearable Multi-Sensors Platforms

A biosignal change is given in function of time or space (McAdams *et al.*, 2010). Some of the standard sensors include body movement (via accelerometer), location (via GPS), temperature, electro-dermal activity (EDA), ECG, heart rate, EMG, EEG, and photoplethysmography (PPG). These sensors are included in a variety of devices and solutions (Swan, 2012).

The multi-sensor platforms allow a wearable approach of medical devices (McAdams *et al.*, 2010). These products include "Holter-type" systems, smartwatches, wristband sensors, wearable sensor patches, brain computer interfaces, wearable systems embedded in textile, smartphone applications and their enhancements and home automation sensors (McAdams *et al.*, 2010, Swan 2012).

The wearable platforms with application in Healthcare and Assisted Living in this section can be divided in two groups:

1. "Holter-type" systems and
2. Wearable Technology:
   2.1. Wearable Sensors and Monitoring Patches;
   2.2. Smartwatches and Wristband Sensors; and
   2.3. Wearable systems embedded in textile.

i. "Holter-Type" Systems

Many multi-sensors platforms systems look like standard Holter monitoring systems. These monitoring systems involve a recording and transmitting device which attached to the person's accessories such as a belt, necklace or is located in some forms of waistcoat. The acquisition system is connected to standard sensors placed in standard locations. A variety of models with different features manufactured by different companies are available below (McAdams *et al.*, 2010).

physioPlux (PLUX wireless biosignals S.A.)

According to the company Plux, the physioPlux (Figure 2, left) is a device that collects and digitizes signals from sensors, transmitting them via Bluetooth® (Connectivity - 10m range, with standard adapter; >100m with high range adapter) to a computer, where are viewed in real time. The analog-to-digital converter (ADC) channels have 12 bits, and its sampling frequency is 1 kHz. The physioPlux has 4 channels for sensors connection, also has a digital port, a terminal for connecting

Figure 2. "Holter-type" systems: left, physioPlux; and right, BITalino

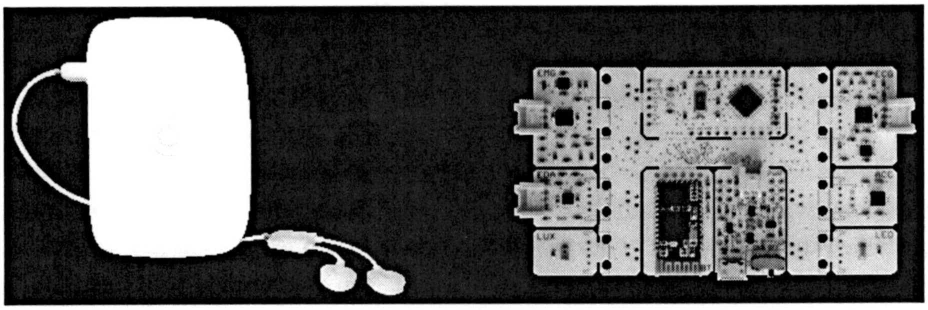

the AC adapter and charge the internal battery (allows a lifespan of approximately 12 hours), and a channel to connect the reference electrode.

Plux has several sensors that can be linked to physiobioPlux such as respiration sensor, respPlux, single button resistive sensor, forcePlux, air pressure, airPlux, angle measurement tool, anglePlux, ambient luminosity, lightPlux, triaxial accelerometer, xyzPlux, ECG sensor (ECG triodes), ecgPlux, electro-dermal activity sensor, edaPlux, peripheral temperature sensor, tempPlux, electromyography sensor, emgPlux, and encephalography sensor, eegPlux (www.plux.info).

The physioPlux system is related with physical activity because it has great potential for free-living applications.

g.MOBIlab+ (g.tec Medical Engineering)

g.MOBIlab+ is a tool for recording multimodal biosignal data on a standard Pocket PC, PC or notebook.

According to the company, this allows investigation of brain-, heart-, and muscle-activity, eye movement, respiration, galvanic skin response, pulse and other body signals. *g.MOBIlab+* is available in two versions: the 8 channel EEG and the multi-purpose version (http://www.gtec.at).

e-Health Sensor Platform for Arduino and Raspberry Pi (Cooking Hacks)

According Cooking Hacks, the e-Health Sensor Platform for Arduino and Raspberry Pi allows users to perform biomedical applications, using nine different sensors, for body monitoring: pulse, oxygen in blood (SPO2), airflow (breathing), body temperature, ECG, glucometer, galvanic skin response (GSR - sweating), blood pressure (sphygmomanometer) and patient position (accelerometer) (Cooking Hacks, 2013).

This physiological information can be sent using Wi-Fi, 3G, GPRS, Bluetooth, 802.15.4 and ZigBee, depending on the application, and data can be sent to the Cloud for storage or visualized in real time in a laptop or Smartphone.

BITalino (PLUX Wireless Biosignals S.A. and Instituto de Telecomunicações)

According to the company Plux, *BITalino* (Figure 2, right) is a low-cost toolkit that claims to allow any developer to create projects and applications with physiological sensors.

BITalino integrates hardware blocks with multiple sensors that can operate as a single system or snapped off into their individual blocks for applications with ECG, EMG, EDA, an accelerometer, and ambient light; and easy to use software (http://www.bitalino.com).

ii. Wearable Technology

The development of wearable technology for monitoring vital signals allows the patient to be continuously monitoring their health conditions, assuming either being at home or walking outside, moving from time to time and place to place, in a comfortable, unobtrusive and independent way. Consequently, a series of benefits and new applications would be taken advantage of by the users including both the patients and the healthcare providers (Zhou *et al.*, 2013).

These systems have some categories: Wearable Sensors and Patches, Smartwatches and Wristband Sensors and Wearable systems embedded in textile.

a. Wearable Sensors and Patches

Advances in sensor technologies, materials and software are driving to the development of a new generation of wearable sensors and medical monitoring device. A notable example is a patch-based wearable sensor that adheres comfortably to the user's skin and continuously gathers physiological and lifestyle information (Praskah, 2012).

Metria™ (Avery Dennison® Medical Solutions)

The platform is based on advanced adhesives, materials and manufacturing processes in combination with a personal monitoring device for continuous physiologic monitoring developed by Proteus Biomedical, Inc. According to the company, the patch will incorporate multiple sensors including ECG and an accelerometer that will allow measurement, during day-to-day activity, such as exercising or taking a shower, of heart rate, activity, sleep and other physiologic metrics (Avery Dennison Corporation, 2013).

Actiheart Monitor (CamNtech Ltd and CamNtechInc)

According to the company, *Actiheart* is a chest-worn monitoring device that records heart rate, Inter-Beat-Interval (IBI), and physical activity. It is designed for capturing the heart rate variability (HRV) data and for calculating and measuring Activity Energy Expenditure (CamNtech Ltd and CamNtechInc, 2012).

b. Smartwatches and Wristband Sensors

Currently, there are a growing number of other health and fitness wristband devices: Wrist-worn devices, Arm-worn devices, Chest harnesses and Head bands and caps. The market for wearable health and fitness wristbands and smartwatches is about to boom, especially now that 'open' platform is about to be released.

EKG Glove™ (IneedMD, Inc.)

The *EKG Glove*™ (Figure 3, top left) is, according to IneedMD Inc., a medical device that replaces the cumbersome cables, electrodes and plugs typically used to perform an ECG. The *EKG Glove*™ is disposable, portable and can easily connect to most industry standard ECG recording devices typically used in private practice, hospitals, emergency services and home health care (IneedMD Inc., 2012).

According the company, for obtaining the tracing, a care giver needs to connect this medical device to an ECG machine or wireless transmission device, insert his right hand into glove and properly positioned the glove over the patient's chest.

Angel Sensor (Seraphim Sense Ltd.)

Angel sensor's (Figure 3, top right) is a wristband platform that monitors pulse, temperature, activity and blood oxygen level. *Angel* is able to send this vital information to applications on smartphone, laptop and possibly even treadmill. According to Seraphim Sense Ltd., *Angel* is the first device designed for developers, with open communication protocols, API/SDK and sensor data streams (http://www.angelsensor.com).

A-PULSE CASPro® (HealthSTATS International)

PULSE CASPro®, developed by HealthSTATS International, is a simple and yet revolutionary device for the measurement of Central Aortic Systolic Pressure (CASP) in clinical environment or home setting. According the developers, it is empowered by Evidence-Based Blood Pressure (EVBP) technology; a FDA listed and patented technology using modified applanation tonometry on the radial artery at the wrist (HealthSTATS, 2010). The system consists of four main elements: 1) PULSE CASPro® monitor; 2) Wrist sensor

Figure 3. Smartwatches and wristband sensors: top left, EKG Glove™; top right, Angel Sensor; bottom left, LifeShirt; and bottom right, Easy Ambulatory EEG System

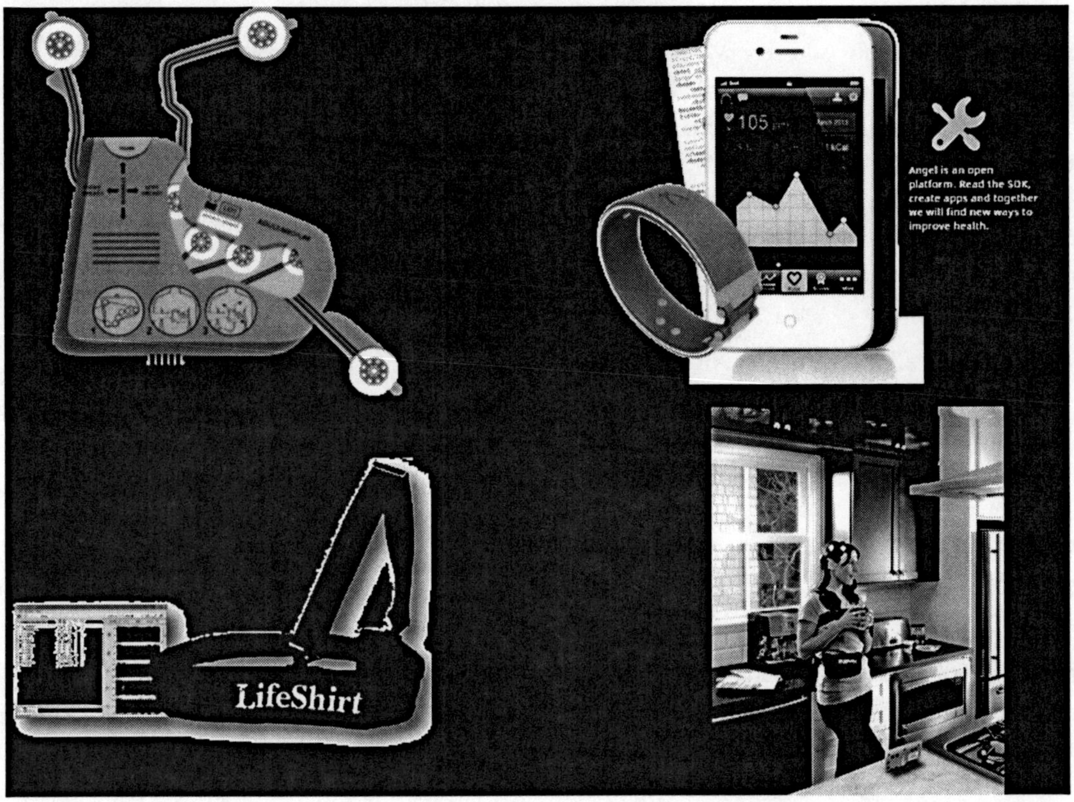

module; 3) PULSE CASP® software; and 4) Integrated oscillometric blood pressure module for calibration.

ez430Chronos (Texas Instruments)

The *eZ430-Chronos* software development tool developed by Texas Instruments(Texas Instruments, 2014) is a highly integrated, wearable, wireless development system that is based on the MCU CC430F6137. It may be used as a reference platform for watch systems, a personal display for personal area networks, or as a wireless sensor node for remote data collection. Based on the MCU CC430F6137 sub-1-GHz RF SoC, the *eZ430-Chronos* is a complete development system featuring a 96-segment LCD display, an integrated pressure sensor, and a three-axis accelerometer for motion sensitive control. The integrated wireless interface allows the *eZ430-Chronos* to act as a central hub for nearby wireless sensors such as pedometers and heart rate monitors. The *eZ430-Chronos* offers temperature and battery voltage measurement and is complete with a USB-based CC1111 wireless interface to a PC.

The sports watch firmware (default) provides a broad set of features. Besides basic watch functions such as time, date, alarm and stopwatch, advanced sports watch features such as an altimeter, heart rate monitor, calorie, vertical speed and distance information are available. The internal accelerometer provides acceleration data on the watch LCD and allows controlling a PC by transferring the sensor's measurements.

BodyMedia FIT (BodyMedia, Inc.)

According to the company,*BodyMedia FIT* is an on-body monitoring system that consists of the armband monitor, online Activity Manager, an optional Display and free downloadable applications for mobile device users. The system measure the intensity of workouts, calories burned during daily activities and also monitors the quality of your sleep (BodyMedia Inc., 2013).

LifeShirt (Vivonoetics)

The *LifeShirt* (Figure 3, bottom left) is a washable shirt system with embedded sensors: respiratory sensors, a three-lead, single channel ECG, and a three-axis accelerometer (Vivonoetics, 2013).

CoughSense (Ubiquitous Computing Lab – University of Washington)

The Ubiquitous Computing Lab (University of Washington) developed algorithms for using audio recorded from a mobile phone microphone to count the number of cough episodes an individual has and the number of coughs within each episode (Larson *et al.*, 2011).

This system could be used to track and monitoring cough frequency for a single person or, when networked, trends across an entire population using nothing more than an individual's existing mobile phone.

Easy Ambulatory EEG System (Cadwell Laboratories Inc.)

The Easy Ambulatory system (Figure 3, bottom right) allows full EEG and polysomnography (PSG) data acquisition outside traditional laboratory. The Easy Ambulatory system not only continuously collects data for extended periods of time, but it allows performing longer term studies over multiple days in a cost effective manner and can also be connected to a computer during acquisition to examine real time data (http://www.cadwell.com).

c. Wearable Systems Embedded in Textile

In the past decade, a variety of noninvasive sensors have been developed for measuring and monitoring various physiological parameters such as ECG, EEG, EDA, respiration, etc. Some of those sensors are in form of wearable devices such as wrist bands, as those mentioned in the previous section, while others are embedded into textile, known as E-textile or smart fabrics. These section presents recently developed solutions that use textile-embedded sensors inside clothes, such as fiber, yarn and fabric structure (Chen *et al.*, 2011).

Great strides have been made in the category of capture vital signals with wearable systems, especially in a system integrated into textiles. There are a number of research and commercial projects in this area.

VitalJacket (Biodevices)

VitalJacket (Figure 4, top right) is a medical device combining wearable technology and mainstream biomedical engineering solutions, reliable cardio monitor. According to the company, the *VitalJacket* can be worn by the patient allowing at least 72 hours of continuous exams enables physicians to do a correct assessment of cardiac problems in an everyday life environment (http://www.vitaljacket.com).

Smart-Clothing (University of Beira Interior - Portugal)

In the University of Beira Interior - Portugal, a project called *Smart-Clothing* ended in 2009. The main areas addressed by the Smart-Clothing Project are Obstetrics and Sports activity (Figure 4, top left). The objective of this project was to obtain a universal obstetric tracing, allowing for the identification of sudden changes in the fetus health, by continuously monitoring the fetus movements and the Fetal Heart Rate (FHR) frequency (Borges *et al.*, 2010).

Figure 4. Wearable systems embedded in textile: top left, VitalJacket; top right, Smart-Clothing; bottom left, Armband integrating textile electrodes; and bottom right, Moticon

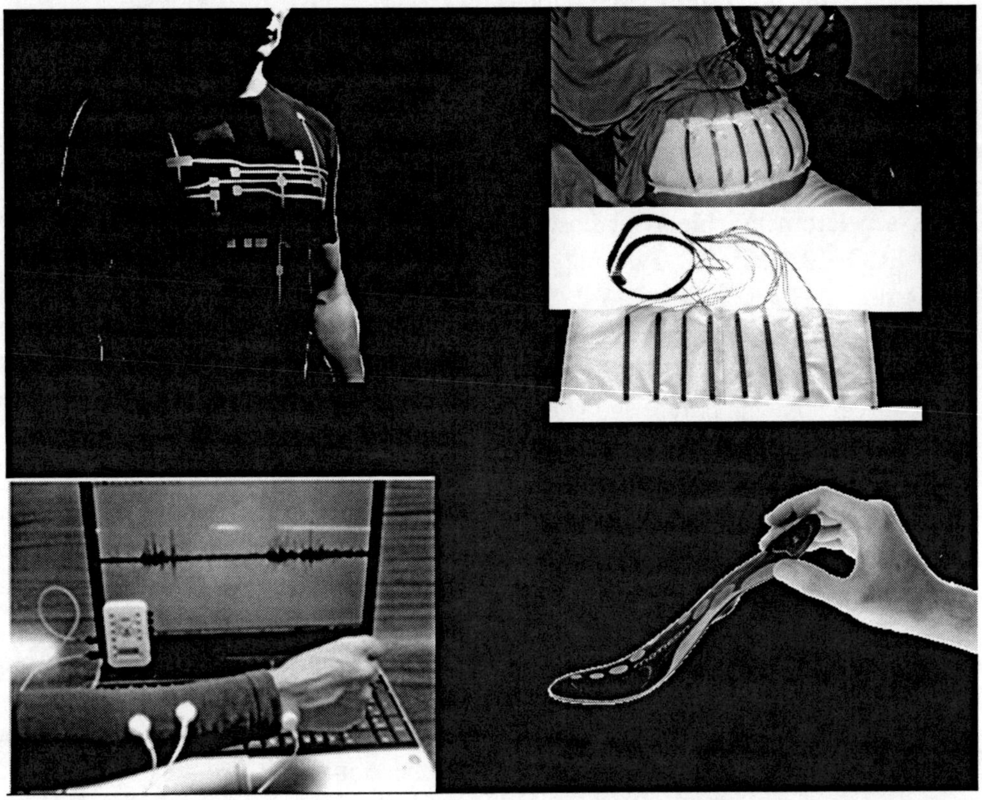

Armband integrating textile electrodes (University of Beira Interior - Portugal)

The Department of Textile Science and Technology (University of Beira Interior, Portugal) developed an armband made of plain weave fabric, integrating embroidery textile electrodes of stainless steel (SS) and elastics to conform to human forearms (Figure 4, bottom left) (Trindade *et al.*, 2010).

The fabric integrates stitched conductive threads of SS/cotton and snaps fasteners interconnecting the textile electrodes to a *bioPlux* signal processing electronic module. The electronic module connects through shielded cables to a portable unit, which can be held in a pocket, and transmit wirelessly to a PC located anywhere in the room where the person is, for real time monitoring and recording of the processed signals.

EMG signals obtained with an armband integrating textile electrodes, worn by a volunteer and processed by a wireless portable unit exhibited comparable quality to those obtained with bipolar Ag/AgCI electrodes (Trindade *et al.*, 2010).

Moticon (Moticon GmbH)

Moticon is the world's first fully integrated and wireless sensor insole (Figure 4, bottom right), according to the company. The insole can be used in any shoe to measure the distribution and motion parameters for patients and athletes. The wireless sensor insole is currently used for daily patient monitoring, rehabilitation, and for status training in sports. The sensor insole, which is fitted with firmware that communicates with PC software via a USB radio stick, is easy to use and doesn't require special training (http://www.moticon.de).

Micro-Electro Mechanical Systems

Micro-Electro Mechanical System (MEMS) are an innovative technology for sensors design based on miniaturized mechanical and electromechanical elements using microfabrication techniques (https://www.memsnet.org). Recently MEMS technology has been used for design of sensors such as accelerometer, blood glucose, blood pressure, ECG, EEG, EMG, gyroscope, pulse oximetry, etc.

One of the main advantages in using this type of sensors embedded into clothes fabrics is the alleviation of electrical contacts failure and skin irritation problems resulting from the long-term usage of silver chloride traditional disposable electrodes. Compared to the conventional electrodes, they are also much more flexible, since their shape can be adapted to human motion.

iii. Self-Management Online Platforms

Training and supporting patients in the self-management of their health condition has shown improvements in the quality of life and reduction in unplanned hospital admissions.

The use of Information and Communication Technologies (ICT) in the form of e-health is expected to lead to improvements in healthcare quality and efficiency, and has brought up an increasing emphasis on promoting self-care and self-management by patients, and a more general promotion of healthy behaviors (Murray, 2012).

As well as delivering greater choice and control for patients, supported self-management increases patients' health education, so that they are better able to understand and engage with their health, and their activation.

Internet users living with chronic disease are slightly more likely than other Internet users to access health information online and more likely to share acquired health information with others, so Internet-mediated chronic disease self-monitoring and self-management platforms may exhibit great potential to reach a broad population of chronic patients (Stellefson *et al.*, 2013).

These web platforms are related to Web 2.0 concept, which consists in the information sharing between people. This has the advantage of, being applied to healthcare, allowing the user to share his experiences and give and get support about the health condition.

Furthermore, online discussion forums provide an open-access space for chronic disease patients to exchange information and learn about how to control disease exacerbations. Additionally, available evidence shows that online self-help groups can enhance social capital in ways that do not undermine, and might in some cases strengthen, hyper personal connections between patients and providers (Stellefson *et al.*, 2013).

Following, some of these platforms are presented. They are often considered as social networks and many can be used with mobile resources and applications.

- **Patients Like Me:** A health data-sharing platform that allows users to compare treatments, symptoms and experiences with people with the same or similar conditions, and take control of their health. It also allows sharing experiences, giving and getting support to improve the life of others and their own; and track their health, creating health charts over time and contribute to research that can advance medicine research. (http://www.patientslikeme.com)
- **Patients Innovation:** A recent Portuguese online platform developed with the purpose of exchanging solutions and strategies for patients and caregivers to deal with the challenges imposed by their health conditions, including new or modified devices or

aids, strategies, behaviors, treatments, adaptations or low-cost alternatives to existing solutions. (https://patient-innovation.com/)

- **Cure Together:** A social platform that has the purpose of bringing together people with certain medical conditions to better understand their bodies and going toward the cure. In this platform the users discuss symptoms and compare health data and which treatments work best for them. The users can see several personal and medical data: rate symptoms they have, treatments they have tried and what they think causes or triggers their condition. The users can also track the daily health status, weight, calories, physical activity and sleep. With this patient-contributed data, new research is made taking into account a range of experiences. (http://curetogether.com)
- **Daily Strength:** A network platform where users share their knowledge, experiences and support. In this platform, users can track goals, discuss several themes, have expert advice and treatments reviews. The platform has free support groups for issues ranging from mental health to cancer to children's health and parenting. (http://www.dailystrength.org)
- **Inspire:** An online platform for build a health and wellness community for patients and caregivers, patient advocacy organizations and life science organizations. The users of the group "Patients & caregivers" can share their health status and health concerns through discussions and blogging. (http://corp.inspire.com)

The Life science organizations can access to patients population for studies and research including market research, clinical trial recruitment, issues analysis, opinion surveys and promotion of brand awareness.

The patient advocacy organizations can provide safety for the online communities in which patients, families, friends and caregivers connect with one another for support and information.

- **HealthVault:** An online platform, hosted by Microsoft, which allows to gather, store, use, and share health information.The platform allows the user to organize the family health information (health records, medications, allergies, health history), prepare for doctor visits and unexpected emergencies, create a complete picture of health status (share medical image or upload medical data) and achieve fitness goals (weight control, exercise motivation). (https://www.healthvault.com)
- **Everyday Health:** A platform to help the self-management of all family health conditions and overall well-being through personalized advice, tools, and communities. The platform has information on various health topics and the user can check a symptom, count calories, make a meal plan, find an expert or look up a drug. (http://www.everydayhealth.com)
- **CarePages:** An online community to share the challenges, hopes and triumphs of people facing or that have faced life-changing health events. *CarePages* allows the creation of personalized websites, through which members can relate their stories, post photos and update friends and family. In turn, people who care send messages of love and encouragement. (https://www.carepages.com)
- **Healthline:** An online repository of medical information aiming to promote a healthy lifestyle and facilitate disease prevention, as well as to offer clinically significant, medically reviewed information for those who are seeking answers to their health questions. In addition to the Health Topics,

it has several tools available as Symptom Checker, Body Maps, Doctor Search, etc. (http://www.healthline.com)

- **WebMD:** Provides health information, supportive communities and in-depth reference material about health subjects. The health information on WebMD can be useful for patients, as well as for physicians and other health providers. WebMD provides information about the most common conditions, as well as a symptom checker and a pill identifier, and allows creating profiles for the family members. Furthermore, it has content on several matters from healthy living to pregnancy and parenting. (http://www.webmd.com)
- **Patients Fusion:** Built to patients and doctors. Patients can find doctors, book doctor appointments, access their health records and latest updates from lab results to prescriptions, read reviews and manage the spending. Doctors can grow their practice with *Patients Fusion* with free online scheduling. (http://www.patientfusion.com)
- **HealthTap:** An interactive health network consisting in a web platform and mobile application that connect doctors with patients, provide education to those who seek it and disseminate trusted, vetted, peer-reviewed health information. The aim of *HealthTap* is to improve people's health and well-being by providing users with personalized health information and free online answers from thousands of doctors, improving people's knowledge about health and keep them more informed on health decisions; for doctors, it is a tool to better serve existing patients, find new ones and build reputation, by demonstrating their expertise and contributing to the improvement of online health information quality. (https://www.healthtap.com)
- **eVida**is a platform that allows a rapid development and integration of wide range of applications for health and quality of life systems.
- **TICE.Healthy:** Based on Open Source software and standards thus facilitating the interoperability and the integration of systems. (https://evida.pt)
- **TICE.Healthyproject (2011-2014):** A project funded by the European Union and the Portuguese government, anchored in the TICE.PT program – Center for Competitiveness and Technology, Center for Information, Communication and Electronics Technologies (http://tice.pt), (http://tice.healthy.ipn.pt).

4. SECURITY AND PRIVACY OF HEALTH DATA

The use of information systems able to replace the traditional paper-based format raised some issues regarding the security and privacy of the data stored in them (Dong *et al.*, 2012). Particularly for health care systems, privacy and security are very complex issues, and the addition of a large number of sensors and devices results in additional challenges (Acampora *et al.*, 2013).

Mechanisms to improve security should be present in systems to prevent disclosure, data manipulation, removal or destruction without clear permission to do so, like specific security policies, passwords protection, secure communications, and so on. To have a certainty that the information is protected, a good practice is to periodically examine the network integrity and security.

Privacy ensures that data isn't seen by other people besides the ones that have authorization to access it, for instance, another health provider, another patient, etc. To respect the privacy, the necessary permissions to access the e-health system should only be given with consent from the patient.

Some authors agree that these issues are two of the main concerns that need to be dealt with to have an effective information governance architecture (Accenture, 2010), and they really stand out in one of the most used e-health information system, cloud storage.

But the use of information systems also has some clear advantages, like the standardization of health data using Digital Imaging Communications in Medicine (DICOM) and Health Level Seven (HL7) (among others) that brings easy communication amidst different systems thanks to its interoperability.

DICOM standard specifies protocols used to exchange medical images with encapsulated information like timestamps, operators identification, patients, identification, etc. between several information systems and health-care providers. Thanks to that, images created using DICOM can be viewed in any system, without concerning where they were produced (Minnesota e-Health Initiative and the Minnesota Department of Health, 2013).

The HL7 organization is not-for-profit, and is accredited by the American National Standards Institutes (ANSI). HL7 defines how to translate and exchange health data between several systems. This can be achieved using the provided framework, which is capable of sharing, merging, withdrawing and trading data according to previously defined standards.

5. OPEN RESEARCH ISSUES AND FUTURE TRENDS

Paying close attention to the evolution of the health market, there are some clear trends in eHealth(AbuKhousa, Mohamed & Al-Jaroodi, 2012). While relying on ICT, eHealth benefits from the effects brought forth by the still valid Moore Law that roughly claims that each 18 months, the number of transistors per integrated circuit doubles.

This invariably means more processing power on smaller devices, a fact that can be witnessed in devices, such as the physioPlux and the BITalino, not to mention the commodity devices, such as the wearable ECG monitoring and respiratory bands from sports equipment manufacturers.

Regarding miniaturization and smaller devices, two major achievements are still unmet: the construction of easy to charge, durable and light batteries, and the invention of self-chargeable, energy harvesting sensors and devices. There is strong ongoing research on both these challenges, and it is expectable that the 2010 decade does not end without these products becoming a commodity too. Combining low-power electronics with secure communication protocols, and using long life, maybe self-rechargingbatteries, all the elements will be united to the development of truly ubiquitous computing and therefore, pervasive eHealth devices.

The miniaturization of electrical devices and the widespread use of wireless networks have empowered the development of Body Area Networks (BANs).A BAN consists of a set of mobile and small size intercommunicating sensors, which are either wearable or can be implanted into the human body for monitoring vital signs and/or environmental parameters and movements. The use of BANs in healthcare applications has shown to be beneficial due to its communication efficiency and cost-effectiveness. Physiological signals obtained by body sensors can be effectively processed to obtain reliable and accurate physiological estimations and, at the same time, the ultralow power consumption provision of such sensors makes their batteries long-lasting (Acampora *et al.*, 2013). Furthermore, BANs are scalable and integrable with other network infrastructures, such as Wireless Sensor Networks (WSNs), radio frequency identification tags (RFID), Bluetooth Low Energy (BLE), etc.

Yet, the sensors' limited resources in terms of energy, bandwidth, memory, and computational capability are a research challenge to overcome so BANs can be widely used. Also, since the performance of BANs is closely related to people's health, it is important to have safe sensor networks in which the requirements of medical data privacy, confidentiality, authentication, and integrity should be satisfied. The lack of security in the operation and communication of resource-constrained medical sensor nodes in BANs has been an obstacle to move the technology forward (Zhang *et al.*, 2012).

Besides BAN, sensors are being embedded into environments, resulting in intelligent and proactive living environments capable of supporting and enhancing daily life. In particular, Wireless Mesh Sensor Networks (WMSNs) could be used for designing unobtrusive, interconnected, adaptable, dynamic and intelligent environments where processors and sensors are embedded in everyday objects (Acampora *et al.*, 2013).

Until these monitoring and therapeutic devices are not autonomous, small and cheap, the promise of the Internet of Things, or as some companies like to name it not, the Internet of Everything, will not be fulfilled. And of course, e-health devices are an important part of this future Internet, because the drive and need to permanent and reliable monitoring of our bodies as a mean to reach a higher quality in life is very strong.

When this happens, and to some extent, it has been happening for a while, the data will start to pile in the servers, and we will need to find a manner to address the enormous volume of bio-physiological, behavioral, positional, informational, genetic and epigenetic, and social interaction data, among others. Making sense of this volume of data is a task for the computer science area termed Big Data.

The number of Internet websites related to a particular disease or condition, or to a particular life-style or philosophy, will also grow. The aim of these sites is to provide the Internet, the end user and the health care providers, a view of similar experiences at all levels, medication experiments and treatment, contributing strongly to what has been common to call the empowered user paradigm. Through these websites, the knowledge is no longer only on the side of the healthcare professionals such as physicians, pharmacists, nurses and so on, but increasingly on the side of the patient, who often arrives at a consultation with a self-diagnosis. Unfortunately, often this is an ill-formed diagnostic, and here lies the true challenge to this type of information sharing websites, to define what is trustworthy and what is just misinformation and repeated misconception. The mechanisms to expunge the malignant information may again be a task for Big Data, if we have the necessary number of data items and we apply some basic statistical concepts.

A final trend must not be discarded, and this is related to the use of a wider variety of sensors. The last few years we have seen a number of sensors being created, and many of them integrated into mobile phones, cars, domestic appliances and so on. The mass use of invasive body sensors has been halted by two reasons, the first related to the problems that energizing these sensors carry, and the second related to regulatory and legal issues.

Combining all the previous aforementioned trends, the future of e-health, we dare say, will be permanent and pervasive Personalized Health Care Services and in particular, Personalized Medicine. Using pervasive sensing and reliable communication channels, with virtually inexhaustible or self-chargeable light weight batteries, with a strong Internet infrastructure that provides not only the communication and data transmission means, but also the hosting and processing of the Peta Bytes of data each of us will generate, storing them in the Cloud alongside with the Big Data applications that will crunch this data to find the hidden patterns of our body health status. This will allow for making precise, time sensible decisions regarding the correction of behaviors and lifestyles, the administration of drugs and medicines, ultimately translated into a type of supervision over our health state that would be equivalent to having a well-trained and informed team of doctors permanently monitoring our bio-signals and living by our side.

ACKNOWLEDGMENT

This work was supported by FCT projectPEst-OE/EEI/L A0008/2013 (Este trabalho foi suportado pelo projecto FCT PEst-OE/EEI/LA0008/2013). The authors would also like to acknowledge the contribution of the COST Action IC1303 – AAPELE – Architectures, Algorithms and Protocols

REFERENCES

Abdel-Aal, R. (2004). Abductive Network Committees for Improved Classification of Medical Data. *Methods of Information in Medicine*, *43*(2), 192–201. PMID:15136869

Abdel-Aal, R. (2005). Improved Classification of Medical Data Using Abductive Network Committees Trained on Different Feature Subsets. *Computer Methods and Programs in Biomedicine*, *80*(2), 141–153. doi:10.1016/j.cmpb.2005.08.001 PMID:16169631

AbuKhousa, E., Mohamed, N., & Al-Jaroodi, J. (2012). e-Health Cloud: Opportunities and Challenges. *Future Internet*, *4*(3), 621–645. doi:10.3390/fi4030621

Acampora, G., Cook, D. J., Rashidi, P., & Vasilakos, A. V. (2013). A Survey on Ambient Intelligence in Health Care. *Proceedings of the IEEE*, *101*(12), 2470–2494. doi:10.1109/JPROC.2013.2262913 PMID:24431472

Accenture. (2010). *Information Governance The Foundation for Effective e-Health.* White Paper. Retrieved from http://www.accenture.com/SiteCollectionDocuments/PDF/Accenture_100473_InfoGovPoV_Final.pdf

Alwan, A., Armstrong, T., Bettcher, D., Branca, F., Chisholm, D., Ezzati, M., et al. (2011). Global status report on noncommunicable diseases. *World Health Organization (WHO).* Retrieved from http://www.who.int/nmh/publications/ncd_report2010/en/

Ambient Assisted Living (AAL). (2012). *Success Stories.* Retrieved from http://www.aal-europe.eu/success-stories/

Avery Dennison Corporation. (2013). *Metria*™. Retrieved January from http://www.averydennison.com/en/home/technologies/creative-showcase/metria-wearable-sensor.html

Blaya, J. A., Fraser, H. S. F., & Holt, B. (2010). E-Health Technologies Show Promise In Developing Countries. *Health Affairs*, *29*(2), 244–251. doi:10.1377/hlthaff.2009.0894 PMID:20348068

BodyMedia, Inc. (2013). *BodyMedia FIT.* Retrieved from http://www.bodymedia.com/the_interface.html

Borges, L. M., Araújo, P., Lebres, A. S., Rente, A., Salvado, R., & Velez, F. J. et al. (2010). Wearable sensors for foetal movement monitoring in low risk pregnancies. In S. C. Mukhopadhyay & A. Lay-Ekuakille (Eds.), *Wearable and Autonomous Biomedical Devices and Systems for Smart Environment: Issues and Characterization* (pp. 115–136). Springer. doi:10.1007/978-3-642-15687-8_6

Boulos, M. N. K., Lou, R. C., Anastasiou, A., Nugent, C. D., Alexandersson, J., & Zimmermann, G. et al. (2009). Connectivity for Healthcare and Well-Being Management: Examples from Six European Projects. *International Journal of Environmental Research and Public Health*, *6*(7), 1947–1971. doi:10.3390/ijerph6071947 PMID:19742164

Boulos, M.N.K, Rocha, A., Martins, A., Vicente, M.E., Bolz, A., Feld, R., & …, Kinirons, M. (2007). CAALYX: A new generation of location-based services in healthcare. *International Journal of Health Geographics*, *6*(9). PMID:17352802

Boulos, M. N. K., Wheeler, S., Tavares, C., & Jones, R. (2011). How smartphones are changing the face of mobile and participatory healthcare: An overview, with example from eCAALYX. *Biomedical Engineering Online*, *10*(24). PMID:21466669

CamNtech Ltd and CamNtech Inc. (2012). *Actiheart*. Retrieved from http://www.camntech.com/products/actiheart/actiheart-overview

Centre de Recerca I Inovació de Catalunya (CRIC). (2012) *Softcare: Unobtrusive plug and play kit for chronic condition based on customized behaviour recognition*. Retrieved from http://www.cric.cat/project-detail/16/

Chen, M., Gonzalez, S., Vasilakos, A., Cao, H., & Leung, V. C. M. (2011). Body Area Networks: A Survey. *Journal Mobile Network Application*, *16*(2), 171–193. doi:10.1007/s11036-010-0260-8

Cooking Hacks. (2013). *e-Health Sensor Platform for Arduino and Rasperry Pi* [Biometric/Medical Applications]. Retrieved from http://www.cooking-hacks.com/documentation/tutorials/ehealth-v1-biometric-sensor-platform-arduino-raspberry-pi-medical/

Cuno, S., Glickman, Y., Baboshin, A., Haritou, M., Serretti, A., Androulidakis, A., & Calati, R. (2011). Management, Monitoring and Supporting Dementia Patients at Home by ALADDIN. In *Proceedings of eChallenges e-2011*. IIMC International Information Management Corporation.

Dong, N., Jonker, H., & Pang, J. (2012). Challenges in eHealth: From Enabling to Enforcing Privacy. In Z. Liu & A. Wassyng (Eds.), *Foundations of Health Informatics Engineering and System* (pp. 195–206). Springer. doi:10.1007/978-3-642-32355-3_12

Handford, R. (2013). *Telefonica reveals future plans following Parkinson's trial*. Retrieved from http://www.mobileworldlive.com/telefonica-announces-results-future-plans-following-parkinsons-trial

Haritou, M., Glickman, Y., Androulidakis, A., Xefteris, S., Anastasiou, A., & Baboshin, A. et al. (2012). A Technology Platform for a Novel Home Care Delivery Service to Patients with Dementia. *Journal of Medical Imaging and Health Informatics*, *2*(1), 1–7. doi:10.1166/jmihi.2012.1060

Health Stats. (2010). *PULSE CASPro®*. Retrieved from http://www.healthstats.com/index3.php?page=product_apulsepro

Hendeby, G., Bleser, G., Lamprinos, I., & Stricker, D. (2010). Healthy Aging using Physical Activity Monitoring. In *Proceedings of AALIANCE Conference*. Malaga, Spain: AALIANCE.

Ineed MD, Inc. (2012). *EKG Glove™*. Retrieved from http://www.ineedmd.com/public/features.html

IS-ACTIVE Project– Inertial Sensing System for Advanced Chronic Condition Monitoring and RiskPrevention. (2010). *WP2 – Architecture, Architecture Specification* (Deliverable D2.2). Retrieved from http://www.is-active.eu/deliverables/

Larson, E., Lee, T., Liu, S., Rosenfeld, M., & Patel, S. N. (2011). Accurate and Privacy Preserving Cough Sensing using a Low-Cost Microphone. In *Proceedings of the 13th International Conference on Ubiquitous Computing* (UbiComp 2011). Beijing, China: ACM. doi:10.1145/2030112.2030163

McAdams, E., Krupaviciute, A., Gehin, C., Dittmar, A., Delhomme, G., & Rubel, P. et al. (2011). Wearable Electronic Systems: Applications to Medical Diagnostics/Monitoring. In A. Bonfiglio & D. De Rossi (Eds.), *Wearable Monitoring Systems* (pp. 179–203). Springer. doi:10.1007/978-1-4419-7384-9_9

Minnesota e-Health Initiative and the Minnesota Department of Health. (2013). *Glossary of Selected Terms and Acronyms*. White Paper. Retrieved from http://www.health.state.mn.us/e-health/glossary/ehealthglossary.pdf

Murray, E. (2012). Web-Based Interventions for Behavior Change andSelf-Management: Potential, Pitfalls, and Progress. *Medicine 2.0, 1*(2e3).

Prakash, D. (2012). *New Patch-Based Wearable Sensor Combines Advanced Skin Adhesive and Sensor Technologies*. Retrieved from http://www.mdtmag.com/articles/2012/07/new-patch-based-wearable-sensor-combines-advanced-skin-adhesives-and-sensor-technologies

Ragesh, G. K., & Baskaran, K. (2012). A Survey on Futuristic Health Care System: WBANs. *Procedia Engineering, 30*, 889–896. doi:10.1016/j.proeng.2012.01.942

REMOTE Project. (2012). *Remote health and social care for independent living of isolated elderly with chronic conditions*. Retrieved from http://www.remote-project.eu/

ROSETTA Project. (2012a). Retrieved from http://www.aal-rosetta.eu/

ROSETTA Project. (2012b). *Guidance and Awareness Services for Independent Living* (Flyer). Retrieved from http://www.aal-rosetta.eu/Site_rosetta/docs/ROSETTA_Flyer_e_IESE-100118.pdf

Sáez, I., Oliveras, M., Ciudad, M. J., Fort, I., Llopart, J. R., & Haritou, M., & the Aladdin Research Consortium. (2011). *A Technology Platform for the Assisted Living of Dementia Elderly Individuals and their Carers*. Paper presented at the 7th Congress of the European Union Geriatric Medicine Society (EUGMS). Malaga, Spain.

Sánchez-Tato, I., Senciales, J. C., Salinas, J., Fanucci, L., Pardini, G., Costalli, F., et al. (2010). Health @ Home: A telecare system for patients with chronic heart failure. In *Proceedings of Fifth International Conference on Broadband and Biomedical Communications (IB2Com)*. Malaga, Spain: IB2Com. doi:10.1109/IB-2COM.2010.5723634

Saponara, S., Donati, M., Bacchillone, T., Fanucci, L., Sanchez-Tato, I., Carmona, C., & Barba, P. (2012). Remote monitoring of vital signs in patients with chronic heart failure: Sensor devices and data analysis perspective. In *Proceedings of Sensors Applications Symposium (SAS) 2012*. Brescia, Italy: SAS. doi:10.1109/SAS.2012.6166310

Stellefson, M., Chaney, B., Barry, A.E., Chavarria, E., Tennant, B., Walsh-Childers, K., Sriram,P.S, Zagora, J. (2013). Web 2.0 Chronic Disease Self-Management for Older Adults: A Systematic Review. *Journal of Medical Internet Research, 15*(2e35).

Swan, M. (2012). Sensor Mania! The Internet of Things, Wearable Computing, Objective Metrics, and the Quantified Self 2.0. *Journal of Sensor and Actuator Networks, 1*(3), 217–253. doi:10.3390/jsan1030217

Texas Instruments. (2014). *eZ430-Chronos™ Development Tool*. Retrieved from http://www.ti.com/tool/ez430-chronos

Trindade, I. G., Lucas, J., Miguel, R., Alpuim, P., Carvalho, M., & Garcia, N. M. (2010). Lightweight Portable Sensors for Health Care. In *Proceedings of 12th IEEE International Conference on e-Health Networking Applications and Services (Healthcom)*. Lyon, France: IEEE. doi:10.1109/HEALTH.2010.5556575

Vivonoetics. (2013). *LifeShirt*. Retrieved from http://vivonoetics.com/products/sensors/lifeshirt/

Waterworth, J. A., Ballesteros, S., & Peter, C. (2009). User-sensitive Home-based Systems for Successful Ageing. In *Proceedings of 2nd Conference on Human Systems Interactions*. Catania, Italy: Academic Press.

Zhang, Z., Wang, H., Vasilakos, A. V., & Fang, H. (2012). ECG-Cryptography and Authentication in Body Area Networks. *IEEE Transactions on Information Technology in Biomedicine*, *16*(6), 1070–1078. doi:10.1109/TITB.2012.2206115 PMID:22752143

Zhou, J., Cao, Z., Dong, X., Lin, X., & Vasilakos, A. V. (2013). Securing m-Healthcare Scial Networks: Challenges, Countermeasures and Future Directions. *IEEE Wireless Communications*, *20*(4), 12–21. doi:10.1109/MWC.2013.6590046

KEY TERMS AND DEFINITIONS

Ambient Assisted Living: New area that use of information and communication technology to enable new products, services, and processes that help to provide safe, healthy, lives for the aged and for people in recovery.

Chronic Diseases: Diseases that have one or more of the following characteristics: they are permanent; they produce inability or residual disability, are caused by irreversible pathological changes, require special training of the patient for rehabilitation, or may require long periods of supervision, observation or care.

E-Health: Healthcare practice supported by information and communication technologies and electronic processes.

Multi-Sensors Platforms: Integrated technology that enables ubiquitous presence of sensing, computing and communication capabilities and hence, enable a large number of application domains.

Tele-Monitoring: Healthcare practice involving remotely monitoring of patients who are not at the same location as the health care provider.

Section 5

Government-to-Business and Citizen Communications and Services

Chapter 17
Evaluating E-Government Initiatives:
An Approach Based upon the Appropriation of Tangible and Intangible Benefits

Antonio Juarez Alencar
Federal University of Rio de Janeiro (UFRJ), Brazil

Eber Assis Schmitz
Federal University of Rio de Janeiro (UFRJ), Brazil

Marcelo Carvalho Fernandes
Federal University of Rio de Janeiro (UFRJ), Brazil

Alexandre Luis Correa
Federal University of the State of Rio de Janeiro (UNIRIO), Brazil

ABSTRACT

Over the last decade, governments around the word have made substantial investments in e-government initiatives with the aim of improving the efficiency and effectiveness of public services. While some of these initiatives are aimed at improving tax collection and reducing running costs, the main benefits that they provide are intangibles such as greater taxpayer satisfaction and increased transparency in government decisions. This chapter presents a method to analyse e-government initiatives. The method takes into consideration that these initiatives are frequently comprised of several projects that are divided into a number of subprojects. Moreover, it evaluates e-government initiatives through a balanced view of the tangible and intangible benefits they provide. All of this is made clear with the support of a real-world inspired example.

INTRODUCTION

In many countries the interest of civil servants in information and communication technology (ICT) goes back to the very beginning of the commercial electronic computer era in the 1950's. For example, in the United States the first electronic computer to be commercially available, the UNIVAC I, was bought by the US Census Bureau, which used it to predict the results of elections and analyse economic time series. The next six UNIVAC sever built were also bought by US government agencies,

DOI: 10.4018/978-1-4666-7266-6.ch017

such as the Air Force, the Army Map Service, the Atomic Energy Commission and the Navy (Campbell-Kelly, Aspray, Ensmenger, & Yost, 2013). Government has also been an early adopter of ICT in Canada, the United Kingdom, Germany, Brazil and many other countries (Frauenfelder, 2013; Raum, 2008; Vardalas, 2001).

Nevertheless, the role that ICT has played in both the private and public sectors has changed quite considerably over the course of time. From a machine that is able to perform calculations at high speed, computers have been used as an aid to capture, store and transform information efficiently, and as an enabler of process automation. Also, they have been used to build support tools for data analysis and better decision making.

As a result, in many markets ICT has become an important element in business strategy. Moreover, nowadays the very existence of numerous companies depends on ICT, especially those that thrive on the virtual world, such as search-engine service providers, e-book editing and publishing companies, digital marketing agencies and on-line distance learning institutions (Barnes & Hunt, 2013).

In the public sector ICT has allowed for the construction of numerous computerized systems with the view of improving the efficiency, effectiveness, transparency and accountability of public services. Moreover, such systems facilitate the interaction between citizens and government, government and businesses, government and civil servants, government and its agencies, and also among the different branches of government at municipal, state and federal levels. In the literature these computerized systems are usually referred to as e-government, or e-gov for short (Almarabeh & AbuAli, 2010; Wahid, 2012).

All of this has instigated the development of a large number of concepts, techniques and methods to support the analysis of ICT investments (Peffers & Santos, 2013). Despite government being one of the biggest investors in ICT in developed and developing nations, the vast majority of the methods proposed so far are aimed at the private sector (Kundra, 2010; Wilkin, Campbell, & Moore, 2013).

Because the private and public sectors differ substantially in their goals, culture and management structure, it would be naive to simply apply methods developed to analyse investment in one sector to the other (Campbell, McDonald, & Sethibe, 2010; Rosacker & Rosacker, 2010).

This chapter presents a method to better analyse e-gov initiatives. The method is based upon the ideas of Thomas L. Saaty (2013) on the evaluation of intangibles and Mark Denne and Jane Cleland-Huang (2013) on the incremental funding of ICT projects. The method addresses many relevant questions concerning the investment in e-gov initiatives that have been neglected by others (see the RELATED WORK section in this respect). As a consequence, it provides civil servants with a tool that allows them to make better investment decisions.

The remainder of this chapter is organized as follows. The RELATED WORK section reviews meaningful contributions to the improvement of e-gov evaluation methods and identifies their shortcomings. The BACKGROUND section presents a review of the principal concepts, methods and techniques used in the subsequent sections. The EXAMPLE section introduces the method with the help of a reasonably complex example. The METHOD section describes the method presented in this chapter in more formal terms. The CONCLUSION section presents the conclusion of this chapter.

RELATED WORK

Over the course of time many valuable proposals to augment the coverage, effectiveness and precision of e-gov evaluation methods have been presented. For example, Raus et al. (Raus, Liu, & Kipp, 2010) have devised a value assessment framework that can be used to access business-to-government ICT innovations. The framework incorporates the value perspectives of both the private and public sectors, and the needs and requirements of various stakeholders, facilitating the assessment of ICT innovations.

According to Raus et al. the framework is composed of two main parts. The first considers stakeholders' goals and the business areas that require monitoring to build a value matrix. The matrix not only creates a structure in which different assessment value categories can be properly compared, but also it facilitates the understanding of what ICT dimensions are most worthy of having their value assessed. The second part of the framework adopts a multi-step procedure to guide stakeholders through the process of deriving assessment criteria, accessing the ICT innovation value and communicating the result of the evaluation to interested parties. According to the authors, the combination of the two parts allows the framework to be applied in an efficient and effective manner.

Srivastava, on the other hand, suggests the use of a different framework to evaluate the impact of e-government initiatives (Srivastava, 2011). Srivastava's framework takes into consideration two important dimensions of ICT initiatives in the public sector, i.e. the government and the citizen dimensions. The former is concerned with the policy making process, the effectiveness of the managerial structure and the compliance by organizations and the general public with rules and legislation. The latter considers the financial, political, social, ideological, and stewardship aspects of e-gov initiatives.

Srivastava claims that the returns yielded by e-gov initiatives can be more thoroughly analysed by considering the value they create with respect to these two dimensions. Moreover, he argues that the impact on the government and the citizen dimensions stems from improving the efficiency and effectiveness of targeted process at local, state, and central levels.

Guclu and Bilgen recommend the use of a multi-dimension model for assessing government information systems (IS) initiatives (Guclu & Bilgen, 2011). The model combines four dimensions of value creation:

1. **Agency Value:** The financial and nonfinancial savings provided by the initiative,
2. **User Value:** The benefits yielded to the general public by the IS,
3. **Political Value:** The improvement in perception of how well the government performs its designated role in society, and
4. **Social Value:** How strongly the initiative contributes to improve the well-being of the general population, the fight against exclusion and marginalization, the creation of a sense of belonging, the promotion of trust, and upward mobility.

According to Guclu and Bilgenthe assessment model allows not only for the ex-ante assessment of the value of IS initiatives, but also their ex-post effectiveness and impact on society. Moreover, the authors claim that the model can be used for the continuous monitoring of IS initiatives during their development and implementation. Real world data obtained from a portfolio of IS projects run by the Turkish government is presented to demonstrate the use of the model.

A group of researchers led by Neuronihas developed a framework to assess the value and cost effectiveness of e-government initiatives (Neuroni, Rascon, Spichiger, & Riedl, 2010). The framework advocates the use of a four-step process. The first step consists in eliciting the goals of the initiative, together with the context in which it is going to be developed.

The second step involves the financial evaluation of the initiative. In this step the net present value (NPV) of the initiative is estimated. Flexibility is added to the financial evaluation through the use of real options. In this context, real options refers to a financial appraisal technique that takes into account the possibility of either expanding or calling off a project, if certain conditions are met. Neuroni et al. claim that the use of real options allowsus to capture the flexibility that is intrinsic to ICT projects in the public sector. See Larrabee and Voss (2013) for a thorough introduction to real options concepts and techniques.

In a third step, qualitative variables are used to identify the intangible benefits provided by the initiative. Finally, in the fourth step the findings of the previous steps are consolidated and different projects are compared for possible selection. Neuroni et al. show how their model can be used in practise by presenting a case study involving the Swiss government.

Finally, Tan et al.(Tan, Theodorou, & Over, 2009) sanction the adoption of an e-gov investment management model as a means of unveiling what investment decisions are to be made, who should make those decisions, how these decisions are to be made and how they should be monitored and controlled. Hence, the model provides an integrated approach to selection, evaluation, monitoring and control of e-gov investments across their lifecycle.

Moreover, Tan's investment model advocates the use of a structured process to assure that investments are well thought-out, are cost effective, support the strategic plan, minimize risk and maximize return on investment. The process is divided into three phases:

1. **Preselect Phase:** In which needs are identified, analysed, and documented,
2. **Select Phase:** Which is concerned with the identification of the e-gov investments that best support current mission, strategic goals and mandates, and
3. **Monitoring and Control Phase:** Which ensures that e-gov investments are developed and deployed using disciplined, well-managed and consistent practices.

Cao et al. and Peffers and Santos present reviews of the existing literature on return on investments made in e–gov projects, and of different approaches to assessing such returns (Cao, Mohan, Ramesh, & Sarkar, 2013; Peffers & Santos, 2013).

However, all the proposals presented so far fall short on one or more of the following points:

1. Acknowledging that it is often the case that a single e-gov initiative leads to several projects that are naturally divided into subprojects (Rose & Grant, 2010),
2. Accepting that some of these projects and subprojects do provide financial returns when they are completed, while others simply lay down the infrastructure needed by the e-gov initiative (Doria, Alencar, Schmitz, Correa, & Vital, 2012),
3. Taking advantage of the fact that the financial returns yielded by some e-gov projects and subprojects can be used to finance the development of other system parts (Doria, Alencar, Schmitz, Correa, & Vital, 2012),
4. Considering that the order in which return-provider and infrastructure-provider projects and subprojects are developed may considerably change the value of the e-gov initiative as a whole (Kukreja, Payyavula, Boehm, & Padmanabhuni, 2012), and
5. Taking into account that e-gov initiatives may yield both tangible and intangible benefits (Barbosa, Pozzebon, & Diniz, 2013).

The method proposed in this chapter addresses questions 1 to 5. As a result, it provides decision makers with a tool that allows for better investment decisions with respect to e-gov initiatives, especially those that rely solely on taxpayer's money.

BACKGROUND

Tangible and Intangible Benefits

In financial terms an asset is an economic resource, i.e. something of value that can be controlled or owned. For example, flats, shares in companies, software, and plane tickets are common examples of valuable economic resources. In fact, as they can be controlled or owned, they are all examples of assets.

It should be noted that the value of an asset derives from the benefits that it provides to its controllers or owners. A flat, for instance, can be sold, leased or rented out. The payment made for the right to use a property as its owner or tenant can be used to pay for other products and services (Amadi-Echendu et al., 2010).

Some of the benefits provided by an asset are intangibles (i.e. they are drawn from subjective perceptions of reality that do not have an easily quantifiable financial embodiment). For example, the pride of graduating from a prestigious university or the feeling of happiness that comes from wining an important competition are examples of intangible benefits that one usually earns through dedication and hard work(Hubbard, 2010).

Because government actions are not directed at making a profit, e-gov initiatives tend to yield a variety of intangibles, including increased taxpayer satisfaction, greater transparency in government decisions and more accountability of how civil servants perform their jobs (Tan, Benbasat, & Cenfetelli, 2010).

Dealing with Intangibles

Because the value of intangible benefits depends on perceptions of reality, their value tends to be difficult to quantify. Nevertheless, according to Saaty the value of intangibles are easier to analyse when they are compared in pairs (Saaty, 2013). For a set E= { E_1, E_2, …, E_n } whose elements can be compared using the same criterion, the pairwise comparison advocated by Saaty leads to the construction of the squared valuation matrix V presented in Table 1.

A closer look at Table 1 reveals that V is a matrix in which all the main diagonal elements are 1s. Furthermore, every element $v_{i,j}$ of V is either drawn from Table 2 or is the reciprocal of an element drawn from that table.

If E_2 is moderately more relevant than E_1, then $v_{2,1} = 3$ and $v_{1,2} = 1/3$. In addition, let E_3 be strongly more relevant than E_1, and just a bit more relevant than E2. In these circumstances, $v_{3,1} = 5$ and $v_{1,3} = 1/5$, and $v_{3,2} = 2$ and $v_{2,3} = 1/2$. The valuation matrix presented in Table 3 captures this

Table 1. Saaty's valuation matrix

Valuation Matrix

$$
V = \begin{array}{cc|cccc}
 & & E_1 & E_2 & & E_n \\
 & & \downarrow & \downarrow & \cdots & \downarrow \\
\hline
E_1 & \rightarrow & 1 & \frac{1}{v_{2,1}} & \cdots & \frac{1}{v_{n,1}} \\
E_2 & \rightarrow & v_{2,1} & 1 & \cdots & \frac{1}{v_{n,2}} \\
\vdots & \vdots & \vdots & \vdots & \vdots & \vdots \\
E_n & \rightarrow & v_{n,1} & v_{n,2} & \cdots & 1
\end{array}
$$

Table 2. The fundamental scale of pairwise comparison proposed by Saaty

Intensity of Relevance	Definition
1	**Equal Relevance:** The two elements are equally relevant when compared to each other
3	**Moderate Relevance:** Experience and judgment moderately favour one element over the other
5	**Strong Relevance:** Experience and judgment strongly favour one element over the other
7	**Very Strong:** An element is favoured very strongly over the other
9	**Extreme Relevance:** The evidence favouring one element over the other is of the highest possible order of affirmation
2,4,6,8	**Intermediate Values:** Should be used when compromise is needed

Table 3. Saaty's valuation matrix regarding the elements E_1, E_2, and E_3

Valuation Matrix				
		E_1 ↓	E_2 ↓	E_3 ↓
E_1	→	1	$\frac{1}{3}$	$\frac{1}{5}$
E_2	→	3	1	$\frac{1}{2}$
E_3	→	5	2	1

information. It should be noted that an element is always equally relevant when compared to itself. As a result, $v_{1,1} = v_{2,2} = v_{3,3} = 1$.

According to (Saaty, 2013), the relevance of the elements that are submitted to the pairwise comparison procedure is given by the components of the normalized main eigenvector of V. Therefore, if $(e_1, e_2, \ldots, e_n)^T$ is this eigenvector, then

$$\sum_{k=1}^{n} e_k = 1$$

and the relevance of an element $E_i \in E$ is given by the vector component e_i. Often e_i is referred to as the relevance index of E_i or $RI(E_i)$.

For example, $(0.110, 0.309, 0.581)^T = (11.0\%, 30.9\%, 58.1\%)^T$ is the normalized main eigenvector of the valuation matrix presented in Table 3. Therefore, $RI(E_1) = 11.0\%$, $RI(E_2) = 30.9\%$ and $RI(E_3) = 58.1\%$. As a result, E_3 is the most relevant element for decision making, E_2 comes in second place and E_1 comes last.

As the evaluation of intangibles relies on subjective perceptions of reality, it is not unusual that valuation matrices present inconsistencies. If these inconsistencies are considerable, then they have to be resolved before the relevance indexes can be used for decision making. According to Saaty (op. cit.) these inconsistencies are easily detected by the consistency ratio (CR). For a given n × n valuation matrix V

$$CR = \frac{Cl}{RND}$$

where CI, the consistency index, is the result of $(\lambda_{max} - n) / (n - 1)$ and RND, the random index, is drawn from Table 4 according to n. Note that λ_{max} is the main eigenvalue of V.

As stated in (Saaty, 2013), for 3 × 3 matrices a $CR \geq 0.05$ indicates that the inconsistencies should be fixed. For 4 × 4 matrices the threshold increases to 0.09, and for 5×5 and larger matrices the threshold is 0.10. The CR of the valuation matrix presented in Table 3 is 0.004. Hence it can be safely used for decision making.

See (Klein, 2013) for a comprehensive introduction to eigenvectors, eigenvalues and their applications in computer science and decision making. Saaty's method is often referred to as AHP (Analytic Hierarchy Process). A survey of the many problems that the AHP has been used to solve can be found in (Sipahi & Timor, 2010).

The Incremental Funding of ICT Projects

According to (Denne & Cleland-Huang, 2004)ICT projects can be divided into two different kinds of

Table 4. The random index table

n	1	2	3	4	5	6	7	8	9
RI	0.00	0.00	0.58	0.90	1.12	1.24	1.32	1.41	1.45

subprojects, i.e. those that provide financial returns to investors as soon as they are finished and those that lay down the infrastructure necessary for the development of other subprojects. Denne and Cleland-Huang have named the former minimum marketable feature subprojects (MMFs) and the latter architectural element (AEs).

As it is claimed by those researchers,the order in which MMFs and AEs are developed may substantially change the value of a project as a whole. For example, consider the diagram presented in Figure 1.

In the diagram *Begin* and *End* are dummy subprojects. They indicate respectively the beginning and end of the development of the whole scheme. They take no time to be built, require no capital investment and yield no final products. Furthermore, A, B, C, D and E are either MMFs or AEs. An arrow going from a subproject to another, i.e. A → B, indicates that the development of the latter can only begin when the former is completed. It should be noted that the dependency relation indicated by the arrows is transitive. Therefore, as B → C, then necessarily A → C. Often transitive dependency relations are not presented in dependency diagrams so as to keep them simple.

As stated by Milton Friedman (1912-2006), the American economist and Nobel Prize laureate: "There's no such thing as a free lunch" (Friedman, Savage, & Becker, 2007).Therefore, all the subprojects in Figure 1 require capital investment in order to be developed (Gentle, 2007). Also, while MMF subprojects provide some financial return when they are completed, AE subprojects do not. All of this is captured by the subproject's cash flow presented in Table 5.

It should be noted that project A requires an initial investment of $50,000 (fifty thousand monetary units) or $50K for short. When A is completed it provides no financial returns. The same pattern is followed by subproject B. Therefore, both A and B are AEs.

However, subproject C follows a different path. Although, it requires an initial investment of $100K, it yields a continuous return of $80K from period 2 to 10. The subprojects D and E follow the same pattern. As a result, all these subprojects are MMFs. It might strike the reader that the flow of financial returns ends at the tenth period. The reasons for this are simple; at this point the whole system becomes obsolete and is replaced by a more up to date technological solution. The period of time from the beginning of the development of a project (or a set of subprojects) until it has to be replaced by a better solution is usually referred to as its window of opportunity.

One should not perform arithmetic operations on monetary figures associated with different time periods without taking a discount rate into consideration. Therefore, in order to be able to compare the financial value of different subprojects, one should use their discounted cash-flow.

Figure 1. Dependency diagram of MMF and AE subprojects

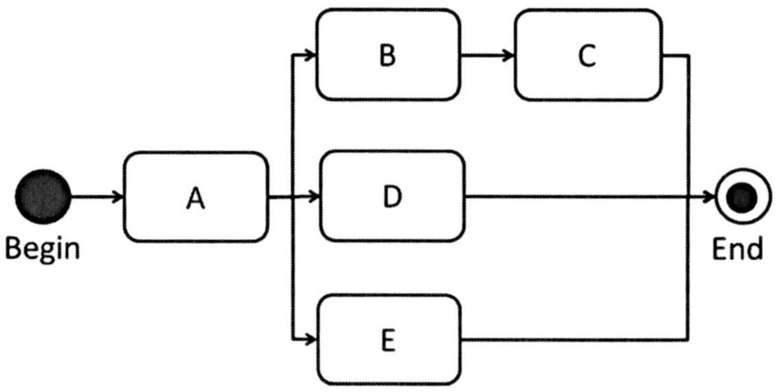

Table 5. Cash flow of MMF and AE subprojects

Subproj.	Period ($ 1.000)									
	1	2	3	4	5	6	7	8	9	10
A	-50	0	0	0	0	0	0	0	0	0
B	-75	0	0	0	0	0	0	0	0	0
C	-100	80	80	80	80	80	80	80	80	80
D	-60	20	20	20	20	20	20	20	20	20
E	-50	40	40	40	40	40	40	40	40	40

Table 6 presents the sum of discounted net cash flow elements of each subproject according to the period in which they are developed. It is assumed that once the development of a subproject starts it cannot be interrupted until the subproject is completed. The sum of the discounted net cash flow elements of a subproject is often referred to as its net present value (NPV).

Therefore, considering an interest rate of 0.8%, if the development of subproject C starts at period 1 it yields a NPV of

$$\$587K = \frac{-\$100K}{(1+0.8\%)^1} + \frac{\$80K}{(1+0.8\%)^2} + \frac{\$80K}{(1+0.8\%)^3} + \cdots + \frac{\$80K}{(1+0.8\%)^{10}}$$

In addition, if the development of C starts in the second period it yields an NPV of $509K, in the third $432K, so on and so forth. The monetary figures presented Table 6 have been rounded to the nearest integer value. In order to facilitate understanding the remaining monetary figures presented in this chapter follow the same convention.

It should be noted that different implementation sequences yield different NPVs. For example, consider the following implementation A → E → B → C → D. It yields an NPV of

$$NPV(A)_1 + NPV(E)_2 + NPV(B)_3 + NPV(C)_4 + NPV(D)_5 =$$

$$-\$50K + \$255K - \$73K + \$355K + \$36K =$$

$$\$523K,$$

where $NPV(\beta)_p$ is the NPV of subproject β, considering that its development starts in period p.

Moreover, the implementation sequence A → E → B → D → C yields a NPV of $465K and A → B → D → E → C yields $405K. Table 7 presents

Table 6. Discounted cash flow of MMF and AE subprojects according to the period when their development starts

Subproj.	Period ($ 1.000)									
	1	2	3	4	5	6	7	8	9	10
A	-50	-49	-49	-48	-48	-48	-47	-47	-47	-46
B	-74	-74	-73	-73	-72	-71	-71	-70	-70	-69
C	587	509	432	355	279	204	129	55	-19	-92
D	112	93	74	55	36	18	-1	-19	-37	-55
E	294	255	216	178	140	102	64	27	-10	-46

Table 7. Possible implementation sequences and their respective NPV

Id	Sequence	NPV ($1.000)
1	A → E → B → C → D	523
2	A → B → C → E → D	520
3	A → B → C → D → E	500
4	A → E → D → B → C	483
5	A → B → E → C → D	482
6	A → E → B → D → C	465
7	A → D → E → B → C	464
8	A → D → B → C → E	463
9	A → B → D → C → E	443
10	A → B → E → D → C	425
11	A → D → B → E → C	425
12	A → B → D → E → C	405

all possible implementation sequences for the subprojects introduced in Figure 1, together with their respective NPV.

This chapter combines the ideas of Saaty (op. cit.) on the evaluation of intangibles and Denne and Huang (op. cit.) on the financial appraisal of ICT projects to devise a method for analysing e-gov initiatives.

AN EXAMPLE

Because "a good example is the best sermon" (Isaacson, 2004), we initially present the method proposed in this chapter with the aid of a real-world inspired example. Readers may wish to refer to the next section, which provides a summary of the method.

Context Information

Consider a large city somewhere in the world. In the context of this chapter this city is referred to as Enki[1]. At present, the mayor of Enki wants to run a few innovative e-gov projects with the view of tackling some of the problems faced by its citizens.

As in most large cities, traffic going towards Enki's city centre is particularly slow in certain periods of the day. To better understand the causes of the problem the mayor ordered a study targeting people who drive their car in the city centre at peak hours. The study revealed that part of the problem stems from the excessive number of drivers who go to the city centre without knowing exactly where they are going to park their cars. If a parking space is not found straight away, drivers tend to go round in circles looking for a place to park. As a result, the number of cars being driven in the city centre streets and avenues increases unnecessarily.

However, a considerable percentage of the parking spaces in the city centre is run by the municipal government. Therefore, the mayor is in a position in which he can act to ease the search for vacant parking spaces and, as a result, make the traffic flow, avoiding congestion points. With this aim in mind he decided to order the development of a mobile application that allows drivers to book in advance the parking space they intend to use. If no parking space can be found on a particular day and time, people will feel compelled to use public transport or to re-plan their trip to the city centre. This mobile application project was named parking-space booking system, or PRK.

Moreover, as soon as the mayor's intention was made public, the private parking-space companies in the city centre expressed the desire to join the PRK project. Therefore, the PRK project has gained a new dimension.

The study also revealed that Enki's drivers are far from being model law-abiding citizens when it comes to traffic legislation. As they frequently break those laws, traffic in congested areas is much worse than it should be. What is more, the mayor has been heavily criticized by both the opposition and the press for doing little about it.

As a result, the mayor's office has decided to provide traffic officers with a mobile system that allows them to enforce traffic legislation by fining law-breaking drives straight away. The system, named motor-vehicle fining system, or FNG, is composed of a computer application, a tablet with a high definition camera and a mobile connection to the Internet. Furthermore, the system allows pictures to be taken from vehicles that are caught breaking the law, making it difficult for car owners to claim that the fine was an unfortunate mistake.

Finally, the mayor's office has been receiving many complaints about the difficulty in obtaining information from municipal agencies and offices. Although Enki's municipal website has plenty of information regarding legislation and services, the elderly tend to find it difficult to navigate. As a result, the mayor has decided to make an intelligent virtual agent (IVA) available on the site.

For those who are not familiar with IVAs it worth mentioning that they are computer programs one may interact with using natural language. When one poses a question the IVA provides an answer obtained from its knowledge base. The answer provided by an IVA may contain text, pictures, sound or a combination of these. An IVA can even redirect the Internet site one is currently looking at to facilitate access to the information one is after. It can also capture and update information stored in different databases (Budakova, 2013). The projects in the mayor's portfolio of e-gov projects are summarized in Table 8.

The Valuation Criteria

In a democratic city like Enki, the mayor is expected to stay in power for a pre-established period of time. Therefore, it is possible that only a subset of the e-gov projects in the mayor's portfolio can be implemented during his administration. Nevertheless, the mayor wants the citizens of Enki to enjoy the maximum possible benefits provided by those e-gov projects while he is in power. Also, as there are many other projects to be run in Enki, funding for the portfolio of e-gov projects is tight and should be used wisely.

To oversee the planning and execution of the portfolio of e-gov projects the mayor has nominated a steering committee composed of specialists in several areas. Before making any recommendations the committee has decided to evaluate the e-gov projects from the perspective of the criteria presented in Table 9.

Because all the criteria presented in Table 9 require judgment based on perceptions of reality, the steering committee decided to adhere to Saaty's ideas on the evaluation of intangibles. Consistent with the current political and financial landscape of Enki, the steering committee considers that the PBL is slightly more relevant than the MDC and moderately more relevant than the ENV. More-

Table 8. Projects in the mayor's portfolio of e-gov projects

Id	Project Description
PRK	**Parking-Space Booking System:** Enables drivers to book in advance parking space in the city centre
FNG	**Motor-Vehicle Fining System:** Allows police officers to fine vehicles that have broken the law
IVA	**Intelligent Virtual Agent:** Provides citizens with an automated system that answers questions about legislation and the services provided by the municipal government

Table 9. The main evaluation criteria

Id	Criterion Definition
PBL	**Intensity of Public Support:** Indicates the amount of support that a project can expect to receive from the general public
MDC	**Volume of Media Coverage:** Describes the anticipated amount of positive media coverage
ENV	**Positive Impact on the Environment:** Reflects the positive impact a project may have on the environment

over, the MDC is slightly more relevant than the ENV. The valuation matrix presented in Table 10 captures this information.

Observe that E = (53.9%, 29.7%, 16.4%)^T is the normalized eigenvector of the valuation matrix presented in Table 10. Therefore, according to the steering committee, the PBL is the most relevant criterion, the MDC comes in second and the ENV is the least relevant.

The Valuation of the E-Gov Projects in the Portfolio

It is importance to keep in mind that distinct projects may perform quite differently when subjected to specific criteria. For example, a project may be quite beneficial for the environment and yet gather little public support. Despite the fact that most electronic equipment contain substances that are dangerous to animals and plants, the sale of mobile phones and tablets has been soaring all over the world. Therefore, one could consider limiting the production of mobile phones. Although imposing a limit on the production of mobiles and other electronic devices could be good for the environment, if such a measure were ever taken it would most certainly be highly unpopular (Eddy, 2013; Gayle, 2012).

Therefore, the decisions to be made about the execution of a portfolio of e-gov projects are made easier by aweighted index. Such an index indicates the combined performance of each project in respect to a set of distinct criteria. As indicated by Saaty, this is accomplished by the weighted relevance index, or WRI. For a given projectP_k,

$$\mathrm{WRI}\left(\mathrm{P_k}\right)=\sum_{i=1}^{n}\mathrm{RI}\left(\mathrm{C_i}\right)\times\mathrm{RI_{Ci}}\left(\mathrm{P_k}\right) \qquad (1)$$

where RI(C_i) is the relevance index of criterion C_i, and $RI_{Ci}(P_k)$,is the relevance of P_k when subjected to criterion C_i.

For example, consider the evaluation criteria introduced in Table 9 and their respective relevance indexes presented in Table 10. Moreover, allow the evaluation matrices presented in Tables 11, 12, and 13 to capture the performance of the e-gov projects in each of those criteria.

It should be noted that the normalized main eigenvector of the valuation matrix presented in Table 11 is (24.9%, 66.9%, 8.8%)^T, indicating that the IVA project scores highly in the PS criterion. According to the steering committee's point of view the IVA is the most relevant project in this criterion. The PRK and IVA projects trail far behind.

Table 10. The relevance of the evaluation criteria (CR = 0.01)

Evaluation Criteria	PBL ↓	MDC ↓	ENV ↓	E(%) ↓
PBL →	1	2	3	53.9
MDC →	$\frac{1}{2}$	1	2	29.7
ENV →	$\frac{1}{3}$	$\frac{1}{2}$	1	16.4

Table 11. Intensity of public support generated by each project (CR = 0.09)

Public Support	PRK ↓	IVA ↓	FNG ↓	E(%) ↓
PRK →	1	$\frac{1}{3}$	3	24.9
IVA →	3	1	7	66.9
FNG →	$\frac{1}{3}$	$\frac{1}{7}$	1	8.8

Table 12. Volume of media coverage generated by each project (CR = 0.03)

Media Coverage	PRK ↓	IVA ↓	FNG ↓	E(%) ↓
PRK →	1	$\frac{1}{3}$	2	20.7
IVA →	3	1	9	70.3
FNG →	$\frac{1}{2}$	$\frac{1}{9}$	1	9.0

Table 13. Evaluation of the projects' positive impact on the environment (CR = 0.02)

Positive Impact	PRK ↓	IVA ↓	FNG ↓	E(%) ↓
PRK →	1	$\frac{1}{5}$	1	13.4
IVA →	5	1	7	74.6
FNG →	1	$\frac{1}{7}$	1	12.0

Moreover, when it comes to receiving positive media coverage and having a positive impact on the environment the IVA is also the most relevant among the projects in the portfolio. The index presented in Table 14 provides a combined view of the performance of the IVA project when subject to the criteria presented in Table 9. In addition, the same Table 14 also presents the combined view of the performance of the remainder of the e-gov projects.

It should be noted that the IVA is the project that has the highest WRI, indicating that it is the most relevant project in the portfolio in terms of the amount of benefits it provides. The WRI of the PRK and FNG projects trail far behind the WRI of the IVA project.If enough capital were available and only one project could be completed during the mayor's administration, clearly the IVA should be the project to be executed.

Dividing Projects into Subprojects

It is widely accepted among software engineers, researchers and practitioners that dividing a project into subproject helps with understanding, planning and maintenance(Fairley, 2008). As a result, the steering committee has decided to breakdown the e-gov projects in the mayor's portfolio into smaller and easier to handle subprojects. For example, Table 15 presents a partition of the PRK project into a number of subprojects. Table 16 and 17 presents the division of the IVA and FNG projects into subprojects.

E-gov subprojects tend to behave in the same way e-gov projects do when it comes to project performance. For instance, the performance of subproject may vary when subjected to differ-

Table 14. The projects' weighted relevance indexes

Project	WRI (%)
PRK	54.5 × 24.3 + 29.7 × 20.7 + 16.4 × 13.4 = 21.4
IVA	54.5× 66.9 + 29.7× 70.3 + 16.4× 74.6 = 69.1
FNG	54.5× 8.8 + 29.7× 9.0 + 16.4× 12.0 = 9.5
Total	100.0

Table 15. Parking-space booking system subprojects

Subproj.	Description
PRK_1	Chooses the remotely-controlled digital parking meters to be used to control the use of parking spaces
PRK_2	Builds the parking meter reservation and control information system
PRK_3	Buys sufficient remotely-controlled digital parking meters and replaces the existing mechanical parking meters.
PRK_4	Integrates the new digital parking meters into the parking-space booking system
PRK_5	Activates the parking meter reservation and control system
PRK_6	Integrates the privately owned parking spaces in the city centre into the control and reservation system
PRK_7	Allows advertising in the PRK system to take place

Table 16. The intelligent virtual-agent system subprojects

Subproj.	Description
IVA_1	Selects the IVA software to be used by the municipal government
IVA_2	Builds the knowledge base of the IVA
IVA_3	Configures the IVA software with the view to fulfilling the municipal government requirements and making it attractive to the general public
IVA_4	Chooses and hires a third party to monitor the IVA performance, and makes the necessary adjustments when necessary
IVA_5	Enables the IVA to interact with its users in pre-selected foreign languages
IVA_5	Develops and deploys the IVA statistical analysis facilities

Table 17. Motor-vehicle fining system

Subproj.	Description
FNG_1	Selects the image capturing and license plate recognition software
FNG_2	Selects the tablet-like device to be used by traffic control officers
FNG_3	Builds the mobile traffic fining system, integrating the image capturing and license plate recognition into the system
FNG_4	Deploys the mobile traffic fining system
FNG_5	Integrates the mobile fining system into the existing traffic fining management system
FNG_6	Acquires the tablet-like devices, loading the mobile fining system application into those devices
FNG_7	Distributes the tablet-like devices, providing traffic control officers with the necessary training

ent criteria. Moreover, their performance in the criteria under consideration may vary with the passage of time. Tables 18, 19, and 20 present the performance of subprojects comprising the FNG project considering each of the criteria introduced in Table 9.

Evaluating Subproject Intangibles

It should be noted that the central column of Table 21 (which is shown in grey background) presents the WRI of each of the FNG's subprojects. The column provides a balanced view of the perfor-

Table 18. Intensity of public support generated by each FNG subproject (CR = 0.05)

Public Support	FNG_1 ↓	FNG_2 ↓	FNG_3 ↓	FNG_4 ↓	FNG_5 ↓	FNG_6 ↓	FNG_7 ↓	E(%) ↓
FNG_1 →	1	1	$\frac{1}{3}$	5	5	3	$\frac{1}{5}$	12.0
FNG_2 →	1	1	$\frac{1}{3}$	5	5	3	$\frac{1}{5}$	12.0
FNG_3 →	3	3	1	7	7	5	$\frac{1}{2}$	25.8
FNG_4 →	$\frac{1}{5}$	$\frac{1}{5}$	$\frac{1}{7}$	1	1	$\frac{1}{7}$	$\frac{1}{9}$	3.0
FNG_5 →	$\frac{1}{5}$	$\frac{1}{5}$	$\frac{1}{9}$	1	1	$\frac{1}{5}$	$\frac{1}{9}$	2.9
FNG_6 →	$\frac{1}{3}$	$\frac{1}{3}$	$\frac{1}{5}$	9	2	1	$\frac{1}{5}$	5.4
FNG_7 →	5	5	2	9	9	5	1	38.7

Table 19. Volume of media coverage yielded by each FNG subproject (CR = 0.04)

Media Coverage	FNG_1 ↓	FNG_2 ↓	FNG_3 ↓	FNG_4 ↓	FNG_5 ↓	FNG_6 ↓	FNG_7 ↓	E(%) ↓
FNG_1 →	1	1	5	5	5	5	$\frac{1}{3}$	21.9
FNG_2 →	1	1	5	5	5	5	$\frac{1}{3}$	21.9
FNG_3 →	$\frac{1}{5}$	$\frac{1}{5}$	1	1	1	1	$\frac{1}{5}$	5.2
FNG_4 →	$\frac{1}{5}$	$\frac{1}{5}$	1	1	1	1	$\frac{1}{5}$	5.2
FNG_5 →	$\frac{1}{5}$	$\frac{1}{5}$	1	1	1	1	$\frac{1}{5}$	5.2
FNG_6 →	$\frac{1}{5}$	$\frac{1}{5}$	1	1	1	1	$\frac{1}{5}$	5.2
FNG_7 →	3	3	5	5	5	5	1	35.6

Table 20. Positive impact on the environment provided by each FNG subproject (CR = 0.03)

Positive Impact								
	FNG_1 ↓	FNG_2 ↓	FNG_3 ↓	FNG_4 ↓	FNG_5 ↓	FNG_6 ↓	FNG_7 ↓	E(%) ↓
FNG_1 →	1	1	5	5	5	5	5	32.7
FNG_2 →	1	1	5	5	5	5	5	32.7
FNG_3 →	$\frac{1}{5}$	$\frac{1}{5}$	1	1	2	1	1	7.5
FNG_4 →	$\frac{1}{5}$	$\frac{1}{5}$	1	1	1	3	1	8.2
FNG_5 →	$\frac{1}{5}$	$\frac{1}{5}$	$\frac{1}{2}$	1	1	1	2	6.9
FNG_6 →	$\frac{1}{5}$	$\frac{1}{5}$	1	$\frac{1}{3}$	1	1	1	5.9
FNG_7 →	$\frac{1}{5}$	3	1	1	$\frac{1}{2}$	1	1	6.1

Table 21. The PSB subprojects' adjusted weighted relevance index

Subproj.	WRI (%)	AWRI = WRI x 9.5%
FNG_1	53.9 × 12.0 + 29.7 × 21.9 + 16.4 × 32.7 = 18.4	1.7
FNG_2	53.9× 12.0 + 29.7× 21.9 + 16.4× 32.7 = 18.4	1.7
FNG_3	53.9× 25.8 + 29.7× 5.2 + 16.4× 7.5 = 16.7	1.6
FNG_4	53.9× 3.0 + 29.7× 5.2 + 16.4× 8.2 = 4.5	0.4
FNG_5	53.9× 2.9 + 29.7× 5.2 + 16.4× 6.9 = 4.2	0.4
FNG_6	53.9× 5.4 + 29.7× 5.2 + 16.4× 5.9 = 5.4	0.5
FNG_7	53.9× 38.7+ 29.7× 35.6 + 16.4× 6.1 = 32.4	3.2
Total	100.0	9.5

mance of those subprojects when the different criteria introduced in Table 9 are considered simultaneously.

In order for the division of projects into subprojects to be consistent, the set of subprojects should provide the same benefits as its source project, i.e. the project that gave birth to it. This constraint is more easily accomplished by replacing the WRI by the adjusted weighted relevance index, or AWRI. In formal terms, the AWRI of a subproject SP_i of a project P_k is given by

$$AWRI(SP_i) = WRI(SP_i) \times WRI(P_k) \qquad (2)$$

The rightmost column of Table 21 introduces the AWRI of each of the FNG's subprojects. The WRI(PRK) is 24.3% and so it is the sum of the AWRI of its subprojects. Table 22 presents the AWRI of the remainder of the subprojects.

The Dependency Relations among Subprojects

When a project is divided into a set of subprojects it is often the case that some dependency relations will hold true among the subprojects. For example,

Table 22. The IVA and FNG subproject's AWRI

Sub-proj.	AWRI	Sub-proj.	AWRI
IVA_1	12.7	PRK_1	1.8
IVA_2	4.4	PRK_2	3.0
IVA_3	23.1	PRK_3	2.7
IVA_4	7.6	PRK_4	1.3
IVA_5	4.6	PRK_5	5.7
IVA_6	14.4	PRK_6	7.0
		PRK_7	2.7
Total	66.9	**Total**	24.3

one cannot realistically expect that the parking space booking system could be deployed before it is actually developed. Therefore, the development of PRK_2 should precede the development of PRK_5 (see Table15). Figure 2 introduces the dependency relations that are required to hold true among the PRK's subprojects in accordance with the view of the steering committee. Figures 3 and 4 introduce the dependency relations among the VIA's and the FNG's subprojects.

It is important to bear in mind that the benefits yielded by the PRK's subprojects can only be fully appropriated if all subprojects are executed. If only a subset of these subprojects is implemented, then the appropriation of benefits in only partial. For example, consider the following partial implementation sequence S of the PRK's subprojects

$$PRK_1 \rightarrow PRK_2 \rightarrow PRK_3 \rightarrow PRK_4 \rightarrow PRK_5$$

For a given source project the benefits yielded by a partial implementation of its subprojects, is given by the sum of the AWRI of the subproject comprising the partial implementation. Therefore,

$$AWRI(PRK_1 + PRK_2 + PRK_3 + PRK_4 + PRK_5) =$$

Figure 2. The PRK subprojects' precedence diagram

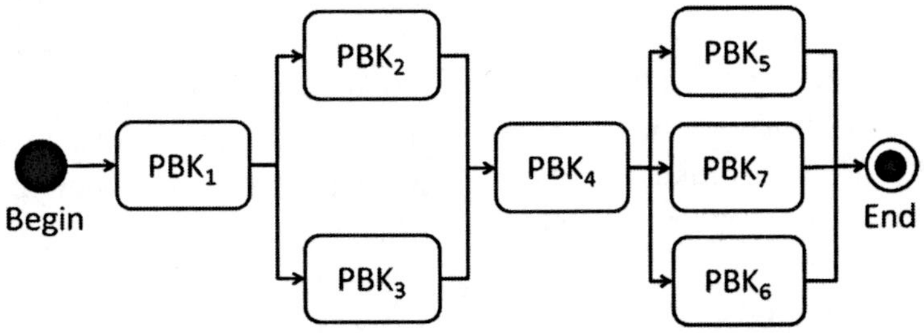

Figure 3. The VIA subproject's precedence diagram

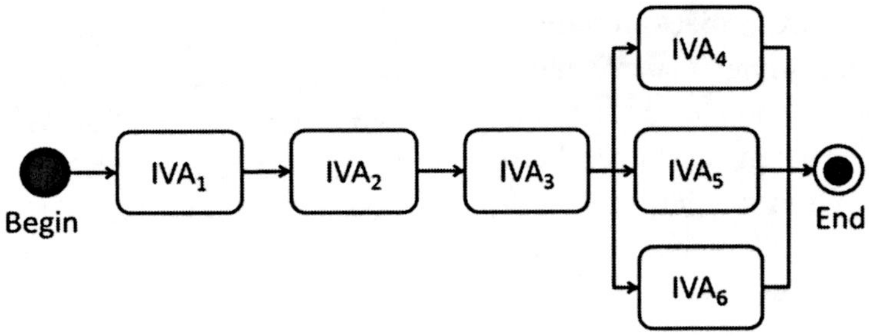

Figure 4. The FNG subproject's precedence diagram

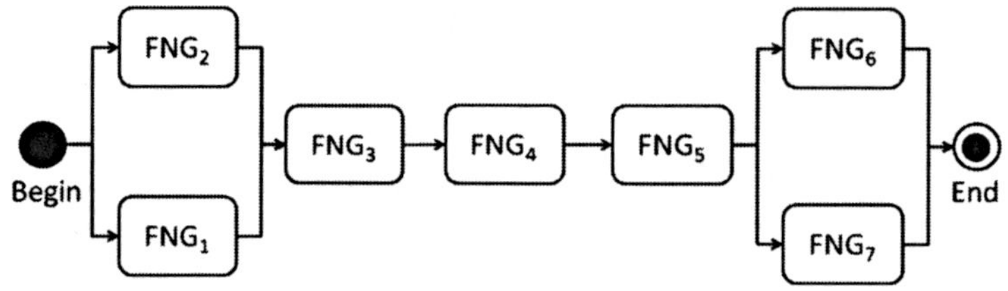

$AWRI(PRK_1) + AWRI(PRK_2) + AWRI(PRK_3) + AWRI(PRK_4) + AWRI(PRK_5) =$

$1.8 + 3.0 + 2.7 + 1.3 + 5.7 =$

14.5

As a result, the partial implementation sequence S yields just 59.7% = 14.5 / 24.3 of all the benefits potentially provided the PRK project (see Table 22 in this respect).Other partial implementation sequences allow for the appropriation of different percentages of the adjusted weighted relevance index of the PRK subprojects.

Project Financing

As there is no free lunch, even public sector e-gov initiatives require some capital investment to be carried out. While some of these initiatives yield financial returns when they are completed, others are only aimed at increasing taxpayer's satisfaction with services. Moreover, the former can be used to finance the development of the latter, thus diminishing the need for capital investment and reducing the risks that every e-gov initiative is naturally exposed to (Doria et al., 2012).

For example, the PRK project introduced in Table 8 does provide some financial return when its development is completed. Not only is payment made easier for the customer, but it is also cheaper for the government to collect. In addition, the PRK project allows the municipal government to charge private parking companies for using the system and to offer paid advertising space on the system's website. Moreover, the new digital parking meter is less expensive to maintain. Therefore, replacing the old mechanical parking meters actually generates some important earnings for the municipal government.

On the other hand, the IVA project is expected to provide no financial returns when implemented. Nevertheless, it is likely to increase taxpayer's satisfaction with the services provided by the municipal government of Enki.

Table 23 presents the investment required by each subproject in the portfolio of e-gov projects together with the return they are expected to provide when their development is finished.

According to the information presented in Table 23 subprojects PRK_5, PRK_6, PRK_7 and FNG_7 are MMFs, as they provide financial returns when they are completed. All the remainder of the subprojects are AEs. In addition, it should be noted that the window of opportunity for the e-gov projects is 24 periods. According to the steering committee this short window of opportunity is a reflection of the current political landscape in Enki.

Identifying the Possible Implementation Sequences

In a democracy the executive branch of government tends to be under constant pressure to provide better services for all. Most of this pressure comes from associations of concerned citizens and professionals, and from people's representatives in the legislative branch. However, as there is a limit to the amount of taxes that one is willing to pay, it is also the case that budget restrictions prevent many

Table 23. The e-gov subproject's cash-flow elements

Subproj.	Period							
	1	2	3	4	5	6	...	24
PRK_1	-15	0	0	0	0	0	...	0
PRK_2	-90	0	0	0	0	0	...	0
PRK_3	-80	0	0	0	0	0	...	0
PRK_4	-20	0	0	0	0	0	...	0
PRK_5	-25	50	100	150	150	150	...	150
PRK_6	-50	75	100	125	200	200	...	200
PRK_7	-30	15	30	45	45	45	...	45
IVA_1	-10	0	0	0	0	0	...	0
IVA_2	-120	0	0	0	0	0	...	0
IVA_3	-50	0	0	0	0	0	...	0
IVA_4	-90	0	0	0	0	0	...	0
IVA_5	-40	0	0	0	0	0	...	0
IVA_6	-30	0	0	0	0	0	...	0
FNG_1	-10	0	0	0	0	0	...	0
FNG_2	-15	0	0	0	0	0	...	0
FNG_3	-70	0	0	0	0	0	...	0
FNG_4	-55	0	0	0	0	0	...	0
FNG_5	-90	0	0	0	0	0	...	0
FNG_6	-30	0	0	0	0	0	...	0
FNG_7	-50	75	100	120	120	120	...	120

public sector projects from being implemented. Therefore, it is not unusual that relevant ideas and projects are put on hold for some time or are implemented only partially.

In addition, fluctuations in the political and social scenario such as changes in voters' behaviour, the proximity of the next election, the action of pressure groups and other potentially threatening events may require that projects in the public sector are run within a specific makespan (MS), i.e. the length of time between the start of the first project activity and the conclusion of the last.

The committee has decided on a 13-period makespan for the project in the portfolio of e-gov projects with $186K of available capital and an interest rate of 0.8% per period. Table 24 shows all possible development sequences for the subprojects in the e-gov portfolio. These comply with the portfolio window of opportunity, allowed make span and available capital for investment (CI). In addition, it shows MS, AWRI, CI and ROI (return on investment) of each implementation sequence.

Identifying the Best Implementation Sequence

There are several sequences listed in Table 24 that bear the same highest AWRI. These sequences deliver the maximum possible benefits considering the restrictions imposed by the political, financial, and social environment in Enki. Nevertheless, the first two sequences yield the same highest ROI. As

Table 24. All possible development sequences for the subprojects in the portfolio of e-gov projects

#	Subproject Implementation Sequences	MS	AWRI (%)	CI ($1K)	ROI (%)
1	$PRK_2 \rightarrow PRK_3 \rightarrow PRK_4 \rightarrow PRK_5 \rightarrow PRK_6 \rightarrow PRK_7 \rightarrow IVA_1 \rightarrow IVA_2 \rightarrow IVA_3 \rightarrow IVA_5 \rightarrow IVA_6 \rightarrow IVA_4$	13	91.2	186	2,876
2	$PRK_2 \rightarrow PRK_3 \rightarrow PRK_4 \rightarrow PRK_5 \rightarrow PRK_6 \rightarrow PRK_7 \rightarrow IVA_1 \rightarrow IVA_2 \rightarrow IVA_3 \rightarrow IVA_6 \rightarrow IVA_5 \rightarrow IVA_4$	13	91.2	186	2,876
3	$PRK_2 \rightarrow PRK_3 \rightarrow PRK_4 \rightarrow PRK_5 \rightarrow PRK_6 \rightarrow PRK_7 \rightarrow IVA_1 \rightarrow IVA_2 \rightarrow IVA_3 \rightarrow IVA_4 \rightarrow IVA_5 \rightarrow IVA_6$	13	91.2	186	2,875
4	$PRK_2 \rightarrow PRK_3 \rightarrow PRK_4 \rightarrow PRK_5 \rightarrow PRK_6 \rightarrow PRK_7 \rightarrow IVA_1 \rightarrow IVA_2 \rightarrow IVA_3 \rightarrow IVA_4 \rightarrow$ IVA6 $\rightarrow$ IVA5	13	91.2	186	2,875
5	$PRK_2 \rightarrow PRK_3 \rightarrow PRK_4 \rightarrow PRK_5 \rightarrow PRK_6 \rightarrow PRK_7 \rightarrow IVA_1 \rightarrow IVA_2 \rightarrow IVA_3 \rightarrow IVA_5 \rightarrow IVA_4 \rightarrow IVA_6$	13	91.2	186	2,875

these sequences provide best return on taxpayer's money, either of them should be used to implement the portfolio of e-gov projects.

It should be noted that none of the subprojects comprising the FNG project are part of these implementation sequences. The reasons for this are quite simple. The FNG subprojects yield on average the lowest AWRI among the projects in the portfolio. Also, these subprojects take too long to provide any financial return.

A SUMMARY OF THE METHOD

When developing e-gov projects government bodies, organizations and agencies may benefit from using the following steps:

Step 1 - Portfolio Selection: Identify the portfolio P of e-gov projects that one is willing to run.

Step 2 - Select the Evaluation Criteria: Select the evaluation criteria C_1, C_2, ..., C_m to be used to analyse the e-gov projects in P.

Step 3 - Prioritize the Evaluation Criteria: Calculate the relevance index (RI) of each evaluation criteria C_1, C_2, ..., C_m.

Step 4 - Work out the Weighted Relative Relevance Index of Each Project: Work out the WRI of each project P_1, P_2, ...,P_n in P.

Step 5 - Partition the Projects: In order to facilitate planning and improve understanding partition the projects P_1, P_2, ...,P_n into a set of subprojects SP = { SP_1, SP_2, ...,SP_k}.

Step 6 - Calculate the AWRI of Each Subproject: Compute the adjusted weighted relative index (AWRI) of each subproject SP_1, SP_2, ...,SP_k.

Step 7 - Capture the Dependency Relations: Determine the dependency relations that are required to hold true among the subprojects SP_1, SP_2, ...,SP_k.

Step 8 - Identify the Constraints: Consider the political, social and economic environment in which the projects in P are going to be run. As a result, determine the proper window of opportunity, allowed makespan, capital available for investment and interest rate to guide the development of the projects in P.

Step 9 - Estimate the Cost of Development and Returns: Establish the cash flow elements of each of the subprojects SP_1, SP_2, ...,SP_k and their respective NPVs with respect to the period in which their development starts.

Step 10 - Calculate the CI and ROI: Generate all possible implementation sequences for the subprojectsSP$_1$, SP_2, ...,SP_k that comply with the constraints identified in Step 8. For each of these subprojects calculate their respective AWRI, CI and ROI.

Step 11 - Identify the Best Implementation Sequence(s): Among all possible implementation sequences, select those that provide the highest AWRI.

Step 12 - Tie-Breaking Criteria: If just one sequence bears the highest AWRI, then this sequence is the logical choice to develop the projects in P, either partly or completely. If two or more implementation sequences bear the highest AWRI, then the one that has the highest ROI is the logical choice to develop the projects in P. If several sequences have the same ROI, then any of these sequences can be used.

CONCLUSION

The widespread availability of ICT has transformed society. Social networks, for example, have allowed citizens to organize themselves in groups that share common interests. Many of these groups intend to promote entertainment and the exchange of knowledge. Nevertheless, others aim at creating a better society for all by campaigning for changes to the law and demanding government action.

Also, ICT has been making government more responsive to the needs, hopes and desires of their citizens. Not only has ICT given a more vigorous voice to citizens, but it has also made the executive branch of government more concerned with the effectiveness and efficiency of the services they provide for all. As a result the number of e-gov initiatives has been rapidly increasing all over the world, especially in developed and developing countries. All of this calls for better e-gov evaluation methods that are better able to deal with the intangibles that are a common concern in government actions and projects.

This work presents a method for the evaluation of e-gov initiatives. The method is based upon the ideas of Saaty on the evaluation of intangibles and the fact that e-gov projects can often be divided into smaller subprojects. In many aspects the method presented in this chapter is superior to other methods that have been put forward so far.

For example, it favours the appropriation of as many intangible benefits as possible within a predefined window of opportunity and project makespan. Moreover, it encourages the use of the financial resources provided by a subproject to fund other system parts. As a result, it allows more intangible benefits to be appropriated with less financial resources. Finally, by reducing the need for capital investment, it reduces the risk exposure that every public-run project is naturally exposed to, due to changes in the social, political, and economic scenario.

FUTURE RESEARCH DIRECTIONS

Flexibility vs. Integrity Restrictions

At this point the reader is most certainly aware that the method presented in this chapter allows for the partial implementation of a portfolio of e-gov projects. Nevertheless, what they may have missed completely are the implications of such implementation flexibility.

For example, consider the project of building a car bridge at the taxpayer's expense. Imagine that this project is divided into two subprojects, the first involving creating the structure of the bridge and the second the deployment of the road surface. Note that, if the project make span is short, the method presented in this chapter allows the building project to be ended when the bridge structure alone is completed.

Therefore, despite the investment made in the construction of the bridge, no vehicle would be able to cross it and no benefit would be appropriated by the general public from its construction. At first sight this may seem a huge flaw in the method. However, the real world is full of projects that were started by one government administration and completed, later on, by another. It is also the case that there are many other examples of government projects whose execution were unexpectedly interrupted for a variety of reasons, never to be resumed again.

As a result, it is difficult to decide what restrictions (if any) should be imposed on the implementation sequences of e-gov projects. More research along these lines would most certainly throw some light on the subject.

Nevertheless, regarding the method presented in this chapter, if one wants to make sure that the execution of a project P_k cannot be interrupted once it starts, it suffices to introduce an integrity restriction in the method establishing that

$$\text{if } SP_i \in Sub(P_k) \wedge SP_i \text{ in } S\text{; then } SP_j \in Sub(P_k) \wedge SP_j \neq SP_j \Rightarrow SP_j \text{ in } S$$

where P_k is a project in the portfolio of e-gov projects under consideration, $Sub(P_k)$ is the set of all subprojects of P_k, S is the selected implementation sequence, and _ *in* _ is an operator that returns true if a subproject can be found in a implementation sequence and false otherwise.

Automation and Difficulties in Using the Method

Although the method presented in this chapter may be used to properly evaluate e-gov initiatives, it requires a considerable knowledge of mathematics and finance. Even though some public officials in decision making positions have such knowledge, others may find it difficult to figure out the eigen values and eigenvectors of Saaty's valuation matrices, calculate their consistency indexes, determine the weighted relevance index of projects, and the adjusted weighted relevance index of subprojects. In addition, in order to make proper use of the method, public officials are required to identify the net present value and return of each possible implementation sequence.

Fortunately, most of what has been presented in this chapter can be made easier to use with the support of an adequate software tool. Such a tool would not only make the life of these decision makers much easier, but also speed up the evaluation process as a whole.

REFERENCES

Almarabeh, T., & AbuAli, A. (2010). A general framework for e-government: Definition maturity challenges, opportunities, and success. *European Journal of Scientific Research*, *39*(1), 29–42.

Amadi-Echendu, J. E., Willett, R., Brown, K., Hope, T., Lee, J., & Mathew, J. … Yang, B.-S. (2010). What Is Engineering Asset Management? In J. E. Amadi-Echendu, K. Brown, R. Willett, & J. Mathew (Eds.), *Definitions, Concepts and Scope of Engineering Asset Management* (pp. 3–16). Springer London. Retrieved from http://link.springer.com/chapter/10.1007/978-1-84996-178-3_1

Barbosa, A. F., Pozzebon, M., & Diniz, E. H. (2013). Rethinking E-Government Performance Assessment from a Citizen Perspective. *Public Administration*, *91*(3), 744–762.

Barnes, S., & Hunt, B. (2013). *E-Commerce and V-Business*. Routledge.

Budakova, Dakovski, & Lyudmil. (2013). The intelligent virtual agents - a new interface to the computer. Saarbrücken: LAP LAMBERT Academic Publishing.

Campbell, J., McDonald, C., & Sethibe, T. (2010). Public and Private Sector IT Governance: Identifying Contextual Differences. *Australasian Journal of Information Systems*, *16*(2). Retrieved from http://dl.acs.org.au/index.php/ajis/article/view/538

Campbell-Kelly, M., Aspray, W., Ensmenger, N., & Yost, J. R. (2013). *Computer a History of the Information Machine*. New York: Westview Press.

Cao, L., Mohan, K., Ramesh, B., & Sarkar, S. (2013). Adapting funding processes for agile IT projects: An empirical investigation. *European Journal of Information Systems*, *22*(2), 191–205. doi:10.1057/ejis.2012.9

Cleland-Huang, J. (2013). Are Requirements Alive and Kicking? *IEEE Software*, *30*(3), 13–15. doi:10.1109/MS.2013.47

Denne, M., & Cleland-Huang, J. (2004). *Software by numbers: low risk, high return development*. Upper Saddle River, NJ: Prentice Hall.

Doria, J. V., Jr., Alencar, A. J., Schmitz, E. A., Correa, A. L., & Vital, I. M., Jr. (2012). On the Merits and Pitfalls of the Incremental Funding Method and Its Software Project Scheduling Algorithms. In K. R. Venugopal & L. M. Patnaik (Eds.), Wireless Networks and Computational Intelligence (pp. 493–502). Springer Berlin Heidelberg. Retrieved from http://link.springer.com/chapter/10.1007/978-3-642-31686-9_57

Eddy, N. (2013, October 21). *Mobile Phone, Tablet Sales Driven by Budget Devices: Gartner. eWeek*. Retrieved November 20, 2013, from http://www.eweek.com/mobile/mobile-phone-tablet-sales-driven-by-budget-devices-gartner.html

Fairley, R. E. (2008). Project Planning Techniques. In Managing and Leading Software Projects (pp. 173–206). John Wiley & Sons, Inc. Retrieved from http://onlinelibrary.wiley.com/doi/10.1002/9780470405697.ch5/summary

Frauenfelder, M. (2013). The computer. London: Carlton.

Friedman, M., Savage, L. J., & Becker, G. S. (2007). *Milton Friedman on economics: selected papers*. Chicago: University of Chicago Press.

Gayle, D. (2012). Chemical breakdown: The toxic substances inside your mobile phone. *Daily Mail Online*. Retrieved November 21, 2013, from http://www.dailymail.co.uk/sciencetech/article-2213366/Chemical-breakdown-What-really-goes-new-iPhone.html

Gentle, M. (2007). *IT success! towards a new model for information technology*. Hoboken, NJ: John Wiley & Sons.

Guclu, A. N., & Bilgen, S. (2011). Modelling and Assessment of the Effectiveness of Government Information Technologies - Value Space Approach with a Public Sector Case Study in Turkey. *The Electronic Journal of Information Systems in Developing Countries, 45*(0).

Hubbard, D. W. (2010). *How to measure anything finding the value of "intangibles" in business*. Hoboken, NJ: Wiley. doi:10.1002/9781118983836

Isaacson, W. (2004). *Benjamin Franklin: an American life*. New York: Simon & Schuster.

Jr, I. M. V., Alencar, A. J., Schmitz, E. A., Correa, A. L., & Jr, J. V. D. (2012). Identifying the Most Efficient Implementation Sequence of IT Projects Broken Down into MMFs and AEs. In K. R. Venugopal & L. M. Patnaik (Eds.), Wireless Networks and Computational Intelligence (pp. 477–486). Springer Berlin Heidelberg. Retrieved from http://link.springer.com/chapter/10.1007/978-3-642-31686-9_55

Klein, P. N. (2013). *Coding the matrix: Linear algebra through applications to computer science*. Academic Press.

Kukreja, N., Payyavula, S. S., Boehm, B., & Padmanabhuni, S. (2012). Selecting an appropriate framework for value-based requirements prioritization. In *Proceedings of Requirements Engineering Conference (RE)*, (pp. 303–308). RE. doi:10.1109/RE.2012.6345819

Kundra, V. (2010). *25 Point Implementation Plan to Reform Federal information Technology Management*. Academic Press.

Larrabee, D. T., & Voss, J. A. (2013). *Valuation techniques discounted cash flow, earnings quality, measures of value added, and real options*. Hoboken, NJ: John Wiley & Sons.

Neuroni, A., Rascon, A., Spichiger, A., & Riedl, R. (2010). Assessing and Evaluating Value and Cost Effectiveness of e-Government Initiatives: Focusing the Step of the Financial Evaluation. In *Proceedings of the 11th Annual International Digital Government Research Conference on Public Administration Online: Challenges and Opportunities* (pp. 105–111). Puebla, Mexico: Digital Government Society of North America.

Peffers, K., & Santos, B. L. D. (2013). Research opportunities in information technology funding and system justification. *European Journal of Information Systems*, *22*(2), 131–138. doi:10.1057/ejis.2012.60

Raum, E. (2008). *The history of the computer*. Chicago, IL: Heinemann Library.

Raus, M., Liu, J., & Kipp, A. (2010). Evaluating IT innovations in a business-to-government context: A framework and its applications. *Government Information Quarterly*, *27*(2), 122–133. doi:10.1016/j.giq.2009.04.007

Rosacker, K. M., & Rosacker, R. E. (2010). Information technology project management within public sector organizations. *Journal of Enterprise Information Management*, *23*(5), 587–594. doi:10.1108/17410391011083047

Rose, W. R., & Grant, G. G. (2010). *Critical issues pertaining to the planning and implementation of e-government initiatives*. Retrieved from http://www.sciencedirect.com/science/article/pii/S0740624X09001105

Saaty, T. L. (2013). *Decision Making for Leaders: The Analytic Hierarchy Process for Decisions in a Complex World (3rd ed.)*. RWS Publications.

Sipahi, S., & Timor, M. (2010). The analytic hierarchy process and analytic network process: An overview of applications. *Management Decision*, *48*(5), 775–808. doi:10.1108/00251741011043920

Srivastava, S. C. (2011). Is e-government providing the promised returns?: A value framework for assessing e-government impact. *Transforming Government: People, Process and Policy*, *5*(2), 107–113.

Tan, A., Theodorou, P., & Over, D. V. (2009). Use of Information Technology Investment Management to Manage State Government Information Technology Investments. In Strategic Information Technology and Portfolio Management. Idea Group Inc (IGI).

Tan, C.-W., Benbasat, I., & Cenfetelli, R. (2010). Understanding the Antecedents and Consequences of E-Government Service Quality: Transactional Frequency as a Moderator of Citizens' Quality Perceptions. In *Proceedings of ECIS 2010*. Retrieved from http://aisel.aisnet.org/ecis2010/115

Vardalas, J. N. (2001). *The Computer Revolution in Canada: Building National Technological Competence (History of Computing)*. The MIT Press.

Wahid, F. (2012). The Current State of Research on eGovernment in Developing Countries: A Literature Review. In H. J. Scholl, M. Janssen, M. A. Wimmer, C. E. Moe, & L. S. Flak (Eds.), *Electronic Government* (pp. 1–12). Springer Berlin Heidelberg. doi:10.1007/978-3-642-33489-4_1

Wilkin, C. L., Campbell, J., & Moore, S. (2013). Creating value through governing IT deployment in a public/private-sector inter-organisational context: A human agency perspective. *European Journal of Information Systems*, *22*(5), 498–511. doi:10.1057/ejis.2012.21

ADDITIONAL READING

Aikins, S. K. (2012). Managing e-government projects concepts, issues and best practices. Hershey, Pa.: IGI Global (701 E. Chocolate Avenue, Hershey, Pennsylvania, 17033, USA). doi:10.4018/978-1-46660-086-7

Aladwani, A. M. (2012). An Exploratory Investigation of Kuwaitis' Views of E-Government Quality (SSRN Scholarly Paper No. ID 2189829). Rochester, NY: Social Science Research Network; Retrieved from http://papers.ssrn.com/abstract=2189829

Anthopoulos, L. G., & Reddick, C. G. (2013). *Government e-Strategic Planning and Management: Practices, Patterns and Roadmaps (Public Administration and Information Technology) (2014 edition.)*. Springer.

Barbosa, B. P., Schmitz, E., & Alencar, A. (2008). Generating software-project investment policies in an uncertain environment. In *IEEE Systems and Information Engineering Design Symposium, 2008. SIEDS 2008* (pp. 178–183). doi:10.1109/SIEDS.2008.4559707

Chen, H. (2008). *Digital government e-government research, case studies and implementation*. Berlin: Springer.

Denne, M., & Cleland-Huang, J. (2004). The incremental funding method: Data-driven software development. *Software, IEEE*, *21*(3), 39–47. doi:10.1109/MS.2004.1293071

Gil García, J. R. (2013a). *E-government success around the world cases, empirical studies, and practical recommendations*.

Gil García, J. R. (2013b). *E-government success factors and measures theories, concepts, and methodologies*. Hershey, PA: Information Science Reference. doi:10.4018/978-1-4666-4058-0

Hadi, F., & Bin Muhaya, F. T. (2011). Essentials for the e-government security. In *2011 International Conference on Information Society (i-Society)* (pp. 237–240).

Homburg, V. (2008). *Understanding e-government: information systems in public administration*. London, New York: Routledge.

Keen, J. M. (2011). *Making Technology Investments Profitable: ROI Road Map from Business Case to Value Realization (2 edition.)*. Wiley.

Kleis, L., Chwelos, P., Ramirez, R. V., & Cockburn, I. (2012, March 1). *Information Technology and Intangible Output: The Impact of IT Investment on Innovation Productivity*. research-article. Retrieved December 18, 2013, from http://pubsonline.informs.org/doi/abs/10.1287/isre.1100.0338

Otenyo, E. E., & Lind, N. S. (2011). e-Government: The Use of Information and Communication Technologies in Administration. Teneo Press.

Papadomichelaki, X., & Mentzas, G. (2012). e-GovQual: A multiple-item scale for assessing e-government service quality. *Government Information Quarterly*, *29*(1), 98–109. doi:10.1016/j.giq.2011.08.011

Read, T. J. (2009). *The IT Value Network: From IT Investment to Stakeholder Value (1 edition.)*. Wiley.

Saaty, T. L. (2013). *Mathematical Principles of Decision Making (Principia Mathematica Decernendi)*. RWS Publications.

Saaty, T. L., & Peniwati, K. (2013). *Group Decision Making: Drawing Out and Reconciling Differences*. RWS Publications.

Sarantis, D., Askounis, D., & Smithson, S. (2009). Critical appraisal on project management approaches in e-Government. In *2009 7th International Conference on ICT and Knowledge Engineering* (pp. 44–49). doi:10.1109/ICTKE.2009.5397335

Satynarayna, J. (2013). *E-Government: The Science of The Possible*. PHI Learning Private Limited.

Zhao, J. J., Zhao, S. Y., & Zhao, S. Y. (2010). Opportunities and threats: A security assessment of state e-government websites. *Government Information Quarterly*, *27*(1), 49–56. doi:10.1016/j.giq.2009.07.004

KEY TERMS AND DEFINITIONS

Analytic Hierarchy Process: A method for decision making based on pairwise comparison of tangible and intangible elements. It was developed by Thomas L. Saaty.

Architectural Element: A software module or ICT project that lays down the infrastructure necessary to build other modules or projects.

Asset: Something of value that can be owned or controlled. For example, houses, boats, computers, etc.

Cash Flow: The flow of money in and out of a business or project.

Information and Communication Technology: A term used to designate the association between computers (hardware), computer systems (software) and communication technology (networks, phone lines, satellites, signal processing, etc.).

Intangible Asset: An asset that does not have a physical or financial embodiment. For example, patents, trademarks, copyrights and software.

Intangible Benefit: A perceived advantage given by the use of an asset that stems from perceptions of reality, which does not have an easily quantifiable financial embodiment.

Interest Rate: A fee that is paid by money borrowers to the money's owner or controller as a form of compensation for its use.

Minimum Marketable Features Modules or Projects: A term coined by Mark Denne and Jane Cleland-Huang to designate modules or ICT projects that generate financial return as soon as it is deployed.

Net Present Value: The sum of the cash flow elements of a business or project brought to its current value by using a proper interest rate.

ENDNOTE

1 Enki is the Sumerian god of intellect, creation and wisdom.

Chapter 18
Impact of Local Self-Government Institutions on Creating a Business-Friendly Environment:
Multi-Criteria Analysis

Jelena Stanković
University of Niš, Faculty of Economics, Serbia

Igor Novaković
University in Pristina/Kosovska Mitrovica, Serbia

ABSTRACT

The chapter objective is to demonstrate application possibilities of Multi-Criteria Analysis (MCA) in the specific local economic development problem in Serbia that refers to assessment of Local Self-Government (LSG) institutions' capabilities to act in order to create business-friendly environments and increase entrepreneurial activities. The primary aim of the chapter is to formulate an adequate multi-criteria model for evaluation of institutional cooperation between business councils, as representatives of local authorities and the business community in observed LSG units. Results indicate inadequate quality and functionality of the business councils, although cooperation has been established between the business councils, as a local government institution, and representatives of business community. Data analysis is conducted using relevant statistical methods. For multi-criteria analysis of subjective preferences of Local Economic Development (LED) offices has been applied Analitic Hierarchy Process (AHP).

INTRODUCTION

Entrepreneurial activities are very important for inclusion of developing local self-government units into national economy. Therefore, increase of entrepreneurial activities is seen as an opportunity for providing growth in developing LSG. A country representative bodies and institutions have a great role in creating business environment. However, they are not the only ones that should be taking actions and making positive environment for business activities. Local governments can

DOI: 10.4018/978-1-4666-7266-6.ch018

also take part in encouraging entrepreneurship and business prosperity. They can create micro climate, which should make their communities recognizable and favourable for entrepreneurs. One of the first steps includes development of local economic strategies and plans with purpose of reducing risks for developing business and creating stable business environment. The chapter summarizes the problems and efforts concerning business environment improvements that local communities in Serbia were facing during the last two decades and the factors that influenced the reduction of business activities (Antic *et al.*, 2013). Local governments in some cities have already realized the importance of local actions and discovering of local comparative advantages for increasing business activities and making better position inside regionally unbalanced Serbian economy (Stankovic *et al.*, in press).

Two of the most influential determinants on business activities are business environment and the state and local government bodies' ability to deal with specific problems in creating stable and favorable business environment. Especially in the period of the recent economic crisis these two factors have been analyzed from many different aspects (e.g. Grilli, 2011; Lavric, 2010; Bumgardner *et al.*, 2011; Nicolescu *et al.*, 2011). Similar conclusions can be found in research conducted by Ciocarlan-Chitucea and Popescu (2010), Norwood (2011), Dunkelberg and Wade (2012) as well as Nicolescu and Nicolescu (2013). The main conclusions of all mentioned scientific papers and studies refer to the multiple influence of the business environment on the business activities and the crucial role of the state institutions in developing and enabling business environment.

Some other studies show that local governments are likely the primary policy makers and regulators that entrepreneurs and small businesses encounter (McFarland *et al.*, 2010). Unfortunately, many local governments do not know the impact of their efforts or what their most effective roles should be. Too often, local regulations can unknowingly create institutional and bureaucratic barriers that impede development and the speed to market for new businesses (Morris & Brennan, 2003; Roxas *et al.*, 2008; Stankovic *et al.*, 2013; Stankovic *et al.*, 2014). Additionally, while most local governments have policies and programs designed to proactively support entrepreneurs and small businesses, these efforts are not necessarily well suited to meet the needs of the types of small businesses most likely to drive economic growth (McFarland & McConnell, 2011a).

Local self-governments are interacting with business activities via its regulations, policies and communicatory and governance processes, as an important factor in supporting new and small business growth. Regulations affect doing business in a community and good communication between local institutions and business comunity helps establish trust, build supportive policies and provide ways to solve problems (McFarland & McConnell, 2011b).

Governments can, given their powers, have considerable influence over the entrepreneurial process by stifling the efforts of those attempting to start a new business. This may be done through onerous bureaucratic requirements, complex regulations or merely slow reaction to requests for decisions required to form a new business. (Reynolds et al., pp. 447)

The speed, efficiency, and complexity of local regulatory processes are indicators of a local government's responsiveness to the needs of business community.

When it comes to Serbia, the competencies of state institutions and local government institutions vary even more drastically (Stankovic *et al.*, 2013). In fact, due to the high level of centralization, the operational capacity of local institutions in the area of creating a favorable business environment is small. On the other hand, previous studies have shown that the business communities are still not perceived by local governments as partners but there is still a distance relationship, where the local authorities are considered as the category of "power" (Stankovic *et al.*, 2012). All jurisdictions of local institutions in the field of local economic development are relatively new and have not yet found the right model of action. In this context, this research aims to identify some key issues of operation (in)efficiency of local institutions and thus improve the relationship between the business community and local government.

Since stimulating local economic development is a relatively recent jurisdiction of towns and municipalities, introduced by the Law on local self-government, the towns and municipalities have for some time been practising activities aimed at stimulating local economic growth. These activities are carried out not only within the Offices for local economic development (or, more exactly, organizational authorities of the town or municipal government which in their area deal in businesses of local economic development) but are also practised by other bodies and departments within the framework of organizational structure of the self-government, such as member of the city or municipal council in charge of economy, the council/committee of Municipal Assembly for economy, the strategic planning committee, the committee for planning capital investment, employment council, socio-economic council, etc. Representatives of economy in local self-government bodies have the opportunity to make statements on certain aspects of the local economic development in some of these forums – for instance, local employment councils gather representatives of local self-governments, national employment service, private entrepreneurs, representatives of centres for social work, representative syndicates and non-governmental organizations. However, bearing in mind that these forums (councils, boards or committees) have been founded with the aim of establishing or better functioning of only one part of the local economic framework (employment, education, defining and following development strategies), the role of these economic representatives is limited only to formulating prepositions and initiatives and following already adopted measures referring to a single particular area. In that way, they do not always have motivation or a long term interest in participating and essentially contributing to activities of these bodies.

The chapter points out the main institutions of LSG units in creating business friendly environment and the effects of their actions, measured through quality rate of Business Councils operation. The respondents (LED offices) have been offered a set of functions of Local Business Council and they are asked to express an opinion on their significance for the improvement of the business environment and the level of compliance in the respective local self-government unit. Since this is a heterogeneous criteria, which include a variety of responsibilities of councils, it is possible to form an adequate multi-criteria model and to determinate relative importance of criteria using AHP method. The analysis in the chapter will quantify the subjective perception of LED offices about business council's functionality.

The result of this chapter is to provide statistically analysed data for determination of relevant criteria for evaluation of different functions of LSG bodies used and their functionality at local level for business climate improvement. In addition, as it is already pointed out, by using AHP methodology it is possible to quantify subjective perception of LED offices about importance of certain criterion for business friendly environment. In that context, AHP is used as methodology for weights derivation when the decision maker is a group. Finally, the chapter will present testing of significant differences between the results of the statistical analysis and the subjective perception of LED offices assessed by AHP method. In order to present these analyses and results the chapter contains the following headings:

1. Legal framework of institutional cooperation between local self-government and business community,

2. Research methodology and hypotheses,
3. Statistical analysis of business council's functionality,
4. Impact of business council activities on business council quality and functionality rating, and
5. Future research directions.

The research presented in the chapter has practical value because it provides information about importance of institutional co-operation between LSG bodies and the business community and it can become valuable guideline for future actions of local self-government authorities in order to increase business friendly environment.

LEGAL FRAMEWORK OF INSTITUTIONAL COOPERATION BETWEEN LOCAL SELF-GOVERNMENT AND BUSINESS COMMUNITY

The Law on Local Self-Government (Official Gazette of Republic of Serbia, No. 129/2007) determines jurisdictions of local self-governments in the area of local economic development as well, which creates a legal basis for local self-governments to actively cooperate with business communities in order to carry out the jurisdictions given. However, this Law does not define obligations or ordered way of institutional cooperation, although other regulations predict establishment of different institutional mechanisms for cooperation between local self-government and business community. Namely, establishment, jurisdictions and functioning of different institutional forms of cooperation between local self-government and business community have been defined by the Law on Employment and Insurance in Case of Unemployment (Official Gazette of Republic of Serbia, No. 36/2009 and 88/2010) as well as the Law on Socio-Economic Council (Official Gazette of Republic of Serbia, No. 125/2004).

Also, several donor development programs and development institutions have promoted different models of institutional cooperation between local self-government authority and business community. Thus, *USAID*[1] through program *Municipal Economic Growth Activity - MEGA* promoted formation of Offices for local economic development within the authority of local self-government, as part of administration which will, among other things, cooperate with the local business community. Founding and functioning of Offices for local economic development in Serbia have been supported by *GTZ*[2], *UNDP*[3] and the like. The same programs proposed and promoted forming of economic (business) councils, representing advisory bodies with the task to establish dialogue and active participation of local business community in creating and carrying out local economic development policy. National Alliance for Local Economic Development (NALED) initiated the process of certifying local self-governments with favourable business environment, which, within the framework of defined criteria, made the existence of Offices for local economic development and economic (business) councils obligatory for local self-governments, which to a great extent, made local self-governments participating in the process create this mechanism of institutional cooperation as well (see Business Friendly Certification South East Europe, 2013 and NALED, Certification program business-friendly municipality, 2012).

In connection with the legal framework for establishing institutional mechanisms of cooperation between local self-government authorities and economy, we have to bear in mind the Law on Economic Chambers (Official Gazette of Republic of Serbia, No. 65/2001, 36/2009 and 99/2011), particularly taking into consideration changes in the "chamber system" in the Republic of Serbia, as well as annulment of obligatory membership of all business entities in economic chambers.

From the foregoing, it can be concluded that there is a valid legal framework that enables the formation of bodies of local governments whose competences would be directly aimed at improving the business environment. Also, in addition to legal solutions, initiatives in this field have solid financial support of donor funds.

RESEARCH METHODOLOGY AND HYPOTHESES

Empirical research was conducted within the framework of cooperation with the Board for local economic development and Network for local economic development of Standing Conference of Towns and Municipalities in Serbia during April and May 2013. The research was carried out on the sample of 56 cities and municipalities in Serbia and consisted of two segments:

1. Research of existence of institutional capacities for local economic development within the government, that is, administration of towns and municipalities and
2. Research of various models and mechanisms of institutional cooperation with business community, where special attention is given to existence, structure and functionality of three possible forms: (1) Local Socio-Economic Council, (2) Local Employment Council and (3) Local Economic, i.e. Business Council.

Total number of questions included in the survey is 31. The questionnaire was sent to all local governments in Serbia (174 LSG units, according to Statistical Office of RS: 150 municipalities, 23 cities and the City of Belgrade as a capital) and 56 of them responded positively and joined the research. The research was conceived as a kind of self-evaluation of local self-government institutions and response to the questionnaire was the responsibility of LED offices. Out of total number of 56 cities and municipalities included in research sample, according to population, 23 belong to small municipalities (up to 20,000 inhabitants), 21 belong to medium-sized (from 20,000 to 80,000), and 12 of them belong to large municipalities (over 80,000 inhabitants), as shown in Table 1.

Within local self-governments surveyed, activities in the area of local economic development are organized in 12 cases through Department for local economic development, in 8 cases through Division for local economic development and in 26 cases through Office for local economic development. In only 5 towns and municipalities local economic development activities are done by Agencies for local economic development as separate legal entities (Table 2).

Table 1. The structure of the surveyed municipalities by size

The Size of Municipality	Number of Municipalities	%
Small (up to 20,000 inhabitants)	23	41.07%
Medium (from 20,000 to 80,000 inhabitants)	21	37.50%
Large (over 80,000 inhabitants)	12	21.43%
Total	56	100.00%

Table 2. Institutional forms on local level that carries the activities of economic development

Institutional Form	Number of Municipalities	%
Department for Local Economic Development	12	21.43%
Division for Local Economic Development	8	14.29%
Office for Local Economic Development	26	46.43%
Agency for Local Economic Development	5	8.93%
	51	91.08%
No local institutional form in the field of LED	5	8.93%
Total	56	100.00%

Based on the given data, it can be concluded that in 51 out of 56 municipalities surveyed (91.08%), exist special organizational authorities to perform activities in the area of local economic development, most commonly organized as Offices for local economic development (46.43%), which shows that local self-government authorities have become aware of their obligation to actively deal with local economic development.

Since there is currently a high level of centralization in Serbia, the authors of this paper have found it necessary to evaluate initially the existence of local self-government bodies in all municipalities that are within its jurisdiction that should deal with local economic development problems. First of all, this applies to small and underdeveloped municipalities in which the existence of these bodies is of great importance. Therefore, the null hypothesis is defined as:

H_0: There is no connection between the size of the municipality and existence of Business Council.

If there is adequate institutional infrastructure at the local level, the paper will also test the functionality of these institutions and their cooperation with the business community through involvement of business representatives in the work of these institutions. In this regard, the authors tested the following hypotheses:

H_1: There is no correlation between the size of the municipality and quality and functionality rating of Business Council, and

H_2: There is no correlation between the fact that the President of the Council is among the business representatives and quality and functionality rating of Business Council.

In order to test the hypothesis, the relevant statistical methods will be applied.

Furthermore, functionality analysis of business councils will be tested through the application of multi-criteria analysis. Namely, through the process of determining the weights, evaluation of all activities performed by the Business Council will be carried out. This part of research refers to following hypothesis:

H_3: Quality rating of Business Council dependent on activities performed by the Business Council in observed municipality and contribution of each activity can be expressed by weights in multi-criteria model.

In order to test the hypothesis H_3, the appropriate methods for determining weights will be applied. Since this is a quantification of the subjective preferences about quality of performance of Business Councils the applied method will be Analytic Hierarchy Process. Data analysis that precedes forming of the pairwise comparison matrix will be performed using the Chi-Square Test.

STATISTICAL ANALYSIS OF BUSINESS COUNCILS FUNCIONALITY[4]

In the observed sample of LSG units, 32 of them have established Economic i.e. The Business Council, which is 57.1 percent (Table 3). Also, one of the municipalities in the sample, Odžaci, had established Business Council in the period from 2010 to 2012 and those experiences will be taken into account in the analysis.

If the size of LSG units in the context of the population is considered, it can be concluded that 75.0% of large municipalities and 63.9% of medium municipalities have established the Business Councils (Table 4). When it comes to small municipalities, the percentage of those who have a Business Council is much smaller and amounts to only 43.5%, which is well below the sample average.

The fact that in small municipalities there is lower percentage that indicates the existence

Table 3. Descriptive statistics: is the Business Council established?

		Frequency	Percent	Valid Percent	Cumulative Percent
Valid	No	24	42.9	42.9	42.9
	Yes	32	57.1	57.1	100.0
	Total	56	100.0	100.0	

Table 4. Cross tabulation analysis between municipality size and existence of Business Council

The Size of the Municipality	Is it Business Council Established?		Total
	No	Yes	
Small - up to 20.000	13	10	23
Count % within municipality size	56.5%	43.5%	100.0%
Medium - from 20.000-80.000	8	13	21
Count % within municipality size	38.1%	61.9%	100.0%
Large - over 80000	3	9	12
Count % within municipality size	25.0%	75.0%	100.0%
Total	24	32	56
Count % within municipality size	42.9%	57.1%	100.0%

of the Business Council, makes null hypothesis justified. For purpose of testing H_0, Chi-Square Test is applied. Chi-Square Test is a well known statistical procedure that refers both to a statistical distribution and to a hypothesis testing procedure that produces a statistic that is approximately distributed as the chi-square distribution. For the purpose of research, Chi-Square Test is used in its second sense. The original procedure dates from Karl Pearson paper published in the 1900s which defined the chi-squared test of goodness of fit (Plackett, 1983).

However, the results of Chi-Square Test (Table 5) clearly show that municipality size does not influence the fact whether Business Council is established (Pearson Chi-Square equals 0.131). Regardless of the circumstances where small municipalities have a lower percentage of those who established Business Council, this difference is not statistically significant and cannot be correlated with the size of the municipality. The null hypothesis has been confirmed by this conclusion.

This finding is very important, in terms of decentralization, because it suggests that the process of establishment of the institutional framework of cooperation between local governments and the business community is taking place in all LSG units. The next issue to be analyzed is relating to the management of Business Council. The very idea and purpose of the establishment of the Business Council is in cooperation between institutions and businesses focused on business enabling environment. In this sense, it is very important to analyze the participation of businessmen in the work and management of the Business Council. Particular question contained in the questionnaire was whether the president of the Business Council from among the business representatives. The answer to this question was given by 33 LSG units, of which 23 or 69.7% have a president of the Business Council among business representatives (Table 6).

If one looks at management structure of the Business Council in relation to the size of the

Table 5. Chi-Squere test results: is there a dependence between the size of the municipality and the fact that the Business Council was established?

	Value	df	Asymp. Sig. (2-sided)
Pearson Chi-Square	4.069[a]	2	**.131**
Likelihood Ratio	4.115	2	.128
Linear-by-Linear Association	3.714	1	.054
N of Valid Cases	56		

1 cells (16.7%) have expected count less than 5. The minimum expected count is 4.93.

Table 6. Descriptive statistics: Whether the president of the Business Council is among the business representatives

		Frequency	Percent	Valid Percent	Cumulative Percent
Valid	No	10	17.9	30.3	30.3
	Yes	23	41.1	69.7	100.0
	Total	33	58.9	100.0	
Missing	System	23	41.1		
	Total	56	100.0		

municipality, it can be concluded that the majority of representatives of business in the position of the president are in the medium-sized municipalities (56.5%), followed by large municipalities with 26.1%. Cross tabulation results between municipality size and the fact that the president of the Business Council is among the business representatives is presented in Table 7.

That is not the case when it comes to small municipalities where the share of business representatives as president of the Business Council is lower.

The results of Chi Square Test indicates that there is a dependence between size of the municipality and this issue in the sense that in most medium and large municipalities have president of the Business Council from among businessmen (Table 8).

The following analysis is related to Business Council quality and functionality assessment. The quantification of perception of LED offices about quality and functionality of Business Council is achieved by applying the Likert scale (Likert, 1931), where the highest level is rated with 5, and the lowest level with 1. Assessment results are presented in Table 9.

Quality and functionality of Business Council were assessed in 30 municipalities. The average rate was 2.97, and the standard deviation is 1.33. Business counsels in medium-sized municipalities have best average rating 3.15, while both other groups are below average of the sample (Table 10).

However, despite the obvious difference in average scores, which can be seen from the cross tabulation analysis, Chi-Square Test shows that there is no statistically significant dependence

Table 7. Cross tabulation analysis between municipality size and the fact that the President of the Council is among the business representatives

The Size of the Municipality	Is it President of the Council among the Business Representatives?		Total
	No	Yes	
Small: Up to 20.000 Count % within municipality size	6 60.0%	4 17.4%	10 30.3%
Medium: From 20.000-80.000 Count % within municipality size	1 10.0%	13 56.5%	14 42.4%
Big: Over 80000 Count % within municipality size	3 30.0%	6 26.1%	9 27.3%
Total Count % within municipality size	10 100.0%	23 100.0%	33 100.0%

Table 8. Chi-Square Test results: Is there dependence between size of the municipality and the fact that the President of the Council is among the business representatives

	Value	df	Asymp. Sig. (2-sided)
Pearson Chi-Square	7.770[a]	2	**.021**
Likelihood Ratio	8.363	2	.015
Linear-by-Linear Association	1.760	1	.185
N of Valid Cases	33		

3 cells (50.0%) have expected count less than 5. The minimum expected count is 2.73.

between the size of the municipality and the average rating of the Business Council in it (Table 11). Therefore, the research hypothesis H_1 is proved.

Finally, the relation of the average quality and functionality rates has been analyzed depending on whether the Business Council is managed by a business representative.

The results show that there is a higher quality and functionality rate in those business councils where the president is among business representatives (Table 12), but the difference is not statistically significant. Therefore, the research hypothesis H_2 is proved, as well.

IMPACT OF BUSINESS COUNCIL ACTIVITIES ON BUSINESS COUNCIL QUALITY AND FUNCTIONALITY RATING

The quality and functionality of the Business Council is reflected in the ability to efficiently and effectively implement activities that contribute to improving the business climate at the local level. Starting from the assumption that there is a finite set of activities carried out by Business Council and that the goal of its work is to create a favorable business environment, the whole problem can be regarded as multi-criteria model where it is necessary to determine the weights of criteria and thus assess the extent to which they contribute to the problem goal.

The problem of relative weights determination exists since the formulation of the first multi-criteria analysis methods. During that period several approaches have been proposed to determine weights (Hwang, 1987; Saaty, 1980). Most of them can be classified depending on the information provided for their assessment in two main groups: (1) subjective and (2) objective approaches. Subjective approaches determine weights that reflect subjective judgment, while

Table 9. Business Council quality and functionality assessment

		Frequency	Percent	Valid Percent
Valid	1.000	6	10.7	20.0
	2.000	5	8.9	16.7
	3.000	6	10.7	20.0
	4.000	10	17.9	33.3
	5.000	3	5.4	10.0
	Total	30	53.6	100.0
Missing	System	26	46.4	
Total		56	100.0	

Table 10. Cross tabulation analysis between municipality size and quality and functionality rates of business councils

The Size of the Municipality	The Quality and Functionality Rates of the Business Councils					Total	Average Rate
	1.000	2.000	3.000	4.000	5.000		
Small: Up to 20.000 Count	3	1	2	3	1	10	2.8000
% within municipality size	30.0%	10.0%	20.0%	30.0%	10.0%	100.0%	
Medium: From 20.000-80.000 Count	2	2	3	4	2	13	3.1538
% within municipality size	15.4%	15.4%	23.1%	30.8%	15.4%	100.0%	
Big: Over 80000 Count	1	2	1	3	0	7	2.8571
% within municipality size	14.3%	28.6%	14.3%	42.9%	.0%	100.0%	
Total Count	6	5	6	10	3	30	2.9667
% within municipality size	20.0%	16.7%	20.0%	33.3%	10.0%	100.0%	

Table 11. Chi-Square Test results: Is there dependence between size of the municipality and quality and functionality rates of business councils

	Value	df	Asymp. Sig. (2-sided)
Pearson Chi-Square	3.130[a]	8	**.926**
Likelihood Ratio	3.669	8	.886
Linear-by-Linear Association	.028	1	.868
N of Valid Cases	30		

objective approaches determine weights by making use of mathematical models and they do not consider subjective judgment (Liu, 2003).

The most popular subjective approaches are the Analytic Hierarchy Process (Saaty, 1977), least squares comparison (Chu *et al.*, 1979), Delphi method (Hwang & Lin, 1987), etc. The objective approaches include methods such are LINMAP - Linear Programming Techniques for Multidimensional Analysis of Privileged (Srinivasan & Shocker, 1973), various computer-aided mathematical models (Pekelman & Sen, 1974), Data Envelopment Analysis (Charnes *et al.*, 1978), the entropy method (Hwang & Yoon, 1981; Van Uden & Kwiesielewicz, 2003; Chen & Lili Qu, 2006), principal component analysis and multi-attribute programming methods (Fan *et al.*, 1999), all statistical methods, etc. Usual application of those methods in the field of local economic development (Wong, 2002) or urban economy (Nel, 2001) is through creating composite indices. The subject of this chapter, in contrast to conventional

Table 12. Group statistics of quality and functionality ratings of Business Council according to the fact that the president of the council is among the business representatives

		N	Mean	Std. Deviation	Std. Error Mean
Is the President of the Council among the business representatives?	No	9	2.88889	1.691482	.563827
	Yes	21	3.00000	1.183216	.258199

application, relates to the implementation of multi-criteria analysis in local economic development problem where weight determination and ranking relevant criteria should be preformed, based on which would be possible, in some of the further research, to make comparison of business councils performance, through creating a composite indices of their quality and functionality.

Testing Dependence between Activities and Quality and Functionality of Business Council

Suppose the Business Council performs *n* different activities with aim to improve business environment and it is necessary to determine the measure of relative importance of each activity, expressed through weights w_j (j=1,2,...,n). A way of quantifying the contribution of activities is the assessment of the quality and functionality of the Business Council. The higher the rating of quality and functionality, the greater the extent of contribution of the Business Council in creating a friendly business environment. The quality and functionality ratings are subjective estimations of the LED offices about degree of performance success of the Business Council.

According to research data, Business Council performs the following activities:

A1: Draws conclusions, recommendations and opinions, it is important to improve the business climate in the community;

A2: Submits the above documents to the Municipal/City Parliament, Municipal/City Council and Municipal President/Mayor with a proposal to take adequate measures;

A3: Prepares a proposal of the Strategic Plan;

A4: Prepares amendments to the Strategic or Action Plan;

A5: Prepares annual implementation plans;

A6: Monitors and evaluates the implementation of projects and tasks of the Strategic Plan;

A7: Provides support to the LED offices in the performance of all functions within their jurisdiction;

A8: Provides support to Municipal President/Mayor and Municipal/City Council in making decisions related to other economic and development programs; and

A9: Gives opinions and suggestions for improvement of the municipal/city government, public enterprises, institutions, organizations and agencies established by the municipality/city in order to enhance conditions for economic activities in the municipality/city.

Each of these activities is categorized as "performed" and labeled with 1, or "not performed" and labeled with 0. In order to connect the category "performed" of certain Business Council activities with its quality and functionality rating, Chi-Square Test was used as a suitable non-parametric test. The results of Chi-Square Test where the dependence between quality and functionality rates was tested and particular activities conducted by Business Council are presented in Table 13.

Based on results presented above, it can be concluded that there is only one activity that is statistically significant for achieving higher quality

Table 13. Chi-Square Test results: testing dependence between quality and functionality rates and particular activities conducted by Business Council

Activity	Frequency of Quality and Functionality Rates in the Group of Business Counsels that are Performing the Observed Activity					Total Number of Business Councils which Perform the Observed Activity	P-Value
	1	2	3	4	5		
A1	4	3	6	10	3	26	0.115
A2	2	1	4	8	3	18	0.053
A3	2	3	3	3	3	14	0.553
A4	2	2	3	3	2	12	0.948
A5	0	1	2	3	2	8	0.203
A6	2	2	1	7	3	15	0.257
A7	1	2	4	7	3	17	0.181
A8	3	0	5	9	3	20	0.001
A9	3	1	3	8	3	18	0.063

and functionality rate of Business Council (p-value for *A8* is 0.001). This suggests that the activity A_8 has the highest level of utility for achieving the goal and this information will be used in forming the decision matrix in the analysis that follows. Also, for all other activities analog estimation logic will be applied - lower p-values mean a stronger connection with the quality and functionality rate, which automatically means greater importance for achieving the goal. Based on this data objectification of preferences will be conducted. Simple additive normalization of expression (1 - p-value) in order to obtain weights assessment, will not give the desired result because utility arising from the perception of statistical significance would be ignored and all activities would be treated equally. By applying a subjective method of determining the weights, the desired goal is achieved - to objectively assessed dependence between activity and quality and functionality rate, has been added new information about the utility of that assessment for achieving the goal of the problem. This procedure will be carried out using the method of Analytic Hierarchy Process.

Analytic Hierarchy Process for Weights Assessment of Business Council Activities

Analytic Hierarchy Process (AHP) is a well-known method of multi-criteria analysis developed by Thomas Saaty in 1980s. The AHP algorithm is defined through set of principals and axioms that delimits the scope of the problem environment (Forman & Gass, 2001). Three basic principles of AHP are (1) decomposition, (2) comparative judgments and (3) hierarchic composition or synthesis of priorities (Saaty, 1994).

The purpose of decomposition is to structure a complex problem into clusters of different hierarchy: criteria, sub-criteria, sub-sub-criteria and so on. At the bottom level are alternatives that should be ranked according to higher levels of hierarchy. The principle of comparative judgments is applied to construct pairwise comparisons of all combinations of elements in a particular cluster with respect to the cluster of the higher level. First knowledge about pairwise comparison method was introduced by Fechner in 1860 and developed sixty years later by Thurstone in 1927. Based on this essential pairwise comparison method, Saaty developed the AHP as a method for multi-criteria decision-making.

These pairwise comparisons are used to assess "local" priorities of the elements in a particular cluster with respect to their higher level cluster. The principle of hierarchical composition or synthesis is applied to the priorities of the elements in each cluster level and creates a kind of "general" priority vector for all elements and all hierarchy levels in the problem.

The theory of AHP method is based on three axioms. The first axiom, the reciprocal axiom refers to forming decision matrix. Based on pairwise comparison reciprocal matrix A_{nxn} has been formed, for each cluster respecting their parent in hierarchy above. The reciprocal matrix has elements $a_{ii} = 1$, (the main diagonal elements are equal to one), while the elements below main diagonal are computed as the reciprocal of the elements above, i.e. $a_{ji} = 1 / a_{ij}$, $i \neq j$, $i, j = 1, 2, ..., n$ (1):

$$\begin{bmatrix} 1 & \cdots & a_{1n} \\ \vdots & \ddots & \vdots \\ 1/a_{1n} & \cdots & 1 \end{bmatrix} \quad (1)$$

The second is homogeneity axiom which suggests that the elements being compared through pairwise comparison should not be too different or there will tend to be larger errors in judgment. On the basis of this axiom it is implied that AHP method is not suitable for problems where there is a large number of criteria or alternatives.

The third axiom states that judgments about, or the priorities of, the elements in a hierarchy do not depend on lower level elements. This axiom is required for the principle of hierarchic composition to be applied. While the first two axioms are, in our experience, completely consonant with real world applications, the third axiom requires careful examination, as it is not uncommon for it to be violated (Forman & Gass, 2001).

The mathematical background of AHP algorithm for calculating the priorities is theory of consistent matrices as well as Perron-Frobenius theory on non-negative matrix (Perron, 1907; Frobenius 1912). Simply, whole algorithm is based on ability of eigenvector to generate true or approximate weights (Saaty, 1987). The AHP algorithm makes a comparison of criteria or alternatives with respect to an observed criterion, in pairwise mode. As a tool for pairwise comparison, AHP uses a fundamental scale of absolute numbers (from 1 to 9) that has been widely accepted in practice and validated by many different experiments in the field of decision theory (Saaty, 1977). This scale has to be a scale that quantifies individual preferences with respect to quantitative and qualitative attributes just as well or better than other scales. The pairwise comparison matrix that refers to activities of Business Council whose relative importance is to be estimated is presented in Table 14.

According to the Perron-Frobenius Theorem, if A is an nxn, non-negative, primitive matrix, then one of its eigenvalues λ_{max} is positive and greater than or equal to (in absolute value) all other eigenvalues, and there is a positive eigenvector W corresponding to that eigenvalue, and that eigenvalue is a simple root (matrix Frobenius root) of the characteristic equation. (Alonso & Lamata, 2006, p. 447):

$$AW = \lambda_{max} W \text{ or } (A - \lambda_{max} I)W = 0 \quad (2)$$

According to eigenvector method, weights could be calculated based on eigenvector W by additive normalization. If the pairwise comparison matrix is perfectly consistent, following statements are valid: (1) for arbitrary i, j and p, $a_{ij} . a_{jp} = a_{ip}$ ($i,j,p=1,..., n$), (2) the comparison matrix determinant is equal to 0 and (3) the matrix Frobenius root i.e. eigenvalue λ_{max} is equal to n and (4) the remaining eigenvalues are equal 0 for any a_{ij}. Thus, the eigenvector corresponding to the λ_{max} is always non-negative and each element of the

Table 14. Pairwise comparison matrix

	A1	A2	A3	A4	A5	A6	A7	A8	A9
A1	1	1/2	4	8	2	3	2	1/2	1
A2	2	1	5	9	2	3	2	1/2	1
A3	1/4	1/5	1	4	1/4	1/3	1/4	1/5	1/5
A4	1/8	1/9	1/4	1	1/8	1/6	1/8	1/9	1/9
A5	1/2	1/2	4	8	1	2	1	1/3	1/2
A6	1/3	1/3	3	6	1/2	1	1/2	1/4	1/4
A7	1/2	1/2	4	8	1	2	1	1/4	0.5
A8	2	2	5	9	3	4	3	1	2
A9	1	1	5	9	2	3	2	1/2	1

eigenvector standardized by additive normalization can be interpreted as relative importance of corresponding criterion (Alonso & Lamata, 2001). In situation of perfect consistency, the comparison matrix satisfies the transitivity property for all pairwise comparisons. However, ideal judgments that decision matrix makes consistent are rare and it is necessary to determine the acceptable level of inconsistency. In this case, Saaty defined the consistency index (*CI*) as follows:

$$CI = \frac{\ddot{e}_{max} - n}{n - 1} \tag{3}$$

as well as consistency ratio:

$$CR = \frac{CI}{RI} \tag{4}$$

where *RI* is the average value of *CI* for random matrices using the Saaty scale. According to Saaty only acceptable inconsistency is if $CR < 0.1$.

For pairwise comparison matrix presented in Table 14, the calculated maximum eigenvalue was $\lambda_{max} = 9.304137$, as well as the corresponding consistency index $CI = 0.0380171$ and consistency ratio $CR = 0.0262187$. The random index value was the one provided by Saaty and Wharton where $RI_{(n=9)} = 1.45$ (data from Table 1. *RI*(n) values from various authors, Alonso & Lamata, 2001, p. 449). The application of eigenvector method determined weights presented in Table 15. Eigenvector solution is calculated by additive normalization procedure, i.e. each weight is calculated as ratio of corresponding coefficient of eigenvector and sum of all elements of eigenvector. The calculations were performed using the software package Mathematica 9.0.

According to results providing support to municipal government bodies (Municipal President/ Mayor and Municipal/City Council) in making decisions related to economic and development programs is the activity which makes Business Council the most efficient and effective in creating a favorable business environment, i.e. achieving greater level of quality and functionality. Activities that follow in significance are submitting proper documents with conclusions, recommendations and opinions, it is important to improve the business climate in the community to municipal government bodies, as well as giving opinions and suggestions for improvement of the municipal government, public enterprises, institutions, organizations and agencies established by the municipality in order to enhance conditions for economic activities.

Table 15. Weights assessment

Activity	Eigenvector	Eigenvector Solution (Weights)	Rank of Activity Importance
A1	0.3571332	0.1398397	4
A2	0.4317899	0.1690724	2
A3	0.0841002	0.0329304	8
A4	0.0374878	0.0146788	9
A5	0.2381119	0.0932355	5
A6	0.1523057	0.0596371	7
A7	0.2381119	0.0932355	5
A8	0.6214303	0.2433283	1
A9	0.3934056	0.1540425	3

FUTURE RESEARCH DIRECTIONS

Future research that would be complementary to the one presented in the chapter will focus on the analysis of other forms of institutional cooperation between local authorities and the business community. Special attention will be paid to the analysis of the work and results of the Socio-Economic Council and the Council for Employment. In this regard it is possible to perform an analog analysis of their activities in order to assess their quality and functionality.

In addition, research will focus on collecting data for the objectification quality and functionality evaluation of these local government bodies. Namely, authors intend to measure the effects of their actions through numbers of open and closed businesses, employment rates, unemployment rates and investments in the territory of the observed LSG unit. Finally, it is important to investigate and review the business community about the quality and functionality of LSG bodies involved in issues of local economic development. By fusion of all those research results, it is possible, by using multi-criteria analysis, to create a composite index which show the comparison and ranking of the business councils in different LSG units, which contained indicators of LED office self-evaluation, as well as attitudes of the business community about the quality and functionality of cooperation.

Nevertheless, further research will focus on global dimension of the local economic issues, considering the analysis of the business environment through international cooperation and relations with neighboring countries.

CONCLUSION

Research conducted for the purposes of this chapter clearly indicates that the LED offices are not largely satisfied with the quality and functionality of the business council (low average quality and functionality rate). On the other hand, if we take into account the response of LSG units, where only one-third of them participated in the survey it can be concluded that there is still no awareness of any local authorities to proactively participate in the improvement of its quality and functionality.

Positive conclusions are related to the fact that the most of LSG units (regardless of size) have formed bodies that would carry out institutional co-operation with the business community.

Also, there are indications of good cooperation with representatives of business and the most of the business councils head are exactly business representatives.

When it comes to activities that are carried out by business councils, their effects are not assessed as significant, because there is a clear statistical correlation only between one activity and quality and functionality rate. The AHP method provided weights that suggest the same conclusion. This clearly indicates that the business councils in observed LSG units in Serbia do not carry out their activities in an efficient and effective manner. Hence, it is necessary to improve the quality and functionality of the business councils in terms of the selection of activities according to the concrete needs and problems of the local economy in observed LSG unit, but also through a more efficient way of carrying out those activities.

REFERENCES

Alonso, J. A., & Lamata, M. T. (2006). Consistency in the Analytic Hierarchy Process: A New Approach. *International Journal of Uncertainty, Fuzziness and Knowledge-based Systems, 14*(4), 445–459. doi:10.1142/S0218488506004114

Antic, L., DJukic, T., Stevanovic, T., Stankovic, J., Bojic, B., & Grabovica, E. (2013). Activity Based Costing and Throughput Accounting in the Function of Making Business Decisions. *Technics Technologies Education Management, 8*(3), 1840–1503.

Bumgardner, M., Buehlmann, U., Schuler, A., & Crissey, J. (2011). Competitive Actions of Small Firms in a Declining Market. *Journal of Small Business Management, 49*(4), 578–598. doi:10.1111/j.1540-627X.2011.00337.x

Business Friendly Certification South East Europe. (2013). *Certification of Business friendly Municipalities in SEE*. Retrieved February 16, 2013 from http://www.bfc-see.org/upload/Document/File/2013_07/BFC_SEE_Brochure.pdf

Charnes, A., Cooper, W. W., & Rhodes, E. (1978). Measuring the Efficiency of Decision Making Units. *European Journal of Operational Research, 12*(6), 429–444. doi:10.1016/0377-2217(78)90138-8

Chen, Y., & Qu, L. (2006). Evaluating the Selection of Logistics Centre Location Using Fuzzy MCDM Model Based on Entropy Weight. In *Proceedings of the Sixth World Congress on Intelligent Control and Automation*, (pp. 7128 – 7132). Academic Press. doi:10.1109/WCICA.2006.1714468

Chu, A. T. W., Kalaba, R. E., & Spingarn, K. (1979). A comparison of two methods for determining the weights of belonging to fuzzy sets. *Journal of Optimization Theory and Applications, 27*(4), 531–538. doi:10.1007/BF00933438

Ciocarlan-Chitucea, A., & Popescu, D. (2010). The SMEs Performances Explained Through Influences of the Economic Context. Study Case: Romania. *Review of International Comparative Management, 12*(6), 195–201.

Dunkelberg, C., & Wade, H. (2012). NFIB Small Business Economic Trends, December 2012. *National Federation of Independent Business*. Available at http://www.nfib.com/portals/0/pdf/sbet/sbet201012.pdf

Fan, Z., Ma, J., & Tian, P. (1999). A subjective and objective integrated approach for the determination of attribute weights. *European Journal of Operational Research, 112*(2), 397–404. doi:10.1016/S0377-2217(98)00141-6

Forman, E. H., & Gass, S. I. (2001). The Analytic Hierarchy Process – An Exposition. *Operations Research, 49*(4), 469–486. doi:10.1287/opre.49.4.469.11231

Forman, E. H., Saaty, T. L., Selly, M. A., & Waldron, R. (1983). Expert Choice. Decision Support Software.

Grilli, L. (2011). When the Going Gets Tough, Do the Tough Get Going? The Pre-Entry Work Experience of Founders and High-tech Start-up Survival during an Industry Crisis. *International Small Business Journal, 29*(6), 626–647. doi:10.1177/0266242610372845

Hwang, C. L., & Lin, M. J. (1987). *Group Decision Making Under Multiple Criteria: Methods and Applications*. Berlin: Springer-Verlag. doi:10.1007/978-3-642-61580-1

Hwang, C. L., & Yoon, K. (1981). *Multiple Attribute Decision Making: Methods and Applications*. Berlin: Springer. doi:10.1007/978-3-642-48318-9

Lavric, V. (2010). The Development of the SMEs Sector in Romania. An Approach Regarding the Dynamics and the Perspectives. *Review of International Comparative Management, 11*(5), 931–939.

Likert, R. (1931). A technique for the measurement of attitudes. *Archives de Psychologie, 22*(140), 1–55.

Liu, C. C. (2003). Simulating Weights Restrictions in Data Envelopment Analysis by the Subjective and Objective Integrated Approach. *Web Journal of Chinese Management Review, 6*(1), 68–78.

Lloyd, L., Mumby, R., & Sear, L. (2010). Entrepreneurship Education: Embedding Practitioner Experience', 2010. *Review of International Comparative Management, 12*(6), 391–403.

Mantel, N. (1963). Chi-Square Tests with One Degree of Freedom; Extensions of the Mantel-Haenszel Procedure. *Journal of the American Statistical Association, 58*(303), 690–700.

McFarland, C., Seeger, K., & Geary, C. (2010). *The Role of Local Elected Officials in Economic Development: Ten Things You Should Know*. Washington, DC: National League of Cities.

McFarland, C. K., & McConnell, J. K. (2011a). *Strategies for Globally Competitive Cities: Local Roles in Foreign Direct Investment and International Trade*. Washington, DC: National League of Cities.

McFarland, C. K., & McConnell, J. K. (2011b). Local Roles in Cultivating a Small Business and Entrepreneurial Culture. In *Proceedings of Conference Small Business and Entrepreneurship during an Economic Recovery*. Retrieved July 8, 2013 from http://www.federalreserve.gov/newsevents/conferences/mcfarland-20111109.pdf

Morris, R. J., & Brennan, G. P. (2003). Creating a Seamless Local Government and Small Business Interface for Better Regional Economic Development Outcomes. *Journal of Small Business Management, 41*(4), 417–426.

National Alliance for Local Economic Development. (2012). *Certification program business-friendly municipality*. Retrieved April 21, 2013 from http://www.naledserbia.org/documents/download/Certification_brochure_ 2012.pdf.

Nel, E. (2001). Local Economic Development: A Review and Assessment of its Current Status in South Africa. Urban Studies, 38(7), 1003–1024.

Nicolescu, O., & Nicolescu, C. (2013). Entrepreneurs' Perceptions of the State Implication in the Business Environment Modelling in Romania. *Transylvanian Review of Administrative Sciences, 38*(E/2013), 106-124.

Nicolescu, O., Verboncu, I., Profiroiu, M., Nicolescu, C., & Anghel, F. (2010). Romanian Management Assessment. Bucharest: Prouniversitaria.

Norwood, S. (2011). *Tatum's Survey of Business Conditions*. Tatum. Retrieved July 7, 2013 from http://www.smallbusinessadvocate.com/small-business-articles/the-tatumsurvey-of-business-conditions-september

Official Gazette of Republic of Serbia. (2001). *Law on Chambers of Commerce*, No. 65/2001, No. 36/2009 and No. 99/2011.

Official Gazette of Republic of Serbia. (2004). *Law on Social - Economic Council*, No. 125/2004.

Official Gazette of Republic of Serbia. (2007). *The Law on Local Self-Government*, No. 129/2007.

Official Gazette of Republic of Serbia. (2009). *Law on Employment and Unemployment Insurance*, No. 36/2009 and No. 88/2010.

Pekelman, D., & Sen, S. K. (1974). Mathematical programming models for the determination of attribute weights. *Management Science, 20*(7), 1217–1229. doi:10.1287/mnsc.20.8.1217

Perron, O. (1907). Zur Theorie der Matrizen. *Math Annales, 64*, 248–263.

Plackett, R. L. (1983). Karl Pearson and the Chi-Squared Test. *International Statistical Review, 51*(1), 59–72. doi:10.2307/1402731

Reynolds, P., Storey, D. J., & Westhead, P. (1994). Cross-National Comparisons of the Variation in New Firm Formation Rates. *Regional Studies, 28*(4), 443–456. doi:10.1080/00343409412331348386

Roxas, H., Lindsay, V., Ashill, N., & Victorio, A. (2008). An Institutional View of Local Entrepreneurial Climate. *Asia-Pacific Social Science Review, 7*(1), 28–44. doi:10.3860/apssr.v7i1.113

Saaty, T. L. (1977). A scaling method for priorities in hierarchical structures. *Journal of Mathematical Psychology, 15*(3), 234–281. doi:10.1016/0022-2496(77)90033-5

Saaty, T. L. (1980). *Multicriteria decision making: the Analytic Hierarchy Process*. New York, NY: McGraw-Hill.

Saaty, T. L. (1987). Rank according to Perron: A new insight. *Mathematics Magazine, 6*(4), 211–213. doi:10.2307/2689340

Saaty, T. L. (1994). *Fundamentals of Decision Making*. Pittsburgh, PA: RWS Publications.

Srinivasan, V., & Shocker, A. D. (1973). Estimating the weights for multiple attributes in a composite criterion using pairwise judgments. *Psychonometrica, 38*(4), 473–493. doi:10.1007/BF02291490

Stankovic, J., Andjelkovic-Pesic, M., & Radenkovic-Jocic, D. (in press). Improving the Business Environment of Cities and Municipalities in Serbia: Experiences and Recommendations. *Themes, 38* (1).

Stankovic, J., Jankovic-Milic, V., & Andjelkovic, M. (2012). The Role of Institutions in Creating Business Friendly Environment. In *Proceedings of the Conference Employment through the Prism of Entrepreneurship*, (pp. 62-69). University of Montenegro.

Stankovic, J., Jankovic-Milic, V., & Andjelkovic-Pesic, M. (2013). Multi-Criteria Analysis of Social Capital Influence on Business Performances. *Actual Problems of Economics, 12* (150), 515-52.

Stankovic, J., Jankovic-Milic, V., & Boskovic, G. (2013). Business Friendly Environment –The Key Task of the Local Self-Government, International Scientific Conference. In *Proceedings of ISC*, (pp. 353-362). ISC.

Stankovic, J., Jankovic-Milic, V., & Radosavljevic, M. (2014). Improving the business environment in cities and municipalities in Serbia. *Matica Srpska Social Sciences Quarterly, 146* (1), 105 -117.

Statistical Office of the Republic of Serbia. (2012). *Municipalities and Regions in the Republic of Serbia in 2012*. Retrieved February 16, 2013 from http://webrzs.stat.gov.rs/WebSite/repository/documents/00/00/54/08/OpstinskigodisnjakRepublike_Srbije_2011.zip

Thurstone, L. L. (1927). A law of comparative judgements. *Psychological Review*, *34*(4), 273–286. doi:10.1037/h0070288

Van Uden, E., & Kwiesielewicz, M. (2003). Evaluating Attribute Significance in AHP Using Shannon Entropy. In *Proceedings of ISAHP*. ISAHP.

Wong, C. (2002). Developing Indicators to Inform Local Economic Development in England. *Urban Studies (Edinburgh, Scotland)*, *39*(10), 1833–1863. doi:10.1080/0042098022000002984

ADDITIONAL READING

Aguaron, J., & Moreno-Jimenez, J. M. (2003). The geometric consistency index: Approximated thresholds. *European Journal of Operational Research*, *147*(1), 137–145. doi:10.1016/S0377-2217(02)00255-2

Alonso, J. A., & Lamata, M. T. (2004). Estimation of the Random Index in the Analytic Hierarchy Process. *Proceedings of Information Processing and Management of Uncertainty in Knowledge-Based Systems*, *1*, 317–322.

Aull-Hyde, R., Erdogan, S., & Duke, J. M. (2006). An experiment on the consistency of aggregated comparison matrices in AHP. *European Journal of Operational Research*, *171*(1), 290–295. doi:10.1016/j.ejor.2004.06.037

Begg, I. (1999). Cities and competitiveness. *Urban Studies (Edinburgh, Scotland)*, *36*(5), 795–809. doi:10.1080/0042098993222

Bennett, R. J., & Krebs, G. (1991). *Local Economic Development: Public–Private Partnership Initiative in Britain and Germany*. London: Belhaven Press.

Blakely, E. J. (1994). *Planning Local Economic Development: Theory and Practice* (2nd ed.). California: Sage.

Chisholm, M. D. I. (1990). *Regions in Recession and Resurgence*. London: Unwin and Hyman.

Clarke, S. E. (1995). Institutional logics and local economic development: A comparative analysis of eight American cities. *International Urban and Regional Research*, *18*(4), 513–533. doi:10.1111/j.1468-2427.1995.tb00526.x

Coombes, M., Raybould, S., & Wong, C. (1992). *Developing Indicators to Assess the Potential for Urban Regeneration*. London: HMSO.

Deas, I., & Giordano, B. (2001). Conceptualising and measuring urban competitiveness in major English cities: An exploratory approach. *Environment & Planning*, *33*(8), 1411–1429. doi:10.1068/a33142

Dikmen, I., & Birgonul, M. T. (2006). An analytic hierarchy process based model for risk and opportunity assessment of international construction projects. *Canadian Journal of Civil Engineering*, *33*(1), 58–68. doi:10.1139/l05-087

Eisenschitz, A., & Gough, J. (1993). *The Politics of Local Economic Policy: The Problems and Possibilities of Local Initiative*. Basingstoke: Macmillan.

Escobar, M. T., & Moreno-Jiménez, J. M. (2000). Reciprocal distributions in the analytic hierarchy process. *European Journal of Operational Research*, *123*(1), 154–174. doi:10.1016/S0377-2217(99)00086-7

European Commission. (1995). *Local development information press*. Brussels: European Commission Directorate General for Regional Policies.

Figueira, J., Greco, S., & Ehrgott, M. (Eds.). (2005). *Multiple Criteria Decision Analysis: State of the Art Survey*. Springer.

Gass, S. I., & Rapcsák, T. (2004). Singular value decomposition in AHP. *European Journal of Operational Research, 154*(3), 573–584. doi:10.1016/S0377-2217(02)00755-5

Ginevičius, R., & Podvezko, V. (2007 a). Some problems of evaluating multicriteria decision methods. *International Journal of Management and Decision Making, 8*(5/6), 527–539. doi:10.1504/IJMDM.2007.013415

Ginevičius, R., & Podvezko, V. (2007 b). Complex assessment of sustainable development of state regions with emphasis on ecological and dwelling conditions. *Ekologija, 53*, 41–48.

Kearns, G., & Philo, C. (1993). *Selling Places: The City as Cultural Capital, Past and Present*. Oxford: Pergamon Press.

Kresl, P. K., & Singh, B. (1999). Competitiveness and the urban economy: Twenty-four large US metropolitan areas. *Urban Studies (Edinburgh, Scotland), 36*(5), 1017–1027. doi:10.1080/0042098993330

Levy, J. M. (1990). What do Local economic developers actually do? *Journal of the American Planning Association, 56*(2), 153–160. doi:10.1080/01944369008975756

Ma, J., Fan, Z.-P., & Huang, L. H. (1999). A subjective and objective integrated approach to determine attribute weights. *European Journal of Operational Research, 112*(2), 397–404. doi:10.1016/S0377-2217(98)00141-6

Mansouri, S. A., Moattar Husseini, S. M., & Newman, S. T. (2000). A review of the modern approaches to multicriteria cell design. *International Journal of Production Research, 38*(5), 1201–1218. doi:10.1080/002075400189095

Munday, M. (1990). *Japanese Manufacturing Investment in Wales*. Cardiff: University of Wales Press.

Ozdemir, M. S. (2005). Validity and inconsistency in the analytic hierarchy process. *Applied Mathematics and Computation, 161*(3), 707–720. doi:10.1016/j.amc.2003.12.099

Peláez, J. I., & Lamata, M. T. (2003). A New Measure of Consistency for Positive Reciprocal Matrices. *Computers & Mathematics with Applications (Oxford, England), 46*(12), 1839–1845. doi:10.1016/S0898-1221(03)90240-9

Phelps, N. A. (1996). *Industry embeddedness and peripheral region development: a review of the literture with illustrations from Wales*. Paper presented to *ACSP–AESOP Joint International Congress*, July, Toronto.

Porter, M. E. (1990). *The Competitive Advantage of Nations*. Basingstoke: Macmillan.

Porter, M. E. (1991). *The Competitive Advantage of Massachusetts*. Boston, MA: Harvard Business School.

Saaty, T. L. (2005). The Analytic Hierarchy and Analytic Network Processes for the Measurement of Intangible Criteria and for Decision-Making, in Figueira, J.; Greco, S.; Ehrgott, M. (Eds.). Multiple Criteria Decision Analysis: State of the Art Surveys. Springer, 345–408.

Viteikiene, M., & Zavadskas, E. K. (2007). Evaluating the sustainability of Vilnius city residential areas. *Journal of Civil Engineering and Management, 13*(2), 149–155.

Young, S., Hood, N., & Peters, E. (1994). Multinational enterprises and regional economic development. *Regional Studies*, *28*(7), 657–678. doi:10.1080/00343409412331348566

Zavadskas, E. K., & Turskis, Z. (2011). Multiple criteria decision making (MCDM) methods in economics: An overview. *Technological and Economic Development of Economy*, *17*(2), 397–427. doi:10.3846/20294913.2011.593291

Zavadskas, E. K., Zakarevičius, A., & Antuchevičienė, J. (2006). Evaluation of ranking accuracy in multi-criteria decisions. *Informatica*, *17*(4), 601–618.

Zavadska,s E.K., Vilutiene, T.,Turskis, Z. & Tamosaitiene, T. (2010). Contractor selection for construction works by applying saw-g and topsis grey techniques, *Journal of Business Economics and Management, 11*(1), 34-55.

KEY TERMS AND DEFINITIONS

Analytic Hierarchy Process: One of the most popular methods of multi-criteria analysis developed by Thomas Saaty in 1980.

Business Council: An advisory body which is aimed at encouraging economic activities at the local level.

Business Environment: An environment in which business operates.

Chi-Square Test: Well known statistical procedure that refers both to a statistical distribution and to a hypothesis testing procedure that produces a statistic that is approximately distributed as the chi-square distribution.

Institutional Cooperation: Official cooperation between local government bodies and the economy sector.

Local Self-Government Institutions: The authorities at the local level.

Multi-Criteria Analysis: A set of methods aimed at selection or ranking alternatives on the basis of two or more relevant criteria.

Statistical Analysis: A set of methods that are used for data analysis.

Weights Assessment: The procedure of determining the relative importance of criteria in the model.

ENDNOTES

1 U.S. Agency for International Development.

2 *GTZ* and then its successor organisation *GIZ* (Deutsche Gesellschaft für Internationale Zusammenarbeit), formed on January 1, 2011 through the merger of DED, GTZ and Inwent.

3 United Nations Development Programme.

4 All of the tables under this heading are the authors' calculation using SPSS.

Chapter 19
Towards a Citizen-Centric E-Government Service Index Model:
Developments and Impediments within the Egyptian Context

Mohamed R. Zakaria
Al Ghurair University, UAE

Tarek R. Gebba
Al Ghurair University, UAE

Mohamed Gamal Aboelmaged
Ain Shams University, Egypt

ABSTRACT

The purpose of this chapter is three-fold. First, it proposes a novel E-Government Service Index (ESI) that is a citizen-centric maturity model. Second, the model uses Egypt's E-Government services as an experimental arena to spot the maturity of the provided services and highlights e-government development in Egypt. Finally, the chapter explores the impediments of citizen-centric e-government implementation within the Egyptian context and recommends specific interventions within the frame of the proposed model.

INTRODUCTION

The emerging role of Information and Communications Technology (ICT) in facilitating and accelerating social, economic and political development has been recognized by most of developing countries. Moreover, ICT has been acknowledged for paving the way towards democratic initiatives through shifting public authorizes towards creating new perceptions about government and governance. An increasing number of federal, state, and local governments are placing plenty of information online, automating administrative processes, procedures, and interacting with citi-

DOI: 10.4018/978-1-4666-7266-6.ch019

zens, businesses and employees through online public services, nevertheless the great opportunities offered by these new technologies remain mostly unutilized. Achieving more improvements in delivery and efficiency of government services necessitates a rethinking of the role of ICT. Essentially, a UN report has indicated that most of governments perceive E-government-as-a-whole concept which focuses on the provision of services at the front-end, supported by integration, consolidation and innovation in back-end processes and systems to achieve greatest cost savings and improved service delivery (UN, 2008).

While the application of information technology in governmental bodies can be traced back to the 1970's, E-Government has been have been developed along with the E-Commerce and internet flourishing era in the late 1990s (Danziger, 2002; Grönlund, 2010; Hiller & Bélanger, 2001).

An assented definition of E-Government is hard to find since every definition adopt such a level of E-Government sophistication ranges from considering E-Government as simple electronic service delivery to a complex infrastructure that transform government role and enforce democratic initiatives. For example, United Nations (UN, 2002) defined E-Government as utilizing the internet and the world-wide-web for delivering government information and services to citizens, while OECD (2003) asserted that E-Government is the use of ICT for better governance. On the other hand, other definitions focus more on goals of E-Government including cost saving, enhanced transparency, improved service delivery and public administration, and enhanced government competency and democratic process (Grönlund, 2010; UN, 2005).

As a communication system, E-Government systems can be divided into two components involves internal communication (IC) subsystems and external communication (XC) subsystems. While the IC subsystem represents the E-business layer (back-end) where knowledge processing and sharing takes place, the XC subsystem embodies the Government Portal (front-end) layer where the public citizens can interact and obtain the necessary services (Zakareya & Zahir, 2005).

Hence, a true advantage of E-Government is not only applying ICT technology but also in answering the needs of public citizens as Figure 1 highlights some of internal and external E-Government contributions (UN, 2008).

A shared conception during the preliminary stages of E-Government development has usually been information technology-oriented to enhance data quality and integrate back-end with front-end systems.

Therefore, there is a need for developing a model that spots the level of E-Government service maturity regarding information technology, stakeholders' interactivity and participation as well as online transaction.

This chapter is an attempt to find an answer for the following questions: (1) are the current maturity models efficient enough to spot deficiencies in E-government services?; (2) How can the proposed E-Government Service Index (ESI) (Zakaria & Gebba, 2012) model overcomes shortages within the current maturity models?; and (3) how can ESI model spot limitations within an E-government program in one of the developing countries?. To answer these questions, this chapter aims at proposing a novel E-Government Service Index (ESI) that is citizen-centric maturity model, using Egypt's E-Government services as an experimental arena to spot the maturity of the provided services, and exploring the impediments of citizen-centric E-Government implementation within the Egyptian context and recommending specific interventions within the frame of the proposed ESI model.

The chapter is organized into eight sections. The second section explores key E-Government maturity models. This is followed by research

Figure 1. Internal and external contributions of e-government
(Adapted from UN, 2008).

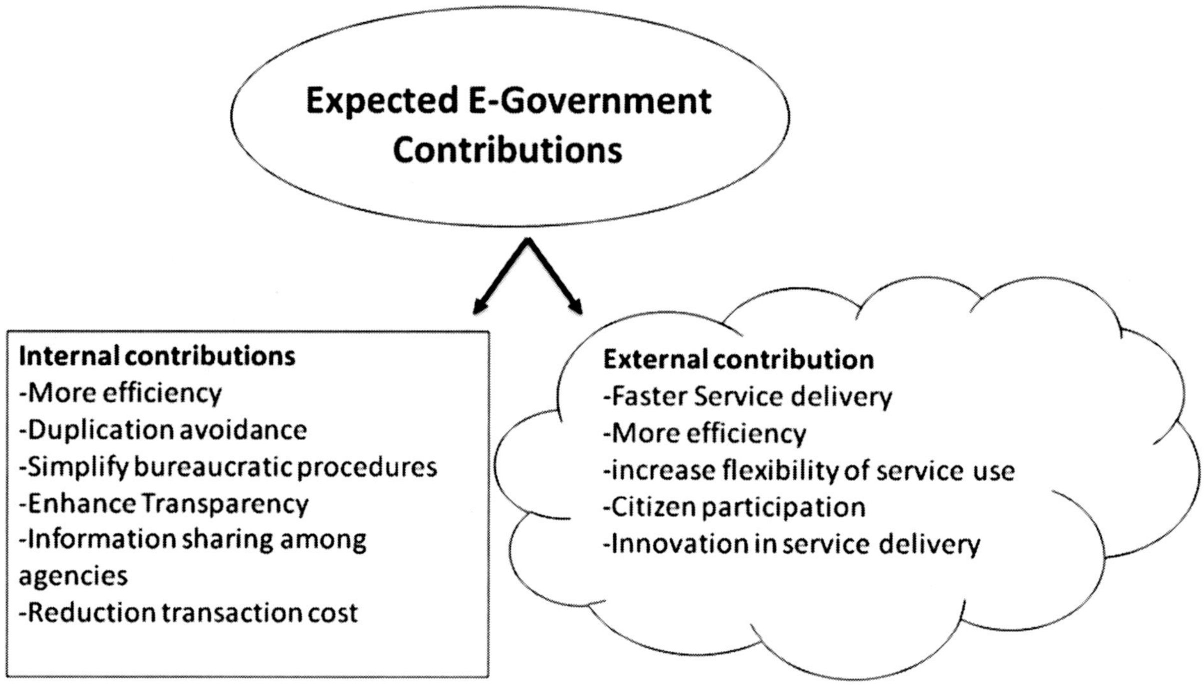

methodology in sections three and four, respectively. Section five presents the development E-Government service index (ESI) model and its application to analyze and spot the maturity level of Egypt's E-Government services. Section six explores the implementation of E-Government in Egypt as well as the impediments to citizen-centric E-Government in Egypt and recommendations for facilitating its implementation. Finally, sections seven and eight focuses on research discussion and conclusion.

E-GOVERNMENT MATURITY MODELS

E-government service delivery capabilities can be assessed by identifying and analyzing e-government maturity. Through literature review for the domain, researchers concluded a classification for the maturity models into: normative models and non-normative models. This classification is based on common characteristics and methodologies of implementation (Coursey & Norris, 2008; Zakaria & Gebba, 2012).

1. Normative Maturity Models

Normative models are stage-based models that reflect an evolutionary methodology of e-government as a number of consecutive stages. These models are usually adopted by international organizations such as United Nations and European Union (Capgemini, 2007; 2010; UN, 2005; 2010). The concept of stage-based models goes back Nolan's (1973) discussions about Information Systems maturity in organizations. Within this view, E-Government system goes via different evolutionary stages from simple to complex online interactive system between government and its stakeholders.

ANAO and SAFAD Models (ANAO, 2000; Statskontoret, 2000)

Australian National Auditing Office (ANAO) has developed a normative maturity model to classify online service delivery of government authorizes. The model is divided into four stages:

1. **Publishing Information:** Where authorities provide citizens with static information as well as downloadable publications with unlimited access;
2. **Interaction Stage:** Where citizens are supplied with search and screening facility and calculation services for government subsidies and debts;
3. **Transaction of Secure Information:** Where only users with registered identification have access to secured governmental information; and
4. **Sharing Information with Other Agencies:** In which information are shared among various governmental agencies such as sharing a new phone number of a citizen among all governmental agencies. Similarly, The Swedish Agency for Administrative Development (SAFAD) has developed another normative maturity model of E-Government that reflects four evolutionary phases including information pivot, interaction, transaction, and integration.

United Nations E-Government Web Evolution Model and EU Benchmarking Model (Capgemini, 2007; 2010; UN, 2005; 2010)

United Nations E-Government web evolution model categorized E-government development into five stages including emerging presence stage, that represents the official online presence of governmental bodies in form of an official static website of a government with links to different ministers and archived information. Such a stage resembles the first stage in all the above mentioned models. *Enhanced presence* is the second stage that provides wider information for public in form of current and archived documents with the ability of searching for documents such as, polices, regulations, laws, etc. However, the direction of information in this stage is tipping to public from the government side only. Third stage, interactive presence, provides public with the services they require in a manner of downloadable forms such as tax and license forms. Fourth, transactional presence that reflects the point at which the government should be able to provide all of its services online and in interactive mode such as online payments of taxes, online application for IDs and passports, issuing official certificates online such as birth certificate. Moreover, such a governmental website should have the ability to provide online tenders, and suppliers can bid online through secure links. Finally, network presence is the stage where governments use web and internet technology not only for providing services electronically but also to participate in decision-making such as, collecting citizens' views about certain laws or policies and voting for elections. Moreover, this stage provides all types of electronic interaction among governmental bodies (G to G) and between government and public (G to P and P to G). In the United Nations report 2010 (UN, 2010), the development stages are reduced to only four: Emerging stage and enhanced stage which resembles the emerging presence and enhanced presence in 2005 maturity model (UN, 2005). Transactional services: is a combination of the interactive, transactional, and network presence. Connected services stage represents seamless integration between applications among government agencies. The EU benchmarking framework is composed of five stages (information, one-way interaction, two-way interaction, transaction, integration). The EU five stages are somehow similar to those of UN where information stage reflects the emerging and enhanced stages in the UN model, while the one-way, two-way interaction stage and transaction stages resemble the interaction stage. Additionally, the personalization stage is close to the connected services stage.

Layne and Lee Model (Layne, 2001)

The model is derived from observing E-Government evolving in USA. Layne and Lee claim that the model initiated from the state level but can be used on federal as well as local level. The model divides the delivery of services into four stages: Catalogue: this stage resembles the publishing information stage at the ANAO model, where the focus is mainly on providing the public with information about the agency and its publications. Transaction: this stage gives public the choice to process governmental services online such as, renewing licenses and paying fines. Vertical integration: This stage reflects the linkage between local level systems and higher level systems. Horizontal integration: this stage reflects the linkage between all systems on the same level.

Hiller and Bélanger Model (Hiller & Bélanger, 2001)

This model divides the E-Government development stages into five stages:

1. **Information:** This stage resembles the first stage in the above two models where agencies are posting static information about their offered services and related publications.
2. **Two-Way Communication:** This stage is the same as the previous one with the advantage of communication between public and agency through e-mails.
3. **Transaction:** According to Hiller and Bélanger (2001), this is the most advanced level of E-Government where the public can process all their requirements online such as renewing license, paying fine and tax. Such stage resembles the transaction stage mentioned in the above two models.
4. **Integration:** Refers to the presence of single entry point to all the services provided by the E-Government.
5. **Political Participation:** Such stage includes online voting and posting comments online. Hiller and Bélanger (2001) claim that this stage belongs to stage two. Nevertheless, the importance of political aspect encourages a separate development stage.

2. Non-Normative Maturity Models

Although stages model tendency has been employed by many parties ranging from governments to international bodies such as UN and EU, it has its own serious flaws (Limba, 2011; Gronlund, 2010; Coursey, 2008; Goldkuhl, 2006; Persson & Goldkuhl, 2005) which are discussed below. Because of the defects and lack of a ground theoretical validation (Chatfield, 2009) of the stages models, new models started to evolve with different conceptions, such as:

Diamond Model (Goldkuhl, 2006)

Diamond Model is based on the idea of services categorization and deconstruction of the stages model inspiration into three polarities regarding e-services integration, security and presence. Moreover, each service class has further subclasses. For example, the service integration stage in stages models is decomposed into two categories in the Diamond Model: Separated and Coordinated. Separated services refer to services not integrated. Whereas coordinated services class refer to integrated services and has further decomposition to fused and aligned subclasses. Aligned services indicate services that are put together in one uniting website but still identifiable as differentiated services, while fused services refer to services that are fully integrated together as one service with no observable differences. The same methodology is used with the other two polarities where each polar has two subcategories opposite in description with further decomposition to other subclasses as shown in Figure 2.

E-Co Model (Lind, 2007)

The E-Co model is a user centric model that is based on four axes: Vision (what e-service is needed?), Current situation (problem awareness), Means of change (tools to achieve the vision) and feedback (evaluation of the degree of closeness to the vision). The model encourages the participation of citizens with respect to the vision as it takes into account citizens' life situations as a point of departure for considering the potential e-service. The naming of the model comes from a perception that the evolvement of e-services is a continuous co-design process taking different stakeholders' values into consideration.

3. Normative vs. Non-Normative Trends

Normative models have been used to classify services in order to evaluate progress of E-Government adoption among countries or among agencies in countries. The classification is based on sequential stages where the higher the stage in order the better it is, additionally higher stages embrace other stages lower in order. As a result, the linear evolution of those stages from basic online presence to full transaction is a central assumption. Such an assumption raised many questions among researchers about the accuracy, guidance and theoretical validity of that type of models

Figure 2. Categorization of e-services based on three polarities
(Adopted from Lind, 2007).

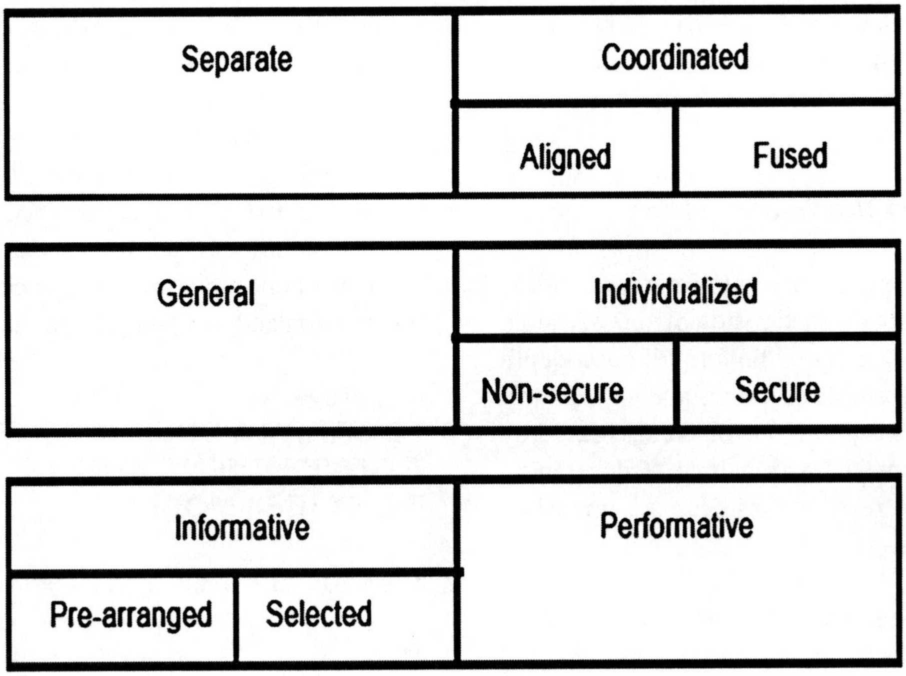

(Coursey, 2008; Goldkuhl, 2006).). On the other hand, non-normative models are based on citizens' needs other than sequential evolution for e-services technological capabilities. As a result, this type of model relies on categorizing e-services where there is no difference between them in terms of better or best e-service. However, non-normative models are complex in implementation because of the lack of experience in applying such type of models, in addition to the difficulty of proper sorting/categorizing for e-services for some model types such as e-diamond model (Ref: Holistic)

Although both trends are different some common features are also found. Limba (2011) conducted a comparative analysis between a number of non-normative models and a normative model. The analysis was based on 6 features: Possible levels of implementation, the main features of different levels, the level of targeting at the client, the level of targeting at organizational inner processes, Feedback (self-assessment opportunity), Technological background for the implementation of the selected model. The result of the analysis concluded that both electronic government normative models and the "E-Diamond" model are proportionally oriented towards a client and towards internal organizational processes.

RESEARCH METHODOLOGY

This research is exploratory in nature. To satisfy the exploratory characteristics of the research, research approach takes the form of an in-depth study of e-government services maturity models in addition to programs and challenges faced by the government in Egypt as one of developing countries. The research has been accomplished through two stages:

1. Investigating maturity models that are widely accepted and implemented by international bodies and governments, and
2. Defining similarities and differences between those models and grouping them.

It has been argued that using the case research method allows for in-depth investigation and rich description, particularly with adopting a single case research methodology (Miles & Hubermann, 1994; Yin, 2003). The conclusions are based on a single organization and therefore it may have limitations in its applicability in other settings. Although, a case study research has been frequently criticized for its lack of rigor, but practitioners also acknowledge such qualitative case-oriented research as it is more useful to communicate the practical usefulness of the research (Benbasat & Zmud, 1999).

The nation that is selected for the case study was one of the first Arab countries to be involved in developing and offering e-government services. The country has a formal process for its e-government program planning and implementation since early 2000. Egypt's e-government portal and all other government websites launched by different ministries have been analyzed. All available documentation materials were provided by the Ministry of Communication and Information Technology, including archival data, such as, e-government strategy in terms of the strategic vision, mission and overall goals and objectives, e-government initiatives, and related governance documentations. Use of multiple-informants and use of archival data helped in crosschecking relevant information and verifying the reliability of data.

TOWARDS A CITIZEN-CENTRIC E-GOVERNMENT SERVICE INDEX (ESI) MODEL

The needs of local authorities systems and national users in different countries around the world vary. Therefore, it is difficult to distinguish one model that would be dominating or overwhelming. Each model has its advantages and disadvantages. Thus, based on the former analyzed models; it would be purposeful to develop more universal maturity model that is suitable for most countries public sectors and based on the following features:

1. **User Centric:** Normative models assumed that stages with higher order in technology complexity are better. Such assumption has no theoretical background (Limba, 2011; Gronlund, 2010; Coursey, 2008; Goldkuhl, 2006). Researchers claim that, in E-Government services, the need for technological complexity must be driven by citizens' need for e-services that fulfill their requirements.
2. **Easy to Implement:** Difficulty of implementation because of the lack of experience is a common obstacle that non-normative models are facing. On the other hand, normative models are widely implemented. However, there are endeavors to create transitional models that help in migrating from the stages methodology to non-normative models such as Holistic model (Limba, 2011). Hence, the new model must take advantage of this wide implementation of normative models.

The E-Government Service Index (ESI) is based on the former two features. The classification of e-services in ESI has been adapted from the stages presentation used in the normative models. The reason for such adaptation is to verify the two ESI basic features through the following:

1. **Categories Labeling:** Normative models have been around for almost a decade. Hence, the stages labeling has been deeply investigated in sense of reflecting e-services level of complexity against citizens' requirements, regardless of the accuracy of the sequential and dependable approach. Thus, citizen's needs regarding e-services are almost standardized around those stages naming. Therefore, categories labeling in ESI is somehow similar to those used for the stages in normative models.
2. **Sorting E-Services:** The re-sorting of e-services based on normative models implementation is much more feasible than creating new e-services classification and this is the main obstacle that non-normative models are facing. Thus, ESI is taking advantage of the wide implementation of the normative models and re-sort the e-services based on citizen's requirements.

The ESI model is composed of four independent categories with extra two sub-categories. The categories reflect the offered e-services with respect to presence, information flow, user interactivity and participation as follows:

1. **No-Presence Category (C0):** This category embraces the "not existing" e-services either through a broken link or through a corresponding page with under construction notation.
2. **Informative Category (C1):** C1 Involves one way directional flow of information from the service provider to the public such as description of steps required to complete an enquiry or form downloading etc. Moreover, it might include search criteria for the published information.
3. **Transactional Category (C2):** C2 represents a two way directional flow of information between the government and public. Furthermore, it is composed of two sub-classes:
    a. **Non-Financial (C2A):** it includes online submission and files uploading
    b. **Financial (C2B):** it represents online payment for the required service.
4. **Participatory Category (C3):** The participatory category incorporates e-services related to customer satisfaction side of the presented service. As a result, service pro-

viders enhance the quality of the offered e-services by investigating public opinion through providing a digital medium such as feedback form, blogs, forums or any other suitable mean. Additionally, C3 embraces e-services used in political activities such as online voting and polling.

To assess the practicality of the ESI model, an E-Government program of a developing country is needed where there is an enormous opportunity for enhancement and change. Additionally, one of the objectives of such E-Government program is to be citizen centric and been evaluated using an international accepted model that belongs to the family of normative models and shows improvement. Based on the former criteria Egypt's E-Government program (Eid, 2009) has been selected. Table 1 provides a full analysis of the offered e-services based on the ESI categorization as shown below.

Table 1. An analysis of Egypt's E-Government services using ESI model

ESI Model			C0	C1	C2		C3
Service Provider	Service	Description			C2A	C2B	
Academy of Scientific Research	National rewards Services	Apply for Different National Rewards	x				
Alexandria Library	Digital Assets Repository	A Gateway to the library's digital collection			x		
	Egypt Memory website	Online shop for products that reflect Egyptian culture throughout different eras (Pharaonic, Roman, Coptic and Islamic).				x	
Cairo Opera House	Cairo Opera House e-Booking Service	This services allows for electronic booking and payment of the Cairo Opera House tickets	x				
Cairo Water Company	Water Bill Enquiry Service	Allows citizens to enquire about the amounts of their monthly water bills, as well as pay for their bills (Cairo Only)				* [x]	
Civil Status Office (Belongs to Ministry of Internal Affairs)	Birth Certificate Extract	Birth Certificate Extract				x	x
	Marriage Document Extract	Marriage Document Extract				x	x
	Family Record Extract	Family Record Extract				x	x
	Divorce Document Extract	Divorce Document Extract				x	x
	Death Document Extract	Death Certificate Extract				x	x
	National ID Extract	National ID Extract				x	x
Delta and Upper Land Transportation companies (Belongs to the holding company for maritime and land transport – belongs to Ministry of Investment)	Bus Reservation Service	Between cities public bus booking service				x	x

continued on following page

Table 1. Continued

ESI Model			C0	C1	C2		C3
Service Provider	**Service**	**Description**			**C2A**	**C2B**	
Document Registration Offices	Real Estate Offices Services	Providing Real estate authority services, including requesting formal certificates and photocopies as well as application tracking	x				
Egypt Air (Belongs to ministry of civil aviation)	Egypt Air e-Ticketing Service	Egypt Air e-Ticketing - Booking online				x	x
Egyptian Company of Telecommunication (Belongs to Ministry of Communications and Information Technology)	Telecom Egypt Services	Telecom Egypt Electronic Services				x	x
Egyptian Customs Authority (Belongs to the ministry of finance)	Customs Tariff Service	Customs Tariff Service		x			
	Customs Services	ImpEx and Manifest services for Ain Sokhna, Alexandria, Cairo, Dekheila, Suez and Port Said ports			x		
Egyptian Organization of Standards and Quality	Egyptian Organization for Standardization and Quality Services	This service allows for the online purchase of: 6. Egyptian quality Standards 7. Publications 8. Egyptian Seal of Quality 9. Egyptian certificates of conformance 10. Egyptian seal of conformance		x			
Egyptian Railway Authority (Belongs to ministry of transport)	Trains Tickets reservation Service	Tickets reservation and online payment for first and second class trips of Egypt National Railways				x	
Egyptian Tax Authority (Belongs to ministry of finance)	Egyptian Tax Services	Delivering numerous services such as submission of tax declaration, new tax card, and tax profile update. Other services include queries about installments, visits and others.			x		
	Submission of tax declaration 2010	Downloading tax form		x			
Ministry of Environment	Environmental Services	Environmental Services		x			
Ministry of Health and Population	Doctors Charging Service	Doctors Charging Office Application, modification, and enrolment results		x			
Ministry of Investment	Investment Dispute Settlement Committee	Publishes all previous decrees by the investment dispute settlement committee. Allows for search by session number or date		x			

continued on following page

Table 1. Continued

ESI Model			C0	C1	C2		C3
Service Provider	Service	Description			C2A	C2B	
Ministry of Justice	Traffic Prosecution Services	Inquire about irregularities service vehicle license, driving licenses			* [x]		
	Court of Cassation Services	Providing court of cassation services (Civil, Crime). These services include inquires about supreme cases and its ruling, reviewing photocopies, also requesting a formal certificates and photocopies. There is also a service for request follow-up.			x		
	Primary courts Services	Applying for getting a specific certificate of primary courts			x		
	Appeal Court Services	Appeal Courts Services Providing Appeal courts services. These services include Inquires about appealed cases and its ruling, reviewing photocopies, also requesting formal certificates and photocopies. There is also a service for request follow-up.			x		
	Legal Portal Services	Egyptian Laws and Legalizations			x		x

continued on following page

By analyzing the above table we conclude the following:

- The Egyptian E-Government portal is offering 43 e-services through twenty three (23) service providers.
- Out of the offered forty three (43) e-services, six (6) e-services fall in the No-Presence category (C0) where links to some of them are broken and others are still under construction.
- The informative category (C1) contains six (6) e-services.
- Thirty one (31) e-service belong to the transactional category (C2) distributed between non-financial (C2A) and financial (C2B) sub-categories.
- Thirteen (13) e-services fall in transactional (C2) and participatory (C3) categories at the same time.

The above analysis reflects the e-services settings in the Egyptian E-Government. The question that arises here is that: Are those settings reflecting the needs of public? The following three examples will illustrate the answer to this question:

1. Ministry of Environment offers information about environmental e-service which falls in the informative category (C1). A domain like environment requires an interaction between government and public. As a result, a question arises here: How does public deliver their opinions and suggestions to the officials

Table 1. Continued

ESI Model			C0	C1	C2		C3
Service Provider	**Service**	**Description**			**C2A**	**C2B**	
Ministry of State Administrative Development	Giza Governorate E-Services	Provide services of centers, cities, districts and neighborhoods through the Internet or by hand delivery			x		
	Ismailia Governorates E-Services	Provide services of centers, cities, districts and neighborhoods through the Internet or by hand delivery			x		
	Cairo Governorate E-Services	Provide services of centers, cities, districts and neighborhoods through the Internet or by hand delivery			x		
	Monofiya Governorates E-Services	Provide services of centers, cities, districts and neighborhoods through the Internet or by hand delivery			x		
	Fayoum Governorate E-Services	Provide services of centers, cities, districts and neighborhoods through the Internet or by hand delivery			x		
	Citizen Relationship management	Receiving citizens complains and inquiries related to governmental organizations through different communication channels E-Gov portal, Call centre, and written demands to be registered on the system			x		x
	Government Entities Maps Service	Providing map locations for the government services providers, allowing the citizens to find the nearest service provider .definite locations will be displayed on the map alongside landmark locations and descriptions	x				
	University Enrollment Service	University Enrolment for high schools and Equivalent certificates graduates. It includes Universities enrolment Application, transfer, modification, and enrolment results			x		
Ministry of Trade and Industry	Qualified Industrial Zone - QIZ Services	Industrial areas electronic registration. Quarter reports about imports and exports.	x				
National Postal Authority	Lost and Found Service	Search for Lost items which are collected in the post offices			x		
Real Estate Finance Fund	Mortgage Financing Fund Services	Provides reduced mortgage rates for limited income individuals			x		x

continued on following page

Table 1. Continued

ESI Model			C0	C1	C2		C3
Service Provider	Service	Description			C2A	C2B	
Supreme Council of Universities	University Hostels Applications	This service allows the user to apply for housing in university hostels and Inquire about the application status			x		
	Equivalence of a scientific degree-certificate	Equivalence of a scientific degree/ certificate for the universities which is not subject to Egyptian law of universities structure	x				
Tourism And Antiquities Police	Tourism Complaints to Tourism and Antiquities Police	Tourism Complaints to Tourism and Antiquities Police			x		x

*[x] refers to applications to certain areas.

in the ministry? Does the e-service need to have the participatory category function?

2. The Egyptian Opera house is planning to provide an online purchase option for opera tickets. Nevertheless, the e-service belongs to the No-Presence category. The question here: Does the e-service have law priority or is it not very demanding to activate?
3. Egyptian Railway Authority provides an online purchasing for railway tickets. However, there is no means for sharing suggestions or sending complaints to the civil servants.

One of the objectives of the Egyptian E-Government program is to tailor citizen-centric e-services (Eid, 2009). Therefore, via applying the ESI model to the Egyptian E-Government portal, the concerned steering committee can re-evaluate the benefits and shortages of the offered e-services and re-sort them by adding new functions that add value to their overall goals as shown above. The following section is an attempt to understand the challenges and development of E-Government approach in Egypt.

E-GOVERNMENT DEVELOPMENT IN THE EGYPTIAN CONTEXT

The Evolution of Egypt's E-Government Program

In mid 1980s, the government of Egypt in its efforts to adapt with the international IT revolution launched some initiatives to build an Information Society, providing citizens, businesses, visitors and other governmental bodies with a convenient collection of information and services to utilize the benefits of the new information era to achieve national goals.

The Information and Decision Support Center (IDSC) was established in 1985 to build up Egypt's IT industry and governmental decision support infrastructure. One of its key objectives was to provide public access to information, with a particular emphasis on facilitating business and investment. Over the past twenty six years, IDSC has successfully executed many IT projects in terms of legislative reform, public sector reform, human resources development and access to the Internet, commercial registration, natural resources management, cultural heritage preservation, urban planning, and sectorial development projects at the ministerial and governorates level, among many other areas. IDSC currently focuses on decision support for the Cabinet (Ministry of State for Administrative Development, 2010).

In 1999, the Ministry for Communications and Information Technology (MoCIT) was formed to build momentum to create an information society and to improve the information infrastructure (Hassanin, 2003). Shortly after its formation, the Ministry revealed the Egyptian National Communications and Information Technology Plan (NCITP) (Hashem, 2002). The NCITP has paved the road for launching the Egyptian Information Society Initiative (EISI), which has been structured around seven major related mechanisms, each developed, when fully executed, to facilitate Egypt's evolution into an Information Society (MoCIT, 2004).

Egypt's E-Government strategy was addressed in terms of its vision, mission, overall goals and objectives. Egypt's E-Government program was launched by MoCIT in partnership with Ministry of State for Administrative Development (MoSAD). This program was divided into two stages. The first stage (2001- 2007) incorporated setting and approving the E-Government strategic plan, implementing and assessing pilot projects, and starting geographical & sectorial deployment of some projects. The second stage (2007-2012) aimed at expanding successful pilot projects on national level, and the development of government administrative body (MoSAD, 2006). The government of Egypt inaugurated E-Government portal (www.egypt.gov.eg) in January 2004. Some services were placed in the portal to pilot test the project such as telephone e-billing, birth certificate, issuing, etc. (Azab, Ali, & Dafoulas, 2006; Azab, Kamel, & Dafoulas, 2009).

Egypt's E-Government stated with the following vision that comprises three main doctrines (MoCIT, 2004) (1) "public-centric service delivery" (the government orientation to develop a one stop-shop e-services approach emphasized on citizens' needs and expectations), (2) "Community participation" (citizens' needs are continuously being analyzed and considered, and private/public sector organizations are active participants in E-Government implementation and management), and (3) "Optimal utilization of government resources" (i.e. productivity, cost reduction, and efficient allocation of resources are among the major expected outcomes from E-Government implementation). To this end, the government developed its mission to put the vision into practice which focused on "introducing better governance, in order to reduce government expenses and to increase the government efficiency" (MoSAD, 2007).

Although, Egypt's E-Government program was initiated by the MoCIT in 2000, the MoSAD that was founded in 1976 with the purpose of enhancing the efficiency of administrative systems and structures and modernizing public services, took over the leading role in E-Government program in 2004. E-Government program management office was established to give support for the program and manage its functions, which include e-services, shared services, operations management, technology services, and change management. These functions are interrelated and integrated, and do not operate independently. In 2004, the MoSAD launched new strategies and developed goals for the development and modernization of government, and for its implementation. More specifically, it has developed the following four interrelated programs:

- **Institutional Development Program:** This program includes policies, plans, regulations and modern management structures, to regulate the wages and incentive systems, to improve the work environment, and to develop human resources.
- **Governmental Services Development Program:** It is targeted at providing citi-

zens, businesses, government employees and other entities with services, throughout the country, in an efficient, effective and convenient shape.

- **Enterprise Resource Planning Program:** This program is aimed to improve the governmental work flows processes, to reduce government expenditures, and to automate government procedures through the effective and efficient usage of information and communication technologies.
- **Establishing and Integrating National Databases Program:** It is targeted to establish an integrated national database, where government bodies and institutions can efficiently and safely exchange information. The efforts to reach out for more interoperability are mainly driven through the Service Development program, but the other programs are benefiting from established interoperability and at the same time structuring the activities of its constant enhancement.

With regard to Governmental Services Development Program, the following objectives have been developed in order to achieve Egypt's E-Government vision and mission (MoCIT, 2007):

- To provide government services to citizens, businesses, travelers, and government agencies, irrespective of location, in a quick and efficient style; to ensure end users' involvement in decision making process.
- To establish a good communication environment that is structured around cutting red tapes, creating easy access to government services and information, establishing efficient and effective technological clubs and centers, and providing government services through one stop-shop in order to robust local and foreign investments.
- To provide comprehensive, accurate, and updated information to support the decision-making process in the public and private sector in general and foster long term planning in particular.
- To implement new public management techniques in the government sector to increase its productivity.
- To reduce government expenses through adopting e-procurement techniques in the public sector.
- To improve the local competitiveness to be compatible with globalization and prepare Egypt's government sector to be integrated in the international economy.

E-Government Readiness in Egypt

E-Readiness is briefly defined as the degree to which a country is prepared to participate in the networked world (McConnell International Report, 2000). The E-Government readiness ranking is a function of three variables or indices; Web measurement index (it reflects the content and delivery of E-Government services); the telecommunications' infrastructure index (reflects the degree to which a country is prepared for e-transformation and e-delivery); and the human capital index (reflects the degree to which citizens are prepared to participate in the networked world). In general, Egypt has made some efforts to improve its E-Government readiness ranking over the last few years. In terms of achievements in communication infrastructures; the connectivity and access have been improved by adopting a number of policy measures, including the deregulation of telecommunication sector with the launching of three mobile operators licenses. In addition, high quality of broadband connections is currently accessible in main cities and business parks, such as the Smart Village. Mobile uptake penetration increased from 25 subscriptions per 100 inhabitants in 2006 to 90 at the end of 2010.

The number of citizens who have access to the internet using a mobile or USB modem has also increased from 7 million at the end of 2009 to 8.6 million at the end of 2010 (Azab et al., 2009; United Nations, 2011).

Regarding human capital aspect, the government has made some achievements through launching some initiatives in several institutions to provide the private sector with ICT engineers and technicians, in particular for the Information Technology Outsourcing (ITO) and Business Process Outsourcing (BPO) sectors. Therefore, the country has been ranked amongst the top ten emerging markets for its IT skills. On the other side, the government has launched some initiatives in education field, such as the Smart Schools Network (around 5% of all schools) and IT clubs. These initiatives have extended computer-based education in the school system. However, still little has been done, if the huge number of both young population (around 12 million undergraduates) and primary and secondary schools (around 52 thousands) is considered (United Nations, 2011).

Given that Egypt's government has made some initiatives to improve its E-Government readiness ranking as mentioned above. But the UN E-Government Survey (2012) E-Government for people ranked Egypt as number 107 worldwide in 2012. Additionally, according to UN E-Government surveys (UN 2005; 2008; 2010 and 2012), it appears that Egypt lags far behind other Arab countries in E-Government readiness as shown in Table1. However, the country was a pioneer among Arab countries in launching its E-Government program in 2000.

Impediments to Citizen-Centric E-Government Implementation in Egypt

This section opens with highlighting generic challenges in developing countries and in the Arab context, as Egypt belongs to the two groups. Then specific challenges faced by Egypt's government are examined in detail. E-Government implementations in developing countries are generally more problematic in comparison to those in the developed nations. Ndou (2004) explored these challenges by conducting an empirical, web-based research of 15 case studies in developing countries, which had launched and implemented E-Government initiatives. The study found that E-Government offers opportunities for governments; however, the ability of developing countries to obtain the full benefits of E-Government is limited and is largely restricted by the existence of a combination of political, legal, social and economic barriers.

In the Arab context, few studies have been conducted in this regard. These studies summarized E-Government challenges in some Arab countries, such as Saudi Arabia, Jordan, and UAE (Abdel Nasser, Faraj, & Wael, 2007; Akemi & Omar, 2009; Almarabeh & Abuali, 2010; Jawahitha & Gwendolyn, 2010; Khasawneh, Jalghaum, Harfoushi, & Obiedat, 2011):

- The lack of awareness regarding E-Government services in Arab societies on the part of citizens and public organizations' employees;

Table 2. Ranking of e-government readiness's for Arab countries adapted from UN Report (2011; 2012)

Country	2008	2010	2012
Egypt	79	86	107
Tunisia	124	66	103
Jordan	50	51	98
Lebanon	74	93	87
Oman	84	82	64
Kuwait	57	50	63
Qatar	53	62	48
Saudi Arabia	70	58	41
Bahrain	42	13	36

- The current government regulations and structures are not appropriate for the requirements of E-Government implementation;
- The lack of trust in accomplishing tasks online amongst government employees;
- The limited number of studies and research regarding E-Government;
- The fear of consequences and results of the process of transition to E-Government;
- The lack of training programs regarding use of computer and Internet;
- The security and privacy concerns (the lack of security of information);
- The shortage of IT skills;
- The fear that E-Government program will result in a decrease in the role of intervention;
- The dominance of English language in Electronic content development;
- The fear that E-Government will lead to reducing the role of employees in accomplishing work.

The above mentioned generic barriers to E-Government in developing and Arab countries are faced by Egypt's government as well. The next part deeply analyses the specific challenges encountered in E-Government implementation in Egypt.

The analysis of other relevant literature, particularly Egypt's E-Government portal, UN E-Government surveys, the assessment of the Egyptian ICT sector conducted by the UN teams, and other E-Government publications reveals that Egypt faces some similar generic challenges to those of developing and Arab countries, and other specific challenges related to the Egyptian context, in its efforts to harvest E-Government opportunities and to modernize government practices. These challenges facing E-Government can be broadly categorized into social, economic, technological issues (MoSAD, 2009). The Authors managed to identify these challenges clearly and proposed a group of recommendations to assist policy makers in Egypt in developing a coherent strategic vision for the future to overcoming the obstacles in the road for developing a successful E-Government. These challenges and recommendations are analyzed and introduced as follows:

Role of the Proposed Model in Dealing with Limitations of Egypt's E-Government Program

The proposed model can spot limitations of present e-government programs and orient to the interventions, which have been revealed and developed through the profound review and analysis of relevant literature in the Egyptian context:

1. The C0 category (No Presence) incorporates some e-services which are neither offered nor active in the Egyptian context, such as tax procedures and documents completion and submission, online tax payment and issuing land property certificates.
   Recommendations:
   a. To urge the Egyptian government to issue e-government regulations to assure the activation of missing e-services such as online tax payment, e-signature draft that permits for acceptance of authenticated documents among different entities, e-voting etc.
   b. Government must work in close cooperation with the private sector and citizens for ensuring secure use of e-government portals.
2. The C1 (Informative Category) incorporates the flow of information from the service provider to the public. This category can spot the following limitations:
   a. The lack of citizen awareness of government regulations and potential benefits of e-government services.

b. Reluctance, mistrust and difficulty of using e-government services
Recommendations:

a. Develop customer–centric strategies and policies, where the greater use of market and demand studies would help to identify citizens' needs with regard to information and services as follows:

b. Plan and implement advertizing campaigns including broadcast media (TV and Radio programs), print media (newspapers and magazines articles and columns), and e-media (Internet materials) where citizens can know and learn about e-government benefits and opportunities. Special treatment must be delivered to those who have difficulties to integrate (disabled, elderly, visitors).

c. Deliver some basic educational materials on e-government at different educational institutions.

3. The C2 (Transactional Category) represents a two way directional flow of information between the government and public. It includes non-financial and financial transactions. This category addresses privacy and security concerns, such as personal data protection and on line payment respectively.
Recommendations:
    a. To develop a comprehensive and secure e-payment framework that allows several payment techniques such as credit cards, prepaid cards, mobile based payment and other payment methods.
4. The C3 (Participatory category) incorporates e-services related to customer satisfaction side of the presented service and political participation. The category can spot limitations related to the absence of citizens' involvement in public decision making process and e-services development.
Recommendations:
    a. To develop a persuasive initiatives by the government to enhance the pro-active interaction between government authorities and citizens with regards to political, economical and social issues.
5. The E-Government Service Index (ESI) is user centric. It grants service providers and users with the effective classification and standardization of e-service categories, which can help to facilitate the integration and prevent e-services duplication among different government bodies. Therefore, the proposed model can highlight different generic limitation such as the lack of e-services standardization among governmental agencies which lead absence of integration and ability of information exchange among governmental bodies.
Recommendations:

The new political orientation of Egypt paves the way for developing political, economic, social and administrative reform programs. The administrative reform program must pay more attention to the following objectives:

a. To harmonize and integrate all governmental bodies' activities to achieve Egypt's e-government vision.
b. To create easy flow and exchange of information among different governmental entities
c. To eliminate red tapes

DISCUSSION

The ESI model is a citizen-centric model, which categorizes the offered e-services complexity as per public need. The model combined the advantages of normative models and non-normative models as follows:

1. **Normative Models:** the advantage of this type of models lies in the easiness of implementation and wide spread adoption. ESI model is built on the concept of re-sorting the stages which are common among this

type of models instead of recreating new classification. Nevertheless, the categories employed by the ESI models are neither sequential nor dependable. As a result, the model can easily be implemented.

2. **Non-Normative Models:** These types of models are more concerned with citizen needs regardless of the linear technological evolution of E-Government as assumed by normative models. The ESI model took the same approach through categorizing e-services as per citizens' needs, as each category has its own characteristic. Moreover, an e-service may combine the features of two or more categories which may result in an accurate description of the offered e-service goals

Researchers claim that the No-Presence category is the first of its type among maturity models. This new category reflects the e-services that intended to be found but for some reason are suspended or delayed on being activated online. This new category is very commonly found among the E-Government programs of developing countries where no other model has paid attention to this dimension.

Finally the ESI model is a scalable model in the sense that the four basic category types utilized by the ESI model are subject to extension/ modification as per new public requirements.

Applying ESI model, the steering committee of an E-Government program can analyze the current status of e-services provide to the public and match the findings with the goals of the program. Based on this matching, the committee can identify which e-services need to be upgraded, added or changed in terms of technological capability. Therefore, the overall objective of the program can be achieved.

The review of Egypt's e-government arena revealed several limitations to present e-government programs, including legal challenges (the lack of E-signature mechanism, security and privacy concerns), social, cultural and economic challenges (e-payment transactions - inconvenience of delivery mechanisms and its effects on reputation of e-services, lack of citizens awareness, participation and study), bureaucratic challenges (lack of integration and information sharing among government bodies) and technical challenges (the lack of unified standards and the overlap among service providers).

The ESI model contributes to spot impediments of e-government implementation within the Egyptian context and recommend specific interventions as discussed earlier. These recommendations can help policy makers in Egypt develop a coherent strategic vision for the future to overcome the barriers to developing a successful e-government.

CONCLUSION

This chapter is an attempt to provide answers for the above raised research questions through exploring various e-government maturity models as presented in section two. Additionally, the chapter proposed a maturity model based on comparative analysis between the explored maturity trends as discussed in section five. As a result, researchers used the model to analyze e-services provided by the Egyptian e-government to spot limitations and provide suitable recommendations as explained in section five and six.

This chapter reveals that Egypt has acknowledged the growing importance of E-Government at different levels since the official inauguration of Egypt's E-Government portal in 2004. The country recognized the role of E-Government in leveraging the economic, cultural and social development; providing effective and convenient services to publics. E-Government became a standard for improving public sector services in Egypt. Nevertheless, E-Government applications are on different levels of maturity with respect to integration between organizational processes and technological capabilities.

REFERENCES

Abdel Nasser, H., Faraj, A., & Wael, A. (2007). Assessing e-Readiness in the Arab Countries: Perceptions Towards ICT Environment in Public Organizations in the State of Kuwait. *The Electronic Journal of E-Government*, *5*(1), 77–86.

Akemi, T., & Omar, A. (2009). A Cross-Country Comparative Analysis of E-Government Service Delivery among Arab Countries. *Information Technology for Development*, *15*(3), 151–170. doi:10.1002/itdj.20124

Almarabeh, T., & AbuAli, A. (2010). A General Framework for E-Government: Definition Maturity Challenges, Opportunities, and Success. *European Journal of Scientific Research*, *39*(1), 29–42.

Azab, N., Ali, M., & Dafoulas, G. (2006). Incorporating CRM in E-Government: Case of Egypt. In *Proceedings of LADIS International Conference e-Commerce*. LADIS.

Azab, N., Kamel, S., & Dafoulas, G. (2009). A Suggested Framework for Assessing Electronic Government Readiness in Egypt. *Electronic Journal of E-Government*, *7*, 11–28.

Benbasat, I., & Zmud, W. (1999). Empirical research in information systems: The practice of relevance. *Management Information Systems Quarterly*, *23*(1), 3–16. doi:10.2307/249403

Chatfield, A., & Alhujran, O. (2009). A cross-country comparative analysis of e-government service delivery among Arab countries. *Information Technology for Development*, *15*(3), 151–170. doi:10.1002/itdj.20124

Coursey, D., & Norris, D. F. (2008). Models of e-government: Are they correct? an empirical assessment'. *Public Administration Review*, *68*(3), 523–536. doi:10.1111/j.1540-6210.2008.00888.x

Danziger, J. N., & Andersen, K. V. (2002). The impacts of information technology in public administration: An analysis of empirical research from the "golden age" of transformation. *International Journal of Public Administration*, *25*(5), 591–625. doi:10.1081/PAD-120003292

Eid, E. E., & AbdEl-Razek, M. M. (2009). E-government theory and implementation case study Egyptian e-government model. In *Proceedings of the International Conference on Administration and Business*. University of Bucharest.

Goldkuhl, G., & Persson, A. (2006). From e-ladder to e-diamond re-conceptualising models for public e-services. In *Proceedings of the 14th European Conference on Information Systems (ECIS2006)*. Göteborgs Universitet.

Grönlund, Å. (2010). Ten years of e-government: The 'end of history' and new beginning. *EGOV*, *2010*, 13–24.

Grönlund, A., & Horan, T. A. (2004). Introducing E-government: History, definitions, and issues. *Communications of the Association for Information Systems*, *15*, 713–729.

Hashem, M. (2002). Bridging the digital divide in Egypt: Facing the challenges. In *Proceedings of UNCTAD E-Commerce First Expert Meeting*. UNCTAD.

Hassanin, L. (2003). Africa ICT policy monitor project. *Egypt ICT Country Report*.

Hiller, J., & Bélanger, F. (2001). *Privacy strategies for electronic government*. PriceWaterHouse Coopers.

Jawahitha, S., & Gwendolyn, R. (2010). Gender Differences in E-Government Adoption in Dubai. *Business Review (Federal Reserve Bank of Philadelphia)*, *16*(2), 120–126.

Khasawneh, S., Jalghaum, Y., Harfoushi, O., & Obiedat, R. (2011). E-Government Program in Jordan: From Inception to Future Plans. *International Journal of Computer Science Issues*, *8*(4), 568–582.

Layne, K., & Lee, J. (2001). Developing Fully Functional E-government: A Four Stage Model. *Government Information Quarterly*, *18*(2), 122–136. doi:10.1016/S0740-624X(01)00066-1

Limba, T. (2011). Peculiarities of designing holistic electronic government services integration model. *Social Technologies*, *1*(2), 344–362.

Lind, M., Forsgren, O., Salomonson, N., & Albinsson, L. (2007). The e-co model – citizens' driving e-service quality. In *Proceedings of the 51st Annual Conference by the International Society for the Systems Sciences: Integrated Systems Sciences: Systems Thinking, Modelling and Practice*. Tokyo Institute of Technology.

Miles, B., & Hubermann, A. (1994). Qualitative Data Analysis: An Expanded Sourcebook. Sage Publications.

Ministry of State Administrative Development. (2009). *Improving Take-Up E-Government Services: Challenges*. Available at: sbedair@ad.gov.eg

Ministry of State for Administrative Development. (2010). *Egyptian Government*. Available at www.egtpt.gov.eg

Ministry of State for Administrative Development. (n.d.). *About MoSAD*. Available at: http://www.msad.gov.eg/About%20MSAD/Programs/

Ndou, V. (2004). E–government for developing countries: Opportunities and challenges. *The Electronic Journal on Information Systems in Developing Countries*, *18*(1), 1–24.

OECD. (2003). The case for e-government: Excerpts from the OECD report: The EGovernment Imperative. *OECD Journal on Budgeting*, *3*(1), 61–96. doi:10.1787/budget-v3-art5-en

Persson, A., & Goldkuhl, G. (2005). Stage-models for public e-services - investigating conceptual foundations. In *Proceedings of 2nd Scandinavian Workshop on e-Government*. Copenhagen, Denmark: Academic Press.

UN Report. (2011). *ICT Policy Review-Egypt*. United Nations Conference on Trade and Development (UNCTAD). Retrieved January, 2011, http://www.mcit.gov.eg/Upcont/Documents

UNReport, . (2012). *UN E-Government Survey 2012: E-Government for People*. New York: United Nations.

Statskontoret. (2000). *The 24/7 agency: criteria for 24/7 agencies in the networked public administration*. Report 2000:41, Statskontoret, Stockholm.

UN. (2002). *Benchmarking e-government: A global perspective. UN Technical Report*. United Nations.

UN. (2005). *Global e-government readiness report: from e-government to e-inclusion*. United Nations.

UN. (2008). *UN e-government survey 2008: From e-government to connected governance*. United Nations.

UN. (2010). *E-government survey*. United Nations.

Yin, B. (2003). *Case Study Research: Design and Methods*. Thousand Oaks, CA: Sage Publications.

Zakareya, E., & Zahir, I. (2005). E-government adoption: Architecture and barriers. *Business Process Management*, *11*(5), 589–611. doi:10.1108/14637150510619902

Zakaria, M. R., & Gebba, T. R. (2012). Towards Categorizing E-Government Services: The Case of Egypt. *International Journal of Business Information and Technology*, *1*(1), 16–28.

KEY TERMS AND DEFINITIONS

Citizen-Centric E-Government: Citizens are the core of any e-government intervention stage.

E-Government Readiness: The degree to which a country is prepared to participate in the networked world.

E-Government Service Index (ESI): A user-centric index that classifies e-governmental services into four independent categories including no-presence, informative, transactional and participatory.

E-Government: Using information and communication technologies (ICT) by government agencies to transform relations with citizens, businesses, and other arms of government.

Information and Communications Technology (ICT): Integrating information processing and content handling functions with communications technology (e.g., telephone lines and wireless signals, enterprise software, audio-visual systems, networks, the internet, and mobile computing) to enable users to access, store, transmit, and manipulate information.

Maturity Models: A type of conceptual modeling to identify key practices to increase the maturity of e-services that are provided by a governmental agency.

Non-Normative Maturity Models: Non-stage based maturity models that are based on citizens' needs rather than sequential evolution for e-services technology.

Normative Maturity Models: Stage-based maturity models that reflect an evolutionary methodology of e-government as a number of consecutive stages.

Compilation of References

Abbasi, A., Chen, H., Salem, A., Abbasi, A., Chen, H., & Salem, A. (2008). Sentiment analysis in multiple languages: Feature selection for opinion classification in Web forums. *ACM Transactions on Information Systems*, *26*(3), 1–34. doi:10.1145/1361684.1361685

Abdel Nasser, H., Faraj, A., & Wael, A. (2007). Assessing e-Readiness in the Arab Countries: Perceptions Towards ICT Environment in Public Organizations in the State of Kuwait. *The Electronic Journal of E-Government*, *5*(1), 77–86.

Abdel-Aal, R. (2004). Abductive Network Committees for Improved Classification of Medical Data. *Methods of Information in Medicine*, *43*(2), 192–201. PMID:15136869

Abdel-Aal, R. (2005). Improved Classification of Medical Data Using Abductive Network Committees Trained on Different Feature Subsets. *Computer Methods and Programs in Biomedicine*, *80*(2), 141–153. doi:10.1016/j.cmpb.2005.08.001 PMID:16169631

Abrahamson, S., Ryder, P., & Unterberg, B. (2013). *Crowdstorm: The Future of Innovation, Ideas, and Problem Solving*. John Wiley & Sons.

AbuKhousa, E., Mohamed, N., & Al-Jaroodi, J. (2012). e-Health Cloud: Opportunities and Challenges. *Future Internet*, *4*(3), 621–645. doi:10.3390/fi4030621

Acampora, G., Cook, D. J., Rashidi, P., & Vasilakos, A. V. (2013). A Survey on Ambient Intelligence in Health Care. *Proceedings of the IEEE*, *101*(12), 2470–2494. doi:10.1109/JPROC.2013.2262913 PMID:24431472

Accenture. (2010). *Information Governance The Foundation for Effective e-Health*. White Paper. Retrieved from http://www.accenture.com/SiteCollectionDocuments/PDF/Accenture_100473_InfoGovPoV_Final.pdf

Aguilar-Saven, R. S. (2004). Business process modeling: Review and framework. *International Journal of Production Economics*, *90*(2), 129–149. doi:10.1016/S0925-5273(03)00102-6

Ahmed, S. A., & Ali, S. M. (2006). People as Partners: Facilitating people's participation in public-private partnership for solid waste management. *Habitat International*, *30*(4), 781–796. doi:10.1016/j.habitatint.2005.09.004

Ahn, M. (2011). Adoption of E-communication applications in U.S. municipalities: The role of political environment, bureaucratic structure, and the nature of applications. *American Review of Public Administration*, *41*(4), 428–452. doi:10.1177/0275074010377654

Aitken, M., & Hage, J. (1971). The organic organization and innovation. *Sociology*, *5*(1), 63–83. doi:10.1177/003803857100500105

Akemi, T., & Omar, A. (2009). A Cross-Country Comparative Analysis of E-Government Service Delivery among Arab Countries. *Information Technology for Development*, *15*(3), 151–170. doi:10.1002/itdj.20124

Albury, D. (2005). Fostering innovation in public services. *Public Money & Management*, *25*, 51–56.

Al-maghrabi, T., Dennis, C., & Halliday, S. V. (2011). Understanding The Factors That Derive Continuance Intention Of E-Shopping In Saudi Arabia: Age Group Differences In Behaviour. *Journal of Enterprise Information Management*, *24*(1), 85–111. doi:10.1108/17410391111097447

Almarabeh, T., & AbuAli, A. (2010). A General Framework for E-Government: Definition Maturity Challenges, Opportunities, and Success. *European Journal of Scientific Research*, *39*(1), 29–42.

Alonso, J. A., & Lamata, M. T. (2006). Consistency in the Analytic Hierarchy Process: A New Approach. *International Journal of Uncertainty, Fuzziness and Knowledge-based Systems, 14*(4), 445–459. doi:10.1142/S0218488506004114

Alshehri, M., Drew, S., & Alfarraj, O. (2012). A Comprehensive Analysis of E-Government services adoption in Saudi Arabia: Obstacles and Challenges. *International Journal of Advanced Computer Science and Applications, 3*(2), 1–6. doi:10.14569/IJACSA.2012.030201

Al-Tawil, M. K., & Sait, M. S. (2007). E-governance-Where We Stand. In *Pro-Poor Public Service Delivery with ICTs-Making local e-governance work towards achieving the Millennium Development Goals*. Retrieved February 2, 2013, from http://www.unapcict.org/ecohub/resources/apdip-e-note-6-2013-icts-for-povertyreduction/at_download/attachment1

Altshuler, A. A., & Behn, R. D. (1997). *Innovation in American Government: Challenges, Opportunities, and Dilemmas*. Washington, DC: Brookings Institution Press.

Alwan, A., Armstrong, T., Bettcher, D., Branca, F., Chisholm, D., Ezzati, M., et al. (2011). Global status report on noncommunicable diseases. *World Health Organization (WHO)*. Retrieved from http://www.who.int/nmh/publications/ncd_report2010/en/

Amadi-Echendu, J. E., Willett, R., Brown, K., Hope, T., Lee, J., & Mathew, J. ... Yang, B.-S. (2010). What Is Engineering Asset Management? In J. E. Amadi-Echendu, K. Brown, R. Willett, & J. Mathew (Eds.), *Definitions, Concepts and Scope of Engineering Asset Management* (pp. 3–16). Springer London. Retrieved from http://link.springer.com/chapter/10.1007/978-1-84996-178-3_1

Ambali, A. R. (2009). E-government Policy: Ground Issues in E-Filing System. *European Journal of Soil Science, 11*(2), 249–266.

Ambient Assisted Living (AAL). (2012). *Success Stories*. Retrieved from http://www.aal-europe.eu/success-stories/

Andersen, K. V., & Henriksen, H. Z. (2006). E-government maturity models: Extension of the Layne and Lee model. *Government Information Quarterly, 23*(2), 236–248. doi:10.1016/j.giq.2005.11.008

Anderson, G. S. (1999). Human morphology and temperature regulation. *International Journal of Biometeorology, 43*(3), 99–109. doi:10.1007/s004840050123 PMID:10639901

Anderson, J. C., & Gerbing, D. W. (1988). Structural Equation Modeling in Practice: A Review and Recommended Two-Step Approach. *Psychological Bulletin, 103*(3), 411–423. doi:10.1037/0033-2909.103.3.411

Ando, B. (2008). A Smart Multisensor Approach to Assist Blind People in Specific Urban Navigation Tasks. *IEEE Transactions on Neural Systems and Rehabilitation Engineering, 16*(6), 592–594. doi:10.1109/TNSRE.2008.2003374 PMID:19144591

Anliker, U., Ward, J. A., Lukowicz, P., Troster, G., Dolveck, F., & Baer, M. et al. (2004). AMON: A wearable multiparameter medical monitoring and alert system. *IEEE Transactions on* Information Technology in Biomedicine, *8*(4), 415–427.

Annual Report Inland Revenue Board of Malaysia. (2010). Retrieved from http://www.hasil.org.my/pdf/pdfam/AR2010_2.pdf

Antic, L., DJukic, T., Stevanovic, T., Stankovic, J., Bojic, B., & Grabovica, E. (2013). Activity Based Costing and Throughput Accounting in the Function of Making Business Decisions. *Technics Technologies Education Management, 8*(3), 1840–1503.

Araujo, R. M., Taher, Y., Heuvel, W. V. D., & Cappelli, C. (2013). Evolving Government-Citizen Ties in Public Service Design and Delivery. In *Proceedings ofIFIP EGOV Conference*, (pp. 19-26). IFIP.

Arendsen, R., Peters, O., ter Hedde, M., & van Dijk, J. (2014). Does e-government reduce the administrative burden of businesses? An assessment of business-to-government systems usage in the Netherlands. *Government Information Quarterly*.

Argyris, C., & Schön, D. A. (1996). *Organizational Learning: A Theory of Action Perspective*. Reading, MA: Addison- Wesley.

Aris, R. M., Christian, D., Hearne, P. Q., Kerr, K., Finkbeiner, W. E., & Balmes, J. R. (1993). Ozone-induced airway inflammation in human subjects as determined by airway lavage and biopsy. *The American Review of Respiratory Disease*, *148*(5), 1363–1372. doi:10.1164/ajrccm/148.5.1363 PMID:8239177

Aristotle. (350 B.C.E). *Aristotle, Politics Book 3 part 11.*

Arthur, W. B. (1994). Inductive reasoning and bounded rationality. *The American Economic Review*, *84*(2), 406–411.

ATOS. (2011). *Open Cities. New Trends for Smart Cities.* Project co-funded by the European Commission within the ICT Policy Support Programme. Dissemination Level. Deliverable D2.2.21 V1.3.

Avery Dennison Corporation. (2013). *Metria™*. Retrieved January from http://www.averydennison.com/en/home/technologies/creative-showcase/metria-wearable-sensor.html

Avgerou, C. (2003). *The link between ICT and economic growth in the discourse of development Organizational information systems in the context of globalization.* Springer. doi:10.1007/978-0-387-35695-2_23

Axelrod, R. (1984). *The Evolution of Cooperation.* Basic Books.

Azab, N., Ali, M., & Dafoulas, G. (2006). Incorporating CRM in E-Government: Case of Egypt. In *Proceedings of LADIS International Conference e-Commerce*. LADIS.

Azab, N., Kamel, S., & Dafoulas, G. (2009). A Suggested Framework for Assessing Electronic Government Readiness in Egypt. *Electronic Journal of E-Government*, *7*, 11–28.

Babu, P., & Murt, N. (1994). Clustering With Evolution Strategies. *Journal of Pattern Recognition*, *27*(2), 321–329. doi:10.1016/0031-3203(94)90063-9

Baccini, M., Biggeri, A., Accetta, G., Kosatsky, T., Katsouyanni, K., & Analitis, A. et al. (2008). Heat effects on mortality in 15 European cities. *Epidemiology (Cambridge, Mass.)*, *19*(5), 711–719. doi:10.1097/EDE.0b013e318176bfcd PMID:18520615

Bae, Y., & Lee, H. (2012). Sentiment analysis of twitter audiences: Measuring the positive or negative influence of popular twitterers. *Journal of the American Society for Information Science and Technology*, *63*(12), 2521–2535. doi:10.1002/asi.22768

Bagozzi, R. P. (2007). The legacy of the technology acceptance model and a proposal for a paradigm shift. *Journal of the Association for Information Systems*, *8*(4), 244–254.

Bailey, A. (2009). Issues affecting the social sustainability of telecentres in developing contexts: A field study of sixteen telecentres in Jamaica. *The Electronic Journal of Information Systems in Developing Countries, 36.*

Bailur, S., Ratan, A., Toyama, K., Veeraraghavan, R., Dhwani, A. N., Premji, A., & Roof, O. (2007). *Review of Research on Rural PC Kiosks.* Retrieved 22/09/2010, from http://groups.csail.mit.edu/cag/ict4dev/papers/Kiosks%20Research.pdf

Bainbridge, D., Dewsnip, M., & Witten, I. H. (2005). Searching digital music libraries. *Information Processing & amp. Management*, *4*(1), 41–56.

Baldwin, C., & Von Hippel, E. (2010). Modeling a paradigm shift: From producer innovation to user and open collaborative innovation. *Harvard Business School Finance Working Paper,* (10-038), 4764-4709.

Ballester, F., Corella, D., Pérez-Hoyos, S., Sáez, M., & Hervás, A. (1997). Mortality as a function of temperature. A study in Valencia, Spain, 1991-1993. *International Journal of Epidemiology*, *26*(3), 551–561. doi:10.1093/ije/26.3.551 PMID:9222780

Barabási, A. L. (2007). The architecture of complexity. *IEEE Control Systems Magazine*, *27*(4), 33–42. doi:10.1109/MCS.2007.384127

Barbosa, A. F., Pozzebon, M., & Diniz, E. H. (2013). Rethinking E-Government Performance Assessment from a Citizen Perspective. *Public Administration*, *91*(3), 744–762.

Barjis, J. (2008). The Importance of Business Process Modeling in Software Systems Design. *Journal of The Science of Computer Programming*, *71*(1), 73–87. doi:10.1016/j.scico.2008.01.002

Barnes, S., & Hunt, B. (2013). *E-Commerce and V-Business*. Routledge.

Bartoli, A., Hernandez-Serrano, J., Soriano, M., Dohler, M., Kountourisz, A., & Barthelz, D. (2011). Security and Privacy in your Smart City. In *Proceedings ofSmart Cities Congress 2011*. Barcelona: IEEE.

Basagana, X., Sartini, C., Barrera-Gómez, J., Dadvand, P., Cunillera, J., & Ostro, B. et al. (2011). Heat waves and cause-specific mortality at all ages. *Epidemiology (Cambridge, Mass.), 22*(6), 765–772. doi:10.1097/EDE.0b013e31823031c5 PMID:21968768

Basu, R., & Samet, J. M. (2002). An exposure assessment study of ambient heat exposure in an elderly population in Baltimore, Maryland. *Environmental Health Perspectives, 110*(12), 1219–1224. doi:10.1289/ehp.021101219 PMID:12460801

Batalha, J. R., Saldiva, P. H., Clarke, R. W., Coull, B. A., Stearns, R. C., & Lawrence, J. et al. (2002). Concentrated ambient air particles induce vasoconstriction of small pulmonary arteries in rats. *Environmental Health Perspectives, 110*(12), 1191–1197. doi:10.1289/ehp.021101191 PMID:12460797

Bateson, G. (1972). *Steps to an Ecology of Mind: Collected Essays inAnthropology, Psychiatry, Evolution, and Epistemology*. University of Chicago Press.

BBC. (2013). *Predicting crime 'cut Medway street violence by 6%'*. Retrieved 14th August, from http://www.bbc.co.uk/news/uk-england-kent-23689715

Bechhofer, S., Harmelen, F.V., Hendler, J., Horrocks, I., McGuinness, D.L, Patel-Schneider, P.F, & Stein, L.A. (2004). OWL web ontology language reference. *W3C Recommendation, 10*.

Becker, J., Kugeler, M., & Rosenman, M. (2003). *Process Management*. Springer. doi:10.1007/978-3-540-24798-2

Belanger, F., & Carter, L. (2006, January). The Effects of the Digital Divide on E-Government: An Empirical Evaluation. In *Proceedings of System Sciences, (Vol. 4*, pp. 81c-81c). IEEE.

Belanger, F., & Carter, L. (2008). Trust and risk in e-Government adoption. *The Journal of Strategic Information Systems, 17*(2), 165–176. doi:10.1016/j.jsis.2007.12.002

Bélanger, F., & Carter, L. (2009). The impact of the digital divide on e-government use. *Communications of theACM, 52*(4), 132–135. doi:10.1145/1498765.1498801

Bellare, M., Micciancio, D., & Warinschi, B. (2003). Foundations of Group Signatures: Formal Definitions, Simplified Requirements, and a Construction Based on General Assumptions. In E. Biham (Ed.), *Advances in Cryptology—EUROCRYPT 2003: International Conference on the Theory and Applications of Cryptographic Techniques* (LNCS), (*vol. 2656*, pp. 614-629). Berlin: Springer. doi:10.1007/3-540-39200-9_38

Bell, M. L., & Davis, D. L. (2001). Reassessment of the lethal London fog of 1952: Novel indicators of acute and chronic consequences of acute exposure to air pollution. *Environmental Health Perspectives, 109*(s3Suppl 3), 389–394. doi:10.1289/ehp.01109s3389 PMID:11427388

Benayoune, F., & Lancieri, L. (2005). Toward a modelization of mobile learners behavior for the design and the evaluation of advanced training systems. *IADIS International Journal on WWW/Internet, 3*(2), 45-58.

Benbasat, I., & Zmud, W. (1999). Empirical research in information systems: The practice of relevance. *Management Information Systems Quarterly, 23*(1), 3–16. doi:10.2307/249403

Bender, J., Fischlin, M., & Kügler, D. (2009). Security Analysis of the PACE Key-Agreement Protocol. In P. Samarati, M. Yung, F. Martinelli, & C. Ardagna (Eds.), *Information Security: 12th International Conference, ISC 2009*, (LNCS), (vol. 5735, pp. 33-48). Berlin: Springer. doi:10.1007/978-3-642-04474-8_3

Berry, F. S., & Berry, W. D. (1990). State Lottery Adoptions as Policy Innovations: An Event History Analysis. *The American Political Science Review, 84*(2), 395–415. doi:10.2307/1963526

Berry, F. S., & Berry, W. D. (1999). Innovation and Diffusion Models in Policy Research. In P. Sabatier (Ed.), *Theories of the Policy Process*. Boulder, CO: Westview Press.

Bertot, J. C., Jaeger, P. T., & Grimes, J. M. (2010). Using ICTs to create a culture of transparency: E-government and social media as openness and anti-corruption tools for societies. *Government Information Quarterly, 27*(3), 264–271. doi:10.1016/j.giq.2010.03.001

Bertot, J. C., Jaeger, P. T., & Hansen, D. (2012). The impact of polices on government social media usage: Issues, challenges, and recommendations. *Government Information Quarterly, 29*(1), 30–40. doi:10.1016/j.giq.2011.04.004

Bessant, J. (2003). *High-Involvement Management: Building and Sustaining Competitive Advantage Through Continuous Change*. Chichester, UK: Wiley.

Bezdek, J. C. (1981). *Pattern Recognition with Fuzzy Objective Function Algoritms*. New York: Plenum Press. doi:10.1007/978-1-4757-0450-1

Bhanti, P., Lehri, S., & Kumar, N. (2012). E-Governance: An Approach towards the integration of higher Education System in India. *International Journal of Emerging Technology and Advanced Engineering, 2* (8), 225-229.

Bhargava, V., Cutler, K., & Ritchie, D. (2011). *Stimulating the Demand for Good Governance*. Academic Press.

Bhatnagar, S. (2003). E-government and access to information. *Global Corruption Report*, 24-32.

Bhatnagar, S., & Singh, N. (2010). *Results from a study of impact of e-government projects in India*. Academic Press.

Bhattacherjee, A. (2001). Understanding Information Systems Continuance: An Expectation-Confirmation Model. *Management Information Systems Quarterly, 25*(3), 351–370. doi:10.2307/3250921

Bhatt, D. L., & Topol, E. J. (2002). Need to test the arterial inflammation hypothesis. *Circulation, 106*(1), 136–140. doi:10.1161/01.CIR.0000021112.29409.A2 PMID:12093783

Bichsel, P., Camenisch, J., Groß, T., & Shoup, V. (2009). Anonymous credentials on a standard java card. In *Proceedings of the 16th ACM Conference on Computer and Communications Security (CCS '09)* (pp. 600-610). New York: ACM. doi:10.1145/1653662.1653734

Bikhchandani, S., Hirshleifer, D., & Welch, I. (1992). A theory of fads, fashion, custom, and cultural change as informational cascades. *Journal of Political Economy, 100*(5), 992–1026. doi:10.1086/261849

Blagojevic, L. M., Bogdanovic, D. C., Jovic, S. J., Milosevic, Z. G., & Dolićanin, Z. C. (2012). Excess winter mortality of Roma population in Serbia, 1992-2007. *Central European Journal of Public Health, 20*(2), 135–138. PMID:22966739

Blaya, J. A., Fraser, H. S. F., & Holt, B. (2010). E-Health Technologies Show Promise In Developing Countries. *Health Affairs, 29*(2), 244–251. doi:10.1377/hlthaff.2009.0894 PMID:20348068

Blumenthal, D., & Tavenner, M. (2010). The "meaningful use" regulation for electronic health records. *The New England Journal of Medicine, 363*(6), 501–504. doi:10.1056/NEJMp1006114 PMID:20647183

Bodhani, A. (2012). Smart Transport. *Engineering and Technology, 7*(6), 70–73. doi:10.1049/et.2012.0611

BodyMedia, Inc. (2013). *BodyMedia FIT*. Retrieved from http://www.bodymedia.com/the_interface.html

BOE. (2007). *LAW 11/2007, of 22 June, on electronic access to Public Services for members of the public*. Available from http://administracionelectronica.gob.es/pae_Home/dms/pae_Home/documentos/Documentacion/pae_BIBLIOTECA_NORMATIVA_ESTATAL_Leyes/LAW_11-2007_22Jun2007_eGov_Spain_NIPO_000-10-075-0.pdf

BOE. (2010). *Spanish National Interoperability Framework*. Royal Decree 4/2010, of January 8th, which regulates the National Interoperability Framework within the e-government scope. Available from http://administracionelectronica.gob.es/ctt/resources/c5df845d-a98c-4854-90c1-4973408b500f?idIniciativa=145&idElemento=71

Boehmke, F. J., & Skinner, P. (2012). State Policy Innovativeness Revisited. *State Politics & Policy Quarterly, 12*(3), 304–330. doi:10.1177/1532440012438890

Bogdanovic, D. C., Milosevic, Z. G., Lazarevic, K. K., Dolićanin, Z. C., Randelovic, D. M., & Bogdanovic, S. D. (2013). The impact of the July 2007 heat wave on daily mortality in Belgrade, Serbia. *Central European Journal of Public Health, 21*(3), 140–145. PMID:24344537

Bogdanovic, D. C., Nikic, D. S., Milosevic, Z. G., & Stankovic, A. M. (2006). Black smoke air pollution and daily non-accidental mortality in Nis, Serbia. *Central European Journal of Medicine*, *1*(3), 292–297. doi:10.2478/s11536-006-0021-z

Bollier, D. (2010). *The Promise and Peril of Big Data*. Washington, DC: The Aspen Institute.

Bonabeau, E., Theraulaz, G., & Dorigo, M. (1999). *Swarm Intelligence: From Natural to Artificial Systems*. Santa Fe Institute Studies in the Sciences of Complexity.

Bonetti, P. O., Lerman, L. O., & Lerman, A. (2003). Endothelial dysfunction: A marker of atherosclerotic risk. *Arteriosclerosis, Thrombosis, and Vascular Biology*, *23*(2), 168–175. doi:10.1161/01.ATV.0000051384.43104.FC PMID:12588755

Bonsón, E., Torres, L., Royo, S., & Flores, F. (2012). Local e-government 2.0: Social media and corporate transparency in municipalities. *Government Information Quarterly*, *29*(2), 123–132. doi:10.1016/j.giq.2011.10.001

Boon, N. Y., Ramayah, T., Ping, T. A., & Lo, M. (2013). Intention to Use E-Government Websites among UniversitiSains Malaysia (USM) Students. In P. Ordóñez de Pablos, J. Lovelle, J. Gayo, & R. Tennyson (Eds.), *E-Procurement Management for Successful Electronic Government Systems* (pp. 169–180). Hershey, PA: Information Science Reference; doi:10.4018/978-1-4666-2119-0.ch011

Borchers, D. (2013, November 1). *Der ePerso hat Geburtstag: Drei Jahre neuer Personalausweis*. Retrieved from Heise Online: http://heise.de/-2037387

Borges, L. M., Araújo, P., Lebres, A. S., Rente, A., Salvado, R., & Velez, F. J. et al. (2010). Wearable sensors for foetal movement monitoring in low risk pregnancies. In S. C. Mukhopadhyay & A. Lay-Ekuakille (Eds.), *Wearable and Autonomous Biomedical Devices and Systems for Smart Environment: Issues and Characterization* (pp. 115–136). Springer. doi:10.1007/978-3-642-15687-8_6

Borins, S. (1998). *Innovating with Integrity*. Washington, DC: Georgetown University Press.

Borins, S. (2001). *The Challenge of Innovating in Government*. Washington, DC: IBM Center for the Business of Government.

Boulos, M., Rocha, A., Martins, A., Vicente, M., Bolz, A., Feld, R., … Kinirons, M. (2007). CAALYX: A new generation of location-based services in healthcare. *International Journal of Health Geographics, 6*(1), 9.

Boulos, M. N. K., Lou, R. C., Anastasiou, A., Nugent, C. D., Alexandersson, J., & Zimmermann, G. et al. (2009). Connectivity for Healthcare and Well-Being Management: Examples from Six European Projects. *International Journal of Environmental Research and Public Health*, *6*(7), 1947–1971. doi:10.3390/ijerph6071947 PMID:19742164

Boulos, M. N. K., Wheeler, S., Tavares, C., & Jones, R. (2011). How smartphones are changing the face of mobile and participatory healthcare: An overview, with example from eCAALYX. *Biomedical Engineering Online*, *10*(24). PMID:21466669

Boulos, M.N.K, Rocha, A., Martins, A., Vicente, M.E., Bolz, A., Feld, R., & …, Kinirons, M. (2007). CAALYX: A new generation of location-based services in healthcare. *International Journal of Health Geographics*, *6*(9). PMID:17352802

Bouthillier, L., Vincent, R., Goegan, P., Adamson, I. Y., Bjarnason, S., & Stewart, M. et al. (1998). Acute effects of inhaled urban particles and ozone: Lung morphology, macrophage activity, and plasma endothelin-1. *American Journal of Pathology*, *153*(6), 1873–1884. doi:10.1016/S0002-9440(10)65701-X PMID:9846977

Boyd, D., & Crawford, K. (2012). Critical Questions for Big Data. *Information Communication and Society*, *15*(5), 662–679. doi:10.1080/1369118X.2012.678878

Boyd, R., & Richerson, P. J. (2005). *The Origin and Evolution of Cultures (Evolution and Cognition)*. Oxford University Press.

BPMN. (2014). Object Management Group. *Business Process Modeling Notation*. Retrieved February 03, 2014, from http://www.omg.org/spec/BPMN/2.0/

Braga, A. L., Zanobetti, A., & Schwartz, J. (2002). The effect of weather on respiratory and cardiovascular deaths in 12 US cities. *Environmental Health Perspectives*, *110*(9), 859–863. doi:10.1289/ehp.02110859 PMID:12204818

Breslow, L. A., & Aha, D.W. (1997). Simplifying decision trees: A survey. *The Knowledge Engineering Review Archive*, *12*(1), 1-40.

Bridge, M., G¨oker, H., McGinty, L., & Smyth, B. (2006). Case-based recommender systems. *The Knowledge Engineering Review*.

Brillantes, A. Jr, & Fernandez, M. T. (2013). Toward A Reform Framework for Good Governance: Focus On Anti-Corruption. *Philippine Journal of Public Administration*, *54*(1-2), 87–127.

Brimblecombe, P. (1987). *The Big Smoke: A History of Air Pollution in London since Medieval Times Methuen*. London, UK.

Brook, R. D., Brook, J. R., Urch, B., Vincent, R., Rajagopalan, S., & Silverman, F. (2002). Inhalation of fine particulate air pollution and ozone causes acute arterial vasoconstriction in healthy adults. *Circulation*, *105*(13), 1534–1536. doi:10.1161/01.CIR.0000013838.94747.64 PMID:11927516

Brown, D. M., Stone, V., Findlay, P., MacNee, W., & Donaldson, K. (2000). Increased inflammation and intracellular calcium caused by ultrafine carbon black is independent of transition metals or other soluble components. *Occupational and Environmental Medicine*, *57*(10), 685–691. doi:10.1136/oem.57.10.685 PMID:10984341

Browning, T. R. (2009). Towards a process architecture framework for product development processes. *Springer*, *12*(1) pp. 1-90.

Brown, T., & Wyatt, J. (2010). Design thinking for social innovation. *Stanford Social Innovation Review*, *8*(1), 30–35.

Brucker, A. D., & Petritsch, H. (2009, June). Extending access control models with break-glass. In *Proceedings of the 14th ACM symposium on Access control models and technologies* (pp. 197-206). ACM. doi:10.1145/1542207.1542239

Brunekreef, B., & Holgate, S. T. (2002). Air pollution and health. *Lancet*, *360*(9341), 1233–1242. doi:10.1016/S0140-6736(02)11274-8 PMID:12401268

Budakova, Dakovski, & Lyudmil. (2013). The intelligent virtual agents - a new interface to the computer. Saarbrücken: LAP LAMBERT Academic Publishing.

Bumgardner, M., Buehlmann, U., Schuler, A., & Crissey, J. (2011). Competitive Actions of Small Firms in a Declining Market. *Journal of Small Business Management*, *49*(4), 578–598. doi:10.1111/j.1540-627X.2011.00337.x

Bundesamt für Sicherheit in der Informationstechnik. (2011, March 10). *Technical Guideline TR-03127: Architecture electronic Identity Card and electronic Resident Permit*. Retrieved January 20, 2014, from https://www.bsi.bund.de/SharedDocs/Downloads/DE/BSI/Publikationen/TechnischeRichtlinien/TR03127/BSI-TR-03127_en_pdf.pdf?__blob=publicationFile

Bundesamt für Sicherheit in der Informationstechnik. (2012, March). *Technical Guideline TR-03110-2, Version 2.10: Advanced Security Mechanisms for Machine Readable Travel Documents Part 2*. Retrieved from https://www.bsi.bund.de/SharedDocs/Downloads/EN/BSI/Publications/TechGuidelines/TR03110/TR-03110_v2.1_P2pdf.pdf?__blob=publicationFile

Bundesamt für Sicherheit in der Informationstechnik. (2013, July). *Technical Guideline TR-03110-3, Version 2.11: Advanced Security Mechanisms for Machine Readable Travel Documents Part 3*. Retrieved from https://www.bsi.bund.de/SharedDocs/Downloads/EN/BSI/Publications/TechGuidelines/TR03110/TR-03110_v2_11_P3pdf.pdf?__blob=publicationFile Bundesverfassungsgericht/Federal

Burnett, R. T., Smith-Doiron, M., Stieb, D., Cakmak, S., & Brook, J. R. (1999). Effects of particulate and gaseous air pollution on cardiorespiratory hospitalizations. *Archives of Environmental Health: An International Journal*, *54*(2), 130–139. doi:10.1080/00039899909602248 PMID:10094292

Business Friendly Certification South East Europe. (2013). *Certification of Business friendly Municipalities in SEE*. Retrieved February 16, 2013 from http://www.bfc-see.org/upload/Document/File/2013_07/BFC_SEE_Brochure.pdf

Cajaiba-Santana, G. (2013). Social innovation: Moving the field forward. A conceptual framework. *Technological Forecasting and Social Change*.

Cakmak, S., Dales, R., Kauri, L. M., Mahmud, M., Van Ryswyk, K., & Vanos, J. et al. (2014). Metal composition of fine particulate air pollution and acute changes in cardiorespiratory physiology. *Environmental Pollution*, *189*, 208–214. doi:10.1016/j.envpol.2014.03.004 PMID:24682071

Calderón-Garcidueñas, L., Franco-Lira, M., Torres-Jardón, R., Henriquez-Roldán, C., Barragán-Mejía, G., & Valencia-Salazar, G. et al. (2007). Pediatric respiratory and systemic effects of chronic air pollution exposure: Nose, lung, heart, and brain pathology. *Toxicologic Pathology, 35*(1), 154–162. doi:10.1080/01926230601059985 PMID:17325984

Cambria, E., Schuller, B., Yunqing, X., & Havasi, C. (2013). New Avenues in Opinion Mining and Sentiment Analysis. *IEEE Intelligent Systems, 28*(2), 15–21. doi:10.1109/MIS.2013.30

CamNtech Ltd and CamNtech Inc. (2012). *Actiheart.* Retrieved from http://www.camntech.com/products/actiheart/actiheart-overview

Campbell, J., McDonald, C., & Sethibe, T. (2010). Public and Private Sector IT Governance: Identifying Contextual Differences. *Australasian Journal of Information Systems, 16*(2). Retrieved from http://dl.acs.org.au/index.php/ajis/article/view/538

Campbell-Kelly, M., Aspray, W., Ensmenger, N., & Yost, J. R. (2013). *Computer a History of the Information Machine*. New York: Westview Press.

Candiello, A., Albarelli, A., & Cortesi, A. (2010). Three-layered QoS for eGovernment web services. In *Proceedings of DGO'2010*, (pp. 217-222). DGO.

Cao, L., Mohan, K., Ramesh, B., & Sarkar, S. (2013). Adapting funding processes for agile IT projects: An empirical investigation. *European Journal of Information Systems, 22*(2), 191–205. doi:10.1057/ejis.2012.9

Cappelli, C., Leite, J. C. S. P., Engiel, P., & Araujo, R. M. (2013). Managing Transparency Guided by a Maturity Model. In *Proceedings of3rd Global Conference on Transparency Research*. Paris: Academic Press.

Carey, I. M., Atkinson, R. W., Kent, A. J., van Staa, T., Cook, D. G., & Anderson, H. R. (2013). Mortality Associations with Long-Term Exposure to Outdoor Air Pollution in a National English Cohort. *American Journal of Respiratory and Critical Care Medicine, 187*(11), 1226–1233. doi:10.1164/rccm.201210-1758OC PMID:23590261

Carter, L., & Belanger, F. (2005). The utilization of e-government services: Citizien trust, innovation and acceptance factors. *Information Systems Journal, 15*(1), 5–25. doi:10.1111/j.1365-2575.2005.00183.x

Carter, L., & Weerakkody, V. (2008). E-government adoption: A cultural comparison. *Information Systems Frontiers, 10*(4), 473–482. doi:10.1007/s10796-008-9103-6

Casserly, M. (2013). MindMixer Acquires VoterTide, Bets Social Tech Can Save Democratic Process. *Entrepreneurship.* Retrieved 31-01-2014, 2014, from http://www.forbes.com/sites/meghancasserly/2013/03/26/mindmixer-acquires-votertide-bets-social-tech-can-save-democratic-process/

Centers for Disease Control and Prevention. (2002). Heat related deaths – four states, July–August 2001 and United States, 1979–1999. *MMWR Mortality and Morbidity Weekly Report, 51*, 528–531.

Centre de Recerca I Inovació de Catalunya (CRIC). (2012) *Softcare: Unobtrusive plug and play kit for chronic condition based on customized behaviour recognition.* Retrieved from http://www.cric.cat/project-detail/16/

Ceron, A., Curini, L., Iacus, S. M., & Porro, G. (2013). Every tweet counts? How sentiment analysis of social media can improve our knowledge of citizens' political preferences with an application to Italy and France. *New Media & Society, 16*(2), 340–358. doi:10.1177/1461444813480466

Chaitin, G. (2006). The Limits Of Reason. *Scientific American, 294*(3), 74–81. doi:10.1038/scientificamerican0306-74 PMID:16502614

Chalmers, D. (2013). Social innovation: An exploration of the barriers faced by innovating organizations in the social economy. *Local Economy, 28*(1), 17–34. doi:10.1177/0269094212463677

Chandra, D. S., & Yokoyama, K. (2011). *The role of good governance in the knowledge-based economic growth of East Asia–A study on Japan, Newly Industrialized Economies*. Graduate School of Economics, Kyushu University.

Chang, I., Li, Y., Hung, W., & Hwang, H. (2005). An empirical study on the impact of quality antecedents on tax payers' acceptance of Internet tax-filing systems. *Government Information Quarterly*, *22*(3), 389–410. doi:10.1016/j.giq.2005.05.002

Chan, N. Y., Stacey, M. T., Smith, A. E., Ebi, K. L., & Wilson, T. F. (2001). An empirical mechanistic framework for heat-related illness. *Climate Research*, *16*(2), 133–143. doi:10.3354/cr016133

Charnes, A., Cooper, W. W., & Rhodes, E. (1978). Measuring the Efficiency of Decision Making Units. *European Journal of Operational Research*, *12*(6), 429–444. doi:10.1016/0377-2217(78)90138-8

Chatfield, A. T. (2009). Public Service Reform through e-Government: A Case Study of 'e-Tax' in Japan. *Electronic. Journal of E-Government*, *7*(2), 135–146.

Chebana, F., Martel, B., Gosselin, P., Giroux, J. X., & Ouarda, T. B. (2013). A general and flexible methodology to define thresholds for heat health watch and warning systems, applied to the province of Québec (Canada). *International Journal of Biometeorology*, *57*(4), 631–644. doi:10.1007/s00484-012-0590-2 PMID:23100100

Chen, Y., & Qu, L. (2006). Evaluating the Selection of Logistics Centre Location Using Fuzzy MCDM Model Based on Entropy Weight. In *Proceedings ofthe Sixth World Congress on Intelligent Control and Automation*, (pp. 7128 – 7132). Academic Press. doi:10.1109/WCICA.2006.1714468

Chen, L. (2008). Design and implementation of intelligent library system. *Library Collections, Acquisitions & Technical Services*, *32*(3–4), 127–141. doi:10.1016/j.lcats.2008.09.001

Chen, M., Gonzalez, S., Vasilakos, A., Cao, H., & Leung, V. C. M. (2011). Body Area Networks: A Survey. *Journal Mobile Network Application*, *16*(2), 171–193. doi:10.1007/s11036-010-0260-8

Chen, S. C., Chen, H. H., & Chen, M. F. (2009). Determinants of Satisfaction and Continuance Intention Towards Self-Service Technologies. *Industrial Management & Data Systems*, *109*(9), 1248–1263. doi:10.1108/02635570911002306

Chen, T. M. (2011). How networks changed the world. *IEEE Network*, *25*(6), 2–3. doi:10.1109/MNET.2011.6085635

Chen, Y. Y., Huang, H. L., Hsu, Y. C., Tseng, H. C., & Lee, Y. C. (2010). Confirmation of Expectations and Satisfaction with the Internet Shopping: The Role of Internet Self-efficacy. *Computer and Information Science*, *3*(3), 14–22. doi:10.5539/cis.v3n3p14

Chesbrough, H. & Vanhaverbeke, W. (2011). Open Innovation and Public Policy in Europe. *Science Business*.

Chesbrough, H. W. (2003). *Open innovation: The new imperative for creating and profiting from technology*. Harvard Business Press.

Chesbrough, H., Vanhaverbeke, W., & West, J. (2008). *Open Innovation: Researching a New Paradigm: Researching a New Paradigm*. Oxford University Press.

Chinosi, M., & Trombetta, A. (2012). BPMN: An introduction to the standard. *Computer Standards & Interfaces*, *34*(1), 124–134. doi:10.1016/j.csi.2011.06.002

Chin, W. W. (1998). Commentary: Issues and Opinion on Structural Equation Modeling. *Management Information Systems Quarterly*, *22*(1), vii–xvi.

Chin, W. W. (2010). How to Write Up and Report PLS Analyses. In V. Esposito Vinzi et al. (Eds.), *Handbook of Partial Least Squares: Concepts, Methods and Applications* (pp. 655–689). Springer Handbooks of Computational Statistics, Springer-Verlag Berlin Heidelberg. doi:10.1007/978-3-540-32827-8_29

Chiu, C. M., Chang, C. C., Cheng, H. L., & Fang, Y. H. (2009). Determinants of Customer Repurchase Intention in Online Shopping. *Online Information Review*, *33*(4), 761–784. doi:10.1108/14684520910985710

Cho, J. S., & Hyun, K. H. (2006). Meta-ontology for automated information integration of parts libraries. *Computer Aided Design*, *38*(7), 713–725. doi:10.1016/j.cad.2006.03.002

Chor, B., Goldreich, O., Kushilevitz, E., & Sudan, M. (1995). Private information retrieval. In *Proceedings of36th Annual Symposium on Foundations of Computer Science* (pp. 41-50). Milwaukee, WI: IEEE.

Chourabi, H., Nam, T., Walker, S., Gil-García, J. R., Mellouli, S., Nahon, K., et al. (2012). Understanding smart cities: an integrative framework. In *Proceedings of 2012 45th Hawaii International Conference on System Sciences* (pp. 2289-2297). Hawaii, HI: IEEE.

Chou, S. W., & Chen, P. Y. (2009). The Influence of Individual Differences on Continuance Intentions of Enterprise Resource Planning (ERP). *International Journal of Human-Computer Studies, 67*(6), 484–496. doi:10.1016/j.ijhcs.2009.01.001

Choy, M., Cheong, M. L. F., Laik, M. N., & Shung, K. P. (2012). US Presidential Election 2012 Prediction using Census Corrected Twitter Model. *CoRR, abs/1211.0938.*

Chu, A. T. W., Kalaba, R. E., & Spingarn, K. (1979). A comparison of two methods for determining the weights of belonging to fuzzy sets. *Journal of Optimization Theory and Applications, 27*(4), 531–538. doi:10.1007/BF00933438

Chung, L., Nixon, B., Yu, E., & Mylopoulos, J. (2000). *Non-Functional Requirements in Software Engineering.* Kluwer Academic Publishers. doi:10.1007/978-1-4615-5269-7

Chun, S. A., & Luna Reyes, L. F. (2012). Social media in government. *Government Information Quarterly, 29*(4), 441–445. doi:10.1016/j.giq.2012.07.003

Church, K., & Gale, W. (1999). Inverse Document Frequency (IDF): A Measure of Deviations from Poisson. In S. Armstrong (Ed.), *Natural Language Processing Using Very Large Corpora* (pp. 283–295). Kower Academic Publishers, Springer. doi:10.1007/978-94-017-2390-9_18

Cimiano, P., Hotho, A., & Staab, S. (2013). *Comparing Conceptual, Divisive and Agglomerative Clustering for Learning Taxonomies from Text.* Bielefeld University. Retrieved October 14, 2013, from http://pub.uni-bielefeld.de/luur

Ciocarlan-Chitucea, A., & Popescu, D. (2010). The SMEs Performances Explained Through Influences of the Economic Context. Study Case: Romania. *Review of International Comparative Management, 12*(6), 195–201.

Cleland-Huang, J. (2013). Are Requirements Alive and Kicking? *IEEE Software, 30*(3), 13–15. doi:10.1109/MS.2013.47

Clinch, J. P., & Healy, J. D. (2000). Housing standards and excess winter mortality. *Journal of Epidemiology and Community Health, 54*(9), 719–720. doi:10.1136/jech.54.9.719 PMID:10942456

Cloutier, J. (2003). *Qu'est-ce que l'innovation sociale?* Crises.

Cochran, W. G. (2007). *Sampling techniques.* John Wiley & Sons.

Coleman, J. S. (1988). Social capital in the creation of human capital. *American Journal of Sociology, 94*(s1), S95–S120. doi:10.1086/228943

Collins, T. (2009). From Ottawa to Lausanne: Much Done but More to Do? *Electronic. Journal of E-Government, 7*(2), 147–154.

Collis, J., & Hussey, R. (2005). Pesquisa em administração: Um guia prático para alunos de graduação e pós-graduação. *The Bookman.*

Concha, G., Astudillo, H., Porrúa, M., & Pimenta, C. (2012). E-Government procurement observatory, maturity model and early measurements. *Government Information Quarterly, 29*(1), 43–50. doi:10.1016/j.giq.2011.08.005

Conrad, J., Al-Kofahi, K., Zhao, Y., & Karypis, G. (2005). Effective Document Clustering for Large Heterogeneous Law Firm Collections. In *Proceedings ofthe Tenth International Conference on Artificial Intelligence and Law* (pp. 177 – 187), Bologna, Italy: ACM. doi:10.1145/1165485.1165513

Conroy, C. (2006). *Telecentre initiatives in rural India: Failed fad or the way forward? Natural resources institute.* University of Greenwich.

Constitutional Court. (2009, March 3). *Judgment of the Second Senate of 3 March 2009 on the basis of the oral hearing of 28 October 2008.* Retrieved January 20, 2014, from https://www.bundesverfassungsgericht.de/entscheidungen/rs20090303_2bvc000307en.html

Cook, M. E. (2000, October). *What Citizens Want From E-Government: Current Practce Research.* Retrieved January 20, 2014, from http://www.netcaucus.info/books/egov2001/pdf/citizen.pdf

Cooking Hacks. (2013). *e-Health Sensor Platform for Arduino and Rasperry Pi* [Biometric/Medical Applications]. Retrieved from http://www.cooking-hacks.com/documentation/tutorials/ehealth-v1-biometric-sensor-platform-arduino-raspberry-pi-medical/

Coradeschi, S., Cesta, A., Cortellessa, G., Coraci, L., Gonzalez, J., Karlsson, L., … Otslund, B. (2013, June). Giraffplus: Combining social interaction and long term monitoring for promoting independent living. In *Proceedings of Human System Interaction (HSI),* (pp. 578-585). IEEE.

Correia, L. M. (2011). *Expert Working Group on Smart Cities Applications and Requirements.* Lisbon: Univ.

Coursey, D., & Norris, D. F. (2008). Models of E-government: Are they correct? an empirical assessment. *Public Administration Review, 68*(3), 523–536. doi:10.1111/j.1540-6210.2008.00888.x

Criado, J. I., Sandoval-Almazan, R., & Gil-Garcia, J. R. (2013). Government innovation through social media. *Government Information Quarterly, 30*(4), 319–326. doi:10.1016/j.giq.2013.10.003

Cull, R. E. (1981). Barometric pressure and other factors in migraine. *Headache: The Journal of Head and Face Pain, 21*(3), 102–104. doi:10.1111/j.1526-4610.1981.hed2103102.x PMID:7263217

Cuno, S., Glickman, Y., Baboshin, A., Haritou, M., Serretti, A., Androulidakis, A., & Calati, R. (2011). Management, Monitoring and Supporting Dementia Patients at Home by ALADDIN. In *Proceedings of eChallenges e-2011.* IIMC International Information Management Corporation.

Curtis, L., Rea, W., Smith-Willis, P., Fenyves, E., & Pan, Y. (2006). Adverse health effects of outdoor air pollutants. *Environment International, 32*(6), 815–830. doi:10.1016/j.envint.2006.03.012 PMID:16730796

Cysneiros, L. M., Yu, E., & Leite, J. C. S. P. (2003). Cataloguing Non Functional requirements as Softgoal Networks. In *Proceedings of 11th International Requirements Engineering Conference,* (pp. 13-20). Monterey, CA: Academic Press.

Dada, D. (2006). The failure of e-government in developing countries: A literature review. *The Electronic Journal of Information Systems in Developing Countries, 26.*

Dahlander, L., & Gann, D. M. (2010). How open is innovation? *Research Policy, 39*(6), 699–709. doi:10.1016/j.respol.2010.01.013

Daigle, C. C., Chalupa, D. C., Gibb, F. R., Morrow, P. E., Oberdörster, G., Utell, M. J., & Frampton, M. W. (2003). Ultrafine particle deposition in humans during rest and exercise. *Inhalation Toxicology, 15*(6), 539–552. doi:10.1080/08958370304468 PMID:12692730

Damnjanovic, Z., Jovanovic, M. M., Bogdanovic, D. C., Smiljkovic, I. D., Ilic, N., & Damnjanovic, I. (2012). Relationship between the Incidence of Idiopathic Lower Extremity Deep Vein Thrombosis and the Location of the Thrombus depending on the Changes in Atmospheric Pressure. *Chirurgia, 107*(4), 483–487. PMID:23025115

Danet, S., Richard, F., Montaye, M., Beauchant, S., Lemaire, B., & Graux, C. et al. (1999). Unhealthy Effects of Atmospheric Temperature and Pressure on the Occurrence of Myocardial Infarction and Coronary Deaths A 10-Year Survey: The Lille-World Health Organization MONICA Project (Monitoring Trends and Determinants in Cardiovascular Disease). *Circulation, 100*(1), e1–e7. doi:10.1161/01.CIR.100.1.e1 PMID:10393689

Danziger, J. N., & Andersen, K. V. (2002). The impacts of information technology in public administration: An analysis of empirical research from the "golden age" of transformation. *International Journal of Public Administration, 25*(5), 591–625. doi:10.1081/PAD-120003292

Davis, D. L. (2003). *When smoke ran like water: Tales of environmental deception and the battle against pollution.* Basic Books.

Davis, F. D. (1989). Perceived usefulness, perceived ease of use, and user acceptance of information technology. *Management Information Systems Quarterly, 13*(3), 319–340. doi:10.2307/249008

Davis, F. D., Bagozzi, R. P., & Warshaw, P. R. (1989). User Acceptance of Computer Technology: A Comparison of Two Theoretical Models. *Management Science, 15*(8), 982–1003. doi:10.1287/mnsc.35.8.982

Davison, B. D. (2002) Predicting Web Actions from HTML Content. In *Proceedings ofThirteenth ACM Conference on Hypertext and Hypermedia (HT'02).* ACM. doi:10.1145/513338.513380

Delfino, R. J., Murphy-Moulton, A. M., Burnett, R. T., Brook, J. R., & Becklake, M. R. (1997). Effects of air pollution on emergency room visits for respiratory illnesses in Montreal, Quebec. *American Journal of Respiratory and Critical Care Medicine*, *155*(2), 568–576. doi:10.1164/ajrccm.155.2.9032196 PMID:9032196

Delyukov, A. A., & Didyk, L. (1999). The effects of extra-low-frequency atmospheric pressure oscillations on human mental activity. *International Journal of Biometeorology*, *43*(1), 31–37. doi:10.1007/s004840050113 PMID:10466018

Deng, L., Turner, D. E., Gehling, R., & Prince, B. (2010). User Experience, Satisfaction, and Continual Usage Intention of IT. *European Journal of Information Systems*, *19*(1), 60–75. doi:10.1057/ejis.2009.50

Denne, M., & Cleland-Huang, J. (2004). *Software by numbers: low risk, high return development*. Upper Saddle River, NJ: Prentice Hall.

Department of Public Expenditure and Reform. (2011). *Public Service Reform Plan*. Retrieved from http://reformplan.per.gov.ie/files/2012/01/Public-Service-Reform-28112011.pdf

Department of Public Expenditure and Reform. (2012). *Supporting public service reform e-government 2012-2015*. Retrieved from http://per.gov.ie/wp-content/uploads/eGovernment-2012-2015.pdf

Deutsche Post. (2014). *Postident*. Retrieved January 20, 2014, from https://www.deutschepost.de/dpag?tab=1&skin=hi&check=yes&lang=de_EN&xmlFile=link1017202_1009859 Directive 1999/93/EC

Devlin, R. B., Ghio, A. J., Kehrl, H., Sanders, G., & Cascio, W. (2003). Elderly humans exposed to concentrated air pollution particles have decreased heart rate variability. *The European Respiratory Journal*, *21*(suppl 40), 76–80. doi:10.1183/09031936.03.00402403 PMID:12762579

Dey, S. K., & Sobhan, A. (2008). Conceptual Framework for Introducing e-Governance in University Administration. In *Proceedings of Conference International Conference on Theory and Practice of Electronic Governance*. doi:10.1145/1509096.1509186

Dhopeshwarkar, R. V., Kern, L. M., O'Donnell, H. C., Edwards, A. M., & Kaushal, R. (2012). Health care consumers' preferences around health information exchange. *Annals of Family Medicine*, *10*(5), 428–434. doi:10.1370/afm.1396 PMID:22966106

Di Caro, L., & Grella, M. (2013). Sentiment analysis via dependency parsing. *Computer Standards & Interfaces*, *35*(5), 442–453. doi:10.1016/j.csi.2012.10.005

Di Maio, A. (2012). Smart Government: Sustainable, Affordable, Innovative. In *Proceedings of Worldwide Government Solutions Forum 2012*. Academic Press.

Díaz-Agudo, B., González-Calero, P.A., Recio-García, J., & Sánchez-Ruiz, A. (2007). Building CBR systems with jColibri. *Journal of Science of Computer Programming*.

Diaz-Galiano, M. C., Martin-Valdivia, M. T., & Urena-Lopez, L. A. (2009). Query expansion with a medical ontology to improve a multimodal information retrieval system. *Computers in Biology and Medicine*, *39*(4), 396–403. doi:10.1016/j.compbiomed.2009.01.012 PMID:19268924

Diirr, B., Araujo, R. M., & Cappelli, C. (2011). Talking about Public Service Processes. In *Proceedings ofInternational Conference on eParticipation*, (vol. 1, pp. 252-261). Academic Press.

Diirr, B., Araujo, R., & Cappelli, C. (2009). An Approach for Defining Digital Democracy Support based on ICT. In *Proceedings of the 13th International Conference on Computer Supported Cooperative Work in Design*. Academic Press. doi:10.1109/CSCWD.2009.4968059

Dilaveris, P., Synetos, A., Giannopoulos, G., Gialafos, E., Pantazis, A., & Stefanadis, C. (2006). CLimate Impacts on Myocardial infarction deaths in the Athens TErritory: The CLIMATE study. *Heart (British Cardiac Society)*, *92*(12), 1747–1751. doi:10.1136/hrt.2006.091884 PMID:16840509

DiMaggio, P. J., & Powell, W. W. (1991). The Iron Cage Revisited: Institutional Isomorphism and Collective Rationality in Organizational Fields. In W. W. Powell & P. J. DiMaggio (Eds.), *The New Institutionalism in Organizational Analysis*. Chicago, IL: University of Chicago Press.

Ding, H. (2004). Towards the metadata integration issues in peer-to-peer based digital libraries. In GCC (LNCS), (Vol. 3251). Berlin, Germany: Springer.

Directive 2006/123/EC. (2006). *European Parliament and of the Council of 12 December 2006 on services in the internal market*. Retrieved from http://eur-lex.europa.eu/LexUriServ/LexUriServ.do?uri=OJ:L:2006:376:0036:0068:en:pdf

Dockery, D. W., Pope, C. A. III, Kanner, R. E., Villegas, M., & Schwartz, J. (1999). Daily changes in oxygen saturation and pulse rate associated with particulate air pollution and barometric pressure. *Research Report (Health Effects Institute)*, (83): 1–19. PMID:10192116

Dockery, D. W., Pope, C. A. III, Xu, X., Spengler, J. D., Ware, J. H., & Fay, M. E. et al. (1993). An asso.ciation between air pollution and mortality in six US cities. *The New England Journal of Medicine*, *329*(24), 1753–1759. doi:10.1056/NEJM199312093292401 PMID:8179653

Dohler, M., Watteine, T., & Alonso-Zárate, J. (2010). *Centre Tecnològic de Telecomunicacions de Catalunya*. Retrieved from http://www.cttc.es/en/event/100423-machine-to-machi.jsp

Doise, W. (2003). Les relations entre groups. In Psychologie social. Puf edit (in French).

Dolowitz, D. P., & Marsh, D. (1998). Policy Transfer: A Framework for Comparative Analysis. In M. Minogue, C. Polidano, & D. Hulme (Eds.), *Beyond the New Public Management: Changing Ideas and Practices in Governance*. Cheltenham, UK: Edwards Elgar.

Dominici, F., McDermott, A., Daniels, M., Zeger, S., & Samet, J. (2002). *A report to the health effects institute: reanalyses of the NMMAPS database*. Baltimore, MD: Department of Biostatisics and Epidemiology, Bloomberg School of Public Health, Johns Hopkins University.

Donaldson, G. (1997). Cold exposure and winter mortality from ischaemic heart disease, cerebrovascular disease, respiratory disease, and all causes in warm and cold regions of Europe. The Eurowinter Group. *Lancet*, *349*(9062), 1341–1346. doi:10.1016/S0140-6736(96)12338-2 PMID:9149695

Donaldson, G. C., & Keatinge, W. R. (1997). Early increases in ischaemic heart disease mortality dissociated from and later changes associated with respiratory mortality after cold weather in south east England. *Journal of Epidemiology and Community Health*, *51*(6), 643–648. doi:10.1136/jech.51.6.643 PMID:9519127

Dong, N., Jonker, H., & Pang, J. (2012). Challenges in eHealth: From Enabling to Enforcing Privacy. In Z. Liu & A. Wassyng (Eds.), *Foundations of Health Informatics Engineering and System* (pp. 195–206). Springer. doi:10.1007/978-3-642-32355-3_12

Donoghue, E. R., Graham, M. A., Jentzen, J. M., Lifschultz, B. D., Luke, J. L., & Mirchandani, H. G. (1997). Criteria for the diagnosis of heat-related deaths: National Association of Medical Examiners: position paper. *The American Journal of Forensic Medicine and Pathology*, *18*(1), 11–14. doi:10.1097/00000433-199703000-00002 PMID:9095294

Doong, H. S., Wang, H. C., & Chen, P. H. (2007).An Empirical Study of Online Reputation System Continuance. In *Proceedings ofInternational Conference on Wireless Communications, Networking and Mobile Computing*, (pp. 3816-3819). Academic Press. doi:10.1109/WICOM.2007.944

Doria, J. V., Jr., Alencar, A. J., Schmitz, E. A., Correa, A. L., & Vital, I. M., Jr. (2012). On the Merits and Pitfalls of the Incremental Funding Method and Its Software Project Scheduling Algorithms. In K. R. Venugopal & L. M. Patnaik (Eds.), Wireless Networks and Computational Intelligence (pp. 493–502). Springer Berlin Heidelberg. Retrieved from http://link.springer.com/chapter/10.1007/978-3-642-31686-9_57

Downe, J., Hartley, J., & Rashman, L. (2004). Evaluating the Extent of Inter-organizational Learning and Change in Local Authorities Through the English Beacon Council Scheme. *Public Management Review*, *6*(4), 531–553. doi:10.1080/1471903042000303328

Driver, E., & Kroeber, L. (1932). Quantitative expression of cultural relationships. *University of Caltfornia Publications in American Archeology and Ethnology*, *31*, 211–256.

Dugan, R. C., & McGranaghan, M. (2011). Sim City. *IEEE Power and Energy Magazine*, *9*(5), 74–81. doi:10.1109/MPE.2011.941867

Dumas, M., La Rosa, M., Mendling, J., & Reijers, H. (2013). *Fundamentals of Business Process Management*. Springer. doi:10.1007/978-3-642-33143-5

Dunkelberg, C., & Wade, H. (2012). NFIB Small Business Economic Trends, December 2012. *National Federation of Independent Business*. Available at http://www.nfib.com/portals/0/pdf/sbet/sbet201012.pdf

Dunn, J. C. (1973). A fuzzy relative of the ISODATA process and its use in detecting compact well-separated clusters. *Journal of Cybernetics*, *3*(3), 32–57. doi:10.1080/01969727308546046

Eck, J. E., & Spelman, W. (1987). *Problem-Solving: Problem-Oriented Policing in Newport News*. Washington, DC: National Institute of Justice, Police Executive Research Forum (PERF).

Eck, J. E., & Rosenbaum, D. (1994). The new police order: effectiveness, equity, and efficiency in community policing. In D. Rosenbaum (Ed.), *The Challenge of Community Policing: Testing the Promise*. Thousands Oaks, CA: SAGE. doi:10.4135/9781483327006.n1

Eddy, N. (2013, October 21). *Mobile Phone, Tablet Sales Driven by Budget Devices: Gartner. eWeek*. Retrieved November 20, 2013, from http://www.eweek.com/mobile/mobile-phone-tablet-sales-driven-by-budget-devices-gartner.html

Eid, E. E., & AbdEl-Razek, M. M. (2009). E-government theory and implementation case study Egyptian e-government model. In *Proceedings ofthe International Conference on Administration and Business*. University of Bucharest.

EIF. (2014, April 21). *European Interoperability Framework Version 2*. Retrieved from http://ec.europa.eu/isa/strategy/doc/annex_ii_eif_en.pdf

Eirinaki, M., Pisal, S., & Singh, J. (2012). Feature-based opinion mining and ranking. *Journal of Computer and System Sciences*, *78*(4), 1175–1184. doi:10.1016/j.jcss.2011.10.007

Elhari, K., & Bounabat, B. (2011). Platform for Assessing Strategic Alignment Using Enterprise Architecture: Application to E-Government Process Assessment. *International Journal of Computer Science, 8* (1).

Elkan, C. (2004). *Clustering with k-means: faster, smarter, cheaper.* Paper presented at the Workshop on Clustering High-Dimensional Data, SIAM International Conference on Data Mining (SDM 2004). Lake Buena Vista, FL.

Engeström, Y. (1999). Activity theory and individual and social transformation. In Y. Engeström, R. Miettinen, & R.-L. Punamäki (Eds.), Perspectives on Activity Theory, (pp. 19-38). Cambridge University Press. doi:10.1017/CBO9780511812774.003

Engiel, P. (2012). *Designing public services business process models for understandability.* (MSc dissertation). Federal University of the State of Rio de Janeiro, Brazil. (in Portuguese)

ENISA. (2012). *Appropiate security measures for smart grids: Guidelines to asses the sophistication of security measures implementation.* Retrieved from http://www.enisa.europa.eu/activities/Resilience-and-CIIP/critical-infrastructure-and-services/smart-grids-and-smart-metering/ENISA-smart-grid-security-recommendations

Enkel, E., Gassmann, O., & Chesbrough, H. (2009). Open R&D and open innovation: Exploring the phenomenon. *Research Management*, *39*(4), 311–316.

EPC. (2014). *Event-Driven Process Chain.* Retrieved February 03, 2014, from http://en.wikipedia.org/wiki/Event-driven_process_chain

Eriksson, H. E., & Penker, M. (2000). *Business modeling with UML.* Chichester, UK: Wiley.

Eriksson, K., & Nilsson, D. (2007). Determinants of the Continued Use of Self-Service Technology: The Case of Internet Banking. *Technovation*, *27*(4), 159–167. doi:10.1016/j.technovation.2006.11.001

Estevez, E., & Janowski, T. (2013). Electronic Governance for Sustainable Development — Conceptual framework and state of research. *Government Information Quarterly*, *30*(1), 94–109. doi:10.1016/j.giq.2012.11.001

European Commission. (1996). The Green Book on Innovation. Luxembourg: European Commission.

European Union. (2009). Decision Num. 922/2009/EC of the European Parliament and the Council of 16 September 2009 on interoperability solutions for European public administrations (ISA). *Official Journal of the European Union,* (L 260), 20-27.

Ezzati, M., Lopez, A. D., Rodgers, A., Vander Hoorn, S., & Murray, C. J. (2002). Selected major risk factors and global and regional burden of disease. *Lancet, 360*(9343), 1347–1360. doi:10.1016/S0140-6736(02)11403-6 PMID:12423980

Faich, G., & Rose, R. (1979). Blizzard morbidity and mortality: Rhode Island, 1978. *American Journal of Public Health, 69*(10), 1050–1052. doi:10.2105/AJPH.69.10.1050 PMID:484759

Fairley, R. E. (2008). Project Planning Techniques. In Managing and Leading Software Projects (pp. 173–206). John Wiley & Sons, Inc. Retrieved from http://onlinelibrary.wiley.com/doi/10.1002/9780470405697.ch5/summary

Falliere, N. O., Murchu, L., & Chien, E. (2011, February). *W32.Stuxnet Dossier: V1.4.* Retrieved 2013 6-April from http://www.symantec.com/content/en/us/enterprise/media/security_response/whitepapers/w32_stuxnet_dossier.pdf

Fang, Z. (2002). E-Government in Digital Era: Concept, Practice and Development. *International Journal of the Computer, the Internet and Management, 10*(2), 1-22.

Fang, Z. (2002). E-Government in Digital Era: Concept, Practice, and Development. *International Journal of the Computer, the Internet and Management, 10*(2), 1–22.

Fan, Z., Ma, J., & Tian, P. (1999). A subjective and objective integrated approach for the determination of attribute weights. *European Journal of Operational Research, 112*(2), 397–404. doi:10.1016/S0377-2217(98)00141-6

Faustini, A., Stafoggia, M., Cappai, G., & Forastiere, F. (2012). Short-term effects of air pollution in a cohort of patients with chronic obstructive pulmonary disease. *Epidemiology (Cambridge, Mass.), 23*(6), 861–879. doi:10.1097/EDE.0b013e31826767c2 PMID:23018970

Federal Ministry of the Interior. (2013). *German National Identity Card.* Retrieved January 20, 2014, from http://www.personalausweisportal.de/EN/Citizens/Applications/applications_node.html

Feki, M. A., Kawsar, F., Boussard, M., & Trappeniers, L. (2013). The Internet of Things: The Next Technological Revolution. *Computer Magazine, 46*(2), 24–25. doi:10.1109/MC.2013.63

Feldman, D., Sung, C., & Rus, D. (2012). The single pixel GPS: learning big data signals from tiny coresets. In *Proceedings of the 20th International Conference on Advances in Geographic Information Systems* (pp. 23-32). ACM. doi:10.1145/2424321.2424325

Fernández Martínez, A., & Llorens, L. (2011). Gobierno de la TI para las Universidades. *CRUE.* Retrieved from http://www.crue.org/Publicaciones/Documents/Gobierno%20TI/gobierno_de_las_TI_para_universidades.pdf

Ferreira, A., Cruz-Correia, R., Antunes, L., Farinha, P., Oliveira-Palhares, E., Chadwick, D. W., & Costa-Pereira, A. (2006, June). How to break access control in a controlled manner. In *Proceedings of Computer-Based Medical Systems, 2006. CBMS 2006. 19th IEEE International Symposium on* (pp. 847-854). IEEE.

Ferreira, J. S. J., Araujo, R. M., & Baião, F. A. (2010) Identifying Ruptures In Business-It Communication Through Business Models. In *Proceedings of12th International Conference on Enterprise Information Systems.* Academic Press.

Fichtlscherer, S., Rosenberger, G., Walter, D. H., Breuer, S., Dimmeler, S., & Zeiher, A. M. (2000). Elevated C-reactive protein levels and impaired endothelial vasoreactivity in patients with coronary artery disease. *Circulation, 102*(9), 1000–1006. doi:10.1161/01.CIR.102.9.1000 PMID:10961964

Finger, M., & Pécoud, G. (2003). *From E-government to E-governance? Towards a Model of E-governance.* Paper presented at the 3rd European Conference on E-government. Dublin, Ireland.

Finnie, G., & Sun, Z. (2002). Similarity and metrics in case-based reasoning. *International Journal of Intelligent Systems, 17*(3), 273–287. doi:10.1002/int.10021

Flichy, P. (2006). Une histoire de la communication moderne, vie publique, vie privée, ed la découverte. Academic Press. (French)

Forman, E. H., Saaty, T. L., Selly, M. A., & Waldron, R. (1983). Expert Choice. Decision Support Software.

Forman, E. H., & Gass, S. I. (2001). The Analytic Hierarchy Process – An Exposition. *Operations Research*, *49*(4), 469–486. doi:10.1287/opre.49.4.469.11231

Fornell, C., & Larcker, D. F. (1981). Evaluating Structural Equation Models with Unobservable Variables and Measurement Error. *JMR, Journal of Marketing Research*, *18*(1), 39–50. doi:10.2307/3151312

Fortuny, E. J., Smedt, T. D., Martens, D., & Daelemans, W. (2012). Media coverage in times of political crisis: A text mining approach. *Expert Systems with Applications*, *39*(14), 11616–11622. doi:10.1016/j.eswa.2012.04.013

Fountain, J. E. (2001). *Building the virtual state: Information technology and institutional change*. Washington, DC: Brookings Institution Press.

Franchini, M., & Mannucci, P. M. (2009). Particulate air pollution and cardiovascular risk: Short-term and long-term effects. *Seminars in Thrombosis and Hemostasis*, *35*(7), 665–670. doi:10.1055/s-0029-1242720 PMID:20013533

Frauenfelder, M. (2013). The computer. London: Carlton.

Friedman, M., Savage, L. J., & Becker, G. S. (2007). *Milton Friedman on economics: selected papers*. Chicago: University of Chicago Press.

Friend, Z. (2013). Predictive Policing: Using Technology to Reduce Crime. *FBI Law Enforcement Bulletin*. Retrieved from http://www.fbi.gov/stats-services/publications/law-enforcement-bulletin/2013/April/

Fu, J. R., Farn, C. K., & Chao, W. P. (2006). Acceptance of Electronic Tax Filing: A Study of Taxpayer Intentions. *Information & Management*, *43*(1), 109–126. doi:10.1016/j.im.2005.04.001

Fukuyama, F. (2013). What Is Governance? *Governance: An International Journal of Policy, Administration and Institutions*, *26*(3), 347–368. doi:10.1111/gove.12035

Fung, A., Graham, M., & Weil, D. (2007). *Full Disclosure: The Perils and Promise of Transparency*. London: Cambridge University Press. doi:10.1017/CBO9780511510533

GAIA - Group for Artificial Intelligence Applications. (2012). *jCOLIBRI project - Distribution of the development environment with LGPL*. Complutense University of Madrid. Retrieved May 18, 2014, from http://gaia.fdi.ucm.es/grupo/projects/

Galindo Cáceres, J. (2011). Las nuevas tecnologías de información y comunicación y las políticas culturales en México: Ingeniería en Comunicación Social del servicio de redes sociales Facebook. *Intercom: Revista Brasileira de Ciências da Comunicação*, *34*, 175–196.

Gant, J. (2008). *Electronic Government for Developing Countries. International Telecommunication Union*. Geneva: ITU.

Garijo, F., Riquelme, J., & Toro, M. (2002). A GRASP algorithm for Clustering. In *Proceedings of IBERAMIA 2002 (LNAI), (vol. 2527*, pp. 214 – 223). Seville, Spain: University of Seville.

Gavaldà, J., & Ribera-Fumaz, R. (2012). Barcelona 5.0: from Knowledge to Smartness? *IN3 Working Paper Series*.

Gayle, D. (2012). Chemical breakdown: The toxic substances inside your mobile phone. *Daily Mail Online*. Retrieved November 21, 2013, from http://www.dailymail.co.uk/sciencetech/article-2213366/Chemical-breakdown-What-really-goes-new-iPhone.html

Geldof, M., & Unwin, T. (2005). *Becoming an information society: The role of new IT in development*. Paper presented at the Wilton Park Conference. New York, NY.

Gentle, M. (2007). *IT success! towards a new model for information technology*. Hoboken, NJ: John Wiley & Sons.

George, O. (1949). Nineteen Eighty-Four (1984). London: Secker and Warburg.

Ghio, A. J., & Devlin, R. B. (2001). Inflammatory lung injury after bronchial instillation of air pollution particles. *American Journal of Respiratory and Critical Care Medicine*, *164*(4), 704–708. doi:10.1164/ajrccm.164.4.2011089 PMID:11520740

Ghio, A. J., Hall, A., Bassett, M. A., Cascio, W. E., & Devlin, R. B. (2003). Exposure to concentrated ambient particles alters hematologic indices in humans. *Inhalation Toxicology*, *15*(14), 1465–1478. doi:10.1080/08958370390249111 PMID:14648359

Glass, K., & Colbaugh, R. (2012). Estimating the sentiment of social media content for security informatics applications. *Security Informatics*, *1*(1), 1–16. doi:10.1186/2190-8532-1-3

Godbole, M. (2001). *Report of the one man committee on good governance*. Academic Press.

Godleski, J. J., Clarke, R. W., Coull, B. A., Saldiva, P. H., Jiang, N. F., Lawrence, J., & Koutrakis, P. (2002). Composition of inhaled urban air particles determines acute pulmonary responses. *The Annals of Occupational Hygiene*, *46*(suppl 1), 419–424. doi:10.1093/annhyg/46.suppl_1.419

Godleski, J. J., Verrier, R. L., Koutrakis, P., Catalano, P., Coull, B., & Reinisch, U. et al. (2000). Mechanisms of morbidity and mortality from exposure to ambient air particles. *Research Report (Health Effects Institute)*, *91*, 5–88. PMID:10817681

Goldkuhl, G., & Persson, A. (2006). From e-ladder to e-diamond re-conceptualising models for public e-services. In *Proceedings of the 14th European Conference on Information Systems (ECIS2006)*. Göteborgs Universitet.

Goldstein, H. (1979). Improving Policing: A Problem-Oriented Approach. *Crime and Delinquency*, *25*(2), 236–258. doi:10.1177/001112877902500207

Gomez-Perez, A., Corcho, A. O., & Fernandez-Lopez, M. (2003). *Ontological Engineering*. Berlin: Springer.

Gong, Y., & Janssen, M. (2012). From policy implementation to business process management: Principles for creating flexibility and agility. *Government Information Quarterly*, *29*(1), 61–71. doi:10.1016/j.giq.2011.08.004

González, S., Díaz, J., Pajares, M. S., Alberdi, J. C., Otero, A., & López, C. (2001). Relationship between atmospheric pressure and mortality in the Madrid Autonomous Region: A time-series study. *International Journal of Biometeorology*, *45*(1), 34–40. doi:10.1007/s004840000076 PMID:11411413

Gopakumar, K. (2006). *E-governance services through Telecentres-Role of Human Intermediary and issues of Trust*. Paper presented at the Information and Communication Technologies and Development, 2006. New York, NY. doi:10.1109/ICTD.2006.301850

Govedarova, D., Stoyanov, S., & Popchev, I. (2008). An Ontology Based CBR Architecture for Knowledge Management in BULCHINO Catalogue. In *Proceedings ofInternational Conference on Computer Systems and Technologies*. Academic Press. doi:10.1145/1500879.1500953

Granovetter, M. (1983). The strength of weak ties: A network theory revisited. *Sociological Theory*, *1*(1), 201–233. doi:10.2307/202051

Grasso, V. F., & Singh, A. (2011). *Early warning systems: State-of-art analysis and future directions. Draft report*. UNEP.

Greenhalgh, T., Robert, G., Macfarlane, F., Bate, P., & Kyriakidou, O. (2004). Diffusion of Innovations in Service Organizations: Systematic Review and Recommendations. *The Milbank Quarterly*, *82*(4), 581–629. doi:10.1111/j.0887-378X.2004.00325.x PMID:15595944

Grilli, L. (2011). When the Going Gets Tough, Do the Tough Get Going? The Pre-Entry Work Experience of Founders and High-tech Start-up Survival during an Industry Crisis. *International Small Business Journal*, *29*(6), 626–647. doi:10.1177/0266242610372845

Grindle, M. (2012). Good governance: The inflation of an idea. *Planning Ideas That Matter: Livability, Territoriality, Governance, and Reflective Practice*, *259*.

Grindle, M. (2004). Good enough governance: Poverty reduction and reform in developing countries. *Governance: An International Journal of Policy, Administration and Institutions*, *17*(4), 525–548. doi:10.1111/j.0952-1895.2004.00256.x

Grönlund, Å. (2010). Ten years of e-government: The 'end of history' and new beginning. *EGOV*, *2010*, 13–24.

Grönlund, A., & Horan, T. A. (2004). Introducing E-government: History, definitions, and issues. *Communications of the Association for Information Systems*, *15*, 713–729.

Guclu, A. N., & Bilgen, S. (2011). Modelling and Assessment of the Effectiveness of Government Information Technologies - Value Space Approach with a Public Sector Case Study in Turkey. *The Electronic Journal of Information Systems in Developing Countries, 45*(0).

Guha, R., McCool, R., & Miller, E. (2003). Semantic search. In *Proceedings of WWW2003.* WWW.

Gurgueira, S. A., Lawrence, J., Coull, B., Murthy, G. G., & González-Flecha, B. (2002). Rapid increases in the steady-state concentration of reactive oxygen species in the lungs and heart after particulate air pollution inhalation. *Environmental Health Perspectives, 110*(8), 749–755. doi:10.1289/ehp.02110749 PMID:12153754

Hage, J., & Dewar, R. (1973). Elite Values Versus Organizational Structure in Predicting Innovation. *Administrative Science Quarterly, 18*(3), 279–290. doi:10.2307/2391664

Hair, J. F., Jr., Black, W. C., Babin, B. J., & Anderson, R. E. (2010).Multivariate Data Analysis: A Global Perspective (7thed.). Pearson Prentice Hall.

Hamerly, G., & Elkan, C. (2002). Alternatives to the k-means algorithm that find better clusterings. In *Proceedings of the Eleventh International Conference on Information and Knowledge Management (CIKM)* (pp. 600-607). ACM. doi:10.1145/584887.584890

Handford, R. (2013). *Telefonica reveals future plans following Parkinson's trial.* Retrieved from http://www.mobileworldlive.com/telefonica-announces-results-future-plans-following-parkinsons-trial

Hansen, A. L., Bi, P., Ryan, P., Nitschke, M., Pisaniello, D., & Tucker, G. (2008a). The effect of heat waves on hospital admissions for renal disease in a temperate city of Australia. *International Journal of Epidemiology, 37*(6), 1359–1365. doi:10.1093/ije/dyn165 PMID:18710886

Hansen, A., Bi, P., Nitschke, M., Ryan, P., Pisaniello, D., & Tucker, G. (2008b). The effect of heat waves on mental health in a temperate Australian city. *Environmental Health Perspectives, 116*(10), 1369–1375. doi:10.1289/ehp.11339 PMID:18941580

Haque, S., & Pathrannarakul, P. (2013). E-Government towards good governance: A global appraisal. *Journal of E-Governance, 36*(1), 25–34.

Harbach, M., Fahl, S., Rieger, M., & Smith, M. (2013). On the Acceptance of Privacy-Preserving Authentication Technology: The Curious Case of National Identity Cards. In E. De Cristofaro & M. Wright (Eds.), *Privacy Enhancing Technologies: 13th International Symposium, PETS 2013* (LNCS), (*vol. 7981*, pp. 245-264). Berlin: Springer. doi:10.1007/978-3-642-39077-7_13

Haritou, M., Glickman, Y., Androulidakis, A., Xefteris, S., Anastasiou, A., & Baboshin, A. et al. (2012). A Technology Platform for a Novel Home Care Delivery Service to Patients with Dementia. *Journal of Medical Imaging and Health Informatics, 2*(1), 1–7. doi:10.1166/jmihi.2012.1060

Harrell, E., & Langton, L. (2013, December). *Victims of Identity Theft, 2012.* Retrieved January 20, 2014, from U.S. Department of Justice, Bureau of Justice Statistics: http://www.bjs.gov/content/pub/pdf/vit12.pdf

Harris, R., Kumar, A., & Balaji, V. (2003). Sustainable telecentres? Two cases from India. *The Digital Challenge: Information Technology in the Development Context, 8*, 124-135.

Harrison, T. M., Guerrero, S., Burke, G. B., Cook, M., Cresswell, A., & Helbig, N. et al. (2011). Open Government and E-Government: Democratic Challenges from a Public Value Perspective. In *Proceedings of the 12th Annual International Digital Government Research Conference* (pp. 1-9). doi:10.1145/2037556.2037597

Hartley, J. (2005). Innovation in Governance and Public Services: Past and Present. *Public Money and Management, 25*, 27–34.

Hashem, M. (2002). Bridging the digital divide in Egypt: Facing the challenges. In *Proceedings of UNCTAD E-Commerce First Expert Meeting.* UNCTAD.

Hasmah, A. (2009). *e-Filing Pays.* Retrieved from http://www.intanbk.intan.my/i-portal/nict/nict/day1/session3parallel1(session3a)/Dato_hasmah_e-filing_Pays.pdf/

Hassanin, L. (2003). Africa ICT policy monitor project. *Egypt ICT Country Report.*

Hatcher, E., Gospodnetic, O., & McCandless, M. (2009). *Lucene in Action.* Greenwich, CT: Manning Publications.

Havenith, G. (2001). Individualized model of human thermoregulation for the simulation of heat stress response. *Journal of Applied Physiology*, *90*(5), 1943–1954. PMID:11299289

Havenith, G. (2003). Interaction of clothing and thermoregulation. *Exogenous Dermatology*, *1*(5), 221–230. doi:10.1159/000068802

Health Stats. (2010). *PULSE CASPro®*. Retrieved from http://www.healthstats.com/index3.php?page=product_apulsepro

Healy, J. D. (2003). Excess winter mortality in Europe: A cross country analysis identifying key risk factors. *Journal of Epidemiology and Community Health*, *57*(10), 784–789. doi:10.1136/jech.57.10.784 PMID:14573581

Heeks, R. (1999). Reinventing Government in the Information Age. In R. Heeks (Ed.), Reinventing Government in the Information Age (pp. 9-21). New York: Routledge.

Heeks, R. (2001). *Understanding e-governance for development*. Institute for Development Policy and Management Manchester.

Heeks, R. (2002). e-Government in Africa: Promise and practice. *Information Polity*, *7*(2), 97–114.

Heeks, R. (2003). *Most eGovernment-for-development projects fail: how can risks be reduced?*. Manchester, UK: Institute for Development Policy and Management, University of Manchester.

Heflin, J. (2004). OWL Web Ontology Language Use Cases and Requirements. *W3C Recommendation.*

Hellström, J. (2011). *Mobile governance: Applications, challenges and scaling-up Mobile Technologies for Conflict Management*. Springer.

Hendeby, G., Bleser, G., Lamprinos, I., & Stricker, D. (2010). Healthy Aging using Physical Activity Monitoring. In *Proceedings of AALIANCE Conference*. Malaga, Spain: AALIANCE.

Hiller, J., & Bélanger, F. (2001). *Privacy strategies for electronic government*. PriceWaterHouse Coopers.

Hiller, J., McMullen, M. S., Chumney, W. M., & Baumer, D. L. (2011). Privacy and security in the implementation of health information technology (electronic health records): US and EU compared. *BUJ Sci. & Tech. L.*, *17*, 1.

HIPAA. (1996). *Health information privacy*. Retrieved from http://www.hhs.gov/ocr/privacy/index.html

Hochbaum, D., & Shmoys, D. (1985). A best possible heuristic for the k-center problem. *Mathematics of Operations Research*, *10*(2), 180–184. doi:10.1287/moor.10.2.180

Hodgkinson, B., Evans, D., & Wood, J. (2003). Maintaining oral hydration in older adults: A systematic review. *International Journal of Nursing Practice*, *9*(3), S19–S28. doi:10.1046/j.1440-172X.2003.00425.x PMID:12801253

Hoek, G., Brunekreef, B., Fischer, P., & van Wijnen, J. (2001). The association between air pollution and heart failure, arrhythmia, embolism, thrombosis, and other cardiovascular causes of death in a time series study. *Epidemiology (Cambridge, Mass.)*, *12*(3), 355–357. doi:10.1097/00001648-200105000-00017 PMID:11337606

Hoek, G., Brunekreef, B., Goldbohm, S., Fischer, P., & van den Brandt, P. A. (2002). Association between mortality and indicators of traffic-related air pollution in the Netherlands: A cohort study. *Lancet*, *360*(9341), 1203–1209. doi:10.1016/S0140-6736(02)11280-3 PMID:12401246

Hofmann, S., Beverungen, D., Räckers, M., & Becker, J. (2013). What makes local governments' online communications successful? Insights from a multi-method analysis of Facebook. *Government Information Quarterly*, *30*(4), 387–396. doi:10.1016/j.giq.2013.05.013

Hong, Y. C., Lee, J. T., Kim, H., & Kwon, H. J. (2002). Air pollution a new risk factor in ischemic stroke mortality. *Stroke*, *33*(9), 2165–2169. doi:10.1161/01.STR.0000026865.52610.5B PMID:12215581

Hood, C. (1986). *The Tools of Government*. London: Chatham House.

Horridge, M., & Knublauch, H. (2004). *A Practical Guide To Building OWL Ontologies Using The Protégé-OWL Plugin and CO-ODE Tools*. The University of Manchester.

Howaldt, J., Schwarz, M., Henning, K., & Hees, F. (2010). *Social innovation: Concepts, research fields and international trends*. IMA/ZLW.

Hubbard, D. W. (2010). *How to measure anything finding the value of "intangibles" in business*. Hoboken, NJ: Wiley. doi:10.1002/9781118983836

Huizingh, E. K. (2011). Open innovation: State of the art and future perspectives. *Technovation*, *31*(1), 2–9. doi:10.1016/j.technovation.2010.10.002

Hundepool, A., Domingo-Ferrer, J., Franconi, L., Giessing, S., Nordholt, E. S., & Spicer, K. (2012). *Statistical Disclosure Control*. John Wiley & Sons, Ltd. doi:10.1002/9781118348239

Hung, A. A., & Plott, C. R. (2001). Information cascades: Replication and an extension to majority rule and conformity-rewarding institutions. *The American Economic Review*, *91*(5), 1508–1520. doi:10.1257/aer.91.5.1508

Hung, M. C., Chang, I. C., & Hwang, H. G. (2011). Exploring Academic Teachers' Continuance Toward The Web-Based Learning System: The Role Of Causal Attributions. *Computers & Education*, *57*(2), 1530–1543. doi:10.1016/j.compedu.2011.02.001

Hussein, R., Mohamed, N., Ahlan, A. R., Mahmud, M., & Aditiawarman, U. (2010). An Integrated Model on Online Tax Adoption in Malaysia. In *Proceedings of European, Mediterranean & Middle Eastern Conference on Information Systems (EMCIS)*, (pp. 1-16). EMCIS.

Hwang, C. L., & Lin, M. J. (1987). *Group Decision Making Under Multiple Criteria: Methods and Applications*. Berlin: Springer-Verlag. doi:10.1007/978-3-642-61580-1

Hwang, C. L., & Yoon, K. (1981). *Multiple Attribute Decision Making: Methods and Applications*. Berlin: Springer. doi:10.1007/978-3-642-48318-9

Hyden, G. (2001). *Governance and Development: Sorting Out the Basics*. World Governance Survey Working Paper, 1.

Ibald-Mulli, A., Stieber, J., Wichmann, H. E., Koenig, W., & Peters, A. (2001). Effects of air pollution on blood pressure: A population-based approach. *American Journal of Public Health*, *91*(4), 571–577. doi:10.2105/AJPH.91.4.571 PMID:11291368

Ibope. (2013a). *89% dos manifestantes não se sentem representados por partidos*. Retrieved October 29, 2013, from http://www.ibope.com.br/pt-br/noticias/Paginas/89-dos-manifestantes-nao-se-sentem-representados-por-partidos.aspx

Ibope. (2013b). *Veja pesquisa completa do Ibope sobre os manifestantes*. Retrieved November 12, 2013, from http://g1.globo.com/brasil/noticia/2013/06/veja-integra-da-pesquisa-do-ibope-sobre-os-manifestantes.html

IDS SCHEER. (2003). Aris method. Author.

Ineed MD, Inc. (2012). *EKG Glove™*. Retrieved from http://www.ineedmd.com/public/features.html

International Bank for Reconstruction and Development. (2011). *What is social capital?* Retrieved from http://go.worldbank.org/K4LUMW43B0

Ipsos, M. O. R. I. (2007). *The use of personal health information in medical research: general public consultation*. London: Medical Research Council.

Isaacson, W. (2004). *Benjamin Franklin: an American life*. New York: Simon & Schuster.

IS-ACTIVE Project– Inertial Sensing System for Advanced Chronic Condition Monitoring and RiskPrevention. (2010). *WP2 – Architecture, Architecture Specification* (Deliverable D2.2). Retrieved from http://www.is-active.eu/deliverables/

Islam, A. K. M. N. (2012). The Role of Perceived System Quality as Educators' Motivation to Continue E-learning System Use. *AIS Transactions on Human-Computer Interaction*, *4*(1), 25–43.

Islam, M. M., & Ahmed, A. M. S. (2007). Understanding E-Governance: A Theoretical Approach. *Asian Affairs*, *29*(4), 29–46.

Jain, A., Murty, M., & Flynn, P. (1999). Data Clustering: A Review. *ACM Computing Surveys*, *31*(3), 255–322. doi:10.1145/331499.331504

Japan Meteorological Agency. (2013). *Smart City Resilience. Learning from Emergency Response and Coordination in Japan.* Retrieved 2013-April from http://www.gsma.com/connectedliving/wp-content/uploads/2013/02/cl_SmartCities_emer_01_131.pdf

Jawahitha, S., & Gwendolyn, R. (2010). Gender Differences in E-Government Adoption in Dubai. *Business Review (Federal Reserve Bank of Philadelphia)*, *16*(2), 120–126.

Jiménez, C. E., & Gascó, M. (2012). Y ahora... gobierno abierto. Nuevos términos en la constante búsqueda por la transparencia y la rendición de cuentas. In *Proceedings ofXVII Congreso Internacional del CLAD sobre la Reforma del Estado y de la Administración Pública.* Cartagena de Indias: CLAD.

Jiménez, C. E., Criado, J. I., & Gascó, M. (2011). Technological e-Government Interoperability. An Analysis of IberoAmerican Countries. IEEE Latin America Transactions, 9 (7), 1112-1117.

Jiménez, C.E. (2013a). "Smart Governance": Una aproximación al concepto de gobernanza inteligente. *Revista Perspectiva.* Dossier. Septiembre de 2013

Jiménez, C. E. (2013b). *Impacto de la Ley Reguladora del Uso de las TIC en la Administración de Justicia.* Barcelona: Centro de Estudios Jurídicos y Formación Especializada.

Jimeno-Yepes, A., Berlanga-Llavori, R., & Rebholz-Schuhmann, D. (2010). Ontology refinement for improved information retrieval. *Information Processing & Management*, *46*(4), 426–435. doi:10.1016/j.ipm.2009.05.008

Johannesson, P., & Perjons, E. (2001). Design principles for process modelling in enterprise application integration. *Information Systems*, *26*(1), 165–184. doi:10.1016/S0306-4379(01)00015-1

Johnson, N. L. (1999). Diversity in decentralized systems: Enabling self-organizing solutions. In *Proceedings ofDecentralization II Conference*. UCLA.

Jones, V., van Halteren, A., Dokovsky, N., Koprinkov, G., Bults, R., Konstantas, D., & Herzog, R. (2006). Mobihealth: Mobile health services based on body area networks. Springer US.

Jovanov, E., Milenkovic, A., Otto, C. & de Groen, P. (2005). A wireless body area network of intelligent motion sensors for computer assisted physical rehabilitation. *Journal ofNeuroEngineering and Rehabilitation*, *2*(1), 6.

Jr, I. M. V., Alencar, A. J., Schmitz, E. A., Correa, A. L., & Jr, J. V. D. (2012). Identifying the Most Efficient Implementation Sequence of IT Projects Broken Down into MMFs and AEs. In K. R. Venugopal & L. M. Patnaik (Eds.), Wireless Networks and Computational Intelligence (pp. 477–486). Springer Berlin Heidelberg. Retrieved from http://link.springer.com/chapter/10.1007/978-3-642-31686-9_55

Jun, K.-N., & Weare, C. (2010). Institutional Motivations in the Adoption of Innovations: The Case of E-Government. *Journal of Public Administration: Research and Theory*, *21*(3), 495–519. doi:10.1093/jopart/muq020

Junker, R., Heinrich, J., Ulbrich, H., Schulte, H., Schönfeld, R., Köhler, E., & Assmann, G. (1998). Relationship between plasma viscosity and the severity of coronary heart disease. *Arteriosclerosis, Thrombosis, and Vascular Biology*, *18*(6), 870–875. doi:10.1161/01.ATV.18.6.870 PMID:9633925

Kahcevi, T. C., & Taskin, H. (2013). Integrated enterprise management system for higher education institutions based on strategic and process management: The case study of Sakarya University. *Procedia: Social and Behavioral Sciences*, *106*, 1505–1513. doi:10.1016/j.sbspro.2013.12.170

Kalkstein, L. S., & Valimont, K. M. (1986). An evaluation of summer discomfort in the United State using a relative climatological index. *Bulletin of the American Meteorological Society*, *67*(7), 842–848. doi:10.1175/1520-0477(1986)067<0842:AEOSDI>2.0.CO;2

Kapur, M., Voiklis, J., Kinzer, C.K., & Black, J. (2006). Insights into the emergence of convergence in group discussions. In *Proceedings of the 7th International Conference on Learning Sciences*. Academic Press.

Katsouyanni, K., Touloumi, G., Samoli, E., Gryparis, A., Le Tertre, A., & Monopolis, Y. et al. (2001). Confounding and effect modification in the short-term effects of ambient particles on total mortality: Results from 29 European cities within the APHEA2 project. *Epidemiology (Cambridge, Mass.)*, *12*(5), 521–531. doi:10.1097/00001648-200109000-00011 PMID:11505171

Kaufmann, D., Kraay, A., & Mastruzzi, M. (2010). The Worldwide Governance Indicators. *Methodology and Analytical Issues*.

Kavanaugh, A. L., Fox, E. A., Sheetz, S. D., Yang, S., Li, L. T., & Shoemaker, D. J. et al. (2012). Social media use by government: From the routine to the critical. *Government Information Quarterly, 29*(4), 480–491. doi:10.1016/j.giq.2012.06.002

Keatinge, W. R., & Donaldson, G. C. (1995). Cardiovascular mortality in winter. *Arctic Medical Research, 54*, 16–18. PMID:8900826

Keatinge, W. R., Donaldson, G. C., Cordioli, E., Martinelli, M., Kunst, A. E., & Mackenbach, J. P. et al. (2000). Heat related mortality in warm and cold regions of Europe: Observational study. *BMJ: British Medical Journal, 321*(7262), 670–673. doi:10.1136/bmj.321.7262.670 PMID:10987770

Kelly, F. J. (2003). Oxidative stress: Its role in air pollution and adverse health effects. *Occupational and Environmental Medicine, 60*(8), 612–616. doi:10.1136/oem.60.8.612 PMID:12883027

Kelly, F. J., Fuller, G. W., Walton, H. A., & Fussell, J. C. (2012). Monitoring air pollution: Use of early warning systems for public health. *Respirology (Carlton, Vic.), 17*(1), 7–19. doi:10.1111/j.1440-1843.2011.02065.x PMID:21942967

Keniston, K., & Kumar, D. (2003). The four digital divides. *Online Erişim, 21*, 2010.

Kent Police Web Site. (2013). *Predictive policing day of action targets burglars*. Retrieved 3rd December, from http://www.kent.police.uk/news/latest_news/131203_predpol_day_a.html

Kent Police. (2013). *Predpol operational review – initial findings*. Kent County Police Corporate Services – Analysis Department.

Khalil, O. E. (2011). E-Government readiness: Does national culture matter? *Government Information Quarterly, 28*(3), 388–399. doi:10.1016/j.giq.2010.06.011

Khanh, N. T. V. (2014). The Critical Factors Affecting E-Government Adoption: A Conceptual Framework in Vietnam. *Computers & Society*. Retrieved from http://arxiv.org/ftp/arxiv/papers/1401/1401.4876.pdf

Khan, S., & Kant, S. (2007). Computation of Initial Modes for K-modes Clustering Algorithm using Evidence Accumulation. In *Proceedings of The Twentieth International Joint Conference on Artificial Intelligence IJCAI-07* (pp 2784-2789). Hyderabad, India: IJCAI.

Khasawneh, S., Jalghaum, Y., Harfoushi, O., & Obiedat, R. (2011). E-Government Program in Jordan: From Inception to Future Plans. *International Journal of Computer Science Issues, 8*(4), 568–582.

Kim, S., & Layne, K. (2001). Making the connection: E-government and public administration education. *Journal of Public Affairs Education*, 229-240.

Kim, B. (2010). An Empirical Investigation of Mobile Data Service Continuance: Incorporating the Theory of Planned Behavior Into The Expectation–Confirmation Model. *Expert Systems with Applications, 37*(10), 7033–7039. doi:10.1016/j.eswa.2010.03.015

Kimberly, J. R., & Evanisko, M. J. (1981). Organizational innovation: The influence of individual, organizational and contextual factors on hospitals adoption of technological and administrative innovations. *Academy of Management Journal, 24*(4), 689–713. doi:10.2307/256170 PMID:10253688

Kim, H. W., Chan, H. C., & Chan, Y. P. (2007). A Balanced Thinking-Feelings Model of Information Systems Continuance. *International Journal of Human-Computer Studies, 65*(6), 511–525. doi:10.1016/j.ijhcs.2006.11.009

Kim, H., Jarochowski, B., & Ryu, D. (2006). A proposal for a home-based health monitoring system for the elderly or disabled. In *Computers Helping People with Special Needs* (pp. 473–479). Springer Berlin Heidelberg. doi:10.1007/11788713_71

Kim, S., Kim, H. J., & Lee, H. (2009). An institutional analysis of an e-government system for anti-corruption: The case of OPEN. *Government Information Quarterly, 26*(1), 42–50. doi:10.1016/j.giq.2008.09.002

Kingdon, J. W. (1995). *Agendas, Alternatives, and Public Policies*. New York: Longman.

King, N. (1992). Modeling the innovation process: An empirical comparison of approaches. *Journal of Occupational and Organizational Psychology, 65*(2), 89–100. doi:10.1111/j.2044-8325.1992.tb00487.x

Klein, P. N. (2013). *Coding the matrix: Linear algebra through applications to computer science*. Academic Press.

Klugman, J., Rodríguez, F., & Choi, H. J. (2011). The HDI 2010: New controversies, old critiques. *The Journal of Economic Inequality, 9*(2), 249–288. doi:10.1007/s10888-011-9178-z

Kokkinakos, P., Koussouris, K., Panopoulos, D., Askounis, D., Ramfos, A., Georgousopoulos, C., & Wittern, E. (2012). Citizens Collaboration and Co-Creation and Public Service Delivery: The COCKPIT Project. *International Journal of Electronic Government Research.*

Kontopoulos, E., Berberidis, C., Dergiades, T., & Bassiliades, N. (2013). Ontology-based sentiment analysis of twitter posts. *Expert Systems with Applications, 40*(10), 4065–4074. doi:10.1016/j.eswa.2013.01.001

Korteland, E., & Bekkers, V. (2008). The Diffusion of Electronic Service Delivery Innovations in Dutch E-policing: The Case of Digital Warning Systems. *Public Management Review, 10*(1), 71–88. doi:10.1080/14719030701763195

Kossel, A. (2010, November 9). *Neuer Personalausweis: AusweisApp mit Lücken.* Retrieved January 20, 2014, from Heise Online: http://heise.de/-1133376

Kovats, R. S., & Koppe, C. (2005). Heatwaves: past and future impacts on health. In *Integration of public health with adaptation to climate change: Lessons learned and new directions*, (pp. 136-160). Academic Press.

Kravchenko, J., Abernethy, A. P., Fawzy, M., & Lyerly, H. K. (2013). Minimization of heatwave morbidity and mortality. *American Journal of Preventive Medicine, 44*(3), 274–282. doi:10.1016/j.amepre.2012.11.015 PMID:23415125

Krippendorff, K. (1980). Clustering. In J. Cappella & P. Monge (Eds.), *Multivariate techniques in human communication research* (pp. 259–307). New York: Academic Press Inc.

Kukreja, N., Payyavula, S. S., Boehm, B., & Padmanabhuni, S. (2012). Selecting an appropriate framework for value-based requirements prioritization. In *Proceedings ofRequirements Engineering Conference (RE),* (pp. 303–308). RE. doi:10.1109/RE.2012.6345819

Kumar, R., & Best, M. (2006). Impact and sustainability of e-government services in developing countries: Lessons learned from Tamil Nadu, India. *The Information Society, 22*(1), 1–12. doi:10.1080/01972240500388149

Kundra, V. (2010). *25 Point Implementation Plan to Reform Federal information Technology Management.* Academic Press.

Kuriyan, R., Toyama, K., & Ray, I. (2006). *Integrating social development andfinancial sustainability: The challenges ofrural computer kiosks in Kerala*. Paper presented at the Information and Communication Technologies and Development, 2006. New York, NY.

Kwak, D. H., McDaniel, S., & Kim, K. T. (2012). Revisiting the Satisfaction-Loyalty Relationship in the Sport Video Gaming Context: The Mediating Role of Consumer Expertise. *Journal of Sports Management, 26*(1), 81–91.

Lancieri, L. (2000). A connectionist approach for evaluating the complexity of interactions in the World Wide Web: The case of News Groups. In *Proceedings ofIEEE International Joint Conference on Neural Network IJCNN 2000*. IEEE.

Lancieri, L. (2004). Reusing Implicit Cooperation: A novel approach to knowledge management. *TripleC, 2*(1), 28-46.

Lancieri, L. (2005) Semantic organization of data networks. In *Proceedings ofIEEE International Conference on Computational Intelligence for Modelling Control and Automation, (CIMCA'2005).* IEEE.

Lancieri, L. (2007). Modelling collective behaviour using traces of individual activity. In *Proceedings of19th International Conference on Systems Research, Informatics and Cybernetics (InterSymp2007).* Academic Press.

Lancieri, L., Lavallard, A., & Manson, P. (2005). E-brainstorming: Optimization of collaborative learning thanks to online questionnaires. In *Proceedings ofIADIS International Conference Cognition and Exploratory Learning in Digital Age (CELDA 2005).* IADIS.

Lane, P. C. R., Clarke, D., & Hender, P. (2012). On developing robust models for favourability analysis: Model choice, feature sets and imbalanced data. *Decision Support Systems, 53*(4), 712–718. doi:10.1016/j.dss.2012.05.028

Larrabee, D. T., & Voss, J. A. (2013). *Valuation techniques discounted cash flow, earnings quality, measures of value added, and real options*. Hoboken, NJ: John Wiley & Sons.

Larson, E., Lee, T., Liu, S., Rosenfeld, M., & Patel, S. N. (2011). Accurate and Privacy Preserving Cough Sensing using a Low-Cost Microphone. In *Proceedings of the13th International Conference onUbiquitous Computing* (UbiComp 2011). Beijing, China: ACM. doi:10.1145/2030112.2030163

Larsson, A. O., & Moe, H. (2011). Studying political microblogging: Twitter users in the 2010 Swedish election campaign. *New Media & Society, 14*(5), 729–747. doi:10.1177/1461444811422894

Lavric, V. (2010). The Development of the SMEs Sector in Romania. An Approach Regarding the Dynamics and the Perspectives. *Review of International Comparative Management, 11*(5), 931–939.

Law 12.527. (2011). *Information Access Law - Regulation of access to information*. Retrieved October 15, 2013, from http://www.planalto.gov.br/ccivil_03/_Ato2011-2014/2011/Lei/L12527.htm

Law 131. (2009). *Transparency Law*. Retrieved October 15, 2013, from https://www.planalto.gov.br/ccivil_03/Leis/LCP/Lcp131.htm

Layne, K., & Lee, J. (2001). Developing Fully Functional E-government: A Four Stage Model. *Government Information Quarterly, 18*(2), 122–136. doi:10.1016/S0740-624X(01)00066-1

Lean, O. K., Zailani, S., Ramayah, T., & Fernando, Y. (2009). Factors Influencing Intention to Use e-Government Services Among Citizens in Malaysia. *International Journal of Information Management, 29*(6), 458–475. doi:10.1016/j.ijinfomgt.2009.03.012

Lee, J., & Lee, H. (2010). The computer-mediated communication network: Exploring the linkage between the online community and social capital. *New Media & Society, 12*(5), 711–727. doi:10.1177/1461444809343568

Lee, M. C. (2010). Explaining and Predicting Users' Continuance Intention Toward e-Learning: An Extension of the Expectation-Confirmation Model. *Computers & Education, 54*(2), 506–516. doi:10.1016/j.compedu.2009.09.002

Leite, J. C. S. P., & Cappelli, C. (2008). Exploring i* Characteristics that Support Software Transparency. In *Proceedings of the 3rd International i* Workshop*, (pp. 51-54). Academic Press.

Lettice, F., & Parekh, M. (2010). The social innovation process: Themes, challenges and implications for practice. *International Journal of Technology Management, 51*(1), 139–158. doi:10.1504/IJTM.2010.033133

Levitt, B., & March, J. G. (1988). Organizational Learning. *Annual Review of Sociology, 14*(1), 319–340. doi:10.1146/annurev.so.14.080188.001535

Lévy, P. (1999). *Collective Intelligence: Mankind's Emerging World in Cyberspace*. Perseus Books.

Lewiński, M., & Mohammed, D. (2012). Deliberate design or unintended consequences: The argumentative uses of Facebook during the Arab spring. *Journal of Public Deliberation, 8*(1), 11.

Lewis, E., Mohler, G., Brantingham, P. J., & Bertozzi, A. L. (2012). Self-exciting point process models of civilian deaths in Iraq. *Security Journal, 25*(3), 244–264. doi:10.1057/sj.2011.21

Liao, C., Palvia, P., & Chen, J. L. (2009). Information Technology Adoption Behavior Life Cycle: Toward a Technology Continuance Theory (TCT). *International Journal of Information Management, 29*(4), 309–320. doi:10.1016/j.ijinfomgt.2009.03.004

Libby, P., Ridker, P. M., & Maseri, A. (2002). Inflammation and atherosclerosis. *Circulation, 105*(9), 1135–1143. doi:10.1161/hc0902.104353 PMID:11877368

Li, G., & Liu, F. (2012). Application of a clustering method on sentiment analysis. *Journal of Information Science, 38*(2), 127–139. doi:10.1177/0165551511432670

Li, G., & Shi, X. (2012). The Determinants of Consumers' Purchase Intention to Online Group-Buying. *Advanced Materials Research, 459*, 372–376.

Likert, R. (1931). A technique for the measurement of attitudes. *Archives de Psychologie, 22*(140), 1–55.

Limayem, M., Hirt, S. G., & Chin, W. W. (2001). Intention Does Not Always Matter: The Contingent Role of Habit on IT Usage Behavior. In *Proceedings of the 9th European Conference on Information Systems*, (pp. 274-286). Academic Press.

Limayem, M., & Cheung, C. M. K. (2008). Understanding Information System Continuance: The Case of Internet-Based Learning Technologies. *Information & Management*, *45*(4), 227–232. doi:10.1016/j.im.2008.02.005

Limayem, M., Hirt, S. G., & Cheung, C. M. K. (2007). How Habit Limits the Predictive Power of Intention: The Case of Information System Continuance. *Management Information Systems Quarterly*, *31*(4), 705–737.

Limba, T. (2011). Peculiarities of designing holistic electronic government services integration model. *Social Technologies*, *1*(2), 344–362.

Lim, M. (2012). Clicks, Cabs, and Coffee Houses: Social Media and Oppositional Movements in Egypt, 2004–2011. *Journal of Communication*, *62*(2), 231–248. doi:10.1111/j.1460-2466.2012.01628.x

Lin, K.M., Chen, N.S., & Fang, K. (2011). Understanding E-Learning Continuance Intention: A Negative Critical Incidents Perspectives. *Behaviour & Information Technology*, 1362 – 3001.

Li, N., Sioutas, C., Cho, A., Schmitz, D., Misra, C., & Sempf, J. et al. (2003). U.ltrafin.e particulate pollutants induce oxidative stress and mitochondrial damage. *Environmental Health Perspectives*, *111*(4), 455–460. doi:10.1289/ehp.6000

Lin, C. S., Wu, S., & Tsai, R. J. (2005). Integrating Perceived Playfulness Into Expectation-Confirmation Model For Web Portal Context. *Information & Management*, *42*(5), 683–693. doi:10.1016/j.im.2004.04.003

Lindén, F. (2009). epSOS, smart open services for European patients from strategies to services—eHealth as the enabler for cross-border healthcare. *Infrastructures for Health Care, 23.*

Linders, D. (2012). From e-government to we-government: Defining a typology for citizen coproduction in the age of social media. *Government Information Quarterly*, *29*(4), 446–454. doi:10.1016/j.giq.2012.06.003

Lind, M., Forsgren, O., Salomonson, N., & Albinsson, L. (2007). The e-co model – citizens' driving e-service quality. In *Proceedings of the 51st Annual Conference by the International Society for the Systems Sciences: Integrated Systems Sciences: Systems Thinking, Modelling and Practice.* Tokyo Institute of Technology.

Lin, M. Y. C., & Ong, C. S. (2010).Understanding Information System Continuance Intention: A Five Factor Model of Personality Perspectives. In *Proceedings of the Pacific Asia Conference on Information System (PACIS)*, (pp. 366-376). PACIS.

Linn, W.S., Gong, H. Jr., Clark, K.W., & Anderson, K.R. (1999). Day-to-day particulate exposures and health changes in Los Angeles area residents with severe lung disease. *Journal of the Air & Waste Management Association*, *49* (9), 108–115.

Linn, W. S., Szlachcic, Y., Gong, H. Jr, Kinney, P. L., & Berhane, K. T. (2000). Air pollution and daily hospital admissions in metropolitan Los Angeles. *Environmental Health Perspectives*, *108*(5), 427–434. doi:10.1289/ehp.00108427 PMID:10811569

Lipsett, M. J. (2001). Ozone. In J. B. Sullivan & G. R. Krieger (Eds.), *Clinical environmental health and toxic exposure* (2nd ed., pp. 806–818). Philadelphia, PA: Lippincott Williams & Wilkins.

Liu, B. (2010). Sentiment Analysis and Subjectivity. Handbook of Natural Language Processing, 2, 627-666.

Liu, C. C. (2003). Simulating Weights Restrictions in Data Envelopment Analysis by the Subjective and Objective Integrated Approach. *Web Journal of Chinese Management Review*, *6*(1), 68–78.

Liu, F., Yin, J., Du, M., Yan, P., Xu, J., Zhu, X., & Yu, J. (2009). Heat-stress-induced damage to porcine small intestinal epithelium associated with downregulation of epithelial growth factor signaling. *Journal of Animal Science*, *87*(6), 1941–1949. doi:10.2527/jas.2008-1624 PMID:19213704

Li, X. Y., Gilmour, P. S., Donaldson, K., & MacNee, W. (1996). Free radical activity and pro-inflammatory effects of particulate air pollution (PM10) in vivo and in vitro. *Thorax*, *51*(12), 1216–1222. doi:10.1136/thx.51.12.1216 PMID:8994518

Lloyd, L., Mumby, R., & Sear, L. (2010). Entrepreneurship Education: Embedding Practitioner Experience', 2010. *Review of International Comparative Management*, *12*(6), 391–403.

Lo, B., Wang, J., & Yang, G. (2005). From imaging networks to behavior profiling: Ubiquitous sensing for managed homecare of the elderly. In *Proceedings of the 3rd International Conference on Pervasive Computing*. Academic Press.

Lönn, C., & Uppström, E. (2013). Process Management Challenges in Swedish Public Sector: A Bottom Up Initiative. EGOV 2013. *LNCS*, *8074*, 212–223.

Loo, W., Yeow, P., & Chong, S. (2009, April). User acceptance of Malaysian government multipurpose smartcard applications. *Government Information Quarterly*, *26*(2), 358–367. doi:10.1016/j.giq.2008.07.004

Loren, J. D. (2011). What is Open Innovation? In A guide to Open Innovation and Crowdsourcing (Vol. 1). Kogan Page.

Luchenski, S., Balasanthiran, A., Marston, C., Sasaki, K., Majeed, A., Bell, D., & Reed, J. E. (2012). Survey of patient and public perceptions of electronic health records for healthcare, policy and research: Study protocol. *BMC Medical Informatics and Decision Making*, *12*(1), 40. doi:10.1186/1472-6947-12-40 PMID:22621621

Luger, G. F. (2002). Artificial Intelligence, Structures and Strategies for Complex Problem Solving (4th ed.). Pearson Education Limited.

Lynn, L. (1997). Innovation and the Public Interest: Insights from the Private Sector. In A. Altchuler & R. Behn (Eds.), *Innovation in American Government*. Washington, DC: Brookings Institution.

Madon, S. (2009). *E-governance for development: A focus on rural India*. Palgrave Macmillan.

Madon, S. (2008). Evaluating the developmental impact of e-governance initiatives: An exploratory framework. ICTs and Indian Social Change: Diffusion, Poverty. *Governance: An International Journal of Policy, Administration and Institutions*, 268.

Magari, S. R., Hauser, R., Schwartz, J., Williams, P. L., Smith, T. J., & Christiani, D. C. (2001). Association of heart rate variability with occupational and environmental exposure to particulate air pollution. *Circulation*, *104*(9), 986–991. doi:10.1161/hc3401.095038 PMID:11524390

Malhotra, C., & Krishnaswamy, G. (2011). Citizens' Expectations from Rural Telecentres: A Case Study of Implementation of Common Service Centres in Mushedpur Village, Haryana, India. World Academy of Science, Engineering and Technology, 53.

Manovich, L. (2011). *Trending: The Promises and the Challenges of Big Social Data*. Retrieved from http://www.manovich.net/DOCS/Manovich_trending_paper.pdf

Mantel, N. (1963). Chi-Square Tests with One Degree of Freedom; Extensions of the Mantel-Haenszel Procedure. *Journal of the American Statistical Association*, *58*(303), 690–700.

Manyika, J., Chui, M., Brown, B., Bughin, J., Dobbs, R., Roxburgh, C., & Hung Byers, A. (2011). *Big Data: The Next Frontier for Innovation, Competition, and Productivity*. McKinsey Global Institute.

MAP. (2014). *Aplicaciones utilizadas para el ejercicio de potestades: Criterios de Seguridad, Normalización y Conservación*. Ministerio de Administraciones Públicas. Retrieved from http://www.csi.map.es/csi/criterios/index.html

Maple, J., & Mitchell, C. (2000). *The Crime Fighter: How You Can Make Your Community Free*. New York: Broadway Books.

Marche, S., & McNiven, J. D. (2003). E-Government and E-Governance: The Future Isn't What It Used to Be. *Canadian Journal of Administrative Sciences*, *20*(1), 74–86. doi:10.1111/j.1936-4490.2003.tb00306.x

March, J. G., & Olsen, J. P. (1989). *Rediscovering Institutions: The Organizational Basis of Politics*. New York: The Free Press.

Markus, M. L., & Jacobson, D. D. (2010). Business Process Governance. In J. vom Brocke & M. Rosemann (Eds.), Handbook on Business Process Management 2, (pp. 201-222). Academic Press.

Martínez-Ballesté, A., Rashwan, H. A., Puig, D., & Paniza Fullana, A. (2012). Towards a trustworthy privacy in pervasive video surveillance systems. In *Proceedings ofIEEE International Conference on Pervasive Computing and Communications Workshops* (pp. 914-919). Lugano: IEEE. doi:10.1109/PerComW.2012.6197644

Martínez-Ballesté, A., Solanas, A., & Pérez-Martínez, A. (2013). The Pursuit of Citizens Privacy: A Privacy-Aware Smart City is Possible. *IEEE Communications Magazine*, *51*(6), 136–141. doi:10.1109/MCOM.2013.6525606

Martin, L. (1999). *All you really need to know to interpret arterial blood gases*. Wolters Kluwer Health.

Matthies, F., & Menne, B. (2009). Prevention and management of health hazards related to heatwaves. *International Journal of Circumpolar Health*, *68*(1). doi:10.3402/ijch.v68i1.18293 PMID:19331238

Mattmann, C., & Zitting, J. (2012). *Tika in Action*. Greenwich, CT: Manning Publications.

McAdams, E., Krupaviciute, A., Gehin, C., Dittmar, A., Delhomme, G., & Rubel, P. et al. (2011). Wearable Electronic Systems: Applications to Medical Diagnostics/Monitoring. In A. Bonfiglio & D. De Rossi (Eds.), *Wearable Monitoring Systems* (pp. 179–203). Springer. doi:10.1007/978-1-4419-7384-9_9

McAfee, A., & Brynjolfsson, E. (2012). Big Data: The Management Revolution. *Harvard Business Review*, (October): 1–9. PMID:23074865

McFarland, C. K., & McConnell, J. K. (2011b). Local Roles in Cultivating a Small Business and Entrepreneurial Culture. In *Proceedings of Conference Small Business and Entrepreneurship during an Economic Recovery*. Retrieved July 8, 2013 from http://www.federalreserve.gov/newsevents/conferences/mcfarland-20111109.pdf

McFarland, C., Seeger, K., & Geary, C. (2010). *The Role of Local Elected Officials in Economic Development: Ten Things You Should Know*. Washington, DC: National League of Cities.

McFarland, C. K., & McConnell, J. K. (2011a). *Strategies for Globally Competitive Cities: Local Roles in Foreign Direct Investment and International Trade*. Washington, DC: National League of Cities.

McNutt, J. G. (1998). Ensuring social justice for the new underclass: community interventions to meet the needs of the new poor. In B. Ebo (Ed.), *The Cyberghetto or Cybertopia: Race, Class, Gender & Marginalization in Cyberspace* (pp. 33–47). New York: Praeger.

Meddie, M. (2006). Rethinking telecentre sustainability: How to implement a social enterprise approach-Lessons from India and Africa. *Journal of Community Informatics*, *2*(3).

Meijer, A., & Thaens, M. (2013). Social media strategies: Understanding the differences between North American police departments. *Government Information Quarterly*, *30*(4), 343–350. doi:10.1016/j.giq.2013.05.023

Melcher, J., Mendling, J., Reijers, H. A., & Seese, D. (2009). On Measuring the Understandability of Process Models. In *Proceedings of1st Workshop on Empirical Research in BPM*. Ulm, Germany: Academic Press.

Melville, A. (2005). *Taxation: Finance Act 2004* (10th ed.). Edinburgh, UK: Prentice Hall, Pearson Education Limited.

Mendling, J., & Strembeck, M. (2008) Influence factors of understanding business process models. In *Proceedings of11th International Conference on Business Information Systems*. Springer-Verlag. doi:10.1007/978-3-540-79396-0_13

Mendling, J., Reijers, H., & Cardoso, J. (2007). What makes process models understandable? Lecture Notes in Computer Science, 4714, 48-63.

Mentes, J. C., & Culp, K. (2003). Reducing hydration-linked events in nursing home residents. *Clinical Nursing Research*, *12*(3), 210–225. doi:10.1177/1054773803252996 PMID:12918647

Mergel, I. (2012). The social media innovation challenge in the public sector.[Article]. *Information Polity: The International Journal of Government & Democracy in the Information Age*, *17*(3/4), 281–292.

Mergel, I. (2013a). A framework for interpreting social media interactions in the public sector. *Government Information Quarterly*, *30*(4), 327–334. doi:10.1016/j.giq.2013.05.015

Mergel, I. (2013b). Social media adoption and resulting tactics in the U.S. federal government. *Government Information Quarterly*, *30*(2), 123–130. doi:10.1016/j.giq.2012.12.004

Michele-Lee Moore, F. R. W., Tjornbo, O., & Holroyd, C. (2012). The loop, the lens, and the lesson: Using resilience theory to examine public policy and social innovation. In A. M. Nicholls (Ed.), Social Innovation Blurring Boundaries to Reconfigure Markets (Vol. 1, pp. 114-136). London: Academic Press.

Michelozzi, P., Kirchmayer, U., Katsouyanni, K., Biggeri, A., McGregor, G., & Menne, B. et al. (2007). Assessment and prevention of acute health effects of weather conditions in Europe, the PHEWE project: Background, objectives, design. *Environmental Health*, *6*(1), 12–21. doi:10.1186/1476-069X-6-12 PMID:17456236

Miklian, J., & Carney, S. (2013). Corruption, Justice and Violence in Democratic India. *SAIS Review*, *33*(1), 37–49. doi:10.1353/sais.2013.0011

Miles, B., & Hubermann, A. (1994). Qualitative Data Analysis: An Expanded Sourcebook. Sage Publications.

Milosević, Z., Bogdanović, D., Jović, S., Stanković, A., Milutinović, S., & Rancić, N. (2010). Influence of air pollution on hospital admissions for cardiovascular and respiratory diseases in Nis, Serbia]. *Vojnosanitetski Pregled. Military-Medical and Pharmaceutical Review*, *67*(6), 473–479. doi:10.2298/VSP1006473M PMID:20629426

Milutinovic, M., & De Decker, B. (2013). Comprehensive eHealth system design for privacy protection. Technical Report (CW Reports), CW643. Department of Computer Science, KU Leuven.

Mindmixer. (2014). *About Mindmixer*. Retrieved 15-01, 2014, from http://www.mindmixer.com/#how

Minelli, M. (2013). *Big Data, Big Analytics, Emerging Business Intelligence and Analytic Trends for Today's Business*. Hoboken, NJ: John Wiley & Sons. doi:10.1002/9781118562260

Ministry of State Administrative Development. (2009). *Improving Take-Up E-Government Services: Challenges*. Available at: sbedair@ad.gov.eg

Ministry of State for Administrative Development. (2010). *Egyptian Government*. Available at www.egtpt.gov.eg

Ministry of State for Administrative Development. (n.d.). *About MoSAD*. Available at: http://www.msad.gov.eg/About%20MSAD/Programs/

Minnesota e-Health Initiative and the Minnesota Department of Health. (2013). *Glossary of Selected Terms and Acronyms*. White Paper. Retrieved from http://www.health.state.mn.us/e-health/glossary/ehealthglossary.pdf

Mishra, G. (2013). *Role of telecenters in empowering citizens: A case study of 'Mahiti Mitra' project in Kutch district of Gujarat, India*. Paper presented at the Global Humanitarian Technology Conference: South Asia Satellite (GHTC-SAS). New York, NY.

Misra, A. (2013). *Empowerment of backward classes through reservation policy with reference to Dr. BR Ambedkar's vision and challenges in current socio-legal milieu*. Academic Press.

Misund, G., & Hoiberg, J. (2003). *Sustainable information technology for global sustainability*. Digital Earth. Paper presented at the Information Resources for Global Sustainability Symposium. New York, NY.

Mitchell, W. J. (2007). *Intelligent cities*. Retrieved from http://www.uoc.edu/uocpapers/5/dt/eng/mitchell.pdf

Monn, C., & Becker, S. (1999). Cytotoxicity and induction of proinflammatory cytokines from human monocytes exposed to fine (PM2.5) and coarse particles (PM10-2.5) in outdoor and indoor air. *Toxicology and Applied Pharmacology*, *155*(3), 245–252. doi:10.1006/taap.1998.8591 PMID:10079210

Montoyo, A., Martínez-Barco, P., & Balahur, A. (2012). Subjectivity and sentiment analysis: An overview of the current state of the area and envisaged developments. *Decision Support Systems*, *53*(4), 675–679. doi:10.1016/j.dss.2012.05.022

Moon, M. J. (2002). The Evolution of E-Government among Municipalities: Rhetoric or Reality? *Public Administration Review*, *62*(4), 424–433. doi:10.1111/0033-3352.00196

Moore, M. (2006). Good Government?. *IDS Bulletin*, *37*(4), 50–56. doi:10.1111/j.1759-5436.2006.tb00286.x

Moore, M. H. (2005). Break-through innovations and continuous improvement: Two different models ofinnovative processes in the public sector. *Public Money and Management*, *25*, 43–50.

Moore, M., & Hartley, J. (2008). Innovations in Governance. *Public Management Review*, *10*(1), 3–20. doi:10.1080/14719030701763161

Moreo, A., Romero, M., Castro, J. L., & Zurita, J. M. (2012). Lexicon-based Comments-oriented News Sentiment Analyzer system. *Expert Systems with Applications*, *39*(10), 9166–9180. doi:10.1016/j.eswa.2012.02.057

Morris, M. D., & McAlpin, M. (1979). *Measuring the Condition of the World's Poor*. New York: Pergamon Press.

Morris, R. D. (2001). Airborne particulates and hospital admissions for cardiovascular disease: A quantitative review of the evidence. *Environmental Health Perspectives*, *109*(s4Suppl 4), 495–500. doi:10.1289/ehp.01109s4495 PMID:11544153

Morris, R. J., & Brennan, G. P. (2003). Creating a Seamless Local Government and Small Business Interface for Better Regional Economic Development Outcomes. *Journal of Small Business Management*, *41*(4), 417–426.

Mossberger, K., Wu, Y., & Crawford, J. (2013). Connecting citizens and local governments? Social media and interactivity in major U.S. cities. *Government Information Quarterly*, *30*(4), 351–358. doi:10.1016/j.giq.2013.05.016

Mostafa, M. M. (2013). More than words: Social networks' text mining for consumer brand sentiments. *Expert Systems with Applications*, *40*(10), 4241–4251. doi:10.1016/j.eswa.2013.01.019

Mouthami, K., Devi, K. N., & Bhaskaran, V. M. (2013). *Sentiment analysis and classification based on textual reviews*. Paper presented at the Information Communication and Embedded Systems (ICICES). New York, NY. doi:10.1109/ICICES.2013.6508366

MPA. (2013). *Access to health records*. Retrieved from http://www.medicalprotection.org/uk/england-factsheets/access-to-health-records

Muehlen, M., & Indulska, M. (2010). Modeling languages for business processes and business rules: A representational Analysis. *Information Systems*, *35*(4), 379–390. doi:10.1016/j.is.2009.02.006

Muhammad Rais, A. K., & Nazariah, M. K. (2003). *E-Government in Malaysia. In Pelanduk Publications (M)*. Sdn Bhd.

Mukae, H., Vincent, R., Quinlan, K., English, D., Hards, J., Hogg, J. C., & van Eeden, S. F. (2001). The effect of repeated exposure to particulate air pollution (PM10) on the bone marrow. *American Journal of Respiratory and Critical Care Medicine*, *163*(1), 201–209. doi:10.1164/ajrccm.163.1.2002039 PMID:11208647

Mukerji, M. (2008). Telecentres in rural India: emergence and a typology. *The Electronic Journal of Information Systems in Developing Countries, 35*.

Mukerji, M. (2013). *ICTs and Development: A Study of Telecentres in Rural India*. Palgrave Macmillan.

Mulgan, G. (2006). The process of social innovation. *Innovations, 1*(2), 145-162.

Mulgan, G., & Albury, D. (2003). *Innovations in the Public Sector*. London: Cabinet Office.

Muñoz-Cañavate, A., & Hípola, P. (2011). Electronic administration in Spain: From its beginnings to the present. *Government Information Quarterly*, *28*(1), 74–90. doi:10.1016/j.giq.2010.05.008

Murray, E. (2012). Web-Based Interventions for Behavior Change andSelf-Management: Potential, Pitfalls, and Progress. *Medicine 2.0, 1*(2e3).

Murray, R., Caulier-Grice, J., & Mulgan, G. (2010). *The open book of social innovation*. National Endowment for Science, Technology and the Art.

Nafstad, P., Skrondal, A., & Bjertness, E. (2001). Mortality and temperature in Oslo, Norway, 1990–1995. *European Journal of Epidemiology*, *17*(7), 621–627. doi:10.1023/A:1015547012242 PMID:12086075

National Alliance for Local Economic Development. (2012). *Certification program business-friendly municipality*. Retrieved April 21, 2013 from http://www.naledserbia.org/documents/download/Certification_brochure_ 2012.pdf.

National Institute of Public Health Surveillance. (2003). *Impact sanitaire de la vague de chaleur en France survenue en août 2003. Rapport d'étape – 29 août 2003.* Saint Maurice, France: National Institute of Public Health Surveillance.

Ndou, V. (2004). E–government for developing countries: Opportunities and challenges. *The Electronic Journal on Information Systems in Developing Countries*, *18*(1), 1–24.

Nel, E. (2001). Local Economic Development: A Review and Assessment of its Current Status in South Africa. Urban Studies, 38(7), 1003–1024.

Nemery, B., Hoet, P. H., & Nemmar, A. (2001). The Meuse Valley fog of 1930: An air pollution disaster. *Lancet*, *357*(9257), 704–708. doi:10.1016/S0140-6736(00)04135-0 PMID:11247570

Nemmar, A., Hoet, P. M., Vanquickenborne, B., Dinsdale, D., Thomeer, M., & Hoylaerts, M. F. et al. (2002a). Passage of inhaled particles into the blood circulation in humans. *Circulation*, *105*(4), 411–414. doi:10.1161/hc0402.104118 PMID:11815420

Nemmar, A., Hoylaerts, M. F., Hoet, P. H., Dinsdale, D., Smith, T., & Xu, H. et al. (2002b). Ultrafi.ne particles affect experimental thrombosis in an in vivo hamster model. *American Journal of Respiratory and Critical Care Medicine*, *166*(7), 998–1004. doi:10.1164/rccm.200110-026OC PMID:12359661

Net!Works European Technology Platform Expert Working Group. (2011). *Smart Cities Applications and Requirements.* Net!Works.

Neuberger, M., Moshammer, H., & Rabczenko, D. (2013). Acute and Subacute Effects of Urban Air Pollution on Cardiopulmonary Emergencies and Mortality: Time Series Studies in Austrian Cities. *International Journal of Environmental Research and Public Health*, *10*(10), 4728–4751. doi:10.3390/ijerph10104728 PMID:24157504

Neumeier, S. (2012). Why do Social Innovations in Rural Development Matter and Should They be Considered More Seriously in Rural Development Research?–Proposal for a Stronger Focus on Social Innovations in Rural Development Research. *Sociologia Ruralis*, *52*(1), 48–69. doi:10.1111/j.1467-9523.2011.00553.x

Neuroni, A., Rascon, A., Spichiger, A., & Riedl, R. (2010). Assessing and Evaluating Value and Cost Effectiveness of e-Government Initiatives: Focusing the Step of the Financial Evaluation. In *Proceedings of the 11th Annual International Digital Government Research Conference on Public Administration Online: Challenges and Opportunities* (pp. 105–111). Puebla, Mexico: Digital Government Society of North America.

New Straits Times (NST). (2012). *15 percent increase in e-Filing, says LHDN.* Retrieved on February 14th, 2013 from http://www.nst.com.my/latest/15-per-cent-increase-in-e-filing-says-lhdn-1.91623

Nicolescu, O., & Nicolescu, C. (2013). Entrepreneurs' Perceptions of the State Implication in the Business Environment Modelling in Romania. *Transylvanian Review of Administrative Sciences, 38*(E/2013), 106-124.

Nicolescu, O., Verboncu, I., Profiroiu, M., Nicolescu, C., & Anghel, F. (2010). Romanian Management Assessment. Bucharest: Prouniversitaria.

Niehaves, B., & Malsch, R. (2009). Democratizing Process Innovation? On Citizen Involvement in Public Sector BPM. In *Proceedings of8th International Conference Egov.* Linz, Austria: Egov. doi:10.1007/978-3-642-03516-6_21

Niehaves, B., Plattfaut, R., & Becker, J. (2013). Business process management capabilities in local governments: A multi-method study. *Government Information Quarterly*, *30*(3), 217–225. doi:10.1016/j.giq.2013.03.002

Nielsen. (2009). *Nielsen Global Online Consumer Survey April 2009*. Retrieved from http://www.nielsen.com/content/dam/corporate/us/en/newswire/uploads/2009/07/pr_global-study_07709.pdf

Nietzsche, F. (1886). Beyond Good and Evil. Penguin Classics.

Nightingale, J. A., Maggs, R., Cullinan, P., Donnelly, L. E., Rogers, D. F., & Kinnersley, R. et al. (2000). Airway. inflammation after controlled exposure to diesel exhaust particulates. *American Journal of Respiratory and Critical Care Medicine*, *162*(1), 161–166. doi:10.1164/ajrccm.162.1.9908092 PMID:10903236

Nikic, D., Bogdanovic, D., Nikolic, M., Stankovic, A., Zivkovic, N., & Djordjevic, A. (2009). Air quality monitoring in NIS (SERBIA) and health impact assessment. *Environmental Monitoring and Assessment*, *158*(1-4), 499–506. doi:10.1007/s10661-008-0599-5 PMID:18951135

Nikić, D., Bogdanović, D., Stanković, A., Nikolić, M., & Milošević, Z. (2008). Impact of air pollution on the rate of hospital admission of children with respiratory diseases. *Vojnosanitetski Pregled. Military-Medical and Pharmaceutical Review*, *65*(11), 814–819. doi:10.2298/VSP0811814N PMID:19069711

NIST. (2010). *Introduction to NISTIR 7628 Guidelines for Smart Grid Cyber Security.* Retrieved from http://csrc.nist.gov/publications/nistir/ir7628/introduction-to-nistir-7628.pdf

Nograšek, J. & Vintar, M. (2014). E-government and organisational transformation of government: Black box revisited? *Government Information Quarterly*.

Norris, P. (2002). *Democratic phoenix: Reinventing political activism*. Cambridge University Press. doi:10.1017/CBO9780511610073

Norwood, S. (2011). *Tatum's Survey of Business Conditions*. Tatum. Retrieved July 7, 2013 from http://www.smallbusinessadvocate.com/small-business-articles/the-tatumsurvey-of-business-conditions-september

Nunomura, E. (2013). A imprensa, o Twitter e as eleições de 2010 no Brasil. *Intercom: Revista Brasileira de Ciências da Comunicação*, *36*, 103–126.

OASIS. (2007). *Business process execution language* (WS-BPEL 2.0). Retrieved from http://docs.oasis-open.org/wsbpel/2.0/wsbpel-v2.0.html

Obama, B. (2009). Transparency and Open Government. *Presidential Documents, 74*(15), 4685-4686.

O'Callaghan, D., Prucha, N., Greene, D., Conway, M., Carthy, J., & Cunningham, P. (2014). Online Social Media in the Syria Conflict: Encompassing the Extremes and the In-Betweens. *arXiv preprint arXiv:1401.7535.*

OECD. (2003). The case for e-government: Excerpts from the OECD report: The EGovernment Imperative. *OECD Journal on Budgeting*, *3*(1), 61–96. doi:10.1787/budget-v3-art5-en

OECD. (2013). Exploring Data-Driven Innovation as a NewSource of Growth: Mapping the Policy Issues Raised by 'BigData'. *OECD Digital Economy Papers, 222.*

Oestmann, S., & Dymond, A. C. (2001). Telecentres—Experiences, lessons and trends. Perspectives on Distance Education. Telecentres: Case Studies and Key Issues. The Commonwealth of Learning.

Office of Climate, Water and Weather Services. (2001). *New wind chill temperature Index*. Washington, DC: Author.

Official Gazette of Republic of Serbia. (2001). *Law on Chambers of Commerce*, No. 65/2001, No. 36/2009 and No. 99/2011.

Official Gazette of Republic of Serbia. (2004). *Law on Social - Economic Council*, No. 125/2004.

Official Gazette of Republic of Serbia. (2007). *The Law on Local Self-Government*, No. 129/2007.

Official Gazette of Republic of Serbia. (2009). *Law on Employment and Unemployment Insurance*, No. 36/2009 and No. 88/2010.

Ohlhorst, F. (2013). *Big Data Analytics: Turning Big Data into Big Money*. Hoboken, NJ: John Wiley& Sons.

Ojo, A., Dzhusupova, Z., & Janowski, T. (2012). *e-Macao Report 199 - Intelligent Governance of Smart Cities.* Research-Practice Gap Analysis.

Okot-Uma, R. W. (2000). *Electronic governance: reinventing good governance*. London: Commonwealth Secretariat.

Oliveira, G. H. M., & Welch, E. W. (2013). Social media use in local government: Linkage of technology, task, and organizational context. *Government Information Quarterly*, *30*(4), 397–405. doi:10.1016/j.giq.2013.05.019

Oliver, R. L. (1980). A Cognitive Model of the Antecedents and Consequences of Satisfaction Decisions. *JMR, Journal of Marketing Research*, *17*(4), 460–469. doi:10.2307/3150499

Ong, C. S., & Day, M. Y. (2010). An Integrated Evaluation Model of User Satisfaction with Social Media Services. In *Proceeding of the International Conference on Information Reuse and Integration (IRI)*, (pp. 195-200). IRI. doi:10.1109/IRI.2010.5558940

Osborne, D., & Gaebler, T. (1993). *Reinventing Government: How the Entrepreneurial Spirit Is Transforming the Public Sector*. London: Plume.

Osborne, S. P. (1998). Naming the beast' defining and classifying service innovations in social policy. *Human Relations*, *30*(9), 1133–1154. doi:10.1177/001872679805100902

Osborne, S. P., & Brown, L. (2011). Innovation, Public Policy and Public Services Delivery in the UK: The Word that Would Be King? *Public Administration*, *89*(4), 1335–1350. doi:10.1111/j.1467-9299.2011.01932.x

Ott, J. C. (2010). Good governance and happiness in nations: Technical quality precedes democracy and quality beats size. *Journal of Happiness Studies*, *11*(3), 353–368. doi:10.1007/s10902-009-9144-7

Otto, C., Milenkovic, A., Sanders, C., & Jovanov, E. (2006). System architecture of a wireless body area sensor network for ubiquitous health monitoring. *Journal of Mobile Multimedia*, *1*(4), 307–326.

Page, S. E. (2008). *The Difference: How the Power of Diversity Creates Better Groups, Firms, Schools, and Societies*. Princeton University Press.

Panagiotakos, D. B., Chrysohoou, C., Pitsavos, C., Nastos, P., Anadiotis, A., & Tentolouris, C. et al. (2004). Climatological variations in daily hospital admissions for acute coronary syndromes. *International Journal of Cardiology*, *94*(2), 229–233. doi:10.1016/j.ijcard.2003.04.050 PMID:15093986

Pang, B., & Lee, L. (2008). Opinion mining and sentiment analysis. *Foundations and Trends in Information Retrieval*, *2*(1-2), 1–135. doi:10.1561/1500000011

Papacharissi, Z., & Oliveira, M. F. (2012). Affective News and Networked Publics: The Rhythms of News Storytelling on #Egypt. *Journal of Communication*, *62*(2), 266–282. doi:10.1111/j.1460-2466.2012.01630.x

Park, S. J., Lim, Y. S., Sams, S., Nam, S. M., & Park, H. W. (2010). Networked Politics on Cyworld: The Text and Sentiment of Korean Political Profiles. *Social Science Computer Review*, *29*(3), 288–299. doi:10.1177/0894439310382509

Parks, W. (1957). The open government principle: Applying the right to know under the Constitution. *The George Washington Law Review*, *26*(1).

Parvanta, C., Roth, Y., & Keller, H. (2013). Crowdsourcing 101 A Few Basics to Make You the Leader of the Pack. *Health Promotion Practice*, *14*(2), 163–167. doi:10.1177/1524839912470654 PMID:23299912

Paterson, L. (2010). *Privacy and Prejudice: Young People's Views on the Development and Use of Electronic Patient Records*. Royal Academy of Engineering.

Paulini, M., Murty, P., & Maher, M. L. (2013). Design processes in collective innovation communities: A study of communication. *CoDesign*, *9*(2), 90–112. doi:10.1080/15710882.2012.716850

Pavlou, P. (2003). Consumer acceptance of electronic commerce: Integrating trust and risk with the technology acceptance model. *International Journal of Electronic Commerce*, *7*, 69–103.

Peffers, K., & Santos, B. L. D. (2013). Research opportunities in information technology funding and system justification. *European Journal of Information Systems*, *22*(2), 131–138. doi:10.1057/ejis.2012.60

Pekelman, D., & Sen, S. K. (1974). Mathematical programming models for the determination of attribute weights. *Management Science*, *20*(7), 1217–1229. doi:10.1287/mnsc.20.8.1217

Pekkanen, J., Peters, A., Hoek, G., Tiittanen, P., Brunekreef, B., & de Hartog, J. et al. (2002). Particulate Air Pollution and Risk of ST-Segment Depression During Repeated Submaximal Exercise Tests Among Subjects With Coronary Heart Disease The Exposure and Risk Assessment for Fine and Ultrafine Particles in Ambient Air (ULTRA) Study. *Circulation*, *106*(8), 933–938. doi:10.1161/01.CIR.0000027561.41736.3C PMID:12186796

Pérez-Martinez, P. A., & Solanas, A. (2011). W3-privacy: the three dimensions of user privacy in LBS. In *Proceedings of12th ACM International Symposium on Mobile Ad Hoc Networking and Computing*. Paris: ACM.

Perron, O. (1907). Zur Theorie der Matrizen. *Math Annales*, *64*, 248–263.

Persinger, M. A. (1980). *The weather matrix and human behavior*. New York: Praeger.

Persson, A., & Goldkuhl, G. (2005). Stage-models for public e-services - investigating conceptual foundations. In *Proceedings of 2nd Scandinavian Workshop on e-Government*. Copenhagen, Denmark: Academic Press.

Peters, A., Dockery, D. W., Muller, J. E., & Mittleman, M. A. (2001b). Increased particulate air pollution and the triggering of myocardial infarction. *Circulation*, *103*(23), 2810–2815. doi:10.1161/01.CIR.103.23.2810 PMID:11401937

Peters, A., Döring, A., Wichmann, H. E., & Koenig, W. (1997). Increased plasma viscosity during an air pollution episode: A link to mortality? *Lancet*, *349*(9065), 1582–1587. doi:10.1016/S0140-6736(97)01211-7 PMID:9174559

Peters, A., Fröhlich, M., Döring, A., Immervoll, T., Wichmann, H. E., & Hutchinson, W. L. et al. (2001a). Particulate air pollution is associated with an acute phase response in men: Results from the MONICA-Augsburg study. *European Heart Journal*, *22*(14), 1198–1204. doi:10.1053/euhj.2000.2483 PMID:11440492

Peters, A., Liu, E., Verrier, R. L., Schwartz, J., Gold, D. R., & Mittleman, M. et al. (2000b). Air pollution and incidence of cardiac arrhythmia. *Epidemiology (Cambridge, Mass.)*, *11*(1), 11–17. doi:10.1097/00001648-200001000-00005 PMID:10615837

Peters, A., Perz, S., Döring, A., Stieber, J., Koenig, W., & Wichmann, H.-E. (2000a). Activation of the autonomic nervous system and blood coagulation in association with an air pollution episode. *Inhalation Toxicology*, *12*, 51–61a. doi:10.1080/08958370050029770

Phalp, K. T., & Shepperd, M. (2000). Quantitative Analysis of Static Models of Processes. *Journal of Systems and Software*, *52*(2-3), 105–112. doi:10.1016/S0164-1212(99)00136-3

Phills, J. A., Deiglmeier, K., & Miller, D. T. (2008). Rediscovering social innovation. *Stanford Social Innovation Review*, *6*(4), 34–43.

Pirard, P., Vandentorren, S., Pascal, M., Laaidi, K., Le Tertre, A., Cassadou, S., & Ledrans, M. (2005). Summary of the mortality impact assessment of the 2003 heat wave in France. *European Communicable Disease Bulletin*, *10*(7), 153-156.

Plackett, R. L. (1983). Karl Pearson and the Chi-Squared Test. *International Statistical Review*, *51*(1), 59–72. doi:10.2307/1402731

Pol, E., & Ville, S. (2009). Social innovation: Buzz word or enduring term? *Journal of Socio-Economics*, *38*(6), 878–885. doi:10.1016/j.socec.2009.02.011

Pollitt, C. (2002). Clarifying convergence: Striking similarities and durable differences in public management reform. *Public Management Review*, *3*(4), 471–492. doi:10.1080/14616670110071847

Pope, C. A. (2000). Epidemiology of fine particulate air pollution and human health: Biologic mechanisms and who's at risk? *Environmental Health Perspectives*, *108*, 713–723. doi:10.2307/3454408 PMID:10931790

Pope, C. A. III, Burnett, R. T., Thurston, G. D., Thun, M. J., Calle, E. E., Krewski, D., & Godleski, J. J. (2004). Cardiovascular mortality and long-term exposure to particulate air pollution: Epidemiological evidence of general pathophysiological pathways of disease. *Circulation*, *109*(1), 71–77. doi:10.1161/01.CIR.0000108927.80044.7F PMID:14676145

Pope, C. A. III, Thun, M. J., Namboodiri, M. M., Dockery, D. W., & Evans, J. S. et al. (1995). Particulate air pollution as a predictor of mortality in a prospective study of US adults. *American Journal of Respiratory and Critical Care Medicine*, *151*(pt1), 669–674. PMID:7881654

Pope, C. A. III, Verrierm, R. L., Lovett, E. G., Larson, A. C., Raizenne, M. E., & Kanner, R. E. et al. (1999). Heart rate variability associated with particulate air pollution. *American Heart Journal*, *138*(pt 1), 890–899. doi:10.1016/S0002-8703(99)70014-1 PMID:10539820

Porter, H. (2004). If you value your freedom, reject this sinister ID card: We should be afraid of future governments, whose nature we can't predict. *The Guardian*. Retrieved from http://www.guardian.co.uk/comment/story/0,1375584,00.html

Prabowo, R., & Thelwall, M. (2009). Sentiment analysis: A combined approach. *Journal of Informetrics*, *3*(2), 143–157. doi:10.1016/j.joi.2009.01.003

Prakash, D. (2012). *New Patch-Based Wearable Sensor Combines Advanced Skin Adhesive and Sensor Technologies*. Retrieved from http://www.mdtmag.com/articles/2012/07/new-patch-based-wearable-sensor-combines-advanced-skin-adhesives-and-sensor-technologies

Prasad, R., & Ray, R. S. (2012). *Telecentres go where mobile phones fear to tread: Evidence from India*. Paper presented at the Regional International Telecommunications Society India Conference. New Delhi, India.

PrêmioIdeia. (2014). *PrizeIdea - A plataform for open social innovation*. Retrieved 22-05, 2014, from http://www.premioideia.com

PROTÉGÉ. (2013, December 16). *The Protégé Ontology Editor and Knowledge Acquisition System*. Retrieved from http://protege.stanford.edu/

Putnam, R. D. (1995). Bowling alone: America's declining social capital. *Journal of Democracy*, *6*(1), 65–78. doi:10.1353/jod.1995.0002

Putnam, R. D. (2007). E pluribus unum: Diversity and community in the twenty-first century the 2006 Johan Skytte Prize Lecture. *Scandinavian Political Studies*, *30*(2), 137–174. doi:10.1111/j.1467-9477.2007.00176.x

Putnam, R. D., Leonardi, R., & Nanetti, R. Y. (1994). *Making democracy work: Civic traditions in modern Italy*. Princeton University Press.

Puyosa, H. (2008). Control systems vulnerability to cyberattacks. *Oilgas*, *41*(475), 71–75.

Quan, D., & Karger, D. R. (2004). How to make a semantic web browser. In *Proceedings of WWW2004*. WWW. doi:10.1145/988672.988707

Ragesh, G. K., & Baskaran, K. (2012). A Survey on Futuristic Health Care System: WBANs. *Procedia Engineering*, *30*, 889–896. doi:10.1016/j.proeng.2012.01.942

Rainie, L., Purcell, K., & Smith, A. (2011). *The social side of the internet*. Pew Internet and American Life Project.

Rainie, H., Rainie, L., & Wellman, B. (2012). *Networked: The new social operating system*. The MIT Press.

Rainie, L., Smith, A., Schlozman, K. L., Brady, H., & Verba, S. (2012). *Social media and political engagement*. Pew Internet & American Life Project.

Raman, V. V. (2008). Examining the "e" in Government and Governance: A Case Study in Alternatives from Bangalore City India. *The Journal of Community Informatics*, *4*(2).

Rashman, L., & Hartley, J. (2002). Leading and learning? Knowledge transfer in the Beacon Council Scheme. *Public Administration*, *80*(3), 523–542. doi:10.1111/1467-9299.00316

Rashman, L., & Radnor, Z. (2005). Learning to Improve: Approaches to Improving Local Government Services. *Public Money and Management*, *25*(1), 19–26.

Raum, E. (2008). *The history of the computer*. Chicago, IL: Heinemann Library.

Raus, M., Liu, J., & Kipp, A. (2010). Evaluating IT innovations in a business-to-government context: A framework and its applications. *Government Information Quarterly*, *27*(2), 122–133. doi:10.1016/j.giq.2009.04.007

Recker, J., & Dreiling, A. (2007). Does it matter which process modelling language we teach or use? an experimental study on understanding process modeling languages without formal education. In *Proceedings of18th Australasian Conference on Information Systems*, (pp. 356-366). Toowoomba, Australia: Academic Press.

REMOTE Project. (2012). *Remote health and social care for independent living of isolated elderly with chronic conditions*. Retrieved from http://www.remote-project.eu/

Reynolds, P., Storey, D. J., & Westhead, P. (1994). Cross-National Comparisons of the Variation in New Firm Formation Rates. *Regional Studies*, *28*(4), 443–456. doi:10.1080/00343409412331348386

Richardson, C., & Miers, D. (2013). *The Forrester Wave™: BPM Suites, Q1*. Academic Press.

Ridker, P. M. (2001). High-sensitivity C-reactive protein: Potential adjunct for global risk assessment in the primary prevention of cardiovascular disease. *Circulation*, *103*(13), 1813–1818. doi:10.1161/01.CIR.103.13.1813 PMID:11282915

Ridker, P. M., Rifai, N., Stampfer, M. J., & Hennekens, C. H. (2000). Plasma concentration of interleukin-6 and the risk of future myocardial infarction among apparently healthy men. *Circulation*, *101*(15), 1767–1772. doi:10.1161/01.CIR.101.15.1767 PMID:10769275

Rijsbergen, K. (1979). *Information Retrieval* (2nd ed.). London: Butterworth-Heinemann.

Ritz, B., Yu, F., Fruin, S., Chapa, G., Shaw, G. M., & Harris, J. A. (2002). Ambient air pollution and risk of birth defects in Southern California. *American Journal of Epidemiology*, *155*(1), 17–25. doi:10.1093/aje/155.1.17 PMID:11772780

Robaldo, L., & Di Caro, L. (2013). OpinionMining-ML. *Computer Standards & Interfaces*, *35*(5), 454–469. doi:10.1016/j.csi.2012.10.004

Robinson, R. (2012). *The Urban Technologist: A personal view of emerging technology and Smarter Cities*. Retrieved from http://theurbantechnologist.com/2012/08/07/five-roads-to-a-smarter-city/

Roca, J. C., Chiu, C. M., & Martinez, F. J. (2006). Understanding e-Learning Continuance Intention: An Extension of the Technology Acceptance Model. *International Journal of Human-Computer Studies*, *64*(8), 683–696. doi:10.1016/j.ijhcs.2006.01.003

Rogers, E. M. (2003). *Diffusion of Innovations*. New York: The Free Press.

Rogers, E. M., & Shukla, P. (2001). The role of Telecenters in development communication and the digital divide. *The Journal of Development Communication*, *2*(12), 26–31.

Roman, R., & Colle, R. (2002). *Themes and issues in telecentre sustainability* (Vol. 10). Institute for Development Policy and Management, University of Manchester.

Rosacker, K. M., & Rosacker, R. E. (2010). Information technology project management within public sector organizations. *Journal of Enterprise Information Management*, *23*(5), 587–594. doi:10.1108/17410391011083047

Rose, W. R., & Grant, G. G. (2010). *Critical issues pertaining to the planning and implementation of e-government initiatives*. Retrieved from http://www.sciencedirect.com/science/article/pii/S0740624X09001105

Rosen, S. (1989). *Weathering*. New York: Evans and Co Inc.

ROSETTA Project. (2012a). Retrieved from http://www.aal-rosetta.eu/

ROSETTA Project. (2012b). *Guidance and Awareness Services for Independent Living* (Flyer). Retrieved from http://www.aal-rosetta.eu/Site_rosetta/docs/ROSETTA_Flyer_e_IESE-100118.pdf

Rose, W. R., & Grant, G. G. (2010). Critical issues pertaining to the planning and implementation of E-Government initiatives. *Government Information Quarterly*, *27*(1), 26–33. doi:10.1016/j.giq.2009.06.002

Ross, J. (2009). Electronic medical records: The promises and challenges. *Journal of Perianesthesia Nursing*, *24*(5), 327–329. doi:10.1016/j.jopan.2009.08.002 PMID:19853820

Roxas, H., Lindsay, V., Ashill, N., & Victorio, A. (2008). An Institutional View of Local Entrepreneurial Climate. *Asia-Pacific Social Science Review*, *7*(1), 28–44. doi:10.3860/apssr.v7i1.113

Rusbridger. (2013). *NSA surveillance goes beyond Orwell's imagination*. Retrieved from http://www.theguardian.com/world/2013/sep/23/orwell-nsa-surveillance-alan-rusbridger

Saaty, T. L. (1977). A scaling method for priorities in hierarchical structures. *Journal of Mathematical Psychology*, *15*(3), 234–281. doi:10.1016/0022-2496(77)90033-5

Saaty, T. L. (1980). *Multicriteria decision making: the Analytic Hierarchy Process*. New York, NY: McGraw-Hill.

Saaty, T. L. (1987). Rank according to Perron: A new insight. *Mathematics Magazine*, *6*(4), 211–213. doi:10.2307/2689340

Saaty, T. L. (1994). *Fundamentals of Decision Making*. Pittsburgh, PA: RWS Publications.

Saaty, T. L. (2013). *Decision Making for Leaders: The Analytic Hierarchy Process for Decisions in a Complex World (3rd ed.)*. RWS Publications.

Sáez, I., Oliveras, M., Ciudad, M. J., Fort, I., Llopart, J. R., & Haritou, M., & the Aladdin Research Consortium. (2011). *A Technology Platform for the Assisted Living of Dementia Elderly Individuals and their Carers*. Paper presented at the 7th Congress of the European Union Geriatric Medicine Society (EUGMS). Malaga, Spain.

Salton, G., & Buckley, C. (1988). Term-weighting approaches in automatic text retrieval. *Information Processing & Management, 24*(5), 513–523. doi:10.1016/0306-4573(88)90021-0

Salvi, S. S., Nordenhall, C., Blomberg, A., Rudell, B., Pourazar, J., & Kelly, F. J. et al. (2000). Acute e.xposure to diesel exhaust increases IL-8 and GRO-alpha production in healthy human airways. *American Journal of Respiratory and Critical Care Medicine, 161*(pt 1), 550–557. doi:10.1164/ajrccm.161.2.9905052 PMID:10673199

Salvi, S., Blomberg, A., Rudell, B., Kelly, F., Sandström, T., Holgate, S. T., & Frew, A. (1999). Acute inflammatory responses in the airways and peripheral blood after short-term exposure to diesel exhaust in healthy human volunteers. *American Journal of Respiratory and Critical Care Medicine, 159*(3), 702–709. doi:10.1164/ajrccm.159.3.9709083 PMID:10051240

Samet, J. M., Dominici, F., Curriero, F. C., Coursac, I., & Zeger, S. L. (2000). Fine particulate air pollution and mortality in 20 U.S. cities, 1987–1994. *The New England Journal of Medicine, 343*(24), 1742–1749. doi:10.1056/NEJM200012143432401 PMID:11114312

Samet, J. M., Hatch, G. E., Horstman, D., Steck-Scott, S., Arab, L., & Bromberg, P. A. et al. (2001). Effect of antioxidant supplementation on ozone-induced lung injury in human subjects. *American Journal of Respiratory and Critical Care Medicine, 164*(5), 819–825. doi:10.1164/ajrccm.164.5.2008003 PMID:11549539

Sánchez-Tato, I., Senciales, J. C., Salinas, J., Fanucci, L., Pardini, G., Costalli, F., et al. (2010). Health @ Home: A telecare system for patients with chronic heart failure. In *Proceedings ofFifth International Conference on Broadband and Biomedical Communications (IB2Com)*. Malaga, Spain: IB2Com. doi:10.1109/IB2COM.2010.5723634

Santos, L. M., Esmin, A. A. A., Zambalde, A. L., & Nobre, F. M. (2011). Twitter, análise de sentimento e desenvolvimento de produtos: Quanto os usuários estão expressando suas opiniões? *Prisma.Com,* (13).

Sapat, A. (2004). Devolution and innovation: The adoption of state environmental policy innovations by administrative agencies. *Public Administration Review, 64*(2), 141–151. doi:10.1111/j.1540-6210.2004.00356.x

Saponara, S., Donati, M., Bacchillone, T., Fanucci, L., Sanchez-Tato, I., Carmona, C., & Barba, P. (2012). Remote monitoring of vital signs in patients with chronic heart failure: Sensor devices and data analysis perspective. In *Proceedings ofSensors Applications Symposium (SAS) 2012*. Brescia, Italy: SAS. doi:10.1109/SAS.2012.6166310

Sasaki, H., & Kiyoki, Y. (2005). A formulation for patenting content-based retrieval processes in digital libraries, *Information Processing &amp. Management, 41*(1), 57–74.

Sathi, A. (2012). *Big Data Analytics*. Boise: MC Press.

Schaanning, J., Finsen, H., Lereim, I., & Saeterhaug, A. (1986). Effects of cold air inhalation combined with prolonged submaximal exercise on airway function in healthy young males. *European Journal of Respiratory Diseases. Supplement, 143*, 74–77. PMID:3462020

Schaffers, H., Komninos, N., Pallot, M., Trousse, B., Nilsson, M., & Oliveira, A. (2011). *Smart cities and the future internet: towards cooperation frameworks for open innovation. In The future internet* (pp. 431–446). Springer. doi:10.1007/978-3-642-20898-0_31

Schifano, P., Cappai, G., De Sario, M., Michelozzi, P., Marino, C., Bargagli, A. M., & Perucci, C. A. (2009). Susceptibility to heat wave-related mortality: A follow-up study of a cohort of elderly in Rome. *Environmental Health, 8*(1), 50. doi:10.1186/1476-069X-8-50 PMID:19909505

Schooley, B. L., & Horan, T. A. (2007). Towards end-to-end government performance management: Case study of interorganizational information integration in emergency medical services (EMS). *Government Information Quarterly, 24*(4), 755–784. doi:10.1016/j.giq.2007.04.001

Schumpeter, J. A. (1961). *The theory of economic development: An inquiry into profits, capital, credit, interest, and the business cycle* (Vol. 55). Transaction Books.

Schuppan, T. (2009). E-Government in developing countries: Experiences from sub-Saharan Africa. *Government Information Quarterly*, *26*(1), 118–127. doi:10.1016/j.giq.2008.01.006

Schwartz, J. (2005). Who is sensitive to extremes of temperature?: A case-only analysis. *Epidemiology (Cambridge, Mass.)*, *16*(1), 67–72. doi:10.1097/01.ede.0000147114.25957.71 PMID:15613947

Schwartz, J., Dockery, D. W., Neas, L. M., Wypij, D., Ware, J. H., & Spengler, J. D. et al. (1994). Acute effects of summer air pollution on respiratory symptom reporting in children. *American Journal of Respiratory and Critical Care Medicine*, *150*(5), 1234–1242. doi:10.1164/ajrccm.150.5.7952546 PMID:7952546

Schwartz, J., Samet, J. M., & Patz, J. A. (2004). Hospital admissions for heart disease: The effects of temperature and humidity. *Epidemiology (Cambridge, Mass.)*, *15*(6), 755–761. doi:10.1097/01.ede.0000134875.15919.0f PMID:15475726

Scott, W. R. (2001). *Institutions and Organizations*. Thousand Oaks, CA: Sage Publications.

Seaton, A., MacNee, W., Donaldson, K., & Godden, D. (1995). Particulate air pollution and acute health effects. *Lancet*, *345*(8943), 176–178. doi:10.1016/S0140-6736(95)90173-6 PMID:7741860

Seaton, A., Soutar, A., Crawford, V., Elton, R., McNerlan, S., & Cherrie, J. et al. (1999). Particulate air pollution and the blood. *Thorax*, *54*(11), 1027–1032. doi:10.1136/thx.54.11.1027 PMID:10525563

SEC. (2003). *Commission Staff Workking Paper: Linking up Europe, the importance of interoperability for egovernment services.* Retrieved from http://europa.eu.int/ISPO/ida/export/files/en/1523.pdf

Seger, D. L., & Welch, L. W. (2001). Carbon monoxide. In J. B. Sullivan & G. R. Krieger (Eds.), *Clinical Environmental Health and Toxic Exposures* (2nd ed., pp. 722–727). Philadelphia, PA: Lippincott Williams & Wilkins.

Seltzer, E., & Mahmoudi, D. (2013). Citizen Participation, Open Innovation, and Crowdsourcing: Challenges and Opportunities for Planning. *Journal of Planning Literature*, *28*(1), 3–18. doi:10.1177/0885412212469112

Semenza, J. C., Wilson, D. J., Parra, J., Bontempo, B. D., Hart, M., Sailor, D. J., & George, L. A. (2008). Public perception and behavior change in relationship to hot weather and air pollution. *Environmental Research*, *107*(3), 401–411. doi:10.1016/j.envres.2008.03.005 PMID:18466894

Sentanin, O. F., Almada Santos, F. C., & Chiappetta Jabbour, C. J. (2008). Business process management in a Brazilian public research centre. *Business Process Management*, *14*(4), 483–496. doi:10.1108/14637150810888037

Sharma, S. K. (2005). Good Governance in Ancient India. *Facets of Good Governance, 1*.

Sharp, A., & Mcdermott, P. (2010). *Workflow Modeling: Tools For Process Improvement And Application Development*. Norwood, MA: Artech House.

Shelfer, K., & Procaccino, J. (2002, July). Smart Card Evolution. *Communications of the ACM*, *45*(7), 83–88. doi:10.1145/514236.514239

Shiau, W. L., Huang, L. C., & Shih, C. H. (2011). Understanding Continuance Intention of Blog Users: A Perspective of Flow and Expectation Confirmation Theory. *Journal of Convergence Information Technology*, *6*(4), 306–317. doi:10.4156/jcit.vol6.issue4.33

Shukla, A., Timblin, C., BeruBe, K., Gordon, T., McKinney, W., & Driscoll, K. et al. (2000). Inhaled particulate matter causes expression of nuclear factor (NF)-kappaB–related genes and oxidant-dependent NF-kappaB activation in vitro. *American Journal of Respiratory Cell and Molecular Biology*, *23*(2), 182–187. doi:10.1165/ajrcmb.23.2.4035 PMID:10919984

Silverman, D. (1971). *The Theory of Organisations: A Sociological Framework*. London: Heinemann.

Simic, G., Jeremic, Z., Kajan, E., Randjelovic, D., & Presnall, A. (2014). A Framework for Delivering e-Government Support. *Acta Polytechnica Hungarica*, *11*(1), 79–96.

Simms, J. R. (2006). Technical and social innovation determinants of behaviour. *Systems Research and Behavioral Science*, *23*(3), 383–393. doi:10.1002/sres.734

Singh, B. P. (2008). The Challenge of Good Governance in India: Need for Innovative Approaches. *Ash Institute for Democratic Governance and Innovation*. Available online: http://www.innovations.harvard.edu/cache/documents/1034/103461.pdf

Singh, J. V., Tucker, D. J., & House, R. J. (1986). Organizational Legitimacy and the Liability of Newness. *Administrative Science Quarterly*, *31*(2), 32–44. doi:10.2307/2392787

Sipahi, S., & Timor, M. (2010). The analytic hierarchy process and analytic network process: An overview of applications. *Management Decision*, *48*(5), 775–808. doi:10.1108/00251741011043920

Škrinjar, R., & Trkman, P. (2013). Increasing process orientation with business process management: Critical practices. *International Journal of Information Management*, *33*(1), 48–60. doi:10.1016/j.ijinfomgt.2012.05.011

Smith, J. B. (1994). *Collective Intelligence in Computer-based Collaboration*. Lawrence Erlbaum Associates.

Smith, R., Guttorp, P., Sheppard, L., Lumley, T., & Ishikawa, N. (2001). *Comments on the Criteria Document for Particulate Matter Air Pollution. NRCSE-TRS No. 066*. Seattle, WA: University of Washington, National Research Center for Statistics and the Environment.

Smoyer, K. E. (1998). A comparative analysis of heat waves and associated mortality in St. Louis, Missouri–1980 and 1995. *International Journal of Biometeorology*, *42*(1), 44–50. doi:10.1007/s004840050082 PMID:9780845

Smrcka, V., & Leznarova, D. (1998). Environmental pollution and occurrence of congenital defects in a 15-year period in a south Moravian district. *Acta Chirurgiae Plasticae*, *40*, 112–114. PMID:9949547

Snead, J. T. (2013). Social media use in the U.S. Executive branch. *Government Information Quarterly*, *30*(1), 56–63. doi:10.1016/j.giq.2012.09.001

Sobaci, M. Z., & Karkin, N. (2013). The use of twitter by mayors in Turkey: Tweets for better public services? *Government Information Quarterly*, *30*(4), 417–425. doi:10.1016/j.giq.2013.05.014

Sobkowicz, P., Kaschesky, M., & Bouchard, G. (2012). Opinion mining in social media: Modeling, simulating, and forecasting political opinions in the web. *Government Information Quarterly*, *29*(4), 470–479. doi:10.1016/j.giq.2012.06.005

Sokal, R., & Sneath, A. (1963). *Principles of numerical taxonomy*. San Francisco, CA: Freeman.

Solanas, A., & Martínez-Ballesté, A. (2008). A TTP-free protocol for location privacy in location-based services. *Computer Communications*, *31*(6), 1181–1191. doi:10.1016/j.comcom.2008.01.007

Sommet, A., Durrieu, G., Lapeyre-Mestre, M., & Montastruc, J. L. (2012). A comparative study of adverse drug reactions during two heat waves that occurred in France in 2003 and 2006. *Pharmacoepidemiology and Drug Safety*, *21*(3), 285–288. doi:10.1002/pds.2307 PMID:22162094

Sorebo, O., & Eikebrokk, T. R. (2008). Explaining IS Continuance in Environments where Usage is Mandatory. *Computers in Human Behavior*, *24*(5), 2357–2371. doi:10.1016/j.chb.2008.02.011

Sørensen, M., Daneshvar, B., Hansen, M., Dragsted, L. O., Hertel, O., Knudsen, L., & Loft, S. (2003). Personal PM2. 5 exposure and markers of oxidative stress in blood. *Environmental Health Perspectives*, *111*(2), 161–166. doi:10.1289/ehp.5646 PMID:12573899

Spreng, R. A., MacKenzie, S. B., & Olshavsky, R. W. (1996). A Reexamination of the Determinants of Consumer Satisfaction. *Journal of Marketing*, *60*(3), 15–32. doi:10.2307/1251839

Sreekumar, T. T., & Vadrevu, S. (2013). Subpolitics and Democracy: The Role of New Media in the 2011 General Elections in Singapore. *Science, Technology & Society*, *18*(2), 231–249. doi:10.1177/0971721813489458

Srinivasan, V., & Shocker, A. D. (1973). Estimating the weights for multiple attributes in a composite criterion using pairwise judgments. *Psychonometrica*, *38*(4), 473–493. doi:10.1007/BF02291490

Srivastava, S. C. (2011). Is e-government providing the promised returns?: A value framework for assessing e-government impact. *Transforming Government: People, Process and Policy*, *5*(2), 107–113.

Staab, S., & Studer, R. (2005). *Handbook on Ontologies*. Berlin: Springer.

Stankovic, A., Nikolic, M., & Bogdanovic, D. (2012). Short-term effects of black smoke on cardiovascular hospitalization in elderly in Niš, Serbia. *Chemical Industry and Chemical Engineering Quarterly, 18*(4-2), 661-665.

Stankovic, J., Andjelkovic-Pesic, M., & Radenkovic-Jocic, D. (in press). Improving the Business Environment of Cities and Municipalities in Serbia: Experiences and Recommendations. *Themes, 38* (1).

Stankovic, J., Jankovic-Milic, V., & Andjelkovic, M. (2012). The Role of Institutions in Creating Business Friendly Environment. In *Proceedings of the Conference Employment through the Prism of Entrepreneurship*, (pp. 62-69). University of Montenegro.

Stankovic, J., Jankovic-Milic, V., & Andjelkovic-Pesic, M. (2013). Multi-Criteria Analysis of Social Capital Influence on Business Performances. *Actual Problems of Economics, 12* (150), 515-52.

Stankovic, J., Jankovic-Milic, V., & Boskovic, G. (2013). Business Friendly Environment–The Key Task of the Local Self-Government, International Scientific Conference. In *Proceedings of ISC*, (pp. 353-362). ISC.

Statistical Office of the Republic of Serbia. (2012). *Municipalities and Regions in the Republic of Serbia in 2012*. Retrieved February 16, 2013 from http://webrzs.stat.gov.rs/WebSite/repository/documents/00/00/54/08/OpstinskigodisnjakRepublike_Srbije_2011.zip

Statskontoret. (2000). *The 24/7 agency: criteria for 24/7 agencies in the networked public administration*. Report 2000:41, Statskontoret, Stockholm.

Statute N° 6.932. (2009). *Provides a simplification of public service to citizens*. Retrieved October 15, 2013, from http://www.planalto.gov.br/ccivil_03/_Ato2007-2010/2009/Decreto/D6932.htm

Stellefson, M., Chaney, B., Barry, A.E., Chavarria, E., Tennant, B., Walsh-Childers, K., Sriram,P.S, Zagora, J. (2013). Web 2.0 Chronic Disease Self-Management for Older Adults: A Systematic Review. *Journal of Medical Internet Research, 15*(2e35).

Stoker, G., & Wilson, D. (1986). Intra-organizational politics in local authorities: Towards a new approach. *Public Administration, 64*(3), 285–302. doi:10.1111/j.1467-9299.1986.tb00623.x

Štolfa, S., & Vondrák, I. (2004). A description of business process modeling as a tool for definition of requirements specification. In Proceedings of System Integration (pp. 463-469). Academic Press.

Strak, M., Hoek, G., Steenhof, M., Kilinc, E., Godri, K. J., & Gosens, I. et al. (2013). Components of ambient air pollution affect thrombin generation in healthy humans: The RAPTES project. *Occupational and Environmental Medicine, 70*(5), 332–340. doi:10.1136/oemed-2012-100992 PMID:23378445

Streib, G., & Willoughby, K. (2005). Local Governments as E-Governments:Meeting the Implementation Challenge. *Public Administration Quarterly, 29*(1), 78–110.

Strykowski, S. & Wojciechowski, R. (2012). Composable Modeling and Execution of Administrative Procedures. In *Advancing Democracy, Government and Governance* (LNCS), (vol. 52-66). Berlin: Springer.

Stuckenschmidt, H., & Harmelen, F. V. (2001). *Ontology-based metadata generation from semi-structured information. In Proceedings of K-CAP* (pp. 163–170). ACM.

Sum, K. W., Zheng, Y. P., & Mak, A. F. T. (2005). Vital sign monitoring for elderly at home: Development of a compound sensor for pulse rate and motion. *Studies in Health Technology and Informatics, 117*, 43. PMID:16282652

Sun, Z., & Finnie, G. (2004). *Intelligent Techniques in E-Commerce: A Case-based Reasoning Perspective*. Heidelberg, Germany: Springer-Verlag. doi:10.1007/978-3-540-40003-5

Sure, Y., & Studer, R. (2005). Semantic Web technologies for digital libraries. Library Management Journal, 26.

Suri, G., & Kaur, S. (2013). A study on e-Governance initiatives in Panjab University. In *Proceedings of Conference 7th International Conference on Education, Management and Technology*. Academic Press.

Suwa, T., Hogg, J. C., Quinlan, K. B., Ohgami, A., Vincent, R., & van Eeden, S. F. (2002). Particulate air pollution induces progression of atherosclerosis. *Journal of the American College of Cardiology, 39*(6), 935–942. doi:10.1016/S0735-1097(02)01715-1 PMID:11897432

Swan, M. (2012). Sensor Mania! The Internet of Things, Wearable Computing, Objective Metrics, and the Quantified Self 2.0. *Journal of Sensor and Actuator Networks, 1*(3), 217–253. doi:10.3390/jsan1030217

Swearingen, K., & Sinha, R. (2002). Interaction Design for Recommender Systems. In *Proceedings of Designing Interactive Systems*. DIS.

Tabar, A., Keshavarz, A., & Aghajan, H. (2006). Smart home care network using sensor fusion and distributed vision-based reasoning. In *Proceedings of the 4th ACM International Workshop on Video Surveillance and Sensor Networks (VSSN'06)*, (pp. 145 – 154). New York, NY: ACM. doi:10.1145/1178782.1178804

Tan, A., Theodorou, P., & Over, D. V. (2009). Use of Information Technology Investment Management to Manage State Government Information Technology Investments. In Strategic Information Technology and Portfolio Management. Idea Group Inc (IGI).

Tan, C.-W., Benbasat, I., & Cenfetelli, R. (2010). Understanding the Antecedents and Consequences of E-Government Service Quality: Transactional Frequency as a Moderator of Citizens' Quality Perceptions. In *Proceedings of ECIS 2010*. Retrieved from http://aisel.aisnet.org/ecis2010/115

Taniar, D., & Rahayu, J. W. (2006). *Web semantics and ontology*. Hershey, PA: Idea Group. doi:10.4018/978-1-59140-905-2

Tan, W. C., Qiu, D., Liam, B. L., Ng, T. P., Lee, S. H., & van EEDEN, S. F. et al. (2000). The human bone marrow response to acute air pollution caused by forest fires. *American Journal of Respiratory and Critical Care Medicine, 161*(4), 1213–1217. doi:10.1164/ajrccm.161.4.9904084 PMID:10764314

Taqiuddin, M. (2011). Strengthening Open Government: India Country Paper. *Better Service Delivery through Open Government and Innovative Policies, 4*.

Task Force of the European Society of Cardiology and the North American Society of Pacing and Electrophysiology. (1996). Heart rate variability: Standards of measurement, physiological interpretation, and clinical use. *Circulation, 93*(5), 1043–1065. doi:10.1161/01.CIR.93.5.1043 PMID:8598068

Taylor, J. B. (1970). Introducing social innovation. *The Journal of Applied Behavioral Science, 6*(1), 69–77. doi:10.1177/002188637000600104

Terry, N. P., & Francis, L. P. (2007). Ensuring the privacy and confidentiality of electronic health records. *U. Ill. L. Rev.*, 681.

Tether, B. S. (2002). Who co-operates for innovation, and why an empirical analysis. *Research Policy, 31*(6), 947–967. doi:10.1016/S0048-7333(01)00172-X

Texas Instruments. (2014). *eZ430-Chronos™ Development Tool*. Retrieved from http://www.ti.com/tool/ez430-chronos

Thomas, C. W. (1998). Maintaining and restoring public trust in government agencies and their employees. *Administration & Society, 30*(2), 166–193. doi:10.1177/0095399798302003

Thompson, V. (1965). Bureaucracy and innovation. *Administrative Science Quarterly, 10*(1), 1–20. doi:10.2307/2391646

Thurstone, L. L. (1927). A law of comparative judgements. *Psychological Review, 34*(4), 273–286. doi:10.1037/h0070288

Tidd, J., Bessant, J., & Pavitt, K. (2005). *Managing Innovation: Integrating Technological, Market and Organizational Change*. Chichester, UK: Wiley.

Todaro, M. (1985). *Economic development in the third world*. New York: Longman.

Tolbert, C. J., Mossberger, K., & McNeal, R. (2008). Institutions, policy innovation, and e-government in the American states. *Public Administration Review*, *68*(3), 549–563. doi:10.1111/j.1540-6210.2008.00890.x

Toledo, C. M., Ale, M. A., Chiotti, O., & Galli, M. R. (2011). An Ontology-driven Document Retrieval Strategy for Organizational Knowledge Management Systems. *Electronic Notes in Theoretical Computer Science*, *281*, 21–34. doi:10.1016/j.entcs.2011.11.023

Toloo, G., FitzGerald, G., Aitken, P., Verrall, K., & Tong, S. (2013). Evaluating the effectiveness of heat warning systems: Systematic review of epidemiological evidence. *International Journal of Public Health*, *58*(5), 667–681. doi:10.1007/s00038-013-0465-2 PMID:23564031

Toussaint, J., & Cheng, K. (2006). Web-based CBR (case-based reasoning) as a tool with the application to tooling selection. *International Journal of Advanced Manufacturing Technology*, *29*(1-2), 24–34. doi:10.1007/s00170-004-2501-0

Toyama, K., Kiri, K., Ratan, M. L., Nileshwar, A., Vedashree, R., & MacGregor, R. F. (2004). *Rural kiosks in India*. MSR Techincal Report.

Trindade, I. G., Lucas, J., Miguel, R., Alpuim, P., Carvalho, M., & Garcia, N. M. (2010). Lightweight Portable Sensors for Health Care. In *Proceedings of12th IEEE International Conference on e-Health Networking Applications and Services (Healthcom)*. Lyon, France: IEEE. doi:10.1109/HEALTH.2010.5556575

Tsai, N., Choi, B., & Perry, M. (2009). Improving the process of E-Government initiative: An in-depth case study of web-based GIS implementation. *Government Information Quarterly*, *26*(2), 368–376. doi:10.1016/j.giq.2008.11.007

Tsai, S. S., Goggins, W. B., Chiu, H. F., & Yang, C. Y. (2003). Evidence for an association between air pollution and daily stroke admissions in Kaohsiung, Taiwan. *Stroke*, *34*(11), 2612–2616. doi:10.1161/01.STR.0000095564.33543.64 PMID:14551399

Tsytsarau, M., & Palpanas, T. (2012). Survey on mining subjective data on the web. *Data Mining and Knowledge Discovery*, *24*(3), 478–514. doi:10.1007/s10618-011-0238-6

Tuček, D., & Basl, J. (2011). Using BPM Principles to increase efficiency of processes in Higher education in the CR. In *Proceedings ofInternational Conference on Education and Education technologies* (WORLD –EDU ´11). Academic Press.

Tumasjan, A., Sprenger, T. O., Sandner, P. G., & Welpe, I. M. (2011). Election Forecasts With Twitter: How 140 Characters Reflect the Political Landscape. *Social Science Computer Review*, *29*(4), 402–418. doi:10.1177/0894439310386557

U.K. Ministry of Health. (1954). *Mortality and morbidity during the London Fog of December 1952. Reports on Public Health and Medical Subjects; No 95*. London: U.K. Ministry of Health.

UN Public Administration Program. (2010). *Human Capital*. Retrieved from http://unpan3.un.org/egovkb/egovernment_overview/humancapital.htm

UN Report. (2011). *ICT Policy Review-Egypt*. United Nations Conference on Trade and Development (UNCTAD). Retrieved January, 2011, http://www.mcit.gov.eg/Upcont/Documents

UN. (2002). *Benchmarking e-government: A global perspective. UN Technical Report*. United Nations.

UN. (2005). *Global e-government readiness report: from e-government to e-inclusion*. United Nations.

UN. (2008). *UN e-government survey 2008: From e-government to connected governance*. United Nations.

UN. (2010). *E-government survey*. United Nations.

UNDESA (United Nations Department of Economic and Social Affairs). (2003). *E-Government Survey 2012: E-Government for the People*. New York: United Nations.

United Nations E-Government Readiness Survey (UNPAN). (2008). *From E-Government to Connected Governance*. Retrieved from http://unpan1.un.org/intradoc/groups/public/documents/un/unpan028607.pdf

United Nations. (2012). *E-Government Survey 2012: E-Government for the people*. Retrieved from http://unpan1.un.org/intradoc/groups/public/documents/un/unpan048065.pdf

UNReport, . (2012). *UN E-Government Survey 2012: E-Government for People*. New York: United Nations.

US Environmental Protection Agency, Office of Research and Development, National Center for Environmental Assessment. (1996). Air Quality Criteria for Ozone and Related Photochemical Oxidants. Washington, DC: US Environmental Protection Agency.

US Executive Office of the President. (2014). *Big Data: Seizing Opportunities, Preserving Values*. Washington, DC: The White House.

Vaidya, J., & Clifton, C. (2004). Privacy-preserving data mining: Why, how and when. *Security & Privacy*, *2*(6), 19–27. doi:10.1109/MSP.2004.108

Valente, T. W. (1995). *Network models of the diffusion of innovations*. Cresskill, NJ: Hampton Press.

Van de Ven, A. H., & Rogers, E. M. (1988). Innovations and organizations: Critical perspectives. *Communication Research*, *15*(5), 632–651. doi:10.1177/009365088015005007

Van Der Aalst, W. M. P., Pesic, M., & Schonenberg, H. (2009). Declarative workflows: Balancing between flexibility and support. *Computer Science Research for Development*, *23*(2), 99–113.

van Eeden, S. F., Tan, W. C., Suwa, T., Mukae, H., Terashima, T., & Fujii, T. et al. (2001). Cytokines involved in the systemic inflammatory response induced by exposure to particulate matter air pollutants (PM10). *American Journal of Respiratory and Critical Care Medicine*, *164*(5), 826–830. doi:10.1164/ajrccm.164.5.2010160 PMID:11549540

Van Uden, E., & Kwiesielewicz, M. (2003). Evaluating Attribute Significance in AHP Using Shannon Entropy. In *Proceedings of ISAHP*. ISAHP.

Vanos, J. K., Hebbern, C., & Cakmak, S. (2014). Risk assessment for cardiovascular and respiratory mortality due to air pollution and synoptic meteorology in 10 Canadian cities. *Environmental Pollution*, *185*, 322–332. doi:10.1016/j.envpol.2013.11.007 PMID:24355413

Vardalas, J. N. (2001). *The Computer Revolution in Canada: Building National Technological Competence (History of Computing)*. The MIT Press.

Vathanophas, V., Krittayaphongphun, N., & Klomsiri, C. (2008). Technology Acceptance Toward e-Government Initiative in Royal Thai Navy. *Transforming Government: People, Process and Policy*, *2*(4), 256–282.

Veilleroy, Y., Eurin, G., Hoogstoel, & Lancieri, L. (2013). Exploring Collective Intelligence in Online Brainstorming. In *Proceedings ofthe Third International Conference on Advanced Collaborative Networks, Systems and Applications (Colla2013)*. Academic Press.

Venkatesh, V., Morris, M. G., Davis, G. B., & Davis, F. D. (2003). User acceptance of information technology: Toward a unified view. *Management Information Systems Quarterly*, *3*, 425–478.

Venkatesh, V., Sykes, T. A., & Venkatraman, S. (2013). Understanding e-Government portal use in rural India: Role of demographic and personality characteristics. *Information Systems Journal*.

Vergidis, K., Tiwari, A., & Majeed, B. (2008). Business process analysis and optimization: beyond reengineering. *IEEE Transactions on* Systems, Man, and Cybernetics, Part C: Applications and Reviews, *38*(1), 69–82.

Veronesi, B., Oortgiesen, M., Roy, J., Carter, J. D., Simon, S. A., & Gavett, S. H. (2000). Vanilloid (capsaicin) receptors influence inflammatory sensitivity in response to particulate matter. *Toxicology and Applied Pharmacology*, *169*(1), 66–76. doi:10.1006/taap.2000.9040 PMID:11076698

Vienna University of Technology. (2007). *European Smart Cities*. Retrieved from http://www.smart-cities.eu/

Vivonoetics. (2013). *LifeShirt*. Retrieved from http://vivonoetics.com/products/sensors/lifeshirt/

Volpato, S., Guralnik, J. M., Ferrucci, L., Balfour, J., Chaves, P., Fried, L. P., & Harris, T. B. (2001). Cardiovascular disease, interleukin-6, and risk of mortality in older women: The Women's Health and Aging Study. *Circulation*, *103*(7), 947–953. doi:10.1161/01.CIR.103.7.947 PMID:11181468

von Schneidemesser, E., & Monks, P. S. (2013). Air quality and climate–synergies and trade-offs. *Environmental Science: Processes & Impacts*, *15*(7), 1315–1325. PMID:23743609

Vukšić, V. B., Bach, M. P., & Popovič, A. (2013). Supporting performance management with business process management and business intelligence: A case analysis of integration and orchestration. *International Journal of Information Management*, *33*(4), 613–619. doi:10.1016/j.ijinfomgt.2013.03.008

W3C. (2014). *RDF Vocabulary Description Language 1.0: RDF Schema*. Retrieved from http://www.w3.org/TR/rdf-schema/

Wahid, F. (2012). The Current State of Research on eGovernment in Developing Countries: A Literature Review. In H. J. Scholl, M. Janssen, M. A. Wimmer, C. E. Moe, & L. S. Flak (Eds.), *Electronic Government* (pp. 1–12). Springer Berlin Heidelberg. doi:10.1007/978-3-642-33489-4_1

Walker, R. M. (2003). Evidence on the Management of Public Service Innovation. *Public Money & Management*, *23*(2), 93–102. doi:10.1080/09540962.2003.10874830

Walser, K., & Schaffroth, M. (2011). BPM and BPMN as Integrating Concepts in eGovernment. *The Swiss eGovernment BPM Ecosystem S-BPM ONE*, 106–120.

Walsh, W. F. (2001). Compstat: An analysis of an emerging police managerial paradigm. *Policing: An International Journal of Police Strategies & Management*, *24*(3), 347–362. doi:10.1108/13639510110401717

Walters, S., Griffiths, R. K., & Ayres, J. G. (1994). Temporal association between hospital admissions for asthma in Birmingham and ambient levels of sulphur dioxide and smoke. *Thorax*, *49*(2), 133–140. doi:10.1136/thx.49.2.133 PMID:8128402

Wangpipatwong, S., Chutimaskul, W., & Papasratorn, B. (2008). Understanding Citizen's Continuance Intention to Use e-Government Website: A Composite View of Technology Acceptance Model and Computer Self-Efficacy. *The Electronic. Journal of E-Government*, *6*(1), 55–64.

Wang, T., Oh, L. B., Wang, K., & Zhang, B. (2010).An Empirical Study of the Impact of Trial Experiences on the Continued Usage of Mobile Newspapers. In *Proceeding of the Pacific Asia Conference on Information Systems (PACIS)*, (pp. 1148-1159). PACIS.

Warnier, V., & Lecocq, X. (2004). L'émergence de la mode dans un secteur: Une stratégie collective. In *Le cas du Prêt-à-Porter: Actes de l'atelier Stratégies collectives*. Academic Press (In French).

Warren, P. (2005). *Applying semantic technologies to a digital library: a case study*. *Library Management Journal*.

Waterworth, J. A., Ballesteros, S., & Peter, C. (2009). User-sensitive Home-based Systems for Successful Ageing. In *Proceedings of2nd Conference on Human Systems Interactions*. Catania, Italy: Academic Press.

Weerakkody, V., Janssen, M., & Dwivedi, Y. K. (2011). Transformational change and business process reengineering (BPR): Lessons from the British and Dutch public sector. *Government Information Quarterly*, *28*(3), 320–328. doi:10.1016/j.giq.2010.07.010

Weisburd, D., Telep, C., Hinkle, J., & Eck, J. (2008). *Effects of Problem-Oriented Policing on Crime and Disorder*. Washington, DC: U.S. Department of Justice. doi:10.4073/csr.2008.14

Weiss, T. G. (2000). Governance, good governance and global governance: Conceptual and actual challenges. *Third World Quarterly*, *21*(5), 795–814. doi:10.1080/713701075

Wellenius, G. A., Coull, B. A., Godleski, J. J., Koutrakis, P., Okabe, K., & Savage, S. T. et al. (2003). Inhalation of concentrated ambient air particles exacerbates myocardial ischemia in conscious dogs. *Environmental Health Perspectives*, *111*(4), 402–408. doi:10.1289/ehp.5775 PMID:12676590

Wellenius, G. A., Saldiva, P. H., Batalha, J. R., Krishna Murthy, G. G., Coull, B. A., Verrier, R. L., & Godleski, J. J. (2002). Electrocardiographic changes during exposure to residual oil fly ash (ROFA) particles in a rat model of myocardial infarction. *Toxicological Sciences*, *66*(2), 327–335. doi:10.1093/toxsci/66.2.327 PMID:11896300

Wenger, E. (2007). *Communities of Practice: Learning, Meaning, and Identity*. Cambridge, MA: Cambridge University Press.

West, D. M. (2005). *Digital government: Technology and public sector performance*. Princeton, NJ: Princeton University Press.

WGI Cross Country Indicators. (2011). Retrieved from http://info.worldbank.org/governance/wgi/index.aspx#doc-cross

White House. (2014). *About SICP - The Community Solutions Agenda*. Retrieved 18-01, 2014, from http://www.whitehouse.gov/administration/eop/sicp/about

WHO. (1987). Air Quality Guidelines for Europe. Copenhagen: WHO Regional Publications.

WHO. (2001). *Air Quality and Health Air Management Information System AMIS 3.0*. Geneva, Switzerland: WHO.

Whyte, A. (1999). *Understanding the role of community telecentres in development: A proposed approach to evaluation*. Paper presented at Telecentre Evaluation: A Global Perspective. Quebec, Canada.

Wilkin, C. L., Campbell, J., & Moore, S. (2013). Creating value through governing IT deployment in a public/private-sector inter-organisational context: A human agency perspective. *European Journal of Information Systems*, *22*(5), 498–511. doi:10.1057/ejis.2012.21

Wilkinson, P., Pattenden, S., Armstrong, B., Fletcher, A., Kovats, R. S., Mangtani, P., & McMichael, A. J. (2004). Vulnerability to winter mortality in elderly people in Britain: Population based study. *BMJ (Clinical Research Ed.)*, *329*(7467), 647–652. doi:10.1136/bmj.38167.589907.55 PMID:15315961

Willem, A., & Buelens, M. (2007). Knowledge sharing in public sector organizations: The effect oforganizational characteristics on interdepartmental knowledge sharing. *Journal of Public Administration: Research and Theory*, *17*(4), 581–606. doi:10.1093/jopart/mul021

Wilson, S. C., & Linders, D. (2011). *The open government directive: a preliminary assessment. In Proceedings of iConference 2011* (pp. 387–394). New York: ACM. doi:10.1145/1940761.1940814

Witten, I. H., & Bainbridge, D. (2003). *How to Build a Digital Libary*. Morgan Kaufmann.

Wobbe, W. (2012). Measuring social innovation and monitoring progress of EU polices. In H.-W. F. J. Howaldt (Ed.), *Challenge Social Innovation: Potentials for Business, Social Entrepreneurship, Welfare and Civil Society*. Berlin: Springer. doi:10.1007/978-3-642-32879-4_19

Wolfe, A. (1994). Organizational innovation: Review, critique and suggested research directions. *Journal of Management Studies*, *31*(3), 405–431. doi:10.1111/j.1467-6486.1994.tb00624.x

Wolfe, C. P. (1981). Social impact assessment. *Impact Assessment Bulletin*, *1*(1), 9–19. doi:10.1080/07349165.1982.9725924

Wong, C. (2002). Developing Indicators to Inform Local Economic Development in England. *Urban Studies (Edinburgh, Scotland)*, *39*(10), 1833–1863. doi:10.1080/0042098022000002984

Woolley, A. W., Chabris, C. F., Pentland, A., Hashmi, N., & Malone, T. W. (2010). Evidence for a Collective Intelligence Factor in the Performance of Human Groups. *Science*, *330*(6004), 686–688. doi:10.1126/science.1193147 PMID:20929725

XPDL. (n.d.). *WfMC, XML process definition language* (XPDL 2.2). Retrieved from http://www.xpdl.org/index.html

Xu, R., & Wuncsh, D. (2008). *Clustering*. Wiley-IEEE Press. doi:10.1002/9780470382776

Yang, D.-H., & Yu, G. (2013). A method of feature selection and sentiment similarity for Chinese microblogs. *Journal of Information Science*, *39*(4), 429–441. doi:10.1177/0165551513480308

Yang, Y., & Chute, C. G. (1994). An Example-Based Mapping Method for Text Categorization and Retrieval. *ACM Transactions on Information Systems*, *12*(3), 252–277. doi:10.1145/183422.183424

Yan, Y., Qian, Y., Sharif, H., & Tripper, D. (2012). A Survey on Cyber Security for Smart Grid Communication. *IEEE Communications Surveys and Tutorials*, *14*(4), 998–1010. doi:10.1109/SURV.2012.010912.00035

Yeow, P., & Loo, W. (2011). Acceptability of ATM and Transit Applications Embedded in Multipurpose Smart Identity Card: An Exploratory Study in Malaysia. In *Applied Technology Integration in Governmental Organizations* (pp. 118–137). New E-Government Research.

Yin, B. (2003). *Case Study Research: Design and Methods*. Thousand Oaks, CA: Sage Publications.

Yoon, S., Elhadad, N., & Bakken, S. (2013). A Practical Approach for Content Mining of Tweets. *American Journal of Preventive Medicine*, *45*(1), 122–129. doi:10.1016/j.amepre.2013.02.025 PMID:23790998

Yu, E., Strohmaier, M., & Deng, X. (2006). Exploring intentional modeling and analysis for enterprise architecture. In *Proceedings of Edoc 2006 Conference Workshop on Trends in Enterprise Architecture Research*. IEEE Computer Science Press. doi:10.1109/EDOCW.2006.36

Yu, Y., Duan, W., & Cao, Q. (2013). The impact of social and conventional media on firm equity value: A sentiment analysis approach. *Decision Support Systems*, *55*(4), 919–926. doi:10.1016/j.dss.2012.12.028

Zakareya, E., & Zahir, I. (2005). E-government adoption: Architecture and barriers. *Business Process Management*, *11*(5), 589–611. doi:10.1108/14637150510619902

Zakaria, M. R., & Gebba, T. R. (2012). Towards Categorizing E-Government Services: The Case of Egypt. *International Journal of Business Information and Technology*, *1*(1), 16–28.

Zambonelli, F. (2012). Toward Sociotechnical Urban Superorganisms. *Computer Magazine*, *45*(8), 76–78. doi:10.1109/MC.2012.280

Zanobetti, A., Schwartz, J., Sher, D., Eagan Bengston, E., Gates, K. A., Bar, M., … Gold, D. (2002). *Blood pressure and heart rate associated with PM2.5 in a cardiac rehabilitation study*. Paper presented at American Thoracic Society 98th Annual Conference. Atlanta, GA.

Zanobetti, A., Schwartz, J., Samoli, E., Gryparis, A., Touloumi, G., & Peacock, J. et al. (2003). The temporal pattern of respiratory and heart disease mortality in response to air pollution. *Environmental Health Perspectives*, *111*(9), 1188–1193. doi:10.1289/ehp.5712 PMID:12842772

Zappavigna, M. (2011). Ambient affiliation: A linguistic perspective on Twitter. *New Media & Society*, *13*(5), 788–806. doi:10.1177/1461444810385097

Zefferer, T. (2010). *STORK Work Item 3.3.5: Smartcard eID comparison*. Retrieved from STORK Project: https://www.eid-stork.eu/index.php?option=com_processes&Itemid=&act=streamDocument&did=1384

Zhang, C., Zeng, D., Li, J., Wang, F.-Y., & Zuo, W. (2009). Sentiment analysis of Chinese documents: From sentence to document level. *Journal of the American Society for Information Science and Technology*, *60*(12), 2474–2487. doi:10.1002/asi.21206

Zhang, P., & He, Z. (2013). A weakly supervised approach to Chinese sentiment classification using partitioned self-training. *Journal of Information Science*, *39*(6), 815–831. doi:10.1177/0165551513480330

Zhang, Y., Li, S., Pan, X., Tong, S., Jaakkola, J. J., & Gasparrini, A. et al. (2014). The effects of ambient temperature on cerebrovascular mortality: An epidemiologic study in four climatic zones in China. *Environmental Health*, *13*(1), 24. doi:10.1186/1476-069X-13-24 PMID:24690204

Zhang, Z., Wang, H., Vasilakos, A. V., & Fang, H. (2012). ECG-Cryptography and Authentication in Body Area Networks. *IEEE Transactions on Information Technology in Biomedicine*, *16*(6), 1070–1078. doi:10.1109/TITB.2012.2206115 PMID:22752143

Zhaohao, S., & Gavin, F. (2005). A Unified Logical Model for CBR-based E-commerce Systems. *International Journal of Intelligent Systems*, *20*(1), 29–46. doi:10.1002/int.20052

Zheng, Y., Cheng, X., Huang, R., & Man, Y. (2006). A Comparative Study on Text Clustering Methods. In X. Li, O. R. Zaiane, & Z. Li (Eds.), *ADMA 2006, (LNAI), (vol. 4093,* pp. 644–651). Berlin: Springer-Verlag. doi:10.1007/11811305_71

Zhou, J., Cao, Z., Dong, X., Lin, X., & Vasilakos, A. V. (2013). Securing m-Healthcare Scial Networks: Challenges, Countermeasures and Future Directions. *IEEE Wireless Communications*, *20*(4), 12–21. doi:10.1109/MWC.2013.6590046

Zou, K., Wang, Z., & Hu, M. (2008). An new initialization method for fuzzy c-means algorithm. *Journal of Fuzzy Optimization and Decision Making*, *7*(4), 409–416. doi:10.1007/s10700-008-9048-8

Zubin, A. (1938). A technique for measuring likemindedness. *Journal of Abnormal and Social Psychology*, *33*(4), 508–516. doi:10.1037/h0055441

Zwicker, J., Fettke, P., & Loos, P. (2010). Business process maturity in public administrations. In J. vom Brocke & M. Rosemann (Eds.), Handbook on business process management, (vol. 2, pp. 369–400). Academic Press.

About the Contributors

Ćemal Dolićanin (emeritus) is currently Director of the State University of Novi Pazar, Serbia. In 2009, he was chosen for a permanent member of South Slovenian Academy of Non-Linear Sciences (JANN). Prof. Dolićanin is exceptionally meritorious for establishment and foundation of the State University in Novi Pazar, the first integrated university in Serbia, where he served as the first rector of that university since 2007. The scientific work of Prof. Dolićanin includes several areas of Mathematics: Non-Euclidean Geometry, Differential Geometry and Topology, Differential Equations, Applied Mathematics, and Numeric Analysis. He has been developed several geometrical and numeric models and also models for researching of effects following the work of complex structures, description of dynamical systems and bifurcations, dynamical behaviour and vibrations, oscillations within acoustic and mechanical systems, wave spreading, copying, non-linear phenomena and others, and this depicts his versatile Mathematical interest. Prof. Dolićanin has published 22 textbooks, 2 monographs, and around 90 scientific papers in international and national journals and at international and domestic conferences, as well. He has managed and participated in realisation of 20 scientific-research projects funded by the Ministry for Science and Technology Republic of Serbia, and also participated in realisation several international projects, where a significant segment make TEMPUS projects (more than 10), and he has been a coordinator in two projects. He has been a coordinator of two MA study programmes organised in cooperation with World University Service (WUS) Austria. Prof. Dolićanin is Editor-in-Chief of the international journal, *Journal of Electrotechnique and Mathematics*, published by Faculty of Technical Sciences, Kosovska Mitrovica (former Electrical Engineering in Pristina), and he is the establisher and Editor-in-Chief of the journal, *Scientific Publications of the State University of Novi Pazar, Series A: Applied Mathematics, Informatics & Mechanics*. During his career, Prof. Dolićanin received several awards, such as diploma "Dr Vojislav Stojanovic" for a special contribution to university education-Association of University Professors and Scientists of Serbia, Plaque "Kapetan Misa Anastasijevic" for establishment and affirmation of university education, Plaque of Faculty of Technical Sciences, University in Novi Sad, for exceptional contribution to development of faculties of technical sciences, Svetosavka Award for his exceptional contribution in development of education and upbringing in the Republic of Serbia in 2012, awarded by the Ministry of Education, Science, and Technical Development, Republic of Serbia, and Devetomajska Award 2013 for his special contribution, tenure, and exceptional development of the university from the State University in Novi Pazar, just to mention a few.

Ejub Kajan teaches at the State University of Novi Pazar, Serbia. He holds a PhD and MSc in Computer Science from University of Niš, Serbia, and diploma degree in Electronic Engineering from University of Split, Croatia. His current research focuses on e-commerce in general, e-commerce architectures, semantic interoperability, social networking, computer networks, and decision support systems. He authored over 100 papers, 4 research books, 2 edited books, 5 chapters in edited books, and 5 textbooks. Prof. Kajan published in various outlets, including ACM, IEEE, and Ivy League Publishing journals, IGI Global and Springer books, as well as in IEEE, IADIS, and WSEAS conference proceeding, etc. He is a Senior Member of the ACM, and a member of IEEE, IADIS, and ISOC. Dr. Kajan is involved in a series of international conferences as a program committee member including, but not limited to prestigious DEXA, FedCSIS, and IADIS conferences. He also serves editorial boards of *International Journal of Distributed Systems and Technologies* (IJDST) and *Journal of Information, Information Technology, and Organization* (JIITO). In the past, he worked as software engineer and general manager in the computer industry.

Dragan Ranđelović teaches at the Academy for Criminalistics and Police Studies in Belgrade and at the Agriculture faculty, University of Priština, as well. He holds a PhD and MSc in Applied Mathematics from University of Priština, 1999, and University of Niš, 1984, respectively, and diploma degree in Electronic Engineering from University of Niš, 1977, Serbia. His current research focuses on decision making in general and decision making methodologies, computer networks and Web technologies, forensics, and decision support systems. He has authored over 100 papers, over 10 research and textbooks, several chapters in edited books. He is a Member of the Serbian Informatics Association and Serbian Association of Engineers and Technicians. Dr. Ranđelović is involved in a series of international conferences as a program committee member. He served on the editorial boards of proceedings from several international conferences. In addition, he holds plenary lectures with invited papers at several international conferences. In the past, he participated in many projects that were supported by Ministry of Sciences Republic of Serbia and currently participates at a few such projects, in one of them as project leader. He was, also, author of many projects in computer industry where he worked as an electronic engineer, researcher in research institute, and general manager in the electronic industry of Niš, Serbia.

Boban Stojanović is professor in Microeconomics at the University of Niš. He holds a PhD and MSc in Economics from University of Belgrade, Serbia, and diploma degree in Economics from University of Niš, Serbia. His current research focuses on theory of monopoly and competition policy. He has authored over 50 papers, 2 research books, several chapters in edited books, and 2 textbooks. He has published in various outlets. He was a visiting professor at the Al-Farabi Kazakh National University Almaty, Kasakhstan. Dr. Stojanović is involved in a series of international conferences. He also serves on the editorial boards of *Journal of Business and Economics* (Akademic Star Publishing) and *Panoeconomicus*. His current positions are Full Professor at the University of Nis, Faculty of Economics, Jean Monnet Program, Key Activity 1 Award, Consortium Member of the TEMPUS Project 158885, Member of the DAAD Scholarship Selection Board.

* * *

Mohamed Gamal Aboelmaged has a PhD in Management Science from Lancaster University, UK, and MA in Public Policy and Administration from Institute of Social Studies, The Netherlands. Currently, he is a Professor of Production and Operations Management at Ain Shams University, Egypt. His research interests include quality management and lean systems, knowledge and innovation management, supply chain management. His work has been published in international journals and conference proceedings such as *Production Planning & Control, International Journal of Quality & Reliability Management, Industrial Management & Data Systems, Business Process Management Journal, Measuring Business Excellence, International Journal of Social Ecology and Sustainable Development, International Journal of Enterprise Network Management,* IEEE International Conference on Management of Innovation and Technology, Information Quality Conference at the Massachusetts Institute of Technology (MIT), British Academy of Management Annual Conference, The Operational Research Society Annual Conference, and Annual Global Information Technology Management World Conference.

Michael J. Ahn is an assistant professor in the Department of Public Policy and Public Affairs at University of Massachusetts Boston. The primary focus of his research is exploring the effects of Information Technology on government performance, accountability and political dynamics. In the past, he has examined: 1) how e-government can be strategically used to enhance the political control over government bureaucracy and provide a leverage for the executive bureaucracy against the legislature, 2) how the changing information environment from texts-based communication to image and video-based communication (such as YouTube) affect the communication and implementation of public policies, and 3) why "political outsiders" (governors) in the state government pursue Web 2.0 applications more actively than those who are "political insiders." Currently, Dr. Ahn is conducting research on emerging technological innovations in government including Open Government, Open Data, and Collaborative Governance, the role of the arts and cultural sector on national branding value, cyber-security, and the role of public sector call centers in our complex information and communication environment ("human-centered e-government"). His articles have appeared in journals such as *Public Administration Review, American Review of Public Administration*, and *Government Information Quarterly*. He received his PhD in Public Administration from Syracuse University in 2007.

Antonio Juarez Alencar is a researcher with the Federal University of Rio de Janeiro (UFRJ), Brazil. He received his BSc in Mathematics and MSc in System Engineering and Computer Science from UFRJ. He holds a DPhil in Computer Science from Oxford University, England. His research interests include economics of software engineering, ICT strategy, and risk analysis.

Celina Micaela Afonso Alexandre is currently a BSc student and researcher in Assisted Living Computing and Telecommunications Laboratory – ALLab, a research laboratory within the Networks Group of the Instituto de Telecomunicações at the University of Beira Interior (UBI), Covilhã, Portugal. His research interests include software developing, computing algorithms and video processing.

Renata Araujo obtained her DSc in Computer Science from the Federal University of Rio de Janeiro (UFRJ) in 2000. She is an Associate Professor at UNIRIO (Federal University of the State of Rio de Janeiro), Brazil. Her experience and research work focus on Information Systems, Software Development Process Improvement, Business Process Management, Computer-Supported Cooperative Work, and e-Democracy. She coordinates the Research and Innovation Group in CiberDemocracy (https://sites.google.com/site/ciberdem/). Her current research concentrates on how to turn organizations more democratic by the use of business process management, collaborative support and social tools.

Alberto Asquer is Lecturer of Public Policy and Management in the Distance Learning programme of the School of Oriental and African Studies, University of London. His research interests are regulation and governance, organizational change and innovation in the public sector, and public management. His works have been published in *Governance, Public Management Review, International Public Management Journal, Annals of Public and Cooperative Economics, Journal of Comparative Policy Analysis, Utilities Policy,* and *Water Policy*. He was Visiting Researcher at CESifo Centre in Munich, Visiting Fellow of the Florence School of Regulation of the European University Institute, and presently acts as Scientific Coordinator of the Turin School of Regulation.

Paulo Henrique de Souza Bermejo has PhD in Knowledge Engineering and Management by the Universidade Federal de Santa Catarina (Brazil), and performed a post-doctoral stage in Information Systems Management and Innovation at Bentley University (USA) in the years of 2011 and 2012. Currently, he is Assistant Professor in the Department of Computer Science at Universidade Federal de Lavras (Brazil) and researches about information technology governance, knowledge management, software innovation, and software engineering. He is author of the book *Gerência de Riscos em Projetos de Software* (*Risk Management in Software Projects*), advocate member of ISACA Association, and Cobit certified. Over his 15-years career, Bermejo has published more than 50 refereed papers on knowledge management and innovation, IT governance and software engineering, and has developed over 25 software products in partnership with public and private institutions. In the period of 2009 to 2011, he worked as Associate Dean for Graduate Studies at Universidade Federal de Lavras. In 2013, Dr. Bermejo started to conduct "productivity scholarship in research" supported by Foundation for Supporting Research in the states of Minas Gerais (Fapemig).

Dragan Bogdanović is Doctor of Medical Sciences, specialist in Medical Statistics and Informatics. He is assistant professor at the Department of Biomedical Sciences, State University of Novi Pazar, Serbia, and also works at the Center for Informatics and Biostatistics of the Public Health Institute Niš, Serbia. He teaches Statistics and Methodology of scientific research at study programs for rehabilitation, sport and physical education, and psychology. Published over 20 papers in SCI/SCIE list scientific journals. Most of these works are related to the assessment of the impact of climate change, meteorological factors, pollutants, and other risk factors on human health.

Claudia Cappelli obtained her DSc degree in Computer Science at PUC-RJ in 2009. She is Assistant Professor at UNIRIO (Federal University of the State of Rio de Janeiro). She is author of many publications in national and international congresses. She coordinates consulting projects at companies and develops projects in the field of Business Process Modeling, Requirements Engineering, and Technology Architecture. She worked as Project Manager, Chief Architect, and Technology Director in some big companies. Her areas of interest are Business Process Management, Enterprise Architecture, Electronic Democracy, and Organizational Transparency.

Alexandre Luis Correa is a Professor of Computer Science with the State of Rio de Janeiro Federal University (UNIRIO). He holds a BSc in Mathematics and a MSc and a DSc in System Engineering and Computer Science from the Federal University of Rio de Janeiro. His research interests include reverse engineering, system validation, and software development modeling tools.

Rafael Couto is currently a Research Fellow at SEGAL - Space & Earth Geodetic Analysis Laboratory, where he is responsible for the development of a GNSS stations network monitoring solution. Rafael is also a collaborator at ALLab – Assisted Living Computing and Telecommunications Lab (Covilhã, Portugal) since Jan. 2010, where he worked on: TICE.Healthy – PPS10; SIMTEV – Web+SMS Interaction System for Lifestyles Monitoring and Training; and WiDIC – Wearable Wireless Device for Interface control. His main interests are related to Ambient Assisted Living (AAL), e-Health, robotics, and aeronautics. Rafael holds a bachelor degree in Informatics Engineering, and he is currently a Master's student in the same field at the University of Beira Interior (Covilhã, Portugal).

Bart De Decker is a professor at the Department of Computer Science of the KU Leuven (Belgium), where he is a member of the research group iMinds-DistriNet. Bart De Decker received a Diploma in Engineering, Computer Science in 1981 and a PhD in 1988 both from the KU Leuven. He is a professor at the KU Leuven since 1988. His main research interests include information security, privacy and anonymity, and more in particular Privacy-Enhancing Technologies (PET), the development of middleware that supports these technologies and the design of privacy-friendly distributed applications. He has co-authored more than 150 research papers presented at international conferences or published in international journals. He has been a PC member of many international security conferences, chaired the Communications and Multimedia Security conference several times, and is currently vice-chair of IFIP TC11 (Security and Privacy Protection in Information Processing Systems).

Priscila Engiel is a DSc student at Pontifical Catholic University (PUC-RJ) in Rio de Janeiro, Brazil. In 2012, she obtained her MSc in Information Systems at the Federal University of State of Rio de Janeiro (UNIRIO). She obtained her degree in Information Systems in the same university in 2009. She has skills and practical experience in business process modeling and management in industry. Her research areas are electronic democracy, transparency, BPM, process understandability, and non functional IS requirements.

Francisco Falcone received a Telecommunications Engineering Degree in 1999 and a PhD in Communication Engineering in 2005, both from the Universidad Pública de Navarra, in Spain. From 1999 to 2000, he was Microwave Commissioning Engineer in Siemens-Italtel, working on the deployment of Amena mobile network (now Orange). From 2000 to 2008, he was Radio Network Engineer in Telefónica Móviles. In 2009, he co-founded TafcoMetawireless, a technological Spin-Off, being its first director. In parallel, he was Assistant Lecturer in the Electrical and Electronic Engineering Department at the Universidad Pública de Navarra (UPNA), and since June 2009, he is Associate Professor at the same university. He is currently the Head of the Department of Electrical and Electronic Engineering at UPNA. He has over 350 publications in the field of complex electromagnetic media, artificial media, and wireless systems analysis and modeling. He has been president of the Asociación Navarra de Ingenieros de Telecomunicación and co-dean of the Colegio Oficial de Ingenieros de Telecomunicación from 2008 to 2011. He has been member of the IEEE MTT-11 committee and the Education Society IEEE Chapter in Spain. He is currently Chair of the IEEE TMC Spain Chapter, member of the IEEE Spain section, and member of the IEEE APS Wave and Propagation Committee. He has been awarded the CST Best Paper award in 2003 and 2005, the best PhD prize from the Colegio Oficial de Ingenieros de Telecomunicación in 2006, best internal instructor in Telefonica in 2008, PhD Award 2004-2006 from the Universidad Pública de Navarra, the Juan López de Peñalver Young Researcher Award granted by the Royal Academy of Engineering of Spain, and the Talgo Prize 2012 for Technological Innovation.

Virginie dos Santos Felizardo is currently a MSc Researcher in Assisted Living Computing and Telecommunications Laboratory – ALLab, a research laboratory within the Networks Group of the Instituto de Telecomunicações at the University of Beira Interior, Covilhã, Portugal. She graduated in Biomedical Sciences (University of Beira Interior, Covilhã, Portugal) and, in 2010, received MSc in Electrotechnical Engineering – Bionic Systems (University of Beira Interior, Covilhã, Portugal). She is involved in research activities in the Department of Electromechanical Engineering at University of Beira Interior, Covilhã, Portugal. Her research interests include sensors for biomedical applications, biomedical instrumentation, health monitoring, medical signal acquisition, analysis, and processing.

Marcelo Carvalho Fernandes is a PhD student with the Federal University of Rio de Janeiro (UFRJ), Brazil. He received his BSc in Computer Science and MSc in Informatics from UFRJ. His research interests include software development methodologies, project management, and economics of software engineering.

Nuno M. Garcia holds a PhD in Computer Science Engineering from the University of Beira Interior (UBI, Covilhã, Portugal) (2008) and he is a 5-year BSc in Mathematics /Informatics also from UBI (1999-2004). He is Assistant Professor at UBI and invited Associate Professor at the School of Communication, Architecture, Arts, and Information Technologies of the Universida de Lusófona de Humanidades e Tecnologias (Lisbon, Portugal). He was founder and is coordinator of the Assisted Living Computing and Telecommunications Laboratory (ALLab), a research group within the Instituto deTelecomunicações at UBI. He was also co-founder and is coordinator of the BSAFE LAB – Law Enforcement, Justice and Public Safety Research, and Technology Transfer Laboratory, a multidisciplinary research laboratory in

UBI. He is the coordinator of the Cisco Academy at UBI and Head of EyeSeeLab in EyeSeeLda (Lisbon, Portugal). He is also Chair of the COST Action IC1303 AAPELE – Architectures, Algorithms, and Platforms for Enhanced Living Environments. He is the main author of several international, European, and Portuguese patents. He is member of the Non-Commercial Users Constituency, a group within GNSO in ICANN. He is also member of ACM SIGBio, ISOC, and IEEE. His main interests include Next-Generation Networks, algorithms for bio-signal processing, distributed and cooperative protocols.

Tarek Roshdy Gebba has a PhD in Management Science from Manchester University, UK, and MSc in Marketing from Menoufia University, Egypt. Currently, he is an Associate Professor of Marketing and Director of Graduate Studies at Al Ghurair University, UAE. His research interests include e-government services, knowledge management governance, online and mobile banking. His work has been published in international journals and conference proceedings such as *International Journal of Business Research and Development, Journal of Applied Finance and Banking, International Journal of Technology and Management, International Journal of Business Information and Technology,* and *The Annual Conference of Advanced Management.*

Federico Gonzalez is the community manager of STC on eGovernment project and associated social networks. MSc on Systems Engineering and Computing Engineer, he participated in the interactive tool developed for teaching operating systems and interested in the processes of public key has been involved in developing online file encryption. He teaches automata theory and computer architecture at UNED University for 8 years. He currently works for public administration as Head of Distribution, and has been involved in the development of IT Governance and he has worked in the areas of technology management and has participated in several projects of implementing new technologies in workplaces, as South Project. He is a member the IEEE TMC Spain Board and member of the IEEE since 2008.

Carlos E. Jimenez, MSc, on Information and Knowledge Society, Postgraduate degree on Information Systems Management, Expert in Law and ICT, and Computer Engineer. His main interests include e-Governance, e-Justice, Interoperability, and Open and Smart Government. In these fields, he has published articles and papers and he has been speaker in international conferences, as the ITU/UNESCO Forum on Smart Sustainable Cities, where he has been appointed speaker by the IEEE Smart Cities Committee in 2014. He has been civil servant since 1991, and nowadays, he forms part of the team in charge of the e-Justice project of the Autonomous Government of Catalonia, project prizewinner in Spain in 2010, 2011, 2012, and 2013. As independent consultant, he has carried out international training and consulting work for organizations such as the Government of Brazil, the international organization CLAD, or the European Commission. He is also a grant researcher in the ICT area for the Center for Legal Studies of the Department of Justice, and he forms part of the e-Government tutors team of several international institutions. Member of the IEEE, IEEE Society of Social Implications of Technology (SSIT), IEEE Computer Society (CS), and the Association for Computing Machinery (ACM); he is founder—and nowadays, Chair—of the IEEE eGovernment STC, 2012-2015 Head of Strategy and New Programs of IEEE Spain, and 2012-2013 Chair of the IEEE Technology Management Council in Spain. He is currently the IEEE representative within the Spanish Open Data Community.

Luigi Lancieri is full-time professor at the University of Lille (France) and head of the NOCE research team since 2009. Formerly, he coordinated a research activity within the Orange Labs (France Telecom R&D, CNET), where he worked for 17 years. His main topics of interest deal with the understanding and the support of human interactions in computer-mediated environments. The measure of the group opinion in social networks or the recommendation systems are some examples of studies he achieved in the past years. More details including a list of publications can be found at http://www.lifl.fr/~lancieri.

Konstansa Lazarević is Doctor of Medical Sciences, specialist in Hygiene and Human Ecology. She is assistant professor at the Department of Biomedical Sciences, State University of Novi Pazar, Serbia. She teaches Human Ecology, Balneoclimatology, and Hygiene at study programs for rehabilitation, sport, and physical education. Works at the Center for Hygiene and Human Ecology of the Institute of Public Health Niš, Serbia, focusing mainly on tesing food safety. Published several papers in SCI/SCIE list scientific journals. Her area of research is Medical Ecology, Dietetics, and Hygiene of Working Environment.

Carlos Leon received the BSc degree in Electronic Physics in 1991 and the PhD degree in Computer Science in 1995, both from the University of Seville, Seville, Spain. He is a professor of Electronic Engineering and Computer Science at the University of Seville since 1991. His research areas include knowledge-based systems and computational intelligence focus on Utilities System Management. He is a Senior Member of the IEEE, Professor of the Chair Telefonica at the University o Seville, since 2009, head of more than 50 research project, financing with public and private companies funds and CIO of the University of Seville for 10 years. Dr. Leon has been author of more than 100 papers and conference contributions.

Antonio Martín is a researcher and author. He has a Computer Science degree and PhD in Intelligence Artificial Applied in Management Knowledge. Dr. Martín is Professor in the Electronic Technology Department and head of research and educational support section in the Computer Service at the Sevilla University in Spain. Professor Martín is an active researcher; he also serves as editorial board member of several journals and conferences; guest editor for journal special issues; chair of conference tracks; and keynote speaker at conferences. His research interests encompass subject areas including data mining, intelligence artificial, knowledge management, software engineering, and expert systems. Professor Martín has published numerous articles in international journals and conference proceedings on these topics, in addition to two books on artificial intelligence and knowledge management.

M. Antonia Martínez-Carreras has a PhD in Computer Science from the University of Murcia (Spain) since 2005. She is a Teaching Assistant Professor for Compilers and Multi-Agent Systems at the University of Murcia. She also participates as a teacher in the Msc of New Technologies in Computer Science, teaching in the courses Software as a Service and Development technologies for ubiquitous systems. Her research area is devoted to Cooperative Systems, CSCW, Groupware, CSCL, Context-Awareness and Interoperability issues. She has been working in the Department of Information and Communication Engineering since 1999 until now, where she was involved in several research projects funded by the European Commission such as ITCOLE, COLAB, and ECOSPACE, a contract to act as a consultant in a Leonardo Project Replika and some national projects such as CAM4HOME. She has contributed to several books such as *Electronic Business Interoperability, Advancing Collaborative Knowledge Environments: New Trends in E-Collaboration*, and *Handbook of e-Business Protocols and Standards*. She has published several papers in national and international conferences and journals.

Teresa Cristina Monteiro Martins is a Master's Degree student at the Universidade Federal de Lavras (Brasil) on which develops researches on Social Innovation and Open Innovation. She is a student at Universidade Federal Fluminense (Brasil) on which studies the Distance education management. She holds a degree in Computer Science with a specialization in Administration of ICT Systems from Universidade Federal de Lavras. Currently, she works at the same University, where holds the office of "administrative technician" and she is a tutor of the Open University of Brazil.

John McNutt is Professor in the School of Public Policy and Administration and Coordinator of the Nonprofit Concentration in the MPA Program at the University of Delaware. Prior to coming to the university in 2007, he was Associate Professor and Coordinator of the Advanced Practice Concentration in Organizations and Communities at the University of South Carolina College of Social Work. He has over 30 years of higher education experience including posts at Boston College Graduate School of Social Work and Indiana University School of Social Work. Before becoming an academic, Dr. McNutt worked in social services, beginning his professional practice career as a VISTA Volunteer in Birmingham, Alabama in 1975. Dr. McNutt's research efforts are in the areas of political use of the Internet and the use and adoption of technology by nonprofit organizations. His over 100 published works include 5 co-authored or co-edited books and many articles, book chapters, reviews, and other works on advocacy, the digital divide, volunteerism, community development technology, and nonprofit organizations, technology, and public participation. His practice specialties are criminal justice and child welfare. He regularly presents at national and international conferences. Dr. McNutt is also a member of the editorial boards of several scholarly journals.

Milica Milutinovic is a Doctoral researcher and a teaching assistant at the Computer Science Department of the KU Leuven University, Belgium. She is a member of the research group iMinds-DistriNet. She has obtained her bachelor and Master's degree at the University of Belgrade, Faculty of Electrical Engineering. Her research interests are security and privacy, with special focus on privacy-preserving identity management. In particular, she is investigating privacy solutions for systems deployed in practice, such as electronic health or value-transfer systems.

Gaurav Mishra is an Assistant Professor at Dhirubhai Ambani Institute of Information and Communication Technology (DA-IICT), India. He is engaged in teaching postgraduate programme in Information and Communication Technology for Agriculture and Rural Development (ICTARD) at DA-IICT. He has PhD from the University of Reading in International and Rural Development. During PhD, he researched on the issues of adoption and development impact of e-governance in rural India. Before pursuing PhD, he worked with the International Crops Research Institute for the Semi-Arid Tropics (ICRISAT), Hyderabad, India, as a research intern, in the area of knowledge management in agriculture. His research interests lie in the area of human computer interaction, technology and development, e-governance, and knowledge management.

Igor Novakovic is assistant professor at the Faculty of Education, University of Kosovska Mitrovica. As well, he is part time employed as professor at Faculty of Management Novi Sad, Serbia, and Business School in Blace, Serbia. He gained professional training abroad: CIBA, Basel, Switzerland, management information systems in 1997; YUCAN, Frankfurt, Germany, vocational training, management information systems in 1998; BBAval, Bezema, Stoll, professional development and management information systems in 1999. His scientific fields of expertise are Electrical and Computer Engineering and Computer Science, Information Systems and Management. He is the author of 2 monographs, 6 books, and 2 additional learning tools. He has been mentor or member of the commissions that evaluated the 46 graduate theses, 15 Master's theses, and 2 Doctoral dissertations. Has published scientific papers in international and national journals in the areas of structuring business rules in development of information systems, the changing role of information systems in organizations, increasing the functionality of tools, charts deployment of e-business applications for supply chain management, theory development, innovation, and competitiveness.

Daniel José Silva Oliveira has bachelor in Public Administration by Universidade Federal de Lavras (Brazil). Currently, he is Master's candidate in the Program of Public Administration at Universidade Federal de Lavras. He has degree in Commercial Management Technology by Centro Universitário do Sul de Minas (Brazil) and specialization in Management and Strategy of Marketing by Faculdades Integradas de Jacarepaguá (Brazil). Since 2008, Oliveira is a civil servant working as administrative technician in education at Communication Department of Instituto Federal de Educação, Ciência e Tecnologia de Minas Gerais (IFMG), Congonhas (Brazil). His areas of interest involve public management, information technology, democracy, accountability, e-government, and social participation.

Daniel Sabugueiro Oliveira is currently a MSc student and researcher in Assisted Living Computing and Telecommunications Laboratory – ALLab, a research laboratory within the Networks Group of the Instituto de Telecomunicações at the University of Beira Interior (UBI), Covilhã, Portugal. He graduated in Computer Science (UBI, Covilhã, Portugal). His research interests include image processing, computing algorithms, and software developing.

Ivan Miguel Serrano Pires is a PhD Student in Computer Science at University of Beira Interior, Covilhã. He obtained MSc degree in Computer Science at the University of Beira Interior, Covilhã. After Master's degree, he worked in some companies in Castelo Branco, working as Web developer, mobile developer, and others. The research area is related to Ambient Assisted Living, working with sensors and mobile technologies.

Hector Puyosa has more than 25 years of experience in service, oil and gas, and plastics industries. He started his career in 1984 as maintenance electronic and automation engineer providing services for companies on food, beverage, paper, and metal transformation sectors. He entered in the plastic business in 1996 as senior process engineer for the design and implementation of the control system for the largest polycarbonate plant built in Spain. He currently works as chemical operation plant manager in Spain. Hector has led a business global initiative on advanced manufacturing system as technical leader setting priorities and direction around MES and control system, identifying focus group activities and developing metrics of success, defining global standards and process/procedure to retain business knowledge. Currently, he is engaged on a technical working group developing cybersecurity standard for industrial control systems. Hector holds PhD degree on Industrial Engineering from the University of Murcia, and he is part-time professors at Polytechnic University of Cartagena, IEEE Senior member, EAB IEEE Spain coordinator.

Thurasamy Ramayah is currently a Professor at the School of Management in USM. He has taught courses in Statistics, Operations Management, Research Methods, Forecasting, and Computer Literacy at undergraduate level. He has also presented numerous papers at local and international conferences having won five "Best Paper" awards. His publications, which exceed 300, have appeared in *Journal of Environmental Management, Technovation, Computers in Human Behavior, Resources, Conservation and Recycling, International Journal of Information Technology & Decision Making (IJITDM), International Journal of Information Management, Lecture Notes in Computer Science, Turkish Online Journal of Education Technology, Journal of Research in Interactive Marketing, Information Development, Journal of Project Management (JoPM), IJITDM, International Journal of Services and Operations Management (IJSOM), Engineering, Construction, and Architectural Management (ECAM),* and *North American Journal of Psychology,* among others. He also serves on the editorial boards and program committee of several international journals and conferences of repute. His full profile can be accessed from http://www.ramayah.com.

Jesus D. Jimenez Re was born in Murcia in 1977. He holds a degree in Computer Sciences from Faculty of Computer Science of University of Murcia, Spain. Since 2003, he has been working in several facets in network security, such as autopsy forensic, IPsec, VPN, and network administration tasks. He has worked as a research engineer in some IST European project, such Euro6ix, POSITIF, and SEINIT. He has worked as teaching assistant professor for the last three years. Currently, he is IT business analyst at IT Department at the University of Murcia, where both their job and research are focused on Business Process Management (BPM), Document Management, and e-Government solutions. Along these years, he has acquired experience in several technologies, protocols, and frameworks as XML-related technologies, Service-Oriented Architectures (SOA), and Business Process Management Notation (BPMN).

Pamela Aparecida dos Santos is an Information Systems undergraduate student at Universidade Federal de Lavras (Brazil). In addition to mandatory academic activities for her degree, she is also involved in undergraduate research projects with research activities in the area of Information Technology (IT) Governance and Open Innovation in Software. She also spoke at the National Forum of IT Governance, presenting results of a research project on IT Governance in Brazil. Along with these activities, she was also involved with the local, student-led computing enterprise society for two years. In 2014, Pamela developed an Android application at Murray State University (USA) to control an autonomous beetletrap, involving conceptualization, coding, debug, and validation of the application.

Eber Assis Schmitz is a Professor of Computer Science with the Federal University of Rio de Janeiro (UFRJ). He holds a BSc in Electrical Engineering from the Federal University of Rio Grande do Sul (UFRGS), an MSc in Electrical Engineering from the Federal University of Rio de Janeiro, and a PhD in Computer Science and Control from the Imperial College of Science Technology and Medicine, London, England. His research interests include software development modeling tools, business process modeling, and stochastic modeling.

Goran Šimić is Assistant Professor at Military Academy, University of Defense, Belgrade, Serbia. He is also head of Center for Simulations and Distance Learning – the unit of Military Academy which is given the status of ADL partnership lab (http://www.adlnet.gov/partnerships/serbia-adl-partnership-lab/). The main area of his interest is software engineering and implementation of artificial intelligence in business systems. His team established the distance-learning platform for providing services for Serbian Ministry of Defense, Serbian Army, but also for international cooperation. He participates in several research projects focused on improving e-Government services, implementation of Web-based e-learning, interoperability between different learning resources and systems, and integration between intelligent tutoring systems and learning management systems. So far, he has authored/co-authored dozens research papers and books. Dr. Šimić is a member of the GoodOldAI research network (http://goodoldai.org/).

Agusti Solanas is the head of the Smart Health Research Group in the Department of Computer Engineering and Mathematics of the Universitat Rovira i Virgili (URV). He received his MSc degree in Computer Engineering from Universitat Rovira i Virgili in 2004 with honors (Outstanding Graduation Award). He received a Diploma of Advanced Studies (Master's) in Telematics Engineering from Universitat Politècnica de Catalunya in 2006 and a PhD in Telematics Engineering from UPC in 2007 with honors. His main fields of activity are smart health, e-health, m-health, privacy, and security. He has authored over 90 publications. He is a member of the ACM and the IEEE.

Christoph Sorge received his diploma degree (Master equivalent) in Information Engineering and Management from the Karlsruhe Institute of Technology in 2004 and his PhD in Computer Science from the same university in 2007. After working as a research scientist at NEC Laboratories Europe, Heidelberg, he joined the University of Paderborn as an assistant professor in 2010. He now holds the professorship for Law and Informatics—endowed by Juris, a company specialized in computer-assisted legal research—at Saarland University, which he joined in April 2014. Christoph Sorge's research interests include IT security and data protection, both from a technical and legal perspective. Moreover, he addresses applications of computer science for legal researchers and practitioners.

Paula Sofia Sousa graduated in Biomedical Sciences at University of Beira Interior (UBI – Covilhã, Portugal) in 2008, and in 2010, she completed the Master's degree in Biomedical Sciences (UBI), in which she demonstrated a great interest in biomedical signal analysis and processing. Currently, she is involved in research activities in the Assisted Living Computing and Telecommunications Laboratory – AALab, a research group within the Network Group of Institute of Telecommunications at the University of Beira Interior, Covilhã, Portugal. Her research interests are based on health monitoring, including biomedical applications and instrumentation, and medical signal acquisition, analysis, and processing.

Jelena Stankovic is an assistant professor at the Faculty of Economics, University of Nis, for narrow scientific field Economic statistics, the application of mathematical, and statistical methods in economic research, and teaches courses in Operational Research, Financial and Actuarial Mathematics, and Decision Theory. She gained the MSc degree at the Faculty of Economics, University of Belgrade, and PhD degree at the Faculty of Economics, University of Nis. In her academic work, she has published 2 monographs, more than 70 papers in scientific and professional journals, and has participated in research conferences at home and abroad. Dr. Stankovic has been working as a researcher on projects funded by the Ministry of Education and Science of Republic of Serbia, as well as international projects. She has specialist training certificate for monitoring and risk analysis in financial institutions organized by FitchRating in 2007 in New York. She is a member of EWG E-CUBE – European Working Group on Experimental Economics, group under the Association of European Operational Research Societies.

Santhanamery Thominathan is currently a senior lecturer at the Faculty of Business Management in Universiti Teknologi Mara Malaysia. She has thought courses in Business, Management, and Economics at diploma and undergraduate level. Prior to this, she was an operation officer for Maybank Berhad from 1996 – 2002. Her experience in banking industry for 6 years was in the area of banking operations and handling customer service. Her publications in the area of technology adoption particularly on e-government have appeared in IGI Global and Technics Technologies Education Management (TTEM). Having experience in banking and education industry for almost 16 years, she would like to collaborate and share her experience in technology management, technology adoption, and operation management area.

M. R. Zakaria has a PhD in E-Learning Systems and Adaptation in general and user modeling in particular from University of Nottingham, UK, and MSc in Information Technology from the same institute. Currently, he is an Assistant Professor at Al Ghurier University, Dubai, UAE. His research interests include Web development, e-government services, and maturity models. His work has been published in international journals and conference proceedings such as *International Journal of Business Information and Technology, International Journal of Technology and Management, New Review of Hypermedia and Multimedia,* International Conference of Engineering Education, International Conference of Adaptive Hypermedia, and ACM Conference on Hypertext and Hypermedia.

Salem Zoughbi is a global advisor for Information and Communication Technology (ICT). Saleem Zoughbi has been providing technical assistance and advisory services to over 30 countries. He focused on development and has been assisting governments on the strategic and policy levels on e-governance, smart cities, national strategies, and ICT development. In addition, he conducts consultancies for major consulting firms such as Booze, PricewaterhouseCoopers, and others in technical missions and projects. He is active in international community of e-governance, strategies and policies of smart governance, mobile government, smart cities and smart sectors, and ICT for development. He focused on development and has been assisting governments on the strategic and policy levels on e-governance, smart cities, national strategies, and ICT development. He worked for the United Nations Economic and Social Commission of Western Asia (UN ESCWA). This included special technical advice in different applications such as the evaluation of national policies and strategies, evaluation of IT departments within a CIO approach that includes business and process re-engineering, planning and evaluation in e-government and e-governance, databases, data centers, and others. He provided a lot of technical advisories to ministries of several countries on public sector information management, enterprise architecture, ICT policies and strategies, national development plans in addition to e-governance and assessment of e-government national strategies and operational initiatives. He worked in 2013 as a senior adviser at the UN eGOV at IIST of the United Nations University in Macao. He is also currently adviser to UN APCIC in UN ESCAP in enterprise architecture providing developing knowledge sharing, capacity building, and running advisory mission to Central and South East Asia and the Pacific. He is a committed member of the IEEE STC eGov committee and coordinates the ICT for development, especially e-governance and smart governance.

Index

A

Administrative Procedure 123
Air Pollution 265-268, 270-275, 280-282, 284-286, 288, 301
Ambient Assisted Living 304, 306, 326
Analytic Hierarchy Process 333, 352, 358, 362, 364, 373
Anonymisation 258, 263
Anonymous Credential 220, 225-226, 255, 257-258, 263-264
Architectural Element 334, 352

B

Big Data 8, 11, 13, 20-21, 24-26, 30, 32-33, 37, 164, 181, 322
Break-the-Glass 258, 260, 264
Business Council 355, 358-361, 363-367, 373
Business Environment 353-357, 361, 363, 366-367, 373
Business Process Management 93-94, 97, 102, 106, 108-110, 113, 117, 120, 123
Business Process Model 94, 106, 108, 110, 113

C

Case-Based Reasoning 192-194, 199-200, 204, 213
Cash Flow 65, 334-335, 352
Catalogue of Procedures 123
Causa Brasil Platform 238, 248
Chi-Square Test 358-360, 363, 373
Chronic Diseases 265, 276, 283, 285, 302, 304, 307, 326
Citizen-Centric E-Government 374-376, 380, 389, 395
Citizen Characteristics 39, 49-50
common service centres (CSCs) 60, 64
Continuance Intention 73, 78-80, 89
Credential Pseudonym 264
Crowdsourcing 149-150, 153, 155, 157, 163
Crowdstorming 149-150, 153, 155, 157, 163

D

Digital Library 213
Digital Signature 109, 116, 224, 229, 264
DiscoverText 238-239, 248

E

Early Warning System 265, 287-288, 301
E-Filing System 73-75, 79, 83-85, 89
E-Government Readiness 388-389, 395
E-Government Service Index (ESI) 374-376, 380-381, 395
Egypt 233, 374-376, 380, 382, 386-392
E-Health 302-304, 313, 318, 320-322, 326
eID card 214-215, 217-226, 229
E-Participation 44, 46-50, 71
E-Services 44, 47-50, 71, 378-382, 384, 386-387, 391-392, 395
Extended Access Control (EAC) 229

F

Facebook 79, 149, 155-156, 233, 238-242, 248-249

G

Gini Coefficient 55
Gross Domestic Product per Capita 55

H

Heat Index 265, 282-283, 301
Hierarchical Clustering 166, 170-172, 188, 191
Human Capital 43-44, 47-48, 50-51, 388-389

I

Innovation Diffusion 20, 24, 30, 32, 37
Institutional Cooperation 353, 356, 367, 373
Intangible Asset 352
Intangible Benefit 352
Interest Rate 335, 345, 352
Internet Penetration 44, 55
Inventory of Procedures 123
Inverse Document Frequency (IDF) 188, 191

K

Knowledge Management 199, 209, 213

L

Local Self-Government Institutions 353, 357, 373

M

Machine Learning 236, 239, 248
Manual Filing 90
Maturity Models 375-376, 378, 380, 392, 395
Mediated Services 136, 143
Microfoundations 38-39, 41, 47, 49-50, 55
Minimum Marketable Features Modules or Projects 352
Multi-Criteria Analysis 353, 358, 361, 363-364, 367, 373
Multi-Sensors Platforms 303-304, 312, 326

N

Natural Language Processing (NLP) 235, 248
Net Present Value 330, 335, 348, 352
Network of Caregivers 264
Non-Normative Maturity Models 378, 395
Normative Maturity Models 376, 395

O

Open Innovation 5, 144-145, 149-153, 155-159, 163
Open Social Innovation 144-145, 151-155, 157-159, 163
Organizational Transparency 93, 95-96, 106

P

Partition Clustering 165-166, 171-174, 188, 191
Password Authenticated Connection Establishment (PACE) 229
Perceived Usefulness 73-75, 77-80, 82-85, 90
Popular Demonstrations in Brazil 249
Predictive Policing 20-21, 25-32, 37
Pseudonym 256-258, 264
Pseudonymous Relationship 264
Public Key Infrastructure (PKI) 218, 229

R

Recommendation System 132, 137, 143
Restricted Identification (RI) 229
Retrieval Information 193-194, 198, 208, 213

S

security and privacy 11-12, 225, 253, 303, 320, 392
Semantic Web 192-194, 204, 209, 213
Sentiment Analysis 231-237, 240, 242-243, 249
Service Oriented Architecture (SOA) 108-109, 113, 115-116, 119-120, 123
Smart City 1-8, 10-13, 16, 19
Smart Government 1-4, 6-8, 16, 19
Social Capital 39-41, 44, 47-50, 55, 63, 66, 318
Social Challenge Ideas 153, 158-159, 163
Social Innovation 39, 144-155, 157-159, 163
Social Media 21, 25, 79, 155, 231-238, 241-243, 248-249
Social Values 40, 44, 47, 50, 146
Soft Clustering 173-176, 191
SOM Clustering 191
Statistical Analysis 204, 209, 258, 355, 358, 373
Symbiosis 125, 132, 143

T

Taxpayers 27, 73-74, 79, 84-85, 89-90
Telecentre 56, 61-62, 64-67, 71-72
Tele-Monitoring 326
Term Frequency (TF) 168, 188, 191
Twitter 233, 238-242, 248-249

U

Understandability 93-97, 99, 101-103, 106

W

Weights Assessment 364, 373
Wind Chill Index 265, 283, 286, 301

CPSIA information can be obtained at www.ICGtesting.com
Printed in the USA
BVOW05*1549120115

382577BV00007B/31/P

9 781466 672666